Mercedes-Benz C-Class
Owners Workshop Manual

Peter T Gill

Models covered

(4780 - 312)

C160, C180, C200, C220, C230 & C270 Saloon, Estate & Coupe (W203 series),
including 'Kompressor' models and special/limited editions

Petrol: 1.8 litre (1796cc), 2.0 litre (1998cc) & 2.3 litre (2295cc)
Turbo-Diesel: 2.2 litre (2148cc) & 2.7 litre (2685cc)

Does NOT cover models with V6 engines or AMG versions
Does NOT cover new C-Class range (W204 series) introduced June 2007

© Haynes Publishing 2009

ABCDE
FGHIJ
KLM

A book in the **Haynes Owners Workshop Manual Series**

ISBN **978 0 85733 953 9**

British Library Cataloguing in Publication Data
A catalogue record for this book is available from the British Library.

Printed in the USA

Haynes Publishing
Sparkford, Yeovil, Somerset BA22 7JJ, England

Haynes North America, Inc
861 Lawrence Drive, Newbury Park, California 91320, USA

Haynes Publishing Nordiska AB
Box 1504, 751 45 UPPSALA, Sverige

Contents

LIVING WITH YOUR MERCEDES-BENZ C-CLASS

Contents

The Mercedes Benz C-Class was launched in the UK in October 1993. Developed from the very successful 190 series, the new C-Class attracted very favourable reviews, featuring as it does the traditional excellent Mercedes design and engineering combined with first-class build quality.

All engines are developments of well-proven engines, which have appeared in many Mercedes-Benz vehicles. The engines covered in this manual are of double overhead camshaft 4-valves-per-cylinder design, mounted longitudinally ('north-south') with the transmission mounted behind the engine. Both manual and automatic transmissions are available

Fully-independent suspension is fitted front and rear, with a Macpherson type front suspension and the multilink rear suspension first seen on the 190 series.

All models feature anti-lock brakes (ABS), power steering, central locking, electric mirrors, and a driver's airbag. As the range has developed, more equipment has been fitted as standard, with the most recent models featuring passenger and side airbags, electric front and rear windows, traction control and cruise control.

Provided that regular servicing is carried out in accordance with the manufacturer's recommendations, the C-Class should prove very reliable and durable. The engine compartment is well-designed, and most of the items requiring frequent attention are easily accessible.

Your Mercedes C-Class manual

The aim of this manual is to help you get the best value from your vehicle. It can do so in several ways. It can help you decide what work must be done (even should you choose to get it done by a garage). It will also provide information on routine maintenance and servicing, and give a logical course of action and diagnosis when random faults occur. However, it is hoped that you will use the manual by tackling the work yourself. On simpler jobs it may even be quicker than booking the car into a garage and going there twice, to leave and collect it. Perhaps most importantly, a lot of money can be saved by avoiding the costs a garage must charge to cover its labour and overheads.

The manual has drawings and descriptions to show the function of the various components so that their layout can be understood. Tasks are described and photographed in a clear step-by-step sequence. The illustrations are numbered by the Section number and paragraph number to which they relate – if there is more than one illustration per paragraph, the sequence is denoted alphabetically.

References to the 'left' or 'right' of the car are in the sense of a person in the driver's seat, facing forwards.

Acknowledgements

Thanks are due to Draper Tools Limited, who provided some of the workshop tools, and to all those people at Sparkford who helped in the production of this manual.

We take great pride in the accuracy of information given in this manual, but vehicle manufacturers make alterations and design changes during the production run of a particular vehicle of which they do not inform us. No liability can be accepted by the authors or publishers for loss, damage or injury caused by any errors in, or omissions from, the information given.

Working on your car can be dangerous. This page shows just some of the potential risks and hazards, with the aim of creating a safety-conscious attitude.

General hazards

Scalding

• Don't remove the radiator or expansion tank cap while the engine is hot.
• Engine oil, automatic transmission fluid or power steering fluid may also be dangerously hot if the engine has recently been running.

Burning

• Beware of burns from the exhaust system and from any part of the engine. Brake discs and drums can also be extremely hot immediately after use.

Crushing

• When working under or near a raised vehicle, always supplement the jack with axle stands, or use drive-on ramps. *Never venture under a car which is only supported by a jack.*

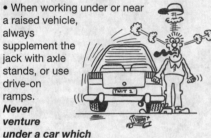

• Take care if loosening or tightening high-torque nuts when the vehicle is on stands. Initial loosening and final tightening should be done with the wheels on the ground.

Fire

• Fuel is highly flammable; fuel vapour is explosive.
• Don't let fuel spill onto a hot engine.
• Do not smoke or allow naked lights (including pilot lights) anywhere near a vehicle being worked on. Also beware of creating sparks (electrically or by use of tools).
• Fuel vapour is heavier than air, so don't work on the fuel system with the vehicle over an inspection pit.
• Another cause of fire is an electrical overload or short-circuit. Take care when repairing or modifying the vehicle wiring.
• Keep a fire extinguisher handy, of a type suitable for use on fuel and electrical fires.

Electric shock

• Ignition HT voltage can be dangerous, especially to people with heart problems or a pacemaker. Don't work on or near the ignition system with the engine running or the ignition switched on.

• Mains voltage is also dangerous. Make sure that any mains-operated equipment is correctly earthed. Mains power points should be protected by a residual current device (RCD) circuit breaker.

Fume or gas intoxication

• Exhaust fumes are poisonous; they often contain carbon monoxide, which is rapidly fatal if inhaled. Never run the engine in a confined space such as a garage with the doors shut.

• Fuel vapour is also poisonous, as are the vapours from some cleaning solvents and paint thinners.

Poisonous or irritant substances

• Avoid skin contact with battery acid and with any fuel, fluid or lubricant, especially antifreeze, brake hydraulic fluid and Diesel fuel. Don't syphon them by mouth. If such a substance is swallowed or gets into the eyes, seek medical advice.
• Prolonged contact with used engine oil can cause skin cancer. Wear gloves or use a barrier cream if necessary. Change out of oil-soaked clothes and do not keep oily rags in your pocket.
• Air conditioning refrigerant forms a poisonous gas if exposed to a naked flame (including a cigarette). It can also cause skin burns on contact.

Asbestos

• Asbestos dust can cause cancer if inhaled or swallowed. Asbestos may be found in gaskets and in brake and clutch linings. When dealing with such components it is safest to assume that they contain asbestos.

Special hazards

Hydrofluoric acid

• This extremely corrosive acid is formed when certain types of synthetic rubber, found in some O-rings, oil seals, fuel hoses etc, are exposed to temperatures above 400ºC. The rubber changes into a charred or sticky substance containing the acid. *Once formed, the acid remains dangerous for years. If it gets onto the skin, it may be necessary to amputate the limb concerned.*
• When dealing with a vehicle which has suffered a fire, or with components salvaged from such a vehicle, wear protective gloves and discard them after use.

The battery

• Batteries contain sulphuric acid, which attacks clothing, eyes and skin. Take care when topping-up or carrying the battery.
• The hydrogen gas given off by the battery is highly explosive. Never cause a spark or allow a naked light nearby. Be careful when connecting and disconnecting battery chargers or jump leads.

Air bags

• Air bags can cause injury if they go off accidentally. Take care when removing the steering wheel and/or facia. Special storage instructions may apply.

Diesel injection equipment

• Diesel injection pumps supply fuel at very high pressure. Take care when working on the fuel injectors and fuel pipes.

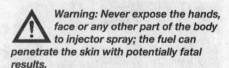 *Warning: Never expose the hands, face or any other part of the body to injector spray; the fuel can penetrate the skin with potentially fatal results.*

Remember...

DO

• Do use eye protection when using power tools, and when working under the vehicle.

• Do wear gloves or use barrier cream to protect your hands when necessary.

• Do get someone to check periodically that all is well when working alone on the vehicle.

• Do keep loose clothing and long hair well out of the way of moving mechanical parts.

• Do remove rings, wristwatch etc, before working on the vehicle – especially the electrical system.

• Do ensure that any lifting or jacking equipment has a safe working load rating adequate for the job.

DON'T

• Don't attempt to lift a heavy component which may be beyond your capability – get assistance.

• Don't rush to finish a job, or take unverified short cuts.

• Don't use ill-fitting tools which may slip and cause injury.

• Don't leave tools or parts lying around where someone can trip over them. Mop up oil and fuel spills at once.

• Don't allow children or pets to play in or near a vehicle being worked on.

The following pages are intended to help in dealing with common roadside emergencies and breakdowns. You will find more detailed fault finding information at the back of the manual, and repair information in the main chapters.

If your car won't start and the starter motor doesn't turn

- ☐ If it's a model with automatic transmission, make sure the selector is in P or N.
- ☐ Remove the battery cover and make sure that the battery terminals are clean and tight.
- ☐ Switch on the headlights and try to start the engine. If the headlights go very dim when you're trying to start, the battery is probably flat. Get out of trouble by jump starting (see next page) using a friend's car.

If your car won't start even though the starter motor turns as normal

- ☐ Is there fuel in the tank?
- ☐ Is there moisture on electrical components under the bonnet? Switch off the ignition, then wipe off any obvious dampness with a dry cloth. Spray a water-repellent aerosol product (WD-40 or equivalent) on ignition and fuel system electrical connectors like those shown in the photos. (Note that diesel engines don't usually suffer from damp).

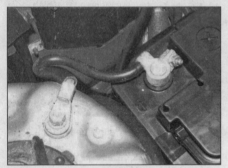

A Check the condition and security of the battery connections.

B Check the fuses in the fusebox located in the engine compartment inside the vehicle.

C Check the wiring to the ignition coil on the top of the engine (petrol models only).

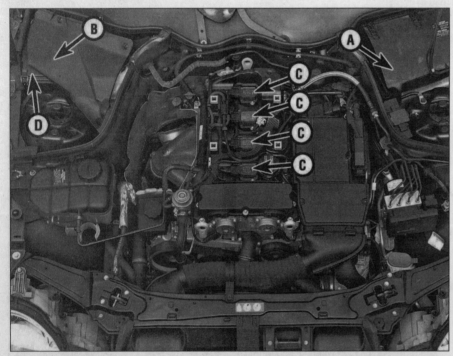

Check that electrical connections are secure (with the ignition switched off) and spray them with a water-dispersant spray like WD-40 if you suspect a problem due to damp

D Check that the ECU wiring is secure.

Check that the fuel lines are secure and no air in the system (diesel model shown).

Jump starting

When jump-starting a car using a booster battery, observe the following precautions:

✔ Before connecting the booster battery, make sure that the ignition is switched off.

✔ Ensure that all electrical equipment (lights, heater, wipers, etc) is switched off.

✔ Take note of any special precautions printed on the battery case.

✔ Make sure that the booster battery is the same voltage as the discharged one in the vehicle.

✔ If the battery is being jump-started from the battery in another vehicle, the two vehicles MUST NOT TOUCH each other.

✔ Make sure that the transmission is in neutral (or PARK, in the case of automatic transmission).

 HAYNES HiNT *Jump starting will get you out of trouble, but you must correct whatever made the battery go flat in the first place. There are three possibilities:*

1 *The battery has been drained by repeated attempts to start, or by leaving the lights on.*

2 *The charging system is not working properly (alternator drivebelt slack or broken, alternator wiring fault or alternator itself faulty).*

3 *The battery itself is at fault (electrolyte low, or battery worn out).*

1 Connect one end of the red jump lead to the positive (+) terminal of the flat battery or to the remote positive terminal located on the fuse/relay box

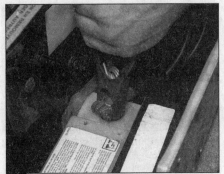

2 Connect the other end of the red lead to the positive (+) terminal of the booster battery.

3 Connect one end of black jump lead to the negative (-) terminal of the booster battery.

4 Connect the other end of the black jump lead to the earth cable on the upper strut mounting

5 Make sure that the jump leads will not come into contact with the cooling fan, drivebelts or other moving parts on the engine.

6 Start the engine, then with the engine running at fast idle speed disconnect the jump leads in the reverse order of connection.

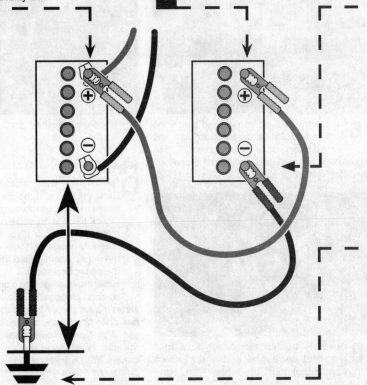

Wheel changing

Note: *Some models have a collapsed tyre to save space. There is an electric air pump stored with the wheel changing tools to inflate the spare tyre when required. Other models have the TYREFIT system which uses sealant on the punctured tyre.*

⚠️ **Warning: Do not change a wheel in a situation where you risk being hit by other traffic. On busy roads, try to stop in a lay-by or a gateway. Be wary of passing traffic while changing the wheel – it is easy to become distracted by the job in hand.**

Preparation

☐ When a puncture occurs, stop as soon as it is safe to do so.
☐ Park on firm level ground, if possible, and well out of the way of other traffic.
☐ Use hazard warning lights if necessary.

☐ If you have one, use a warning triangle to alert other drivers of your presence.
☐ Apply the handbrake and engage first or reverse gear (or P on models with automatic transmission).

☐ Chock the wheel diagonally opposite the one being removed – a couple of large stones will do for this.
☐ If the ground is soft, use a flat piece of wood to spread the load under the jack.

Changing the wheel

1 The spare wheel is stored in the luggage compartment. Raise the floor covering, and lift out the spare wheel and wheel changing tools.

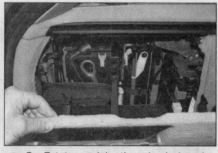

2 On Estate models, the wheel changing tools and jack are stored behind the left-hand rear inner panel.

3 Use the wheelbrace to slacken each wheel bolt by half a turn.

4 Unscrew the plastic retainer and remove the spare wheel.

5 Locate the jack on firm ground below the reinforced point on the sill (don't jack the vehicle at any other point of the sill), then turn the jack handle clockwise until the wheel is raised clear of the ground.

6 Unscrew the wheel bolts and remove the wheel.

Finally...

☐ Remove the wheel chocks.
☐ Stow the jack and tools with the spare wheel in the luggage compartment.
☐ Check the tyre pressure on the wheel just fitted. If it is low, or if you don't have a pressure gauge with you, drive slowly to the nearest garage and inflate the tyre to the correct pressure.
☐ Have the damaged tyre or wheel repaired as soon as possible.

Note: *If a temporary 'space-saver' spare wheel has been fitted, special conditions apply to its use. This type of spare wheel is only intended for use in an emergency, and should not remain fitted any longer than it takes to get the punctured wheel repaired. While the temporary wheel is in use, ensure it is inflated to the correct pressure, do not exceed 50 mph, and avoid harsh acceleration, braking or cornering.*

7 Fit the spare wheel, and screw in the bolts. When fitting a steel spare wheel, shorter bolts will be provided with the spare wheel. Lightly tighten the bolts with the wheelbrace then lower the vehicle to the ground.

8 Securely tighten the wheel bolts in a diagonal sequence and then (where applicable), refit the wheel trim. Note that the wheel bolts should be tightened to the specified torque at the earliest possible opportunity.

Identifying leaks

Puddles on the garage floor or drive, or obvious wetness under the bonnet or underneath the car, suggest a leak that needs investigating. It can sometimes be difficult to decide where the leak is coming from, especially if the engine bay is very dirty already. Leaking oil or fluid can also be blown rearwards by the passage of air under the car, giving a false impression of where the problem lies.

 Warning: Most automotive oils and fluids are poisonous. Wash them off skin, and change out of contaminated clothing, without delay.

 HAYNES HiNT *The smell of a fluid leaking from the car may provide a clue to what's leaking. Some fluids are distinctively coloured. It may help to clean the car carefully and to park it over some clean paper overnight as an aid to locating the source of the leak.*
Remember that some leaks may only occur while the engine is running.

Sump oil

Engine oil may leak from the drain plug...

Oil from filter

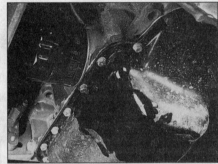

...or from the base of the oil filter.

Gearbox oil

Gearbox oil can leak from the seals at the inboard ends of the driveshafts.

Antifreeze

Leaking antifreeze often leaves a crystalline deposit like this.

Brake fluid

A leak occurring at a wheel is almost certainly brake fluid.

Power steering fluid

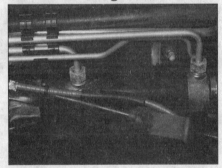

Power steering fluid may leak from the pipe connectors on the steering rack.

Towing

When all else fails, you may find yourself having to get a tow home – or of course you may be helping somebody else. Long-distance recovery should only be done by a garage or breakdown service. For shorter distances, DIY towing using another car is easy enough, but observe the following points:

☐ Use a proper tow-rope – they are not expensive. The vehicle being towed must display an ON TOW sign in its rear window.

☐ Always turn the ignition key to the 'On' position when the vehicle is being towed, so that the steering lock is released, and the direction indicator and brake lights work.

☐ Only attach the tow-rope to the towing eyes provided. The towing eye is supplied as part of the toolkit stored in the luggage compartment. To fit the eye, remove the vent/ cover from the bumper. Screw the eye into position, and tighten using the wheelbrace handle.

☐ Before being towed, release the handbrake and select neutral on the transmission. Automatic transmission models should not be towed for more than 30 miles at a maximum speed of 30 mph.

☐ Note that greater-than-usual pedal pressure will be required to operate the brakes, since the vacuum servo unit is only operational with the engine running.

☐ Because the power steering will not be operational, greater-than-usual steering effort will be required.

☐ Make sure that both drivers know the route before setting off.

☐ The driver of the car being towed must keep the tow-rope taut at all times to avoid snatching.

☐ Only drive at moderate speeds and keep the distance towed to a minimum. Drive smoothly and allow plenty of time for slowing down at junctions.

Introduction

There are some very simple checks which need only take a few minutes to carry out, but which could save you a lot of inconvenience and expense.

These *Weekly checks* require no great skill or special tools, and the small amount of time they take to perform could prove to be very well spent, for example:

☐ Keeping an eye on tyre condition and pressures, will not only help to stop them wearing out prematurely, but could also save your life.

☐ Many breakdowns are caused by electrical problems. Battery-related faults are particularly common, and a quick check on a regular basis will often prevent the majority of these.

☐ If your car develops a brake fluid leak, the first time you might know about it is when your brakes don't work properly. Checking the level regularly will give advance warning of this kind of problem.

☐ If the oil or coolant levels run low, the cost of repairing any engine damage will be far greater than fixing the leak, for example.

Underbonnet check points

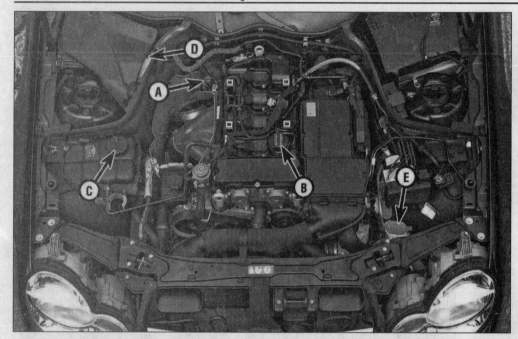

◀ 1.8 litre petrol

A *Engine oil level dipstick*

B *Engine oil filler cap*

C *Coolant expansion tank*

D *Brake/clutch fluid reservoir (under cover)*

E *Screen washer fluid reservoir*

◀ 2.2 litre diesel

A *Engine oil level dipstick*

B *Engine oil filler cap*

C *Coolant expansion tank*

D *Brake/clutch fluid reservoir*

E *Screen washer fluid reservoir*

Engine oil level

Before you start

✔ Make sure that the car is on level ground.
✔ The oil should be at normal operating temperature.
✔ The engine should have been switched off for at least 5 minutes.

HAYNES HINT *If the oil is checked immediately after driving the vehicle, some of the oil will remain in the upper engine components, resulting in an inaccurate reading on the dipstick.*

The correct oil

Modern engines place great demands on their oil. It is very important that the correct oil for your car is used (see *Lubricants and fluids*).

Car care

● If you have to add oil frequently, you should check whether you have any oil leaks. Place some clean paper under the car overnight, and check for stains in the morning. If there are no leaks, then the engine may be burning oil, or the oil may only be leaking when the engine is running.

● Always maintain the level between the upper and lower dipstick marks. If the level is too low, severe engine damage may occur. Oil seal failure may result if the engine is overfilled by adding too much oil.

1 Some models, have a red cap fitted to the dipstick tube and **NOT** a dipstick. On these models, the oil is checked on the multi-function display unit on the Instrument panel. By pressing the up-and-down buttons on the multifunction steering wheel repeatedly, the ENGINE OIL LEVEL, MEASURING NOW! will appear on the display. Follow the instructions shown to achieve the correct oil level.

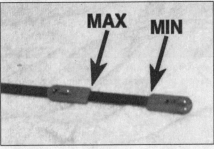
3 Note the level on the end of the dipstick, which should be between the upper (MAX) and lower (MIN) mark. Oil is added through the filler cap aperture. A funnel may help to reduce spillage.

2 On models with a dipstick fitted, the dipstick cap is coloured red for easy identification (see *Underbonnet check points* for exact location). Withdraw the dipstick, and then use a clean rag or paper towel to wipe the oil from it. Insert the clean dipstick into the tube as far as it will go, then withdraw it again.

4 Unscrew the cap and place some cloth rags around the filler cap aperture, then top-up the level. Add the oil slowly, checking the level on the dipstick frequently. Avoid overfilling (see *Car care*).

Coolant level

⚠ *Warning: Do not attempt to remove the expansion tank pressure cap when the engine is hot, as there is a very great risk of scalding. Do not leave open containers of coolant about, as it is poisonous.*

Car care

● With a sealed-type cooling system, adding coolant should not be necessary on a regular basis. If frequent topping-up is required, it is likely there is a leak. Check the radiator, all hoses and joint faces for signs of staining or wetness, and rectify as necessary.

● It is important that antifreeze is used in the cooling system all year round, not just during the winter months. Don't top up with water alone, as the antifreeze will become diluted.

1 The coolant level varies with the temperature of the engine. When the engine is cold, the coolant level should be up to the level marker inside the filler neck of the expansion tank.

2 If topping-up is necessary, wait until the engine is cold. Slowly unscrew the cap to release any pressure present in the cooling system, and remove the cap.

3 Add a mixture of water and the specified antifreeze (see *Lubricants and fluids*) to the expansion tank until the coolant level is halfway between the level marks. Refit the cap and tighten it securely.

Brake and clutch fluid level

Note: *On manual transmission models, the fluid reservoir also supplies the clutch master cylinder with fluid.*

Before you start

✔ Make sure that the car is on level ground.
✔ Cleanliness is of great importance when dealing with the braking system; so take care to clean around the reservoir cap before topping-up. Use only clean brake fluid.

Safety first!

● If the reservoir requires repeated topping-up, this is an indication of a fluid leak somewhere in the system, which should be investigated immediately.

● If a leak is suspected, the car should not be driven until the braking system has been checked. Never take any risks where brakes are concerned.

 Warning: *Brake fluid can harm your eyes and damage painted surfaces, so use extreme caution when handling and pouring it. Do not use fluid which has been standing open for some time, as it absorbs moisture from the air, which can cause a dangerous loss of braking effectiveness.*

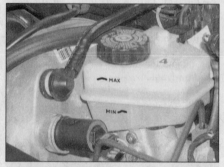

1 The MIN and MAX marks are indicated on the reservoir. The fluid level must be kept between the marks at all times. If topping-up is necessary, first wipe clean the area around the filler cap to prevent dirt entering the hydraulic system.

2 If topping-up is necessary, first wipe clean the area around the filler cap to prevent dirt entering the hydraulic system. Unscrew and remove the reservoir's cap.

3 Carefully add fluid, taking care not to spill it onto the surrounding components (use a funnel). Use only the specified fluid (see *Lubricants and fluids*); mixing different types can cause damage to the system. On completion, securely refit the cap and wipe away any spilt fluid.

Washer fluid level

● Screenwash additives not only keep the windscreen clean during bad weather, they also prevent the washer system freezing in cold weather – which is when you are likely to need it most. Don't top-up using plain water, as the screenwash will become diluted, and will freeze in cold weather.

Caution: *On no account use engine coolant antifreeze in the screen washer system – this may damage the paintwork.*

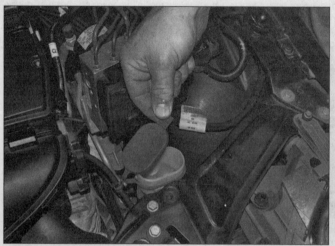

1 The screenwash fluid reservoir is located on the left-hand side (as seen from the driver's seat) of the engine compartment, behind the headlight. Pull up the filler cap to release it from the reservoir.

2 When topping-up the reservoir, a screenwash additive should be added in the quantities recommended on the bottle.

Wiper blades

Note: *It is possible to park the wipers in a Service/Winter position with both wipers pointing upwards to allow unrestricted removal of the blades. To do this, operate the wipers within 10 seconds of switching off the ignition. The wiper arms can now be lifted away from the windscreen.*

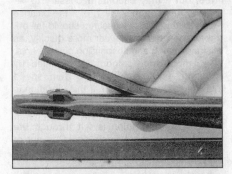

1 Check the condition of the wiper blades; if they are cracked or show any signs of deterioration, or if the glass swept area is smeared, renew them. For maximum clarity of vision, wiper blades should be renewed annually, as a matter of course.

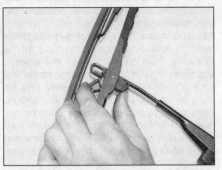

2 To remove a windscreen wiper blade, pull the arm fully away from the screen until it locks. On standard wipers, swivel the blade through 90°, press the locking tab with your fingers, and slide the blade out of the hooked end of the arm.

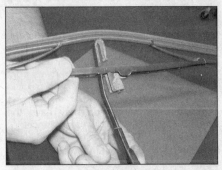

3 Where applicable, don't forget to check the tailgate wiper blade as well. To remove the blade, depress the retaining tab and slide the blade out of the hooked end of the arm.

Battery

Caution: Before carrying out any work on the vehicle battery, read the precautions given in 'Safety first!' at the start of this manual.

✔ Make sure that the battery tray is in good condition, and that the clamp is tight. Corrosion on the tray, retaining clamp and the battery itself can be removed with a solution of water and baking soda. Thoroughly rinse all cleaned areas with water. Any metal parts damaged by corrosion should be covered with a zinc-based primer, then painted.

✔ Periodically (approximately every three months), check the charge condition of the battery as described in Chapter 5A. A 'magic eye' charge indicator is fitted to the standard battery – if the indicator is green in colour, the battery is fully charged, however, if it is colourless, it should be recharged. If it is yellow in colour, the battery should be renewed.

✔ If the battery is flat, and you need to jump start your vehicle, see *Jump starting*.

1 The battery is located in the left-hand rear corner of the engine compartment, below the pollen filter housing. Unclip and remove the filter housing, to gain access to the battery terminals.

2 Check the security and condition of the battery connections. The exterior of the battery should be inspected periodically for damage such as a cracked case or cover.

3 If corrosion (white, fluffy deposits) is evident, remove the cables from the battery terminals (refer to *Disconnecting the battery* in *Reference*), clean them with a small wire brush, then refit them. Automotive stores sell a tool for cleaning the battery post . . .

4 . . . as well as the battery cable clamps.

Tyre condition and pressure

It is very important that tyres are in good condition, and at the correct pressure - having a tyre failure at any speed is highly dangerous. Tyre wear is influenced by driving style - harsh braking and acceleration, or fast cornering, will all produce more rapid tyre wear. As a general rule, the front tyres wear out faster than the rears. Interchanging the tyres from front to rear ("rotating" the tyres) may result in more even wear. However, if this is completely effective, you may have the expense of replacing all four tyres at once! Remove any nails or stones embedded in the tread before they penetrate the tyre to cause deflation. If removal of a nail does reveal that the tyre has been punctured, refit the nail so that its point of penetration is marked. Then immediately change the wheel, and have the tyre repaired by a tyre dealer.

Regularly check the tyres for damage in the form of cuts or bulges, especially in the sidewalls. Periodically remove the wheels, and clean any dirt or mud from the inside and outside surfaces. Examine the wheel rims for signs of rusting, corrosion or other damage. Light alloy wheels are easily damaged by "kerbing" whilst parking; steel wheels may also become dented or buckled. A new wheel is very often the only way to overcome severe damage.

New tyres should be balanced when they are fitted, but it may become necessary to re-balance them as they wear, or if the balance weights fitted to the wheel rim should fall off. Unbalanced tyres will wear more quickly, as will the steering and suspension components. Wheel imbalance is normally signified by vibration, particularly at a certain speed (typically around 50 mph). If this vibration is felt only through the steering, then it is likely that just the front wheels need balancing. If, however, the vibration is felt through the whole car, the rear wheels could be out of balance. Wheel balancing should be carried out by a tyre dealer or garage.

1 *Tread Depth - visual check*
The original tyres have tread wear safety bands (B), which will appear when the tread depth reaches approximately 1.6 mm. The band positions are indicated by a triangular mark on the tyre sidewall (A).

2 *Tread Depth - manual check*
Alternatively, tread wear can be monitored with a simple, inexpensive device known as a tread depth indicator gauge.

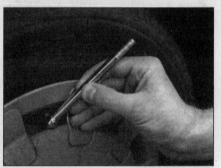

3 *Tyre Pressure Check*
Check the tyre pressures regularly with the tyres cold. Do not adjust the tyre pressures immediately after the vehicle has been used, or an inaccurate setting will result.

Tyre tread wear patterns

Shoulder Wear

Underinflation (wear on both sides)
Under-inflation will cause overheating of the tyre, because the tyre will flex too much, and the tread will not sit correctly on the road surface. This will cause a loss of grip and excessive wear, not to mention the danger of sudden tyre failure due to heat build-up.
Check and adjust pressures
Incorrect wheel camber (wear on one side)
Repair or renew suspension parts
Hard cornering
Reduce speed!

Centre Wear

Overinflation
Over-inflation will cause rapid wear of the centre part of the tyre tread, coupled with reduced grip, harsher ride, and the danger of shock damage occurring in the tyre casing.
Check and adjust pressures

If you sometimes have to inflate your car's tyres to the higher pressures specified for maximum load or sustained high speed, don't forget to reduce the pressures to normal afterwards.

Uneven Wear

Front tyres may wear unevenly as a result of wheel misalignment. Most tyre dealers and garages can check and adjust the wheel alignment (or "tracking") for a modest charge.
Incorrect camber or castor
Repair or renew suspension parts
Malfunctioning suspension
Repair or renew suspension parts
Unbalanced wheel
Balance tyres
Incorrect toe setting
Adjust front wheel alignment
Note: *The feathered edge of the tread which typifies toe wear is best checked by feel.*

Electrical systems

✔ Check all external lights and the horn. Refer to the appropriate Sections of Chapter 12 for details if any of the circuits are found to be inoperative.
✔ Visually check all accessible wiring connectors, harnesses and retaining clips for security, and for signs of chafing or damage.

 HAYNES HiNT *If you need to check your brake lights and indicators unaided, back up to a wall or garage door and operate the lights. The reflected light should show if they are working properly.*

1 If a single indicator light, brake light or headlight has failed, it is likely that a bulb has blown and will need to be renewed. Refer to Chapter 12 for details. If both brake lights have failed, it is possible that the brake light switch operated by the brake pedal has failed. Refer to Chapter 9 for details.

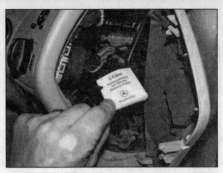

2 If more than one indicator light or headlight has failed, it is likely that either a fuse has blown or that there is a fault in the circuit (see *Electrical fault finding* in Chapter 12). The lighting circuit fuses are in the fusebox behind a cover on the right-hand end of the facia panel. Use a small screwdriver to prise off the cover. There is a fuse location chart located on the top of the fusebox.

3 Additional fuses and fusible links are in the fusebox located in the right-hand side rear of the engine compartment. There is also an additional fusebox located in the left-hand rear panel of the luggage compartment.

4 To renew a blown fuse, pull it from its location in the fusebox, using the plastic pliers provided. Fit a new fuse of the same rating, available from car accessory shops. It is important that you find the reason that the fuse blew (see *Electrical fault finding* in Chapter 12).

Lubricants and fluids

Engine . . . . Multigrade engine oil with a viscosity suited to the ambient temperature **(see illustration)** approved in accordance with MB sheets 229.1 or 229.3

Cooling system . . . . MB 325.0 000 989 08 25 or 000 989 21 25

Manual transmission . . . . Gear oil MB 317 or MB 235.10 transmission oil 001 989 2603

Automatic transmission . . . . MB 236.14 ATF

Braking system . . . . MB 331.0 hydraulic fluid 000 989 08 07 or DOT 4 plus

Power steering . . . . MB 345.0 hydraulic fluid A 001 989 2403

Final drive . . . . Universal hypoid gear oil – SAE 85 W-90 or SAE 75 W-85

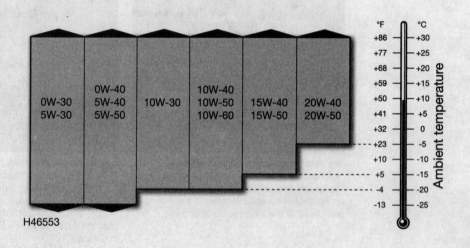

H46553

Tyre pressures

Note: *The recommended tyre pressures for each vehicle are given on a sticker attached to the inside of the fuel filler flap. The pressures given are for the original equipment tyres – the recommended pressures may vary if any other make or type of tyre is fitted; check with the tyre manufacturer or supplier for latest recommendations.*

Chapter 1 Part A:
Routine maintenance & servicing – petrol models

Contents

Degrees of difficulty

Easy, suitable for novice with little experience 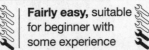	**Fairly easy,** suitable for beginner with some experience	**Fairly difficult,** suitable for competent DIY mechanic 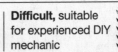	**Difficult,** suitable for experienced DIY mechanic 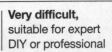	**Very difficult,** suitable for expert DIY or professional

Lubricants and fluids

Refer to *Weekly checks* on page 0•16

Capacities

Engine oil including oil filter

1.8 litre engines	5.5 litres
2.0 and 2.3 litre engines	7.0 litres

Cooling system

All models.	8.6 litres

Transmission

Manual transmission*:

Up to transmission code 716.639	1.2 litres
From transmission code 716.640.	1.5 litres
Automatic transmission	7.5 litres

* See Chapter 7A for transmission codes

Final drive unit

All models.	1.1 litres

Power-assisted steering

All models (approximate)	1.0 litre

Fuel tank

All models:

Total	62 litres
Reserve.	8.0 litres

Windscreen washer reservoir

Models with windscreen washers only.	3.0 litres
Models with heated reservoir and headlamp cleaning system	6.0 litres

Cooling system

Antifreeze mixture:

50% antifreeze	Protection down to –37°C
55% antifreeze	Protection down to –45°C

Note: *Refer to antifreeze manufacturer for latest recommendations.*

Ignition system

Spark plugs:	Type	Electrode gap
1.8 litre engines	Bosch F6MPP332	0.8 mm
	NGK IIFR60	0.8 mm
2.0 and 2.3 litre engines	Bosch F7DPER	0.8 mm
	NGK IFR6D10	1.0 mm

Brakes

Brake pad friction material minimum thickness.	2.0 mm

Torque wrench settings

	Nm	lbf ft
Engine oil drain plug.	30	22
Manual transmission:		
Fluid filler plug	35	26
Fluid drain plug.	30	22
Oil filter cap:		
1.8 litre engines	24	18
2.0 and 2.3 litre engines	25	18
Roadwheel bolts.	110	81
Spark plugs:		
Up to 20/04/04	25	18
From 21/04/04	28	21

The maintenance intervals in this manual are provided with the assumption that you, not the dealer, will be carrying out the work. These are the minimum maintenance intervals recommended by us for vehicles driven daily. If you wish to keep your vehicle in peak condition at all times, you may wish to perform some of these procedures more often. We encourage frequent maintenance, because it enhances the efficiency, performance and resale value of your vehicle.

If the vehicle is driven in dusty areas, used to tow a trailer, or driven frequently at slow speeds (idling in traffic) or mainly for short journeys, shorter maintenance intervals are recommended.

When the vehicle is new, it should be serviced by a dealer service department (or other workshop recognised by the vehicle manufacturer as providing the same standard of service) in order to preserve the warranty. The vehicle manufacturer may reject warranty claims if you are unable to prove that servicing has been carried out as and when specified, using only original equipment parts or parts certified to be of equivalent quality.

Every 250 miles or weekly

☐ Refer to *Weekly checks*

Every 7500 miles or 12 months, whichever comes first

☐ Renew the engine oil and filter (Section 3)

Note: *Frequent oil and filter changes are good for the engine. We recommend changing the oil at least once a year.*

One spanner on display (Service A)

In addition to the items listed above, carry out the following:

☐ Check coolant antifreeze/inhibitor (Section 4)
☐ Lubricate all hinges, locks and sunroof (Section 5)
☐ Check the operation of the windscreen/headlight washer system(s) (as applicable) (Section 6)
☐ Check the operation of the parking brake* (Section 7)
☐ Check the exhaust system and mountings* (Section 8)
☐ Carry out a road test (Section 9)
☐ Reset the service indicator (Section 10)

* Note: *These tasks are not specified by Mercedes as routine maintenance items.*

Two spanners on display (Service B)

In addition to the items listed above, carry out the following:

☐ Check the power steering fluid level (Section 11)
☐ Check the battery condition, security and electrolyte level (Section 12)
☐ Check all underbonnet components and hoses for fluid leaks (Section 13)
☐ Check the auxiliary drivebelt (Section 14)
☐ Check the headlight beam adjustment (Section 15)
☐ Renew the pollen filter (Section 16)
☐ Check front brake pads for wear (Section 17)
☐ Check front brake discs for wear (Section 18)
☐ Check the rear brake pads for wear (Section 19)
☐ Check the rear brake discs for wear (Section 20)
☐ Check the steering and suspension components for condition and security (Section 21)
☐ Check the rear driveshaft gaiters (Section 22)
☐ Check the seat belts (Section 23)
☐ Renew the windscreen wiper blades (Section 24)

Every 2 years

Note: *These tasks are normally performed at the same time as Service A or Service B.*

☐ Check the automatic transmission fluid level* (Section 25)
☐ Check the manual transmission fluid level* (Section 26)
☐ Check final drive unit oil level* (Section 27)
☐ Renew the brake fluid (Section 28)
☐ Check for damage and corrosion (Section 29)

* Note: *These tasks are not specified by Mercedes as routine maintenance items.*

Every 2 years or 30 000 miles, whichever comes first

Note: *This task is normally performed at the same time as Service A or Service B.*

☐ Renew the evaporative emission control charcoal canister (Section 30)

Every 3 years

Note: *This task is normally performed at the same time as Service A or Service B.*

☐ Renew the coolant (Section 31)

Note: *This work is every 15 years/155 000 miles in the Mercedes schedule for later models if the recommended Mercedes coolant antifreeze/inhibitor is used.*

Every 4 years or 50 000 miles, whichever comes first

Note: *This task is normally performed at the same time as Service A or Service B.*

☐ Renew the air filter element (Section 32)
☐ Renew the fuel filter (Section 33)

Every 50 000 miles

Note: *This task is normally performed at the same time as Service A or Service B.*

☐ Check the condition of the propeller shaft rubber coupling (Section 34)

Every 4 years or 55 000 to 65 000 miles, whichever comes first

Note: *This task is normally performed at the same time as Service A or Service B.*

☐ Renew the spark plugs (Section 35)

Underbonnet view of a 1.8 litre model

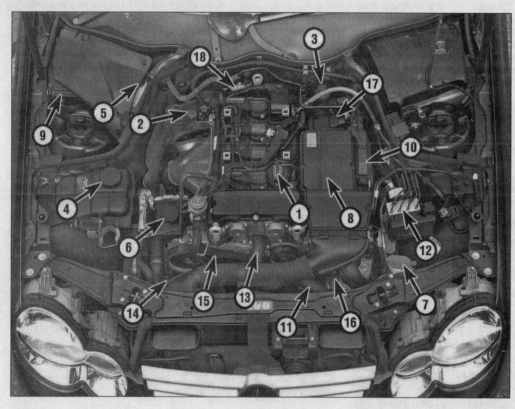

1 Engine oil filler cap
2 Engine oil dipstick
3 Oil filter
4 Coolant expansion tank
5 Brake fluid reservoir
   (under cover)
6 Power steering fluid
   reservoir
7 Windscreen/headlamp
   washer fluid reservoir
8 Air filter
9 Fusebox
10 Engine management ECU
11 Radiator top hose
12 Brake ABS unit
13 Thermostat housing
14 Alternator
15 Auxiliary drivebelt
16 Air conditioning
   compressor
17 Airflow meter
18 Brake vacuum pump

Front underbody view of a 1.8 litre model

1 Engine oil drain plug
2 Alternator
3 Air conditioning
   compressor
4 Anti-roll bar
5 Front suspension lower
   arms
6 Steering track rod
7 Subframe
8 Steering rack
9 Transmission
10 Exhaust system front pipe

Typical rear underbody view

1 Propeller shaft
2 Final drive unit
3 Fuel tank (under plastic cover)
4 Driveshaft
5 Rear suspension radius arm
6 Handbrake cable
7 Rear suspension lower arm
8 Exhaust tailpipe
9 Rear suspension torque strut

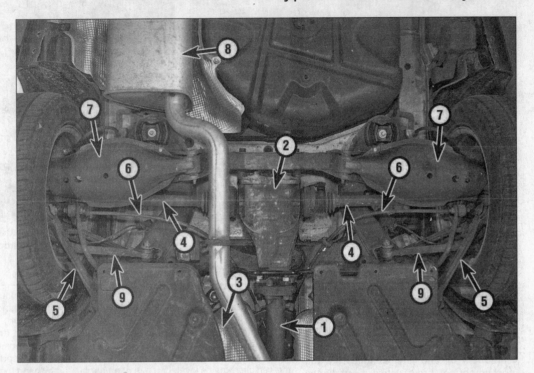

Maintenance procedures

1 Introduction

This Chapter is designed to help the home mechanic maintain his/her vehicle for safety, economy, long life and peak performance.

The Chapter contains a maintenance schedule, followed by Sections dealing with each task in the schedule. Visual checks, adjustments, component renewal and other helpful items are included. Refer to the accompanying illustrations of the engine compartment and the underside of the vehicle for the locations of the various components.

Servicing your vehicle in accordance with the above recommendations and the following Sections will provide a planned maintenance programme, which should result in a long and reliable service life. This is a comprehensive plan, so maintaining some items but not others at the specified service intervals, will not produce the same results.

As you service your vehicle, you will discover that many of the procedures can – and should – be grouped together, because of the particular procedure being performed, or because of the proximity of two otherwise-unrelated components to one another. For example, if the vehicle is raised for any reason, the exhaust can be inspected at the same time as the suspension and steering components.

The first step in this maintenance programme is to prepare yourself before the actual work begins. Read through all the Sections relevant to the work to be carried out, then make a list and gather all the parts and tools required. If a problem is encountered, seek advice from a parts specialist, or a dealer service department.

2 Regular maintenance

If, from the time the vehicle is new, the routine maintenance schedule is followed closely, and frequent checks are made of fluid levels and high-wear items, as suggested throughout this manual, the engine will be kept in relatively good running condition, and the need for additional work will be minimised.

It is possible that there will be times when the engine is running poorly due to the lack of regular maintenance. This is even more likely if a used vehicle, which has not received regular and frequent maintenance checks, is purchased. In such cases, additional work may need to be carried out, outside of the regular maintenance intervals.

If engine wear is suspected, a compression test (refer to Chapter 2A) will provide valuable information regarding the overall performance of the main internal components. Such a test can be used as a basis to decide on the extent of the work to be carried out. If, for example, a compression test indicates serious internal engine wear, conventional maintenance as described in this Chapter will not greatly improve the performance of the engine, and may prove a waste of time and money, unless extensive overhaul work is carried out first.

The following series of operations are those usually required to improve the performance of a generally poor-running engine:

Primary operations

a) Clean, inspect and test the battery (See Weekly checks and Section 12).
b) Check all the engine-related fluids (See Weekly checks).
c) Check the condition of the auxiliary drivebelt (Section 14).
d) Renew the spark plugs (Section 35).
e) Check the condition of the air filter, and renew if necessary (Section 32).
f) Check the fuel filter, and renew if necessary (Section 33).
g) Check the condition of all hoses, and check for fluid leaks (Section 13).

If the above operations are not fully effective, carry out the following secondary operations:

Secondary operations

All items listed under Primary operations, plus the following:

a) Check the charging system (see Part A of Chapter 5).
b) Check the ignition system (see Part B of Chapter 5).
c) Check the fuel system (see Part A of Chapter 4).

3.3 Using a filter cap removal tool – the tool locates on the cap flats

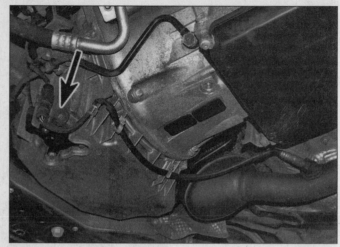

3.5 The sump drain plug is located on the left-hand side of the sump

Every 7500 miles or 12 months

3 Engine oil and filter renewal

1 Frequent oil and filter changes are the most important preventative maintenance procedures which can be undertaken by the DIY owner. As engine oil ages, it becomes diluted and contaminated, which leads to premature engine wear.

2 Before starting this procedure, gather together all the necessary tools and materials. Also make sure that you have plenty of clean rags and newspapers handy, to mop-up any spills. Ideally, the engine oil should be warm, as it will drain better, and more built-up sludge will be removed with it. Take care, however, not to touch the exhaust or any other hot parts of the engine when working under the vehicle. To avoid any possibility of scalding, and to protect yourself from possible skin irritants and other harmful contaminants in used engine oils, it is advisable to wear gloves when carrying out this work. Access to the underside of the vehicle will be greatly improved if it can be raised on a lift, driven onto ramps, or jacked up and supported on axle stands (see *Jacking and vehicle support*). Whichever method is chosen, make sure that the vehicle remains level, or if it is at an angle, so that the drain plug is at the lowest point. Where necessary, remove the undershield from under the engine.

3 Working in the engine compartment, locate the oil filter/housing at the front left-hand side of the engine on 2.0 and 2.3 litre engines, and at the left-hand side rear of the engines on 1.8 litre engines. Place a wad of rag around the housing to absorb any spilt oil, and then unscrew the oil filter cap. It is recommended that a filter removal tool is obtained **(see illustration)** as this can be used to tighten the cap to its specified torque when fitting the new filter element. **Note:** *By removing the cap, the oil will drain from the housing into the sump.*

4 The element is withdrawn with the oil filter cap, and can then be separated and discarded. On early 2.0 and 2.3 litre engines the element is left in the housing and can be removed after the filter cap is removed. Note its fitted position for refitting.

5 Working under the vehicle, unscrew the sump drain plug about half a turn **(see illustration)**. Position the draining container under the drain plug, and then remove the plug completely. If possible, try to keep the plug pressed into the sump while unscrewing it by hand the last couple of turns **(see Haynes Hint)**.

6 Recover the sealing ring from the drain plug.

7 Allow some time for the old oil to drain, noting that it may be necessary to reposition the container as the oil flow slows to a trickle. Remove the oil filler cap from the camshaft cover.

8 After all the oil has drained from the engine, wipe off the drain plug with a clean rag and renew the sealing washer. Clean the area around the drain plug opening, then refit and tighten the plug **(see illustration)**.

9 Remove the old oil and all tools from under the car, then refit the undershield and lower the car to the ground.

10 Wipe out the oil filter housing and cap using a clean rag, then locate the new sealing ring(s) supplied with the new filter **(see illustrations)**.

11 Carefully press the new element into the

HAYNES HINT

As the drain plug releases from the threads, move it away sharply so the stream of oil from the sump runs into the container, not up your sleeve.

3.8 Refitting the oil drain plug together with a new sealing washer

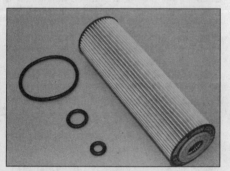

3.10a New oil filter element and seals

3.10b Fit new seals to filter cap – 1.8 litre engine

3.10c Fitting a new O-ring to the groove in the filter cap – 2.0 litre engine

3.11a Fitting the new element in the cap – 1.8 litre engine

3.11b Fitting the new element in the cap – 2.0 litre engine

3.12a Fitting the element and cap – 1.8 litre engine

3.12b Torque setting is stamped on the cap – 1.8 litre engine

cap, making sure that it is fitted correctly **(see illustrations)**.

12 Smear a little oil around the seals and screw the cap and filter in place, then tighten the cap to the specified torque **(see illustrations)**.

13 Where fitted, remove the oil level dipstick then fill the engine, using the correct grade and type of oil (see *Lubricants and fluids*). An oil can spout or funnel may help to reduce spillage. Pour in half the specified quantity of oil first, and then wait a few minutes for the oil to run down into the sump. Continue adding oil a small quantity at a time until the level is up to the lower mark on the dipstick. Finally, top-up the oil level, bringing it up to the upper mark on the dipstick. Insert the dipstick, and refit the filler cap.

14 On models with no dipstick fitted, the oil level is checked on the multifunction display panel on the instrument panel. At this stage pour in 5 litres of oil and then check the level with the display unit.

15 Start the engine and run it for a few

3.12c Fitting the element and cap – 2.0 litre engine

minutes; check for leaks around the oil filter cap and the sump drain plug. Note that there may be a delay of a few seconds before the oil pressure warning light goes out when the engine is first started, as the oil circulates through the engine oil galleries and the new oil filter, before the pressure builds-up.

16 Switch off the engine, and wait at least five minutes for the oil to settle in the sump

3.12d Tightening the oil filter cap to the specified torque

once more. With the new oil circulated and the filter completely full, recheck the level on the dipstick, and add more oil as necessary. On models with no dipstick, check the multifunction display unit on the instrument panel to check the level in the engine.

17 Dispose of the used engine oil safely, with reference to *General repair procedures* in the Reference section of this manual.

One spanner on display (Service A)

4 Coolant antifreeze/ inhibitor check

⚠️ *Warning: Wait until the engine is cold before starting this procedure. Do not allow antifreeze to* *come in contact with your skin, or with the painted surfaces of the vehicle. Rinse off spills immediately with plenty of water.*

1 A tester will be required to check the coolant strength; these can be obtained relatively cheaply from most motor accessory shops.

2 With the engine completely cold, unscrew and remove the filler cap from the coolant expansion tank. Follow the instructions supplied with the tester and check the coolant mixture is sufficient to give protection down to temperatures well below freezing. If the coolant has been renewed at the specified intervals this shouldn't be a problem. However, if the coolant mixture is not strong enough to provide sufficient protection it will

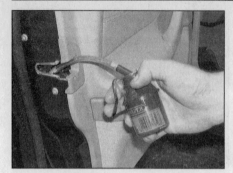

5.1 Lubricating the door locks

be necessary to drain the cooling system and renew the coolant (see Section 31).

3 Once the test is complete, check the coolant level is correct (see *Weekly checks*) then securely refit the pressure cap.

5 Lubricate hinges, locks and sunroof

1 Lubricate the hinges of the bonnet, doors and tailgate with light general-purpose oil. Similarly, lubricate all latches, locks and lock strikers **(see illustration)**. At the same time, check the security and operation of all the locks, adjusting them if necessary (see Chapter 11).

2 Lightly lubricate the bonnet release mechanism and cable with suitable grease.

3 On models with a sunroof, slide the roof fully back and clean the sunroof guide rails. Apply a smear of fresh multipurpose grease to the rails and close the sunroof.

6 Windscreen/headlight washer system check

1 Check that each of the washer jet nozzles are clear and that each nozzle provides a strong jet of washer fluid.

2 On Estate models, the tailgate jet should be aimed to spray at the centre of the screen.

3 The windscreen washer nozzles should be aimed slightly above the centre of the screen.

4 Where fitted, the headlight jet should be

8.2a Check the exhaust clamps . . .

aimed slightly above the horizontal centreline of the headlight. Mercedes technicians use a special tool to adjust the headlight jet after pulling the jet out onto its stop.

5 Especially during the winter months, make sure that the washer fluid frost concentration is sufficient.

7 Parking brake check

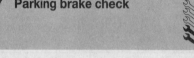

1 Chock the front wheels, then jack up the rear of the car, and support it on axle stands (see *Jacking and vehicle support*).

2 Release the parking brake fully, and select neutral.

3 Have an assistant gradually apply the parking brake, counting the number of clicks from the ratchet, while you check to see at what point the rear wheel begins to drag, and then locks. Repeat this check on the other rear wheel.

4 The rear wheels should both lock at the same point – if not, either the shoes need adjusting, or one of the rear cables is binding.

5 Both rear wheels should be fully locked within five clicks from the ratchet mechanism.

6 When the parking brake is released, both rear wheels should be free to turn. Remember that there will be some drag from the rear axle and propeller shaft, however.

7 If necessary, adjust the parking brake as described in Chapter 9. Check that the parking brake cables are free to move easily and lubricate all exposed linkages/cable pivots.

8 Exhaust system check

1 With the engine cold, check the complete exhaust system from the engine to the end of the tailpipe. The exhaust system is most easily checked with the vehicle raised on a hoist, or suitably supported on axle stands, so that the exhaust components are readily visible and accessible.

2 Check the exhaust pipes and connections for evidence of leaks, severe corrosion and damage. Make sure that all brackets and

8.2b . . . and the rubber mountings

mountings are in good condition, and that all relevant nuts and bolts are tight **(see illustrations)**. Leakage at any of the joints or in other parts of the system will usually show up as a black sooty stain in the vicinity of the leak.

3 Rattles and other noises can often be traced to the exhaust system, especially the brackets and mountings. Try to move the pipes and silencers. If the components are able to come into contact with the body or suspension parts, secure the system with new mountings. Otherwise separate the joints (if possible) and twist the pipes as necessary to provide additional clearance.

9 Road test

Instruments and electrical equipment

1 Check the operation of all instruments and electrical equipment.

2 Make sure that all instruments read correctly, and switch on all electrical equipment in turn, to check that it functions properly.

Steering and suspension

3 Check for any abnormalities in the steering, suspension, handling or road 'feel'.

4 Drive the vehicle, and check that there are no unusual vibrations or noises.

5 Check that the steering feels positive, with no excessive 'sloppiness', or roughness, and check for any suspension noises when cornering and driving over bumps.

Drivetrain

6 Check the performance of the engine, clutch (where applicable), gearbox/transmission, propeller shaft and driveshafts.

7 Listen for any unusual noises from the engine, clutch and gearbox/transmission.

8 Make sure that the engine runs smoothly when idling, and that there is no hesitation when accelerating.

9 Check that, where applicable, the clutch action is smooth and progressive, that the drive is taken up smoothly, and that the pedal travel is not excessive. Also listen for any noises when the clutch pedal is depressed.

10 On manual gearbox models, check that all gears can be engaged smoothly without noise, and that the gear lever action is smooth and not abnormally vague or 'notchy'.

11 On automatic transmission models, make sure that all gearchanges occur smoothly, without snatching, and without an increase in engine speed between changes. Check that all the gear positions can be selected with the vehicle at rest. If any problems are found, they should be referred to a Mercedes-Benz dealer.

Braking system

12 Make sure that the vehicle does not pull

to one side when braking, and that the wheels do not lock when braking hard.

13 Check that there is no vibration through the steering when braking.

14 Check that the parking brake operates correctly without excessive movement of the foot pedal, and that it holds the vehicle stationary on a slope.

15 Test the operation of the brake servo unit as follows. With the engine off, depress the footbrake four or five times to exhaust the vacuum. Hold the brake pedal depressed, and then start the engine. As the engine starts, there should be a noticeable 'give' in the brake pedal as vacuum builds-up. Allow the engine to run for at least two minutes, and then switch it off. If the brake pedal is depressed now, it should be possible to detect a hiss from the servo as the pedal is depressed. After about four or five applications, no further hissing should be heard, and the pedal should feel considerably harder.

10 Service indicator resetting

Mercedes C-Class models are equipped with a Service Indicator System (ASSYST). Approximately one month before a service is due; a spanner will appear on the indicator display together with the remaining distance or time. If the service is not performed on time, the display will flash, letting you know how many days (or km/miles) that the service has been exceeded by. An audible signal also can be heard if the service date has been exceeded.

After carrying out a service, the Mercedes-Benz dealership will reset the Service Indicator. To reset the system yourself, carry out the following.

1 Insert the ignition key and turn it to position 2.

2 By pressing the lower buttons on the left-hand side of the steering wheel, call up the trip meter and total distance on the display in the instrument panel.

3 Press the upper (arrowed) buttons on the left-hand side of the steering wheel, until the service indicator appears on the display.

4 Press and hold the reset button on the left-hand side of the instrument panel for approximately 4 seconds.

5 The display unit in the instrument panel will show *DO YOU WANT TO RESET SERVICE INTERVAL? CONFIRM BY USING RESET BUTTON.*

6 Press and hold the reset button again until an audible signal is heard, the service indicator has now been reset.

7 The distance until the next service will appear on the display.

Two spanners on display (Service B)

11 Power steering fluid level check

1 Park the vehicle on level ground and set the steering wheel straight-ahead. The engine should be turned off; for the check to be accurate, the steering must not be turned once the engine has been stopped.

Caution: The need for frequent topping-up indicates a leak, which should be investigated immediately.

2 The power steering fluid reservoir is located at the front right-hand side of the engine on 1.8 litre petrol models and at the front left-hand side of the engine on all other models **(see illustration)**.

3 A dipstick is incorporated in the filler cap. Wipe clean the top of the fluid reservoir, then unscrew and remove the reservoir cap and dipstick.

4 Wipe the dipstick clean, then screw the reservoir cap fully back into position. Unscrew the cap once more, remove the dipstick and check the fluid level, which should be between the MAX and MIN marks. **Note:** *There are two sets of marks – 20° marks are for checking the fluid when cold, and the 80° marks for fluid at operating temperature (see illustration).*

5 Top-up the fluid level to the MAX mark, using the specified type of fluid (do not overfill the reservoir), then refit and tighten the filler cap.

12 Battery check

1 The battery is located in the left-hand (as seen from the driver's seat) rear corner of the engine compartment **(see illustration)**.

Remove the pollen filter as described in Section 16.

2 Check that both battery terminals are securely attached and are free from corrosion **(see illustration). Note:** *Before disconnecting the terminals from the battery, refer to 'Disconnecting the battery' in the Reference Chapter at the end of this manual. Always remove keys before disconnecting battery – otherwise electronic components may be damaged.*

3 Check the battery casing for signs of damage or cracking and check the battery retaining-clamp is secure **(see illustration)**. If the battery casing is damaged in any way the battery must be renewed (see Chapter 5A).

4 If the vehicle is not fitted with a sealed-for-life maintenance-free battery, check the electrolyte level is between the MAX and MIN level markings on the battery casing. If topping-up is necessary, remove the battery (see Chapter 5A) from the vehicle then remove

11.2 Power steering fluid reservoir – 1.8 litre engine

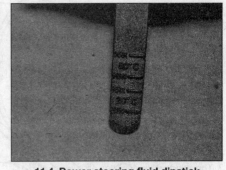

11.4 Power steering fluid dipstick markings

12.1 Battery Location

12.2 Check that the battery terminals are secure

12.3 Battery clamp retaining bolt

the cell caps/cover (as applicable). Using distilled water, top the electrolyte level of each cell up to the MAX level mark then securely refit the cell caps/cover. Ensure the battery has not been overfilled then refit the battery to the vehicle (see Chapter 5A).
5 On completion of the check, refit the pollen filter securely back into position.

13 Hose and fluid leak check

1 Visually inspect the engine joint faces, gaskets and seals for any signs of water or oil leaks. Pay particular attention to the areas around the camshaft cover, cylinder head, oil filter and sump joint faces. Bear in mind

A leak in the cooling system will usually show up as white- or antifreeze-coloured deposits on the area adjoining the leak.

that, over a period of time, some very slight seepage from these areas is to be expected – what you are really looking for is any indication of a serious leak. Should a leak be found, renew the offending gasket or oil seal by referring to the appropriate Chapters in this manual.
2 Also check the security and condition of all the engine-related pipes and hoses. Ensure that all cable-ties or securing clips are in place and in good condition. Clips that are broken or missing can lead to chafing of the hoses, pipes or wiring, which could cause more serious problems in the future.
3 Carefully check the radiator hoses and heater hoses along their entire length. Renew any hose,

which is cracked, swollen or deteriorated. Cracks will show up better if the hose is squeezed. Pay close attention to the hose clips that secure the hoses to the cooling system components. Hose clips can pinch and puncture hoses, resulting in cooling system leaks.
4 Inspect all the cooling system components (hoses, joint faces, etc) for leaks. A leak in the cooling system will usually show up as white- or antifreeze-coloured deposits on the area adjoining the leak **(see Haynes Hint)**. Where any problems of this nature are found on system components, renew the component or gasket with reference to Chapter 3.
5 Where applicable, inspect the automatic transmission fluid cooler hoses for leaks or deterioration.
6 With the vehicle raised, inspect the fuel tank and filler neck for punctures, cracks and other damage. The connection between the filler neck and tank is especially critical. Sometimes a rubber filler neck or connecting hose will leak due to loose retaining clamps or deteriorated rubber.
7 Carefully check all rubber hoses and metal fuel lines leading away from the petrol tank. Check for loose connections, deteriorated hoses, crimped lines, and other damage. Pay particular attention to the vent pipes and hoses, which often loop up around the filler neck and can become blocked or crimped. Follow the lines to the front of the vehicle, carefully inspecting them all the way. Renew damaged sections as necessary.
8 Closely inspect the metal brake pipes, which run along the vehicle under body. If they show signs of excessive corrosion or damage they must be renewed.
9 From within the engine compartment, check the security of all fuel hose attachments and pipe unions, and inspect the fuel hoses and vacuum hoses for kinks, chafing and deterioration.
10 Check the condition of the power steering fluid hoses and pipes.

14 Auxiliary drivebelt check and renewal

Drivebelt checking

1 Due to its function and construction, the auxiliary drivebelt is prone to failure after a period of time, and should be inspected periodically to prevent problems.
2 There are two lengths of drivebelt fitted, one for models with air conditioning and a shorter version for models without **(see illustration)**. The drivebelt is of multi-rib type and drives the alternator, power steering pump, coolant pump and, where fitted, the air conditioning compressor and air intake compressor. The belt is automatically tensioned by an idler pulley, which incorporates a damper to cushion engine pulses.
3 If desired to improve access for belt

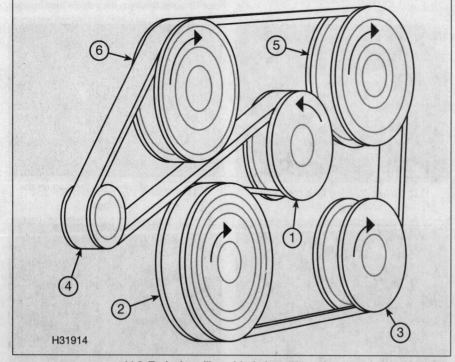

H31914

14.2 Typical auxiliary drivebelt configuration

1 *Tensioner pulley*
2 *Crankshaft pulley*
3 *Air conditioning compressor*
4 *Alternator*
5 *Power steering pump pulley*
6 *Coolant pump pulley*

inspection, remove the engine covers from the top of the engine and cooling fan cowl as described in Chapter 3.

4 With the engine stopped, check the drivebelt for cracks and separation of the belt plies. Also check for fraying and glazing, which gives the belt a shiny appearance. Both sides of the belts should be inspected, which means the belt will have to be twisted to check the underside. Turn the engine using a socket on the crankshaft pulley bolt so that the whole of the belt can be inspected.

5 Where removed, refit the engine covers and cooling fan cowl.

Drivebelt renewal

6 To improve access, remove the engine covers from the top of the engine and the cooling fan cowling.

7 Where applicable, unclip and remove the air intake hose from across the front of the engine (see illustration).

8 On Kompressor models, release the retaining clips and remove the charge air hoses from the wide band silencer in the charge air system across the front of the engine. Undo the retaining bolts and remove the wide band silencer from the engine compartment (see illustrations).

9 On 2.0 and 2.3 litre engines, engage a spanner or socket with the nut in the centre of the tensioner pulley, then lever the tensioner anti-clockwise to relieve the tension in the belt (see illustration).

10 On 1.8 litre engines, engage a Torx T60 bit/socket with the tensioner body; below the pulley, and then lever the tensioner anti-

14.7 Remove the air ducting

14.8b . . . remove the upper hose . . .

clockwise to relieve the tension in the belt (see illustrations).

11 Hold the tensioner in position with the spanner/socket, and slide the belt from the pulleys. If necessary, the tensioner can be retained in its released position by inserting a

14.8a Undo the retaining clips (arrowed) . . .

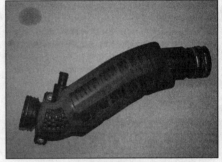

14.8c . . . and unbolt the charge air silencer

suitable bolt or metal dowel through the holes provided (see illustration).

12 Fit the new belt around the pulleys, starting with the crankshaft pulley. Check that the belt is correctly seated on all the pulleys (see illustration). Where applicable,

14.9 Removing the auxiliary drivebelt

14.10a Use a Torx bit . . .

14.10b . . . to slacken the tension on the belt

14.10c Position of Torx recess for adjuster

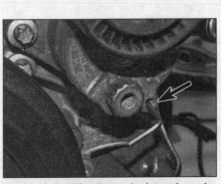

14.11 Using Allen key to lock tensioner in position

14.12 Fitting the belt around the power steering pulley

16.4a Release the three securing clips . . .

16.4b . . . then unclip the washer pipe from the side of the housing

16.5 Removing the pollen filter element

remove the metal dowel/bolt from the tensioner.

13 Release the spanner/socket, and allow the tensioner to move into position against the belt.

14 Where removed, refit the viscous cooling fan and cowl as described in Chapter 3.

15 Headlight beam adjustment check

Accurate adjustment of the headlight beam is only possible using optical beam-setting equipment, and a Mercedes-Benz dealer or service station should therefore carry out this work with the necessary facilities.

Details of the headlight adjuster system are given in Chapter 12, Section 12.

16 Pollen filter renewal

1 The air entering the vehicle's ventilation system is passed through a very fine pleated-paper air filter element, which removes particles of pollen, dust and other airborne foreign matter. To ensure its continued effectiveness, this filter's element must be renewed at regular intervals. Failure to renew the element will also result in greatly reduced

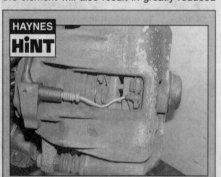

HAYNES HINT

For a quick check, the thickness of the friction material of the brake pad can be measured through the aperture in the caliper body.

airflow into the passenger compartment, reducing demisting and ventilation capability.

2 The filter housing is located in the left-hand (as seen from the driver's seat) rear corner of the engine compartment, above the battery.

3 Open the bonnet and clean around the air filter housing to prevent dirt ingress.

4 Release the three retaining clips at the rear of the filter housing and remove the cover from the housing **(see illustrations)**. Unclip the windscreen washer pipe from the side of the filter housing.

5 Withdraw the pollen filter element from its location in the filter housing; noting which way round it is fitted **(see illustration)**.

6 Fit the new filter into position in the filter housing, noting any direction-of-fitting markings, which may be present. Refit the cover to the housing and secure with the retaining clips.

17 Front brake pad check

1 Firmly apply the parking brake, and then jack up the front of the car and support it securely on axle stands (see *Jacking and vehicle support*). Remove the front roadwheels **(see Haynes Hint)**.

2 For a comprehensive check, the brake pads should be removed and cleaned. The operation of the caliper can then also be checked, and the condition of the brake disc itself can be fully examined on both sides. Refer to Chapter 9 for further information.

3 If any pad's friction material is worn to the specified thickness or less; *all four pads must be renewed as a set.*

18 Front brake disc check

Refer to Chapter 9, Section 6.

19 Rear brake pad check

1 Chock the front wheels, then jack up the

rear of the car and support it securely on axle stands (see *Jacking and vehicle support*). Remove the rear road wheels.

2 As with the front brake pads, the thickness of pad linings can be checked quickly through the aperture at the rear of the caliper.

3 For a comprehensive check, the brake pads should be removed and cleaned. The operation of the caliper can then also be checked, and the condition of the brake disc itself can be fully examined on both sides. Refer to Chapter 9 for further information.

4 If any pad's friction material is worn to the specified thickness or less; *all four pads must be renewed as a set.*

20 Rear brake disc check

Refer to Chapter 9, Section 7.

21 Steering and suspension check

Front suspension and steering

1 Raise the front of the vehicle, and securely support it on axle stands (see *Jacking and vehicle support*).

2 Visually inspect the balljoint dust covers and the steering linkage gaiters for splits, chafing or deterioration. Any wear of these components will cause loss of lubricant, together with dirt and water entry, resulting in rapid deterioration of the balljoints. Also check that the steering box mountings are tightened to the specified torque settings (see Chapter 10).

3 Check the power steering fluid hoses for chafing or deterioration, and the pipe and hose unions for fluid leaks. Also check for signs of fluid leakage under pressure from the steering box, which would indicate failed fluid seals within the steering box.

4 Grasp the roadwheel at the 12 o'clock and 6 o'clock positions, and try to rock it **(see illustration)**. Very slight free play may be felt, but if the movement is appreciable, further investigation is necessary to determine the source. Continue rocking the wheel while

21.4 Check for wear in the hub bearings by grasping the wheel and trying to rock it

22.1a Check the driveshaft inner CV joints . . .

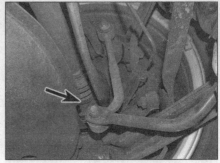

22.1b . . . and outer CV joints

an assistant depresses the footbrake. If the movement is now eliminated or significantly reduced, it is likely that the hub bearings are at fault. If the free play is still evident with the footbrake depressed, then there is wear in the suspension joints or mountings. Note that the front hub bearings are adjustable (See Chapter 10).

5 Now grasp the wheel at the 9 o'clock and 3 o'clock positions, and try to rock it as before. Any movement felt now may again be caused by wear in the hub bearings or the steering track rod balljoints. If the inner or outer balljoint is worn, the visual movement will be obvious.

6 Using a large screwdriver or flat bar, check for wear in the suspension mounting bushes by levering between the relevant suspension component and its attachment point. Some movement is to be expected as the mountings are made of rubber, but excessive wear should be obvious. Also check the condition of any visible rubber bushes, looking for splits, cracks or contamination of the rubber.

7 With the car standing on its wheels, have an assistant turn the steering wheel back-and-forth about an eighth of a turn each way. There should be very little lost movement between the steering wheel and roadwheels. If this is not the case, closely observe the linkage joints and mountings previously described, but in addition, check the steering column universal joint/coupling for wear, and the steering box itself.

Shock absorbers

8 Check for any signs of fluid leakage around the shock absorber body, or from the rubber gaiter around the piston rod. Should any fluid be noticed, the shock absorber is defective internally, and should be renewed. **Note:** *Shock absorbers should always be renewed in pairs on the same axle.*

9 The efficiency of the shock absorber may be checked by bouncing the vehicle at each corner. Generally speaking, the body will return to its normal position and stop after being depressed. If it rises and returns on a rebound, the shock absorber is probably suspect. Examine also the shock absorber upper and lower mountings for any signs of wear.

22 Driveshaft gaiter check

1 With the vehicle raised and securely supported on stands, slowly rotate the rear roadwheel. Inspect the condition of the outer constant velocity (CV) joint rubber gaiters, squeezing the gaiters to open out the folds. Check for signs of cracking, splits or deterioration of the rubber, which may allow the grease to escape, and lead to water and grit entry into the joint. Also check the security and condition of the retaining clips. Repeat these checks on the inner CV joints **(see illustrations)**. If any damage or deterioration is found, the gaiters should be renewed (see Chapter 8).

2 At the same time, check the general condition of the CV joints themselves by first holding the driveshaft and attempting to rotate the wheel. Repeat this check by holding the inner joint and attempting to rotate the driveshaft. Any appreciable movement indicates wear in the joints, wear in the driveshaft splines, or a loose driveshaft retaining nut.

23 Seat belt check

1 Carefully examine the seat belt webbing for cuts or any signs of serious fraying or deterioration. If the seat belt is of the retractable type, pull the belt all the way out from its reel, and examine the full extent of the webbing.

2 Fasten and unfasten the belt, ensuring that the locking mechanism holds securely and releases properly when intended. If the belt is of the retractable type, check also that the retracting mechanism operates correctly when the belt is released.

3 Check the security of all seat belt mountings and attachments which are accessible, without removing any trim or other components, from inside the vehicle.

24 Windscreen wiper blade renewal

Mercedes-Benz recommend that the windscreen wiper blades should be renewed at this interval, regardless of their apparent condition. Refer to *Weekly checks* for details.

Every 2 years

25 Automatic transmission fluid level check

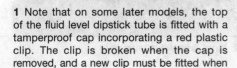

1 Note that on some later models, the top of the fluid level dipstick tube is fitted with a tamperproof cap incorporating a red plastic clip. The clip is broken when the cap is removed, and a new clip must be fitted when the cap is refitted. The dipstick is **not** fitted inside the tube, but must be obtained as a separate tool (number 140 589 15 21 00) from a Mercedes-Benz dealer. The alternative is to take the vehicle to a dealer for the fluid level check.

2 In order to check the automatic transmission fluid level, the transmission must be at operating temperature (fluid temperature 80°C). Operating temperature is reached after driving for approximately 10 miles. **Do not** attempt to check the fluid level on a cold transmission.

3 With the transmission at operating temperature, ensure that the vehicle is parked on level ground.

4 With the engine running at idle speed, ensure that the transmission selector lever is in position P, and apply the parking brake.

5 Where applicable, pull out the locking pin securing the dipstick in its tube.

25.6a Pull out the automatic transmission fluid level dipstick . . .

25.6b . . . and wipe with a clean cloth

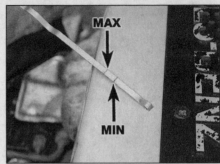

25.7 The fluid level should be between the MIN and MAX marks

25.8 Topping-up the automatic transmission hydraulic fluid

6 Remove the fluid level dipstick and wipe it with a lint-free cloth, then re-insert it **(see illustrations)**.

7 Pull out the dipstick once more, and read off the fluid level. The level should be between the MIN and MAX marks **(see illustration)**.

8 If topping-up is necessary, top-up through the filler tube **(see illustration)**, using fluid of the specified type (see *Lubricants and fluids*). **Do not** overfill the transmission – the fluid level must not be above the MAX mark.

9 On completion, refit the dipstick or filler tube cap (as applicable). Fit a new tamperproof clip where necessary **(see illustration)**.

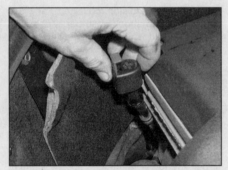

25.9 Fit the filler tube cap, then depress the tamperproof clip

26 Manual transmission fluid level check

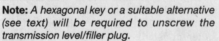

Note: *A hexagonal key or a suitable alternative (see text) will be required to unscrew the transmission level/filler plug.*

1 Jack up the front and rear of the vehicle and support it on axle stands (see *Jacking and vehicle support*); ensure the vehicle is level.

2 Place a suitable container beneath the transmission level/filler plug, located on

the right-hand side of the transmission. A hexagonal key should be used to unscrew the plug, but a tool can be improvised using a long nut, or a length of hexagonal bar and a spanner **(see illustration)**.

3 The fluid level should just be up to the bottom of the level/filler plug hole.

4 If necessary, top-up the level until fluid just begins to run out of the level/filler plug hole (see *Lubricants and fluids*).

5 When the level is correct, refit the plug, and tighten securely.

27 Final drive unit oil level check

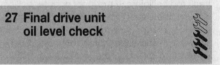

1 Either position the vehicle over an inspection pit, or jack up the front and rear of the vehicle and support it on axle stands (see *Jacking and vehicle support*). The vehicle must be level for the check to be accurate.

2 Clean the area around the filler/level plug on the left-hand side of the final drive unit **(see illustration)**, then slacken and remove the plug from the housing (refer to Chapter 8, Section 2).

3 The oil level should be up to the lower edge of the filler/level plug aperture.

26.2 Using a long nut and a spanner to unscrew the transmission fluid level/filler plug

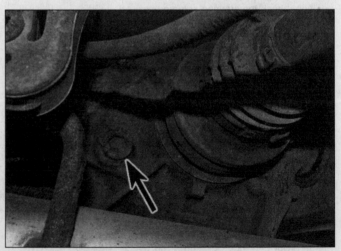

27.2 Final drive filler/level plug

4 If necessary, top-up using the specified type of lubricant until the oil level is correct (see *Lubricants and fluids*). Fill the final drive until oil starts to flow out and allow excess oil to drain out.

5 Once the final drive unit oil level is correct, refit the filler/level plug and tighten it securely. Lower the vehicle to the ground.

6 Note that frequent need for topping-up indicates a leakage, possibly through an oil seal. The cause should be investigated and rectified.

28 Brake fluid renewal

⚠️ **Warning: Brake hydraulic fluid can harm your eyes and damage painted surfaces, so use extreme caution when handling and pouring it. Do not use fluid that has been standing open for some time, as it absorbs moisture from the air. Excess moisture can cause a dangerous loss of braking effectiveness.**

1 The procedure is similar to that for the bleeding of the hydraulic system as described in Chapter 9, except that the brake fluid reservoir should be emptied by syphoning, using a clean poultry baster or similar before starting, and allowance should be made for the old fluid to be expelled when bleeding a section of the circuit.

2 Working as described in Chapter 9, open the first bleed screw in the sequence, and pump the brake pedal gently until nearly all the old fluid has been emptied from the master cylinder reservoir.

3 Top-up to the MAX level with new fluid, and continue pumping until only the new fluid remains in the reservoir, and new fluid can be seen emerging from the bleed screw. Tighten the screw, and top the reservoir level up to the MAX level line.

4 Work through all the remaining bleed screws in the sequence until new fluid can be seen at all of them. Be careful to keep the master cylinder reservoir topped-up to above the MIN level at all times, or air may enter the system and greatly increase the length of the task.

5 When the operation is complete, check that all bleed screws are securely tightened, and that their dust caps are refitted. Wash off all traces of spilt fluid, and recheck the master cylinder reservoir fluid level.

6 Check the operation of the brakes before taking the car on the road.

29 Underbody check

Note: *This check should be carried out by a Mercedes-Benz dealer in order to validate the vehicle corrosion warranty.*

1 With the vehicle raised and securely supported, carry out a thorough check of the vehicle underbody sealant for signs of damage. If any area of the underbody sealant shows visible damage, the affected area should be repaired to prevent possible problems with corrosion occurring at a later date.

2 Thoroughly check the underbody for signs of corrosion.

3 Lower the car to the ground.

Every 2 years or 30 000 miles

30 Evaporative emission control charcoal canister renewal

1 Refer to Chapter 4C, Section 2.

Every 3 years

31 Coolant renewal

⚠️ **Warning: Wait until the engine is cold before starting this procedure. Do not allow antifreeze to come in contact with your skin, or with the painted surfaces of the vehicle. Rinse off spills immediately with plenty of water. Never leave antifreeze lying around in an open container, or in a puddle in the driveway or on the garage floor. Children and pets are attracted by its sweet smell, but antifreeze can be fatal if ingested.**

Cooling system draining

1 After allowing the engine to cool completely, cover the pressure cap with a wad of rag, and slowly turn the cap anti-clockwise to relieve the pressure in the cooling system (a hissing sound will normally be heard). Wait until any pressure remaining in the system is released, then continue to turn the cap until it can be removed **(see illustration)**.

2 Position a suitable container beneath the radiator, and then slacken the drain plug on the bottom left-hand corner of the radiator. Allow the coolant to drain into the container **(see illustration)**.

3 Reposition the container so that it lies beneath the engine block drain plug, which is located on the side of the cylinder block **(see illustration)**. (Certain engines are fitted with a drain plug with an integral nozzle, to which a length of rubber hose can be connected.) Open the drain plug by turning it with an open-ended spanner and allow the coolant to drain into the container.

31.1 Removing the pressure cap from the coolant expansion tank

31.2 Unscrew the radiator drain plug from below

31.3 Cylinder block drain plug

4 Once all the coolant has drained, remove the drain hoses and close the cylinder block and radiator drain plugs.

Cooling system flushing

5 If coolant renewal has been neglected, or if the antifreeze mixture has become diluted, then in time the cooling system may gradually lose efficiency as the coolant passages become restricted due to rust, scale deposits, and other sediment. Flushing the system clean can restore the cooling system efficiency.
6 The radiator should be flushed independently of the engine, to avoid unnecessary contamination.

Radiator flushing

7 To flush the radiator disconnect the top and bottom hoses and any other relevant hoses from the radiator, with reference to Chapter 3.
8 Insert a garden hose into the radiator top inlet. Direct a flow of clean water through the radiator, and continue flushing until clean water emerges from the radiator bottom outlet.
9 If after a reasonable period, the water still does not run clear, the radiator can be flushed with a good proprietary cooling system cleaning agent. It is important that the manufacturer's instructions are followed carefully. If the contamination is particularly bad, insert the hose in the radiator bottom outlet, and reverse-flush the radiator.

Engine flushing

10 To flush the engine, remove the thermostat as described in Chapter 3, and then temporarily refit the thermostat cover. Adjust the heater control to the maximum setting.
11 With the top and bottom hoses disconnected from the radiator, insert a garden hose into the radiator top hose. Direct a clean flow of water through the engine, and continue flushing until clean water emerges from the radiator bottom hose.
12 On completion of flushing, refit the thermostat and reconnect the hoses with reference to Chapter 3.

Cooling system refilling

13 Before attempting to fill the cooling system, make sure that all hoses and clips are in good condition, and that the clips are tight. Note that an antifreeze mixture must be used all year round, to prevent corrosion of the engine components (see following sub-Section).
14 Remove the pressure cap, and fill the system by slowly pouring the coolant into the expansion tank (or radiator header tank) to prevent airlocks from forming.
15 If the coolant is being renewed, begin by pouring in a couple of litres of water, followed by the correct quantity of antifreeze, then top-up with more water.
16 Once the level in the expansion tank/ header tank starts to rise, squeeze the radiator top and bottom hoses to help expel any trapped air in the system. Once all the air is expelled, top-up the coolant level to the MAX mark. Refit the pressure cap securely.
17 Start the engine and run it until the thermostat opens – the radiator top hose will begin to heat up as coolant flows through it to the top of the radiator.
18 Check for leaks, particularly around disturbed components. Check the coolant level in the expansion tank/header tank, and top-up if necessary. Note that the system must be cold before an accurate level is indicated. If the pressure cap is removed while the engine is still warm, cover the cap with a thick cloth, and unscrew the cap slowly to gradually relieve the system pressure (a hissing sound will normally be heard). Wait until any pressure remaining in the system is released, then continue to turn the cap until it can be removed.

Antifreeze mixture

19 The antifreeze should always be renewed at the specified intervals. This is necessary not only to maintain the antifreeze properties, but also to prevent corrosion, which would otherwise occur as the corrosion inhibitors become progressively less effective.
20 Always use an ethylene glycol based antifreeze, which is suitable for use in mixed-metal cooling systems. The quantity of antifreeze and levels of protection are indicated in the *Specifications*.
21 Before adding antifreeze, the cooling system should be completely drained, preferably flushed, and all hoses checked for condition and security.
22 After filling with antifreeze, a label should be attached to the expansion tank or header tank, stating the type and concentration of antifreeze used, and the date installed. Any subsequent topping-up should be made with the same type and concentration of antifreeze.
Caution: Do not use engine antifreeze in the windscreen/tailgate washer system, as it will cause damage to the vehicle paintwork. A screen wash additive should be added to the washer system in the quantities stated on the bottle.

Every 4 years or 50 000 miles

32 Air filter element renewal

1 Undo the retaining screws from around the top of the air cleaner cover **(see illustration)**.
2 Lift the cover from the air cleaner, and then withdraw the element, noting how it is fitted **(see illustration)**.

3 Wipe clean the interior surfaces of the cover and main body, using a dampened cloth.
4 Locate the new element in the main body, making sure it is seated correctly, then refit the cover and secure with the retaining screws.

**32.1 Undo the retaining screws –
1.8 litre engine**

**32.2 Removing the air filter element –
1.8 litre engine**

33 Fuel filter renewal

Refer to the information in Chapter 4A, Section 3.

Every 50 000 miles

34 Propeller shaft rubber coupling condition check

1 Chock the front wheels, then jack up the rear of the vehicle and support it on axle stands.

2 Carefully check the propeller shaft front and rear rubber couplings for signs of damage and deterioration (see illustrations). Look for deterioration in the form of splitting, cracking or perishing. Damage may also be caused by oil or grease contamination. Rotate one of the rear wheels to check all around the rubber couplings.

3 To check the centre rubber coupling, undo the retaining nuts and remove the heat shield(s) from above the exhaust system (see illustration).

4 If any of the couplings require renewal, refer to Chapter 8 for a description of the renewal procedure.

34.2a Check the front rubber coupling . . .

34.2b . . . and rear rubber coupling

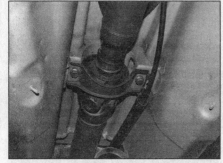

34.3 Remove heat shield to access the centre coupling

Every 4 years or 55 000 to 65 000 miles

35 Spark plug renewal

1 The correct functioning of the spark plugs is vital for the correct running and efficiency of the engine. It is essential that the plugs fitted are appropriate for the engine (a suitable type is specified at the beginning of this Chapter). If this type is used and the engine is in good condition, the spark plugs should not need attention between scheduled renewal intervals. Spark plug cleaning is rarely necessary, and should not be attempted unless specialised equipment is available, as damage can easily be caused to the firing ends.

2 Open the bonnet and unclip the cover (where applicable) from the top of the engine (see illustration).

3 On 2.0 and 2.3 litre engines, undo the three retaining screws and remove the cover from the centre of the cylinder head cover.

4 Note the routing of the wiring to the ignition coils and disconnect the connectors from the ignition coils (see illustration).

5 Undo the retaining screws and withdraw the coils from the top of the spark plugs (see illustrations).

6 Unscrew the plugs using a spark plug

35.2 Remove the engine cover

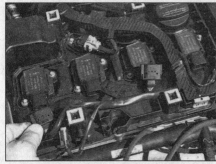

35.4 Disconnect the wiring connectors

35.5a Remove the retaining bolts . . .

35.5b . . . and withdraw the ignition coil

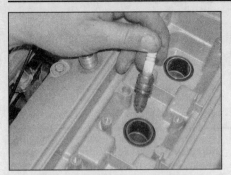

35.6 Removing the spark plugs

35.11 Measuring the spark plug electrode gap, using a feeler blade

35.12 Set the spark plug gap by carefully bending the electrode, using an adjusting tool

spanner, suitable box spanner or a deep socket and extension bar **(see illustration)**. Keep the socket aligned with the spark plug – if it is forcibly moved to one side, the ceramic insulator may be broken off. As each plug is removed, examine it as follows.

7 Examination of the spark plugs will give a good indication of the condition of the engine. If the insulator nose of the spark plug is clean and white, with no deposits, this is indicative of a weak mixture or too hot a plug (a hot plug transfers heat away from the electrode slowly, a cold plug transfers heat away quickly).

8 If the tip and insulator nose are covered with hard black-looking deposits, then this is indicative that the mixture is too rich. Should the plug be black and oily, and then it is likely that the engine is fairly worn, as well as the mixture being too rich.

9 If the insulator nose is covered with light tan to greyish-brown deposits, then the mixture is correct and it is likely that the engine is in good condition.

10 The spark plug electrode gap is of considerable importance as, if it is too large or too small, the size of the spark and its efficiency will be seriously impaired. The gap should be set to the value given in the *Specifications* at the beginning of this Chapter. **Note:** *The electrode gap on multi-electrode spark plugs cannot be adjusted.*

11 To set the gap, measure it with a feeler blade and then bend open, or closed, the outer plug electrode until the correct gap is achieved. The centre electrode should never be bent, as this may crack the insulator and cause plug failure, if nothing worse. If using feeler blades, the gap is correct when the appropriate-size blade is a firm sliding fit **(see illustration)**.

12 Special spark plug electrode gap adjusting tools are available from most motor accessory shops, or from some spark plug manufacturers **(see illustration)**.

13 Before fitting the spark plugs **(see Haynes Hint)**, check that the threaded connector sleeves are tight, and that the plug exterior surfaces and threads are clean.

14 Tighten the plug to the specified torque using the spark plug socket and a torque wrench. Refit the remaining spark plugs in the same manner.

15 The remaining procedure is a reversal of removal.

HAYNES HiNT

It is very often difficult to insert spark plugs into their holes without cross-threading them. To avoid this possibility, fit a short length of 5/16 inch internal diameter rubber hose (arrowed) over the end of the spark plug. The flexible hose acts as a universal joint to help align the plug with the plug hole. Should the plug begin to cross-thread, the hose will slip on the spark plug, preventing thread damage to the cylinder head.

Chapter 1 Part B:
Routine maintenance & servicing – diesel models

Contents

Degrees of difficulty

Easy, suitable for novice with little experience 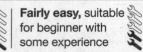	**Fairly easy,** suitable for beginner with some experience 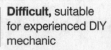	**Fairly difficult,** suitable for competent DIY mechanic 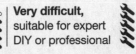	**Difficult,** suitable for experienced DIY mechanic	**Very difficult,** suitable for expert DIY or professional

Lubricants and fluids

Refer to *Weekly checks* on page 0•16

Capacities

Engine oil

All engines . . . . 6.5 litres

Cooling system

All models. . . . . 8.6 litres

Transmission

Manual transmission*:

   Up to transmission code 716.639 . . . . 1.2 litres

   From transmission code 716.640. . . . . 1.5 litres

Automatic transmission . . . . 7.5 litres

* See Chapter 7A for transmission codes

Final drive unit

All models. . . . . 1.1 litres

Power-assisted steering

All models (approximate) . . . . 1.0 litre

Fuel tank

All models:

   Total . . . . 62.0 litres

   Reserve. . . . . 8.0 litres

Windscreen washer reservoir

Models with windscreen washer only . . . . 3.0 litres

Models with heated reservoir and headlamp cleaning system . . . . 6.0 litres

Cooling system

Antifreeze mixture:

   50% antifreeze . . . . Protection down to –37°C

   55% antifreeze . . . . Protection down to –45°C

Note: *Refer to antifreeze manufacturer for latest recommendations.*

Brakes

Brake pad friction material minimum thickness. . . . . 2.0 mm

Torque wrench settings

	Nm	lbf ft
Cylinder head trim panel cover	10	7
Coolant drain plug in crankcase.	30	22
Engine oil drain plug (M14).	30	22
Glow plug	19	14
Oil filter cap	25	18
Roadwheel bolts.	110	81

The maintenance intervals in this manual are provided with the assumption that you, not the dealer, will be carrying out the work. These are the minimum maintenance intervals recommended by us for vehicles driven daily. If you wish to keep your vehicle in peak condition at all times, you may wish to perform some of these procedures more often. We encourage frequent maintenance, because it enhances the efficiency, performance and resale value of your vehicle.

If the vehicle is driven in dusty areas, used to tow a trailer, or driven frequently at slow speeds (idling in traffic) or mainly for short journeys, shorter maintenance intervals are recommended.

When the vehicle is new, it should be serviced by a dealer service department (or other workshop recognised by the vehicle manufacturer as providing the same standard of service) in order to preserve the warranty. The vehicle manufacturer may reject warranty claims if you are unable to prove that servicing has been carried out as and when specified, using only original equipment parts or parts certified to be of equivalent quality.

Every 250 miles or weekly

☐ Refer to *Weekly checks*

Every 7500 miles or 12 months, whichever comes first

☐ Renew the engine oil and filter (Section 3)

Note: *Frequent oil and filter changes are good for the engine. We recommend changing the oil at least once a year.*

One spanner on display (Service A)

In addition to the items listed above, carry out the following:

☐ Check coolant antifreeze/inhibitor (Section 4)
☐ Lubricate all hinges, locks and sunroof (Section 5)
☐ Check the operation of the windscreen/headlight washer system(s) (as applicable) (Section 6)
☐ Check the operation of the parking brake* (Section 7)
☐ Check the exhaust system and mountings* (Section 8)
☐ Carry out a road test (Section 9)
☐ Reset the service indicator (Section 10)

* Note: *These tasks are not specified by Mercedes as routine maintenance items.*

Two spanners on display (Service B)

In addition to the items listed above, carry out the following:

☐ Check the power steering fluid level (Section 11)
☐ Check the battery condition, security and electrolyte level (Section 12)
☐ Check all underbonnet components and hoses for fluid leaks (Section 13)
☐ Check the auxiliary drivebelt (Section 14)
☐ Check the headlight beam adjustment (Section 15)
☐ Renew the pollen filter (Section 16)
☐ Check front brake pads for wear (Section 17)
☐ Check front brake discs for wear (Section 18)
☐ Check the rear brake pads for wear (Section 19)
☐ Check the rear brake discs for wear (Section 20)
☐ Check the steering and suspension components for condition and security (Section 21)
☐ Check the rear driveshaft gaiters (Section 22)
☐ Check the seat belts (Section 23)
☐ Renew the windscreen wiper blades (Section 24)

Every 2 years

Note: *These tasks are normally performed at the same time as Service A or Service B.*

☐ Check the automatic transmission fluid level* (Section 25)
☐ Check the manual transmission fluid level* (Section 26)
☐ Check final drive unit oil level* (Section 27)
☐ Renew the brake fluid (Section 28)
☐ Check for damage and corrosion (Section 29)

* Note: *These tasks are not specified by Mercedes as routine maintenance items.*

Every 3 years

Note: *This task is normally performed at the same time as Service A or Service B.*

☐ Renew the coolant (Section 30)

Note: *This work is every 15 years/155 000 miles in the Mercedes schedule for later models if the recommended Mercedes coolant antifreeze/inhibitor is used.*

Every 4 years or 35 000 miles, whichever comes first

Note: *This task is normally performed at the same time as Service A or Service B.*

☐ Renew the fuel filter (Section 31)

Every 4 years or 50 000 miles, whichever comes first

Note: *This task is normally performed at the same time as Service A or Service B.*

☐ Renew the air filter element (Section 32)

Every 50 000 miles

Note: *This task is normally performed at the same time as Service A or Service B.*

☐ Check the condition of the propeller shaft rubber coupling (Section 33)

Underbonnet view of a 2.2 litre turbo-diesel model

1   Engine oil filler cap
2   Engine oil dipstick
3   Oil filter
4   Coolant expansion tank
5   Brake fluid reservoir
6   Power steering fluid reservoir
7   Windscreen/headlamp washer fluid reservoir
8   Air filter
9   Fusebox
10 Engine management ECU and wiring connector box
11 Radiator top hose
12 Brake ABS unit
13 Fuel injector rail
14 Fuel high-pressure pump
15 Inlet manifold
16 Air duct to intercooler
17 Fuel filter
18 EGR unit
19 Turbocharger (below air filter housing)
20 Brake vacuum pump

Front underbody view of a 2.2 litre turbo-diesel model

1   Engine oil drain plug
2   Air conditioning compressor
3   Anti-roll bar
4   Front suspension lower arms
5   Steering track rod
6   Subframe/crossmember
7   Steering rack
8   Transmission
9   Exhaust system front pipe/silencer

Rear underbody view of a 2.2 litre turbo-diesel model

1 Propeller shaft
2 Final drive unit
3 Fuel tank (under plastic cover)
4 Driveshaft
5 Rear suspension radius arm
6 Handbrake cable
7 Rear suspension lower arm
8 Exhaust tailpipe
9 Rear suspension torque strut

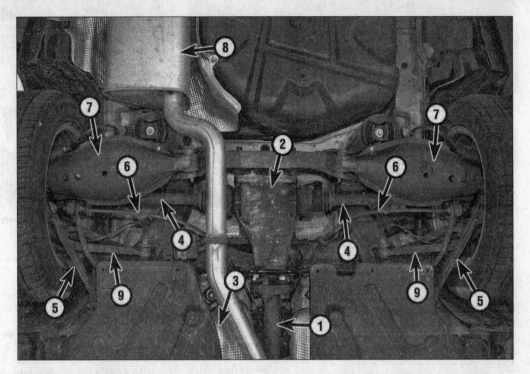

Maintenance procedures

1 Introduction

This Chapter is designed to help the home mechanic maintain his/her vehicle for safety, economy, long life and peak performance.

The Chapter contains a maintenance schedule, followed by Sections dealing specifically with each task in the schedule. Visual checks, adjustments, component renewal and other helpful items are included. Refer to the accompanying illustrations of the engine compartment and the underside of the vehicle for the locations of the various components.

Servicing your vehicle in accordance with the above recommendations and the following Sections will provide a planned maintenance programme, which should result in a long and reliable service life. This is a comprehensive plan, so maintaining some items, but not others at the specified service intervals, will not produce the same results.

As you service your vehicle, you will discover that many of the procedures can – and should – be grouped together, because of the particular procedure being performed, or because of the proximity of two otherwise-unrelated components to one another. For example, if the vehicle is raised for any reason, the exhaust can be inspected at the same time as the suspension and steering components.

The first step in this maintenance programme is to prepare yourself before the actual work begins. Read through all the Sections relevant to the work to be carried out, then make a list and gather all the parts and tools required. If a problem is encountered, seek advice from a parts specialist, or a dealer service department.

2 Regular maintenance

If, from the time the vehicle is new, the routine maintenance schedule is followed closely, and frequent checks are made of fluid levels and high-wear items, as suggested throughout this manual, the engine will be kept in relatively good running condition, and the need for additional work will be minimised.

It is possible that there will be times when the engine is running poorly due to the lack of regular maintenance. This is even more likely if a used vehicle, which has not received regular and frequent maintenance checks, is purchased. In such cases, additional work may need to be carried out, outside of the regular maintenance intervals.

If engine wear is suspected, a compression test (refer to Chapter 2B) will provide valuable information regarding the overall performance of the main internal components. Such a test can be used as a basis to decide on the extent of the work to be carried out. If, for example, a compression test indicates serious internal engine wear, conventional maintenance as described in this Chapter will not greatly improve the performance of the engine, and may prove a waste of time and money, unless extensive overhaul work is carried out first.

The following series of operations are those most often required to improve the performance of a generally poor-running engine:

Primary operations

a) Clean, inspect and test the battery (See Weekly checks and Section 12).
b) Check all the engine-related fluids (See Weekly checks).
c) Check the condition and tension of the auxiliary drivebelt (Section 14).
d) Check the condition of the air filter, and renew if necessary (Section 33).
e) Check the fuel filter, and renew if necessary (Section 31).
f) Check the condition of all hoses, and check for fluid leaks (Section 13).

If the above operations do not prove fully effective, carry out the following secondary operations:

Secondary operations

All items listed under Primary operations, plus the following:

a) Check the charging system (see Part A of Chapter 5).
b) Check the fuel system (see Part B of Chapter 4).
c) Check the preheating system (see Part C of Chapter 5).

3.3a Remove the engine covers (612 type engine)

3.3b Oil filter location (646 type engine)

Every 7500 miles or 12 months

3 Engine oil and filter renewal

1 Frequent oil and filter changes are the most important preventative maintenance procedures, which can be undertaken by the DIY owner. As engine oil ages, it becomes diluted and contaminated, which leads to premature engine wear.

2 Before starting this procedure, gather together all the necessary tools and materials. Also make sure that you have plenty of clean rags and newspapers handy, to mop-up any spills. Ideally, the engine oil should be warm, as it will drain better, and more built-up sludge will be removed with it. Take care, however, not to touch the exhaust or any other hot parts of the engine when working under the vehicle. To avoid any possibility of scalding, and to protect yourself from possible skin irritants and other harmful contaminants in used engine oils, it is advisable to wear gloves when carrying out this work. Access to the underside of the vehicle will be greatly improved if it can be raised on a lift, driven onto ramps, or jacked up and supported on axle stands (see *Jacking and vehicle support*). Whichever method is chosen, make sure that

the vehicle remains level, or if it is at an angle, so that the drain plug is at the lowest point. Where necessary, remove the under tray from under the engine.

3 Working in the engine compartment, on 611 and 612 engines, undo the retaining bolts and remove the engine trim panel cover **(see illustration)**. On 646 engines unclip the cover from the top of the engine. Locate the oil filter/housing on the front left-hand side of the engine **(see illustration)**. Place a wad of rag around the housing to absorb any spilt oil, and then unscrew the oil filter cap. **Note:** *By removing the cap, the oil will drain from the housing into the sump.*

4 Lift the old oil filter element out from the housing, and discard it.

5 Working under the vehicle, unscrew the sump drain plug about half a turn. Position the draining container under the drain plug, and then remove the plug completely **(see illustration)**. If possible, try to keep the plug pressed into the sump while unscrewing it by hand the last couple of turns **(see Haynes Hint)**.

6 Recover the sealing ring from the drain plug.

3.5 Draining the engine oil

HAYNES HINT

As the drain plug releases from the threads, move it away sharply so the stream of oil from the sump runs into the container, not up your sleeve.

7 Allow some time for the old oil to drain, noting that it may be necessary to reposition the container as the oil flow slows to a trickle. Remove the oil filler cap from the camshaft cover.

8 After all the oil has drained from the engine, wipe off the drain plug with a clean rag and renew the sealing washer. Clean the area around the drain plug opening, then refit and tighten the plug.

9 Remove the old oil and all tools from under the car, then refit the undershield and lower the car to the ground.

10 Wipe out the oil filter housing and cap using a clean rag, then fit a new oil filter element to the housing.

11 Fit a new O-ring to the cap then refit it and tighten the nuts or cap as applicable.

12 Remove the oil level dipstick then fill the engine, using the correct grade and type of oil (see *Lubricants and fluids*). An oil can spout or funnel may help to reduce spillage. Pour in half the specified quantity of oil first, and then wait a few minutes for the oil to run to the sump. Continue adding oil a small quantity at a time until the level is up to the lower mark on the dipstick. Finally, bring the level up to the upper mark on the dipstick. Insert the dipstick, and refit the filler cap.

13 Start the engine and run it for a few minutes; check for leaks around the oil filter cap and the sump drain plug. Note that there may be a delay of a few seconds before the oil pressure warning light goes out when the engine is first started, as the oil circulates through the engine oil galleries and the new oil filter before the pressure builds-up.

14 Switch off the engine, and wait a few minutes for the oil to settle in the sump once more. With the new oil circulated and the filter completely full, recheck the level on the dipstick, and add more oil as necessary.

15 Dispose of the used engine oil safely, with reference to *General repair procedures* in the Reference section of this manual.

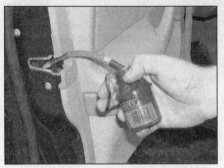

5.1 Lubricating the door locks

8.2a Check the exhaust clamps . . .

8.2b . . . and the rubber mountings

One spanner on display (Service A)

4 Coolant antifreeze/ inhibitor check

⚠ *Warning: Wait until the engine is cold before starting this procedure. Do not allow antifreeze to come in contact with your skin, or with the painted surfaces of the vehicle. Rinse off spills immediately with plenty of water.*

1 A tester will be required to check the coolant strength; these can be obtained relatively cheaply from most motor accessory shops.
2 With the engine completely cold, unscrew and remove the filler cap from the coolant expansion tank. Follow the instructions supplied with the tester and check the coolant mixture is sufficient to give protection down to temperatures well below freezing. If the coolant has been renewed at the specified intervals this shouldn't be a problem. However, if the coolant mixture is not strong enough to provide sufficient protection it will be necessary to drain the cooling system and renew the coolant (see Section 30).
3 Once the test is complete, check the coolant level is correct (see *Weekly checks*) then securely refit the expansion tank cap.

5 Lubricate hinges, locks and sunroof

1 Lubricate the hinges of the bonnet, doors and tailgate with light general-purpose oil. Similarly, lubricate all latches, locks and lock strikers **(see illustration)**. At the same time, check the security and operation of all the locks, adjusting them if necessary (see Chapter 11).
2 Lightly lubricate the bonnet release mechanism and cable with suitable grease.
3 On models with a sunroof, slide the roof fully back and clean the sunroof guide rails. Apply a smear of fresh multipurpose grease to the rails and close the sunroof.

6 Windscreen/headlight washer system check

1 Check that each of the washer jet nozzles are clear and that each nozzle provides a strong jet of washer fluid.
2 On Estate models, the tailgate jet should be aimed to spray at the centre of the screen.
3 The windscreen washer nozzles should be aimed slightly above the centre of the screen.
4 Where fitted, the headlight jet should be aimed slightly above the horizontal centreline of the headlight. Mercedes technicians use a special tool to adjust the headlight jet after pulling the jet out onto its stop.
5 Especially during the winter months, make sure that the washer fluid frost concentration is sufficient.

7 Parking brake check

1 Chock the front wheels, then jack up the rear of the car, and support it on axle stands (see *Jacking and vehicle support*).
2 Release the parking brake fully, and select neutral.
3 Have an assistant gradually apply the parking brake, counting the number of clicks from the ratchet, while you check to see at what point the rear wheel begins to drag, and then locks. Repeat this check on the other rear wheel.
4 The rear wheels should both lock at the same point – if not, either the shoes need adjusting, or one of the rear cables is binding.
5 Both rear wheels should be fully locked within five clicks from the ratchet mechanism.
6 When the parking brake is released, both rear wheels should be free to turn. Remember that there will be some drag from the rear axle and propeller shaft, however.
7 If necessary, adjust the parking brake as described in Chapter 9. Check that the parking brake cables are free to move easily and lubricate all exposed linkages/cable pivots.

8 Exhaust system check

1 With the engine cold, check the complete exhaust system from the engine to the end of the tailpipe. The exhaust system is most easily checked with the vehicle raised on a hoist, or suitably supported on axle stands, so that the exhaust components are readily visible and accessible.
2 Check the exhaust pipes and connections for evidence of leaks, severe corrosion and damage. Make sure that all brackets and mountings are in good condition, and that all relevant nuts and bolts are tight **(see illustrations)**. Leakage at any of the joints or in other parts of the system will usually show up as a black sooty stain in the vicinity of the leak.
3 Rattles and other noises can often be traced to the exhaust system, especially the brackets and mountings. Try to move the pipes and silencers. If the components are able to come into contact with the body or suspension parts, secure the system with new mountings. Otherwise separate the joints (if possible) and twist the pipes as necessary to provide additional clearance.

9 Road test

Instruments and electrical equipment

1 Check the operation of all instruments and electrical equipment.
2 Make sure that all instruments read correctly, and switch on all electrical equipment in turn, to check that it functions properly.

Steering and suspension

3 Check for any abnormalities in the steering, suspension, handling or road 'feel'.
4 Drive the vehicle, and check that there are no unusual vibrations or noises.

5 Check that the steering feels positive, with no excessive 'sloppiness', or roughness, and check for any suspension noises when cornering and driving over bumps.

Drivetrain

6 Check the performance of the engine, clutch (where applicable), gearbox/transmission, propeller shaft and driveshafts.

7 Listen for any unusual noises from the engine, clutch and gearbox/transmission.

8 Make sure that the engine runs smoothly when idling, and that there is no hesitation when accelerating.

9 Check that, where applicable, the clutch action is smooth and progressive, that the drive is taken up smoothly, and that the pedal travel is not excessive. Also listen for any noises when the clutch pedal is depressed.

10 On manual gearbox models, check that all gears can be engaged smoothly without noise, and that the gear lever action is smooth and not abnormally vague or 'notchy'.

11 On automatic transmission models, make sure that all gearchanges occur smoothly, without snatching, and without an increase in engine speed between changes. Check that all the gear positions can be selected with the vehicle at rest. If any problems are found, they should be referred to a Mercedes-Benz dealer.

Braking system

12 Make sure that the vehicle does not pull to one side when braking, and that the wheels do not lock when braking hard.

13 Check that there is no vibration through the steering when braking.

14 Check that the parking brake operates correctly without excessive movement of the foot pedal, and that it holds the vehicle stationary on a slope.

15 Test the operation of the brake servo unit as follows. With the engine off, depress the footbrake four or five times to exhaust the vacuum. Hold the brake pedal depressed, and then start the engine. As the engine starts, there should be a noticeable 'give' in the brake pedal as vacuum builds-up. Allow the engine to run for at least two minutes, and then switch it off. If the brake pedal is depressed now, it should be possible to detect a hiss from the servo as the pedal is depressed. After about four or five applications, no further hissing should be heard, and the pedal should feel considerably harder.

10 Service indicator resetting
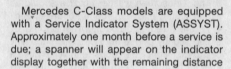

Mercedes C-Class models are equipped with a Service Indicator System (ASSYST). Approximately one month before a service is due; a spanner will appear on the indicator display together with the remaining distance or time. If the service is not performed on time, the display will flash, letting you know how many days (or km/miles) that the service has been exceeded by. An audible signal also can be heard if the service date has been exceeded.

After carrying out a service, the Mercedes-Benz dealership will reset the Service Indicator. To reset the system yourself, carry out the following.

1 *Insert the ignition key and turn it to position 2.*
2 *By pressing the lower buttons on the left-hand side of the steering wheel, call up the trip meter and total distance on the display in the instrument panel.*
3 *Press the upper (arrowed) buttons on the left-hand side of the steering wheel, until the service indicator appears on the display.*
4 *Press and hold the reset button on the left-hand side of the instrument panel for approximately 4 seconds.*
5 *The display unit in the instrument panel will show DO YOU WANT TO RESET SERVICE INTERVAL? CONFIRM BY USING RESET BUTTON.*
6 *Press and hold the reset button again until an audible signal is heard, the service indicator has now been reset.*
7 *The distance until the next service will appear on the display.*

Two spanners on display (Service B)

11 Power steering fluid level check

1 Park the vehicle on level ground and set the steering wheel straight-ahead. The engine should be turned off; for the check to be accurate, the steering must not be turned once the engine has been stopped.

Caution: The need for frequent topping-up indicates a leak, which should be investigated immediately.
2 The power steering fluid reservoir is located at the front left-hand side of the engine.
3 A dipstick is incorporated in the filler cap. Wipe clean the top of the fluid reservoir, then unscrew and remove the reservoir cap and dipstick **(see illustration)**.
4 Wipe the dipstick clean, then screw the reservoir cap fully back into position. Unscrew the cap once more, remove the dipstick and check the fluid level, which should be between the MAX and MIN marks. **Note:** *There are two sets of marks – 20° marks are for checking the fluid when cold, and the 80° marks for fluid at operating temperature **(see illustration)**.*
5 Top-up the fluid level to the MAX mark, using the specified type of fluid (do not overfill the reservoir), then refit and tighten the filler cap **(see illustration)**.

11.3 Power steering fluid dipstick

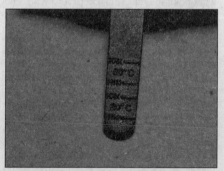
11.4 Power steering fluid dipstick markings

11.5 Topping-up the power steering fluid

12.1 Battery location

12.2 Check that the battery terminals are secure

12.3 Battery clamp retaining bolt

12 Battery check

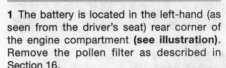

1 The battery is located in the left-hand (as seen from the driver's seat) rear corner of the engine compartment **(see illustration)**. Remove the pollen filter as described in Section 16.

2 Check that both battery terminals are securely attached and are free from corrosion **(see illustration)**. Note: *Before disconnecting the terminals from the battery, refer to 'Disconnecting the battery' in the Reference Chapter at the end of this manual. Always remove keys before disconnecting battery – otherwise electronic components may be damaged.*

3 Check the battery casing for signs of damage or cracking and check the battery retaining-clamp is secure **(see illustration)**. If the battery casing is damaged in any way the battery must be renewed (see Chapter 5A).

4 If the vehicle is not fitted with a sealed-for-life maintenance-free battery, check the electrolyte level is between the MAX and MIN level markings on the battery casing. If topping-up is necessary, remove the battery (see Chapter 5A) from the vehicle then remove the cell caps/cover (as applicable). Using distilled water, top the electrolyte level of each cell up to the MAX level mark then securely refit the cell caps/cover. Ensure the battery has not been overfilled then refit the battery to the vehicle (see Chapter 5A).

5 On completion of the check, refit the pollen filter securely back into position.

13 Hose and fluid leak check

1 Visually inspect the engine joint faces, gaskets and seals for any signs of water or oil leaks. Pay particular attention to the areas around the camshaft cover, cylinder head, oil filter and sump joint faces. Bear in mind that, over a period of time, some very slight seepage from these areas is to be expected – what you are really looking for is any indication of a serious leak. Should a leak be found, renew the offending gasket or oil seal by referring to the appropriate Chapters in this manual.

2 Also check the security and condition of all the engine-related pipes and hoses. Ensure that all cable-ties or securing clips are in place and in good condition. Clips that are broken or missing can lead to chafing of the hoses, pipes or wiring, which could cause more serious problems in the future.

3 Carefully check the radiator hoses and heater hoses along their entire length. Renew any hose which is cracked, swollen or deteriorated. Cracks will show up better if the hose is squeezed. Pay close attention to the hose clips that secure the hoses to the cooling system components. Hose clips can pinch and puncture hoses, resulting in cooling system leaks.

4 Inspect all the cooling system components (hoses, joint faces, etc) for leaks. A leak in the cooling system will usually show up as white- or antifreeze-coloured deposits on the area adjoining the leak **(see Haynes Hint)**. Where any problems of this nature are found on system components, renew the component or gasket with reference to Chapter 3.

5 Where applicable, inspect the automatic transmission fluid cooler hoses for leaks or deterioration.

6 With the vehicle raised, inspect the fuel tank and filler neck for punctures, cracks and other damage. The connection between the filler neck and tank is especially critical. Sometimes a rubber filler neck or connecting

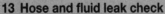
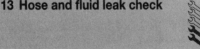

A leak in the cooling system will usually show up as white- or antifreeze-coloured deposits on the area adjoining the leak.

hose will leak due to loose retaining clamps or deteriorated rubber.

7 Carefully check all rubber hoses and metal fuel lines leading away from the petrol tank. Check for loose connections, deteriorated hoses, crimped lines, and other damage. Pay particular attention to the vent pipes and hoses, which often loop up around the filler neck and can become blocked or crimped. Follow the lines to the front of the vehicle, carefully inspecting them all the way. Renew damaged sections as necessary.

8 Closely inspect the metal brake pipes, which run along the vehicle underbody. If they show signs of excessive corrosion or damage they must be renewed.

9 From within the engine compartment, check the security of all fuel hose attachments and pipe unions, and inspect the fuel hoses and vacuum hoses for kinks, chafing and deterioration.

10 Check the condition of the power steering fluid hoses and pipes.

14 Auxiliary drivebelt check and renewal

Drivebelt checking

1 Due to their function and construction, the belts are prone to failure after a period of time, and should be inspected periodically to prevent problems.

2 The number of belts used on a particular vehicle depends on the accessories fitted **(see illustrations)**. Drivebelts are used to drive

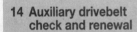
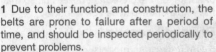
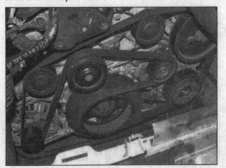

14.2 Auxiliary drivebelt configurations (646 type engine)

14.7a Release the tension on the belt . . .

14.7b . . . using either a Torx bit or a 12-point socket

15 Headlight beam adjustment check

Accurate adjustment of the headlight beam is only possible using optical beam-setting equipment, and a Mercedes-Benz dealer or service station should therefore carry out this work with the necessary facilities.

Details of the headlight adjuster system are given in Chapter 12, Section 12.

16 Pollen filter renewal

14.8 Using an Allen key to lock the tensioner in position

14.9 Fitting the belt around the tensioner

the coolant pump, alternator, power steering pump and air conditioning compressor.

3 To improve access for belt inspection, if desired, remove the viscous cooling fan and cowl as described in Chapter 3.

4 With the engine stopped, using your fingers (and an electric torch if necessary), move along the belts, checking for cracks and separation of the belt plies. Also check for fraying and glazing, which gives the belt a shiny appearance. Both sides of the belts should be inspected, which means the belt will have to be twisted to check the underside. If necessary turn the engine using a spanner or socket on the crankshaft pulley bolt so that the whole of the belt can be inspected.

Drivebelt renewal

5 On 5-cylinder models, to make access easier, remove the cooling fan and shroud, as described in Chapter 3.

6 Where applicable, remove the engine covers from the top of the engine and the cooling fan cowling to improve access.

7 Engage a socket or Torx T60 bit/socket with the tensioner body below the pulley, and then lever the tensioner anti-clockwise to relieve the tension in the belt (see illustrations).

8 Hold the tensioner in position with the spanner/socket, and slide the belt from the pulleys. If necessary, the tensioner can be retained in its released position by inserting a suitable bolt or metal dowel through the holes provided (see illustration).

9 Fit the new belt around the pulleys, starting with the crankshaft pulley. Check that the belt is correctly seated on all the pulleys (see illustration). Where applicable, remove the metal dowel/bolt from the tensioner.

10 Release the spanner/socket, and allow the tensioner to move into position against the belt.

1 The air entering the vehicle's ventilation system is passed through a very fine pleated-paper air filter element, which removes particles of pollen, dust and other airborne foreign matter. To ensure its continued effectiveness, this filter's element must be renewed at regular intervals. Failure to renew the element will also result in greatly reduced airflow into the passenger compartment, reducing demisting and ventilation capability.

2 The filter housing is located in the left-hand (as seen from the driver's seat) rear corner of the engine compartment, above the battery.

3 Open the bonnet and clean around the air filter housing to prevent dirt ingress.

4 Release the three retaining clips at the rear of the filter housing and remove the cover from the housing (see illustrations). Unclip the windscreen washer pipe from the side of the filter housing.

5 Withdraw the pollen filter element from its location in the filter housing; noting which way round it is fitted (see illustration).

6 Fit the new filter into position in the filter housing, noting any direction-of-fitting markings which may be present. Refit the cover to the housing and secure with the retaining clips.

16.4a Release the three securing clips . . .

16.4b . . . then unclip the washer pipe from the side of the housing

16.5 Removing the pollen filter element

17 Front brake pad check

1 Firmly apply the parking brake, and then jack up the front of the car and support it securely on axle stands (see *Jacking and vehicle support*). Remove the front roadwheels **(see Haynes Hint)**.

2 For a comprehensive check, the brake pads should be removed and cleaned. The operation of the caliper can then also be checked, and the condition of the brake disc itself can be fully examined on both sides. Refer to Chapter 9 for further information.

3 If any pad's friction material is worn to the specified thickness or less; *all four pads must be renewed as a set.*

18 Front brake disc check

Refer to Chapter 9, Section 6.

19 Rear brake pad check

1 Chock the front wheels, then jack up the rear of the car and support it securely on axle stands (see *Jacking and vehicle support*). Remove the rear road wheels.

2 As with the front brake pads, the thickness of pad linings can be checked quickly through the aperture at the rear of the caliper.

3 For a comprehensive check, the brake pads should be removed and cleaned. The operation of the caliper can then also be checked, and the condition of the brake disc itself can be fully examined on both sides. Refer to Chapter 9 for further information.

4 If any pad's friction material is worn to the specified thickness or less; *all four pads must be renewed as a set.*

20 Rear brake disc check

Refer to Chapter 9, Section 7.

21 Steering and suspension check

Front suspension and steering

1 Raise the front of the vehicle, and securely support it on axle stands (see *Jacking and vehicle support*).

2 Visually inspect the balljoint dust covers and the steering linkage gaiters for splits, chafing or deterioration. Any wear of these components

For a quick check, the thickness of the friction material of the brake pad can be measured through the aperture in the caliper body.

will cause loss of lubricant, together with dirt and water entry, resulting in rapid deterioration of the balljoints. Also check that the steering box mountings are tightened to the specified torque settings (see Chapter 10).

3 Check the power steering fluid hoses for chafing or deterioration, and the pipe and hose unions for fluid leaks. Also check for signs of fluid leakage under pressure from the steering box, which would indicate failed fluid seals within the steering box.

4 Grasp the roadwheel at the 12 o'clock and 6 o'clock positions, and try to rock it **(see illustration)**. Very slight free play may be felt, but if the movement is appreciable, further investigation is necessary to determine the source. Continue rocking the wheel while an assistant depresses the footbrake. If the movement is now eliminated or significantly reduced, it is likely that the hub bearings are at fault. If the free play is still evident with the footbrake depressed, then there is wear in the suspension joints or mountings. Note that the front hub bearings are adjustable (See Chapter 10).

5 Now grasp the wheel at the 9 o'clock and 3 o'clock positions, and try to rock it as before. Any movement felt now may again be caused by wear in the hub bearings or the steering track rod balljoints. If the inner or outer balljoint is worn, the visual movement will be obvious.

6 Using a large screwdriver or flat bar, check for wear in the suspension mounting bushes

21.4 Check for wear in the hub bearings by grasping the wheel and trying to rock it

by levering between the relevant suspension component and its attachment point. Some movement is to be expected as the mountings are made of rubber, but excessive wear should be obvious. Also check the condition of any visible rubber bushes, looking for splits, cracks or contamination of the rubber.

7 With the car standing on its wheels, have an assistant turn the steering wheel back-and-forth about an eighth of a turn each way. There should be very little lost movement between the steering wheel and roadwheels. If this is not the case, closely observe the linkage joints and mountings previously described, but in addition, check the steering column universal joint/coupling for wear, and the steering box itself.

Shock absorber

8 Check for any signs of fluid leakage around the shock absorber body, or from the rubber gaiter around the piston rod. Should any fluid be noticed, the shock absorber is defective internally, and should be renewed. **Note:** *Shock absorbers should always be renewed in pairs on the same axle.*

9 The efficiency of the shock absorber may be checked by bouncing the vehicle at each corner. Generally speaking, the body will return to its normal position and stop after being depressed. If it rises and returns on a rebound, the shock absorber is probably suspect. Examine also the shock absorber upper and lower mountings for any signs of wear.

22 Driveshaft gaiter check

1 With the vehicle raised and securely supported on stands, slowly rotate the rear roadwheel. Inspect the condition of the outer constant velocity (CV) joint rubber gaiters, squeezing the gaiters to open out the folds. Check for signs of cracking, splits or deterioration of the rubber, which may allow the grease to escape, and lead to water and grit entry into the joint. Also check the security and condition of the retaining clips. Repeat these checks on the inner CV joints **(see illustrations)**. If any damage or deterioration

22.1a Check the driveshaft inner CV joints . . .

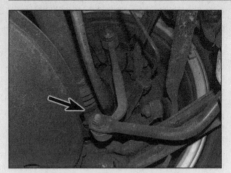

22.1b ... and outer CV joints

is found, the gaiters should be renewed (see Chapter 8).

2 At the same time, check the general condition of the CV joints themselves by first holding the driveshaft and attempting to rotate the wheel. Repeat this check by holding the inner joint and attempting to rotate the driveshaft. Any appreciable movement indicates wear in the joints, wear in the driveshaft splines, or a loose driveshaft retaining nut.

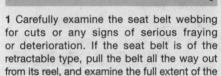

23 Seat belt check

1 Carefully examine the seat belt webbing for cuts or any signs of serious fraying or deterioration. If the seat belt is of the retractable type, pull the belt all the way out from its reel, and examine the full extent of the webbing.

2 Fasten and unfasten the belt, ensuring that the locking mechanism holds securely and releases properly when intended. If the belt is of the retractable type, check also that the retracting mechanism operates correctly when the belt is released.

3 Check the security of all seat belt mountings and attachments which are accessible, without removing any trim or other components, from inside the vehicle.

24 Windscreen wiper blade renewal

Mercedes-Benz recommend that the windscreen wiper blades should be renewed at this interval, regardless of their apparent condition. Refer to *Weekly checks* for details.

Every 2 years

25 Automatic transmission fluid level check

1 Note that on some later models, the top of the fluid level dipstick tube is fitted with a tamperproof cap incorporating a red plastic clip. The clip is broken when the cap is removed, and a new clip must be fitted when the cap is refitted. The dipstick is **not** fitted inside the tube, but must be obtained as a separate tool (number 140 589 15 21 00) from a Mercedes-Benz dealer. The alternative is to take the vehicle to a dealer for the fluid level check.

2 In order to check the automatic transmission fluid level, the transmission must be at operating temperature (fluid temperature 80°C). Operating temperature is reached after driving for approximately 10 miles. **Do not** attempt to check the fluid level on a cold transmission.

3 With the transmission at operating temperature, ensure that the vehicle is parked on level ground.

4 With the engine running at idle speed, ensure that the transmission selector lever is in position P, and apply the parking brake.

5 Where applicable, pull out the locking pin securing the dipstick in its tube.

6 Remove the fluid level dipstick and wipe it with a lint-free cloth, then re-insert it **(see illustrations)**.

7 Pull out the dipstick once more, and read off the fluid level. The level should be between the MIN and MAX marks **(see illustration)**.

8 If topping-up is necessary, top-up through the filler tube **(see illustration)** using fluid of the specified type (see *Lubricants and fluids*). **Do not** overfill the transmission – the fluid level must not be above the MAX mark.

9 On completion, refit the dipstick or filler tube cap (as applicable). Fit a new tamperproof clip where necessary **(see illustration)**.

26 Manual transmission fluid level check

Note: *A hexagonal key, or a suitable alternative (see text) will be required to unscrew the transmission level/filler plug.*

1 Jack up the front and rear of the vehicle and support it on axle stands (see *Jacking and vehicle support*); ensure the vehicle is level.

2 Place a suitable container beneath the transmission level/filler plug, located on

25.6a Pull out the automatic transmission fluid level dipstick ...

25.6b ... and wipe with a clean cloth

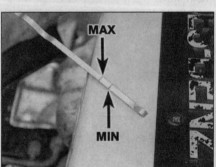

25.7 The fluid level should be between the MIN and MAX marks

25.8 Topping-up the automatic transmission hydraulic fluid

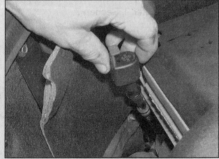

25.9 Fit the filler tube cap, then depress the tamperproof clip

26.2 Using a long nut and a spanner to unscrew the transmission fluid level/filler plug

the right-hand side of the transmission. A hexagonal key should be used to unscrew the plug, but a tool can be improvised using a long nut, or a length of hexagonal bar and a spanner **(see illustration)**.

3 The fluid level should just be up to the bottom of the level/filler plug hole.

4 If necessary, top-up the level until fluid just begins to run out of the level/filler plug hole (see *Lubricants and fluids*).

5 When the level is correct, refit the plug, and tighten securely.

27 Final drive unit oil level check

1 Either position the vehicle over an inspection pit, or jack up the front and rear of the vehicle and support it on axle stands (see *Jacking and vehicle support*). The vehicle must be level for the check to be accurate.

2 Clean the area around the filler/level plug on the left-hand side of the final drive unit **(see illustration)**, then slacken and remove the plug from the housing (refer to Chapter 8, Section 2).

3 The oil level should be up to the lower edge of the filler/level plug aperture.

4 If necessary, top-up using the specified

type of lubricant until the oil level is correct (see *Lubricants and fluids*). Fill the final drive until oil starts to flow out and allow excess oil to drain out.

5 Once the final drive unit oil level is correct, refit the filler/level plug and tighten it securely. Lower the vehicle to the ground.

6 Note that frequent need for topping-up indicates a leakage, possibly through an oil seal. The cause should be investigated and rectified.

28 Brake fluid renewal

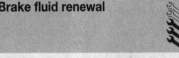

⚠️ *Warning: Brake hydraulic fluid can harm your eyes and damage painted surfaces, so use extreme caution when handling and pouring it. Do not use fluid that has been standing open for some time, as it absorbs moisture from the air. Excess moisture can cause a dangerous loss of braking effectiveness.*

1 The procedure is similar to that for the bleeding of the hydraulic system as described in Chapter 9, except that the brake fluid reservoir should be emptied by syphoning, using a clean poultry baster or similar before starting, and allowance should be made for the old fluid to be expelled when bleeding a section of the circuit.

2 Working as described in Chapter 9, open the first bleed screw in the sequence, and pump the brake pedal gently until nearly all the old fluid has been emptied from the master cylinder reservoir.

3 Top-up to the MAX level with new fluid, and continue pumping until only the new fluid remains in the reservoir, and new fluid can be seen emerging from the bleed screw. Tighten the screw, and top the reservoir level up to the MAX level line.

4 Work through all the remaining bleed screws in the sequence until new fluid can be seen

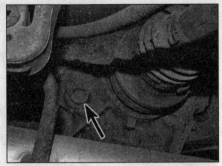

27.2 Final drive oil filler/level plug

at all of them. Be careful to keep the master cylinder reservoir topped-up to above the MIN level at all times, or air may enter the system and greatly increase the length of the task.

5 When the operation is complete, check that all bleed screws are securely tightened, and that their dust caps are refitted. Wash off all traces of spilt fluid, and recheck the master cylinder reservoir fluid level.

6 Check the operation of the brakes before taking the car on the road.

29 Underbody check

Note: *This check should be carried out by a Mercedes-Benz dealer in order to validate the vehicle corrosion warranty.*

1 With the vehicle raised and securely supported, carry out a thorough check of the vehicle underbody sealant for signs of damage. If any area of the underbody sealant shows visible damage, the affected area should be repaired to prevent possible problems with corrosion occurring at a later date.

2 Thoroughly check the underbody for signs of corrosion.

3 Lower the car to the ground.

Every 3 years

30 Coolant renewal

⚠️ *Warning: Wait until the engine is cold before starting this procedure. Do not allow antifreeze to come in contact with your skin, or with the painted surfaces of the vehicle. Rinse off spills immediately with plenty of water. Never leave antifreeze lying around in an open container, or in a puddle in the driveway or on the garage floor. Children and pets are attracted by*

its sweet smell, but antifreeze can be fatal if ingested.

Cooling system draining

1 After allowing the engine to cool completely, cover the pressure cap with a wad of rag, and slowly turn the cap anti-clockwise to relieve the pressure in the cooling system (a hissing sound will normally be heard). Wait until any pressure remaining in the system is released, then continue to turn the cap until it can be removed **(see illustration)**.

2 Position a suitable container beneath the radiator, and then slacken the drain plug on the bottom left-hand corner of the radiator.

30.1 Removing the pressure cap from the coolant expansion tank

30.2 Remove the radiator drain plug

30.3 Cylinder block drain plug

Allow the coolant to drain into the container **(see illustration)**.

3 Reposition the container so that it lies beneath the engine block drain plug, which is located on the side of the cylinder block **(see illustration)**. (Certain engines are fitted with a drain plug with an integral nozzle, to which a length of rubber hose can be connected.) Open the drain plug by turning it with an open-ended spanner and allow the coolant to drain into the container.

4 Once all the coolant has drained, remove the drain hoses and close the cylinder block and radiator drain plugs.

Cooling system flushing

5 If coolant renewal has been neglected, or if the antifreeze mixture has become diluted, then in time, the cooling system may gradually lose efficiency, as the coolant passages become restricted due to rust, scale deposits, and other sediment. The cooling system efficiency can be restored by flushing the system clean.

6 The radiator should be flushed independently of the engine, to avoid unnecessary contamination.

Radiator flushing

7 To flush the radiator disconnect the top and bottom hoses and any other relevant hoses from the radiator, with reference to Chapter 3.

8 Insert a garden hose into the radiator top inlet. Direct a flow of clean water through the radiator, and continue flushing until clean water emerges from the radiator bottom outlet.

9 If after a reasonable period, the water still does not run clear, the radiator can be flushed with a good proprietary cooling system cleaning agent. It is important that the manufacturer's instructions are followed carefully. If the contamination is particularly bad, insert the hose in the radiator bottom outlet, and reverse-flush the radiator.

Engine flushing

10 To flush the engine, remove the thermostat

as described in Chapter 3, and then temporarily refit the thermostat cover. Adjust the heater control to the maximum setting.

11 With the top and bottom hoses disconnected from the radiator, insert a garden hose into the radiator top hose. Direct a clean flow of water through the engine, and continue flushing until clean water emerges from the radiator bottom hose.

12 On completion of flushing, refit the thermostat and reconnect the hoses with reference to Chapter 3.

Cooling system refilling

13 Before attempting to fill the cooling system, make sure that all hoses and clips are in good condition, and that the clips are tight. Note that an antifreeze mixture must be used all year round, to prevent corrosion of the engine components (see following sub-Section).

14 Remove the pressure cap, and fill the system by slowly pouring the coolant into the expansion tank to prevent airlocks from forming.

15 If the coolant is being renewed, begin by pouring in a couple of litres of water, followed by the correct quantity of antifreeze, then top-up with more water.

16 Once the level in the expansion tank/ header tank starts to rise, squeeze the radiator top and bottom hoses to help expel any trapped air in the system. Once all the air is expelled, top-up the coolant level to the MAX mark. Refit the pressure cap securely.

17 Where applicable, unscrew the plug from the coolant sensor housing, on the upper surface of the cylinder head. As soon as coolant starts to flow out, refit the plug and tighten it. If none flows out, pour coolant into the hole vacated by the plug until it begins to flow back out. Refit the plug and tighten it securely. This removes any airlocks in the cooling system that might inhibit the operation of the coolant sensor(s).

18 Start the engine and run it until the

thermostat opens – the radiator top hose will begin to heat up as coolant flows through it of the radiator when this happens.

19 Check for leaks, particularly around disturbed components. Check the coolant level in the expansion tank/header tank, and top-up if necessary. Note that the system must be cold before an accurate level is indicated. If the pressure cap is removed while the engine is still warm, cover the cap with a thick cloth, and unscrew the cap slowly to gradually relieve the system pressure (a hissing sound will normally be heard). Wait until any pressure remaining in the system is released, then continue to turn the cap until it can be removed.

Antifreeze mixture

20 The antifreeze should always be renewed at the specified intervals. This is necessary not only to maintain the antifreeze properties, but also to prevent corrosion, which would otherwise occur as the corrosion inhibitors become progressively less effective.

21 Always use an ethylene glycol based antifreeze, which is suitable for use in mixed-metal cooling systems. The quantity of antifreeze and levels of protection are indicated in the Specifications.

22 Before adding antifreeze, the cooling system should be completely drained, preferably flushed, and all hoses checked for condition and security.

23 After filling with antifreeze, a label should be attached to the expansion tank or header tank, stating the type and concentration of antifreeze used, and the date installed. Any subsequent topping-up should be made with the same type and concentration of antifreeze.

24 Do not use engine antifreeze in the windscreen/tailgate washer system, as it will cause damage to the vehicle paintwork. A screenwash additive should be added to the washer system in the quantities stated on the bottle.

Every 4 years or 35 000 miles

31 Fuel filter renewal

1 The fuel filter is located to the left-hand side of the cylinder head **(see illustration)**. To minimise fuel spillage, pad the surrounding area with absorbent rags.
2 Release the securing clips and disconnect the fuel hoses from the top of the fuel filter. Note the fitted positions for refitting; one of the fuel hoses has a larger diameter than the other. Plug the ends of the fuel hoses to prevent dirt ingress **(see illustrations)**.
3 Slacken the retaining bolt from down the side of the filter, and then withdraw the filter from its mounting bracket **(see illustration)**.
4 Remove the filter canister from the engine bay, keeping the mating face upwards to minimise fuel spillage.
5 Take the new fuel filter canister and fit it into the mounting bracket and tighten the retaining bolt.
6 Refit the fuel hoses to the top of the fuel filter in their correct positions (as noted on removal), making sure they are secure.
7 Start and run the engine at idle and check around the fuel filter for fuel leaks. **Note:** *The fuel pump is self-priming, but it may take a few seconds of cranking before the engine starts.*
8 Raise the engine speed to about 2000 rpm several times, and then allow the engine to

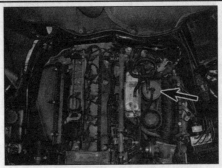

31.1 Fuel filter location

31.2a Remove the fuel filter hoses . . .

31.2b . . . and plug the ends

31.3 Fuel filter retaining clamp bolt

idle again. This should bleed the air bubbles from the filter canister, but if the engine idle is at all rough or hesitant, repeat the action until the fuel system clears itself.

Every 4 years or 75 000 miles

32 Air filter element renewal

1 Where applicable remove the cover(s) from the top of the engine.

611 and 612 type engines

2 Undo the retaining bolts from the top edge of the air filter housing **(see illustration)**.
3 Disconnect the wiring connector from the airflow sensor **(see illustration)**.

4 Slacken the retaining clip and remove the air intake pipe from the air cleaner cover **(see illustration)**.
5 Lift off the air cleaner cover, releasing it from the three locating lugs at the lower end of the cover **(see illustration)**.
6 Remove the filter element from the air

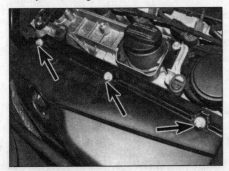

32.2 Undo the retaining bolts . . .

32.3 . . . disconnect the wiring connector . . .

32.4 . . . remove the air intake pipe . . .

32.5 . . . lift off the filter cover . . .

32.6 . . . and remove the air filter element

32.12a Release the retaining clips . . .

cleaner housing, noting its fitted position **(see illustration)**.

7 Brush out all traces of dirt and debris from inside the air cleaner. Take care to prevent debris from falling down the intake orifice.

8 Lay the new filter element in position in the air cleaner housing as noted on removal.

9 Refit the air cleaner cover making sure the lower lugs are located correctly **(see illustration 32.5)**, then fit the retaining bolts and tighten them securely.

10 Refit the air intake pipe to the air cleaner upper cover and tighten the retaining clip.

11 Reconnect the wiring plug to the airflow sensor.

646 type engines

12 Release the spring clips and release the air cleaner cover **(see illustrations)**.

13 Remove the filter element from the air cleaner cover, noting its fitted position **(see illustration)**.

32.12b . . . and lift off the filter cover

32.13 Remove the air filter element

14 Brush out all traces of dirt and debris from inside the air cleaner.

15 Lay a new filter element in position in the air cleaner housing.

16 Check the rubber seal in the channel that runs around the edge of the air cleaner housing and fit the air cleaner cover.

17 Secure the cover in position with the spring clips.

Every 50 000 miles

33 Propeller shaft rubber coupling condition check

1 Chock the front wheels, then jack up the rear of the vehicle and support it on axle stands.

2 Carefully check the propeller shaft front and rear rubber couplings for signs of damage and deterioration **(see illustrations)**. Look for deterioration in the form of splitting, cracking or perishing. Damage may also be caused by oil or grease contamination. Rotate one of the rear wheels to check all around the rubber couplings.

3 To check the centre rubber coupling, undo the retaining nuts and remove the heat shield(s) from above the exhaust system **(see illustration)**.

4 If any of the couplings require renewal, refer to Chapter 8 for a description of the renewal procedure.

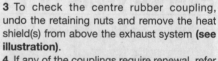

33.2a Check the front rubber coupling . . .

33.2b . . . and rear rubber coupling

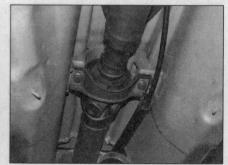

33.3 Remove heat shield to access the centre coupling

Chapter 2 Part A:
Petrol engine in-car repair procedures

Contents

Degrees of difficulty

Easy, suitable for novice with little experience		**Fairly easy,** suitable for beginner with some experience		**Fairly difficult,** suitable for competent DIY mechanic		**Difficult,** suitable for experienced DIY mechanic		**Very difficult,** suitable for expert DIY or professional	

Specifications

General

Engine code*:
  1.8 litre engine:
    2002 to 2006 . . . . 271.948
    2002 to 2007 . . . . 271.940, 271.942 or 271.946
    2004 to 2007 . . . . 271.921
  2.0 litre engine . . . . 111.951 or 111.955
  2.3 litre engine 111.981
Displacement:
  1.8 litre engine . . . . 1796 cc
  2.0 litre engines . . . . 1998 cc
  2.3 litre engines . . . . 2295 cc
Bore:
  1.8 litre engines . . . . 82.0 mm
  2.0 litre engines . . . . 89.9 mm
  2.3 litre engines . . . . 90.9 mm
Stroke:
  1.8 litre engines . . . . 85.0 mm
  2.0 litre engine . . . . 78.7 mm
  2.3 litre engines . . . . 88.4 mm
Direction of engine rotation . . . . Clockwise (viewed from front of vehicle)
No 1 cylinder location. . . . . Timing chain end
Firing order 1-3-4-2
Compression ratio:
  1.8 litre engine:
    271.921 . . . . N/A
    271.940 . . . . 9.5 : 1
    271.942 . . . . 10.3 : 1
    271.946 . . . . 10.2 : 1
    271.948 . . . . 8.7 : 1
  2.0 litre engine:
    111.951 . . . . 10.6 : 1
    111.955 . . . . 9.5 : 1
  2.3 litre engine . . . . 9.0 : 1

* See 'Vehicle identification numbers' for information about the engine code

Cylinder head bolts

111 type engines:
Length when new	102.0 mm
Maximum length	105.0 mm

271 type engines:
Length when new	165.0 mm
Maximum length	167.5 mm

Lubrication system

Oil pressure (at temperature 90°C):

111 type engines:
At idle (minimum)	0.3 bar
At 3000 rpm (minimum)	3.0 bar

271 type engines:
At 650 rpm	0.5 bar
At 1000 rpm	0.9 bar
At 2000 rpm	1.7 bar
At 4000 rpm	3.6 bar

Torque wrench settings

	Nm	lbf ft
Armature centre bolt:		
Stage 1	5	4
Stage 2	Angle-tighten a further 90°	
Auxiliary drivebelt tensioner	25	18
Auxiliary drivebelt tensioner damper strut bolts	10	7
Auxiliary drivebelt tensioner pulley bolt	25	18
Big-end bearing cap bolts:		
111 type engines:		
Stage 1	5	4
Stage 2	25	18
Stage 3	Angle-tighten a further 90°	
271 type engines:		
Stage 1	5	4
Stage 2	15	10
Stage 3	Angle-tighten a further 90°	
Camshaft bearing cap (111 type engines)	21	15
Camshaft bearing lower housing (271 type engines)	14	10
Camshaft bearing upper housing (271 type engines):		
Stage 1	10	7
Stage 2	Angle-tighten a further 90°	
Camshaft cover bolts	10	7
Camshaft sprocket bolts:		
Stage 1	20	15
Stage 2	Angle-tighten a further 60°	
Crankshaft pulley bolt:		
111 type engines	300	221
271 type engines:		
Stage 1	200	148
Stage 2	Angle-tighten a further 90°	
Crankshaft rear oil seal housing bolts	10	7
Cylinder head bolts:		
111 type engines:		
Stage 1	55	41
Stage 2	Angle-tighten a further 90°	
Stage 3	Angle-tighten a further 90°	
271 type engines:		
Stage 1	45	33
Stage 2	Angle-tighten a further 90°	
Stage 3	Angle-tighten a further 90°	
Cylinder head to front timing cover:		
111 type engines:		
M6	10	7
M8	25	18
271 type engines	20	15
Driveplate:		
Stage 1	45	33
Stage 2	Angle-tighten a further 90°	

Torque wrench settings (continued)

	Nm	lbf ft
Engine-to-transmission bolts:		
Manual transmission:		
M10 x 40 mm bolts	55	41
M10 x 90 mm bolts	45	33
Automatic transmission:		
M10 bolts	55	41
M12 bolts	65	48
Flywheel:		
Stage 1	45	33
Stage 2	Angle-tighten a further 90°	
Front engine mounting bracket to cylinder block	20	15
Front engine mountings to crossmember (lower)	35	26
Front engine mountings to mounting brackets (upper)	50	37
Hub/plate to camshaft flange:		
Stage 1	20	15
Stage 2	Angle-tighten a further 60°	
Main bearing cap bolts:		
111 type engines:		
Stage 1	55	41
Stage 2	Angle-tighten a further 95°	
271 type engines:		
Stage 1	30	22
Stage 2	Angle-tighten a further 90°	
Oil drain plug	30	22
Oil filter cap	25	18
Oil pump mounting bolts	20	15
Piston-to-hub/plate nut	65	48
Sump to crankcase:		
M6	10	7
M8	20	15
Sump to transmission	40	30
Thermostat housing:		
M6 bolts	10	7
M8 bolts	25	18
Timing chain front cover bolts	25	18
Timing chain upper guide bolts	10	7
Timing chain tensioner:		
111 type engines:		
Tensioner body	80	59
Tensioner end piece	40	30
271 type engines	40	30

1 General information

How to use this Chapter

This Part of Chapter 2 describes the repair procedures that can reasonably be carried out on the engine while it remains in the vehicle. If the engine has been removed from the vehicle and is being dismantled as described in Part C, any preliminary dismantling procedures can be ignored.

Note that, while it may be possible to overhaul items such as the piston/connecting rod assemblies while the engine is in the car, such tasks are not usually carried out as separate operations. Usually, several additional procedures are required (not to mention the cleaning of components and oilways); for this reason, all such tasks are classed as major overhaul procedures, and are described in Part C of this Chapter.

Part C describes the removal of the engine/transmission from the car, and the full overhaul procedures that can then be carried out.

Engine description

The engine is of four-cylinder in-line double overhead camshaft design, mounted in-line ('north-south') with the transmission on the rear of the engine.

The crankshaft is supported in five main bearings within the cast iron cylinder block. Crankshaft endfloat is controlled by thrustwashers fitted on either side of the centre main bearing.

The connecting rods are attached to the crankshaft by horizontally-split big-end bearings, and to the pistons by fully-floating gudgeon pins retained in the pistons by circlips. The alloy pistons are fitted with three piston rings; two compression and one oil control.

The camshafts are driven from the crankshaft sprocket by a double-row chain. A variable valve timing device is fitted to certain engines.

The device consists of a piston located inside the inlet camshaft sprocket. The piston is splined to the sprocket and to the hub/plate with an intermediate gear, and the splines are helical to provide the necessary amount of advance or retard. An armature on the front of the device is operated by a solenoid located on the cylinder head front cover. The engine management ECU activates the solenoid, and the armature pulls out an internal plunger which uncovers oil supply holes to supply oil pressure to one side of the piston. The piston moves along the helical splines and the inlet camshaft valve timing is advanced or retarded. When the solenoid is de-activated, an internal spring forces the plunger back to uncover different oil supply holes in order to direct oil pressure to the other side of the piston.

The camshafts are supported in five bearings in the aluminium alloy cylinder head. The camshafts actuate the valves via hydraulically-operated tappets.

The oil pump is chain-driven from a sprocket on the front of the crankshaft.

3.3 Inserting a bolt through the hole in the camshaft front bearing cap and into the flange

Operations with engine in vehicle

The following operations can be carried out without having to remove the engine from the vehicle:

a) Removal and refitting of the cylinder head.
b) Removal and refitting of the timing chain and sprockets.
c) Removal and refitting of the camshafts.
d) Removal and refitting of the sump.
e) Removal and refitting of the big-end bearings, connecting rods, and pistons*.
f) Removal and refitting of the oil pump.
g) Renewal of the engine/transmission mountings.
h) Removal and refitting of the flywheel/driveplate.

* Although it is possible to remove these components with the engine in place, for reasons of access and cleanliness it is recommended that the engine is removed.

2 Compression test – description and interpretation

1 When engine performance is down, or if misfiring occurs which cannot be attributed to the ignition or fuel systems, a compression test can provide diagnostic clues as to the engine's condition. If the test is performed regularly, it can give warning of trouble before any other symptoms become apparent.
2 The engine must be fully warmed-up to normal operating temperature, the battery must be fully-charged, and all the spark plugs must be removed (Chapter 1A). The aid of an assistant will also be required.
3 Disable the ignition system by removing the fuel pump relay, to ensure that no fuel is injected as the engine is cranked.
4 Fit a compression tester to the No 1 cylinder spark plug hole – the type of tester which screws into the plug thread is to be preferred.
5 Have the assistant hold the throttle wide open, and crank the engine on the starter motor. After one or two revolutions, the compression pressure should build-up to a maximum figure, and then stabilise. Record the highest reading obtained.
6 Repeat the test on the remaining cylinders, recording the pressure in each.
7 All cylinders should produce very similar pressures; a difference of more than 1.5 bars between any two cylinders indicates a fault. Note that the compression should build-up quickly in a healthy engine. Low compression on the first stroke, followed by gradually increasing pressure on successive strokes, indicates worn piston rings. A low compression reading on the first stroke, which does not build-up during successive strokes, indicates leaking valves or a blown head gasket (a cracked head could also be the cause). Deposits on the undersides of the valve heads can also cause low compression.
8 If the pressure in any cylinder is low, carry out the following test to isolate the cause. Introduce a teaspoonful of clean oil into that cylinder through its spark plug hole, and repeat the test.
9 If the addition of oil temporarily improves the compression pressure, this indicates that bore or piston wear is responsible for the pressure loss. No improvement suggests that leaking or burnt valves, or a blown head gasket, may be to blame.
10 A low reading from two adjacent cylinders is almost certainly due to the head gasket having blown between them; the presence of coolant in the engine oil will confirm this.
11 If one cylinder is about 20 percent lower than the others and the engine has a slightly rough idle; a worn camshaft lobe could be the cause.
12 On completion of the test, refit the spark plugs (see Chapter 1A) and fuel pump relay.

3 Engine assembly and valve timing marks – general information and usage

111 type engines

1 Valve timing on the 111 series engine is set up at 20° ATDC, and not at TDC. At this position, tension from the valve springs is reduced, enabling, for example, the camshafts to be removed without the danger of the timing chain jumping across the camshaft sprocket teeth.
2 Using a spanner on the crankshaft pulley bolt, turn the engine until the 20° ATDC mark on the pulley is aligned with the timing pointer on the timing cover. To check that the engine is positioned correctly, remove the oil filler cap and check that the No 1 cylinder inlet camshaft lobes are facing upwards at an angle. If they are not, turn the engine one complete turn and align the marks again.
3 If necessary, the camshafts can be locked in position by first removing the air cleaner (Chapter 4A) and camshaft cover (Section 4 of this Chapter). Check that the timing holes in the camshaft front bearing caps are aligned with the holes in the camshaft front drive flanges. Mercedes-Benz technicians use a special U-shaped tool to do this, however, the use of two suitable drill bits inserted through the holes will be sufficient (see illustration).
4 If the timing chain is worn and stretched, it is possible that the timing holes may not align correctly with the crankshaft set at 20° ATDC. In this instance, it is permissible for the inlet camshaft to align between 20° and 30° ATDC, and for the exhaust camshaft to align between 25° and 35° ATDC. Note that incorrect fitting of the timing chain by one tooth on a camshaft sprocket will result in a change in crankshaft angle of approximately 20°.

271 type engines

5 Top dead centre (TDC) is the highest point in its travel up-and-down its cylinder bore that each piston reaches as the crankshaft rotates. While each piston reaches TDC both at the top of the compression stroke and again at the top of the exhaust stroke, for the purpose of timing the engine, TDC refers to the No 1 piston position at the top of its compression stroke.
6 No 1 piston and cylinder are at the front (timing chain) end of the engine. Note that the crankshaft rotates clockwise when viewed from the front of the vehicle.
7 Switch off the ignition and all electrical consumers, and remove the ignition key. Remove all four spark plugs as described in Chapter 1A.
8 Remove the camshaft cover as described in Section 4.
9 Turn the engine with a socket (27mm) on the crankshaft pulley bolt until the TDC markings on the front pulley align with the TDC mark on the timing chain cover (see illustrations).

3.9a Turn the engine using a socket and bar . . .

3.9b . . . to set the timing marks

3.10 Camshaft alignment marks

4.3 Disconnect the camshaft sensor – 271 type engine

4.4a Disconnect the wiring connector . . .

10 In this position the alignment marks on the camshafts should be in line with the markings on No 1 camshaft bearing caps (see illustration). The camshaft lobes on No 1 cylinder should be facing upwards, the engine is now at TDC on No 1 piston.

11 Refitting of components, is the reversal of the removal procedure with reference to the relevant Chapters

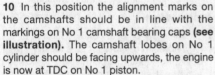

4 Camshaft cover – removal and refitting

4.4b . . . and unclip the PCV valve

4.5 Removing the cover from over the thermostat housing

Removal

1 On 111 type engines, undo the retaining bolts and remove the cover from down the centre of the camshaft cover. On 271 type engines, unclip the plastic cover from the top of the engine.

2 Disconnect the wiring connectors from the ignition coils, undo the retaining bolts and withdraw the ignition coils from the top of the spark plugs. Refer to Chapter 1A for further information.

3 Disconnect the wiring connector from the camshaft position sensor (see illustration).

4 On 271 type engines, disconnect the wiring connector, and then unclip the PCV valve from the camshaft cover (see illustrations).

5 On 111 type engines, remove the plastic cover from the front of the camshaft cover (see illustration).

6 On 111 type engines, undo the retaining bolt and disconnect the earth cable from the camshaft cover.

7 Unclip the wiring loom from the top of the camshaft cover and move it to one side (see illustration). Check around the cover for any hoses or wiring connectors still attached and remove if required.

8 Unscrew the bolts and lift the camshaft cover from the top of the cylinder head (see illustration). Recover the gasket from the groove in the cover.

Refitting

9 Clean the surfaces of the camshaft cover and cylinder head.

10 On 111 type engines, if necessary the spark plug tube seals can be renewed. Use

a screwdriver to prise them out from the camshaft cover, and then use a suitable metal tube to drive the new ones into position. The outer metal perimeters of the seals are quite

4.7 Unclip the wiring harness from the cover

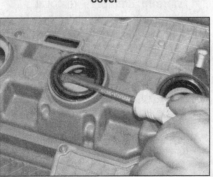

4.10a Prising the spark plug tube seals from the camshaft cover

thin, and it will be necessary to use an exact fitting metal tube (see illustrations).

11 On 271 type engines, renew the four seals down the centre of the camshaft cover

4.8 Removing the camshaft cover

4.10b Using a socket to drive in the new spark plug tube seals

4.11 Fit new seals to the spark plug recess

4.12 Fit new gasket to the camshaft cover

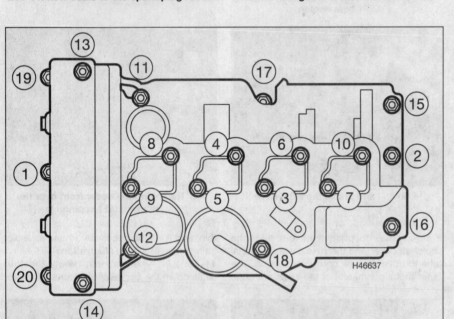

4.13 Camshaft cover tightening sequence – 271 type engine

for the spark plug access holes **(see illustration)**

12 Locate the new gasket in the camshaft cover outer groove, then position the cover on the cylinder head. Insert the retaining bolts and hand-tighten them at this stage. Make sure that the gasket is still correctly located in the cover groove. To do this, feel around the rear of the cylinder head **(see illustration)**.

13 Fully tighten the bolts to the specified

5.5 Removing the crankshaft pulley bolt and dished washers – 111 type engine

torque setting. On 271 type engines, follow the correct sequence for tightening **(see illustration)**.

14 Complete the installation by reversing the removal procedure. When all components are refitted, start the engine and check carefully around the camshaft cover for any oil leaks.

5 Crankshaft pulley/vibration damper – removal, inspection and refitting

Removal

1 To gain better access, remove the fan and shroud from the rear of the radiator with reference to Chapter 3.

2 Remove the auxiliary drivebelt, with reference to Chapter 1A.

3 Working under the front of the vehicle, undo the retaining bolts and remove the engine undershield.

4 The crankshaft must now be held stationary while the pulley bolt is loosened. The bolt is tightened to a high torque. Mercedes-Benz

technicians remove the starter motor and use a special tool which is bolted to the transmission and locks the flywheel. It may be possible to insert a wide-bladed screwdriver between the starter ring gear teeth to prevent the engine from turning.

5 Unscrew the crankshaft pulley bolt then slide the pulley from the front of the crankshaft. Note the location of the washers under the head of the bolt, as they need to be fitted in the same position on refitting **(see illustration)**. If the pulley is tight on the crankshaft, use a suitable puller to remove it. A two-legged puller, which locates in the pulley holes, is ideal.

6 If necessary, remove the Woodruff key from the groove in the nose of the crankshaft.

Inspection

7 Examine the oil seal contact surface of the pulley/vibration damper for an excessive wear groove. If evident, it is permissible to position the oil seal slightly further into the timing chain cover so that it runs on the unworn area of the pulley. Alternatively, the pulley should be renewed. The oil seal in the timing cover must be renewed as a matter of course with reference to Section 14.

Refitting

8 Locate the Woodruff key in the groove in the nose of the crankshaft. Make sure that it is firmly pressed into position, and that its outer edge is parallel with the crankshaft so that the pulley/vibration damper will engage with it easily.

9 Wipe clean and lightly oil the seal contact surface of the pulley, and then slide it fully onto the crankshaft, engaging it with the Woodruff key.

10 Lightly oil the threads of the crankshaft pulley bolt and the washers, and then locate the washer(s) correctly onto the bolt, as noted on removal. Insert the bolt and tighten it to the specified torque while holding the crankshaft stationary as for removal. If necessary, refit the starter motor.

11 Refit the auxiliary drivebelt with reference to Chapter 1A.

12 Refit the fan and shroud to the rear of the radiator with reference to Chapter 3.

13 Where applicable, refit the engine undershield.

6 Timing chain cover – removal and refitting

Removal

1 Disconnect the battery negative (earth) lead and position it away from the terminal.

2 Remove the camshaft cover as described in Section 4.

3 To improve access, remove the fan and shroud from the rear of the radiator, as described in Chapter 3.

4 Remove the auxiliary drivebelt (and air

6.6a Unbolt the thermostat housing . . .

6.6b . . . and recover the O-ring seal –
111 type engine

6.6c Disconnect the coolant hose . . .

6.6d . . . and unbolt the thermostat
housing – 271 type engine

6.9 Withdraw the coolant pump from the
timing chain cover – 111 type engine

6.10 Remove the front cover from the
cylinder head – 271 type engine

conditioning compressor drivebelt where fitted) with reference to Chapter 1A.

5 Drain the cooling system as described in Chapter 1A.

6 Disconnect the upper radiator hose and unbolt the thermostat housing from the front of the cylinder head. Recover the O-ring seal **(see illustrations)**.

7 Disconnect the lower radiator hose from the coolant pump.

8 Undo the retaining bolts and remove the pulley from the front of the coolant pump. Hold the pulley stationary with an oil filter strap or with the auxiliary drivebelt.

9 Remove the coolant pump from the front cover, as described in Chapter 3 **(see illustration)**.

10 Disconnect any wiring connectors from the front of the engine and move to one side, then unbolt the front cover from the cylinder head **(see illustration)**.

11 Unbolt the alternator from its mounting bracket on the front of the engine and move it to one side.

12 Unbolt the auxiliary drivebelt tensioner from the timing chain cover **(see illustration)**.

13 Unbolt the pulley from the power steering pump. Hold the pulley stationary with an oil filter strap or with the auxiliary drivebelt.

14 Unbolt the power steering pump and position it to the left-hand side of the engine compartment. **Do not** disconnect the hydraulic lines from the pump.

15 On models with air conditioning, unbolt the compressor from the engine with reference to Chapter 3 and support it to one side. **Do not** disconnect the refrigerant lines from the compressor.

16 Using a socket on the crankshaft pulley bolt, turn the engine until the timing marks are aligned, as described in Section 3.

17 Use a dab of paint or a marker pen to mark

the timing chain and the inlet and exhaust camshaft sprockets in relation to each other. This is necessary to ensure the chain is refitted correctly and the valve timing maintained.

18 Remove the crankshaft pulley as described in Section 5.

19 Remove the sump as described in Section 11.

20 Remove the timing chain tensioner, as described in Section 8.

271 type engines

21 Undo the mounting bolt and remove the auxiliary belt idler pulley from the engine front cover **(see illustration)**.

22 Remove the blanking plug and then undo the bolt from the left-hand timing chain sliding rail **(see illustration)**.

23 Unscrew and remove the upper bolts securing the timing cover to the cylinder head.

24 Unscrew the remaining bolts and remove

6.12 Remove the auxiliary drivebelt
tensioner from the left-hand side of the
engine – 111 type engine

6.21 Remove the idler pulley

6.22 Remove chain guide pin blanking
plug - arrowed

6.28 Using a universal slide hammer and bolt to remove the guide rail pin from the front of the cylinder head

the timing chain cover from the front of the engine, taking care not to damage the front part of the cylinder head gasket. To ensure the bolts are refitted in the correct locations, make a drawing of their positions, or use a dab of paint on them to identify them. If the location dowels are loose, remove them also.

25 It is recommended that the crankshaft front oil seal be renewed with reference to Section 14.

111 type engines

26 Hold the exhaust camshaft stationary using a spanner on the flats provided, and then unscrew the three bolts and remove the sprocket from the location peg on the camshaft flange. Release the sprocket from the timing chain. **Note:** *The sprocket retaining bolts must be renewed every time they are removed.*

27 Remove the inlet camshaft sprocket as described in Section 8.

28 Pull the guide rail pin from the front of the cylinder head. Mercedes-Benz technicians use a slide hammer tool which is screwed into the pin, however a universal slide hammer and bolt can be used **(see illustration)**, or alternatively it may be possible make up a removal tool using a long bolt, nut, large washers and metal tube. Locate the metal tube over the guide rail pin, and fit the nut to the bolt followed by the washers. Screw the bolt into the pin through the tube, and then tighten the nut against the washers to extract the pin. **Note:** *If the pin has not been removed for some time, it can be very tight.*

6.30 Removing the air conditioning compressor mounting plate

29 Unscrew and remove the 4 upper bolts securing the timing cover to the cylinder head.

30 Unbolt the air conditioning compressor mounting plate from the lower left-hand end of the timing chain cover **(see illustration)**.

31 Unscrew the remaining bolts and remove the timing chain cover from the front of the engine **(see illustration)**, taking care not to damage the front part of the cylinder head gasket. To ensure the bolts are refitted in the correct locations, make a drawing of their positions, or use a dab of paint on them to identify them. Remove the O-ring seals from their location on the inside of the cover. If the location dowels are loose, remove them also.

32 With the timing cover removed, use a pair of pliers to extract the chain tensioner oil reservoir non-return valve from the front of cylinder block. Clean it and inspect for wear and damage, and if necessary, renew it. Then locate the oil reservoir non-return valve back in its location in the front of the cylinder block.

33 It is recommended that the crankshaft front oil seal be renewed with reference to Section 14.

Refitting

34 Clean away all traces of old sealant, then apply new sealant to the mating surfaces of the timing cover, and where applicable, fit new O-ring seals; make sure that no sealant is allowed to enter the oil supply chamber for the chain tensioner. If removed, refit the location dowels in the cylinder block. Clean the front part of the cylinder head gasket, which contacts the timing cover.

35 Pull up the timing chain tightly so that it is located on the guides, and then locate the timing cover on the front of the engine **Note:** *If the chain is not pulled up, there is the possibility of a loop forming near the crankshaft sprocket.*

36 Insert the cover bolts in their previously-noted positions and tighten to the specified torque.

37 Complete the rest of the installation by reversing the removal procedure, referring to the relevant Chapters. When all components are refitted, start the engine and check carefully around the timing chain cover and sump for any oil leaks. Also check for coolant leaks.

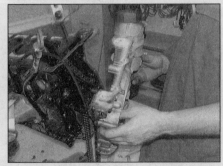

6.31 Removing the timing chain cover from the front of the engine

7 Timing chain – inspection and renewal

Inspection

1 Remove the air cleaner assembly as described in Chapter 4A.

2 Remove the camshaft cover as described in Section 4.

3 Using a socket on the crankshaft pulley/vibration damper hub bolt, turn the engine so that the whole length of the chain can be progressively viewed at the camshaft sprocket.

4 The chain should be renewed if the sprocket or chain is worn, indicated by excessive lateral play between the links, and excessive noise in operation. It is wise to renew the chain in any case if the engine is to be dismantled for overhaul. Note that the rollers on a very badly worn chain may be slightly grooved. To avoid future problems, if there is any doubt at all about the condition of the chain, renew it.

Renewal

Note 1: *This following procedure, uses a chain breaker/riveter to renew the chain without removing the front timing chain cover, a second person will be required to assist fitting the timing chain.*

Note 2: *If the chain needs to be renewed as a complete assembly, then remove the front timing chain cover as described in Section 6.*

5 Disconnect the battery negative (earth) lead and position it away from the terminal.

6 If not already done, proceed as described in paragraphs 1 and 2.

7 Remove the spark plugs as described in Chapter 1A.

8 Using a socket on the crankshaft pulley bolt, turn the engine until the timing marks are aligned, as described in Section 3.

9 Remove the timing chain tensioner as described in Section 8.

10 With the engine still in the ATDC or TDC position (as applicable), use a couple of cable-ties to keep the timing chain on the camshaft sprocket. Put some clean rag into the timing chain recess to prevent anything dropping down into the engine.

11 Use the chain breaker to press out one of the timing chain pins and split the timing chain.

12 Connect the new timing chain to the old chain and press the chain link pin back into position. **Note:** *Make sure the new chain is connected to the front part of the chain, as the engine has to be turned clockwise, in the direction of rotation to feed the chain around the sprockets.*

13 With the new chain connected securely to the old chain, take a firm hold of both ends of the chain and remove the cable-ties from the camshaft sprocket. Remove the clean rag from around the timing chain before turning the engine.

14 With the aid of an assistant, turn the engine in the direction of rotation. Keeping the timing chain taut feed it around the crankshaft sprocket, until the new chain comes all the way around to the camshaft sprocket.

15 Cable-tie both ends of the timing chain back to the camshaft sprocket, and refit the clean rag back into the timing chain recess.

16 Use the chain breaker to press out the timing chain pin and split the old timing chain from the new timing chain. **Note:** *Make sure the chain is pulled tight on the lower section of the engine, and the upper section slack to allow for the fitting of the chain tensioner.*

17 Check that the timing marks on the crankshaft pulley and timing chain cover are aligned, and the marks on the camshaft and camshaft bearing caps are still aligned correctly.

18 Fit the new timing chain link, using the timing chain riveter to connect the two ends of the chain securely. Always read the instructions that come with the chain riveter, as there are many different types available. The link pins need to be riveted securely, to prevent the chain coming apart.

19 Remove the clean rag from the timing chain recess, and fit the timing chain tensioner, with reference to Section 8. With the tensioner now fitted, check the timing marks are still in line.

20 Rotate the engine two complete turns and check the timing marks come back in alignment. Refer to Section 3 to check timing mark alignment is correct.

21 Refit the camshaft cover with reference to Section 4.

22 Refit the spark plugs as described in Chapter 1A.

23 Refit the air cleaner assembly.

24 Reconnect the battery negative lead.

8 Timing chain tensioner and camshaft sprockets – removal, inspection and refitting

111 type engine tensioner

Removal

1 Remove the top cover from the air cleaner and the air cleaner-to-throttle housing air duct.

2 Using a spanner on the crankshaft pulley bolt, turn the engine until the 20° ATDC mark on the pulley is aligned with the timing pointer on the timing cover. This will release any tension from the timing chain and ensure that it will not jump across any of the camshaft sprocket teeth when the tensioner is removed. To check that the engine is positioned correctly, remove the oil filler cap and check that the No 1 cylinder inlet camshaft lobes are both facing upwards at an angle.

3 Cover the alternator with a cloth rag as a precaution against anything falling into it.

4 Using an Allen key unscrew the timing chain tensioner end piece approximately one turn **(see illustration)**.

5 Unscrew the tensioner from the cylinder head and recover the washer **(see illustrations)**. **Note:** *Once the tensioner has been*

unscrewed, it must be completely dismantled and reset. **Do not** *attempt to retighten the tensioner in its housing at this stage, otherwise the timing chain will be overtensioned.*

6 Completely unscrew the end piece from the tensioner. Recover the seal.

7 Remove the filler pin and main compression spring.

8 Push out the thrust pin and detent spring **(see illustration)**.

Inspection

9 Thoroughly clean the tensioner components, and examine them for signs of damage or wear.

10 Check the condition of the springs, and renew if necessary.

11 Note that the oil reservoir of the timing chain tensioner is located in the front of the cylinder block, and is accessed by removing the timing cover. See Section 6 for more details.

12 Apply clean engine oil to the components as they are being reassembled.

Refitting

13 Insert the thrust pin and detent spring into the outer end of the tensioner housing until the pin's inner end is flush with the inner end of the housing.

14 Refit the tensioner together with a new washer, and tighten it to the specified torque **(see illustration)**.

15 Locate a new washer on the end piece and make sure it remains in position by using a little grease **(see illustration)**.

16 Insert the main compression spring, filler

8.4 Unscrew the timing chain tensioner end piece approximately one turn . . .

8.5a . . . then unscrew the tensioner . . .

8.5b . . . and remove it from the cylinder head

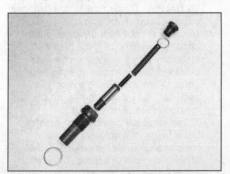

8.8 Timing chain tensioner components

8.14 Refit the tensioner together with a new washer

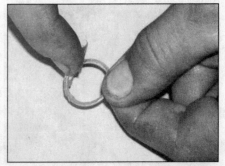

8.15 Use a little grease to hold the new washer on the end piece

8.16 Insert the main compression spring and filler pin

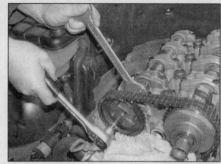

8.31a Hold the exhaust camshaft stationary while loosening the sprocket bolts

8.31b Releasing the exhaust camshaft sprocket from the timing chain

pin, and end piece, press in and screw on a few threads **(see illustration)**.

17 Tighten the end piece to the specified torque.

18 Refit the top cover to the air cleaner.

271 type engine tensioner

Removal

19 Remove the alternator as described in Chapter 5A.

20 Unscrew the tensioner from the right-hand side of the timing chain cover

Inspection

21 The tensioner is a complete unit and cannot be stripped down, if there is any fault with the tensioner, it will need to be renewed.

Refitting

22 Refit the tensioner together with a new sealing washer, and tighten it to the specified torque.

23 Refit the alternator with reference to Chapter 5A.

Camshaft sprockets

Removal

24 Remove the camshaft cover as described in Section 4.

25 Drain the cooling system as described in Chapter 1A.

26 Disconnect the upper radiator hose, then unbolt the thermostat housing from the front cover and recover the O-ring seal.

27 Unbolt the front cover from the cylinder head, and where applicable, recover the sealing ring. Check that the location dowels remain in the cover.

28 Using a spanner on the crankshaft pulley bolt, turn the engine until the timing marks are aligned with the timing mark on the timing cover, as described in Section 3. On engines with a variable valve timing device fitted to the front of

the inlet camshaft, the device must be in its retarded position (ie, when viewed from the rear, the dog in the upper cut-out must be on the left-hand side of the cut-out). On 111 type engines, insert suitable drills or metal dowels through the holes in the camshaft front bearing caps to lock the camshafts. In this position the camshafts are not under any tension when the timing chain is removed. Note that it may be necessary to turn the crankshaft between 20° and 30° ATDC in order to get both camshaft sprockets aligned with the bearing cap holes (refer to Section 3).

29 Use a dab of paint or a marker pen to mark the timing chain and the inlet and exhaust camshaft sprockets in relation to each other. This is necessary to ensure the chain is refitted correctly and the valve timing maintained.

30 Remove the chain tensioner as described earlier in this Section, then unbolt the upper chain guide from the front of the cylinder head.

31 On engines without variable valve timing, hold the camshaft stationary using a spanner on the flats provided, then unscrew the three Torx bolts and remove the sprocket from the location peg on the camshaft flange. Release the sprocket from the timing chain **(see illustrations)**. **Note:** *The sprocket retaining bolts must be renewed every time they are removed.* Tie the timing chain to one side.

32 On engines with a variable valve timing device on the front of the camshaft, use the following procedure to remove the sprocket.

 a) *Counterhold the armature (using a spanner on the flats provided) at the front of the inlet camshaft, and unscrew the securing bolt. Withdraw the armature **(see illustration)**. Discard the bolt, a new one must be used on refitting.*

 b) *Unscrew the nut from the front of the camshaft while holding the camshaft stationary with a spanner on the flats provided, then withdraw the stepped collar. When unscrewing the nut, the camshaft can be counterheld on the flats provided **(see illustrations)**.*

 c) *At this stage the piston of the variable valve timing device must be held on the camshaft while the outer sprocket is removed from its splines. To do this, either screw on a flanged nut or use a washer together with the collar securing nut. With the nut in position, slide the*

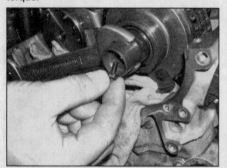

8.32a Counterhold the armature and unscrew the bolt

8.32b Unscrew the nut . . .

8.32c . . . and withdraw the stepped collar

8.32d Using a flanged nut to hold the piston on the camshaft while removing the sprocket

8.32e Releasing the timing chain from the inlet camshaft sprocket

8.32f Unscrew the temporary nut . . .

8.32g . . . and withdraw the piston and spring

8.32h Unscrew the bolts . . .

8.32i . . . and remove the hub/plate from the inlet camshaft flange

8.32j Extract the circlip . . .

sprocket from the splined centre hub, at the same time releasing the timing chain from the sprocket teeth **(see illustrations)**. Tie the chain to one side using string or wire.

d) Unscrew the temporary nut, and then withdraw the piston, followed by the spring. Note that the smaller end of the spring locates on the inner hub of the device **(see illustrations)**.

e) Hold the inlet camshaft stationary using a spanner on the flats provided, then unscrew the three Torx bolts and remove the hub/plate from the location pin on the camshaft flange **(see illustrations)**. **Note:** The sprocket retaining bolts must be renewed every time they are removed.

f) If desired, working at the rear of the hub/plate remove the circlip, and withdraw the control plunger and spring **(see illustrations)**.

33 Note that the timing chain cannot become disengaged from the crankshaft sprocket, since the timing cover incorporates a retaining stub, however, it is recommended that the chain is kept tensioned by tying it to one side. Note that the timing cover also incorporates an upper retaining stub, so that it is impossible for the chain to drop completely into the timing cover cavity with the timing cover in position.

34 If necessary, remove the locating pins from the ends of the camshafts.

Inspection

35 Examine the teeth on the inlet and exhaust sprockets for wear. Each tooth forms an inverted V. If worn, the side of each tooth under tension will be slightly concave in shape when compared with the other side of the tooth (ie, the teeth will have a 'hooked' appearance). If the teeth appear worn, the sprockets must be renewed.

Refitting

36 Refit the locating pins to the camshafts.

37 On engines without variable valve timing, engage the timing chain with the exhaust camshaft sprocket, then refit the sprocket to the camshaft, insert the new bolts, and tighten to the specified torque and angle while holding the camshaft stationary with a spanner on the flats provided **(see illustration)**.

38 On engines with variable valve timing, refit the camshaft sprocket using the following procedure.

a) Refit the control plunger and spring to the hub/plate and secure with the circlip.

b) Refit the hub/plate on the camshaft flange, insert the new bolts, and tighten to the specified torque and angle while holding the camshaft stationary with a spanner on the flats provided **(see illustrations)**.

8.32k . . . and remove the control plunger and spring

8.37 Engage the timing chain with the exhaust camshaft sprocket

8.38a Refit the hub/plate on the camshaft flange . . .

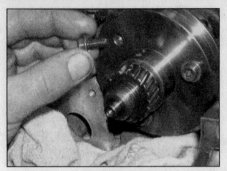

8.38b . . . insert the new bolts . . .

8.38c . . . and tighten the bolts to the specified torque and angle

8.38d Refit the spring and piston . . .

8.38e . . . and temporarily hold with a nut

8.38f Slide on the inlet sprocket and engage it with the timing chain . . .

the timing chain with the sprocket making sure that the previously-made marks are aligned with each other.

e) Unscrew the temporary nut, then refit the stepped collar followed by the retaining nut. Tighten the nut to the specified torque while holding the camshaft stationary with a spanner on the flats provided (see illustrations).

f) Refit the armature, insert the new bolt, and tighten to the specified torque while counterholding the armature with a spanner on the flats provided (see illustrations).

39 Refit the upper timing chain guide to the front of the cylinder head, and tighten the bolts to the specified torque, then refit the tensioner as described earlier in this Section.

40 On 111 type engines, remove the locking drills/dowels then refit the front cover together with a new O-ring and tighten the bolts to the specified torque.

c) Locate the spring on the hub (small end first) and refit the piston on the hub/plate. It is necessary to press the piston against the tension of the spring when locating it on the splines – note that there is a master spline to ensure correct alignment.

Fit a temporary nut to hold the piston on the hub/plate (see illustrations).

d) Slide the inlet sprocket onto the piston hub splines – note there is a master spline to ensure correct alignment (see illustration). At the same time engage

8.38g . . . refit the stepped collar . . .

8.38h . . . and nut . . .

8.38i . . . refit the armature . . .

8.38j . . . and bolt . . .

8.38k . . . torque-tighten . . .

8.38l . . . and angle-tighten the bolt

9.5 Remove the thermostat housing pipe – 271 type engine

9.6 Remove the cylinder head front cover – 271 type engine

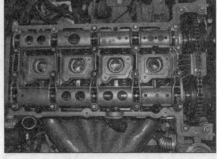

9.13 Camshaft upper housing retaining bolts (20) – 271 type engine

41 Refit the thermostat housing together with a new O-ring seal.

42 Refit the camshaft cover as described in Section 4.

9 Camshafts and hydraulic tappets – removal, inspection and refitting

Removal

1 Disconnect the battery negative (earth) lead and position it away from the terminal.

2 Remove the camshaft cover as described in Section 4.

3 At this stage it is possible to carry out a basic check of the hydraulic tappets. Turn the engine as necessary so that the heel of the first camshaft lobe is positioned over the hydraulic tappet. Using a wooden or plastic tool, press down on the tappet and check that it feels firm. If it moves down, the internal components are not sealing correctly and the tappet must be renewed. Check the tappet of the second valve on that cylinder, and then turn the engine as necessary to check the remaining tappets. **Note:** *Do not use excessive force to depress the tappets; otherwise the valves may open, giving a false indication.*

4 Drain the cooling system as described in Chapter 1A.

5 Disconnect the coolant hose, and then unbolt the thermostat housing from the cylinder head front cover **(see illustration)**. Recover the O-ring.

6 Disconnect the wiring from the variable valve timing coil(s), and then unbolt the front cover from the front of the cylinder head. Where applicable, recover the sealing ring **(see illustration)**.

7 Use a dab of paint or a marker pen to mark the timing chain and the inlet and exhaust camshaft sprockets in relation to each other. This is necessary to ensure the chain is refitted correctly and the valve timing maintained. If not already marked, identify each camshaft with an I for inlet and E for exhaust.

8 Remove the chain tensioner as described in Section 8.

9 Unbolt the timing chain upper guide from the front of the cylinder head. On 271 type

engines, this is part of the camshaft upper housing.

10 If required, remove the sprockets from the inlet and exhaust camshafts with reference to Section 8. **Note:** *The sprocket retaining bolts must be renewed every time they are removed.*

11 With reference to Section 3, use a socket on the crankshaft pulley bolt, and turn the engine until the timing mark on the pulley is aligned with the timing mark on the timing cover. Turn the crankshaft past TDC by approximately 30°, this will ensure that the camshafts can be rotated without the valves touching the tops of the pistons.

12 On 111 type engines, note that the camshaft bearing caps are numbered from 1 to 10, starting at the front of the exhaust camshaft. Progressively unscrew the bearing cap bolts then remove the caps from the inlet and exhaust camshafts.

13 On 271 type engines, the camshafts have an upper bearing housing which covers the both camshafts. Progressively unscrew the upper bearing housing working from the outside to the inside. Then remove the housing from the inlet and exhaust camshafts **(see illustration)**.

14 Note the angled position of the camshaft lobes of No 1 cylinder as an aid to refitting, then carefully lift the inlet and exhaust camshafts from the cylinder head.

15 Obtain sixteen small, clean containers, and number them 1 to 16 or a large container split into 16 different sections.

16 On 111 type engines, use a rubber sucker to withdraw each hydraulic tappet in turn from

the cylinder head, invert it to prevent oil loss, and place it in its respective container, which should then be filled with clean engine oil **(see illustrations)**. **Note:** *Do not use a magnet to withdraw the tappets, as this will magnetise the upper surface, causing swarf to be attracted to it.* Do not interchange the hydraulic tappets, or their rate of wear will be much increased. Do not allow them to lose oil or they will take a long time to refill on restarting the engine.

17 On 271 type engines, lift out the roller/rocker arm complete with hydraulic tappet from the cylinder head, and place it in its respective container, which should then be filled with clean engine oil. Do not interchange the roller/rocker arm and hydraulic tappets, or their rate of wear will be much increased. Do not allow them to lose oil or they may take a long time to refill on restarting the engine.

Inspection

18 With the camshafts, roller/rocker arms and hydraulic tappets removed, check all components for signs of obvious wear (scoring, pitting, etc) and for ovality, and renew if necessary. Clean all the components thoroughly before making the check.

19 Measure the outside diameter of each tappet – take measurements at the top and bottom of each tappet, then a second set at right-angles to the first; if any measurement is significantly different from the others, the tappet is tapered or oval (as applicable) and must be renewed. If the tappets or the cylinder head bores are excessively worn, new tappets and/or a new cylinder head will be required.

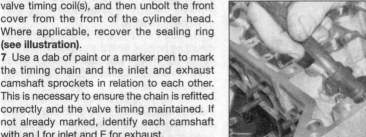

9.16a Use a rubber sucker . . .

9.16b . . . to remove the hydraulic tappets from the cylinder head

10.8 Disconnecting the coolant hose from the left-hand rear of the cylinder head

10.9 Disconnecting the wiring from the coolant temperature sensor

10.10 Disconnecting the radiator top hose

20 If the engine's valve components have sounded noisy, particularly if the noise persists after initial start-up from cold, there is reason to suspect a faulty hydraulic tappet. Only a good mechanic experienced in these engines can tell whether the noise level is typical, or if renewal of one or more of the tappets is warranted. If faulty tappets are diagnosed, and the engine's service history is unknown, it is always worth trying the effect of renewing the engine oil and filter (see Chapter 1A), using *only* good-quality engine oil of the recommended viscosity and specification, before going to the expense of renewing the any of the tappets.

21 Visually examine the camshaft lobes for score marks, pitting, and evidence of overheating (blue, discoloured areas). Look for flaking away of the hardened surface layer of each lobe. If any such signs are evident, renew the component concerned.

22 Examine the camshaft bearing journals and the cylinder head bearing surfaces for signs of obvious wear or pitting. If any such signs are evident, renew the component concerned. On 271 type engines, check the upper and lower camshaft bearing housings for wear.

23 Using a micrometer, measure the diameter of each journal at several points. If the diameter of any one journal is excessive between each measurement, renew the camshaft.

Refitting

24 Locate the hydraulic tappets/roller rocker arms in their respective bores in the cylinder head.

25 Lubricate the camshaft journals with fresh engine oil, then locate the inlet and exhaust camshafts in the cylinder head in their positions noted on removal. Check the timing marks on the camshafts are aligned as described in Section 3. On 111 type engines, the timing holes in the front bearing caps and camshaft flanges must be aligned with each other.

26 Locate the bearing caps/upper camshaft housing in their original positions, and then insert the bolts and progressively tighten them to the specified torque. The tightening procedure must be carried out carefully so that the camshafts are not unduly stressed. On 271 type engines, gradually tighten the bolts in the upper camshaft bearing housing, starting from the centre and spiralling outwards.

27 On 111 type engines, turn the engine slightly anti-clockwise until the 20° ATDC timing mark on the pulley is aligned with the timing mark on the timing cover.

28 On 271 type engines, turn the crankshaft 30° anti-clockwise back to the TDC position.

29 Refit the sprockets and timing chain to the inlet and exhaust camshafts with reference to Section 8.

30 Refit the timing chain guide to the front of the cylinder head and tighten the bolts securely.

31 Refit the chain tensioner as described in Section 8.

32 Apply suitable sealant to the mating surfaces, then refit the front cover to the front of the cylinder head together with a new O-ring. Tighten the bolts to the specified torque. Reconnect the wiring to the variable valve timing coil.

33 Refit the thermostat housing together with a new O-ring and tighten the bolts securely. Reconnect the by-pass hose and tighten the clip.

34 Refit the camshaft cover as described in Section 4.

35 Refill and bleed the cooling system with reference to Chapter 1A.

---

10 Cylinder head – removal, inspection and refitting

Note: *A new cylinder head gasket will be required on refitting, and new cylinder head bolts may be required – see text. Ensure that*

10.14 Using a universal slide hammer and bolt to remove the guide rail pin from the front of the cylinder head

the engine is cold before attempting to remove the cylinder head.

Removal

1 Remove the covers from the top of the engine and make a note of the routing of any wiring and hoses around the cylinder head to aid refitting.

2 Disconnect the battery negative (earth) lead and position it away from the terminal.

3 Raise the bonnet to the fully open position, as described in Chapter 11.

4 Drain the cooling system as described in Chapter 1A. Also unscrew the crankcase drain plug located on the side of the cylinder block, and drain the coolant.

5 Refer to Chapter 4C and disconnect the exhaust downpipe from the exhaust manifold. If required, remove the complete manifold from the cylinder head with reference to Chapter 4C. A new exhaust gasket will be required.

6 Remove the camshaft cover as described in Section 4 and the spark plugs as described in Chapter 1A.

7 Unbolt the inlet manifold from the left-hand side of the cylinder head and support to one side with reference to Chapter 4A. It may be necessary to completely remove the inlet manifold on some models.

8 Slacken the securing clip and disconnect the coolant hose from the left-hand rear of the cylinder head **(see illustration)**.

9 Disconnect the wiring connector from the coolant temperature sensor **(see illustration)**.

10 Slacken the securing clips and disconnect the coolant hoses from the cylinder head **(see illustration)**.

11 Remove the camshafts, camshaft housings (where applicable) and hydraulic tappets as described in Section 9.

12 Unbolt the engine oil level dipstick tube mounting bracket from the cylinder head.

13 On automatic transmission models, unbolt the transmission fluid level dipstick tube from the cylinder head.

14 Pull the guide rail pin from the front of the cylinder head. Mercedes-Benz technicians use a slide hammer tool which is screwed into the pin, however a universal slide hammer and bolt can be used **(see illustration)**, or alternatively it may be possible make up a removal tool using a long bolt, nut, large washers and metal tube. Locate the metal tube over the guide rail pin, and fit the nut to the bolt followed by the washers. Screw the bolt into the pin through the tube, and then tighten the nut against the washers to extract the pin. **Note:** *If the pin has not been removed for some time, it can be very tight.*

15 Unscrew and remove the four upper bolts securing the timing cover to the cylinder head. The bolts are located in the recess at the front of the cylinder head **(see illustration)**.

16 Make sure that the engine is cold, then progressively unscrew the cylinder head bolts in two stages, using the **reverse** sequence to the tightening sequence **(see illustration 10.32a)**.

17 With the help of an assistant, lift the cylinder head (complete with exhaust manifold, where applicable) from the block and remove from the engine compartment. If it is stuck, do not attempt to prise the head from the block with a screwdriver or similar tool as the mating surfaces will be damaged. Rock the head from side-to-side to release it. As the head is being removed, take care not to damage the timing chain guide rails.

18 Recover the cylinder head gasket. If necessary, remove the location dowels from the block.

Inspection

19 Refer to Chapter 2C for details of cylinder head dismantling and reassembly. Where applicable, the exhaust manifold can be removed with reference to Chapter 4C.

20 The mating faces of the cylinder head and block must be perfectly clean before refitting the head. Use a scraper to remove all traces of gasket and carbon, and also clean the tops of the pistons. Take particular care with the aluminium cylinder head, as the soft metal is easily damaged. Also make sure that debris is not allowed to enter the oil and water passages. Using adhesive tape and paper, seal the water, oil and bolt holes in the cylinder block. To prevent carbon entering the gap between the pistons and bores, smear a little grease in the gap. After cleaning each piston, rotate the crankshaft so that the piston moves **down** the bore, and then wipe out the grease and carbon with a cloth rag.

21 Check the block and head for nicks, deep scratches and other damage. If very slight, they may be removed carefully with a file. More serious damage may be repaired by machining, but this is a specialist job.

22 If warpage of the cylinder head is suspected, use a straight-edge to check it for distortion, with reference to Chapter 2C.

23 Clean out the bolt holes in the block using a pipe cleaner or rag and a screwdriver. Make sure that all oil and water is removed, otherwise there is a possibility of the block being cracked by hydraulic pressure when the bolts are tightened.

24 Examine the bolt threads and the threads in the cylinder block for damage. If necessary, use the correct size tap to chase out the threads in the block.

25 The manufacturers recommend that the cylinder head bolts are measured, to determine

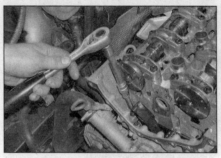

10.15 Removing the four upper bolts securing the timing cover to the cylinder head

10.29 Locate the new cylinder head gasket on the cylinder block

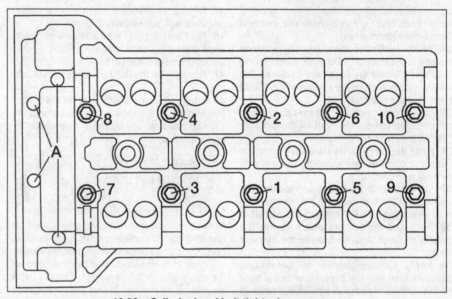

10.32a Cylinder head bolt tightening sequence

A Bolts securing cylinder head to timing cover

whether renewal is necessary; however, some owners may wish to renew all the bolts as a matter of course.

26 Measure the length of each bolt from the base of the head to the end of the shank. If the bolt length is greater than the maximum specified, the bolts should be renewed.

27 Reassemble the cylinder head with reference to Chapter 2C. Where applicable, refit the exhaust manifold together with a new gasket with reference to Chapter 4C.

Refitting

Note: *A new cylinder head gasket will be required on refitting. The new gasket will be supplied in a sealed wrapper – do not remove the wrapper until the gasket is about to be fitted.*

28 If removed, refit the location dowels in the block.

29 Fit the new gasket over the dowels on the cylinder block, ensuring that it is fitted the correct way round **(see illustration)**.

30 Carefully lower the cylinder head onto the block, while guiding the aperture in the front of the head over the timing chain guide rails. If necessary, engage the help of an assistant to hold the rails.

31 Oil the threads and the contact faces of the cylinder head bolts, and then insert them and screw them into the cylinder block by hand.

32 Tighten the cylinder head bolts in the order shown **(see illustration)**. Tighten the bolts in the stages given in the Specifications – ie, tighten all bolts to the Stage 1 torque, then tighten all bolts to the Stage 2 angle, and finally tighten all the bolts to the Stage 3 angle **(see illustration)**.

10.32b Angle-tightening the cylinder head bolts

10.33 Torque-tightening the timing cover-to-cylinder head upper bolts

10.34a Apply sealant to the guide rail pin . . .

10.34b . . . then drive it into the front of the cylinder head

33 Insert the cylinder head-to-timing cover upper bolts and tighten them to the specified torque **(see illustration)**.

34 Apply sealant to the guide rail pin, then insert it in the front of the cylinder head making sure that it enters the top of the guide rail. Tap it fully into position using a soft metal drift and hammer **(see illustrations)**.

35 On 111 type engines, refit the upper timing chain guide rail to the front of the cylinder head with reference to Section 8.

36 Refit the camshafts, camshaft housings (where applicable) and hydraulic tappets with reference to Section 9.

37 On automatic transmission models, refit and tighten the bolt securing the transmission fluid level dipstick tube to the cylinder head.

38 Refit and tighten the bolt securing the engine oil level dipstick tube to the cylinder head.

39 Apply suitable sealant to the mating surfaces then refit the front cover to the front of the cylinder head and tighten the bolts to the specified torque.

40 Reconnect the wiring to the camshaft position sensor(s) and variable valve timing coil(s), and secure it with a cable-tie.

41 Refit the thermostat housing together with a new O-ring and tighten the bolts, then reconnect the hoses and tighten the clips.

42 Refit the camshaft cover with reference to Section 4 and the spark plugs as described in Chapter 1A.

43 Refit the coolant hose to the rear of the cylinder head and tighten the clip.

44 Refit the inlet manifold to the cylinder head with reference to Chapter 4A.

45 Where applicable, refit the exhaust manifold with reference to Chapter 4C.

46 Refit and tighten the radiator and crank-case drain plug, then refill the cooling system as described in Chapter 1A.

47 Reconnect the battery negative (earth) lead.

48 When all components are refitted, start the engine and check carefully around the cylinder head for any oil leaks. Also check for coolant leaks.

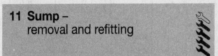

11 Sump – removal and refitting

Note: *A suitable hoist and lifting tackle will be required for this operation. To carry out this procedure, the front suspension crossmember will need to be lowered, to allow enough room for the sump to be removed. On 111 type engines, a new sump gasket will be required on refitting, for 271 type engines, sealant will be required.*

Removal

1 Apply the parking brake, then jack up the front of the vehicle and support it on axle stands (see *Jacking and vehicle support*). Remove both front roadwheels.

2 Drain the engine oil as described in Chapter 1A. On completion, check the copper washer and renew it if necessary, then refit the drain plug and tighten to the specified torque.

3 Lower the front suspension crossmember with reference to Chapter 10.

4 Remove the cooling fan and shroud from the rear of the radiator, with reference to Chapter 3.

5 Refer to Chapter 4C and detach the exhaust downpipe from the manifold, then unbolt the exhaust mounting from the transmission and support the exhaust on an axle stand.

6 Disconnect the wiring from the oil level sensor. If necessary, the sensor may be removed from the sump **(see illustrations)**.

7 Attach a suitable hoist to the engine and take the weight of the engine.

8 Unscrew the bolts from the bottom of the engine mountings at each side of the engine **(see illustration)**.

9 Unscrew the bolts securing the transmission to the rear engine mounting bracket. Leave the bracket attached to the underbody.

10 Raise the engine and transmission as far as possible. Make sure it is adequately supported, as the next procedure involves working beneath the engine.

11 Unscrew the bolts securing the transmission to the rear of the sump, then unscrew the remaining sump-to-engine bolts and lower the sump from the cylinder block **(see illustration)**. Note the location of the bolts as some are of different lengths. Where applicable, recover the gasket. If the sump is stuck, use a hide or wooden mallet to tap its sides in order to release it. Do not drive a screwdriver between the sump and cylinder block as this may damage the mating surfaces.

12 It is recommended that the oil and oil filter are renewed whenever the sump is removed. Before refitting the sump, it is a good idea to remove the oil filter in order to allow the oil to

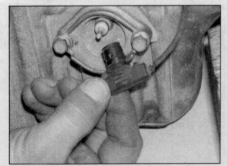

11.6a Disconnecting the wiring from the oil level sensor

11.6b Recover the O-ring seal

11.8 Engine mounting lower bolt

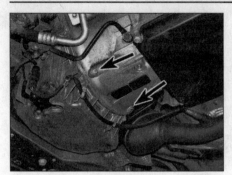

11.11 Sump-to-transmission mounting bolts

11.14a Locate the new gasket on the crankcase . . .

11.14b . . . and then refit the sump

drain from the cylinder block oil gallery and internal oilways.

Refitting

13 Thoroughly clean the mating surfaces of the sump and cylinder block.

14 On 111 type engines, smear a little grease on the block and fit the gasket making sure that all of the holes align correctly. Refit the sump then insert all of the bolts finger-tight **(see illustrations)**.

15 On 271 type engines, ensure that the cylinder block mating face of the sump is free from all traces of old sealant, oil and grease, and then apply a 1.5 to 2.5 mm thick bead of silicone sealant (A 003 989 98 20 or equivalent) to the sump. Note that the sealant should be run around the inside of the bolt holes in the sump. The sump must be fitted within 10 minutes of applying the sealant. Refit the sump then insert all of the bolts finger-tight.

16 The bolts securing the transmission to the sump can now be tightened to the specified torque. This will ensure the rear of the sump is correctly aligned with the transmission, as if it is not aligned correctly, vibration and noise may occur.

17 Tighten the remaining sump bolts to the specified torque.

18 Complete the rest of the installation by reversing the removal procedure, referring to the relevant Chapters.

19 Renew the oil filter and refill the engine with clean engine oil with reference to Chapter 1A.

20 When all components are refitted, start the engine and check carefully around the sump for any oil leaks.

12 Oil pump – removal, inspection and refitting

Removal

1 Remove the sump as described in Section 11. Note that this involves suspending the engine with a hoist.

111 type engines

2 The sprocket is pressed onto the driveshaft, and the sprocket must be disengaged from the chain as the oil pump is being removed.

3 Unscrew the mounting bolts, withdraw the oil pump from the bottom of the crankcase, and recover the O-ring seal **(see illustrations)**. Note, the oil pump mounting bolts also secure the baffle plate, and it may be helpful to loosen some of the baffle bolts to release the oil pump. Disengage the sprocket from the chain as the pump is being removed.

271 type engines

4 The oil pump is bolted to the rear of the balance shaft assembly. The balance shaft assembly does not have to be removed or the drive chain disturbed.

5 Undo the retaining bolts and remove the access cover from the oil pump.

6 Slacken and remove the retaining bolt on the smaller oil pump gear and remove the gear from the oil pump housing. To slacken this bolt, counterhold the balance shaft with an open-ended spanner.

7 Undo the oil pump mounting bolts and withdraw it from the balance shaft, disengaging it from the oil feed pipe. **Note:** *One of the mounting bolts is behind the large oil pump drive gear inside the housing, turn the gear until the bolt can be accessed through one of its recesses.*

Inspection

8 Thoroughly clean all components, and examine them for wear and damage. If there is any sign of excessive wear or damage, renew the appropriate component(s).

9 Examine the drive chain for wear and damage. If necessary, renew the chain.

10 Where required, reassemble the oil pump using a reversal of the dismantling procedure, lubricating each component with fresh engine oil before fitting.

11 With the oil pump upright, add fresh engine oil into the upper aperture while turning the pump shaft slowly **(see illustration)**. This will prime the oil pump so that normal oil pressure will be resumed as soon as possible after starting the engine.

Refitting

12 Locate the oil pump on the crankcase together with a new O-ring seal, and insert the mounting bolts.

13 On 111 type engines, engage the sprocket with the chain while locating the pump on the crankcase.

14 Refit the sump as described in Section 11. **Note:** *On 111 type engines, check that the baffle bolts are tight first.*

12.3a Withdraw the oil pump from the bottom of the crankcase while disengaging the drive chain

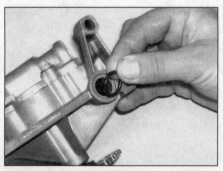

12.3b Recover the O-ring seal from the oil pump

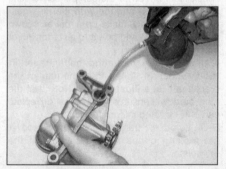

12.11 Priming the oil pump before refitting it

13.3 Flywheel/driveplate holding tool made from a piece of metal

13.4a Unscrew the bolts . . .

13.4b . . . and remove the flywheel from the rear of the crankshaft

13.7 Spigot bearing in the centre of the flywheel

13.12 Angle-tightening the flywheel bolts

13 Flywheel/driveplate – removal, inspection and refitting

Note: *The flywheel/driveplate mounting bolts must be renewed on refitting.*

Removal

1 Remove the manual transmission (Chapter 7A) or automatic transmission (Chapter 7B).
2 On manual transmission models, remove the clutch as described in Chapter 6.
3 The flywheel/driveplate must be held stationary while the mounting bolts are loosened. To do this, have an assistant insert a wide-bladed screwdriver in the starter ring gear teeth through the access hole in the rear of the sump. On manual transmission models, Mercedes-Benz technicians use a special tool bolted to the sump incorporating serrations which engage with the ring gear teeth. Alternatively, make up a tool as shown **(see illustration)** and bolt it to a starter motor mounting hole.
4 Unscrew the mounting bolts, then lift the flywheel/driveplate from the rear of the crankshaft **(see illustrations)**. Note that the location dowel ensures the flywheel/driveplate can only be fitted in one position.
5 On automatic transmission models recover the locking plates from each side of the driveplate.

Inspection

6 If the teeth on the flywheel/driveplate starter ring gear are badly worn, it may be possible to fit a new ring gear, however this work should be entrusted to a Mercedes-Benz dealer who will have the necessary equipment to heat the new gear to the critical temperature in order to fit it. Overheating the gear will affect its hardness, resulting in rapid wear. The old gear may be removed by drilling it and using a cold chisel to split it. Take care not to drill into the flywheel/driveplate.
7 On manual transmission models, if the clutch friction face of the flywheel is deeply scored, cracked or otherwise damaged, the flywheel must be renewed. However, it may be possible to have it surface-ground, but seek the advice of an engine reconditioning specialist. Check the condition of the spigot bearing in the centre of the flywheel or in the end of the crankshaft, and renew if necessary **(see illustration)**.

14.3 Prising out the crankshaft front oil seal

8 It is recommended that the flywheel/driveplate securing bolts are renewed whenever removed.

Refitting

9 Commence refitting by cleaning the mating faces of the crankshaft and flywheel/driveplate.
10 Make sure that the location dowel is in position in the end of the crankshaft. On automatic transmission models, fit the locking plate onto the crankshaft.
11 Locate the flywheel/driveplate onto the crankshaft, then insert the new mounting bolts (and further locking plate on automatic transmission models) and hand-tighten them.
12 Lock the flywheel/driveplate using the method employed during removal, then tighten the securing bolts progressively in a diagonal sequence to the specified torque first, then tighten all the bolts by the specified angle **(see illustration)**.
13 On manual transmission models, refit the clutch as described in Chapter 6.
14 Refit the manual transmission (Chapter 7A) or automatic transmission (Chapter 7B).

14 Crankshaft oil seals – renewal

Crankshaft front oil seal

1 Remove the crankshaft pulley/vibration damper and inspect it as described in Section 5.
2 Measure and note the fitted depth of the oil seal in the timing chain cover.
3 Prise the oil seal from the cover using a hooked instrument **(see illustration)**. Alternatively, drill a small hole in the oil seal, and use a self-tapping screw and a pair of pliers to remove it.
4 Clean the seal location in the timing cover, and also clean the oil seal contact surface on the crankshaft pulley/vibration damper. Examine the seal contact surface of the pulley/vibration damper for an excessive wear groove. If evident, refer to Section 5.
5 Dip the new oil seal in clean engine oil, and press it into the timing chain cover (open end first) to the previously-noted depth, using a suitable tube or socket **(see illustrations)**.

14.5a Locate the new oil seal in the timing cover . . .

14.5b . . . and drive it into position using a socket or metal tube

14.8 Removing the crankshaft rear oil seal

6 Refit the crankshaft pulley/vibration damper as described in Section 5.

Crankshaft rear oil seal

Note: *The rear oil seal is integral with the oil seal housing and should be renewed whenever it is removed.*

7 Remove the flywheel/driveplate as described in Section 13.

8 Unscrew the retaining bolts and remove the oil seal/housing from the cylinder block **(see illustration)**.

9 New oil seal/housings are supplied with a plastic sleeve on the inside of the seal to aid refitting of the seal over the end of the crankshaft. DO NOT remove the plastic fitting sleeve until the oil seal housing is in its fitted position.

10 Ensure that the cylinder block mating face of the oil seal housing is free from all traces of old sealant, oil and grease, and then apply a 1.5 to 2.5 mm thick bead of silicone sealant (A 003 989 98 20 or equivalent) to the oil seal housing. Note that the sealant should be run around the inside of the bolt holes in the oil seal housing. It must be fitted within 10 minutes of applying the sealant. Also apply sealant at the area where the sump, oil seal housing and cylinder block meet.

11 Fit the new oil seal housing over the crankshaft and onto the cylinder block, keeping the plastic sleeve in position.

12 Fit the retaining bolts and tighten them to the specified torque setting.

13 Remove the plastic fitting sleeve from the new oil seal housing.

14 Refit the flywheel/driveplate with reference to Section 13.

15 Crankshaft spigot bearing – renewal

1 A two-mass flywheel is fitted with the bearing located in the centre of the flywheel. On high-mileage engines, the bearing may become dry and noisy, noticeable when the clutch is disengaged with a gear selected. To renew the bearing, proceed as follows.

2 Remove the clutch as described in Chapter 6.

3 It is possible to view the needle rollers of the bearing inside the centre of the flywheel.

4 Remove the flywheel as described in Section 13.

5 Note the fitted depth of the needle bearing to ensure correct fitting.

6 Press or drive out the bearing, noting its fitted position.

7 Press or drive in the new bearing, using a metal tube on the outer part which locates in the flywheel. Make sure the bearing is fitted correctly as noted on removal.

8 Refit the flywheel as described in Section 13.

9 Refit the clutch as described in Chapter 6.

16 Engine/transmission mountings – inspection and renewal

Inspection

1 Three engine/transmission mountings are used, one on either side of the engine, and one under the rear of the transmission.

2 For improved access, raise the front of the vehicle and support it securely on axle stands (see *Jacking and vehicle support*).

3 Check the condition of the mounting rubber to see if it is cracked, hardened or separated from the metal at any point. Renew the mounting if any such damage or deterioration is evident. The mountings contain hydraulic oil, and must be renewed if oil leakage is evident.

4 Check that all the mounting bolts are securely tightened.

5 Using a large screwdriver or metal bar,

16.8 Vibration damper fitted to some models

check for wear in the mounting by carefully levering against it to check for free play. Where this is not possible, enlist the aid of an assistant to move the engine/transmission back-and-forth, or from side-to-side, while you observe the mounting. If excessive free play is found, check first that the fasteners are correctly secured, and then renew any worn components as required.

Renewal

Front engine mountings

6 Support the engine, either using a hoist and lifting tackle connected to the engine lifting brackets, or by positioning a jack and interposed block of wood under the sump. Ensure that the engine is adequately supported before proceeding.

7 Depending on which engine mounting requires removal, it may be necessary to remove the alternator or supercharger/ Kompressor to make access easier. See the relevant Chapters to remove any other components.

8 Unscrew and remove the engine mounting upper bolt. Depending on model, remove the vibration damper from the top of the engine mounting **(see illustration)**.

9 If working on the right-hand engine mounting, remove the heat shield from the top of the engine mounting **(see illustration)**.

10 Working under the vehicle, remove the engine undershield and undo the engine mounting lower bolt **(see illustration)**.

11 Raise the engine as necessary, taking care not to stretch any hoses or wiring, and

16.9 Removing the heat shield

16.10 Engine mounting lower bolt

16.11 Engine mounting bracket retaining bolts

16.12 Engine mounting locating lug

16.15a Unscrew the rear mounting bolts . . .

16.15b . . . and the lower mounting bracket bolts . . .

16.15c . . . and remove, noting the position of the earth cable

remove the mounting. If necessary, unbolt the mounting bracket from the side of the cylinder block **(see illustration)**.

12 Refitting is a reversal of removal, but make sure that the location lug on the top of the mounting engages the cut-out in the mounting bracket **(see illustration)**, and tighten the mounting bolts to the specified torque.

Rear engine/transmission mounting

13 Raise the front of the vehicle and support it securely on axle stands (see *Jacking and vehicle support*).

14 Support the transmission using a jack and interposed block of wood.

15 Unbolt the mounting bracket from the underbody, then unscrew the bolts securing

the mounting rubber to the rear of the transmission. Lower the bracket together with the mounting from the underbody **(see illustrations)**.

16 The mounting rubber can then be unbolted from the bracket.

17 Refitting is a reversal of removal.

Chapter 2 Part B:
Diesel engine in-car repair procedures

Contents

Degrees of difficulty

Easy, suitable for novice with little experience	**Fairly easy,** suitable for beginner with some experience	**Fairly difficult,** suitable for competent DIY mechanic	**Difficult,** suitable for experienced DIY mechanic	**Very difficult,** suitable for expert DIY or professional

Specifications

General

Engine code*:
2.2 litre engine	611.962, 646.962 or 646.963
2.7 litre engine	612.962

Displacement:
2.2 litre engine	2148 cc
2.7 litre engine	2685 cc
Bore	88.0 mm
Stroke.	88.3 mm
Direction of engine rotation	Clockwise (viewed from front of vehicle)
No 1 cylinder location.	Timing chain end

Firing order:
2.2 litre engine	1-3-4-2
2.7 litre engine	1-2-4-5-3

Compression pressures:
New compression pressure	29.0 to 35.0 bars
Minimum compression pressure	18.0 bars (approximately)
Maximum difference between cylinders.	3.0 bars
Compression ratio (all engines)	18.0:1

See 'Vehicle identification numbers' for information about the engine code

Cylinder head bolts

Thread diameter.	M12
Length when new.	102.0 mm
Maximum length.	104.0 mm

Lubrication system

Oil pressure (at temperature 90°C):
611 and 612 type engines:
At idle (minimum)	0.3 bar
At 3000 rpm (minimum)	3.0 bar

646 type engines:
At idle (minimum)	0.7 bar
At 3200 rpm (minimum)	2.5 bar

Torque wrench settings

	Nm	lbf ft
Air conditioning pump to bracket	20	15
Auxiliary drivebelt idler pulley bolt	30	22
Auxiliary drivebelt tensioner damper strut bolts:		
Lower bolt	20	15
Upper bolt	25	18
Big-end bearing cap bolts:		
Stage 1	5	4
Stage 2	25	18
Stage 3	Angle-tighten a further 90°	
Camshaft bearing cap	10	7
Camshaft cover bolts	10	7
Camshaft housing to cylinder head	15	11
Camshaft sprocket	18	13
Coolant pump and housing	10	7
Crankshaft pulley/vibration damper and hub:		
8.8 bolt:		
Stage 1	200	148
Stage 2	Angle-tighten a further 90°	
10.9 bolt:		
Stage 1	325	240
Stage 2	Angle-tighten a further 90°	
12.9 bolt:		
Stage 1	200	148
Stage 2	Angle-tighten a further 90°	
Stage 3	Angle-tighten a further 90°	
Crankshaft rear oil seal housing bolts	10	7
Cylinder block coolant drain plug	30	22
Cylinder head front cover	14	10
Cylinder head-to-timing cover bolts (M8 bolts)	20	15
Cylinder head bolts:		
611 and 612 engines (M12 bolts):		
Stage 1	60	44
Stage 2	Angle-tighten a further 90°	
Stage 3	Angle-tighten a further 90°	
646 engines (M12 bolts):		
Stage 1	15	11
Stage 2	60	44
Stage 3	Angle-tighten a further 90°	
Stage 4	Angle-tighten a further 90°	
Dipstick tube-to-cylinder head bolt	14	10
Driveplate bolts:		
Stage 1	45	33
Stage 2	Angle-tighten a further 90°	
Engine cover trim bolts	10	7
Engine-to-transmission bolts:		
Manual transmission:		
M10 x 40 mm bolts	55	41
M10 x 90 mm bolts	45	33
Automatic transmission:		
M10 bolts	55	41
M12 bolts	65	48
Exhaust manifold to turbocharger	30	22
Flywheel bolts:		
Stage 1	45	33
Stage 2	Angle-tighten a further 90°	
Front engine mounting bolts:		
To axle carrier	35	26
M8	25	18
M10	40	30
Fuel injector retaining plate bolt:		
Stage 1	7	5
Stage 2	Angle-tighten a further 90°	
Stage 3	Angle-tighten a further 90°	
Fuel injection pipe union nuts	23	17
Main bearing cap bolts:		
Stage 1	55	41
Stage 2	Angle-tighten a further 90°	

Torque wrench settings (continued)

	Nm	lbf ft
Oil drain plug:		
M14 plug	30	22
Oil filter cap	25	18
Oil feed line to cylinder head	9	7
Oil feed line to turbocharger:		
Screw fitting	30	22
Banjo bolt	18	13
Oil level sensor to crankcase	20	15
Oil pressure sensor to oil filter	15	11
Oil pump mounting bolts	18	13
Oil pump relief valve plug	50	37
Power steering pump to housing	20	15
Rear engine mounting crossmember to underbody	40	30
Rear engine mounting to transmission crossmember	25	18
Sump (oil pan) bolts to crankcase:		
M6	9	7
M8	20	15
Timing chain cover bolts:		
M6 bolts	10	7
M8 bolts	20	15
Timing chain tensioner	80	59
Transmission bellhousing bolts to sump	40	30
Turbocharger support bracket bolt	30	22

1 General information

How to use this Chapter

This Part of Chapter 2 describes the repair procedures that can reasonably be carried out on the engine while it remains in the vehicle. If the engine has been removed from the vehicle and is being dismantled as described in Part C, any preliminary dismantling procedures can be ignored.

Note that, while it may be possible physically to overhaul items such as the piston/connecting rod assemblies while the engine is in the car, such tasks are not usually carried out as separate operations. Usually, several additional procedures are required (not to mention the cleaning of components and oilways); for this reason, all such tasks are classed as major overhaul procedures, and are described in Part C of this Chapter.

Part C describes the removal of the engine/transmission from the car, and the full overhaul procedures that can then be carried out.

Engine description

The 4- and 5-cylinder diesel engines fitted are fundamentally the same, the only significant difference being the number of cylinders.

The engines are of in-line double overhead camshaft design, mounted in-line ('north-south') at the front of the vehicle with the transmission mounted on the rear of the engine.

On 4-cylinder engines, the crankshaft is supported in five main bearing within the cast iron cylinder block. Crankshaft endfloat is controlled by thrustwashers fitted on either side of No 3 main bearing. Similarly, on 5-cylinder engines the crankshaft is supported in six main bearings, and the endfloat thrustwashers are fitted either side of No 4 bearing location.

The connecting rods are attached to the crankshaft by horizontally-split big-end bearings, and to the pistons by fully-floating gudgeon pins retained by circlips. The alloy pistons are fitted with three piston rings; two compression and one oil control.

The exhaust camshaft is driven from the crankshaft sprocket by a double-row chain, and the inlet camshaft is gear-driven from the exhaust camshaft. The camshaft also drives the fuel injection pump.

The camshaft is supported in bearings in the cylinder head, and actuates the valves directly, via hydraulic valve lifters.

The oil pump is chain-driven from the front of the crankshaft. An oil cooler is located on the oil filter housing at the left-hand front of the cylinder block.

Operations with engine in vehicle

The following operations can be carried out without having to remove the engine from the vehicle:

a) Removal and refitting of the cylinder head.
b) Removal and refitting of the timing chain and sprockets.
c) Removal and refitting of the camshaft.
d) Removal and refitting of the sump.
e) Removal and refitting of the big-end bearings, connecting rods, and pistons*.
f) Removal and refitting of the oil pump.
g) Renewal of the engine/transmission mountings.
h) Removal and refitting of the flywheel/driveplate.

Although it is possible to remove these components with the engine in place, for reasons of access and cleanliness it is recommended that the engine be removed.

2 Compression and leakdown tests – description and interpretation

Compression test

Note: *A compression tester designed for diesel engines must be used for this test.*

1 When engine performance is down, a compression test can provide diagnostic clues as to the engine's condition. If the test is performed regularly, it can give warning of trouble before any other symptoms become apparent.

2 A compression tester specifically intended for diesel engines must be used, because of the higher pressures involved. The tester is connected to an adapter, which screws into the glow plug or injector hole. On these engines, an adapter suitable for use in the injector holes is preferable. It is unlikely to be worthwhile buying such a tester for occasional use, but it may be possible to borrow or hire one – if not, have the test performed by a garage.

3 Unless specific instructions to the contrary are supplied with the tester, observe the following points.

a) The battery must be in a good state of charge, the air filter must be clean, and the engine should be at normal operating temperature.
b) All the injectors or glow plugs should be removed before starting the test.
c) The stop solenoid must be disconnected, to prevent the engine from running or fuel from being discharged.

4 There is no need to hold the accelerator pedal down during the test, because the diesel engine air inlet is not throttled.

5 Crank the engine on the starter motor. After one or two revolutions, the compression

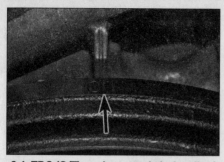

3.4 TDC (O/T) mark on crankshaft pulley/ vibration damper aligned with pointer on timing chain cover

3.5a Camshaft gear alignment marks . . .

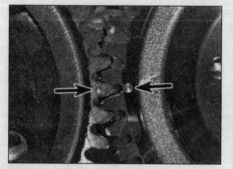

3.5b . . . aligned through the centre of the camshafts

3.6 Insert drill bit to lock camshaft

pressure should build-up to a maximum figure, and then stabilise. Record the highest reading obtained.

6 Repeat the test on the remaining cylinders, recording the pressure in each.

7 The cause of poor compression is less easy to establish on a diesel engine than on a petrol one. The effect of introducing oil into the cylinders ('wet' testing) is not conclusive, because there is a risk that the oil will sit in the swirl chamber or in the recess in the piston crown instead of passing to the rings. However, the following can be used as a rough guide to diagnosis.

8 All cylinders should produce very similar pressures; if there is a large difference, then this indicates a fault. Note that the compression should build-up quickly in a healthy engine; low compression on the first stroke, followed by gradually increasing

4.1 Remove the engine covers

pressure on successive strokes, indicates worn piston rings. A low compression reading on the first stroke, which does not build-up during successive strokes, indicates leaking valves or a blown head gasket (a cracked head could also be the cause). Deposits on the undersides of the valve heads can also cause low compression.

9 A low reading from two adjacent cylinders is almost certainly due to the head gasket having blown between them; the presence of coolant in the engine oil will confirm this.

10 If the compression reading is unusually high, the combustion chambers are probably coated with carbon deposits. If this is the case, the cylinder head should be removed and decarbonised.

11 On completion of the test, refit the injectors or the glow plugs, and reconnect the stop solenoid.

Leakdown test

12 A leakdown test measures the rate at which compressed air fed into the cylinder is lost. It is an alternative to a compression test, and in many ways is better, since the escaping air provides easy identification of where a pressure loss is occurring (piston rings, valves or head gasket).

13 The equipment needed for leakdown testing is unlikely to be available to the home mechanic. If poor compression is suspected, have the test performed by a suitably-equipped garage.

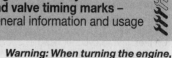

3 Engine assembly and valve timing marks – general information and usage

⚠ *Warning: When turning the engine, do not turn the engine using the camshaft sprocket bolts, and do not turn the engine backwards (ie, anti-clockwise).*

1 Top Dead Centre (TDC) is the highest point in the cylinder that each piston reaches as it travels up and down when the crankshaft turns. Each piston reaches TDC at the end of the compression stroke and again at the end of the exhaust stroke, but for valve timing TDC refers to the No 1 piston position on the compression stroke. No 1 piston is at the timing chain end of the engine.

2 Positioning No 1 piston at TDC is an essential part of many procedures, such as timing chain removal and camshaft removal.

3 Remove the camshaft cover as described in Section 4.

4 Using a socket on the crankshaft pulley/ vibration damper hub bolt, turn the crankshaft clockwise until the O/T (TDC) mark on the crankshaft pulley/vibration damper is aligned with the pointer on the timing chain cover (**see illustration**). For access to the bolt, it may be necessary to remove the fan unit and radiator shroud as described in Chapter 3.

5 In this position the alignment indentations (two 1.5 mm dots) on the camshaft gears (timing chain side) should be next to each other and aligned with the centre points of the camshafts (**see illustrations**). The camshaft lobes on No 1 cylinder should be facing upwards.

6 If necessary, the camshafts can be locked in position. The inlet camshaft gear has a timing hole, which aligns with a hole in the camshaft front bearing cap, and a suitable close-fitting drill should be inserted to lock the camshaft (**see illustration**). **Note:** *Do not use this method to lock the engine, while slackening any retaining bolts.*

7 With the camshafts aligned as described, No 1 piston is at TDC on its firing stroke.

4 Camshaft cover – removal and refitting

Removal

1 On 611 and 612 engines, undo the retaining bolts and withdraw the plastic cover from the top of the engine. On 646 engines, unclip the plastic cover at the rear corners of the trim panel and unclip it from the top of the engine (**see illustration**).

2 Remove the air cleaner/filter housing as described in Chapter 4B.

3 On 646 engines, undo the retaining bolts and remove the heat shield from the top of the exhaust manifold (**see illustrations**). Also

4.3a Remove the heat shield . . .

4.3b . . . and the rear mounting bracket

4.5 Disconnect the breather hose

4.6 Disconnect the camshaft sensor

4.8 Unclip the wiring harness

4.9 Remove the camshaft cover

remove the mounting bracket from the rear of the camshaft cover.

4 On automatic transmission models, undo the retaining bolt from the transmission dipstick guide tube at the left-hand rear of the cylinder head.

5 Disconnect the crankcase ventilation hose at the front of the camshaft cover (see illustration).

6 Where applicable, disconnect the wiring connector from the shutoff valve and camshaft sensor (see illustration).

7 Remove the fuel injectors and injector pipes, as described in Chapter 4B.

8 Undo the retaining bolts and release the wiring loom from the top of the camshaft cover (see illustration).

9 Unscrew the bolts then lift the camshaft cover away from the cylinder head (see illustration).

10 Remove the cover gaskets and discard; new ones will be required for refitting.

Refitting

11 Clean the joint surfaces of the cover and cylinder head, then locate the new gaskets in the grooves in the camshaft cover (see illustrations).

12 Position the camshaft cover with gaskets on the cylinder head, then insert the bolts and tighten them progressively. Do not fully tighten at this point as the fuel injectors will need to centralise in the cover.

13 Refit the fuel injectors and fuel lines and tighten the union nuts to the specified torque.

14 Tighten the camshaft cover bolts to their specified torque setting.

15 Complete the rest of the installation by reversing the removal procedure, referring to the relevant Chapters. When all components are refitted, start the engine and check

carefully around the camshaft cover for any oil leaks.

5 Crankshaft pulley/ vibration damper and hub – removal and refitting

Removal

1 To gain better access, remove the fan and shroud from the rear of the radiator with reference to Chapter 3.

2 Remove the auxiliary drivebelt, with reference to Chapter 1B.

3 Working under the front of the vehicle, undo the retaining bolts and remove the engine undershield.

4 The crankshaft must now be held stationary while the pulley bolt is loosened. The bolt is tightened to a high torque. Mercedes-Benz technicians remove the starter motor and use a special tool which is bolted to the transmission and locks the flywheel. It may be possible to insert a wide-bladed screwdriver between the starter ring gear teeth to prevent the engine from turning.

5 Unscrew the crankshaft pulley bolt then slide the pulley from the front of the crankshaft. Note the location of the washers under the head of the bolt, as they need to be fitted in the same position on refitting (see illustration). If the pulley is tight on the crankshaft, use a suitable puller to remove it. A two-legged puller, which locates in the pulley holes, is ideal.

6 If necessary, remove the Woodruff key from the groove in the nose of the crankshaft.

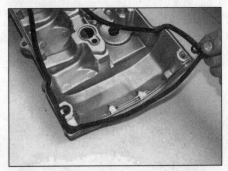

4.11a Fit new camshaft cover gasket . . .

4.11b . . . and fuel injector recess gaskets

5.5 Remove the bolt and washer

5.8 Make sure Woodruff key is located securely

Inspection

7 Examine the oil seal contact surface of the pulley/vibration damper for an excessive wear groove. If evident, it is permissible to position the oil seal slightly further into the timing chain cover so that it runs on the unworn area of the pulley. Alternatively, the pulley should be renewed. The oil seal in the timing cover must be renewed as a matter of course with reference to Section 14.

Refitting

8 Locate the Woodruff key in the groove in the nose of the crankshaft. Make sure that it is firmly pressed into position, and that its outer edge is parallel with the crankshaft so that the pulley/vibration damper will engage with it easily **(see illustration)**.

9 Wipe clean and lightly oil the seal contact surface of the pulley, and then slide it fully onto the crankshaft, engaging it with the Woodruff key.

6.5a Release the retaining clip . . .

10 Lightly oil the threads of the crankshaft pulley bolt and the washers, and then locate the washer(s) correctly onto the bolt, as noted on removal. Insert the bolt and tighten it to the specified torque while holding the crankshaft stationary as for removal. If necessary, refit the starter motor.

11 Refit the auxiliary drivebelt with reference to Chapter 1B.

12 Refit the fan and shroud to the rear of the radiator with reference to Chapter 3.

13 Where applicable, refit the engine under-shield.

6 Timing chain cover – removal and refitting

Note: *The timing chain cover is located between the cylinder head and the sump; take care not to damage any of these gaskets.*

6.5b . . . and remove air the duct

Removal

1 Disconnect the battery negative (earth) lead and position it away from the terminal.

2 Apply the parking brake, then jack up the front of the vehicle and support it on axle stands (see *Jacking and vehicle support*). Remove the engine compartment undershield.

3 Drain the engine oil from the sump and remove the oil filter as described in Chapter 1B.

4 Remove the camshaft cover as described in Section 4.

5 On turbocharged models, remove the air ducts from between the intercooler and intake manifold **(see illustration)**.

6 Remove the cooling fan and shroud from the rear of the radiator as described in Chapter 3.

7 Using a piece of thin plywood or similar, cover the radiator/condenser to protect it from any damage **(see illustration)**.

8 Refer to Section 3 and set the engine at TDC compression on No 1 cylinder. Ideally the crankshaft should be locked in this position during the removal of the timing chain cover. Mercedes-Benz technicians remove the starter motor and use a special tool to lock the teeth of the starter ring gear.

9 On 5-cylinder (612) engines with automatic transmission, disconnect the hydraulic line from the left-hand engine mounting.

10 Drain the cooling system as described in Chapter 1B.

11 On 611 and 612 engines, remove the thermostat housing as described in Chapter 3.

12 Remove the cover plate from the front of the cylinder head as described in Section 15.

13 Remove the high-pressure fuel pump as described in Chapter 4B.

14 Slacken the retaining bolts on the power steering pump pulley **(see illustration)**, and then remove the auxiliary drivebelt as described in Chapter 1B.

15 Remove the pulley and then unbolt the power steering pump and position it to the side of the engine compartment. **Do not** disconnect the hydraulic lines from the pump. Refer to Chapter 10 for further information.

16 Disconnect the wiring connector from the air conditioning compressor and then unbolt the compressor and position it to the side of the engine compartment **(see illustration)**.

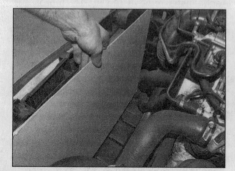

6.7 Protect the radiator with a piece of board

6.14 Slacken the retaining bolts

6.16 Fasten the compressor to one side

6.18 Disconnect the hose from the coolant pump

6.19a Unclip the plastic cap . . .

6.19b . . . and remove the bolt

6.22 Timing chain tensioner

6.23a Unclip the plastic cap . . .

6.23b . . . and remove the bolt

Do not disconnect the refrigerant lines from the compressor. Refer to Chapter 3 for further information.

17 Disconnect the coolant hose from the oil/water heat exchanger at the rear of the oil filter housing. On automatic transmission models, also disconnect the transmission oil lines from the heat exchanger.

18 Disconnect the two coolant hoses from the coolant pump **(see illustration)**.

19 Remove the plastic cap and then undo the retaining bolt and remove the auxiliary belt idler pulley from the coolant pump **(see illustrations)**.

20 Remove the coolant pump as described in Chapter 3.

21 Remove the alternator with reference to Chapter 5A.

22 With the engine set at TDC, slacken and remove the timing chain tensioner from the right-hand front of the engine **(see illustration)**. Discard the sealing washer, as a new one will be required for refitting.

23 Remove the plastic cap and then undo the retaining bolt and remove the auxiliary belt idler pulley from the oil filter housing **(see illustrations)**.

24 Undo the retaining bolts and remove the auxiliary belt tensioner from the front cover **(see illustration)**

25 Remove the crankshaft pulley/vibration damper/hub as described in Section 5.

26 Unscrew and remove the bolts securing the sump to the bottom of the timing chain cover. Slacken the remaining sump bolts by 2 or 3 turns.

27 Working through the aperture in the top

of the cylinder head, unscrew the two bolts securing the timing chain cover to the cylinder head **(see illustration)**.

28 Unscrew the bolts and remove the timing chain cover from the front of the engine, taking care not to damage the front parts of the cylinder head gasket and sump gasket. If required, to ensure the bolts are refitted in their correct locations, make a drawing of their positions, or use a dab of paint on them to identify them. If the two location dowels are loose, remove them also.

29 With the timing chain cover removed, it is recommended that the crankshaft front oil seal be renewed with reference to Section 14.

Refitting

30 Commence refitting by thoroughly cleaning away all traces of old sealant from the mating faces of the timing chain cover and cylinder block. Also clean the areas of the

6.24 Tensioner mounting bolts

cylinder head gasket and sump gasket which contact the timing chain cover.

31 Carefully check the condition of the cylinder head gasket. If the gasket has been damaged during the removal procedure, the cylinder head should be removed in order to renew the gasket, as described in Section 10.

32 Similarly, carefully check the condition of the sump gasket. If the gasket has been damaged during the removal procedure, the sump should be removed in order to renew the gasket, as described in Section 11.

33 Apply sealant to the cylinder block mating face of the timing chain cover. Make sure that the two location dowels are correctly fitted **(see illustration)**.

34 Coat the lips of the crankshaft oil seal with clean engine oil, then slide the cover into position over the crankshaft. Take care not to damage the oil seal lips and the cylinder head and sump gaskets as the cover is fitted.

6.27 Timing chain cover upper mounting bolts

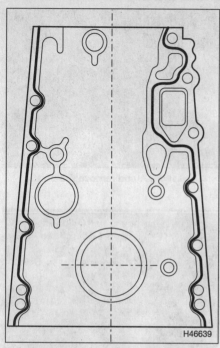

6.33 Apply sealant (2 mm bead) on the inside of the bolt holes

35 Insert all the retaining bolts, including the two upper ones, in their original positions and hand-tighten them. First, progressively tighten the bolts securing the timing chain cover to the cylinder block to the specified torque, and then tighten the two upper bolts to the specified torque.

36 Insert the bolts securing the sump to the bottom of the timing chain cover. Progressively tighten all the sump bolts to the specified torque.

37 Complete the rest of the installation by reversing the removal procedure, referring to the relevant Chapters.

38 Refill the engine with the correct grade and quantity of oil, as described in Chapter 1B.

39 Reconnect the battery negative lead.

40 When all components are refitted, start the engine and check carefully around the front of the engine any oil leaks, or coolant leaks.

41 Refit the engine compartment undershield and lower the car to the ground.

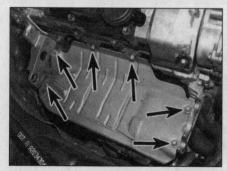

8.6 Undo the heat shield retaining bolts

7 Timing chain – inspection and renewal

Inspection

1 Remove the camshaft cover as described in Section 4.

2 Using a socket on the crankshaft pulley/vibration damper hub bolt, turn the engine so that the whole length of the chain can be progressively viewed at the camshaft sprocket.

3 The chain should be renewed if the sprocket is worn or if the chain is worn (indicated by excessive lateral play between the links, and excessive noise in operation). Note that the rollers on a very badly worn chain may be slightly grooved. To avoid future problems, if there is any doubt at all about the condition of the chain, renew it.

Renewal

Note 1: *This following procedure, uses a chain breaker/riveter to renew the chain without removing the front timing chain cover, a second person will be required to assist fitting the timing chain. Ensure that all tools are available, as well as a new chain and new connecting link before proceeding.*

Note 2: *If the chain needs to be renewed as a complete assembly, then remove the front timing chain cover as described in Section 6.*

4 Disconnect the battery negative (earth) lead and position it away from the terminal.

5 If not already done, remove the camshaft cover as described in Section 4.

6 Remove the cover plate from the front of the cylinder head as described in Section 15.

7 Remove the fan and shroud, as described in Chapter 3.

8 Using a socket on the crankshaft pulley bolt, turn the engine until the timing marks are aligned, as described in Section 3.

9 Remove the timing chain tensioner as described in Section 8.

10 With the engine still in the TDC position, use a couple of cable-ties to keep the timing chain on the camshaft sprocket. Put some clean rag into the timing chain recess to prevent anything dropping down into the engine.

11 Use the chain breaker to press out one of the timing chain pins and split the timing chain.

12 Connect the new timing chain to the old chain and press the chain link pin back into position. **Note:** *Make sure the new chain is connected to the front part of the chain, as the engine has to be turned clockwise, in the direction of rotation to feed the chain around the sprockets.*

13 With the new chain connected securely to the old chain, take a firm hold of both ends of the chain and remove the cable-ties from the camshaft sprocket. Remove the clean rag from around the timing chain before turning the engine.

14 With the aid of an assistant, turn the engine in the direction of rotation. Keeping the timing chain taut feed it around the crankshaft sprocket, until the new chain comes all the way around to the camshaft sprocket.

15 Cable-tie both ends of the timing chain back to the camshaft sprocket, and refit the clean rag back into the timing chain recess.

16 Use the chain breaker to press out the timing chain pin and split the old timing chain from the new timing chain. **Note:** *Make sure the chain is pulled tight on the lower section of the engine, and the upper section slack to allow for the fitting of the chain tensioner.*

17 Check that the TDC marks on the crankshaft pulley and timing chain cover are aligned, and the marks on the camshaft and camshaft bearing caps are still aligned correctly.

18 Fit the new timing chain link, using the timing chain riveter to connect the two ends of the chain securely. Always read the instructions that come with the chain riveter, as there are many different types available. The link pins need to be riveted securely, to prevent the chain coming apart.

19 Remove the clean rag from the timing chain recess, and fit the timing chain tensioner, with reference to Section 8. With the tensioner now fitted, check the timing marks are still in line.

20 Rotate the engine two complete turns and check the timing marks come back in alignment. Refer to Section 3 to check timing mark alignment is correct.

21 Refit the camshaft cover with reference to Section 4.

22 Refit the air cleaner assembly.

23 Reconnect the battery negative lead.

8 Timing chain tensioner, sprockets and guides – removal, inspection and refitting

Timing chain tensioner removal

1 Refer to Section 3 and set the engine to TDC on No 1 cylinder.

2 Remove the air cleaner/filter housing as described in Chapter 4B.

611 and 612 engines

3 Disconnect the breather hose from the top of the camshaft cover. Undo the retaining bolt from the top of the engine oil dipstick tube and move the tube to one side.

4 Undo the retaining bolts and remove the fuel electric shut-off valve from the front of the cylinder head and move it to one side.

5 Unscrew the tensioner from the right-hand side of the timing chain cover. Recover the sealing ring and discard; a new one will be required for refitting.

646 engines

6 Undo the retaining bolts and remove the heat shield **(see illustration)**.

8.7 Removing the tensioner

8.11 Lock the camshaft using a drill bit

8.15 Unbolt the sprocket from the camshaft

7 Unscrew the tensioner from the right-hand side of the timing chain cover **(see illustration)**. Recover the sealing ring and discard; a new one will be required for refitting.

Timing chain tensioner inspection

8 Do not attempt to dismantle the tensioner assembly. If it is suspected that the tensioner is worn or faulty, the complete unit should be renewed.

Timing chain tensioner refitting

9 Locate a new sealing ring on the tensioner, then screw it into position in the cylinder head and tighten to the specified torque.
10 Refitting is the reversal of the removal procedure, referring to the relevant Chapters, where applicable. When all components are refitted, start the engine and check carefully around the tensioner for any oil leaks.

Camshaft sprocket

Removal

11 Refer to Section 3 and set the engine to TDC on No 1 cylinder. Lock the inlet camshaft as described by inserting a drill through the camshaft front bearing cap into the gear **(see illustration)**.
12 Remove the cover plate from the front of the cylinder head as described in Section 15.
13 Use a dab of paint or a marker pen to mark the timing chain and the exhaust camshaft sprocket in relation to each other. This will help ensure that the chain is refitted correctly and the valve timing maintained.
14 Remove the timing chain tensioner as described earlier in this Section.
15 Hold the exhaust camshaft (timing chain) sprocket stationary using a suitable tool located in the sprocket cut-outs, then loosen the bolts securing the sprocket to the camshaft **(see illustration)**. **Do not** rely only on the drill located in the inlet camshaft sprocket to hold the sprocket.
16 At this stage the crankshaft sprocket will still be at TDC, and the crankshaft must not be turned until the camshaft sprocket has been refitted. Use a length of wire to tie the upper part of the timing chain to the cylinder head to ensure the chain remains on the sprockets.
17 Remove the sprockets from their location

dowel on the camshaft flange. Remove the timing chain sprocket from the timing chain, and if required remove the dowel from the flange in the end of the camshaft. **Note: The sprocket bolts must be renewed every time they are removed.**

Inspection

18 Examine the teeth on the sprockets for wear. Each tooth forms an inverted V. If worn, the side of each tooth under tension will be slightly concave in shape when compared with the other side of the tooth (ie, the teeth will have a hooked appearance). If the teeth appear worn, the sprocket must be renewed.

Refitting

19 Ensure that the camshaft and crankshaft timing marks are still aligned, as described in Section 3. If a new sprocket is being fitted, transfer the chain alignment mark from the old sprocket to the new.
20 Fit the location dowel to the hole in the exhaust camshaft flange.
21 Engage the sprocket with the chain, aligning the marks made on the chain and sprocket before removal, then locate the sprocket on the camshaft flange and engage it with the dowel.
22 Insert the bolts and tighten them to the specified torque while holding the sprocket stationary using the used tool for removal. Remove the wire used to tie the chain to the cylinder head.
23 Refit the timing chain tensioner as described earlier in this Section.
24 Using a socket on the crankshaft pulley/ vibration damper hub bolt, turn the crankshaft through two complete revolutions, and check that the crankshaft and camshaft timing marks are still aligned with No 1 piston at TDC, as described in Section 3.
25 Remove the inlet camshaft locking drill, then refit the camshaft cover with reference to Section 4.

Crankshaft sprocket

Removal

Note: A puller may be required to remove the sprocket.
26 Remove the timing chain cover as described in Section 6. This procedure includes removal of the crankshaft pulley/

vibration damper and Woodruff key, and the setting of the engine to its TDC position.
27 Remove the sump as described in Section 11.
28 Hold the oil pump sprocket on the oil pump stationary using a suitable tool engaged with the sprocket holes, then unscrew and remove the mounting bolts. Remove the sprocket from the oil pump drive flange and unhook the drive chain from the crankshaft sprocket on the front of the crankshaft. **Note: The oil pump chain drive sprocket is incorporated into the crankshaft sprocket.**
29 Remove the camshaft sprocket as described previously in this Section, however, in addition to marking the timing chain in relation to the camshaft sprocket, also mark it in relation to the injection pump sprocket and crankshaft sprocket. This is necessary to ensure the valve timing and injection pump timing is maintained, since it will also be difficult to ascertain the TDC position of the crankshaft with the timing chain cover removed.
30 Unhook the timing chain from the crank-shaft sprocket and injection pump sprocket.
31 Slide the crankshaft sprocket from the front of the crankshaft. If it is tight, use a suitable puller, taking care not to damage the sprocket teeth. Alternatively, use two levers against the front of the cylinder block, positioning the levers diagonally opposite each other.
32 Recover the Woodruff key from the groove in the crankshaft.

Inspection

33 Refer to paragraph 18.

Refitting

34 Locate the Woodruff key in the crankshaft groove, making sure that the upper edge is parallel with the surface of the crankshaft.
35 Slide the crankshaft sprocket onto the front of the crankshaft and engage it with the Woodruff key. If necessary, use a suitable metal tube to tap it into position.
36 Engage the timing chain with the crankshaft sprocket and injection pump sprocket, making sure that the previously-made marks are aligned with each other, then pull the chain up through the aperture at the front of the cylinder head.

9.2 Check the markings on the bearing caps

9.3 Note the position of the bearing caps

37 Refit the camshaft sprocket as described earlier in this Section, making sure that the previously-made marks on the chain and sprocket are aligned with each other. Check that the alignment marks are still correctly aligned.

38 Refit the oil pump drive chain and sprocket with reference to Section 12.

39 Refit the sump with reference to Section 11.

40 Refit the timing chain cover and crankshaft pulley/vibration damper as described in Section 6.

Tensioner rail

Removal

41 Remove the cylinder head as described in Section 10.

42 Remove the timing chain cover as described in Section 6.

43 Remove the timing chain tensioner as described previously in this Section.

44 Remove the tensioner rail from its pin.

9.7 Lubricate the camshaft bearing housing

9.8a Lower the camshaft into position . . .

Inspection

45 Examine the tensioner rail for signs of excessive wear, damage or cracks, and renew if necessary.

Refitting

46 Locate the tensioner rail on the pin.

47 Refit the timing chain tensioner as described previously in this Section.

48 Refit the timing chain cover as described in Section 6.

49 Refit the cylinder head as described in Section 10.

---

9 Camshafts, camshaft housing and hydraulic tappets –
removal, inspection and refitting

Camshafts removal

1 Remove the exhaust camshaft sprocket as described in Section 8. Making sure that the timing chain remains engaged with the crankshaft sprocket, using wire to tie it to one side.

2 The camshaft bearing caps are numbered from the timing chain end of the engine (**see illustration**). Check the bearing caps to ensure that marks are present, and if necessary make suitable marks using quick-drying paint or a centre-punch.

3 The camshaft bearing cap bolts must now be slackened according to the following information, and the camshafts removed.

⚠️ Warning: It is absolutely essential to observe the correct sequence when slackening the camshaft

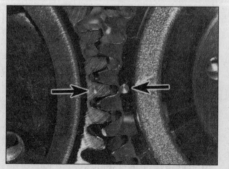

9.8b . . . and align the timing marks

bearing cap bolts, because the camshafts are very sensitive to fracturing.

4-cylinder engine

a) Progressively slacken and then remove the bolts from bearing caps 1, 3 and 5.

b) Lift off bearing caps 1, 3 and 5, keeping them in order (**see illustration**). Note that the bearing caps locate on dowels – if they are stuck, tap gently using a soft-faced mallet.

c) Progressively slacken the bearing cap bolts for bearing caps 2 and 4, in one-turn stages until all pressure on the camshaft is relieved. Take care not to allow uneven pressure on the camshaft as the bolts are unscrewed.

d) Lift off bearing caps 2 and 4, again keeping them in order.

e) Lift the inlet and exhaust camshafts from the camshaft housing and recover the thrustwashers from No 3 bearing location.

5-cylinder engine

a) Progressively slacken and then remove the bolts from bearing caps 1, 3, 4 and 6.

b) Lift off bearing caps 1, 3, 4 and 6, keeping them in order. Note that the bearing caps locate on dowels – if they are stuck, tap gently using a soft-faced mallet.

c) Progressively slacken the bearing cap bolts for bearing caps 2 and 5, in one-turn stages until all pressure on the camshafts is relieved. Take great care not to allow uneven pressure on the camshafts as the bolts are unscrewed.

d) Lift off the bearing caps 2 and 5, again keeping them in order.

e) Lift the inlet and exhaust camshafts from the camshaft housing and recover the thrustwashers from No 3 bearing location.

Camshafts inspection

4 Thoroughly clean the camshafts and the housing/caps.

5 Examine the camshaft journals and cam lobes for any sign of scoring, wear grooves or pitting, and if apparent, renew the relevant camshaft. Any damage of this nature may be attributable to a blocked oil passage in the cylinder head, and careful examination should be carried out to determine the cause.

6 Examine the bearing surfaces in the camshaft housing and bearing caps for excessive wear and scoring. If evident, renew the components together with the camshafts.

Camshafts refitting

7 Lubricate the camshaft journals and the bearing locations in the camshaft housing/caps with clean engine oil (**see illustration**). Also lubricate the hydraulic tappets.

8 Locate the inlet camshaft in the left-hand side of the camshaft housing, and then locate the exhaust camshaft in the right-hand side, at the same time engaging the gears at the fronts of the camshafts so that the timing marks are aligned (**see illustrations**), see Section 3.

9 Locate the bearing caps in position over the camshafts and tighten the securing

9.12 Remove the hydraulic tappets, noting their position

9.13 Removing the camshaft lower housing

9.18 Lubricate the hydraulic tappets with clean oil

bolts according to the following information, ensuring that the bearing caps are fitted to their original locations.

⚠️ **Warning: It is absolutely essential to observe the correct sequence when tightening the camshaft bearing cap bolts, in order to avoid damage to the camshaft.**

4-cylinder engine

a) Fit bearing caps 2 and 4, then insert the bolts, and tighten them progressively in one-turn stages to the specified torque. Take care not to allow uneven pressure on the camshaft as the bolts are tightened.
b) Fit bearing caps 1, 3 and 5, then insert the bolts, and tighten them progressively in one-turn stages to the specified torque.

5-cylinder engines

a) Fit bearing caps 2 and 5, then insert the bolts, and tighten them progressively in one-turn stages to the specified torque. Take care not to allow uneven pressure on the camshaft as the bolts are tightened.
b) Fit bearing caps 1, 3, 4 and 6, then insert the bolts, and tighten them progressively in one-turn stages to the specified torque.

10 Refit the exhaust camshaft sprocket as described in Section 8.

Camshaft lower housing and hydraulic tappets

Removal

11 Remove the camshafts as described earlier in this Section. This procedure includes removal of the camshaft cover and cylinder head front cover.
12 Obtain a container with 16 or 20 compartments and number the compartments to indicate the location of the hydraulic tappets. Remove each hydraulic tappet in turn from the camshaft housing and store them in the container **(see illustration)**.
13 Lift the camshaft lower housing from the cylinder head **(see illustration)**.

Inspection

14 Clean the camshaft housing and cylinder head and check for damage and wear. Also refer to paragraphs 4 to 6.
15 The operation of the removed hydraulic tappets can be checked as follows.

a) Press down firmly on the top of each tappet, using a blunt instrument such as a wooden hammer handle, for approximately 10 seconds.
b) Note how far the piston moves when depressed.
c) Repeat the operation for all the tappets in turn.
d) If any one tappet can be depressed more easily than the others, renew it.

16 Check the hydraulic tappets and the bores in the camshaft lower housing for wear and scoring. If any serious damage or wear is evident, the camshaft housing and tappets must be renewed.

Refitting

17 Locate the lower housing back into position on the cylinder head.
18 Lubricate the hydraulic tappet bores in the camshaft housing with clean engine oil, then locate each hydraulic tappet in its original position in the housing **(see illustration)**.
19 Complete the rest of the installation by reversing the removal procedure, referring to the relevant Chapters. When all components are refitted, start the engine and check carefully around the camshaft cover for any oil leaks.

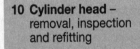

10 Cylinder head – removal, inspection and refitting 🔧🔧🔧

Note: New cylinder head bolts may be required – see text.

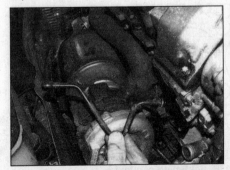

10.9 Remove the turbo oil feed pipe

Removal

1 Ensure that the engine is cold before attempting to remove the cylinder head.
2 Apply the parking brake, then jack up the front of the vehicle and support it on axle stands (see Jacking and vehicle support).
3 Disconnect the battery negative (earth) lead and position it away from the terminal.
4 Raise the bonnet to the fully open position.
5 Drain the engine oil and the coolant as described in Chapter 1B.
6 Remove the camshafts, hydraulic tappets and lower housing, as described in Section 9.
7 Remove the thermostat housing from the right-hand side front of the cylinder head, as described in Chapter 3.
8 Remove the inlet manifold as described in Chapter 4B.
9 Undo the retaining bolts and remove the oil feed pipe to the turbocharger from the cylinder head **(see illustration)**.
10 Undo the retaining bolts from the turbocharger to the exhaust manifold **(see illustration)**.
11 Undo the retaining nut from the exhaust mounting bracket at the rear of the exhaust manifold **(see illustration)**.
12 Using a socket through the cylinder head aperture, unscrew and remove the two bolts securing the timing chain cover to the cylinder head **(see illustration)**.
13 Make a final check to ensure that all relevant hoses and wires have been disconnected from the cylinder head.
14 Progressively loosen the cylinder head

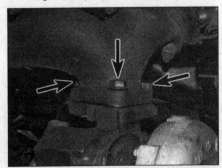

10.10 Turbo-to-manifold retaining bolts

10.11 Exhaust mounting bracket

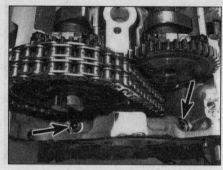

10.12 Cylinder head to timing chain cover bolts

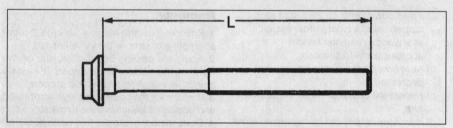

10.26 Measure the length (L) of the cylinder head bolts

See Specifications for maximum length

bolts, working in the **reverse** order to the tightening sequence (**see illustration 10.31**). Remove all cylinder head bolts.

15 Release the cylinder head from the cylinder block and locating dowels by rocking it. Do not prise between the mating faces of the cylinder head and block, as this may damage the gasket faces.

16 With the aid of an assistant, carefully lift the cylinder head, complete with exhaust manifold, from the block, and manoeuvre it out from the engine compartment.

17 Recover the cylinder head gasket.

18 If necessary, remove the exhaust manifold from the cylinder head.

Inspection

19 Refer to Chapter 2C for details of cylinder head dismantling and reassembly.

20 The mating faces of the cylinder head and block must be perfectly clean before refitting the head. Use a scraper to remove all traces of gasket and carbon, and also clean the tops of the pistons. Take particular care with the cylinder head, as the metal is easily damaged. Also make sure that debris is not allowed to enter the oil and water passages. Using adhesive tape and paper, seal the water, oil and bolt holes in the cylinder block. To prevent carbon entering the gap between the pistons and bores, smear a little grease in the gap. After cleaning each piston, rotate the crankshaft so that the piston moves **down** the bore, and then wipe out the grease and carbon with a cloth rag.

21 Check the block and head for nicks, deep scratches and other damage. If very slight, they may be removed from the cylinder block carefully with a file. More serious damage may be repaired by machining, but this is a specialist job.

22 If warpage of the cylinder head is suspected, use a straight-edge to check it for distortion, with reference to Chapter 2C.

23 Clean out the bolt holes in the block using a pipe cleaner or thin rag and a screwdriver. Make sure that all oil and water is removed, otherwise there is a possibility of the block being cracked by hydraulic pressure when the bolts are tightened.

24 Examine the bolt threads and the threads in the cylinder block for damage. If necessary, use the correct size tap to chase out the threads in the block.

25 The manufacturers recommend that the cylinder head bolts are measured, to determine whether renewal is necessary; however, some owners may wish to renew all the bolts as a matter of course.

26 Measure the length of each bolt from the base of the head to the end of the shank (**see illustration**). If the bolt length is greater than the maximum specified, the bolts should be renewed.

27 Reassemble the cylinder head with reference to Chapter 2C. Where applicable, refit the exhaust manifold together with a new gasket.

Refitting

28 Locate the new cylinder head gasket on the block, making sure that it is the correct way up and positioned over the location dowels.

29 With the aid of an assistant, lower the cylinder head carefully onto the block.

30 Oil the threads and the cylinder head contact faces of the cylinder head bolts, then insert them and screw them into the cylinder block by hand. Ensure that the bolts are fitted to their correct locations as noted on removal.

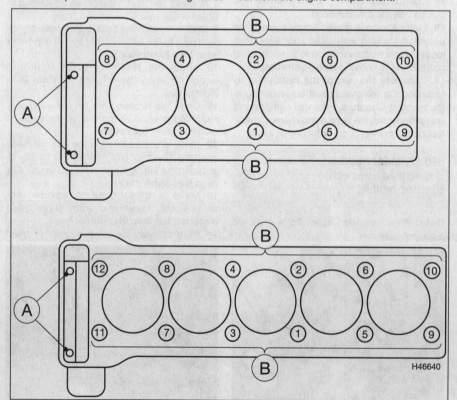

10.31 Cylinder head bolt (B) tightening sequence

A Bolts securing cylinder head to timing chain cover

H46640

31 Tighten the cylinder head bolts in the order shown **(see illustration)**, and in the stages given in the Specifications – ie, tighten all bolts to the Stage 1 torque, then tighten all bolts to the Stage 2 torque, and so on.

32 Tighten the two bolts securing the timing chain cover to the cylinder head at the front of the engine.

33 Refit the turbocharger to the exhaust manifold and tighten the retaining bolts.

34 Refit the retaining nut to the exhaust mounting bracket at the rear of the exhaust manifold.

35 Refit the oil feed pipe to the turbocharger from the cylinder head.

36 Refit the inlet manifold, as described in Chapter 4B.

37 Refit the thermostat housing, as described in Chapter 3.

38 Refit the camshafts, hydraulic tappets and lower housing, as described in Section 9.

39 Refill the cooling system and refill the engine with oil with reference to Chapter 1B.

40 Reconnect the battery negative lead.

41 When all components are refitted, start the engine and check carefully around the engine for any oil leaks, or coolant leaks.

42 Refit the engine compartment undershield and lower the car to the ground.

11 Sump –
removed and refitting

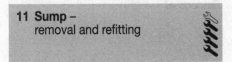

Note: *A suitable hoist and lifting tackle will be required for this operation. To carry out this procedure, the front suspension crossmember will need to be lowered, to allow enough room for the sump to be removed. A new sump gasket will be required on refitting.*

Removal

1 Apply the parking brake, then jack up the front of the vehicle and support it on axle stands (see *Jacking and vehicle support*). Remove both front road wheels.

2 Drain the engine oil as described in Chapter 1B. On completion, check the copper

11.6 Disconnect the wiring connector from the oil level sensor

washer and renew it if necessary, then refit the drain plug and tighten to the specified torque.

3 Lower the front suspension crossmember with reference to Chapter 10.

4 Remove the cooling fan and shroud from the rear of the radiator, with reference to Chapter 3.

5 Refer to Chapter 4C and detach the exhaust downpipe from the manifold, then unbolt the exhaust mounting from the transmission and support the exhaust on an axle stand.

6 Disconnect the wiring from the oil level sensor. If necessary, the sensor may be removed from the sump **(see illustration)**.

7 Attach a suitable hoist to the engine and take the weight of the engine.

8 Unscrew the bolts from the bottom of the engine mountings at each side of the engine **(see illustration)**.

9 Unscrew the bolts securing the transmission to the rear engine-mounting bracket. Leave the bracket attached to the underbody.

10 Raise the engine and transmission as far as possible. Make sure it is adequately supported, as the next procedure involves working beneath the engine.

11 Unscrew the bolts securing the transmission to the rear of the sump, then unscrew the remaining sump-to-engine bolts and lower the sump from the cylinder block **(see illustration)**. Note the location of the bolts as some are of different lengths. Where applicable, recover the gasket. If the

11.8 Engine mounting lower mounting bolt

11.11 Sump-to-transmission bolts

sump is stuck, use a hide or wooden mallet to tap its sides in order to release it. Do not drive a screwdriver between the sump and cylinder block as this may damage the mating surfaces.

12 It is recommended that the oil and oil filter are renewed whenever the sump is removed. Before refitting the sump, it is a good idea to remove the oil filter in order to allow the oil to drain from the cylinder block oil gallery and internal oilways.

Refitting

13 Thoroughly clean the mating surfaces of the sump and cylinder block.

14 Place the gasket onto the sump and align it with the bolt holes in the cylinder block **(see illustrations)**.

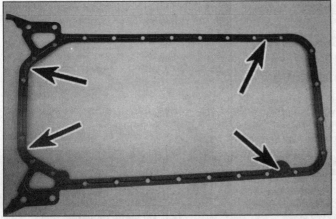

11.14a Note points where sealant is located on gasket

11.14b Fit sump using new gasket

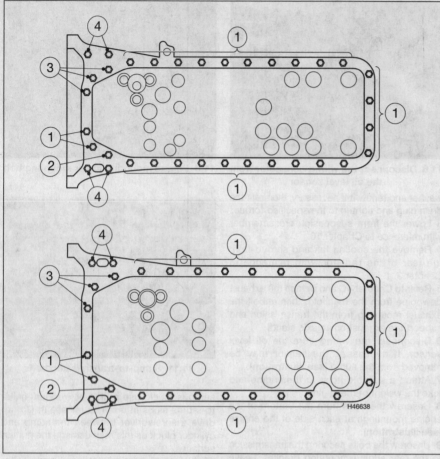

**11.15a Sump bolt locations
(611 and 612 engine)**

| 1 M6x20 bolt | 3 M6x110 bolt |
| 2 M6x40 bolt | 4 M8x40 bolt |

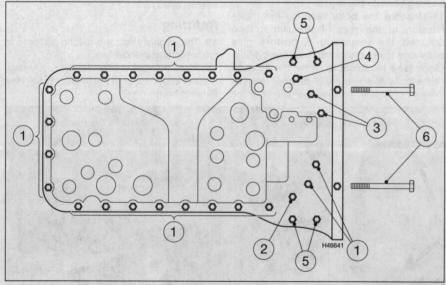

**11.15b Sump bolt locations
(646 engine)**

| 1 M6x20 bolt | 3 M6x80 bolt | 5 M8x40 bolt |
| 2 M6x40 bolt | 4 M6x90 bolt | 6 M10x40 bolt |

15 With the sump in place, insert all of the bolts finger-tight **(see illustrations)**. Make sure all bolts are fitted in the correct position as noted on removal.

16 The bolts can now be tightened securing the transmission to the sump to the specified torque. This will ensure the rear of the sump is correctly aligned with the transmission, as if it is not aligned correctly, vibration and noise may occur.

17 Tighten the remaining sump bolts to the specified torque.

18 Complete the rest of the installation by reversing the removal procedure, referring to the relevant Chapters.

19 Renew the oil filter and refill the engine with clean engine oil with reference to Chapter 1B.

20 When all components are refitted, start the engine and check carefully around the sump for any oil leaks.

12 Oil pump –
removal, inspection and refitting

Note: *It is not necessary to remove the oil pump from the crankcase to remove the oil pressure relief valve components.*

Removal

1 Remove the sump as described in Section 11. Note that this involves suspending the engine with a hoist.

2 The sprocket must be disengaged from the chain as the oil pump is being removed.

3 Unscrew the mounting bolts, withdraw the oil pump from the bottom of the crankcase, and recover the O-ring seal **(see illustration)**.

4 Press against the chain tensioner and disengage the sprocket from the chain as the pump is being removed **(see illustration)**.

Inspection

5 With the exception of the oil pressure relief valve components, the oil pump is a sealed unit. To remove the oil pressure relief valve components, proceed as follows.

6 Unscrew the relief valve plug, in the side of the timing chain cover **(see illustration)**. Take care, as the plug will be pushed out by the spring pressure when it reaches the end of the

12.3 Oil pump mounting bolts

threads. **Note:** *if a sealing ring is present it will need to be renewed on refitting.*

7 Withdraw the spring, guide pin and piston, noting the orientation of the piston.

8 Thoroughly clean all components, and examine them for wear and damage. If there is any sign of excessive wear or damage, renew the appropriate component(s) – pay particular attention to the spring.

9 Also clean the oil pump intake strainer thoroughly, however, **do not** immerse the oil pump in cleaning solvent.

10 Examine the drive chain for wear and damage. If necessary, renew the chain as described later in this Section.

11 Reassemble the oil pressure relief valve using a reversal of the dismantling procedure, lubricating each component with fresh engine oil before fitting. Tighten the relief valve plug to the specified torque.

12 With the oil pump upright, pour fresh engine oil into the upper aperture while turning the pump shaft slowly. This will prime the oil pump so that normal oil pressure will be resumed as soon as possible after starting the engine.

Refitting

13 Check that the sprocket is engaged with the drive chain correctly and then locate the oil pump onto the crankcase. Insert the mounting bolts and tighten the bolts to the specified torque.

14 Refit the sump as described in Section 11.

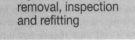

13 Flywheel/driveplate – removal, inspection and refitting

Note: *The flywheel/driveplate mounting bolts must be renewed on refitting.*

Removal

1 Remove the manual transmission (Chapter 7A) or automatic transmission (Chapter 7B).

2 On manual transmission models, remove the clutch as described in Chapter 6.

3 The flywheel/driveplate must be held stationary while the mounting bolts are loosened. To do this, have an assistant insert a wide-bladed screwdriver in the starter ring gear teeth through the access hole in the rear of the sump. On manual transmission models, Mercedes-Benz technicians use a special tool bolted to the sump incorporating serrations which engage with the ring gear teeth. Alternatively, make up a tool as shown **(see illustration)** and bolt it to a starter motor mounting hole.

4 Unscrew the mounting bolts, then lift the flywheel/driveplate from the rear of the crankshaft **(see illustrations)**. Note that the location dowel ensures the flywheel/driveplate can only be fitted in one position.

5 On automatic transmission models recover the locking plates from each side of the driveplate.

12.4 Press against the chain tensioner

12.6 Relief valve retaining plug

Inspection

6 If the teeth on the flywheel/driveplate starter ring gear are badly worn, it may be possible to fit a new ring gear, however this work should be entrusted to a Mercedes-Benz dealer who will have the necessary equipment to heat the new gear to the critical temperature in order to fit it. Overheating the gear will affect its hardness, resulting in rapid wear. The old gear may be removed by drilling it and using a cold chisel to split it. Take care not to drill into the flywheel/driveplate.

7 On manual transmission models, if the clutch friction face of the flywheel is deeply scored, cracked or otherwise damaged, the flywheel must be renewed. However, it may be possible to have it surface-ground, but seek the advice of an engine reconditioning specialist. Check the condition of the spigot bearing in the centre of the flywheel or in the end of the crankshaft, and renew if necessary **(see illustration)**.

8 It is recommended that the flywheel/driveplate securing bolts are renewed whenever removed.

Refitting

9 Commence refitting by cleaning the mating faces of the crankshaft and flywheel/driveplate.

10 Make sure that the location dowel is in position in the end of the crankshaft. On automatic transmission models, fit the locking plate onto the crankshaft.

11 Locate the flywheel/driveplate onto the crankshaft, then insert the new mounting bolts (and further locking plate on automatic transmission models) and hand-tighten them.

12 Lock the flywheel/driveplate using the method employed during removal, then tighten the securing bolts progressively in

13.3 Lock the flywheel in position

13.4a Remove the flywheel

13.4b Location dowel for refitting flywheel

13.7 Spigot bearing fitted in the flywheel

13.12 Use an angle gauge to tighten the retaining bolts

a diagonal sequence to the specified torque first, then tighten all the bolts by the specified angle **(see illustration)**.

13 On manual transmission models, refit the clutch as described in Chapter 6.

14 Refit the manual transmission (Chapter 7A) or automatic transmission (Chapter 7B).

14 Crankshaft oil seals – renewal
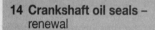

Crankshaft front oil seal

1 Remove the crankshaft pulley/vibration damper and inspect it as described in Section 5.

2 Measure and note the fitted depth of the oil seal in the timing chain cover.

3 Prise the oil seal from the cover using a hooked instrument. Alternatively, drill a small hole in the oil seal, and use a self-tapping screw and a pair of pliers to remove it.

4 Clean the seal location in the timing cover, and also clean the oil seal contact surface on the crankshaft pulley/vibration damper. Examine the seal contact surface of the pulley/vibration damper for an excessive wear groove. If evident, refer to Section 5.

5 Dip the new oil seal in clean engine oil, and press it into the timing chain cover (open end first) to the previously-noted depth, using a suitable tube or socket.

6 Refit the crankshaft pulley/vibration damper as described in Section 5.

14.8 Rear crankshaft oil seal/housing bolts

Crankshaft rear oil seal

Note: *The rear oil seal is integral with the oil seal housing and should be renewed whenever it is removed.*

7 Remove the flywheel/driveplate as described in Section 13.

8 Unscrew the retaining bolts and remove the oil seal/housing from the cylinder block **(see illustration)**.

9 New oil seal/housings are supplied with a plastic sleeve on the inside of the seal to aid refitting of the seal over the end of the crankshaft. DO NOT remove the plastic fitting sleeve until the oil seal housing is in its fitted position.

10 Ensure that the cylinder block mating face of the oil seal housing is free from all traces of old sealant, oil and grease, and then apply a 1.5 to 2.5 mm thick bead of silicone sealant (A 003 989 98 20 or equivalent) to the oil seal housing. Note that the sealant should be run around the inside of the bolt holes in the oil seal housing. It must be fitted within 10 minutes of applying the sealant. Also apply sealant at the area where the sump, oil seal housing and cylinder block meet.

11 Fit the new oil seal housing over the crankshaft and onto the cylinder block, keeping the plastic sleeve in position.

12 Fit the retaining bolts and tighten them to the specified torque setting.

13 Remove the plastic fitting sleeve from the new oil seal housing.

14 Refit the flywheel/driveplate with reference to Section 13.

15 Cylinder head front cover – removal and refitting

1 Disconnect the battery negative (earth) lead and position it away from the terminal.

2 Remove the camshaft cover as described in Section 4.

3 Remove the brake vacuum pump as described in Chapter 9.

611 and 612 engines

4 Remove the timing chain tensioner as described in Section 8.

5 Remove the fuel pre-delivery pump as described in Chapter 4B.

6 Undo the retaining bolts from cover on the front of the cylinder head.

7 Using a screwdriver release the locking ratchet in the upper timing chain slide rail, and then withdraw the cover from the front of the cylinder head.

646 engines

8 Undo the retaining bolt and remove the bracket from the left-hand side front of the cylinder head.

9 Undo the retaining bolts and remove the cover from the front of the cylinder head, noting the position of the locating dowels. **Note:** *The slide rail is attached to the rear of*

the front cover and will be removed with the cover.

10 To remove the slide rail from the cover, insert a screwdriver to release the locking ratchet in the timing chain slide rail, and then withdraw it from the front cover. **Note:** *This only needs to be removed if renewing the front cover or slide rail.*

16 Engine/transmission mountings – inspection and renewal

Inspection

1 Three engine/transmission mountings are used, one on either side of the engine, and one under the rear of the transmission.

2 For improved access, raise the front of the vehicle and support it securely on axle stands (see *Jacking and vehicle support*).

3 Check the condition of the mounting rubber to see if it is cracked, hardened or separated from the metal at any point. Renew the mounting if any such damage or deterioration is evident. The mountings contain hydraulic oil, and must be renewed if oil leakage is evident.

4 Check that all the mounting bolts are securely tightened.

5 Using a large screwdriver or metal bar, check for wear in the mounting by carefully levering against it to check for free play. Where this is not possible, enlist the aid of an assistant to move the engine/transmission back-and-forth, or from side-to-side, while you observe the mounting. If excessive free play is found, check first that the fasteners are correctly secured, and then renew any worn components as required.

Renewal

Front engine mountings

6 Support the engine, either using a hoist and lifting tackle connected to the engine lifting brackets, or by positioning a jack and interposed block of wood under the sump. Ensure that the engine is adequately supported before proceeding.

7 Depending on which engine mounting requires removal, it may be necessary to remove the alternator or turbocharger to make access easier. See the relevant Chapters to remove any other components.

8 Unscrew and remove the engine mounting upper bolt. Depending on model, remove the vibration damper from the top of the engine mounting **(see illustration)**.

9 If working on the right-hand engine mounting, below the exhaust manifold/turbo, remove the heat shield from the top of the engine mounting **(see illustration)**.

10 Working under the vehicle, remove the engine undershield and undo the engine mounting lower bolt **(see illustration)**.

11 Raise the engine as necessary, taking care not to stretch any hoses or wiring, and

16.8 Vibration damper fitted to some models

16.9 Removing the heat shield

16.10 Engine mounting lower bolt

16.11 Engine mounting bracket retaining bolts

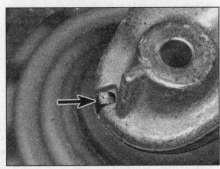

16.12 Engine mounting locating lug

16.15a Unscrew the rear mounting bolts . . .

16.15b . . . and the lower mounting bracket bolts . . .

16.15c . . . and remove, noting the position of the earth cable

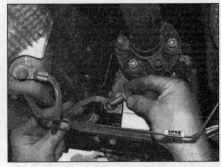

16.17 Earth cable fitted to the rear mounting

remove the mounting. If necessary, unbolt the mounting bracket from the side of the cylinder block **(see illustration)**.

12 Refitting is a reversal of removal, but make sure that the location lug on the top of the mounting engages the cut-out in the mounting bracket **(see illustration)**, and tighten the mounting bolts to the specified torque.

Rear engine/transmission mounting

13 Raise the front of the vehicle and support it securely on axle stands (see *Jacking and vehicle support*).

14 Support the transmission using a jack and interposed block of wood.

15 Unbolt the mounting bracket from the underbody, then unscrew the bolts securing the mounting rubber to the rear of the transmission. Lower the bracket together with the mounting from the underbody **(see illustrations)**.

16 The mounting rubber can then be unbolted from the bracket.

17 Refitting is a reversal of removal, making sure that the earth cable is bolted to the transmission **(see illustration)**.

Chapter 2 Part C:
Engine removal
and general engine overhaul procedures

Contents

Degrees of difficulty

Easy, suitable for novice with little experience	**Fairly easy,** suitable for beginner with some experience	**Fairly difficult,** suitable for competent DIY mechanic	**Difficult,** suitable for experienced DIY mechanic	**Very difficult,** suitable for expert DIY or professional

Specifications

Cylinder head
Maximum gasket face distortion:
  Longitudinal . . . . 0.08 mm
  Transverse . . . . 0.00 mm
Minimum height after machining*:
  Petrol engines**:
    111 type engines . . . . 135.5 mm
  Diesel engines:
    646 type engines . . . . 126.65 mm
Swirl chamber protrusion (diesel engines) . . . . 7.6 to 8.1 mm

* **Note:** *The total thickness of metal removed from the cylinder head and cylinder block mating faces combined must not exceed 0.5 mm for petrol engines or 0.4 mm for diesel engines.*
** **Note:** *The cylinder head and crankcase on 271 type petrol engines cannot be reground.*

Cylinder block
Maximum cylinder bore ovality:
  Petrol engines. . . . . 0.05 mm
  Diesel engines . . . . 0.07 mm
Maximum cylinder bore taper:
  Petrol engines. . . . . 0.05 mm
  Diesel engines . . . . 0.07 mm
Maximum gasket face distortion:
  Petrol engines. . . . . 0.03 mm
  Diesel engines . . . . 0.03 mm

Valves
Valve seat width . . . . 0.9 to 1.1 mm
Valve seat angle . . . . 45°

Pistons
Piston protrusion (diesel engines):
  Minimum. . . . . 0.38 mm
  Maximum . . . . 0.62 mm
Gudgeon pin clearance in small end bush. 0.007 to 0.018 mm

Piston rings

End gaps:
  Petrol engines:
    Top compression ring . . . .   0.30 to 1.00 mm
    Second compression ring . . . .   0.25 to 0.80 mm
    Oil control ring . . . .   0.25 to 0.80 mm
  Diesel engines:
    Top compression ring . . . .   0.22 to 0.42 mm
    Second compression ring . . . .   0.20 to 0.40 mm
    Oil control ring . . . .   0.20 to 0.40 mm
Clearance in grooves:
  Petrol engines:
    Top compression ring . . . .   0.03 to 0.07 mm
    Second compression ring . . . .   0.015 to 0.040 mm
    Oil control ring . . . .   0.010 to 0.045 mm
  Diesel engines:
    Top compression ring . . . .   0.12 to 0.16 mm
    Second compression ring . . . .   0.05 to 0.09 mm
    Oil control ring . . . .   0.03 to 0.07 mm

Connecting rod (big-end) bolts

271 type engines:
  Length when new . . . .   38.0 mm
  Maximum length . . . .   38.4 mm

Crankshaft main bearing cap bolts

111 type petrol engines:
  Length when new . . . .   62.8 mm
  Maximum length . . . .   63.8 mm
611 and 612 type diesel engines:
  Length when new . . . .   62.0 mm
  Maximum length . . . .   63.8 mm

Crankshaft

Endfloat:
  Petrol engines . . . .   0.300 mm
  Diesel engines . . . .   0.300 mm
Endfloat thrustwasher thicknesses . . . .   2.15, 2.20, 2.25, 2.35 and 2.40 mm
Radial play of crankshaft in main bearings:
  Petrol engines . . . .   0.015 to 0.03 mm
  Diesel engines . . . .   0.080 mm
Radial play of big-end bearings on crankshaft:
  Petrol engines . . . .   0.03 to 0.05 mm
  Diesel engines . . . .   0.080 mm

Torque wrench settings

See Chapters 2A (petrol) and 2B (diesel)

---

1 General information

Included in this Part of Chapter 2 are details of removing the engine from the car and general overhaul procedures for the cylinder head, cylinder block/crankcase and all other engine internal components.

The information given ranges from advice concerning preparation for an overhaul and the purchase of parts, to detailed step-by-step procedures covering removal, inspection, renovation and refitting of engine internal components.

After Section 9, all instructions are based on the assumption that the engine has been removed from the car. For information concerning in-car engine repair, as well as the removal and refitting of those external components necessary for full overhaul, refer to Part A or B of this Chapter, as applicable, and to Section 6. Ignore any preliminary dismantling operations described in Parts A or B that are no longer relevant once the engine has been removed from the car.

2 Engine overhaul – general information

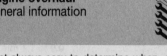

1 It is not always easy to determine when, or if, an engine should be completely overhauled, as a number of factors must be considered.
2 High mileage is not necessarily an indication that an overhaul is needed, while low mileage does not preclude the need for an overhaul. Frequency of servicing is probably the most important consideration. An engine which has had regular and frequent oil and filter changes, as well as other required maintenance, should give many thousands of miles of reliable service. Conversely, a neglected engine may require an overhaul very early in its life.
3 Excessive oil consumption is an indication that piston rings, valve seals and/or valve guides are in need of attention. Make sure that oil leaks are not responsible before deciding that the rings and/or guides are worn. Perform a compression test, as described in Part A or B of this Chapter (as applicable), to determine the likely cause of the problem.
4 Check the oil pressure with a gauge fitted in place of the oil pressure switch, and compare it with that specified in Part A or B. If it is extremely low, the main and big-end bearings, and/or the oil pump, are probably worn out.
5 Loss of power, rough running, knocking or

metallic engine noises, excessive valve gear noise, and high fuel consumption may also point to the need for an overhaul, especially if they are all present at the same time. If a complete service does not remedy the situation, major mechanical work is the only solution.

6 A full engine overhaul involves restoring all internal parts to the specification of a new engine. During a complete overhaul, the pistons and the piston rings are renewed, and the cylinder bores are reconditioned. New main and big-end bearings are generally fitted; if necessary, the crankshaft may be reground, to compensate for wear in the journals. The valves are also serviced as well, since they are usually in less-than-perfect condition at this point. Always pay careful attention to the condition of the oil pump when overhauling the engine, and renew it if there is any doubt as to its serviceability. The end result should be an as-new engine that will give many trouble-free miles.

Note: *Critical cooling system components such as the hoses, thermostat and coolant pump should be renewed when an engine is overhauled. The radiator should be checked carefully, to ensure that it is not clogged or leaking. Also, it is a good idea to renew the oil pump whenever the engine is overhauled.*

7 Before beginning the engine overhaul, read through the entire procedure, to familiarise yourself with the scope and requirements of the job. Overhauling an engine is not difficult if you follow carefully all of the instructions, have the necessary tools and equipment, and pay close attention to all specifications. It can, however, be time-consuming. Plan on the car being off the road for a minimum of two weeks, especially if parts must be taken to an engineering works for repair or reconditioning. Check on the availability of parts and make sure that any necessary special tools and equipment are obtained in advance. Most work can be done with typical hand tools, although a number of precision measuring tools are required for inspecting parts to determine if they must be renewed. Often the engineering works will handle the inspection of parts and offer advice concerning reconditioning and renewal.

Note: *Always wait until the engine has been completely dismantled, and until all components (especially the cylinder block/crankcase and the crankshaft) have been inspected, before deciding what service and repair operations must be performed by an engineering works. The condition of these components will be the major factor to consider when determining whether to overhaul the original engine, or to buy a reconditioned unit. Do not, therefore, purchase parts or have overhaul work done on other components until they have been thoroughly inspected. As a general rule, time is the primary cost of an overhaul, so it does not pay to fit worn or sub-standard parts.*

8 As a final note, to ensure maximum life and minimum trouble from a reconditioned engine, everything must be assembled with care, in a spotlessly-clean environment.

3 Engine removal –
methods and precautions

1 If you have decided that the engine must be removed for overhaul or major repair work, several preliminary steps should be taken.
2 Locating a suitable place to work is extremely important. Adequate workspace, along with storage space for the car, will be needed. If a workshop or garage is not available, at the very least, a flat, level, clean work surface is required.
3 Cleaning the engine compartment and engine/transmission before beginning the removal procedure will help keep tools clean and organised.
4 An engine hoist will also be necessary. Make sure the equipment is rated in excess of the weight of the engine (and transmission if both are being removed). Safety is of primary importance, considering the potential hazards involved in lifting the engine out of the car.
5 If this is the first time you have removed an engine, an assistant should ideally be available. Advice and aid from someone more experienced would also be helpful. There are many instances when one person cannot simultaneously perform all of the operations required when lifting the engine out of the vehicle.
6 Plan the operation ahead of time. Before starting work, arrange for the hire of or obtain all of the tools and equipment you will need. Some of the equipment necessary to perform engine removal and installation safely and with relative ease (in addition to an engine hoist) is as follows: a heavy duty trolley jack, complete sets of spanners and sockets (see *Tools and working facilities*), wooden blocks, and plenty of rags and cleaning solvent for mopping-up spilled oil, coolant and fuel. If the hoist must be hired, make sure that you arrange for it in advance, and perform all of the operations possible without it beforehand. This will save you money and time.
7 Plan for the car to be out of use for quite a while. An engineering works will be required to perform some of the work, which the do-it-yourselfer cannot accomplish without special equipment. These places often have a busy schedule, so it would be a good idea to consult them before removing the engine, in order to accurately estimate the amount of time required to rebuild or repair components that may need work.
8 Always be extremely careful when removing and refitting the engine. Serious injury can result from careless actions. Plan ahead and take your time, and a job of this nature, although major, can be accomplished successfully.
9 On all models, the engine is removed by lifting the assembly out from above the vehicle **(see illustration)**.

3.9 Lifting the engine out from the vehicle

4 Petrol engine –
removal and refitting

Note: *A suitable hoist and lifting tackle will be required for this operation.*

Removal

1 Disconnect the battery negative (earth) lead and position it away from the terminal.
2 Apply the parking brake, then jack up the front of the vehicle and support it on axle stands (see *Jacking and vehicle support*). Allow sufficient height for the hoist to lift the engine out of the engine compartment. Alternatively, the car can be lowered to the ground just before attaching the hoist. With the car raised, remove the engine compartment undershield.
3 Drain the cooling system and remove the radiator as described in Chapters 1A and 3. Unscrew the drain plug from the cylinder block and drain the coolant into a suitable container. On completion refit the plug and tighten.
4 Where fitted, remove the fan and shroud, with reference to Chapter 3. It may be useful to remove the radiator completely, to prevent any damage to it.
5 If necessary, drain the oil from the engine as described in Chapter 1A.
6 Remove the air mass meter as described in Chapter 4A, Section 9.
7 Remove the air mass meter-to-throttle body air duct, and also the air cleaner cover (see Chapter 4A).
8 On models with air conditioning, remove the guard plate from the condenser, then position a piece of strong card or similar over the condenser to protect it as the engine is being removed.
9 On the right-hand rear of the engine compartment, disconnect the engine main wiring, and position the connector on the engine.
10 Where applicable, disconnect the vacuum line from the PMS control unit and also disconnect the hose(s) from the fuel evaporative purge valve.
11 Temporarily remove the fuel tank filler cap and refit it in order to release any pressure, then depressurise the fuel system with reference to Chapter 4A.
12 Unscrew the union nuts and disconnect the fuel feed and return lines from the fuel rail.

4.26 Lifting the engine from the engine compartment

Tape over or plug the lines and apertures to prevent entry of dust and dirt.

13 Disconnect the vacuum line from the inlet manifold/throttle body.

14 Disconnect the brake vacuum line at the inlet manifold/throttle body.

15 On automatic transmission models, disconnect the vacuum lines from the switchover valve.

16 Remove the auxiliary drivebelt with reference to Chapter 1A.

17 Refer to Chapter 10 and unbolt the power steering pump from the side of the engine. Tie the pump to one side in an upright position to prevent the fluid escaping.

18 On models with air conditioning, unbolt the air conditioning compressor and tie it to one side away from the engine. If preferred, the compressor can be unbolted as the engine is being lifted from the engine compartment. **Do not** disconnect the refrigerant lines from the compressor.

⚠️ **Warning: The refrigeration circuit contains pressurised liquid refrigerant. For this reason, disconnection of any part of the system without specialised knowledge and equipment is not recommended.**

19 Loosen the clips and disconnect the coolant hose from the rear of the cylinder head, also disconnect the hoses located on the coolant pump.

20 Remove the front part of the exhaust system as described in Chapter 4C.

Removal without transmission

21 Remove the inlet and exhaust manifolds as described in Chapters 4A and 4C.

4.35 Lifting the engine and transmission from the engine compartment

22 Support the weight of the transmission with a trolley jack and interposed piece of wood.

23 Attach a suitable hoist to the two lifting eyes, and take the weight of the engine.

24 Unscrew and remove the bolts securing the engine front mountings to the suspension crossmember. Alternatively, the mountings can be removed completely.

25 Unscrew the bolts securing the transmission to the rear of the engine, noting the location of any mounting brackets or earth cables. Access to the upper mounting bolts is best achieved from the rear of the transmission with an extensions and a socket.

26 With the help of an assistant, draw the engine forwards from the transmission until the transmission input shaft is clear of the clutch, then lift the engine from the engine compartment, taking care not to damage the surrounding components and wiring **(see illustration)**. Move the hoist forwards and lower the engine to the ground.

Removal with transmission

27 Remove the exhaust heat shield from the underbody, then unbolt the front of the propeller shaft from the flexible joint on the rear of the transmission (refer to Chapter 8).

28 Unbolt the earth cable from the transmission. Also disconnect all wiring plugs from the transmission.

29 On manual transmission models, fit a hose clamp to the hydraulic line leading to the clutch slave cylinder on the transmission (see Chapter 6). Unscrew the union nut and detach the hydraulic line from the slave cylinder. Tape over or plug the line and slave cylinder to prevent entry of dust and dirt. Alternatively, unscrew the slave cylinder mounting bolt and also unscrew the hydraulic pipe support from the left-hand side of the transmission bellhousing, then tie the pipe and slave cylinder to the transmission tunnel.

30 On manual transmission models, disconnect the gearchange levers from the transmission as described in Chapter 7A.

31 On automatic transmission models, disconnect the selector rod from the transmission as described in Chapter 7B. Where applicable, also disconnect the park lock interlock cable.

32 Attach a suitable hoist to the two lifting eyes, and take the weight of the engine and transmission. The hoist chains should be positioned so that the front of the engine will be tilted upwards slightly.

33 Temporarily support the transmission, then unscrew the bolts securing the engine rear mounting bracket to the underbody. If necessary, the complete bracket may be removed from the transmission.

34 Unscrew the lower bolts from the engine front mountings.

35 With the help of an assistant, lift and tilt the engine and transmission to withdraw it from the engine compartment, taking care not to damage the surrounding components and wiring **(see illustration)**. It will be necessary to

move the hoist forwards and guide the engine and transmission up through the engine compartment, taking care not to damage the surrounding components. Move the hoist forwards and lower the engine/transmission assembly to the ground.

36 To remove the transmission from the engine, refer to Chapters 7A or 7B as necessary.

Refitting

37 Before refitting the engine, check the condition of the engine/transmission mountings. In particular, check if they are compressed, are damaged or split, or have signs of oil leakage. If necessary, renew them with reference to Chapter 2A.

38 The refitting procedure is a reversal of removal, noting the following additional information.

a) Tighten all nuts and bolts to the specified torque wrench settings, where given.

b) On automatic transmission models, adjust the selector rod as described in Chapter 7B.

c) On manual transmission models, bleed the clutch hydraulic system as described in Chapter 6.

d) Reconnect the propeller shaft to the flange on the rear of the transmission with reference to Chapter 8.

e) Refill the power steering fluid reservoir with fresh fluid and bleed the system as described in Chapter 10.

f) Ensure that all wiring, hoses and brackets are positioned and routed as noted before removal.

g) Reconnect and if necessary adjust the accelerator cable with reference to Chapter 4A.

h) On completion, refill the engine with oil, and refill the cooling system as described in Chapter 1A.

5 Diesel engine – removal and refitting

Note: *A suitable hoist and lifting tackle will be required for this operation.*

Removal

1 Disconnect the battery negative (earth) lead and position it away from the terminal.

2 Apply the parking brake, then jack up the front of the vehicle and support it on axle stands (see *Jacking and vehicle support*). Allow sufficient height for the hoist to lift the engine out of the engine compartment. Alternatively, the car can be lowered to the ground just before attaching the hoist. With the car raised, remove the engine compartment undershield.

3 On turbocharged models, disconnect and remove the left- and right-hand air ducts to the intercooler. If necessary, remove the intercooler as described in Chapter 4B.

4 Drain the cooling system, then remove

the radiator and cooling fan as described in Chapters 1B and 3.

5 If necessary, drain the oil from the engine as described in Chapter 1B.

6 Remove the auxiliary drivebelt as described in Chapter 1B.

7 On air conditioning models, position a piece of strong card or similar over the condenser to protect it as the engine is being removed.

8 Identify then disconnect the vacuum hoses from the brake vacuum pump, inlet manifold, brake servo unit, and vacuum control valve.

9 Loosen the clips and disconnect the coolant hoses from the rear of the cylinder head and from the thermostat housing on the front, left-hand side of the cylinder head.

10 Refer to Chapter 10 and unbolt the power steering pump from the left-hand side of the engine. Tie the pump to one side, in an upright position to prevent the fluid escaping **(see illustration)**.

11 On the right-hand rear of the engine compartment, disconnect the engine main wiring, and position the connectors on the engine.

12 Briefly remove the filler cap from the fuel tank to relieve any pressure or vacuum, then unscrew the union nuts and disconnect the fuel supply and return lines from the injection pump.

13 On models with air conditioning, unbolt the compressor from the mounting bracket on the left-hand side of the engine, and support it to one side **(see illustration)**. **Do not** disconnect the refrigerant line from the compressor.

⚠️ *Warning: The refrigeration circuit contains pressurised liquid refrigerant. For this reason, disconnection of any part of the system without specialised knowledge and equipment is not recommended.*

14 Remove the front section of the exhaust system as described in Chapter 4C.

Removal without transmission

15 On automatic transmission models, disconnect the control pressure cable and position it to one side.

16 Support the weight of the transmission with a trolley jack and interposed piece of wood.

17 Attach a suitable hoist to the two lifting eyes, and take the weight of the engine.

18 Unscrew and remove the bolts securing the engine mountings to the suspension crossmember. Alternatively, the mountings can be removed completely.

19 Unscrew the bolts securing the transmission to the rear of the engine, noting the location of any mounting brackets or earth cables. Access to the upper mounting bolts is best achieved from the rear of the transmission with an extensions and a socket.

20 With the help of an assistant, draw the engine forwards from the transmission until the transmission input shaft is clear of the clutch, then lift the engine from the engine compartment, taking care not to damage the surrounding components and wiring. Move

the hoist forwards and lower the engine to the ground.

Removal with transmission

21 Remove the exhaust heat shield from the underbody, then unbolt the front of the propeller shaft from the flexible joint on the rear of the transmission (refer to Chapter 8).

22 Unbolt the earth cable from the transmission. Also disconnect all wiring plugs from the transmission.

23 On manual transmission models, fit a hose clamp to the hydraulic line leading to the clutch slave cylinder on the transmission (see Chapter 6). Unscrew the union nut and detach the hydraulic line from the slave cylinder. Tape over or plug the line and slave cylinder to prevent entry of dust and dirt. Alternatively, unscrew the slave cylinder mounting bolt and also unscrew the hydraulic pipe support from the left-hand side of the transmission bellhousing, then tie the pipe and slave cylinder to the transmission tunnel.

24 On manual transmission models, disconnect the gearchange levers from the transmission as described in Chapter 7A.

25 On automatic transmission models, disconnect the selector rod from the transmission as described in Chapter 7B. Where applicable, also disconnect the park lock interlock cable.

26 Attach a suitable hoist to the two lifting eyes, and take the weight of the engine and transmission. The hoist chains should be positioned so that the front of the engine will be tilted upwards slightly.

27 Temporarily support the transmission, then unscrew the bolts securing the engine rear mounting bracket to the underbody. If necessary, the complete bracket may be removed from the transmission.

28 Unscrew the lower bolts from the engine front mountings.

29 With the help of an assistant, lift and tilt the engine and transmission to withdraw it from the engine compartment, taking care not to damage the surrounding components and wiring. It will be necessary to move the hoist forwards and guide the engine and transmission up through the engine compartment, taking care not to damage the surrounding components. Move the hoist forwards and lower the engine/transmission assembly to the ground.

30 To remove the transmission from the engine, refer to Chapters 7A or 7B as necessary.

Refitting

31 Before refitting the engine and transmission, check the condition of the engine/transmission mountings. In particular, check if they are compressed, are damaged or split, or have signs of oil leakage. If necessary, renew them with reference to Chapter 2B.

32 The reconnection and refitting procedures are a reversal of removal, noting the following additional information.

a) *Tighten all nuts and bolts to the specified torque wrench settings, where given.*

5.10 Fasten the power steering pump to the inner wing

b) *On automatic transmission models, adjust the selector rod as described in Chapter 7B.*

c) *On manual transmission models, bleed the clutch hydraulic system as described in Chapter 6.*

d) *Reconnect the propeller shaft to the flange on the rear of the transmission with reference to Chapter 8.*

e) *Refill the power steering fluid reservoir with fresh fluid and bleed the system as described in Chapter 10.*

f) *Ensure that all wiring, hoses and brackets are positioned and routed as noted before removal.*

g) *Reconnect and if necessary adjust the accelerator cable with reference to Chapter 4B.*

h) *On completion, refill the engine with oil, and refill the cooling system as described in Chapter 1B.*

6 Engine overhaul – dismantling sequence

1 It is much easier to dismantle and work on the engine if it is mounted on a portable engine stand. These stands can often be hired from a tool hire shop. Before the engine is mounted on a stand, the flywheel/driveplate should be removed, so that the stand bolts can be tightened into the end of the cylinder block/crankcase.

2 If a stand is not available, it is possible to dismantle the engine with it blocked up on a sturdy workbench, or on the floor. Be extra

5.13 Fasten the compressor to one side

6.3a Remove the engine mounting brackets . . .

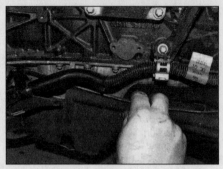

6.3b . . . wiring brackets and insulation . . .

6.3c . . . and remove the dipstick tube

careful not to tip or drop the engine when working without a stand.

3 If you are going to obtain a reconditioned engine, all the external components around the engine must be removed first, so that they can be transferred to the new engine (just as they will if you are doing a complete engine overhaul yourself). These components include the following **(see illustrations)**.

a) *Ancillary unit mounting brackets (oil filter, alternator, power steering pump, engine mountings, crankcase breather housing, etc).*
b) *Thermostat and housing (Chapter 3).*
c) *Dipstick tube.*
d) *All electrical switches and sensors.*
e) *Inlet and exhaust manifolds (Chapters 4A, 4B and 4C).*
f) *Ignition coils and spark plugs – petrol engines (Chapter 1A and 5B)*
g) *Injectors and fuel pipes – diesel engines (Chapter 1B and 4B)*

Note: *When removing the external components from the engine, pay close attention to details that may be helpful or important during refitting. Note the fitted position of gaskets, seals, spacers, pins, washers, bolts, and other small items.*

4 If you are obtaining a 'short' engine (which consists of the engine cylinder block/crankcase, crankshaft, pistons and connecting rods all assembled), then the cylinder head, sump, oil pump, and timing chain will have to be removed also.

5 If you are planning a complete overhaul, the engine can be dismantled, and the internal components removed, in the order given below, referring to Part A or B of this Chapter unless otherwise stated.

a) *Inlet and exhaust manifolds (Chapter 4A, 4B or 4C).*
b) *Timing chain, sprockets and tensioner.*
c) *Cylinder head.*

d) *Flywheel/driveplate.*
e) *Sump.*
f) *Oil pump.*
g) *Piston/connecting rod assemblies (Section 13).*
h) *Crankshaft (Section 11).*

6 Before beginning the dismantling and overhaul procedures, make sure that you have all of the correct tools necessary. Refer to *Tools and working facilities* for further information.

7 Cylinder head – dismantling

Note: *New and reconditioned cylinder heads are available from the manufacturer, and from engine overhaul specialists. Be aware that some specialist tools are required for the dismantling and inspection procedures, and new components may not be readily available. It may therefore be more practical and economical for the home mechanic to purchase a reconditioned head, rather than dismantle, inspect and recondition the original head. A valve spring compressor tool will be required for this operation.*

Petrol engines

1 Remove the cylinder head as described in Part A of this Chapter.

2 Remove the inlet and exhaust manifolds as described in Chapters 4A and 4C.

3 Remove the camshafts and hydraulic tappets as described in Part A of this Chapter.

4 Unscrew the spark plugs from the cylinder head.

5 Using a valve spring compressor, compress the spring on each valve in turn until the split collets can be removed. Release the compressor, and lift off the spring cap and spring **(see illustrations)**. If, when the valve spring compressor is screwed down, the spring cap refuses to free and expose the split collets, gently tap the top of the tool, directly over the spring cap, with a light hammer. This will free the retainer.

6 Using a pair of pliers or special removal tool, carefully extract the valve stem oil seal from the top of the guide, then lift off the spring seat **(see illustrations)**.

7.5a Removing the valve spring cap . . .

7.5b . . . and spring

7.6a Using a special tool to remove the valve stem oil seal

7.6b Removing the valve spring seat

7 Withdraw the valve through the combustion chamber **(see illustration)**.

8 It is essential that each valve is stored with its collets, cap, spring, and spring seat. The valves should also be kept in their correct sequence, unless they are so badly worn that they are to be renewed. If they are going to be kept and used again, place each valve assembly in a labelled polythene bag or similar small container **(see illustration)**. Label each bag No 1 inlet, No 1 exhaust, No 2 inlet, No 2 exhaust, etc, noting that No 1 valve is nearest to the timing chain end of the engine.

Diesel engines

9 Remove the cylinder head as described in Part B of this Chapter.

10 Remove the exhaust manifold as described in Chapter 4C.

11 If desired, remove the glow plugs as described in Chapter 5C.

12 Proceed as described in paragraphs 5 to 8.

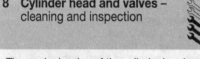

8   Cylinder head and valves –
cleaning and inspection

1 Thorough cleaning of the cylinder head and valve components, followed by a detailed inspection, will enable you to decide how much valve service work must be carried out during the engine overhaul. **Note:** *If the engine has been severely overheated, it is best to assume that the cylinder head is warped – check carefully for signs of this.*

Cleaning

2 Scrape away all traces of old gasket material from the cylinder head.

3 Scrape away the carbon from the combustion chambers and ports, then wash the cylinder head thoroughly with paraffin or a suitable solvent.

4 Scrape off any heavy carbon deposits that may have formed on the valves, then use a power-operated wire brush to remove deposits from the valve heads and stems.

Inspection

Note: *Be sure to perform all the following inspection procedures before concluding that the services of a machine shop or engine overhaul specialist are required. Make a list of all items that require attention.*

Cylinder head

5 Inspect the head very carefully for cracks, evidence of coolant leakage, and other damage. If cracks are found, a new cylinder head should be obtained.

6 Use a straight-edge and feeler blade to check that the cylinder head gasket surface is not distorted **(see illustration)**. If it is, it may be possible to have it machined, provided that the cylinder head is not reduced to less than the specified height. Note also that, on diesel engines, the swirl chamber protrusion must be

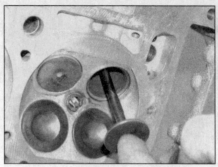

7.7 Removing a valve from the combustion chamber

checked whenever the cylinder head surface is machined – see paragraphs 11 to 13.

7 Examine the valve seats in each of the combustion chambers. If they are severely pitted, cracked, or burned, they will need to be renewed or recut by an engine overhaul specialist. If they are only slightly pitted, this can be removed by grinding-in the valve heads and seats with fine valve-grinding compound, as described later in this Section. If the valve seats are recut, check that the valve recess dimensions, measured between the plane of the cylinder head sealing face and the centre of the valve head, are maintained within the specified limits.

8 Check the valve guides for wear by inserting the relevant valve, and checking for side-to-side motion of the valve. A very small amount of movement is acceptable. If the movement seems excessive, remove the valve. Measure the valve stem diameter (see later in this Section), and renew the valve if it is worn. If the valve stem is not worn, the wear must be in the valve guide, and the guide must be renewed. The renewal of new valve guides should be entrusted to a Mercedes-Benz dealer or engine overhaul specialist, who will have the necessary tools available.

9 If renewing the valve guides, the valve seats should be recut or reground only *after* the guides have been fitted.

10 Examine the camshaft bearing surfaces in the cylinder head and the bearing caps for signs of wear or damage. If the bearings are excessively worn, consult a Mercedes-Benz dealer, or an engine overhaul specialist for further advice.

Swirl chambers (diesel engines)

11 When inspecting the cylinder head, the swirl chamber protrusion should be checked – this is particularly important if the cylinder head face has been machined. If the swirl chamber protrusion is too great, the pistons may hit the swirl chambers when the engine is running, causing expensive damage.

12 Measure the protrusion of the swirl chamber from the sealing face of the cylinder head. If the protrusion is greater than the specified maximum, the protrusion can be altered by removing the swirl chamber and fitting sealing spacers of varying thickness to achieve the specified protrusion.

13 Removal and refitting of the swirl chambers, and fitting of the appropriate spacers should be entrusted to a Mercedes-Benz dealer, or an engine overhaul specialist, due to the special tools required.

Valves

⚠ **Warning: The exhaust valves on most petrol and diesel engines are filled with sodium to improve their heat transfer. Sodium is a highly reactive substance, and will ignite or explode spontaneously on contact with water (including water vapour in the air). These valves must NOT be disposed of as ordinary scrap. Seek advice from a Mercedes-Benz dealer when disposing of the valves.**

14 Examine the head of each valve for pitting, burning, cracks, and general wear. Check the valve stem for scoring and wear ridges. Rotate the valve, and check for any obvious indication that it is bent. Look for pits or excessive wear on the tip of each valve stem. Renew any valve that shows any such signs of wear or damage.

15 If the valve appears satisfactory at this stage, measure the valve stem diameter at several points using a micrometer **(see illustration)**. Any significant difference in the readings obtained indicates wear of the valve stem. Should any of these conditions be apparent, the valve(s) must be renewed.

16 If the valves are in satisfactory condition, they should be ground (lapped) into their respective seats, to ensure a smooth, gas-tight seal. If the seat is only lightly pitted, or if it has

7.8 Store the valve components in a labelled bag

8.6 Use a straight-edge and feeler blade to check the cylinder head gasket face for distortion

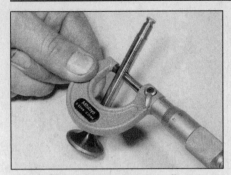

8.15 Measuring a valve stem diameter

8.18 Using a suction valve-grinding tool to grind in a valve

been recut, fine grinding compound should be used to produce the required finish. Coarse valve-grinding compound should not be used, unless a seat is badly burned or deeply pitted. If this is the case, the cylinder head and valves should be inspected, to decide whether seat recutting, or even the renewal of the valve or seat insert (where possible) is required.

17 Valve grinding is carried out as follows. Place the cylinder head upside-down on a bench.

18 Smear a trace of (the appropriate grade of) valve-grinding compound on the seat face, and press a suction grinding tool onto the valve head **(see illustration)**. With a semi-rotary action, grind the valve head to its seat, lifting the valve occasionally to redistribute the grinding compound. A light spring placed under the valve head will greatly ease this operation.

19 If coarse grinding compound is being

used, work only until a dull, matt even surface is produced on both the valve seat and the valve, then wipe off the used compound, and repeat the process with fine compound. When a smooth unbroken ring of light grey matt finish is produced on both the valve and seat, the grinding operation is complete. *Do not grind-in the valves any further than absolutely necessary, or the seat will be prematurely sunk into the cylinder head.*

20 When all the valves have been ground-in, carefully wash off *all* traces of grinding compound using paraffin or a suitable solvent, before reassembling the cylinder head.

Valve components

21 Examine the valve springs for signs of damage and discoloration. Compare the length of the valve springs with that of a new component, where possible, and if necessary renew the springs.

22 Stand each spring on a flat surface, and

check it for squareness. If any of the springs are damaged, distorted or have lost their tension, obtain a complete new set of springs. It is normal to renew the valve springs as a matter of course if a major overhaul is being carried out.

23 Renew the valve stem oil seals regardless of their apparent condition.

Hydraulic tappets

24 Refer to Part A or B of this Chapter for further details.

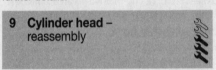

9 Cylinder head – reassembly

Note: *New valve stem oil seals should be fitted.*

Petrol engines

1 Lubricate the stems of the valves, and insert the valves into their original locations **(see illustration)**. If new valves are being fitted, insert them into the locations to which they have been ground.

2 Refit the spring seat.

3 Working on the first valve, dip the new valve stem seal in fresh engine oil. New seals are normally supplied with protective sleeves, which should be fitted to the tops of the valve stems to prevent the collet grooves from damaging the oil seals. If no sleeves are supplied, wind a little thin tape round the top of the valve stems to protect the seals. Carefully locate the seal over the valve and onto the guide. Take care not to damage the seal as it is passed over the valve stem. Use a suitable socket or tube to press the seal firmly onto the guide **(see illustrations)**. Remove the sleeve from the valve stem.

4 Locate the valve spring on top of the seat, then refit the spring cap. On engines where the spring is tapered, make sure that the large diameter end of the spring locates on the seat.

5 Fit the compressor tool, then compress the valve spring and locate the split collets in the recess in the valve stem **(see illustration)**. Release the compressor, then repeat the procedure on the remaining valves.

6 With all the valves installed, support the cylinder head on blocks of wood and, using

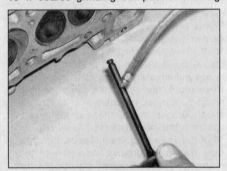

9.1 Lubricate the stems of the valves before inserting them

9.3a Locate the protective sleeve on the valve stem . . .

9.3b . . . then oil the new valve stem seal . . .

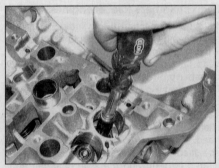

9.3c . . . and press it onto the valve guide

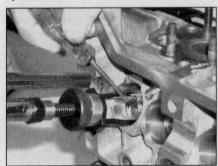

9.5 Fitting the split collets

a hammer and interposed block of wood, tap the end of each valve stem to settle the components.

7 Refit and tighten the spark plugs (refer to Chapter 1A).

8 Refit the hydraulic tappets and camshafts as described in Part A of this Chapter.

9 Refit the inlet and exhaust manifolds as described in Chapters 4A and 4C.

10 Refit the cylinder head as described in Part A of this Chapter.

Diesel engines

11 Proceed as described in paragraphs 1 to 6.

12 Where applicable, refit the glow plugs as described in Chapter 5C.

13 Refit the exhaust manifold as described in Chapter 4C.

14 Refit the cylinder head as described in Part B of this Chapter.

10 Piston/connecting rod assembly – removal

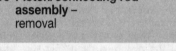

1 Remove the cylinder head, sump and oil pump as described in Part A or B of this Chapter (as applicable). Where fitted, unbolt and remove the oil baffle plate from the crankcase.

2 If there is a pronounced wear ridge at the top of any bore, it may be necessary to remove it with a scraper or ridge reamer, to avoid piston damage during removal. Such a ridge indicates excessive wear of the cylinder bore.

3 Check the connecting rods and big-end caps for identification marks. Both rods and caps should be marked with the cylinder number on the inlet manifold side of each assembly. Note that No 1 cylinder is at the timing chain end of the engine. If no marks are present, using a hammer and centre-punch, paint or similar, mark each connecting rod and big-end bearing cap with its respective cylinder number on the flat-machined surface provided – note on which side of the connecting rods the marks are made.

4 Similarly, check the piston crowns for a direction marking. An arrow on each piston crown should point towards the timing chain end of the engine. On some engines, this mark may be obscured by carbon build-up, in which case the piston crown should be cleaned to check for a mark. In some cases, the direction arrow may have worn off, in which case a suitable mark should be made on the piston crown using a scriber – do not deeply score the piston crown, but ensure that the mark is easily visible.

5 Turn the crankshaft to bring piston Nos 1 and 4 (4-cylinder engines) or No 1 (5-cylinder engine), as applicable, to BDC (bottom dead centre).

6 Unscrew the bolts from No 1 piston big-end bearing cap. Take off the cap, and recover the bottom half bearing shell. If the bearing shells are to be re-used, tape the cap and the shell together.

7 Using a hammer handle, push the piston up through the bore, and remove it from the top of the cylinder block. On diesel engines, take care not to damage the piston cooling oil spay jets in the cylinder block as the piston/connecting rod assembly is removed. Recover the bearing shell, and tape it to the connecting rod for safekeeping.

8 Loosely refit the big-end cap to the connecting rod, and secure with the bolts – this will help to keep the components in their correct order.

9 On 4-cylinder engines, remove No 4 piston assembly in the same way before turning the crankshaft.

10 Turn the crankshaft as necessary to bring the remaining pistons to BDC, and remove them in the same manner.

11 Crankshaft – removal

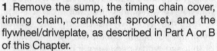

1 Remove the sump, the timing chain cover, timing chain, crankshaft sprocket, and the flywheel/driveplate, as described in Part A or B of this Chapter.

2 Unbolt the crankshaft rear oil seal housing from the cylinder block **(see illustration)**.

3 Remove the pistons and connecting rods, as described in Section 10. If no work is to be done on the pistons and connecting rods, there is no need to remove the cylinder head, or to push the pistons out of the cylinder bores. The pistons should just be pushed far enough up the bores so that they are positioned clear of the crankshaft journals.

4 Check the crankshaft endfloat as described in Section 14, then proceed as follows.

5 On 4-cylinder engines, the crankshaft main bearing caps should be numbered 1 to 5 on the inlet side of the engine, starting from the timing chain end of the engine. Similarly, on the 5-cylinder engine, the main bearing caps should be numbered 1 to 6. If the bearing caps are not marked, mark them accordingly using a centre-punch. Note the orientation of the markings to ensure correct refitting.

6 Unscrew and remove the main bearing cap retaining bolts, and lift off each bearing cap **(see illustration)**. Recover the lower bearing shells, and tape them to their respective caps for safe-keeping.

7 Recover the lower endfloat control thrustwasher halves from either side of the appropriate bearing cap, noting their positions, as follows.

   4-cylinder engine –
      centre (No 3) main bearing.
   5-cylinder engine –
      No 4 main bearing.

8 Lift the crankshaft from the crankcase.

9 Recover the upper bearing shells from the cylinder block, and tape them to their respective caps for safe-keeping. Similarly, recover the upper thrustwasher halves, noting their orientation.

11.2 Crankshaft rear oil seal housing

12 Cylinder block/crankcase – cleaning and inspection

Cleaning

1 Remove all external components, brackets and electrical switches/sensors from the block. Note the position of any mounting brackets before removal. For complete cleaning, the core plugs should ideally be removed. Drill a small hole in the plugs, and then insert a self-tapping screw into the hole. Pull out the plugs by pulling on the screw with a pair of grips, or by using a slide hammer.

2 Scrape all traces of gasket from the cylinder block/crankcase, taking care not to damage the gasket/sealing surfaces.

3 Where applicable, remove the oil gallery plugs, and use new plugs when the engine is reassembled.

4 If the castings are extremely dirty, they should be steam-cleaned.

5 After the castings have been steam-cleaned, clean all oil holes and oil galleries one more time. Flush all internal passages with warm water until the water runs clear. Dry thoroughly, and apply a light film of oil to all mating surfaces, to prevent rusting. Also oil the cylinder bores. If you have access to compressed air, use it to speed up the drying process, and to blow out all the oil holes and galleries.

> ⚠ **Warning: Wear eye protection when using compressed air.**

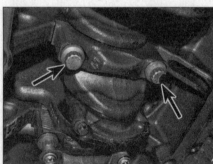

11.6 Main bearing cap bolts

12.7 Piston oil spray jet – where fitted

12.8 Clean damaged threads using a tap

13 Piston/connecting rod assembly –
cleaning and inspection

Cleaning

1 Before the inspection process can begin, the piston/connecting rod assemblies must be cleaned, and the original piston rings removed from the pistons.

2 Carefully expand the old rings over the top of the pistons. The use of two or three old feeler blades will be helpful in preventing the rings dropping into empty grooves **(see illustration)**. Be careful not to scratch the piston with the ends of the ring. The rings are brittle, and will snap if they are spread too far. They are also very sharp – protect your hands and fingers. Note that the third ring incorporates an expander. Always remove the rings from the top of the piston. Keep each set of rings with its piston if the old rings are to be re-used. Note which way up each ring is fitted to ensure correct refitting.

3 Scrape away all traces of carbon from the top of the piston. A hand-held wire brush (or a piece of fine emery cloth) can be used, once the majority of the deposits have been scraped away.

4 Remove the carbon from the ring grooves in the piston, using an old ring. Break the ring in half to do this (be careful not to cut your fingers – piston rings are sharp). Be careful to remove only the carbon deposits – do not remove any metal, and do not nick or scratch the sides of the ring grooves.

5 Once the deposits have been removed, clean the piston/connecting rod assembly with paraffin or a suitable solvent, and dry thoroughly. Make sure that the oil return holes in the ring grooves are clear.

Inspection

6 If the pistons and cylinder bores are not damaged or worn excessively, and if the cylinder block does not need to be rebored, the original pistons can be refitted. Measure the piston diameters, and check that they are within limits for the corresponding bore diameters. If the piston-to-bore clearance is excessive, the block will have to be rebored, and new pistons and rings fitted. Normal piston wear shows up as even vertical wear on the piston thrust surfaces, and slight looseness of the top ring in its groove. New piston rings should always be used when the engine is reassembled. Note that the piston and bore size grades are stamped on the piston crowns, and on the adjacent cylinder head mating face of the cylinder block.

7 Carefully inspect each piston for cracks around the skirt, around the gudgeon pin holes, and at the piston ring 'lands' (between the ring grooves).

8 Look for scoring and scuffing on the piston skirt, holes in the piston crown, and burned areas at the edge of the crown. If the skirt is scored or scuffed, the engine may have been

6 If the castings are not very dirty, you can do an adequate cleaning job with hot (as hot as you can stand!), soapy water and a stiff brush. Take plenty of time, and do a thorough job. Regardless of the cleaning method used, be sure to clean all oil holes and galleries very thoroughly, and to dry all components well. Protect the cylinder bores as described above, to prevent rusting.

7 Where applicable, the piston oil spray jets can be removed from the cylinder block for cleaning, however a special tool is required and it is recommended that an engine overhaul specialist carry out the work **(see illustration)**. The tool for removing the jets consists of an adapter, which engages the base of the jet, and a slide hammer screwed into the adapter. Renew any jets which show signs of damage. Check the oil spray hole and oil passages for blockage.

8 All threaded holes must be clean, to ensure accurate torque readings during reassembly. To clean the threads, run the correct-size tap into each of the holes to remove rust, corrosion, thread sealant or sludge, and to restore damaged threads **(see illustration)**. If possible, use compressed air to clear the holes of debris produced by this operation.

9 Ensure that all threaded holes in the cylinder block are dry.

10 After coating the mating surfaces of the new core plugs with suitable sealant, fit them to the cylinder block. Make sure that they are driven in straight and seated correctly, or leakage could result.

11 Where applicable, fit the new oil gallery plugs.

12 If the engine is not going to be

13.2 Using a feeler blade to help remove a piston ring

reassembled right away, cover it with a large plastic bag to keep it clean; protect all mating surfaces and the cylinder bores as described above, to prevent rusting.

Inspection

13 Visually check the cylinder block/crankcase for cracks and corrosion. Look for stripped threads in the threaded holes. If there has been any history of internal water leakage, it may be worthwhile having an engine overhaul specialist check the cylinder block/crankcase with special equipment. If defects are found, have them repaired if possible, or renew the assembly.

14 Check each cylinder bore for scuffing and scoring. Check for signs of a wear ridge at the top of the cylinder, indicating that the bore is excessively worn.

15 If the cylinder walls are badly scored or scuffed, then the cylinders will have to be rebored by a suitably qualified specialist, and new oversize pistons will have to be fitted. A Mercedes-Benz dealer or engineering workshop will normally be able to supply suitable oversize pistons when carrying out the reboring work.

16 Inspect the upper surface of the cylinder block for damage. Use a straight-edge and feeler blade to check that the cylinder head gasket surface is not distorted. Note also that on diesel engines, the piston protrusion must be checked whenever the cylinder head surface is machined – see paragraph 18.

17 After checking the cylinder block/crankcase, refit the items removed in paragraph 1.

Piston protrusion (diesel engines)

18 When inspecting the cylinder block, the piston protrusion should be checked – this is particularly important if the cylinder head face has been machined. If the piston protrusion is too great, the pistons may hit the swirl chambers when the engine is running, causing expensive damage.

19 Measure the protrusion of the piston from the sealing face of the cylinder head (a dial gauge should be used if possible). If the protrusion is greater than the specified maximum, consult a Mercedes-Benz dealer or an engine-reconditioning specialist for advice – it is likely that the cylinder block will have to be renewed.

suffering from overheating, and/or abnormal combustion, which caused excessively high operating temperatures. The cooling and lubrication systems should be checked thoroughly. Scorch marks on the sides of the pistons show that blow-by has occurred. A hole in the piston crown, or burned areas at the edge of the piston crown, indicates that abnormal combustion (pre-ignition, knocking or detonation) has been occurring. If any of the above problems exist, the causes must be investigated and corrected, or the damage will occur again. The causes may include incorrect ignition/injection pump timing, inlet air leaks or incorrect air/fuel mixture (petrol engines), or a faulty fuel injector (diesel engines).

9 Corrosion of the piston, in the form of pitting, indicates that coolant has been leaking into the combustion chamber and/or the crankcase. Again, the cause must be corrected, or the problem may persist in the rebuilt engine.

10 New pistons can be purchased from a Mercedes-Benz dealer or motor factor.

11 Examine each connecting rod carefully for signs of damage, such as cracks around the big-end and small-end bearings. Check that the rod is not bent or distorted. Damage is highly unlikely, unless the engine has been seized or badly overheated. Detailed checking of the connecting rod assembly can only be carried out by a Mercedes-Benz dealer or engine repair specialist with the necessary equipment.

12 The gudgeon pins are of the floating type, secured in position by two circlips. The pistons and connecting rods can be separated as follows.

13 Using a small screwdriver, prise out the circlips, and push out the gudgeon pin **(see illustrations)**. Hand pressure should be sufficient to remove the pin. Identify the piston and rod to ensure correct reassembly. Discard the circlips – new ones must be used on refitting.

14 Examine the gudgeon pin and connecting rod small-end bearing for signs of wear or damage. It should be possible to push the gudgeon pin through the connecting rod bush by hand, without noticeable play. Wear can be cured by renewing both the pin and bush. Bush renewal, however, is a specialist job – press facilities are required, and the new bush must be reamed accurately.

15 The connecting rods themselves should not be in need of renewal, unless seizure or some other major mechanical failure has occurred. Check the alignment of the connecting rods visually, and if the rods are not straight, take them to an engine overhaul specialist for a more detailed check.

16 Examine all components, and obtain any new parts from your Mercedes-Benz dealer. If new pistons are purchased, they will be supplied complete with gudgeon pins and circlips. Circlips can also be purchased individually.

17 Position the piston in relation to the connecting rod as noted on removal.

18 Apply a smear of clean engine oil to the gudgeon pin. Slide it into the piston and through the connecting rod small-end. Check

13.13a Prise out the circlips . . .

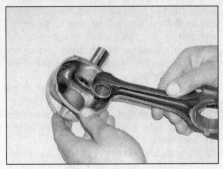

13.13b . . . then press out the gudgeon pin and separate the connecting rod

that the piston pivots freely on the rod, then secure the gudgeon pin in position with two new circlips. Ensure that each circlip is correctly located in its groove in the piston.

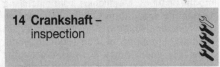

14 Crankshaft – inspection

Checking crankshaft endfloat

1 If the crankshaft endfloat is to be checked, this must be done when the crankshaft is still installed in the cylinder block/crankcase, but is free to move.

2 Check the endfloat using a dial gauge in contact with the end of the crankshaft. Push the crankshaft fully one way, and then zero the gauge. Push the crankshaft fully the other way, and check the endfloat. The result can be compared with the specified amount, and will give an indication as to whether new thrustwasher halves are required **(see illustration)**. Note that all thrustwashers must be of the same thickness – refer to the Specifications for the thicknesses of thrustwashers available.

3 If a dial gauge is not available, feeler blades can be used. First push the crankshaft fully towards the flywheel/driveplate end of the engine, and then use feeler blades to measure the gap between the web of No 3 crankpin and the thrustwasher halves on 4-cylinder engines, or between the web of No 4 crankpin and the thrustwasher halves on the 5-cylinder engine.

Inspection

4 Clean the crankshaft using paraffin or a suitable solvent, and dry it, preferably with compressed air if available. Be sure to clean the oil holes with a pipe cleaner or similar probe, to ensure that they are not obstructed.

 Warning: Wear eye protection when using compressed air.

5 Check the main and big-end bearing journals for uneven wear, scoring, pitting and cracking.

6 Big-end bearing wear is accompanied by distinct metallic knocking when the engine is running (particularly noticeable when the engine is pulling from low speed) and some loss of oil pressure.

7 Main bearing wear is accompanied by severe engine vibration and rumble – getting progressively worse as engine speed increases – and again by loss of oil pressure.

8 Check the bearing journal for roughness by running a finger lightly over the bearing surface. Any roughness (which will be accompanied by obvious bearing wear) indicates that the crankshaft requires regrinding (where possible) or renewal.

9 If the crankshaft has been reground, check for burrs around the crankshaft oil holes (the holes are usually chamfered, so burrs should not be a problem unless regrinding has been carried out carelessly). Remove any burrs with a fine file or scraper, and thoroughly clean the oil holes.

10 Using a micrometer, measure the diameter of the main and big-end bearing journals **(see illustration)**. By measuring the diameter at

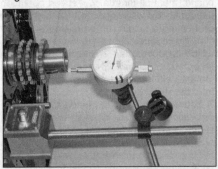

14.2 Checking the crankshaft endfloat using a dial gauge

14.10 Measuring a big-end bearing journal diameter with a micrometer

a number of points around each journal's circumference, you will be able to determine whether or not the journal is out-of-round. Take the measurement at each end of the journal, near the webs, to determine if the journal is tapered.

11 Check the oil seal contact surfaces of the crankshaft for wear and damage. If the seal has worn a deep groove in the surface of the crankshaft, refer to Part A or B of this Chapter (as applicable).

12 If the crankshaft journals have not previously been reground, it may be possible to have the crankshaft reconditioned, and to fit undersize shells (see Section 18). If no undersize shells are available and the crankshaft has worn beyond repair, it will have to be renewed. Consult your Mercedes-Benz dealer or engine specialist for further information on parts availability.

13 Where the transmission input shaft spigot bearing is located in the end of the crankshaft, examine it for smooth running. If necessary renew it.

15 Main and big-end bearings, and bearing cap bolts – inspection

Bearings

1 Even though the main and big-end bearings should be renewed during the engine overhaul, the old bearings should be retained for close examination, as they may reveal valuable information about the condition of the engine. The bearing shells are graded by thickness.

2 Bearing failure can occur due to lack of lubrication, the presence of dirt or other foreign particles, overloading the engine, or corrosion **(see illustration)**. Regardless of the

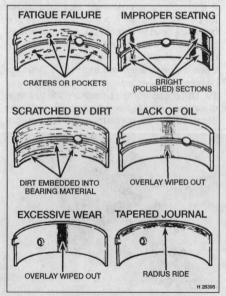

FATIGUE FAILURE — CRATERS OR POCKETS

IMPROPER SEATING — BRIGHT (POLISHED) SECTIONS

SCRATCHED BY DIRT — DIRT EMBEDDED INTO BEARING MATERIAL

LACK OF OIL — OVERLAY WIPED OUT

EXCESSIVE WEAR — OVERLAY WIPED OUT

TAPERED JOURNAL — RADIUS RIDE

H 28395

15.2 Typical bearing failures

cause of bearing failure, the cause must be corrected before the engine is reassembled to prevent it from happening again.

3 When examining the bearing shells, remove them from the cylinder block/crankcase, the connecting rods and the connecting rod big-end bearing caps. Lay them out on a clean surface in the same general position as their location in the engine. This will enable you to match any bearing problems with the corresponding crankshaft journal. *Do not* touch any shell's bearing surface with your fingers while checking it, or the delicate surface may be scratched.

4 Dirt and other foreign matter get into the engine in a variety of ways. It may be left in the engine during assembly, or it may pass through filters or the crankcase ventilation system. It may get into the oil, and from there into the bearings. Metal chips from machining operations and normal engine wear are often present. Abrasives are sometimes left in engine components after reconditioning, especially when parts are not thoroughly cleaned using the proper cleaning methods. Whatever the source, these foreign objects often end up embedded in the soft bearing material, and are easily recognised. Large particles will not embed in the bearing, and will score or gouge the bearing and journal. The best prevention for this cause of bearing failure is to clean all parts thoroughly, and keep everything spotlessly clean during engine assembly. Frequent and regular engine oil and filter changes are also recommended.

5 Lack of lubrication (or lubrication breakdown) has a number of interrelated causes. Excessive heat (which thins the oil), overloading (which squeezes the oil from the bearing face) and oil leakage (from excessive bearing clearances, worn oil pump or high engine speeds) all contribute to lubrication breakdown. Blocked oil passages, which may be the result of misaligned oil holes in a bearing shell, will also oil-starve a bearing, and destroy it. When lack of lubrication is the cause of bearing failure, the bearing material is wiped or extruded from the steel backing of the bearing. Temperatures may increase to the point where the steel backing turns blue from overheating.

6 Driving habits can have a definite effect on bearing life. Full-throttle, low-speed operation (labouring the engine) puts very high loads on bearings, tending to squeeze out the oil film. These loads cause the bearings to flex, which produces fine cracks in the bearing face (fatigue failure). Eventually, the bearing material will loosen in pieces, and tear away from the steel backing.

7 Short-distance driving leads to corrosion of bearings, because insufficient engine heat is produced to drive off the condensed water and corrosive gases. These products collect in the engine oil, forming acid and sludge. As the oil is carried to the engine bearings, the acid attacks and corrodes the bearing material.

8 Incorrect bearing installation during engine

assembly will lead to bearing failure as well. Tight-fitting bearings leave insufficient bearing running clearance, and will result in oil starvation. Dirt or foreign particles trapped behind a bearing shell result in high spots on the bearing, which lead to failure.

9 *Do not* touch any shell's bearing surface with your fingers during reassembly; there is a risk of scratching the delicate surface, or of depositing particles of dirt on it.

10 As mentioned at the beginning of this Section, the bearing shells should be renewed as a matter of course during engine overhaul; to do otherwise is false economy. Refer to Sections 18 and 19 for details of bearing shell selection.

Main bearing cap bolts

11 On some models, the manufacturers recommend that the main bearing cap bolts are measured to determine whether renewal is necessary; however, some owners may wish to renew all the bolts as a matter of course.

12 Where applicable, measure the length of each bolt from the base of the head to the end of the shank **(see illustration)**. If the bolt length is greater than the maximum specified, the bolts should be renewed.

Big-end bearing cap bolts

13 On some models, the manufacturers recommend that the big-end bearing cap bolts are measured to determine whether renewal is necessary, however, some owners may wish to renew all the bolts as a matter of course. It is strongly recommended that the bolts be renewed when reassembling the engine.

14 Press or tap the bolts out from the connecting rods.

15 Where applicable, measure the length of each bolt from the base of the head to the end of the shank. If the bolt length is greater than the maximum specified, the bolts should be renewed.

16 Engine overhaul – reassembly sequence

1 Before reassembly begins, ensure that all new parts have been obtained, and that all necessary tools are available. Read through

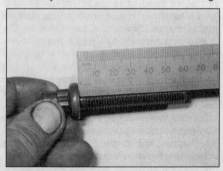

15.12 Measuring a main bearing cap bolt

the entire procedure to familiarise yourself with the work involved, and to ensure that all items necessary for reassembly of the engine are at hand. In addition to all normal tools and materials, thread-locking compound will be needed. A suitable tube of liquid sealant will also be required for the joint faces that are fitted without gaskets.

2 In order to save time and avoid problems, engine reassembly can be carried out in the following order, referring to Part A or B of this Chapter unless otherwise stated. Where applicable, use new gaskets and seals when refitting the various components.

a) *Crankshaft (Section 18).*
b) *Piston/connecting rod assemblies (Section 19).*
c) *Oil pump.*
d) *Sump.*
e) *Flywheel/driveplate.*
f) *Cylinder head.*
g) *Timing chain, tensioner and sprockets.*
h) *Engine external components.*

3 At this stage, all engine components should be absolutely clean and dry, with all faults repaired. The components should be laid out (or in individual containers) on a completely clean work surface.

17 Piston rings – refitting

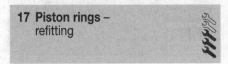

1 Before fitting new piston rings, the ring end gaps must be checked as follows.
2 Lay out the piston/connecting rod assemblies and the new piston ring sets, so that the ring sets will be matched with the same piston and cylinder during the end gap measurement and subsequent engine reassembly.
3 Insert the top ring into the first cylinder, and push it down the bore using the top of the piston. This will ensure that the ring remains square with the cylinder walls. Position the ring near the bottom of the cylinder bore, at the lower limit of ring travel. Note that the top and second compression rings are different. The second ring is easily identified by the step on its lower surface.
4 Measure the end gap using feeler blades.
5 Repeat the procedure with the ring at the top of the cylinder bore, at the upper limit of its travel **(see illustration)**, and compare the measurements with the figures given in the Specifications.
6 If the gap is too small (unlikely if genuine Mercedes-Benz parts are used), it must be enlarged, or the ring ends may contact each other during engine operation, causing serious damage. Ideally, new piston rings providing the correct end gap should be fitted. As a last resort, the end gap can be increased by filing the ring ends very carefully with a fine file. Mount the file in a vice equipped with soft jaws, slip the ring over the file with the ends contacting the file face, and slowly move the

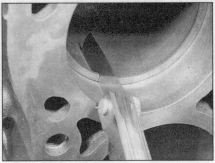

17.5 Measuring a piston ring end-gap

ring to remove material from the ends. Take care, as piston rings are sharp, and are easily broken.
7 With new piston rings, it is unlikely that the end gap will be too large. If the gaps are too large, check that you have the correct rings for your engine and for the particular cylinder bore size.
8 Repeat the checking procedure for each ring in the first cylinder, and then for the rings in the remaining cylinders. Remember to keep rings, pistons and cylinders matched up.
9 Once the ring end gaps have been checked and if necessary corrected, the rings can be fitted to the pistons.
10 Fit the piston rings using the same technique as for removal. Fit the bottom (oil control) ring first, and work up. When fitting the oil control ring, first insert the wire expander, then fit the ring with its gap positioned 180° from the protruding wire ends of the expander. Ensure that the rings are fitted the correct way up – the top surface of the rings is normally marked TOP **(see illustration)**. Arrange the gaps of the top and second compression rings 120° either side of the oil control ring gap, but make sure that none of the rings gaps are positioned over the gudgeon pin hole. **Note:** *Always follow any instructions supplied with the new piston ring sets – different manufacturers may specify different procedures. Do not mix up the top and second compression rings, as they have different cross-sections.*

18 Crankshaft – refitting and main bearing running clearance check

Selection of new bearing shells

1 If the original crankshaft is in good condition and is being refitted, new main bearing shells, which are the same size as the removed shells, should be fitted.
2 If the crankshaft has been reground, undersize bearing shells must be fitted. The engine-reconditioning specialist normally supplies the appropriate shells.

Main bearing clearance check

3 The running clearance check can be carried

17.10 Fitting the oil control ring expander

out using the original bearing shells. However, it is preferable to use a new set, since the results obtained will be more conclusive in determining wear of the crankshaft journals.
4 Clean the backs of the bearing shells, and the bearing locations in both the cylinder block/crankcase and the main bearing caps.
5 Press the bearing shells into their locations, ensuring that the tab on each shell engages in the notch in the cylinder block/crankcase or bearing cap **(see illustration)**. Take care not to touch any shell's bearing surface with your fingers. If the original bearing shells are being used for the check, ensure that they are refitted in their original locations. Note that the bearings shells with oil grooves fit in the cylinder block, and the plain bearing shells fit in the bearing caps.
6 The running clearance can be checked, although this will be difficult to achieve without a range of internal micrometers or internal/ external expanding calipers. Refit the main bearing caps to the cylinder block/crankcase, with bearing shells in place. With the original cap retaining bolts tightened to the specified torque, measure the internal diameter of each assembled pair of bearing shells. If the diameter of each corresponding crankshaft journal is measured and then subtracted from the bearing internal diameter, the result will be the main bearing running clearance.

Final crankshaft refitting

Note: *It is recommended that new main bearing cap bolts be used when finally refitting the crankshaft.*

18.5 Ensure that the tab on each bearing shell (arrowed) engages with the notch in the cap

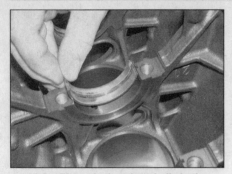

18.9a Place the bearing shells in the crankcase . . .

18.9b . . . and lubricate them with clean engine oil

18.10 Fitting the upper thrustwasher halves

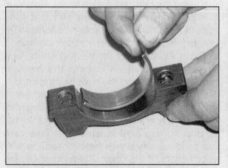

18.12a Locate the main bearing shells in the caps . . .

18.12b . . . and lubricate them with clean engine oil

7 Carefully lift the crankshaft out of the cylinder block once more, and wipe off the surfaces of the bearing shells in the crankcase and bearing caps.

8 Where applicable, ensure that the oil spray jets are fitted to the cylinder block.

9 Place the bearing shells in their locations as described earlier. If new shells are being fitted, ensure that all traces of protective grease are cleaned off using paraffin. Wipe dry the shells and connecting rods with a lint-free cloth. Liberally lubricate each bearing shell in the

cylinder block/crankcase and cap with clean engine oil **(see illustrations)**.

10 Fit the upper thrustwasher halves to the appropriate bearing location in the cylinder block as follows **(see illustration)**.

4-cylinder engines –
  centre (No 3) main bearing.
5-cylinder engine –
  No 4 main bearing.

Ensure that the oil grooves in the thrustwasher halves face out towards the crankshaft journals.

> **HAYNES HINT** *Use a little grease to hold the thrustwasher halves in position.*

11 The crankshaft can now be lowered into position.

12 Lubricate the lower bearing shells in the main bearing caps with clean engine oil. Make sure that the locating lugs on the shells engage with the corresponding recesses in the caps **(see illustrations)**.

13 Fit the main bearing caps to their correct locations, ensuring that they are fitted the correct way round. Ensure that the thrustwasher halves are in place on the appropriate bearing cap **(see illustrations)**.

14 Lightly lubricate the bolt threads, then fit the main bearing cap bolts **(see illustrations)**. Where applicable, ensure that the oil pick-up pipe support bracket is in place on the relevant bolts, as noted before removal. Tighten the bolts by hand only at this stage.

15 Progressively tighten the main bearing cap bolts to the specified torque, starting with the centre bearing cap and working outwards. Observe the two tightening stages given in the Specifications **(see illustrations)**. If the bolts are angle-tightened, it is recommended that an angle-measuring gauge be used during this stage of the tightening, to ensure accuracy. If a gauge is not available, use a dab of white paint to make alignment marks between the bolt and bearing cap prior to tightening; the marks can then be used to check that the bolt has been rotated sufficiently during tightening.

16 Check that the crankshaft rotates freely.

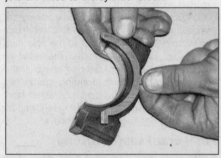

18.13a Fitting a thrustwasher half to a main bearing cap (use a little grease to hold the washer in position)

18.13b Fitting No 3 main bearing cap

18.14a Lightly lubricate the main bearing cap bolts . . .

18.14b . . . then insert them

17 Fit a new crankshaft rear oil seal to the housing, then refit the housing, using a new gasket, or suitable sealant, as applicable.
18 Refit the piston/connecting rod assemblies as described in Section 19.
19 Refit the flywheel/driveplate, crankshaft sprocket, timing chain, timing chain cover and sump, as described in Part A or B of this Chapter.

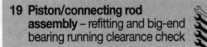

19 Piston/connecting rod assembly – refitting and big-end bearing running clearance check

Selection of new bearing shells

1 If the big-end journals on the crankshaft are in good condition, new big-end bearing shells, which are the same size as the removed shells, should be fitted.
2 If the crankshaft has been reground, undersize bearing shells must be fitted. The engine-reconditioning specialist normally supplies the appropriate shells.

Big-end bearing clearance check

3 Clean the backs of the bearing shells, and the bearing locations in both the connecting rod and bearing cap.
4 Press the bearing shells into their locations, ensuring that the tab on each shell engages in the notch in the connecting rod and cap **(see illustrations)**. Take care not to touch the bearing surface of the shell with your fingers. If the original bearing shells are being used for the check, ensure that they are refitted in their original locations.
5 The running clearance can be checked, although this will be difficult to achieve without a range of internal micrometers or internal/external expanding calipers. Refit the big-end bearing cap to the connecting rod, using the marks made or noted on removal to ensure that they are fitted the correct way around, with the bearing shells in place. With the original cap retaining bolts or nuts (as applicable) correctly tightened, use an internal micrometer or vernier caliper to measure the internal diameter of each assembled pair of bearing shells. If the diameter of each corresponding crankshaft

18.15a Torque-tightening the main bearing cap bolts

18.15b Angle-tightening the main bearing cap bolts

journal is measured, and then subtracted from the bearing internal diameter, the result will be the big-end bearing running clearance.

Piston/connecting rod refitting

Note: *A piston ring compressor tool will be required for this operation. Note that the following procedure assumes that the main bearing caps are in place.*
6 Ensure that the bearing shells are correctly fitted as described earlier. If new shells are being fitted, ensure that all traces of the protective grease are cleaned off using paraffin. Wipe dry the shells and connecting rods with a lint-free cloth.
7 Lubricate the cylinder bores, the pistons, and piston rings, then lay out each piston/connecting rod assembly in its respective position **(see illustrations)**.

19.4a Inserting the bearing shells in the conrod . . .

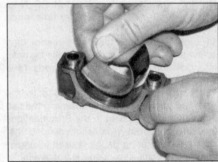

19.4b . . . and big-end bearing cap

8 Start with assembly No 1. Make sure that the piston rings are still spaced as described in Section 17, and then clamp them in position with a piston ring compressor **(see illustration)**.
9 Insert the piston/connecting rod assembly into the top of cylinder No 1. Ensure that the arrow on the piston crown points towards the timing chain end of the engine, and that the identifying marks on the connecting rods and big-end caps are positioned as noted before removal. Using a block of wood or hammer handle against the piston crown, tap the assembly into the cylinder until the piston crown is flush with the top of the cylinder **(see illustration)**. Where applicable, take care not to damage the piston cooling oil spray jets as the piston/connecting rod assemblies are refitted.
10 Ensure that the bearing shell is still

19.7a Lubricating the pistons and rings . . .

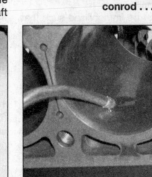

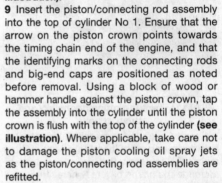

19.7b . . . and cylinder bores

19.8 Fitting a piston ring compressor to the piston

19.9 Inserting a piston in its cylinder bore

19.10 Refitting the big-end bearing cap

19.11 Fitting the big-end bearing cap bolts

19.12a Torque-tightening the big-end bearing bolts

19.12b Angle-tightening the big-end bearing bolts

correctly installed. Liberally lubricate the crankpin and both bearing shells. Taking care not to mark the cylinder bores or damage the piston oil jets (where fitted), pull the piston /connecting rod assembly down the bore and onto the crankpin. Refit the big-end bearing cap **(see illustration)**. Note that the bearing shell locating tabs must abut each other.

11 Lightly lubricate the bolt threads, then screw the big-end bearing cap bolts by hand into position in the connecting rods **(see illustration)**.

12 Progressively tighten the bolts to the specified torque and angle, observing the two tightening stages given in the Specifications **(see illustrations)**. It is recommended that an angle-measuring gauge is used to angle-tighten the bolts. If a gauge is not available, use a dab of white paint to make alignment marks between the bolt and bearing cap prior to tightening; the marks can then be used to check that the bolt has been rotated sufficiently during tightening.

13 Once the bearing cap bolts have been correctly tightened, rotate the crankshaft and check that it turns freely. Some stiffness is to be expected if new components have been fitted, but there should be no signs of binding or tight spots.

14 Refit the remaining piston/connecting rod assemblies in the same way.

15 Refit the oil pump, sump and cylinder head as described in Part A or B of this Chapter (as applicable).

20 Engine – initial start-up after overhaul

1 Refit the remainder of the engine components in the correct order listed in this Chapter. Refit the engine to the vehicle as described in the relevant Section of this Chapter. Double-check the engine oil and coolant levels, and make a final check that everything has been reconnected. Make sure that there are no tools or rags left in the engine compartment.

2 Where necessary, reconnect the battery leads with reference to *Disconnecting the battery* at the rear of this manual.

Petrol engines

3 Remove the spark plugs, referring to Chapter 1A for details.

4 The engine must be immobilised such that it can be turned over using the starter motor without starting – disable the fuel pump by unplugging the fuel pump power relay from the relay board with reference to Chapter 12, and also disable the ignition system by disconnecting the wiring from the DIS module or coils, as applicable.

Caution: To prevent damage to the catalytic converter, it is important to disable the fuel system.

5 Turn the engine using the starter motor until the oil pressure-warning lamp goes out. If the lamp fails to extinguish after several seconds

of cranking, check the engine oil level and oil filter security. Assuming these are correct, check the security of the oil pressure switch wiring – do not progress any further until you are satisfied that oil is being pumped around the engine at sufficient pressure.

6 Refit the spark plugs, and reconnect the wiring to the fuel pump relay and DIS module or coils, as applicable.

Diesel engines

7 Disconnect the injector harness wiring plug at the right-hand rear of the engine compartment – refer to Chapter 4B for details.

8 Turn the engine using the starter motor until the oil pressure warning lamp goes out.

9 If the lamp fails to extinguish after several seconds of cranking, check the engine oil level and oil filter security. Assuming these are correct, check the security of the oil pressure switch cabling – do not progress any further until you are satisfied that oil is being pumped around the engine at sufficient pressure.

10 Reconnect the injector wiring plug.

All engines

11 Start the engine, but be aware that as fuel system components have been disturbed, the cranking time may be a little longer than usual.

12 While the engine is idling, check for fuel, water and oil leaks. Don't be alarmed if there are some odd smells and the occasional plume of smoke as components heat up and burn off oil deposits.

13 Assuming all is well; keep the engine idling until hot water is felt circulating through the top hose.

14 After a few minutes, recheck the oil and coolant levels, and top-up as necessary.

15 There is no need to retighten the cylinder head bolts once the engine has been run following reassembly.

16 If new pistons, rings or crankshaft bearings have been fitted, the engine must be treated as new, and run-in for the first 600 miles. *Do not* operate the engine at full-throttle, or allow it to labour at low engine speeds in any gear. It is recommended that the engine oil and filter are changed at the end of this period.

Chapter 3
Cooling, heating and ventilation systems

Contents

Degrees of difficulty

Easy, suitable for novice with little experience	**Fairly easy,** suitable for beginner with some experience	**Fairly difficult,** suitable for competent DIY mechanic	**Difficult,** suitable for experienced DIY mechanic	**Very difficult,** suitable for expert DIY or professional

Specifications

System type.. Sealed cooling system with auxiliary belt driven coolant pump. The system also has a thermostat and an electrically-operated fan, which is operated by the electronic control unit (ECU), via information from the temperature sensor

General

Pressure cap opening pressure .... 1.4 bar
Thermostat:
  111 type petrol engines:
    Opening commences.................................. $87 \pm 2°C$
    Fully open.. 102°C
  271 type petrol engines:
    Opening commences.................................. $90 \pm 2°C$
    Fully open.. 105°C
  Diesel engines:
    Opening commences.................................. $80 \pm 2°C$
    Fully open.. 100°C
Coolant:
  Type .... See end of *Weekly checks* on page 0•16
  Cooling system total capacity:
    271 type petrol engines .... 8.0 litres
    111 type petrol engines .... 8.5 litres
    611 type diesel engines .... 11.9 litres
    612 type diesel engines .... 12.4 litres
    646 type diesel engines .... 12.0 litres

Torque wrench settings

	Nm	lbf ft
Alternator mounting bracket bolts	45	33
Automatic transmission fluid cooler unions	20	15
Belt tensioner damper bolts	25	18
Belt guide pulley bolt	35	26
Coolant pump mounting bolts:		
Petrol engines:		
M6 bolts	10	7
M8 bolts	20	15
Diesel engines:		
M6 bolts	14	10
M8 bolts	20	15
Coolant pump pulley bolts	10	7
Cylinder block drain plug	30	22
Receiver/drier plug (models up to 04/2004)	20	15
Thermostat cover bolts:		
All except 111 type petrol engines	9	7
111 type petrol engines:		
M6 bolts	10	7
M8 bolts	25	18
Thermostat housing mounting bolts	10	7

1 General information and precautions

General information

The cooling system is of pressurised type, comprising a pump, an aluminium crossflow radiator, an electric cooling fan, and a thermostat. The system functions as follows. Cold coolant from the radiator passes through the hose to the coolant pump, where it is pumped around the cylinder block and head passages. After cooling the cylinder bores, combustion surfaces and valve seats, the coolant reaches the underside of the thermostat, which is initially closed. The coolant passes through the heater and is returned through the cylinder block to the coolant pump.

When the engine is cold, the coolant circulates only through the cylinder block, cylinder head, expansion tank and heater. When the coolant reaches a predetermined temperature, the thermostat opens and the coolant passes through to the radiator. As the coolant circulates through the radiator, it is cooled by the inrush of air when the car is in forward motion. Airflow is supplemented by the action of the electric fan as necessary. Upon reaching the bottom of the radiator, the coolant is now cooled and the cycle is repeated.

The coolant pump is mounted externally on the front of the engine, and is driven by the auxiliary drivebelt.

Coolant temperature information for the gauge mounted in the instrument panel, and for the fuel system, is provided by temperature sensors mounted in the thermostat housing or in the cylinder head, depending on model. A coolant level switch is fitted to bottom of the radiator expansion tank.

An electric cooling fan is fitted and serves a dual purpose, regulating both the engine coolant temperature and that of the air conditioning refrigerant in the condenser (which is mounted in front of the radiator). Partly because of these two roles, the fan is controlled via an electronic unit.

All models have a remote-mounted coolant expansion tank, which is located on the right-hand side of the engine compartment and collects the coolant, which is displaced from the system as it expands due to the rise in temperature. The displaced coolant is returned to the radiator as the system cools.

On models with automatic transmission, the transmission fluid passes through a heat exchanger in front of the radiator, which cools the fluid before returning it to the transmission (see illustration).

Similarly, diesel models are equipped with a heat exchanger attached to either the oil filter housing (646 type engines) or on top of the inlet manifold (611 and 612 type engines). A supply of coolant is fed to the heat exchanger to cool the oil (see illustrations).

Although not strictly part of the cooling system, note that the power steering fluid rigid pipes pass in front of the radiator (see illustration), and are cooled by the inrush of air when the car is moving, thus cooling the fluid.

1.7 Automatic transmission heat exchanger

1.8a Oil cooler (646 type diesel engine)

1.8b Oil cooler (612 type diesel engine)

1.9 Power steering fluid cooler

The vehicle interior heater operates by means of coolant from the engine cooling system. Coolant flow through the heater matrix is regulated by solenoid valves, which are controlled by a temperature sensor at the front of the heater unit. Unusually, the heater matrix is divided into two separate sections, for the driver and front seat passenger. Accordingly, two solenoid valves are fitted into the coolant pipes which lead to the heater, providing independent control of coolant flow through the matrix halves (a further main supply valve is fitted on air conditioning models). Temperature control is further achieved by blending cool air from outside the vehicle (or from the air conditioning system) with the warm air from the heater matrix, in the desired ratio.

Refer to Sections 11 and 12 for information on the air conditioning system.

Precautions

⚠️ *Warning: Do not attempt to remove the pressure cap, or disturb any part of the cooling system, while the engine is hot, as there is a high risk of scalding. If the pressure cap must be removed before the engine and radiator have fully cooled (even though this is not recommended), the pressure in the cooling system must first be relieved. Cover the cap with a thick layer of cloth, to avoid scalding, and slowly unscrew the pressure cap until a hissing sound is heard (be prepared to refit the cap quickly if bubbling noises are heard and hot coolant starts to come out). When the hissing stops, indicating that the pressure has reduced, slowly unscrew the pressure cap until it can be removed; if more hissing sounds are heard, wait until they have stopped before unscrewing the cap completely. At all times, keep your face well away from the pressure cap opening, and protect your hands.*

⚠️ *Warning: Do not allow antifreeze to come into contact with your skin, or with the painted surfaces of the vehicle. Rinse off spills immediately with plenty of water. Never leave antifreeze lying around in an open container, or in a puddle in the driveway or on the garage floor. Children and pets are attracted by its sweet smell, but antifreeze can be fatal if ingested.*

⚠️ *Warning: The cooling fan could cut in even if the engine is not running (if the ignition is on). Be careful to keep your hands, hair, and any loose clothing well clear when working in the engine compartments.*

2 Cooling system hoses – disconnection and renewal

1 The number, routing and pattern of hoses will vary according to model, but the same basic procedure applies. Before commencing

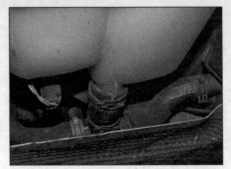

2.3a Expansion tank hoses with spring clip type

work, make sure that the new hoses are to hand, along with new hose clips if needed. It is good practice to renew the hose clips at the same time as the hoses.

2 Drain the cooling system as described in Chapter 1A or 1B, saving the coolant if it is fit for re-use. Squirt a little penetrating oil onto the hose clips if they are corroded.

3 Release the hose clips from the hose concerned. The clip most commonly used on the Mercedes-Benz is the spring clip, which is released by squeezing its tags together with pliers, at the same time working the clip away from the hose stub **(see illustration)**. The worm-drive clip is released by turning its screw anti-clockwise **(see illustration)**. The 'sardine-can' clips are not re-usable, and are best cut off with snips or side cutters.

4 Unclip any wires, cables or other hoses, which may be attached to the hose being removed. Make notes for reference when reassembling, if necessary.

5 Release the hose from its stubs with a twisting motion. Be careful not to damage the stubs on delicate components such as the radiator, or thermostat housings. If the hose is stuck fast, the best course is often to cut it off using a sharp knife, but again be careful not to damage the stubs.

6 Before fitting the new hose, smear the stubs with washing-up liquid or a suitable rubber lubricant to aid fitting. Do not use oil or grease, which may attack the rubber.

7 Fit the hose clips over the ends of the hose, and then fit the hose over its stubs. Work the hose into position. When satisfied, locate and tighten the hose clips.

3.2a Bottom hose retaining clip

2.3b Coolant pump hose with worm-drive clip

8 Refill the cooling system as described in Chapter 1A or 1B. Run the engine, and check that there are no leaks.

9 Recheck the tightness of the hose clips on any new hoses after a few hundred miles.

10 Top-up the coolant level if necessary (see *Weekly checks*).

3 Radiator – removal, inspection and refitting

Removal

1 Refer to Chapter 1A or 1B and drain the cooling system.

2 Slacken the retaining clips and disconnect the coolant hoses from the radiator **(see illustrations)**.

3 Undo the retaining bolts and remove the front crossmember from across the top of the radiator. Move it to one side, leaving the bonnet release cable still connected **(see illustrations)**.

4 Remove the electric cooling fan and shroud, as described in Section 5.

5 Remove the front bumper as described in Chapter 11.

6 On turbo models, disconnect the charge air hoses from the charge air intercooler and disconnect it from the bottom of the radiator.

7 On air conditioned models, unclip the radiator from the condenser and carefully lower the condenser out of the way taking care not to damage the refrigerant lines. Fasten the condenser securely to prevent any damage.

3.2b Release the clip and pull out hose

3.3a Release the plastic lugs . . .

3.3b . . . and remove the crossmember

8 On automatic transmission models, clamp the transmission fluid cooler hoses, ideally using proprietary hose clamps. Unscrew the hose unions from the side of the radiator (do not confuse the cooler hoses with the air conditioning pipes, where applicable). Carefully withdraw and cover the hoses, to prevent dirt ingress.

9 Carefully lift the radiator upwards out of its lower mountings, and withdraw it from the car. Take care not to damage the radiator fins as the radiator is removed.

Inspection

10 Clear the radiator core of flies, small leaves or other debris by brushing or hosing. Check the condition of all hoses, clips, mountings and retaining spring clips, and renew as necessary.

11 Carefully examine the radiator for signs of leaks, corrosion of the alloy core, or damage to the plastic side, top or bottom compartments, as applicable. Should the radiator require attention, this work should be left to a specialist due to the nature of its construction.

Refitting

12 Refitting the radiator is the reverse sequence to removal, noting the following points:

 a) *Ensure that the lower mounting lugs properly engage with the rubber mountings, and that (where applicable) the locating studs are pressed fully home.*

 b) *Make sure that the radiator and fan shroud retaining clips are a secure fit.*

4.14 Unclip and remove the thermostat housing cover

 c) *On automatic transmission models, tighten the radiator fluid cooler unions to the specified torque.*

 d) *After fitting, fill the cooling system as described in Chapter 1A or 1B.*

 e) *On automatic transmission models, check the transmission fluid level as described in Chapter 1A or 1B.*

4 Thermostat – removal, testing and refitting

1 As the thermostat ages, it will become slower to react to changes in water temperature. Ultimately, the unit may stick in the open or closed position, and this causes problems. A thermostat which is stuck open will result in a very slow warm-up; a thermostat that is stuck shut will lead to rapid overheating.

2 Before assuming that the thermostat is to blame for a cooling system problem, check the coolant level. If the system is draining due to a leak, or has not been properly filled, there may be an airlock in the system (refer to the coolant renewal procedure in the relevant part of Chapter 1).

3 If the engine seems to be taking a long time to warm up (based on heater output or temperature gauge operation), the thermostat is probably stuck open.

4 Equally, a lengthy warm-up period might suggest that the thermostat is missing – it may have been removed or inadvertently omitted by a previous owner or mechanic. Don't drive the vehicle without a thermostat – the engine

4.15 Disconnect the inlet air pipe

management system's ECU will then stay in warm-up mode for longer than necessary, causing emissions and fuel economy to suffer.

5 If the engine runs hot, use your hand to check the temperature of the radiator top hose. If the hose isn't hot, but the engine is, the thermostat is probably stuck closed, preventing the coolant inside the engine from escaping to the radiator – renew the thermostat. Again, this problem may also be due to an airlock (refer to the coolant renewal procedure in the relevant part of Chapter 1).

6 If the radiator top hose is hot, it means that the coolant is flowing and the thermostat is open. Consult the *Fault finding* section at the end of this manual to assist in tracing possible cooling system faults.

7 To gain a rough idea of whether the thermostat is working properly when the engine is warming-up, without dismantling the system, proceed as follows.

8 With the engine completely cold, start the engine and let it idle, while checking the temperature of the radiator top hose. Periodically check the temperature indicated on the coolant temperature gauge – if overheating is indicated, switch the engine off immediately.

9 The top hose should feel cold for some time as the engine warms-up, and should then get warm quite quickly as the thermostat opens.

10 The above is not a precise or definitive test of thermostat operation, but if the system does not perform as described, remove and test the thermostat as described below.

Removal

11 The thermostat is located in a housing, which is bolted to front left-hand side of the cylinder head, on diesel models and to the front of the cylinder head on petrol models. On some models, the thermostat and cover are one unit – do not attempt to separate the thermostat from the cover, or it will be damaged.

12 Disconnect the battery negative cable and position it away from the terminal.

13 Remove the engine plastic covers and drain the cooling system as described in Chapter 1A or 1B.

14 Where applicable, unclip the plastic trim panel from the front of the cylinder head on top of the thermostat housing **(see illustration)**.

15 Depending on model, remove air inlet trunking from across the front of the engine **(see illustration)**

16 Slacken the clip(s) and detach the coolant hose(s) from the thermostat housing **(see illustrations)**.

17 On diesel models, disconnect the wiring connector from the temperature sensor in the thermostat housing **(see illustration)**.

18 On 646 diesel engines, undo the retaining bolt and remove the engine cover mounting bracket from the thermostat housing **(see illustrations)**.

19 On petrol models, unscrew the securing bolts, and remove the thermostat cover

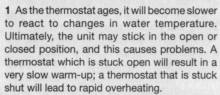

Cooling, heating and ventilation systems 3•5

4.16a Disconnect the hose from the thermostat housing (271 type petrol engine)

4.16b Disconnect the hose from the thermostat housing (646 type diesel engine)

4.17 Disconnect the wiring from the temperature sensor (646 type diesel engine)

from the housing. If the cover is stuck to the housing, tap it gently, or carefully rock it back-and-forth to free it – do not lever between the mating faces. Recover the O-ring seal and discard; a new one will be required for refitting **(see illustrations)**.

20 On diesel models, unscrew the securing bolts, and remove the thermostat housing. On 611 and 612 diesel engines, take care not to damage the bypass pipe below the housing as it is removed. Recover the O-ring seal from the bypass pipe and discard; a new one will be required when refitting **(see illustration)**.

Testing

21 Check the temperature marking stamped on the thermostat, or refer to the opening temperature quoted in this Chapter's Specifications.

22 Using a thermometer and container of water, heat the water until the temperature corresponds with the temperature marking stamped on the thermostat.

23 Suspend the (closed) thermostat on a length of string in the water, and check that maximum opening occurs within two minutes.

24 Remove the thermostat and allow it to cool down; check that it closes fully.

25 If the thermostat does not open and close as described, or if it sticks in either position, it must be renewed. If there is any question about the operation of the thermostat, renew it.

Refitting

26 Commence refitting by thoroughly cleaning the mating faces of the cover and the housing.

4.18a Undo the mounting bolt . . .

27 Lay a new seal in position on the housing, ensuring that it is correctly seated **(see illustration)**.

28 If removed, refit the thermostat to the housing, noting the correct fitted position **(see illustration)**.

4.19a Remove the housing . . .

4.18b . . . and remove the bracket (646 type diesel engine)

29 Fit the thermostat and housing (where applicable), then refit the securing bolts, and tighten to the specified torque.

30 Further refitting is a reversal of removal. Refill the cooling system as described in Chapter 1A or 1B.

4.19b . . . and withdraw the thermostat (271 type petrol engine)

4.20 Remove the thermostat housing (646 type diesel engine)

4.27 Fit new seal to housing (646 type diesel engine)

4.28 Locate the thermostat in the housing (271 type petrol engine)

5.4 Radiator fan wiring connector

5.5a Release the retaining clips . . .

5.5b . . . remove the locating peg . . .

5.5c . . . and release the lugs

5.6 Fan shroud retaining clip

5.7 Lift out the fan and shroud

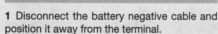

5 Cooling fan – removal and refitting

1 Disconnect the battery negative cable and position it away from the terminal.
2 On diesel models, refer to Chapter 1A or 1B and drain the cooling system, then disconnect the upper and lower coolant hoses from the radiator.
3 If required, to make access easier on diesel models, remove the air filter housing as described in Chapter 4B.
4 Release the retaining clip and prise the cooling fan wiring plug to disconnect it **(see illustration)**.
5 Undo the retaining bolts and remove the front crossmember from across the top of the radiator. Release the plastic retaining clips from along the top of the crossmember and

6.1 Coolant level sensor

pull out the two radiator locating pegs **(see illustrations)**. Move it to one side, leaving the bonnet release cable still connected.
6 Release the retaining clips at each side of the radiator and unclip the fan shroud from the radiator **(see illustration)**
7 Carefully lift out the cooling fan assembly, and remove it from the engine compartment **(see illustration)**.
8 If required, the fan motor can be removed from the shroud by removing the retaining screws, while the fan itself is secured to the motor by a circlip.
9 Refitting is a reversal of removal.

6 Cooling system electrical switches – removal and refitting

Coolant level sensor

1 The sensor is mounted in the base of the coolant expansion tank **(see illustration)**.
2 Refer to the relevant part of Chapter 1 and partially drain the cooling system, so that only the expansion tank is emptied.
3 Ensure that the ignition is switched off, and then unplug the wiring from the coolant level switch at the connector.
4 Turn the sensor anti-clockwise a quarter of a turn, and pull to remove it from the expansion tank. Check the sealing ring, renew if required.
5 Refit the level sensor by following the removal procedure in reverse, noting the following points:

a) Fit a new O-ring seal to the sensor body, if required.
b) On completion, where necessary top-up the cooling system as described in Chapter 1A, 1B, or Weekly checks.

Engine coolant temperature (ECT) sensor

Petrol models

6 On 111 type engines, the coolant temperature sensor is screwed into the thermostat housing on the front of the engine **(see illustration)**.
7 On 271 type engines, the coolant temperature sensor is located in the coolant pipe on the right-hand side of the cylinder head **(see illustration)**.
8 Unclip and remove the plastic covers from the top of the engine, and on 111 type engines unclip the small plastic cover over the thermostat housing **(see illustration)**.

6.6 Coolant temperature sensor

6.7 Coolant temperature sensor

6.8 Unclip and remove the plastic cover from the thermostat housing

6.11a Disconnect the wiring connector . . .

6.11b . . . and remove securing clip

6.14 Coolant temperature sensor

6.16 Disconnect the wiring connector

9 Ensure that the engine is cold, then refer to Chapter 1A and partially drain the cooling system. Alternatively, if the system is not drained, be prepared for some coolant loss when the sensor is removed.
10 On 111 type engines, disconnect the wiring connector from the sensor, then unscrew the sensor and remove it from the housing. Recover the sealing ring.
11 On 271 type engines, disconnect the wiring connector from the sensor, release the retaining clip and pull the sensor to remove it from the coolant pipe **(see illustrations)**. Recover the sealing ring.
12 Clean the sensor, and the location in the housing. Check the condition of the sealing ring, and fit a new one if necessary.
13 Refitting is a reversal of removal, noting the following points:
 a) *Use a smear of sealant on the threads (where applicable), and tighten it securely.*

 b) *On 271 type engines, make sure the retaining clip is located securely.*
 c) *On completion, top-up the cooling system as described in Chapter 1A or Weekly checks.*

Diesel models

14 The coolant temperature sensor is located in the thermostat housing, on the left- hand side of the engine, at the front **(see illustration)**.
15 Ensure that the engine is cold, then refer to Chapter 1B and partially drain the cooling system.
16 Ensure that the ignition is switched off, and then unplug the wiring from the sensor at the connector **(see illustration)**.
17 Release the retaining clip and pull the sensor to remove it from the thermostat housing. Recover the sealing ring.
18 Refitting is a reversal of removal, noting the following points:
 a) *Use a new sealing ring.*

 b) *On completion, top-up the cooling system as described in Chapter 1B or Weekly checks.*

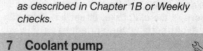
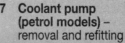

7 Coolant pump (petrol models) – removal and refitting

Removal

1 Disconnect the battery negative cable and position it away from the terminal.
2 Refer to Chapter 1A and drain the cooling system.
3 On Kompressor models, undo the retaining clips and remove the air inlet silencer from across the front of the engine **(see illustrations)**.
4 On 111 type engines, slacken the hose clips and disconnect the coolant hoses from the ports on the coolant pump, noting their fitted position.

7.3a Release the securing clip . . .

7.3b . . . and remove the lower intake hose

7.3c Remove the upper hose . . .

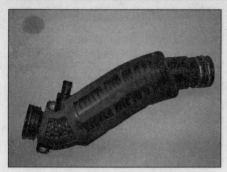

7.3d ... and remove the air intake silencer

7.7 Remove the coolant pump pulley

7.8 Coolant pump retaining bolts

5 Slacken, but do not remove, the bolts securing the coolant pump pulley.
6 Remove the auxiliary drivebelt as described in Chapter 1A.
7 Remove the bolts and washers, and take off the coolant pump pulley **(see illustration)**.
8 Loosen and remove the bolts securing the coolant pump, noting their locations, as they are of different lengths and sizes **(see illustration)**.
9 Withdraw the pump, and recover the O-ring gasket. Discard the O-ring gasket, as a new one will be required when refitting.

Refitting

10 Carefully clean the coolant pump and cylinder block mating surfaces, removing all traces of the old gasket or sealant. Take care to avoid scoring the surfaces, as this will cause leakage.

11 Refit the coolant pump by following the removal procedure in reverse, noting these points:
  a) If the pump is to be refitted using a bead of sealant instead of a gasket, apply the sealant in an even bead to the pump body only. Do not apply an excessive amount, as any excess may enter the pump and then the cooling system itself, which could block the radiator passages.
  b) Fit a new O-ring gasket when refitting the pump.
  c) Tighten the pump bolts in a diagonal sequence to the correct torque, noting the different figures for the different size bolts used.
  d) Refit and tension the auxiliary drivebelt with reference to Chapter 1A.
  e) On completion, refill the cooling system with reference to Chapter 1A.

8 Coolant pump (diesel models) – removal and refitting

Removal

1 Disconnect the battery negative cable and position it away from the terminal.
2 Refer to Chapter 1B and drain the cooling system.
3 Remove the plastic trim covers from the top of the engine.
4 On 5-cylinder engines, remove the cooling fan as described in Section 5.
5 Slacken the hose clips and disconnect the coolant hoses from the ports on the coolant pump, noting their fitted position.
6 Remove the auxiliary drivebelt as described in Chapter 1B.
7 Remove the plastic cap and remove the guide pulley from the oil filter lower housing **(see illustrations)**. **Note:** *One of the coolant pump retaining bolts is positioned behind the guide pulley.*
8 Remove the plastic cap and remove the guide pulley from the top of the coolant pump housing **(see illustrations)**. **Note:** *One of the coolant pump retaining bolts is positioned behind the guide pulley.*
9 On 611 and 612 engines, wrap a cloth around the fuel lines on the fuel shut-off valve, release the securing clips and disconnect the fuel lines from the valve.

⚠️ *Warning: Observe the precautions in Chapter 4B, Section 1, before working on any component in the fuel system.*

10 Loosen and remove the bolts securing the coolant pump, noting their locations, as they are of different lengths and sizes **(see illustration)**.
11 Withdraw the pump, and recover the gasket **(see illustration)**. Discard the gasket, as a new one will be required when refitting.

Refitting

12 Carefully clean the coolant pump and cylinder block mating surfaces, removing all traces of the old gasket or sealant. Take care to avoid scoring the surfaces, as this will cause leakage.

8.7a Unclip the plastic cap ...

8.7b ... and remove the idler pulley

8.8a Unclip the plastic cap ...

8.8b ... and remove the idler pulley

8.10 Coolant pump retaining bolts – note the different sizes

8.11 Removing the coolant pump

8.13 Fit new coolant pump gasket

13 Refit the coolant pump by following the removal procedure in reverse, noting these points:

a) *If the pump is to be refitted using a bead of sealant instead of a gasket, apply the sealant in an even bead to the pump body only. Do not apply an excessive amount, as any excess may enter the pump and then the cooling system itself, which could block the radiator passages.*

b) *Fit a new gasket when refitting the pump* **(see illustration).**

c) *Tighten the pump bolts in a diagonal sequence to the correct torque, noting the different figures for the different size bolts used.*

d) *Refit and tension the auxiliary drivebelt with reference to Chapter 1B.*

e) *On completion, refill the cooling system with reference to Chapter 1B.*

9 Thermostat housing (111 type petrol engines) – removal and refitting

Removal

1 Disconnect the battery negative cable and position it away from the terminal. Drain the cooling system as described in Chapter 1A.

2 Remove the cooling fan as described in Section 5 – this is not essential, but it does improve working room.

3 Unclip and remove the plastic cover fitted over the housing.

4 Disconnect the coolant hose(s) from the housing.

5 Noting the location of each, disconnect the wiring and vacuum connections from the switches and sensors on the housing – refer to Section 6 if necessary.

6 Where fitted, unbolt the drivebelt tensioner damper from the end of the housing, and move it to one side **(see illustration).**

7 Unscrew and remove the five housing mounting bolts, noting their locations as they are of different lengths. Two of the bolts are used to secure the engine front lifting eye **(see illustration).**

8 Loosen the hose clip from the pipe at the base of the housing **(see illustration).**

9 Remove the housing from the engine, lifting the pipe stub out of the hose and recovering the O-ring seal **(see illustrations).**

Refitting

10 Refitting is a reversal of removal. Tighten the housing bolts to the specified torque.

10 Heater/ventilation components – removal and refitting

1 Before working on any of the heater ventilation components, disconnect the battery negative cable and position it away from the terminal.

Heater control panel

2 Remove the centre console and ashtray as described in Chapter 11.

3 Remove the two screws from below the heater control panel **(see illustration).**

9.6 Unbolt the drivebelt tensioner damper from the housing

9.7 Two of the thermostat housing bolts also secure the engine lifting eye

9.8 Loosen the hose clip under the thermostat location

9.9a Remove the housing from the front of the engine, noting the O-ring seal (arrowed) . . .

9.9b . . . and lifting it out of the hose

10.3 Undo the two retaining screws . . .

10.4 . . . and carefully remove the control panel

10.8 Disconnect the motor wiring connector

10.9 Heater motor retaining screws

10.10 Remove the rubber grommet

10.11 Control unit retaining screws

4 Carefully prise the heater control panel out of the facia panel, releasing it from the upper retaining clips (see illustration).

5 Noting their locations, disconnect the wiring from the switches, and remove the panel complete with switches.

6 Refitting is a reversal of removal, making sure the heater panel is located in the upper retaining clips correctly.

Heater blower motor

Note: *The heater blower motor and control unit are removed complete with lower part of the heater housing.*

7 Remove the passenger lower facia panel from under the glovebox to gain access to the heater blower motor. Refer to Chapter 11 for further information.

8 Disconnect the wiring connector from the heater motor (see illustration).

9 Unscrew the heater motor retaining screws,

and withdraw it from the upper housing (see illustration).

10 To remove the fan and motor out from the lower housing, remove the rubber grommet from the housing and undo the retaining screw (see illustration). The fan and motor can now be removed from the lower housing.

11 To remove the control unit from the lower housing, first remove the fan and motor as described in paragraph 10, and then remove the two retaining screws (see illustration).

12 Refitting is a reversal of removal, making sure that all wiring connections are securely remade. Operate the fan before refitting the lower trim panel to check it is fitted correctly.

Heater matrix

 Warning: On models fitted with air conditioning, the air conditioning refrigerant MUST be discharged prior to removal – see Section 11.

13 Drain the cooling system as described in the relevant part of Chapter 1.

14 Remove the centre console, as described in Chapter 11.

15 Pull back the carpet in the passenger side footwell to access the air duct that runs to the rear footwell.

16 Release the retaining clips at the heater housing and remove the passenger side air duct from the housing.

17 Position some rags below the heater pipe connections, as there will still be some coolant spillage, either now or when the heater matrix is removed.

18 Release the securing clips on the pipes into the heater matrix (see illustrations), and then carefully pull out the pipes. Discard the securing clips as new ones will be required for refitting.

19 Undo the retaining screws from the mounting bracket and withdraw the heater matrix from the heater housing (see illustration).

10.18a Release the securing clips . . .

10.18b . . . and disconnect the heater pipes

10.19 Undo the two bracket retaining screws

20 Refitting is a reversal of removal, noting the following points:

a) *On completion, refill the cooling system as described in the relevant part of Chapter 1.*

b) *Run the engine and check the heater operation. It is not unknown for a heater not to work initially, due to the formation of an airlock (especially when a new heater matrix has been fitted). Follow the advice on dealing with airlocks given in the coolant renewal Section of Chapter 1A or 1B.*

Facia vents

Side vents

21 Using a small screwdriver inserted through the vent grilles, release the tabs securing the vent to the facia.

22 Unscrew and remove the screws in each facia vent.

23 Refitting is a reversal of removal.

Centre vents

24 Unclip the cover from the top of the facia panel. Where applicable, disconnect the wiring connector from the parktronic sensor.

25 Working inside the aperture, remove the four retaining screws.

26 Pull the centre air vents out from the facia panel.

27 Refitting is a reversal of removal.

Heater control motors and solenoid valves

28 There are a number of actuator motors and solenoid valves fitted to the heater housing behind the facia panel. To access these, remove the relevant panels as described in Chapter 11.

29 Disconnect the wiring plug from the relevant actuator motor or solenoid valve unit.

30 Undo the retaining screws and disconnect the actuator/valve from the heater housing.

31 Refitting is a reversal of removal.

---

11 Air conditioning system –
general information
and precautions

An air conditioning system is fitted as standard equipment on later high-specification models, and was available as an optional extra on some lower-specification models. In conjunction with the heater, the system enables any reasonable air temperature to be achieved inside the car, it also reduces the humidity of the incoming air, aiding demisting even when cooling is not required.

The refrigeration circuit of the air conditioning system functions in a similar way to a domestic refrigerator. A compressor, belt-driven from the crankshaft pulley, draws refrigerant in its gaseous state from an evaporator. The refrigerant heats up as a result of being compressed, but is then passed through a condenser (mounted in front of the engine radiator) where it loses heat and enters its liquid state. After dehydration, the refrigerant is passed through an evaporator (mounted alongside the heater/ventilation unit) where it is allowed to expand and reverts to being gas. This change of state has the effect of absorbing heat from the air passing over the evaporator fins, reducing its temperature. This cool air is mixed with warm air from the heater unit to achieve the desired cabin temperature. The refrigerant is directed back to the compressor and the cycle is then repeated.

Various subsidiary controls and sensors protect the system against excessive temperature and pressures. Additionally, engine idle speed is increased when the system is in use to compensate for the additional load imposed by the compressor. Electronic sensors detect the rotational speed differential between the engine and the compressor – if this becomes too great (due to a malfunctioning compressor), the compressor clutch is disengaged, to preserve the drivebelt.

Note: *The air conditioning electronic control system can only be tested using dedicated equipment. For this reason, it is recommended that problems with the operation of the air conditioning system are referred to a Mercedes-Benz dealer for diagnosis.*

⚠ *Warning: The refrigeration circuit contains pressurised liquid refrigerant. The refrigerant is potentially dangerous, and should only be handled by qualified persons. Refrigerant that is allowed to come into contact with the skin will cause severe frostbite. It is not itself poisonous, but in the presence of a naked flame (including inhalation through a lighted cigarette), it forms a poisonous gas. Uncontrolled discharging of the refrigerant is dangerous and is also extremely damaging to the environment. For these reasons, disconnection of any part of the system without specialised knowledge and equipment is not recommended.*

• *Do not allow refrigerant lines to be exposed to temperatures in excess of 110°C, for example during welding or paint-drying operations.*

• *Do not operate the air conditioning system if it is known to be short of refrigerant, or component damage may result.*

12.4 Open flap to access receiver/drier

---

12 Air conditioning system components –
removal and refitting

⚠ *Warning: Refer to the previous Section before proceeding. Before carrying out any of the procedures detailed below, the air conditioning system MUST be professionally discharged by a garage or air conditioning specialist.*

Note: *The car may be driven once the system has been discharged, but the air conditioning system should NOT be switched on, as this will cause damage to the compressor. The safest option is to have the system discharged where the car is to be worked on, and not move the car until the system has been recharged. With air conditioning becoming an increasingly common fitment, mobile air conditioning specialists are becoming more widespread.*

Receiver/drier

1 The receiver/drier stores refrigerant and removes moisture from the system. When any major air conditioning component (compressor, condenser or evaporator) is renewed, or the system has been apart and exposed to air for any length of time, the receiver/drier must be renewed. This is to ensure correct functioning of the air conditioning system.

2 The receiver/dryer is mounted at the front of the engine compartment, on the right-hand side of the condenser on models up to 04/2004. On later models, it is mounted below the condenser to the left-hand side (left as seen from the driver's seat).

3 Gloves must be worn when disconnecting the refrigerant lines, even though the system will have been discharged at this point (refer to the warning at the start of this Section). Where applicable, recover the O-ring seals – new ones must be used when refitting. Cover the pipe ends, to prevent the entry of foreign matter.

Models up to 04/2004

4 Open the bonnet and lift up the plastic flap on the right-hand side of the radiator **(see illustration)**.

5 With the system discharged, unscrew the plug from the top of the condenser and withdraw the receiver/drier out through the top of the condenser.

6 If the receiver/drier is being renewed, add 20 cc of clean refrigerant oil to the new receiver/drier. This will maintain the correct oil level in the system after the repairs are completed.

7 If fitting a new receiver/drier, do not open the packaging until you are ready to install the unit into the condenser.

8 Fit the receiver/drier back into the condenser, cylinder end down (shaft end up). Refit the plug cap to the condenser and tighten to the specified torque setting.

9 Have the system professionally recharged before attempting to use it.

12.11 Pull down the plastic cover

12.12 Remove the securing bracket

12.13 Receiver/drier retaining screws

12.18 Undo the pipe retaining nut

Models from 04/004

10 Apply the parking brake, then jack up the front of the vehicle and support it on axle stands (see *Jacking and vehicle support*). Remove the plastic shield from under the engine.

11 Release the retaining clips and pull down the plastic cover from the receiver/drier **(see illustration)**.

12 Undo the retaining screw and remove the pipe securing bracket from the end of the receiver/drier **(see illustration)**.

13 Undo the two retaining screws and remove the receiver/drier from the bottom of the radiator **(see illustration)**. Plug the end of the lines, to prevent the ingress of dirt.

14 Refitting is a reversal of removal, noting the following points:

a) Use new O-ring seals when reconnecting the refrigerant lines, and tighten the unions securely.

b) Lubricate the O-ring seals with clean refrigerant oil.

c) If the receiver/drier is being renewed, add 20 cc of clean refrigerant oil to the new receiver/drier. This will maintain the correct oil level in the system after the repairs are completed.

d) Have the system professionally recharged before attempting to use it.

Condenser

15 Remove the radiator as described in Section 3.

16 Gloves must be worn when disconnecting the refrigerant lines, even though the system will have been discharged at this point (refer to the warning at the start of this Section).

17 Remove the receiver/drier as described earlier in the Section.

18 Unscrew the unions on the two pipes at the base of the condenser, and disconnect

them **(see illustration)**. Recover the O-ring seals – new ones must be used when refitting. Cover the pipe ends, to prevent the entry of foreign matter.

19 Carefully lift the condenser out of its lower mountings, and remove it from the car, taking care not to damage the fins or pipework.

20 Refitting is a reversal of removal, noting the following points:

a) Use new O-ring seals when reconnecting the refrigerant lines, and tighten the unions securely.

b) Lubricate the O-ring seals with clean refrigerant oil.

c) Renew the receiver drier, see paragraph 1 in this Section.

d) Have the system professionally recharged before attempting to use it.

Compressor

21 Disconnect the battery negative cable and position it away from the terminal.

22 Apply the parking brake, then jack up the front of the vehicle and support it on axle stands (see *Jacking and vehicle support*). Remove the plastic shield from under the engine.

23 Remove the auxiliary drivebelt as described in the relevant part of Chapter 1.

24 Undo the retaining bolt and disconnect the refrigerant line bracket from the transmission housing **(see illustration)**.

25 Support the compressor (it is a heavy unit) and remove the mounting bolts. Depending on the exact type of compressor, and on the engine to which it is fitted, there will be either three or four mounting bolts. Lift the compressor and move it forward to access the refrigerant lines and wiring connector.

26 If the compressor is being removed as part of another procedure (such as engine removal), it is sufficient to remove the mounting bolts and tie the compressor up to one side **(see illustration)** without disconnecting the refrigerant lines. If the compressor is being removed completely, proceed as follows.

27 Gloves must be worn when disconnecting the refrigerant lines, even though the system will have been discharged at this point (refer to the warning at the start of this Section). Unscrew the unions on the two pipes on the compressor, and disconnect them. Recover

12.24 Disconnect the pipes from the transmission

12.26 Fasten the compressor to one side

12.28 Disconnect the wiring connector

the O-ring seals – new ones must be used when refitting. Cover the pipe ends, to prevent the entry of foreign matter.

28 Disconnect the wiring plug from the top of the compressor **(see illustration)**.

29 It is advisable to cover the openings on the compressor while it is removed, to reduce oil loss and to prevent foreign matter from entering.

30 Refitting is a reversal of removal, noting the following points:

a) *Use new O-ring seals when reconnecting the refrigerant lines, and tighten the unions securely.*

b) *Tighten the mounting bolts securely.*

c) *Renew the receiver drier, see paragraph 1 in this Section.*

d) *Have the system professionally recharged before attempting to use it.*

Chapter 4 Part A:
Fuel system – petrol engine

Contents

Degrees of difficulty

Easy, suitable for novice with little experience		Fairly easy, suitable for beginner with some experience		Fairly difficult, suitable for competent DIY mechanic		Difficult, suitable for experienced DIY mechanic		Very difficult, suitable for expert DIY or professional	

Specifications

General
System type:
1.8 litre engines	Siemens ME-SIM 4
2.0 litre engines	Siemens ME-SIM 4 or Bosch ME-SFI
2.3 litre engines	Siemens ME-SIM 4

Torque wrench settings	Nm	lbf ft
Camshaft position sensor	8	6
Crankshaft position sensor	8	6
Fuel gauge sender unit retaining ring	85	63
Fuel rail to cylinder head:		
111 type engines	25	18
271 type engines	14	10
Idle speed control actuator/throttle body	9	7
Inlet manifold-to-cylinder head bolts/nuts:		
111 type engines	20	15
271 type engines	14	10
Knock sensor	20	15
Lambda (oxygen) sensors:		
111 type engines	55	41
271 type engines	50	37

1.3 Fuel pump/level sender

1 General information and precautions

The electronic engine management systems primarily control the fuel injection and ignition. This chapter deals mainly with the fuel system components; the ignition system components are dealt with in Chapter 5B.

The major components of the fuel system are a fuel tank, an electric fuel pump, a fuel filter, fuel supply and return lines, a throttle body, a fuel rail, a fuel pressure regulator, four electronic fuel injectors, and an Electronic Control Unit (ECU), together with its associated sensors, actuators and wiring. The overall function of each of these components is outlined below.

The fuel tank is mounted horizontally beneath the vehicle. A fuel pump/level sender unit is mounted in the top of the fuel tank and consists of the fuel inlet filter, the pump and the fuel level sensor. This can be accessed by removing the rear seat cushion, and then removing the access cover in the rear floor panel (see illustration). The fuel filter is located at the rear of the fuel tank on the left-hand side. The fuel pressure regulator is an integral part of the fuel filter.

The fuel pump delivers a constant supply of fuel through a filter to the fuel rail, at a slightly higher pressure than required – the fuel pressure regulator maintains a constant fuel pressure to the fuel injectors and returns excess fuel to the tank via the return line. This constant flow system also helps to reduce fuel temperature and prevents vaporisation.

The fuel injectors are electromagnetic valves, opened and closed by the Electronic Control Unit (ECU), which calculates the injection timing and duration according to engine speed, crankshaft position, throttle position, inlet air mass flow rate, inlet air temperature, coolant temperature and exhaust gas oxygen content information, received from sensors mounted on and around the engine.

Inlet air is drawn into the engine through the air cleaner, which contains a renewable paper and mesh filter element. From there, the air is drawn through the air mass meter. Details of the Kompressor system and supercharger is given in Sections 12 and 13.

Idle speed control is achieved by the ignition system, which gives fine control of the idle speed by altering the ignition timing.

Depending on model, the exhaust gas oxygen content is constantly monitored by the ECU via the lambda sensor(s), which are mounted in the exhaust pipe, in front (and at the rear) of the catalytic converter. The ECU then uses this information to modify the injection timing and duration to maintain the optimum air/fuel ratio – a result of this is that manual adjustment of the idle exhaust CO content is not necessary or possible. In addition, all models are fitted with a catalytic converter in the exhaust system – see Chapter 4C for details.

It should be noted that fault diagnosis of the engine management system described in this Chapter is only possible with dedicated electronic test equipment. Problems with the systems operation should therefore be referred to a Mercedes-Benz dealer for assessment. Once the fault has been identified, the removal/refitting sequences detailed in the following Sections will then allow the appropriate component(s) to be renewed as required.

Precautions

⚠ **Warning: Many of the procedures in this Chapter require the removal of fuel lines and connections, which may result in some fuel spillage. Before carrying out any operation on the fuel system, refer to the precautions given in Safety first! at the beginning of this manual, and follow them implicitly. Always switch off the ignition before working on the fuel system. Petrol is a highly dangerous and volatile liquid, and the precautions necessary when handling it cannot be overstressed.**

Note: *Residual pressure will remain in the fuel lines long after the vehicle was last used. Before disconnecting any fuel line, first depressurise the fuel system as described in Section 10.*

2 Air cleaner housing and filter element – removal and refitting

Air filter element

1 Remove the air filter from the air cleaner housing as described in Chapter 1A.

Air cleaner housing

111 type engines

2 At the front of the air filter housing, rotate the air inlet pipe collar anti-clockwise, and then disconnect it from the air filter housing.

3 Where applicable, disconnect the wiring connector from the Mass Air Flow/Inlet Air Temperature (MAF/IAT) sensor.

4 Slacken the hose clip and disconnect the inlet hose from the right-hand side of the air cleaner housing.

5 Undo the retaining bolt on the left-hand side front of the air cleaner housing and lift the air cleaner housing out from the engine compartment.

6 Refitting is a reversal of removal.

271 type engines

7 Open the bonnet and remove the air inlet pipe from the front of the air cleaner housing (see illustration).

8 Disconnect the battery negative (earth) lead and position it away from the terminal.

9 Release the locking clips and disconnect the wiring connectors from the ECU attached to the air filter housing (see illustration).

10 Disconnect the wiring connector from the mass airflow (MAF) sensor at the rear of the air filter housing (see illustration).

11 Disconnect the wiring connector from the altitude sensor on the side of the air filter housing (see illustration).

2.7 Remove the air intake pipe

2.9 Disconnect the ECU wiring connectors

2.10 Disconnect the MAF sensor wiring connector

12 Remove the cable ties from the mounting brackets and move the wiring loom to one side **(see illustration)**.

13 Disconnect the breather hose from the air filter housing, and undo the two retaining bolts at the rear of the housing **(see illustration)**.

14 Slide the air filter housing to the rear to disengage the locating pegs, and then remove it from the engine compartment **(see illustration)**.

15 Refitting is a reversal of removal.

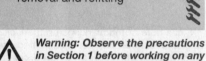

3 Fuel filter –
removal and refitting

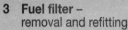

⚠ **Warning: Observe the precautions in Section 1 before working on any component in the fuel system.**

Removal

1 The fuel filter is mounted in the fuel supply line, adjacent to the fuel tank **(see illustration)**. Access is from the underside of the vehicle.

2 Temporarily remove the fuel tank filler cap in order to release pressure from the fuel system (refer to Section 10 and depressurise the fuel system if necessary). Disconnect the battery negative (earth) lead and position it away from the terminal.

3 With the vehicle parked on a level surface, apply the parking brake and chock the front roadwheels. Raise the rear of the vehicle and support it securely on axle stands (see *Jacking and vehicle support*).

4 Remove the screws and lower the protective cover away from under the fuel filter.

5 Clamp the flexible fuel supply hose to the fuel pump, and the fuel filter outlet hose using proprietary hose clamps. Position a suitable container beneath the filter to catch any spilled fuel.

6 Undo (or loosen) the central screw and release the mounting clamp plate from the bottom of the fuel filter.

7 Note the positional arrow on the filter body indicating the correct location, then release the clips and disconnect the inlet and outlet hoses from each end of the filter **(see illustration)**. Withdraw the filter from under the car. Where necessary, recover the insulation sleeve. **Note:** *Some early models may be fitted with a union*

2.11 Disconnect the altitude sensor wiring connector

2.13 Rear mounting bolts

nut and bolt, together with copper washers, instead of normal hose fittings.

Refitting

8 Refitting is a reversal of removal, but where necessary renew any hoses if damaged.

9 When fitting the hoses, make sure that the direction arrow on the filter is pointing the correct way, as noted on removal

10 Make sure the hose clips are secure, and renew the hose clips if required **(see illustration)**.

4 Fuel pump/gauge
sender unit –
removal and refitting

⚠ **Warning: Observe the precautions in Section 1 before working on any component in the fuel system.**
Note: *There are two fuel gauge sender units*

2.12 Release the wiring harness

2.14 Remove the air filter housing

in the fuel tank, which are connected to each other by fuel lines inside the fuel tank. One sender unit is in the right-hand side of the fuel tank which has the pump built into it, and the other is in the left-hand side of the fuel tank.

Removal

1 Disconnect the battery negative (earth) lead and position it away from the terminal.

2 Before carrying out this procedure, make sure that the fuel tank is less than three-quarters full.

3 Remove the rear seat cushion (with reference to Chapter 11), and pull back the soundproofing **(see illustration)**.

4 Undo the retaining screws and remove the access cover from the floor panel **(see illustration)**.

5 On the left-hand fuel gauge sender unit, disconnect the fuel gauge wiring from the sender unit, and then release the retaining

3.1 Fuel filter location under the vehicle

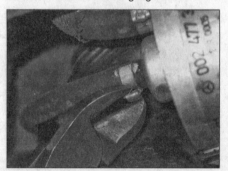

3.7 Release the retaining clips

3.10 Using crimping pliers to secure clips

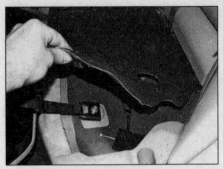

4.3 Remove the under seat soundproofing

4.4 Access cover in floor panel

4.5 Note the fuel line direction arrows

4.6a Using special tool . . .

4.6b . . . to remove the retaining ring

7 Make note of the markings on the locking ring and sender unit to aid refitting **(see illustrations)**, with the rings removed, carefully withdraw the sender units from the fuel tank. Recover the gaskets.

8 To disengage the fuel lines inside the tank with the sender unit, release the locking clips and pull the pipe connection apart **(see illustrations)**. Take care not to damage the fuel sender unit.

Refitting

9 Refitting is a reversal of removal, but always renew the sender unit gaskets, and tighten the retaining rings to the specified torque. Making sure that the marks noted on removal are aligned.

clips and disconnect the fuel lines, noting which way around they are fitted **(see illustration)**. **Note:** *Depending on model, there maybe a different number of fuel lines and wiring connectors.*

6 The retaining rings must now be loosened

and removed. To do this, Mercedes-Benz technicians use a special tool, which engages the holes in the ring **(see illustrations)**. Ideally, this tool should be obtained, however it should be possible to fabricate a home-made version using metal bar and suitable-sized bolts.

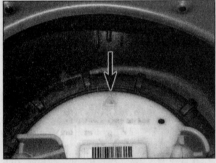

4.7a Note the markings . . .

4.7b . . . for refitting

5 Fuel pump – removal and refitting

⚠️ *Warning: Observe the precautions in Section 1 before working on any component in the fuel system.*

1 The fuel pump is part of the fuel gauge sender unit and cannot be renewed as a separate unit; to remove the fuel pump/sender unit follow the procedure in Section 4.

6 Fuel tank – removal and refitting

⚠️ *Warning: Observe the precautions in Section 1 before working on any component in the fuel system.*

Note: *Removing the fuel tank is difficult, as the rear suspension assembly will need to be lowered. Refer to Chapter 10, to support and lower the rear suspension, to leave enough room to remove the fuel tank. As this means supporting the vehicle on stands, lowering the rear suspension and removing a fuel tank, we do not recommend this as a job to be done at home.*

Removal

1 The fuel tank must be emptied before the operation can be started. This is best achieved by waiting until the tank is almost empty through the course of normal driving.

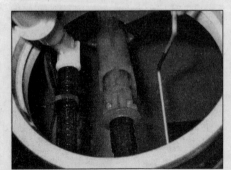

4.8a Lower connections on sender unit . . .

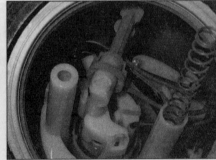

4.8b . . . and upper connection

6.7 Remove heat shields

6.8 Disconnect the handbrake cables

6.18 Fuel tank retaining nut – one shown

2 Park the vehicle on a level surface and chock the front roadwheels. Raise the rear of the vehicle, support it securely on axle stands (see *Jacking and vehicle support*) and remove the rear roadwheels.

> ⚠️ *Warning: The use of an inspection pit is not advised; petrol vapours are heavier than air and can quickly build-up on the floor of the pit, causing a potential hazard.*

3 Disconnect the battery negative (earth) lead and position it away from the terminal.
4 Remove the fuel gauge/pump sender unit as described in Section 4.
5 Remove the two plastic covers from under each side of the vehicle.
6 Remove the exhaust system as described in Chapter 4C.
7 Undo the retaining nuts and remove the exhaust system heat shields from under the vehicle **(see illustration)**.
8 With reference to Chapter 9, remove the rear handbrake cables from the brake cable equaliser under the centre of the vehicle **(see illustration)**.
9 Remove the both rear wheels and remove the brake calipers, carefully tie the calipers to one side. Refer to Chapter 9 for more information.
10 Remove the anti-roll bar as described in Chapter 10.
11 Locate the wiring connectors for the rear wheel speed sensors and brake pad warning wiring (where fitted) and disconnect.
12 Undo the retaining bolts and disconnect the driveshafts from the differential flanges, refer to Chapter 8 for further information.

13 Remove the rear coil springs as described in Chapter 10.
14 Support the rear suspension assembly with an adjustable trolley jack. Make sure the assembly is located securely on the jack head; a frame may need to be made to support it.
15 Remove the four large bolts from the rear suspension crossmember and carefully lower it.
16 Undo the retaining screws and remove the splash shield from under the right-hand rear wheel arch.
17 Slacken the hose clips from the filler neck, vent hose and overflow shut-off hose and disconnect the hoses, from under the right-hand wheel arch.
18 With the aid of an assistant, support the fuel tank and remove the straps from under the fuel tank **(see illustration)**.
19 Lower the tank and check that there are no more hoses or wiring still attached, then remove the fuel tank out from the side of the vehicle.
20 Swill the tank out with clean fuel. If the tank shows signs of leakage, it should be renewed.

> ⚠️ *Warning: Do not attempt to repair the tank yourself by welding, soldering or brazing. The tank will contain an explosive mixture of air and fuel vapour, even when emptied of liquid fuel.*

Refitting

21 Refit the fuel tank by reversing the removal procedure, but tighten all fixings to the correct torque, where specified.

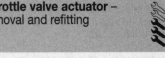

7 Throttle valve actuator – removal and refitting

> ⚠️ *Warning: Observe the precautions in Section 1 before working on any component in the fuel system.*
> **Caution: Never soak the throttle valve actuator in solvent or any type of carburettor cleaner. Also do not use spray carburettor cleaners or silicone lubricants on any part of the throttle body.**

111 type engines

1 Remove the plastic trim cover from the top of the engine.
2 Loosen the hose clip and remove the air inlet pipe from the throttle valve actuator.
3 Disconnect the wiring connector from the actuator.
4 Unscrew the mounting bolts and withdraw the throttle body from the inlet manifold.
5 Remove the gasket/O-ring seal and discard it, a new one will be required for refitting.
6 Refitting is a reversal of removal, noting the following points:
  a) *Wipe clean the gasket-mating surface.*
  b) *Fit new gasket/O-ring seal.*
  c) *Tighten the mounting bolts securely.*

271 type engines

7 Remove the air cleaner housing as described in Section 2.
8 Disconnect the wiring connector from the throttle valve actuator **(see illustration)**.
9 Loosen the hose clip and remove the air

7.8 Disconnect the wiring connector

7.9a Disconnect the hose . . .

7.9b . . . and the sealing collar

7.10a Undo the four retaining bolts . . .   **7.10b . . . and remove the throttle body**   **7.11 Note the fitted position of the seal**

inlet pipe, and then withdraw the sealing collar from the throttle body **(see illustrations)**. Check the sealing collar for any damage, renew if required.

10 Unscrew the four mounting bolts and withdraw the throttle body from the inlet manifold **(see illustrations)**.

11 Remove the O-ring seal and discard it, a new one will be required for refitting **(see illustration)**.

12 Refitting is a reversal of removal, but tighten the mounting bolts securely. Also make sure the new O-ring seal is fitted correctly.

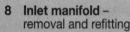
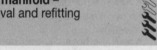

8 Inlet manifold – removal and refitting

Warning: Observe the precautions in Section 1 before working on any component in the fuel system.

1 Disconnect the battery negative (earth) lead and position it away from the terminal. Remove the plastic cover from the top of the engine.

2 Remove the air cleaner housing as described in Section 2.

3 Remove the throttle valve actuator as described in Section 7.

111 type engines

4 Disconnect the vacuum pipes from the switchover valve, remove the mounting bracket and remove the valve from the top of the inlet manifold.

5 Disconnect the wiring connector from the camshaft position sensor.

6 Remove the fuel rail and injectors as described in Section 9.

7 Release the retaining clips and remove the wiring harness to one side.

8 Press the retaining clips and disconnect the brake vacuum hose from the inlet manifold.

9 Disconnect the wiring connector from the pressure sensor on the inlet manifold.

10 Unscrew the mounting bolts/nuts securing the inlet manifold to the cylinder head, noting their fitted position. Remove the inlet manifold from the engine compartment. **Note:** *It may be necessary to disconnect the wiring connector at the air conditioning compressor and unclip the wiring, moving it to one side, to completely withdraw the manifold.*

11 Refitting is a reversal of removal, but use new gaskets/seals where applicable and tighten all nuts and bolts to the specified torque.

271 type engines

12 Disconnect the wiring connector from the charge air temperature sensor **(see illustration)**.

13 Disconnect the ventilation hoses from the inlet manifold **(see illustration)**.

14 Remove the fuel rail and injectors as described in Section 9.

15 Disconnect the wiring connector from the pressure sensor at the rear of the manifold **(see illustration)**.

16 Unscrew the mounting bolts securing the inlet manifold to the cylinder head, noting their fitted position. Remove the inlet manifold from the engine compartment **(see illustration)**. **Note:** *It will be necessary to carefully secure the wiring harness to one side, to allow the manifold to be removed.*

17 Refitting is a reversal of removal, but use new gaskets/seals where applicable and tighten all nuts and bolts to the specified torque.

8.12 Charge air temperature sensor wiring   **8.13 Disconnect breather hose**

8.15 Disconnect pressure sensor connector   **8.16 Manifold retaining bolts – two shown**

9 Fuel injection system components – removal and refitting

Warning: Observe the precautions in Section 1 before working on any component in the fuel system.

Note: *If the ignition is switched on with a sensor disconnected, a fault may be registered in the memory of the system electronic control unit (ECU). If this occurs, the system may enter an 'emergency running' mode which could affect driveability and economy. Therefore, on completion of any procedures described in*

9.8a Remove the MAF sensor from the housing . . .

9.8b . . . and the air inlet pipe

9.14 Disconnect the MAP sensor wiring connector

this Section, it is advisable to have the system checked by a Mercedes-Benz dealer and any faults in memory erased.

Note: *Refer to Section 12 for details of component fault diagnosis. If any of the following components are being removed because of a fault, it will be necessary to erase the fault from the ECU memory on completion.*

Mass airflow (MAF) sensor

111 type engines

1 Remove the plastic trim cover from the top of the engine.

2 Disconnect the wiring connector from the mass airflow sensor.

3 Slacken the hose clip and disconnect the inlet ducting from the mass airflow sensor. If required undo the retaining bolt from mounting bracket on the air inlet ducting and move it to one side.

4 Undo the retaining bolts that secure the mass airflow sensor to the inlet duct and remove it from the engine compartment.

5 Refitting is a reversal of removal; fit a new O-ring seal, if required.

271 type engines

6 The MAF sensor is located on the rear of the air cleaner housing on the left-hand side of the engine compartment.

7 Remove the air cleaner housing as described in Section 2.

8 Undo the retaining bolts that secure the mass airflow sensor and remove it from the air cleaner housing **(see illustrations)**. If required undo the retaining screws and remove the MAF sensor from the air inlet pipe.

9 Refitting is a reversal of removal; fit a new O-ring seal, if required.

Engine coolant temperature (ECT) sensor

10 Refer to Chapter 3, Section 6, for the removal and refitting procedure for the coolant temperature sensor.

Intake air temperature (IAT) sensor

11 The intake air temperature sensor is an integral part of the mass air flow (MAF) sensor, see paragraphs 1 to 9.

Manifold absolute pressure (MAP) sensor

12 The MAP sensor is located on the left-hand rear of the inlet manifold.

13 To make access easier, remove the air cleaner housing as described in Section 2.

14 Disconnect the wiring connector from the sensor **(see illustration)**.

15 Undo the two retaining screws and remove the sensor from the inlet manifold.

16 Refitting is a reversal of removal.

Altitude sensor

271 type engines

17 The altitude sensor is located on the left-hand side of the air cleaner housing.

18 Disconnect the wiring connector from the sensor **(see illustration)**.

19 Undo the two retaining screws and remove the sensor from the air cleaner housing.

9.18 Disconnect the altitude sensor wiring connector

9.22 Disconnect the wiring connector . . .

20 Refitting is a reversal of removal.

Charge air pressure sensor

271 type engines

21 The charge air pressure sensor is fitted in the inlet manifold, behind the mass airflow meter (MAF) sensor **(see illustration)**.

22 Disconnect the wiring connector from the sensor **(see illustration)**.

23 Press the retaining clips at each side of the sensor together and withdraw the sensor from the inlet manifold **(see illustration)**.

24 Refitting is a reversal of removal.

Electronic control unit (ECU)

Caution: Electronic Control Units (ECUs) contain components that are sensitive to the levels of static electricity generated by a person during normal activity. Once the multiway harness connector has been unplugged, the exposed ECU connector

9.21 Charge air pressure sensor

9.23 . . . and unclip sensor

9.26 Remove the fusebox cover

9.27 Disconnect the ECU connectors

9.31a Release the locking clips . . .

9.31b . . . and disconnect the wiring harness

9.32 ECU retaining screws

remove the ECU from the air cleaner housing **(see illustration)**. If required, to make access easier, remove the air cleaner housing as described in Section 2.

33 Refitting is a reversal of removal.

Lambda (oxygen) sensors

34 There are two lambda (oxygen) sensors fitted to the exhaust system. One is between the exhaust manifold and the catalytic converter and the other is in the front pipe below the catalytic converter **(see illustrations)**. First make sure that the ignition is switched off, before removal.

> **HAYNES HINT** *It may be easier to remove the sensor while the exhaust is hot, as the exhaust pipe will contract when cool, making it more difficult to remove the sensor.*

> ⚠️ *Warning: Be careful not to burn yourself, as the exhaust system may still be hot.*

35 To remove the lower sensor, apply the parking brake, and then jack up the front of the vehicle and support it on axle stands (see *Jacking and vehicle support*).

36 Trace the wiring from the lambda sensor and disconnect the wiring connector, unclip the wiring from the retaining clips along its length as it is removed **(see illustration)**

37 Using an open-ended spanner or a special socket, unscrew the lambda sensor from the manifold. **Note:** *As a flying lead remains*

pins can freely conduct stray static electricity to these components, damaging or even destroying them – the damage will be invisible and may not manifest itself immediately. Expensive repairs can be avoided by observing the following basic handling rules:

• *Handle a disconnected ECU by its case only; do not allow fingers or tools to come into contact with the pins.*

• *When carrying an ECU, earth yourself from time to time, by touching a metal object such as an unpainted water pipe, this will discharge any potentially damaging static that may have built-up.*

• *Do not leave the ECU unplugged from its connector for any longer than is absolutely necessary.*

111 type engines

25 The ECU is located in the fusebox at the right-hand side rear of the bulkhead (left-hand side on LHD models). First, make sure that the ignition is switched off, and the earth lead is disconnected from the battery negative terminal.

26 Release the retaining clips and remove the cover from the fusebox **(see illustration)**.

27 Disconnect the two wiring plugs from the ECU **(see illustration)**.

28 The ECU can now be withdrawn from the bulkhead.

29 Refitting is a reversal of removal.

271 type engines

30 The ECU is located on the left-hand side of the air cleaner housing. First, make sure that the ignition is switched off, and the earth lead is disconnected from the battery negative terminal.

31 Pull out the locking clips to release the wiring plugs, and then disconnect from the ECU **(see illustrations)**.

32 Undo the four retaining screws and

9.34a Upper lambda (oxygen) sensor . . .

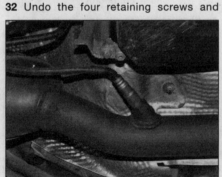

9.34b . . . and lower lambda (oxygen) sensor

9.36 Wiring connector from lambda (oxygen) sensor

connected to the sensor after is has been disconnected, if the correct size spanner is not available, a slotted socket will be required to remove the sensor **(see illustration)**. Take care not to damage the wiring or the sensor tip as it withdrawn.

38 Apply a little high-temperature, anti-seize grease to the sensor threads – avoid contaminating the probe tip. Refit the sensor and tighten it to the specified correct torque. The remaining refitting procedure is a reversal of removal.

Fuel rail and injectors

111 type engines

39 Remove the plastic trim cover from the top of the engine.

40 Refer to Section 10 and depressurise the fuel system. Disconnect the battery negative (earth) lead and position it away from the terminal.

41 Unscrew the union nut and disconnect the fuel feed line from the fuel rail.

42 Disconnect the wiring plugs from the injectors **(see illustration)**. To do this, depress the wire clips.

43 Disconnect the wiring connector from the camshaft position sensor.

44 Unscrew the fuel rail mounting bolts and carefully pull out the fuel rail, together with the injectors, from the cylinder head. Recover the lower O-ring seals from the injectors **(see illustrations)**. Check O-rings for damage and renew if required.

45 To remove an injector from the fuel rail assembly, extract the relevant locking clip and withdraw the injector from its housing. Recover the upper O-ring seal **(see illustrations)**.

46 Refitting is a reversal of removal, but renew the injector O-ring seals and oil them lightly before fitting. Tighten the fuel rail mounting bolts to the specified torque. When refitting an injector to the fuel rail, ensure the locking clip engages with the corresponding retaining lugs on the injector body.

271 type engines

47 Remove the plastic trim cover from the top of the engine.

48 Remove the air cleaner housing as described in Section 2.

49 Refer to Section 10 and depressurise the fuel system. Disconnect the battery negative (earth) lead and position it away from the terminal.

50 Undo the retaining screws and move the engine wiring harness to one side **(see illustrations)**.

51 Unscrew the union nut and disconnect the fuel feed line from the fuel rail **(see illustration)**.

9.37 Using a slotted socket to remove the sensor

9.42 Disconnecting the wiring from the fuel injectors

9.44a Withdraw the fuel rail and injectors from the inlet manifold . . .

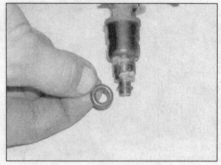

9.44b . . . and recover the lower O-ring seals

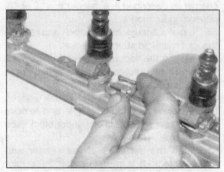

9.45a Extract the locking clip . . .

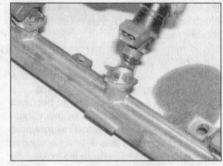

9.45b . . . withdraw the injector from the its housing . . .

9.45c . . . and recover the upper O-ring seal

9.50a Undo the two retaining screws . . .

9.50b . . . and move the wiring harness

9.51 Fuel feed line to rail

9.52 Disconnect the fuel injectors

9.53a Undo the mounting bolts . . .

9.53b . . . and withdraw the fuel rail

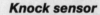

9.54a Remove the securing clip . . .

9.54b . . . and remove the injector

52 Disconnect the wiring plugs from the injectors **(see illustration)**. To do this, depress the wire clips.
53 Unscrew the fuel rail mounting bolts and carefully pull out the fuel rail together with the injectors from the cylinder head. Recover the lower O-ring seals from the injectors **(see illustration)**. Check O-rings for damage and renew if required.
54 To remove an injector from the fuel rail assembly, extract the relevant locking clip and withdraw the injector from its housing. Recover the upper O-ring seal **(see illustrations)**.
55 Refitting is a reversal of removal, but renew the injector O-ring seals and oil them lightly before fitting. Tighten the fuel rail mounting bolts to the specified torque. When refitting an injector to the fuel rail, ensure the locking clip engages with the corresponding retaining lugs on the injector body.

Knock sensor

56 The knock sensor is located on the left-hand side of the cylinder block, just above the starter motor.
57 On Kompressor models, remove the super-charger as described in either Section 12 or 13, depending on model.
58 To make access easier unbolt and remove the inlet manifold support bracket.
59 Release the securing clip and disconnect the wiring connector from the sensor **(see illustration)**.
60 Note the position of the knock sensor, then unscrew the mounting bolt, and remove the knock sensor from the cylinder block **(see illustration)**.
61 Clean the surfaces of the sensor and cylinder block. It is important that the sensor makes good contact with the cylinder block and is tightened to the correct torque, also

clean the threads of the mounting hole and bolt.
62 Locate the knock sensor on the cylinder block with the wiring socket in the previously-noted position, then insert the bolt and tighten to the specified torque.
63 The remainder of the refitting procedure is the reversal of removal.

Crankshaft position (CKP) sensor

Note: *If a new crankshaft position sensor is fitted, Mercedes technicians will need to re-initialise it using special equipment (STAR DIAGNOSIS unit). If the engine does not run correctly when installed, take the vehicle to your nearest dealer.*
64 The crankshaft position sensor is located on the left-hand rear of the cylinder block, above to the starter motor. Disconnect the battery negative (earth) lead and position it away from the terminal.
65 Apply the parking brake, and then jack up the front of the vehicle and support it on axle stands (see *Jacking and vehicle support*). Undo the retaining bolts and remove the plastic shield from under the engine.
66 Release the retaining clip and disconnect the wiring connector from the sensor **(see illustrations)**.
67 Unscrew the mounting bolt and remove the crankshaft position sensor.
68 Refitting is a reversal of removal, but tighten the mounting bolt to the specified torque.

Camshaft position (CMP) sensor

69 Disconnect the battery negative (earth)

9.59 Disconnecting the wiring from the knock sensor

9.60 Knock sensor mounting bolt

9.66a Release the securing clip . . .

9.66b . . . and disconnect the wiring connector

9.69 Unclip the engine cover

lead and position it away from the terminal. Where applicable, remove the engine plastic cover from the top of the engine (see illustration).

111 type engines

70 The camshaft position sensor is located on the left-hand side of the camshaft cover.

71 Disconnect the wiring connector from the camshaft sensor.

72 Unscrew the bolt securing the sensor to the camshaft cover, then withdraw the sensor, together with the O-ring.

73 Refitting is a reversal of removal, but tighten the mounting bolt to the specified torque.

271 type engines

74 There are two camshaft position sensors on these engines, one on the inlet side of the camshaft covers and one on the exhaust side in the cylinder head (see illustrations).

75 Disconnect the wiring connector from the camshaft sensor (see illustrations).

76 Unscrew the bolt securing the sensor to the camshaft cover, then withdraw the sensor, together with the O-ring.

77 Refitting is a reversal of removal, but tighten the mounting bolt to the specified torque.

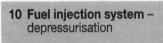

10 Fuel injection system – depressurisation

⚠️ **Warning: Observe the precautions in Section 1 before working on any component in the fuel system. Note that the following procedure will merely relieve the pressure in the fuel system – remember that fuel will still be present in the system components and take precautions accordingly before disconnecting any of them.**

1 The fuel injection system referred to in this Section is defined as the fuel pump/sender unit(s), the fuel filter, the fuel rail, the fuel injectors, the fuel pressure regulator and the metal pipes and flexible hoses of the fuel lines between these components. All these contain fuel, which will be under pressure while the engine is running and/or while the ignition is switched

on. The pressure will remain for some time after the ignition has been switched off and must be relieved before any of these components are disturbed for servicing work. Ideally, for safety reasons, the engine should be allowed to cool completely before work commences.

2 Briefly remove and refit the fuel tank filler cap to release any pressure/vacuum in the tank.

3 On early models, a pressure release valve is located at the front of the fuel rail, beneath a dust cap. The valve is of Schrader type, as found on roadwheels, and ideally an adapter with a drain tube should be fitted to release the pressure. Alternatively, wrap some cloth rag around the valve and depress the valve core with a screwdriver to release the pressure. Make sure that fuel is not allowed to drip onto hot engine components.

4 An alternative method of releasing the pressure is as follows. Refer to Chapter 12,

9.74a Inlet camshaft position sensor

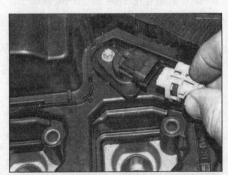

9.75a Disconnect the inlet sensor wiring connector

and locate the fuel pump relay. Remove the relay, and then crank the engine for a few seconds. The engine may fire and run for a while, but continue cranking until it stops. The fuel injectors should have opened enough times during cranking to reduce the line fuel pressure. Place a suitable container beneath the relevant connection/union to be disconnected, and have a large rag ready to soak up any escaping fuel not being caught by the container. It is advisable to clamp off the fuel supply hose to the fuel rail using a proprietary hose clamp. Slowly loosen the connection or union nut (as applicable) to avoid a sudden release of pressure and position the rag around the connection to catch any fuel spray which may be expelled. Once the pressure has been released, disconnect the fuel line and insert plugs to minimise fuel loss and prevent the entry of dirt into the fuel system.

9.74b Exhaust camshaft position sensor

9.75b Disconnect the exhaust sensor wiring connector

11 Idle speed, exhaust CO content and fault diagnosis

Experienced home mechanics equipped with an accurate tachometer and a carefully-calibrated exhaust gas analyser may be able to check the exhaust gas CO content and the engine idle speed, although the vehicle must be taken to a suitably-equipped Mercedes-Benz dealer or fuel injection specialist for assessment. Neither the air/fuel mixture (exhaust gas CO content) nor the engine idle speed are manually-adjustable.

A diagnostics socket, located under the driver's side facia panel **(see illustration)**, next to the bonnet release lever, is incorporated in the engine management system wiring harness, to which dedicated electronic test equipment can be connected. The test equipment is capable of 'interrogating' the engine management system ECU electronically and accessing its internal fault log. In this manner, faults can be pinpointed quickly and simply, even if their occurrence is intermittent. Testing all the system components individually in an attempt to locate the fault by elimination is a time consuming operation that is unlikely to be fruitful (particularly if the fault occurs dynamically), and also carries high risk of damage to the ECU's internal components.

12 Supercharger system (111 type engines) – general information and component renewal

General

1 The supercharger is belt driven, and is mounted on the right-hand side of the engine. An electromagnetic clutch (like the clutch used on an air conditioning compressor) disengages the supercharger when no boost is needed, and engages it when the boost is needed. The system is intercooled; the intercooler is located across the lower front part of the engine compartment. Outside air is routed from the air filter housing into the supercharger, where it is pressurised before travelling through the intercooler. From the intercooler, the compressed air is directed through the mass air flow/intake air temperature (MAF/IAT) sensor, and then through the throttle valve actuator and into the inlet manifold.

2 On later engines, the supercharger runs all the time and boost is governed by the ECU-controlled air flap actuator. When the air flap actuator is closed, all the boosted air goes through the intercooler to the inlet manifold. When the flap is open, boosted air coming out of the blower is recirculated into the resonance body. When the flap is anywhere between fully closed and fully open, the amount of boost is proportional to the angle of the flap, which means that the manifold pressure can be anywhere between almost full boost and

11.2 Diagnostic socket location

inlet manifold vacuum. The ECU determines the position of the flap in relation to the engine load, engine speed, etc.

Component renewal

Resonance body and recirculated air flap actuator

Note: *The recirculated air flap actuator is located below the resonance body, which functions as a reservoir for redirected boosted inlet air when the air flap is open.*

3 Remove the plastic covers from the top of the engine. Disconnect the battery negative (earth) lead and position it away from the terminal.

4 Undo the two retaining bolts from the inlet and pressure connections on the resonance body.

5 Disconnect the two vent hoses from the resonance body (one hose goes to the camshaft cover and the other one goes to the engine block).

6 Slacken the hose clip and disconnect the inlet and pressure connections from the recirculated air flap actuator. To make access easier remove the air filter housing as described in Section 2.

7 Pull the air flap actuator upwards until the wiring connector can be disconnected from the air flap actuator. With the wiring disconnected, remove the resonance body and air flap actuator out from the engine compartment. Retrieve the O-ring seal(s) and check condition, renew if required.

8 The resonance body and recirculated air flap actuator can now be separated if required.

9 Refitting is a reversal of the removal procedure.

Inlet and pressure connections

10 Remove the resonance body and recirculated air flap actuator as described in paragraphs 3 to 8.

11 Undo the retaining bolt and disconnect the coolant hose from the inlet and pressure connection.

12 Disconnect the air duct that connects the output end of the inlet and pressure connection to the inlet pipe of the intercooler.

13 Disconnect the vent line from the inlet and pressure connection.

14 Remove the four retaining bolts and remove the inlet and pressure connection from the

supercharger. Recover the gasket and discard, a new one will be required for refitting.

15 Refitting is a reversal of the removal procedure.

Supercharger

16 Remove the air filter housing as described in Section 2.

17 Remove the inlet and pressure connection as described in paragraphs 10 to 14.

18 Remove the auxiliary drivebelt as described in Chapter 1A.

19 Undo the mounting bolts and remove the supercharger from the engine compartment.

20 Refitting is a reversal of the removal procedure.

Intercooler

21 Apply the parking brake, and then jack up the front of the vehicle and support it on axle stands (see *Jacking and vehicle support*). Undo the retaining bolts and remove the plastic shield from under the engine.

22 Slacken the hose clips and disconnect the inlet and outlet air hoses from each side of the intercooler.

23 Undo the mounting bolts and remove the intercooler from under the vehicle.

24 Refitting is a reversal of the removal procedure.

Charge air duct

Note: *The charge air duct is the long L-shaped air duct that connects the outlet pipe of the intercooler to the mass airflow/intake air temperature (MAF/IAT) sensor.*

25 Remove the air filter housing as described in Section 2.

26 Disconnect the wiring connector from the MAF/IAT sensor.

27 Slacken the hose clip and disconnect the hose from the MAF/IAT sensor to the air scoop.

28 Release the spring clip and remove the charge air duct from the outlet side of the intercooler.

29 Undo the mounting bolts and remove the MAF/IAT sensor from the charge air duct.

30 Inspect the O-ring seals at each end of the charge air duct and renew if required.

31 Refitting is a reversal of the removal procedure.

13 Supercharger system (271 type engines) – general information and component renewal

General

1 The supercharger is belt-driven and is mounted on the left-hand side of the engine. The system uses a recirculated air flap actuator, inlet and pressure connections, inlet manifold, intercooler, wide band silencer and supercharger.

Component renewal

Wide band silencer

Note: *The wide band silencer is a noise damper fitted inline in the charge air duct (the*

13. 2 Remove the air inlet pipe

13.3 Remove the air vent hose

13.4a Release the securing clip . . .

13.4b . . . and remove the lower air pipe

13.5a Slacken the retaining clip . . .

13.5b . . . and remove the upper air pipe

pressurised duct that takes boosted air from the supercharger's pressure damper to the to the intercooler). The charge air duct/wide band silencer assembly is located across the front of the engine. The upper end is on the left-hand side and is connected to the supercharger. The right-hand end is at the lower part of the engine compartment and is connected to the inlet side of the intercooler.

2 Release the retaining clips and remove the air inlet ducting from across the front of the engine compartment **(see illustration)**.

3 Slacken the hose clip and disconnect the hose from the top of the wide band silencer **(see illustration)**.

4 Release the retaining clip and disconnect the charge air pipe from the lower part of the wide band silencer **(see illustrations)**.

5 Slacken the retaining clip and disconnect the charge air pipe from the upper part of the wide band silencer **(see illustrations)**.

6 Undo the two wide band silencer mounting bolts and remove it from the engine compartment **(see illustration)**.

7 Refitting is a reversal of the removal procedure.

Compressor assembly

Note: *The compressor assembly is made up of the supercharger, the inlet and pressure connection and the air flap actuator.*

8 Remove the wide band silencer as described in paragraphs 2 to 6.

9 Remove the auxiliary drivebelt as described in Chapter 1A.

10 Remove the inlet manifold as described in Section 8.

11 Working under the vehicle, undo the supercharger rear lower mounting bolt **(see illustration)**. To make access easier, apply the parking brake, and jack up the front of the vehicle and support it on axle stands (see *Jacking and vehicle support*). Undo the

retaining bolts and remove the plastic shield from under the engine.

12 Undo the supercharger front mounting bolts **(see illustration)**.

13 Remove the rear upper mounting bolt and disconnect the earth cable **(see illustration)**.

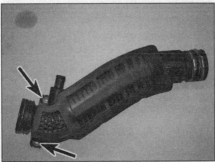

13.6 Air intake silencer mounting bolt holes

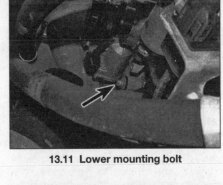

13.11 Lower mounting bolt

13.12 Front upper mounting bolts

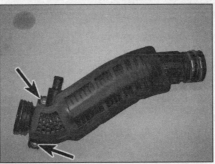

13.13 Rear upper mounting bolt and earth cable

13.14a Disconnect the wiring connector . . .

13.14b . . . and remove the compressor

13.15a Undo the bolts . . .

13.15b . . . and split the supercharger from the actuator . . .

13.15c . . . renew the gasket

13.15d Inlet air pressure unit

14 Lift the compressor assembly upwards and rotate it through 180°, disconnect the wiring connector from the actuator **(see illustrations)**, and remove the assembly from the engine compartment.

15 To remove the supercharger from the air flap actuator or the inlet and pressure connection, undo the retaining bolts and remove. Discard any gaskets, as new ones will be required for refitting **(see illustrations)**.

16 Refitting is a reversal of the removal procedure.

Air recirculation flap actuator

17 The compressor assembly is made up of the supercharger, the inlet and pressure connection and the air recirculation flap actuator. See paragraphs 8 to 15 for removal and refitting procedure.

Inlet and pressure connections

18 The compressor assembly is made up of the supercharger, the inlet and pressure connection and the air recirculation flap actuator. See paragraphs 8 to 15 for removal and refitting procedure.

Intercooler

Note*: The intercooler is located at the lower front end of the vehicle, directly behind the bumper cover.*

19 Apply the parking brake, and then jack up the front of the vehicle and support it on axle stands (see *Jacking and vehicle support*).

Undo the retaining bolts and remove the plastic shield from under the engine.

20 Remove the front bumper cover as described in Chapter 11.

21 Release the securing clips and disconnect the inlet and outlet air hoses from each side of the intercooler. Retrieve the O-ring seal(s) and check condition, renew if required.

22 Unclip the intercooler from the underside of the radiator, and disengage it from the lugs on the sides of the radiator.

23 Lift up the intercooler, complete with air scoop across the top and remove it from the engine compartment.

24 Refitting is a reversal of the removal procedure.

Chapter 4 Part B:
Fuel system – diesel engine

Contents

Degrees of difficulty

Easy, suitable for novice with little experience	**Fairly easy,** suitable for beginner with some experience	**Fairly difficult,** suitable for competent DIY mechanic	**Difficult,** suitable for experienced DIY mechanic	**Very difficult,** suitable for expert DIY or professional

Specifications

General

Injection	Indirect
Idle speed (electronic idle speed control):	
4-cylinder engine	690 to 790 rpm
5-cylinder engine	610 to 710 rpm
Smoke test opacity	1.5

Torque wrench settings

	Nm	lbf ft
Camshaft bearing cap	10	7
Camshaft cover	10	7
Camshaft sprocket	18	13
Fuel gauge sender unit retaining ring	85	63
Fuel injection high-pressure pipe union nuts	14	10
Fuel injection high-pressure pump mounting bolts	14	10
Fuel injector clamp retaining bolt:		
Stage 1	7	5
Stage 2	Angle-tighten a further 90°	
Stage 3	Angle-tighten a further 90°	
Fuel pipe union nuts to fuel rail and injectors	23	17
Fuel pre-delivery pump mounting bolts	10	7
Fuel rail mounting bolts	14	10
Fuel tank support straps:		
Right- and left-hand straps	40	30
Centre strap/bracket	20	15
Inlet manifold bolts	16	12
Inlet manifold support bracket bolts:		
611 and 612 engines	10	7
646 engines:		
To manifold	20	15
To engine	40	30

2.3 Disconnect the breather hose

1 General information and precautions

General information

The major components of the fuel system are a fuel tank, gauge sender unit, a fuel injection pump and lift pump, engine-bay mounted filter, fuel supply and return lines and one fuel injector per cylinder.

The injection pump is driven at half crankshaft speed by the timing chain. Fuel is drawn from the fuel tank, through the filter, to the injection pump, which then distributes the fuel under very high pressure to the injectors via separate delivery pipes.

The basic injection timing is set by the position of the injection pump on its mounting bracket. When the engine is running, the injection timing is advanced and retarded electronically. In addition, an injection-timing device is incorporated in the pump drive sprocket.

The injectors are spring-loaded mechanical valves, which open when the pressure of the fuel supplied to them exceeds a specific limit. Fuel is then sprayed from the injector nozzle into the cylinder via a pre-chamber (indirect injection).

Engine idle speed is controlled electronically, responding to engine load. The system increases the idle speed when the power steering, air conditioning, or automatic transmission systems are operative, in addition

to increased idle speed under cold start conditions. The engine speed is monitored by an electronic control unit via a sensor mounted at the flywheel, and coolant temperature via a sensor threaded into the cylinder head. The ECU compares the actual engine speed with a mapped value stored in memory. If the two are different, the ECU drives an electromagnetic actuator, which mechanically pre-loads the injection pump governor to alter the engine idle speed accordingly.

On turbocharged models, the operation of the diesel fuel injection system is identical to that of the normally-aspirated engines, however, the inlet charge pressure (turbo-boost) and exhaust gas recirculation systems are also controlled by the ECU. Air inlet temperature is monitored by a sensor inside the air duct located above the right-hand side of the radiator.

Precautions

⚠ *Warning: Many of the procedures in this Chapter require the removal of fuel lines and connections, which may result in some fuel spillage. Before carrying out any operation on the fuel system, refer to the precautions given in Safety first! at the beginning of this manual, and follow them implicitly. Always switch off the ignition before working on the fuel system.*

⚠ *Warning: When working on any part of the fuel system, avoid direct skin contact with diesel fuel – wear protective clothing and gloves when handling fuel system components. Ensure the work area is well-ventilated. Fuel injectors operate at extremely high pressures and the jet of fuel produced at the nozzle is capable of piercing skin, with potentially fatal results. When working with pressurised injectors, take great to avoid exposing any part of the body to the fuel spray. It is recommended that any pressure testing of the fuel system components should be carried out by a diesel fuel injection specialist.*

Caution: Do not allow diesel fuel to come into contact with coolant hoses – wipe off accidental spillage immediately. Hoses that have been contaminated with fuel for an

extended period should be renewed. Diesel fuel systems are particularly sensitive to contamination from dirt, air and water. Pay particular attention to cleanliness when working on any part of the fuel system, to prevent the ingress of dirt. Thoroughly clean the area around fuel unions before disconnecting them. Store dismantled components in sealed containers to prevent contamination and the formation of condensation. Only use lint-free cloths and clean fuel for component cleansing.

2 Air cleaner housing and filter element – removal and refitting

Air filter element

1 Remove the air filter from the air cleaner housing as described in Chapter 1B.

Air cleaner housing

611 and 612 engines

2 Remove the air filter element as described in Chapter 1B.

3 Slacken the hose clip and detach the ducting from the front of the air cleaner housing and the breather pipe from the camshaft cover **(see illustration)**.

4 Undo the retaining bolts from inside the lower part of the housing and then unclip the upper part of the housing from the camshaft cover **(see illustrations)**. Remove the lower housing from the engine compartment. As the housing is removed, recover the washers from the mounting bolts.

5 Refitting is a reversal of removal. On completion, refit the air filter element as described in Chapter 1B.

646 engines

6 Remove the air filter element as described in Chapter 1B.

7 Slacken the hose clip and detach the ducting from the front of the air cleaner housing **(see illustration)**.

8 Disconnect the wiring connectors from the mass airflow (MAF) sensor and pressure sensor on the front of the air filter housing.

9 Pull the air cleaner housing upwards and

2.4a Undo the two retaining bolts . . .

2.4b . . . unclip the rubber clips . . .

2.4c . . . and remove the housing

2.7 Disconnect the air intake pipe

2.9a Lift out the housing . . .

2.9b . . . and disconnect it from the rear mounting

then forward to release it from the rear rubber mounting **(see illustrations)**.

10 Refitting is a reversal of removal. On completion, refit the air filter element as described in Chapter 1B.

---

3 Fuel gauge sender unit – removal and refitting

⚠ **Warning: Observe the precautions in Section 1 before working on any component in the fuel system.**

Note: *There are two fuel gauge sender units in the fuel tank, which are connected to each other by fuel lines inside the fuel tank. One sender unit is in the right-hand side of the fuel tank which has a pump built into it, and the other is in the left-hand side of the fuel tank.*

Removal

1 Disconnect the battery negative (earth) lead and position it away from the terminal.

2 Before carrying out this procedure, make sure that the fuel tank is less than three-quarters full.

3 Remove the rear seat cushion (with reference to Chapter11), and pull back the soundproofing **(see illustration)**.

4 Undo the retaining screws and remove the access cover(s) from the floor panel **(see illustration)**.

5 Disconnect the fuel gauge wiring from the sender unit, and then release the retaining clips and disconnect the fuel lines, noting which way around they are fitted **(see**

illustration). **Note:** *Depending on model, there maybe a different number of fuel lines and wiring connectors.*

6 The retaining rings must now be loosened and removed. To do this, Mercedes-Benz technicians use a special tool, which engages

the holes in the ring **(see illustrations)**. Ideally, this tool should be obtained, however it should be possible to fabricate a home-made version using metal bar and suitable-sized bolts.

7 Make note of the markings on the locking ring to aid refitting **(see illustrations)**, with the

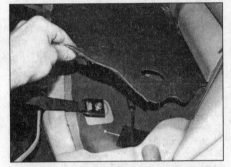

3.3 Remove the under seat soundproofing

3.4 Access cover in floor panel

3.5 Note the fuel line direction arrows

3.6a Using special tool . . .

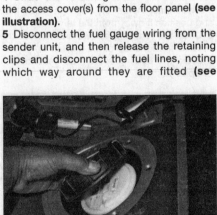

3.6b . . . to remove the retaining ring

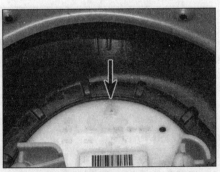

3.7a Note the markings . . .

3.7b . . . for refitting

3.8a Lower connections on sender unit . . .

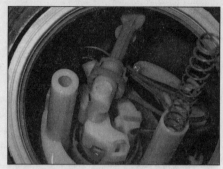

3.8b . . . and upper connection

rings removed, carefully withdraw the sender units from the fuel tank. Recover the sealing gaskets.

8 To disengage the fuel lines inside the tank with the sender unit, release the locking tab and pull the pipe connection apart **(see illustrations)**. Take care not to damage the fuel sender unit.

Refitting

9 Refitting is a reversal of removal, but always renew the sender unit sealing gaskets, and tighten the retaining rings to the specified torque. Making sure that the marks noted on removal are aligned.

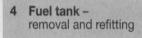

4 Fuel tank –
removal and refitting

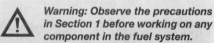

⚠️ **Warning: Observe the precautions in Section 1 before working on any component in the fuel system.**

Note: *Removing the fuel tank is difficult, as the rear suspension assembly will need to be lowered. Refer to Chapter 10, to support and lower the rear suspension, to leave enough room to remove the fuel tank. As this means supporting the vehicle on stands, lowering the rear suspension and removing a fuel tank, we do not recommend this as a job to be done at home.*

Removal

1 The fuel tank must be emptied before the operation can be started. This is best achieved by waiting until the tank is almost empty through the course of normal driving.

2 Park the vehicle on a level surface and chock the front roadwheels. Raise the rear of the vehicle, support it securely on axle stands (see *Jacking and vehicle support*) and remove the rear roadwheels.

⚠️ **Warning: The use of an inspection pit is not advised; petrol vapours are heavier than air and can quickly build-up on the floor of the pit, causing a potential hazard.**

3 Disconnect the battery negative (earth) lead and position it away from the terminal.

4 Remove the fuel gauge/pump sender unit as described in Section 3.

5 Remove the two plastic covers from under each side of the vehicle.

6 Remove the exhaust system as described in Chapter 4C.

7 Undo the retaining nuts and remove the exhaust system heat shields from under the vehicle **(see illustration)**.

8 With reference to Chapter 9, remove the rear handbrake cables from the brake cable equaliser under the centre of the vehicle **(see illustration)**.

9 Remove the both rear wheels and remove the brake calipers, carefully tie the calipers to one side. Refer to Chapter 9 for more information.

10 Remove the anti-roll bar as described in Chapter 10.

11 Locate the wiring connectors for the rear wheel speed sensors and brake pad warning wiring (where fitted) and disconnect.

12 Undo the retaining bolts and disconnect

the driveshafts from the differential flanges, refer to Chapter 8 for further information.

13 Remove the rear coil springs as described in Chapter 10.

14 Support the rear suspension assembly with an adjustable trolley jack. Make sure the assembly is located securely on the jack head; a frame may need to be made to support it.

15 Remove the four large bolts from the rear suspension crossmember and carefully lower it.

16 Undo the retaining screws and remove the splash shield from under the right-hand rear wheel arch.

17 Slacken the hose clips from the filler neck, vent hose and overflow shut-off hose and disconnect the hoses, from under the right-hand wheel arch.

18 With the aid of an assistant, support the fuel tank and remove the straps from under the fuel tank **(see illustration)**.

19 Lower the tank and check that there are no more hoses or wiring still attached, then remove the fuel tank out from the side of the vehicle.

20 Swill the tank out with clean fuel. If the tank shows signs of leakage, it should be renewed.

⚠️ **Warning: Do not attempt to repair the tank yourself by welding, soldering or brazing. The tank will contain an explosive mixture of air and fuel vapour, even when emptied of liquid fuel.**

Refitting

21 Refit the fuel tank by reversing the removal procedure, but tighten all fixings to the correct torque, where specified.

5 Inlet manifold –
removal and refitting

1 Disconnect the battery negative (earth) lead and position it away from the terminal.

2 Undo the retaining screws and remove the cover(s) from the top of the engine.

3 Drain the cooling system as described in Chapter 1B.

4.7 Remove heat shields

4.8 Disconnect the handbrake cables

4.18 Fuel tank retaining nut – one shown

611 and 612 engines

4 Remove the fuel rail as described in Section 8.

5 Undo the retaining bolts and remove the fuel cooler from the top of the inlet manifold **(see illustration)**

6 Remove the fuel filter as described in Chapter 1B.

7 Release the retaining clip and disconnect the charge air hose from the mixing chamber **(see illustration)**.

8 Undo the mounting bolts and move the power steering reservoir to one side. On some models, the pipes may need to be disconnected to allow for the reservoir to be moved.

9 Undo the retaining bolts and remove the support bracket from the front of the inlet manifold.

10 Where applicable, undo the retaining screw from the engine wiring harness along the top of the inlet manifold.

11 Disconnect the coolant hose from the exhaust gas recirculation valve.

12 Undo the retaining bolts and remove the fuel preheater from the housing at the rear of the inlet manifold **(see illustration)**

13 Disconnect the coolant heater hose from the rear of the bulkhead.

14 Disconnect the vacuum hose from the vacuum pump **(see illustration)**.

15 Undo the retaining bolts and remove the support bracket from the under the inlet manifold.

16 Remove the thermostat housing as described in Chapter 3.

17 Progressively unscrew the inlet manifold mounting bolts, and then lift it away from the cylinder head. Discard the O-ring seals as new seals will be required for refitting.

18 Refitting is a reversal of removal, but fit new O-ring seals. Tighten the inlet manifold securing bolts to the specified torque.

646 engines

19 Disconnect the wiring connectors from the oil sensor, crankshaft position sensor, pressure sensor, intake port shut-off motor and exhaust gas recirculation cooler.

20 Disconnect the wiring connector from the starter motor solenoid.

21 Undo the mounting bolts and move the power steering reservoir to one side.

22 Undo the retaining bolts and remove

5.5 Remove the fuel cooler

5.7 Release the retaining clip

5.12 Fuel preheater mounting bolts

the upper mounting bracket from the inlet manifold **(see illustrations)**.

23 Remove the fuel rail and fuel lines as described in Section 8.

24 Remove the thermostat housing as described in Chapter 3.

25 Remove the fuel filter (see Chapter 1B).

5.14 Disconnect the brake vacuum hose

26 Release the retaining clips and disconnect the charge air hose and vent hoses from the mixing chamber **(see illustration)**.

27 Undo the retaining bolts and remove the exhaust gas recirculation valve from the rear of the inlet manifold **(see illustration)**.

28 Release the retaining clips along the length

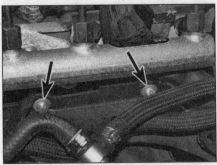

5.22a Undo the inner mounting bolts . . .

5.22b . . . outer front mounting bolt . . .

5.22c . . . and remove the mounting bracket

5.26 Disconnect the air hose

5.27 Remove EGR valve

5.28 Release the wiring harness

5.29 Remove the oil level tube

5.30a Undo the front mounting bolts . . .

5.30b . . . rear mounting bolt . . .

5.30c . . . and remove the lower mounting bracket

of the wiring harness and move it to one side **(see illustration)**.

29 Undo the retaining bolts and withdraw the oil level dipstick tube from between the branches on the inlet manifold **(see illustration)**.

30 Undo the retaining bolts and remove the

mounting bracket that supports the lower part of the inlet manifold **(see illustrations)**.

31 Progressively unscrew the inlet manifold mounting bolts, and then lift it away from the cylinder head **(see illustration)**. Recover the O-ring seals.

5.31 Remove the inlet manifold

5.32 Fit new O-ring seals to the manifold

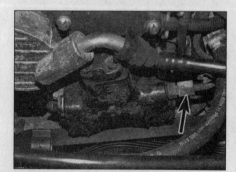

6.4 Disconnect the high-pressure fuel pipe

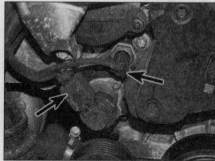

6.9 Disconnect the wiring connectors

32 Refitting is a reversal of removal, but fit new O-ring seals **(see illustration)**. Tighten the inlet manifold securing bolts to the specified torque.

6 Fuel injection pump – removal and refitting

> **Warning: Observe the precautions in Section 1 before working on any component in the fuel system.**

Removal

1 Disconnect the battery negative (earth) lead and position it away from the terminal.

2 Remove the plastic cover from the top of the engine.

611 and 612 engines

3 Remove the auxiliary drivebelt as described in Chapter 1B.

4 Disconnect the high-pressure fuel pipe from the pump **(see illustration)**. Be prepared for an amount of fuel loss – pad the surrounding area with absorbent rags. Tape over or plug the apertures in the injection pump and the fuel pipe to prevent entry of dust and dirt. **Note:** *Undo the fuel pipe retaining nut and do not undo the nut nearest the fuel pump. Use a spanner on the nut nearest the pump to hold the pipe in position, while slackening the fuel pipe retaining nut.*

5 Undo the retaining bolt and remove the bracket to disengage the fuel return pipe from the fuel pump.

6 Undo the retaining bolts and remove the electric shut-off valve from below the brake vacuum pump

7 Undo the retaining bolts and remove the high-pressure fuel pump from the front of the cylinder head. As the pump is removed, retrieve the drivegear from the end of the shaft.

8 Recover the O-ring seal from the rear of the injection pump and discard it – a new one must be used on refitting.

646 engines

9 Disconnect the wiring connectors from the fuel temperature sensor and the quantity control valve on the front of the cylinder head **(see illustration)**.

10 Release the securing clips and disconnect the fuel feed and return lines from the fuel

6.10 Disconnect the fuel pipes

6.11a Undo the bracket retaining bolt . . .

6.11b . . . and disconnect the fuel pipe

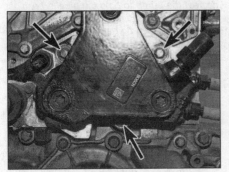

6.12a Undo the retaining bolts . . .

6.12b . . . and remove the fuel pump

6.15a Fit new O-ring seal . . .

6.15b . . . and fit drivegear

pump **(see illustration)**. Be prepared for an amount of fuel loss – pad the surrounding area with absorbent rags. Tape over or plug the apertures in the injection pump and the fuel pipe to prevent entry of dust and dirt.

11 Undo the retaining bolt from the fuel pipe retaining bracket and disconnect the high-pressure fuel pipe from the pump **(see illustrations)**. Be prepared for an amount of fuel loss – pad the surrounding area with absorbent rags. Tape over or plug the apertures in the injection pump and the fuel pipe to prevent entry of dust and dirt. **Note:** *Undo the fuel pipe retaining nut and do not undo the nut nearest the fuel pump. Use a spanner on the nut nearest the pump to hold the pipe in position, while slackening the fuel pipe retaining nut.*

12 Undo the retaining bolts and remove the high-pressure fuel pump from the front of the cylinder head **(see illustrations)**. As the pump is removed, retrieve the drivegear from the end of the shaft.

13 Recover the O-ring seal from the rear of the injection pump and discard it – a new one must be used on refitting.

14 If required the fuel temperature sensor can be unscrewed from the fuel pump housing to remove. The quantity control valve can be removed from the fuel pump housing by undoing the three retaining screws and removing.

Refitting

15 Refit the pump by following the removal procedure in reverse, noting these points:
a) Fit a new O-ring seal to the injection pump mating face and lubricate it lightly with clean engine oil **(see illustration)**.
b) Make sure the drivegear is located

correctly on the shaft before refitting **(see illustration)**.
c) Counterhold the fuel pump nut, when tightening the high-pressure fuel pipe.
d) Tighten the injection pump mounting bolts to the specified torque.

7 Fuel pre-delivery pump – removal and refitting

⚠ Warning: Observe the precautions in Section 1 before working on any component in the fuel system.
Note: *The fuel pre-delivery pump is only fitted to 611 and 612 type engines.*

Removal

1 Disconnect the battery negative cable and position it away from the terminal.

2 Remove the plastic cover from the top of the engine.

7.4a Release the securing clips

3 Remove the brake vacuum pump from the front of the cylinder head as described in Chapter 9.

4 Release the retaining clips and disconnect the feed and return fuel pipes from the pre-delivery pump **(see illustrations)**. Be prepared for an amount of fuel loss – pad the

7.4b Note the direction arrows for refitting

7.5 Pre-delivery pump mounting bolts

surrounding area with absorbent rags. Tape over or plug the apertures in the injection pump and the fuel pipe to prevent entry of dust and dirt. Note their fitted position for refitting.

5 Slacken and withdraw the retaining bolts, then pull the lift pump away from the front of the cylinder head **(see illustration)**. Recover the sealing gasket.

Refitting

6 Refitting is a reversal of removal, noting the following points:

a) *Use a new sealing gasket when refitting the pre-delivery pump.*

b) *Refit the brake vacuum pump with reference to Chapter 9.*

c) *On completion, tighten the pump retaining bolts to their specified torque setting.*

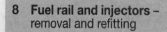

8 Fuel rail and injectors – removal and refitting

⚠️ *Warning: Exercise extreme caution when working on the fuel injectors. Never expose the hands or any part of the body to injector spray, as the high working pressure can cause the fuel to penetrate the skin, with possibly fatal results. You are strongly advised to have any work which involves testing the injectors under pressure carried out by a dealer or fuel injection specialist. Refer to the precautions given in Section 1 of this Chapter before proceeding.*

Note: *Take care not to allow dirt into the fuel rail, injectors or fuel pipes during this procedure. Keep the fuel pipes and injectors identified for position to ensure correct refitting. As the fuel pipes are removed, plug the ends of the pipes, injectors and fuel rail to prevent dirt ingress.*

Fuel rail

1 Remove the plastic trim covers from the top of the engine.

2 Disconnect the wiring connectors from the pressure sensor and the pressure regulator valve at each end of the fuel rail **(see illustrations)**.

3 Slacken and disconnect the injector fuel pipes from the fuel rail, it may be necessary to slacken the pipes at the injectors, to allow for better movement. Make a note of their fitted position, as they will need to be refitted in the

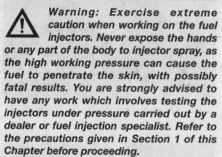

same position on refitting **(see illustration)**. Be prepared for an amount of fuel loss – pad the surrounding area with absorbent rags. Tape over or plug the apertures in the injectors and fuel pipes to prevent entry of dust and dirt.

4 Undo the retaining bolt from the fuel pipe retaining bracket and disconnect the high-pressure fuel pipe from the pump **(see illustrations)**. Be prepared for an amount of fuel loss – pad the surrounding area with absorbent rags. Tape over or plug the apertures in the injection pump and the fuel pipe to prevent entry of dust and dirt. **Note:** *Undo the fuel pipe retaining nut and do not undo the nut nearest the fuel pump. Use a spanner on the nut nearest the pump to hold the pipe in position, while slackening the fuel pipe retaining nut.*

5 Undo the banjo bolt and disconnect the fuel return pipe and leak-off pipes from the rear the fuel rail **(see illustration)**. Discard sealing rings, as new ones will be required for refitting.

6 Working your way along the fuel rail, unclip and disconnect any wiring or pipes that are still attached to the fuel rail. Note their fitted position to aid refitting.

7 Undo the retaining bolts and withdraw the fuel rail from the top of the engine compartment **(see illustration)**.

8 Refitting is a reversal of removal, using new O-ring seals/washers where applicable. Tighten the mounting bolts and union nuts to the specified torque.

Fuel injectors

Note: *Injectors deteriorate with prolonged use, and it is reasonable to expect them to*

8.2a Disconnect the sensor wiring connector

8.2b Disconnect the sensor wiring connector

8.3 Disconnect the fuel injector pipes

8.4a Unbolt the mounting bracket . . .

8.4b . . . and undo the fuel pipe from the pump

8.5 Undo the banjo bolt from the rail

8.7 Removing the fuel rail

8.10 Disconnect the fuel injector wiring connectors

8.11 Remove the injector fuel pipes

need reconditioning after 60 000 miles or so. Accurate testing, overhaul and calibration of the injectors must be left to a specialist. Do not drop the injectors or allow the needles at their tips to become damaged. The injectors are precision-made to fine limits, and must not be handled roughly.

Caution: The injector clamping-bracket retaining bolt can be tight and thread damage or bolt breaking can occur. Bolt repair or Helicoil may be required; this may need to be done by a specialist. A puller will also be required for pulling the injectors out from the cylinder head.

9 Remove the plastic trim covers from the top of the engine.

10 Disconnect the wiring connectors from each of the fuel injectors **(see illustration)**.

11 Slacken and disconnect the fuel pipes from the top of the injectors, it may be necessary to slacken the pipes at the fuel rail, to allow for better movement. Make a note of their fitted position, as they will need to be refitted in the same position on refitting **(see illustration)**. Be prepared for an amount of fuel loss – pad the surrounding area with absorbent rags. Tape over or plug the apertures in the injectors and fuel pipes to prevent entry of dust and dirt.

12 Release and disconnect the fuel leak-off pipes from the top of the four injectors **(see illustrations)**. Discard the securing clips, as new ones will be required on refitting.

13 Slacken and remove the injector clamp mounting bracket retaining bolts (see warning above) from between the injectors **(see illustrations)**. Discard the mounting bolts, as new ones will be required when refitting.

14 If required use a slide hammer/puller to withdraw the injectors from the cylinder head, making sure it is in the vertical position **(see illustration)**. Recover the sealing rings/washers and discard. New ones must be used for refitting.

8.12a Release the retaining clips . . .

8.13a Injector retaining bolts (two shown)

15 Refitting is a reversal of removal, using new sealing rings. Fit new clamp mounting bracket retaining bolts and tighten them to the specified torque. Apply special high-temperature grease from Mercedes to prevent the injectors from getting tight in the bore **(see illustrations)**.

8.12b . . . and remove the fuel return pipes

8.13b Remove the injector clamp

8.14 Withdraw the injector

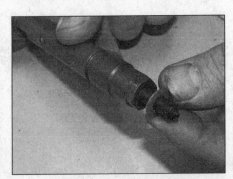

8.15a Fit new sealing washer . . .

8.15b . . . and apply high-temperature grease

9.2 Remove the fusebox cover

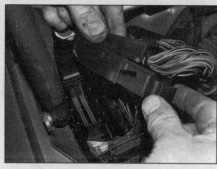

9.3 Release the locking clips

9 Electronic control unit (ECU) – removal and refitting

Caution: Electronic Control Units (ECUs) contain components that are sensitive to the levels of static electricity generated by a person during normal activity. Once the multiway harness connector has been unplugged, the exposed ECU connector pins can freely conduct stray static electricity to these components, damaging or even destroying them – the damage will be invisible and may not manifest itself immediately. Expensive repairs can be avoided by observing the following basic handling rules:

• *Handle a disconnected ECU by its case only; do not allow fingers or tools to come into contact with the pins.*
• *When carrying an ECU, earth yourself from time to time, by touching a metal object such as an unpainted water pipe, this will discharge any potentially damaging static that may have built-up.*
• *Do not leave the ECU unplugged from its connector for any longer than is absolutely necessary.*

1 The ECU is located in the fusebox at the right-hand side rear of the bulkhead (left-hand side on LHD models). First, make sure that the ignition is switched off, and the earth lead is disconnected from the battery negative terminal.
2 Release the retaining clips and remove the cover from the fusebox **(see illustration)**.

3 Disconnect the two wiring plugs from the ECU **(see illustration)**.
4 The ECU can now be withdrawn from the bulkhead.
5 Refitting is a reversal of removal.

10 Intercooler – removal and refitting

Note: *The intercooler is located at the lower front end of the vehicle, directly behind the bumper cover.*

1 Apply the parking brake, and then jack up the front of the vehicle and support it on axle stands (see *Jacking and vehicle support*). Undo the retaining bolts and remove the plastic shield from under the engine.
2 Remove the front bumper cover as described in Chapter 11.
3 Release the securing clips and disconnect the inlet and outlet air hoses from each side of the intercooler. Retrieve the O-ring seal(s) and check condition, renew if required.
4 Unclip the intercooler from the underside of the radiator, and disengage it from the lugs on the sides of the radiator.
5 Lift up the intercooler, complete with air scoop across the top, and remove it from the engine compartment.
6 Refitting is a reversal of the removal procedure.

Chapter 4 Part C:
Emission control and exhaust systems

Contents

Degrees of difficulty

Easy, suitable for novice with little experience	**Fairly easy,** suitable for beginner with some experience 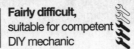	**Fairly difficult,** suitable for competent DIY mechanic	**Difficult,** suitable for experienced DIY mechanic	**Very difficult,** suitable for expert DIY or professional

Specifications

Torque wrench settings	Nm	lbf ft
Exhaust manifold to cylinder head	35	26
Exhaust manifold to front pipe	20	15
Exhaust mounting to transmission (diesel models)	20	15
Lambda (oxygen) sensor	50	37
Turbocharger hose clips	3	2
Turbocharger to exhaust manifold	20	15
Turbocharger to front exhaust pipe	20	15

1 General information

Emission control systems

All petrol engine models are designed to use unleaded petrol only, and are controlled by engine management systems that are programmed to give the best compromise between driveability, fuel consumption and exhaust gas emission. In addition, a number of systems are fitted that help to minimise other harmful emissions: a crankcase emission control system recycles crankcase blow-by gases, a catalytic converter reduces exhaust gas pollutants, and an evaporative loss emission control system reduces the release of gaseous hydrocarbons from the fuel tank. In addition, certain models are fitted with an air injection system that helps to reduce the exhaust gas pollutants produced by partially burnt fuel.

All diesel models have a crankcase emission control system and catalytic converter.

Crankcase emission control

To reduce the emission of unburned hydrocarbons from the crankcase into the atmosphere, the engine is sealed and the blow-by gases and oil vapour are drawn from inside the crankcase, through an oil separator, into the inlet tract to be burned by the engine during normal combustion. According to the speed of the engine, the gases are drawn through a restrictor into the cylinder head or into the inlet duct leading to the throttle body.

Exhaust emission control

Petrol models

To minimise the amount of pollutants which escape into the atmosphere, a catalytic converter is fitted in the exhaust system. The fuelling system is of the closed-loop type, in which a lambda (oxygen) sensor in the exhaust system provides the fuel injection system ECU with constant feedback, enabling the ECU to adjust the air/fuel mixture to optimise combustion.

The lambda sensor has a heating element built-in that is controlled by the ECU through the lambda sensor relay to quickly bring the sensor's tip to its optimum operating temperature. The sensor's tip is sensitive to oxygen and relays a voltage signal to the ECU that varies according on the amount of oxygen in the exhaust gas. If the inlet air/fuel mixture is too rich, the exhaust gases are low in oxygen so the sensor sends a low voltage signal, the voltage increasing as the mixture weakens and the amount of oxygen rises in the exhaust gases. Peak conversion efficiency of all major pollutants occurs if the inlet air/fuel mixture is maintained at the chemically correct ratio for the complete combustion of petrol of 14.7 parts (by weight) of air to 1 part of fuel (the 'stoichiometric' ratio). The sensor output voltage alters in a large step at this point, and the ECU uses the signal change as a reference point for correcting the inlet air/fuel mixture accordingly by altering the fuel injector pulse width. The system is referred to as 'closed-loop', because the exhaust gas oxygen content is constantly monitored in order to adjust the air/fuel mixture.

On certain export models, air injection is employed to help reduce the production of gaseous hydrocarbons and carbon monoxide. A mechanical air pump, driven from the auxiliary drivebelt, forces air into the exhaust manifold where it mixes with the partially burnt fuel particles. The oxygen-rich air combines with pollutants and allows further oxidation to take place, converting a proportion of the hydrocarbons and carbon monoxide into harmless carbon dioxide and water vapour.

Diesel models

An oxidation catalyst is fitted in the exhaust system on diesel-engined models. This has the effect of removing a large proportion of the hydrocarbons and carbon monoxide present in the exhaust gas.

Evaporative loss emission control

Petrol models

To minimise the escape of hydrocarbons from the fuel system into the atmosphere, an evaporative loss emission control system is

**2.2 Location of purge valve –
271 type engine**

fitted to all petrol models. The fuel tank filler cap is sealed and charcoal canister is mounted inside the rear wheel arch to collect the petrol vapours released from the fuel contained in the fuel tank.

The canister stores the gases until they can be drawn via the purge valve into the throttle body by inlet manifold depression, and then burned by the engine during normal combustion.

The flow of fuel vapour from the charcoal canister through the purge valve to the throttle body is controlled by a thermo-valve, which prevents the purge valve from opening until the coolant temperature exceeds a preset limit. This is to ensure that the engine runs correctly when it is cold and to protect the catalytic converter from the effects of an over-rich mixture. In addition, because the purge valve is controlled by manifold vacuum, the charcoal canister is only purged when the engine is under load. This prevents an over-rich mixture from being supplied at idle, preserving idle speed stability and low speed driveability.

Exhaust systems

The exhaust system comprises the exhaust manifold (and turbocharger on turbo-diesel engines), downpipe and catalytic converter, and tailpipe and silencers. On some models the manifold and downpipe are integral. The system is suspended beneath the vehicle by rubber mountings.

The turbocharger fitted to turbo-diesel engined models is oil-cooled and has an integral charge pressure limiting valve.

2.8 Disconnect the wiring connector . . .

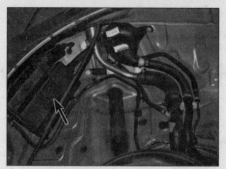

2.5 Location of charcoal canister

---

2 Evaporative loss emission control system – information and component renewal

General information

1 The major components of the evaporative loss emission control system consist of a purge valve, a thermo-valve, an activated charcoal filter canister and vacuum hoses. Fuel gases from the fuel tank and channelled to the charcoal canister, then drawn into the inlet manifold via the idle speed control actuator.

2 The purge valve is fitted in the engine compartment on top of the camshaft cover **(see illustration)**. The charcoal canister is mounted on a bracket inside the right-hand rear wheel housing.

Charcoal canister

Removal

3 Chock the front roadwheels, and then jack up the rear of the vehicle and support on axle stands (see *Jacking and vehicle support*). Remove the right-hand rear roadwheel.
4 Remove the right-hand rear wheel arch liner.
5 Disconnect the inlet and outlet pipes from the charcoal canister **(see illustration)**.
6 Unscrew the mounting bolts and remove the charcoal canister from under the wheel arch.

Refitting

7 Refitting is a reversal of removal.

2.9 . . . and the hoses

Purge valve

Removal

8 Disconnect the wiring from the purge valve **(see illustration)**.
9 Disconnect the hoses from the purge valve **(see illustration)**, noting their order of connection to avoid confusion during refitting.
10 Release the valve from its clip and remove it from the engine bay.

Refitting

11 Refitting is a reversal of removal.

3 Crankcase emission control system – general information

1 The crankcase emission control system consists of a hose that connects the crankcase vent to the inlet ports of the cylinder head, a hose connecting the camshaft cover to the inlet air duct, a restrictor valve and an oil separator unit. When the engine is operating in the idle speed to mid part-load speed, the blow-by gases in the crankcase are drawn through an oil separator and hose with a restrictor to the inlet ports of the cylinder head, where it is mixed with fresh air entering the engine through the inlet manifold. When the engine is operating at mid part-load to full-load speed, the blow-by gases are drawn through the camshaft cover through a hose into the inlet air duct leading to the throttle body.
2 The components of this system require no attention other than to check at regular intervals that the hoses are free of blockages and undamaged.

4 Exhaust manifold – removal and refitting

Removal

1 Apply the parking brake, then jack up the front of the vehicle and support it on axle stands (see *Jacking and vehicle support*). Remove the engine compartment undershield.

Petrol models

2 On some models, it may be necessary to disconnect the wiring for the lambda sensor, trace the wiring and disconnect the wiring connector from under the engine.
3 Unscrew the flange bolts securing the exhaust front pipe to the exhaust manifold, and then unbolt the mounting bracket from the transmission. Recover the gasket **(see illustration)**.
4 Unbolt the hot air shroud from the exhaust manifold **(see illustration)**.
5 Progressively unscrew the nuts securing the exhaust manifold to the cylinder head **(see illustration)**.
6 Withdraw the exhaust manifold from the studs on the cylinder head, and recover the gasket.

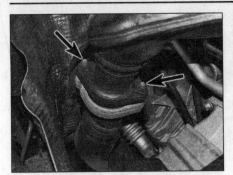

4.3 Unbolt the flange bolts

4.4 Remove the heat shield

4.5 Manifold upper retaining nuts

Diesel models

7 Remove the air cleaner housing as described in Chapter 4B.

8 Unscrew the retaining bolts and remove the heat shield from above the exhaust manifold **(see illustration)**.

9 Undo the retaining bolts and remove the air cleaner housing mounting brackets from the cylinder head **(see illustrations)**.

10 Undo the bolts securing the exhaust manifold to the turbocharger **(see illustration)**.

11 Slacken and remove the bolt from the mounting bracket at the rear of the catalytic converter **(see illustration)**.

12 Progressively unscrew the nuts securing the exhaust manifold to the cylinder head.

13 Withdraw the exhaust manifold from the studs on the cylinder head, and recover the gasket.

Refitting

14 Before refitting the exhaust manifold, check the studs in the cylinder head and renew them if necessary. The nuts should be renewed as a matter of course.

15 Refitting is a reversal of removal, but fit a new gasket and progressively tighten the mounting nuts to the specified torque.

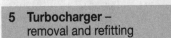

5 Turbocharger – removal and refitting

General information

1 The turbocharger is mounted on the exhaust manifold. Lubrication is provided by a dedicated oil supply pipe that runs from a tapping on the cylinder head **(see**

4.8 Remove the heat shield

illustration). Oil is returned to the sump via a return pipe that connects to the side of the cylinder block. The turbocharger unit has an integral wastegate valve, which is controlled by an electronic unit **(see illustration)**, which is bolted to a bracket below the turbocharger.

4.9a Remove the front . . .

4.9b . . . and rear mounting bracket

4.10 Manifold-to-turbo bolts

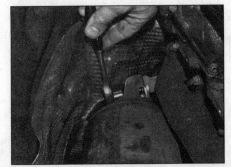

4.11 Remove the exhaust rear mounting bracket

5.1a Turbo oil supply pipe

5.1b Turbo wastegate ECU

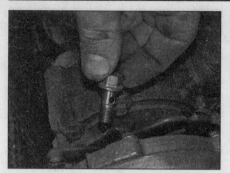

5.8a Undo the banjo bolt . . .

5.8b . . . and remove the oil supply pipe

5.9a Disconnect the charge air hose . . .

5.9b . . . and remove the elbow

5.10 Undo the front support bracket bolt

5.11 Clamp retaining bolt

2 The turbocharger's internal components rotate at very high speed and as such are very sensitive to contamination; a great deal of damage can be caused by small particles of dirt, particularly if they strike the delicate turbine blades. Refer to the *Caution* and *Warning* notes given below before working on or removing the turbocharger unit.

Caution: Thoroughly clean the area around all oil pipe unions before disconnecting them, to prevent the ingress of dirt. Store dismantled components in a sealed container to prevent contamination. Cover the turbocharger air inlet ducts to prevent debris entering and clean using lint-free cloths only.

⚠ *Warning: Do not run the engine with the turbocharger air inlet hose disconnected, since the depression at the inlet can build up very suddenly if the engine speed is raised, and there is the risk of foreign objects being sucked in and then ejected at very high speed.*

Removal

3 Disconnect the battery negative (earth) lead and position it away from the terminal. The battery is located in the rear luggage compartment.

4 Apply the parking brake, then jack up the front of the vehicle and support it on axle stands (see *Jacking and vehicle support*). Remove the engine compartment undershield.

5 Remove the air cleaner housing as described in Chapter 4B.

6 Unscrew the retaining bolts and remove the heat shield from above the exhaust manifold.

7 Undo the retaining bolts and remove the air cleaner housing mounting brackets from the cylinder head.

8 Unscrew the union nuts and remove the oil supply pipe from the turbocharger and cylinder head (see illustrations).

9 Loosen the securing clip and remove the intercooler charge air hose from the turbocharger, then undo the retaining bolts and remove the elbow from the turbocharger (see illustrations).

10 Undo the retaining bolt from the bracket at the front of the turbocharger (see illustration).

11 Undo the retaining bolt from the catalytic converter retaining clamp (see illustration).

12 Undo the retaining bolt from the bracket at the rear of the turbocharger (see illustration).

13 Position a container beneath the oil drain pipe, then unscrew the bolts and remove the pipe and flange from the turbocharger. Recover the gaskets; a new one will be required for refitting. If required the pipe can be withdrawn from the cylinder block; retrieve the rubber seal and renew if required (see illustrations).

5.12 Undo the rear support bracket bolt

5.13a Oil drain pipe gasket . . .

5.13b . . . and cylinder block seal

14 Undo the bolts securing the exhaust manifold to the turbocharger, and then manoeuvre the turbocharger from the engine compartment. As the turbo is removed, disconnect the wiring connector from the wastegate control unit **(see illustrations)**. Recover the gasket; a new one will be required for refitting.

Refitting

15 Refitting is a reversal of removal, but before reconnecting the oil supply pipe to the turbocharger, prime the oil inlet port with clean engine oil. Tighten all nuts and bolts securely, and to the specified torque where given. When the engine is first started, allow it to idle for at least one minute to allow the oil to circulate around the turbocharger bearings. Fit new seals and gaskets, where required **(see illustration)**.

6	Exhaust system – general information and component renewal

General information

1 Depending on model, the exhaust system is made up of an exhaust manifold, a catalytic converter, front silencer (diesel models), a front pipe and a rear tailpipe incorporating one or two silencers. Either one or two lambda sensors (oxygen sensors) are located in the exhaust system.

2 The exhaust system is suspended along its entire length by rubber mountings **(see illustration)**, which are secured to the underside of the vehicle. The downpipe is secured to the transmission by means of a bracket and rubber pad.

3 The catalytic converter is attached to the exhaust manifold either by a flange joint or, on turbocharger models, by a joint and sealing ring secured by a clamp. On petrol models, the catalytic converter is part of the exhaust front pipe, so follow the procedure for removal of the front pipe.

Removal

4 Each exhaust section can be removed individually or, alternatively, the complete system can be removed as a unit.

5 Before removing any part of the system, first jack up the front or rear of the car, as applicable, and support it on axle stands (see *Jacking and vehicle support*). Alternatively (or if the complete exhaust system is being removed) position the car over an inspection pit or on car ramps.

Front pipe

6 On petrol models unscrew and remove the bolts securing the front pipe to the manifold. On diesel models remove the clamp securing the front pipe to the silencer **(see illustrations)**. Recover the sealing olive.

7 Unscrew the bolts and separate the front pipe from the rear exhaust pipe, recover the gasket where applicable.

8 Unbolt the front pipe from the bracket on the rear of the transmission, then withdraw it from under the car **(see illustration)**.

Front silencer (diesel models)

9 Remove the clamp securing the front pipe to the front silencer **(see illustration)**. Recover the sealing olive.

5.14a Manifold-to-turbo bolts

5.14c Disconnect the ECU on removal

5.14b New gasket will be needed

5.15 Fit new sealing ring between turbo and catalytic converter

6.2 Exhaust rubber mounting

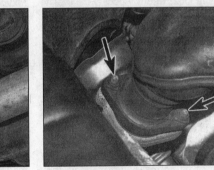
6.6a Front pipe to manifold bolts – 1.8 litre petrol engine

6.6b Front pipe to silencer clamp – 2.2 litre diesel engine

6.8 Exhaust mounting bracket retaining nuts

6.9 Front pipe-to-front silencer clamp

6.11 Remove the exhaust front silencer

6.17 Remove the heat shield

6.19 Undo the retaining clamp bolt

6.20 Remove the rear bracket

10 Undo the retaining nut from the mounting bracket on the side of the transmission.
11 Remove the clamp securing the front silencer to the catalytic converter, and withdraw the front silencer from under the vehicle (see illustration). Recover the sealing olive.

Catalytic converter (petrol models)

Note: *Catalytic converters must not be disposed of as normal scrap metal as they contain precious metal, which can be recycled.*
12 The catalytic converter is part of the exhaust front pipe, so follow the procedure in paragraphs 6 to 8, for removal of the front pipe.

Catalytic converter (diesel models)

Note: *Catalytic converters must not be disposed of as normal scrap metal as they contain precious metal, which can be recycled.*

13 Support the exhaust system on an axle stand or block of wood.
14 Undo the exhaust clamp and disconnect the front pipe from the catalytic converter.
15 Trace the wiring from the lambda (oxygen) sensor(s) and disconnect the block connectors.
16 Remove the air cleaner housing as described in Chapter 4B.
17 Unscrew the retaining bolts and remove the heat shield from above the exhaust manifold (see illustration).
18 Undo the retaining bolts and remove the air cleaner housing mounting brackets from the cylinder head.
19 Undo the retaining bolt from the catalytic converter retaining clamp (see illustration).
20 Slacken and remove the bolt from the mounting bracket at the rear of the catalytic converter (see illustration).

21 Withdraw the catalytic converter from the engine compartment (see illustration).

Rear pipe and silencers

22 Unscrew the bolts and separate the front and rear sections of the exhaust system (see illustration). Recover the sealing olive.
23 Support the rear pipe and silencers, and then release the rubber mountings. Lower the exhaust and remove it from under the vehicle.

Complete system

24 Unscrew and remove the clamp bolts securing the catalytic converter/front pipe to the exhaust manifold/turbocharger, separate and, where necessary, recover the gasket.
25 Release the rubber mounting along the length of the exhaust, and then unbolt the mounting bracket from the transmission.
26 With the help of an assistant, support the rear of the exhaust system, then unhook the rubber mountings and lower the system to the floor. Withdraw it from under the vehicle.

Refitting

27 Each section is refitted by a reverse of the removal sequence, noting the following points.
a) *Ensure that all traces of corrosion have been removed from the flanges and renew all necessary gaskets.*
b) *Inspect the rubber mountings for signs of damage or deterioration and renew as necessary.*
c) *Renew the sealing olive between the front pipe/front silencer and catalytic converter.*
d) *Make sure all mounting brackets are refitted securely.*
e) *Prior to tightening the exhaust system joints, ensure that all rubber mountings are correctly located and that there is adequate clearance between the exhaust system and vehicle underbody.*

7 Catalytic converters – general information and precautions

The catalytic converter is a reliable and simple device, with no moving parts and as such requires no maintenance. There are, however, some facts of which an owner

6.21 Remove the catalytic converter

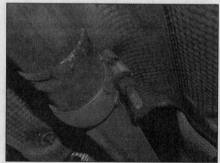

6.22 Front section-to-rear section retaining clamp

should be aware if the converter is to function properly for its full service life.

Petrol models

a) DO NOT use leaded petrol (or LRP) in a car equipped with a catalytic converter – the lead will coat the precious metals, reducing their converting efficiency and will eventually destroy the converter.

b) Always keep the ignition and fuel systems well maintained in accordance with the manufacturer's schedule.

c) If the engine develops a misfire, do not drive the car at all (or at least as little as possible) until the fault is cured.

d) DO NOT push- or tow-start the car – this will soak the catalytic converter in unburned fuel, causing it to overheat when the engine does start.

e) DO NOT switch off the ignition at high engine speeds.

f) DO NOT use fuel or engine oil additives – these may contain substances harmful to the catalytic converter.

g) DO NOT continue to use the car if the engine burns oil to the extent of leaving a visible trail of blue smoke.

h) Remember that the catalytic converter operates at very high temperatures. DO NOT, therefore, park the car in dry undergrowth, over long grass or piles of dead leaves after a long run.

i) Remember that the catalytic converter is FRAGILE – do not strike it with tools during servicing work.

j) The catalytic converter, used on a well-maintained and well-driven car, should last for between 50 000 and 100 000 miles – if the converter is no longer effective it must be renewed.

Diesel models

Refer to the information given in Parts f, g, h, i and j of the petrol models information given above.

Notes

Chapter 5 Part A:
Starting and charging systems

Contents

Degrees of difficulty

Easy, suitable for novice with little experience	**Fairly easy,** suitable for beginner with some experience	**Fairly difficult,** suitable for competent DIY mechanic	**Difficult,** suitable for experienced DIY mechanic	**Very difficult,** suitable for expert DIY or professional

Specifications

General
System type . . . .   12 volt, negative earth

Battery
Charge condition:
    Poor . . . .   12.5 volts
    Normal . . . .   12.6 volts
    Good . . . .   12.7 volts

Alternator
Minimum brush length . . . .   5.0 mm

Torque wrench settings

	Nm	lbf ft
Alternator mounting bolt.	42	31
Starter motor main cable nut	14	10
Starter motor mounting bolt.	42	31

1 General information and precautions

General information

1 The engine electrical system consists mainly of the charging and starting systems. Because of their engine-related functions, these components are covered separately from the body electrical devices such as the lights, instruments, etc (which are covered in Chapter 12). On petrol engine models refer to Part B of this Chapter for information on the ignition system, and on diesel models refer to Part C for information on the preheating system.

2 The electrical system is of the 12 volt negative earth type.

3 The battery may be of the low maintenance or maintenance-free (sealed for life) type and is charged by the alternator, which is belt-driven from the crankshaft pulley.

4 The starter motor is of the pre-engaged type incorporating an integral solenoid. On starting, the solenoid moves the drive pinion into engagement with the flywheel ring gear before the starter motor is energised. Once the engine has started, a one-way clutch prevents the motor armature being driven by the engine until the pinion disengages from the flywheel.

Precautions

5 Further details of the various systems are given in the relevant Sections of this Chapter. While some repair procedures are given, the usual course of action is to renew the component concerned.

6 It is necessary to take extra care when working on the electrical system to avoid damage to semi-conductor devices (diodes and transistors), and to avoid the risk of personal injury. In addition to the precautions given in *Safety first!* at the beginning of this manual, observe the following when working on the system.

• *Always remove rings, watches, etc, before working on the electrical system*. Even with the battery disconnected, capacitive discharge could occur if a component's live terminal is earthed through a metal object. This could cause a shock or nasty burn.

• *Do not reverse the battery connections*. Components such as the alternator, electronic control units, or any other components having semi-conductor circuitry could be irreparably damaged.

• If the engine is being started using jump leads and a slave battery, connect the batteries *positive-to-positive* and *negative-to-negative* (see *Jump Starting*). This also applies when connecting a battery charger.

• Never disconnect the battery terminals, the alternator, any electrical wiring or any test instruments when the engine is running.

• Do not allow the engine to turn the alternator when the alternator is not connected.

• Never test for alternator output by 'flashing' the output lead to earth.

3.1 Release the retaining clips

• Never use an ohmmeter of the type incorporating a hand-cranked generator for circuit or continuity testing.
• Always ensure that the battery negative lead is disconnected when working on the electrical system.
• Before using electric-arc welding equipment on the car, disconnect the battery, alternator and components such as the fuel injection/ ignition electronic control unit to protect them from the risk of damage.

The radio/CD unit fitted as standard equipment by Mercedes-Benz is equipped with a built-in security code to deter thieves. If the power source to the unit is cut, the anti-theft system will activate. Even if the power source is immediately reconnected, the radio/CD unit will not function until the correct security code has been entered. Therefore, if you do not know the correct security code for the radio/CD unit do not disconnect the battery negative terminal of the battery or remove the radio/CD unit from the vehicle. Refer to your Mercedes-Benz dealer for further information on whether the unit fitted to your car has a security code.

2 Battery –
testing and charging

Testing

Standard and low maintenance battery

1 If the vehicle covers a small annual mileage,

3.2 Disconnect the earth lead

it is worthwhile checking the specific gravity of the electrolyte every three months to determine the state of charge of the battery. Use a hydrometer to make the check and compare the results with the following table. The temperatures quoted in the table are ambient (air) temperatures. Note that the specific gravity readings assume an electrolyte temperature of 15°C; for every 10°C below 15°C subtract 0.007. For every 10°C above 15°C add 0.007.

	Ambient temperature	
	Above 25°C	Below 25°C
Fully-charged	1.210 to 1.230	1.270 to 1.290
70% charged	1.170 to 1.190	1.230 to 1.250
Discharged	1.050 to 1.070	1.110 to 1.130

2 If the battery condition is suspect, first check the specific gravity of electrolyte in each cell. A variation of 0.040 or more between any cells indicates loss of electrolyte or deterioration of the internal plates.
3 If the specific gravity variation is 0.040 or more, the battery should be renewed. If the cell variation is satisfactory but the battery is discharged, it should be charged as described later in this Section.

Maintenance-free battery

4 In cases where a 'sealed for life' maintenance-free battery is fitted, topping-up and testing of the electrolyte in each cell is not possible. The condition of the battery can therefore only be tested using a battery condition indicator or a voltmeter.
5 Certain models may be fitted with a maintenance-free battery with a built-in charge condition indicator. The indicator is located in the top of the battery casing, and indicates the condition of the battery from its colour. If the indicator shows green, then the battery is in a good state of charge. If the indicator turns darker, eventually to black, then the battery requires charging, as described later in this Section. If the indicator shows clear/yellow, then the electrolyte level in the battery is too low to allow further use, and the battery should be renewed. **Do not** attempt to charge, load or jump start a battery when the indicator shows clear/yellow.

All battery types

6 If testing the battery using a voltmeter, connect the voltmeter across the battery and compare the result with those given in the *Specifications* under 'charge condition'. The test is only accurate if the battery has not been subjected to any kind of charge for the previous six hours. If this is not the case, switch on the headlights for 30 seconds, then wait four to five minutes before testing the battery after switching off the headlights. All other electrical circuits must be switched off, so check that the doors and tailgate are fully shut when making the test.
7 If the voltage reading is less than 12.2 volts, then the battery is discharged, whilst a reading of 12.2 to 12.4 volts indicates a partially-discharged condition.

8 If the battery is to be charged, remove it from the vehicle and charge it as described later in this Section.

Charging

Note: *The following is intended as a guide only. Always refer to the manufacturer's recommendations (often printed on a label attached to the battery) before charging a battery.*

Standard and low maintenance battery

9 Charge the battery at a rate equivalent to 10% of the battery capacity (eg, for a 46 Ah battery charge at 4.6 A) and continue to charge the battery at this rate until no further rise in specific gravity is noted over a four hour period.
10 Alternatively, a trickle charger charging at the rate of 1.5 amps can safely be used overnight.
11 Specially rapid 'boost' charges that are claimed to restore the power of the battery in 1 to 2 hours are not recommended, as they can cause serious damage to the battery plates through overheating.
12 While charging the battery, note that the temperature of the electrolyte should never exceed 38°C.

Maintenance-free battery

13 This battery type takes considerably longer to fully recharge than the standard type, the time taken being dependent on the extent of discharge, but it can take anything up to three days.
14 A constant voltage type charger is required to be set, when connected, to 13.9 to 14.9 volts with a charger current below 25 amps. Using this method, the battery should be useable within three hours, giving a voltage reading of 12.5 volts, but this is for a partially-discharged battery and, as mentioned, full charging can take considerably longer.
15 If the battery is to be charged from a fully-discharged state (condition reading less than 12.2 volts), have it recharged by your Mercedes-Benz dealer or local automotive electrician, as the charge rate is higher and constant supervision during charging is necessary.

3 Battery –
removal and refitting

Removal

1 The battery is located in the left-hand rear corner of the engine compartment. Open the bonnet, release the retaining clips and remove the air intake housing from above the battery **(see illustration)**.
2 Loosen the clamp bolt and disconnect the battery negative cable from the terminal **(see illustration)**.
3 Loosen the clamp bolt and disconnect the battery positive cable from the terminal.

4 Unscrew the bolt and remove the clamp plate securing the battery to the inner wing panel **(see illustration)**.

5 Lift the battery out from the engine compartment.

Refitting

6 Refitting is a reversal of removal. Tighten the battery clamp plate bolt securely.

4 Alternator/charging system – testing in vehicle

Note: *Refer to the precautions given in Safety first! and in Section 1 of this Chapter before starting work.*

1 If the ignition warning light fails to illuminate when the ignition is switched on, first check the alternator wiring connections for security. If satisfactory, check that the warning light bulb has not blown, and that the bulbholder is secure in its location in the instrument panel. If the light still fails to illuminate, check the continuity of the warning light feed wire from the alternator to the bulbholder. If all is satisfactory, the alternator is at fault and should be renewed or taken to an auto-electrician for testing and repair.

2 If the ignition warning light illuminates when the engine is running, stop the engine and check that the drivebelt is intact and that the alternator connections are secure. If all is so far satisfactory, check the alternator brushes and slip-rings as described in Section 6. If the fault persists, the alternator should be renewed, or taken to an auto-electrician for testing and repair.

3 If the alternator output is suspect even though the warning light functions correctly, the regulated voltage may be checked as follows.

4 Connect a voltmeter across the battery terminals and start the engine.

5 Increase the engine speed until the voltmeter reading remains steady; the reading should be approximately 12 to 13 volts, and no more than 14 volts.

6 Switch on as many electrical accessories (eg, the headlights, heated rear window and heater blower) as possible, and check that the

3.4 Battery clamp mounting bolt

alternator maintains the regulated voltage at around 13 to 14 volts.

7 If the regulated voltage is not as stated, the fault may be due to worn brushes, weak brush springs, a faulty voltage regulator, a faulty diode, a severed phase winding or worn or damaged slip-rings. The brushes and slip-rings may be checked (see Section 6), but if the fault persists, the alternator should be renewed or taken to an auto-electrician for testing and repair.

5 Alternator – removal and refitting

Removal

1 The alternator is bolted to the right-hand side of the engine block and is driven by the auxiliary belt.

5.6 Move the power steering pump to one side

2 Disconnect the battery negative (earth) lead and position it away from the terminal.

3 Apply the parking brake, then jack up the front of the vehicle and support it on axle stands (see *Jacking and vehicle support*). Remove the engine compartment undershield.

4 Detach the auxiliary drivebelt from the alternator pulley with reference to Chapter 1A or 1B.

5 Remove the air filter housing as described in Chapter 4A or 4B.

Petrol engines

6 To make access easier, unbolt the power steering pump/reservoir from the cylinder head and move it to one side **(see illustration)**.

7 Unscrew and remove first the lower mounting bolts, and then the upper mounting bolts. Withdraw the alternator forwards to access the wiring connectors on the rear of the alternator **(see illustration)**.

Diesel engines

8 Undo the retaining bolts and remove the heat shield from above the exhaust manifold **(see illustration)**.

9 Undo the mounting bracket bolts and remove the air intake pipe from turbocharger **(see illustrations)**.

10 Unscrew and remove the mounting bolts, and remove the turbocharger support bracket **(see illustration)**.

11 Unscrew and remove the two lower mounting bolts, and then the two upper mounting bolts **(see illustration)**

5.7 Alternator upper mounting bolts

5.8 Remove the heat shield

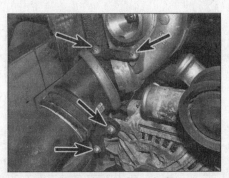

5.9a Undo the retaining bolts . . .

5.9b . . . and remove the air charge elbow

5.10 Unbolt the support bracket

5.11 Alternator upper mounting bolts

5.12 Remove the alternator

5.13 Remove plastic cap . . .

5.14 . . . and disconnect the wiring connectors

12 Withdraw the alternator forwards to access the wiring connectors on the rear of the alternator **(see illustration)**.

All engines

13 Prise off the protective cap and unscrew the nut securing the battery positive lead to the alternator terminal **(see illustration)**. Position the lead to one side.

14 Release the locking clip and disconnect the wiring connector from the alternator terminal **(see illustration)**.

15 If necessary, remove the brush holder/ voltage regulator module as described in Section 6.

Refitting

16 Refitting is a reversal of removal. Refer to Chapter 1A or 1B for details of refitting the auxiliary drivebelt.

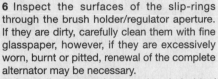

6 Alternator brush holder/ regulator module – renewal

1 Remove the alternator as described in Section 5.

2 Place the alternator on a clean work surface, with the pulley facing down.

3 Undo the two screws, then remove the plastic cover from the rear of the alternator **(see illustrations)**.

4 Undo the three screws securing the brush holder/voltage regulator module to the alternator, then withdraw the module **(see illustration)**.

5 Measure the free length of the brush contacts, check the measurement with the *Specifications*; renew the module if the brushes are worn below the minimum limit.

6 Inspect the surfaces of the slip-rings through the brush holder/regulator aperture. If they are dirty, carefully clean them with fine glasspaper, however, if they are excessively worn, burnt or pitted, renewal of the complete alternator may be necessary.

7 Carefully locate the new brush holder/ regulator on the alternator, taking care not to break the carbon brushes, then insert and tighten the retaining screws. The new holder may incorporate pins, which retain the brushes retracted while the holder is being fitted and the screws inserted, after which the pins are removed to release the brushes against the slip-rings.

8 Refit the plastic cover to the alternator and retain with the three screws.

9 Refit the alternator with reference to Section 5.

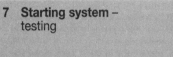

7 Starting system – testing

Note: *Refer to the precautions given in Safety first! and in Section 1 of this Chapter before starting work.*

1 If the starter motor fails to operate when the ignition key is turned to the appropriate position, the following possible causes may be responsible.

a) The battery is faulty.

b) The electrical connections between the switch, solenoid, battery and starter motor are somewhere failing to pass

6.3a Undo the retaining bolts . . .

6.3b . . . and remove the rear cover

6.4 Voltage regulator/brush holder retaining bolts

the necessary current from the battery through the starter to earth.
c) The solenoid is faulty.
d) The starter motor is mechanically or electrically defective.

2 To check the battery, switch on the headlights. If they dim after a few seconds, this indicates that the battery is discharged – recharge (see Section 2) or renew the battery. If the headlights glow brightly, operate the ignition switch and observe the lights. If they dim, then this indicates that current is reaching the starter motor; therefore the fault must lie in the starter motor. If the lights continue to glow brightly (and no clicking sound can be heard from the starter motor solenoid), this indicates that there is a fault in the circuit or solenoid – see following paragraphs. If the starter motor turns slowly when operated, but the battery is in good condition, then this indicates that either the starter motor is faulty, or there is considerable resistance somewhere in the circuit.

3 If a fault in the circuit is suspected, disconnect the battery leads (including the earth connection to the body), the starter/solenoid wiring and the engine/transmission earth strap. Thoroughly clean the connections, and reconnect the leads and wiring, then use a voltmeter or test lamp to check that full battery voltage is available at the battery positive lead connection to the solenoid, and that the earth is sound. Smear petroleum jelly around the battery terminals to prevent corrosion – corroded connections are amongst the most frequent causes of electrical system faults.

4 If the battery and all connections are in good condition, check the circuit by disconnecting the trigger wire from the solenoid terminal. Connect a voltmeter or test lamp between the wire end and a good earth (such as the battery negative terminal), and check that the wire is live when the ignition switch is turned to the 'start' position. If it is, then the circuit is sound – if not the circuit wiring can be checked as described in Chapter 12.

5 The solenoid contacts can be checked by connecting a voltmeter or test lamp between the battery positive feed connection on the starter side of the solenoid and earth. When the ignition switch is turned to the 'start' position, there should be a reading or lighted bulb, as applicable. If there is no reading or lighted bulb, the solenoid is faulty and should be renewed.

6 If the circuit and solenoid are proved sound, the fault must lie in the starter motor. Begin checking the starter motor by removing it and having the brushes checked. If the fault does not lie in the brushes, the motor windings

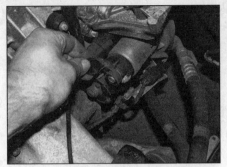

8.4a Remove the retaining nut . . .

8.4b . . . and remove the wiring terminal

8.5 Disconnect the low voltage wire

must be faulty. In this event, it may be possible to have the starter motor overhauled by a specialist, but check on the availability and cost of spares before proceeding, as it may prove more economical to obtain a new or exchange motor.

8 Starter motor – removal and refitting

Removal

1 The starter motor is bolted to the transmission bellhousing, at the rear of the engine on the left-hand side. Access is best achieved from under the front of the car, although on petrol engine models without air conditioning, the starter motor can be removed from above.

2 Disconnect the battery negative (earth) lead and position it away from the terminal.

3 Apply the parking brake, then jack up the front of the vehicle and support it on axle stands (see Jacking and vehicle support). Remove the engine compartment undershield.

4 Remove the cap then unscrew the nut and disconnect the main cable from the terminal on the starter solenoid (see illustrations).

8.8 Unbolt the cable support bracket

5 Disconnect the smaller, trigger wire from the solenoid (see illustration).

6 Release the wiring from the clips on the starter motor. Where necessary, unbolt the support.

7 Using socket extensions above the transmission, unscrew the upper starter mounting bolts, and then unscrew the lower mounting bolts.

8 Remove the starter motor from the transmission bellhousing and withdraw from under the car. On diesel engines, unbolt and remove the cable support and move the cable to one side (see illustration).

Refitting

9 Refitting is a reversal of removal.

9 Starter motor – overhaul

If the starter motor is thought to be defective, it should be removed from the vehicle and taken to an auto-electrician for assessment. In the majority of cases, new starter motor brushes can be fitted at a reasonable cost. However, check the cost of repairs first as it may prove more economical to purchase a new or exchange motor.

Chapter 5 Part B:
Ignition system – petrol engines

Contents

Degrees of difficulty

Easy, suitable for novice with little experience	**Fairly easy,** suitable for beginner with some experience	**Fairly difficult,** suitable for competent DIY mechanic	**Difficult,** suitable for experienced DIY mechanic	**Very difficult,** suitable for expert DIY or professional

Specifications

General

System type	Sequential, closed-loop fuel injection/ignition system

Ignition coil(s)

Primary winding resistance	0.3 to 0.6 ohms
Secondary winding resistance	5.2 to 8.5 k ohms

Spark plugs

Type and electrode gap	See Chapter 1A
Spark plug connector resistance	700 to 1300 ohms

Sensors

Crankshaft position sensor resistance..........................	680 to 1200 ohms
Camshaft position sensor resistance..........................	900 to 1600 ohms
Coolant temperature sensor:	
Approximate electrical resistance:	
At 80°C..	325 ohms
At 40°C..	1170 ohms
At 10°C..	3700 ohms
Inlet air temperature sensor:	
Approximate electrical resistance:	
At 80°C..	620 ohms
At 40°C..	2600 ohms
At 10°C..	9670 ohms

Torque wrench settings

	Nm	lbf ft
Camshaft position sensor	8	6
Crankshaft position sensor	8	6
Knock sensor..	20	15
Spark plugs:		
Up to 20/04/04	25	18
From 21/04/04	28	21

1 General information

The systems fitted to Mercedes-Benz C-Class models covered in this manual are self-contained engine management systems, which control both the fuel injection and ignition. This Chapter deals with the ignition system components only – refer to Chapter 4A for details of the fuel injection system components.

The main components of the system comprise the spark plugs, electronic ignition coils and an electronic control unit (ECU) together with associated sensors and wiring. The basic operation is as follows: the ECU supplies a voltage to the input stage of the ignition coil, which causes the primary windings to be energised. The LT (low tension) supply voltage is periodically interrupted by the ECU and this results in the collapse of the primary magnetic field, which then induces a much larger HT (high tension) voltage in the

coil's secondary windings. This HT voltage is directed to the spark plug in the cylinder currently on its ignition stroke. The spark plug electrodes form a gap small enough for the HT voltage to arc across, and the resulting spark ignites the fuel/air mixture in the cylinder. The timing of this sequence of events is critical and is regulated solely by the ECU.

The ECU calculates and controls the ignition timing and dwell angle primarily according to engine speed, crankshaft position and inlet manifold depression information, received

2.3 Location of diagnostic socket

from sensors mounted on and around the engine. Other parameters that affect ignition timing are throttle position (idle and full throttle positions are sensed via a changeover switch), inlet air temperature and coolant temperature. Again, these are monitored via sensors mounted on the engine.

It should be noted that comprehensive fault diagnosis of all the engine management systems described in this Chapter is only possible with dedicated electronic test equipment. Problems with the systems operation that cannot be pin-pointed by following the basic guidelines in Section 2 should therefore be referred to a Mercedes-Benz dealer for assessment. Once the fault has been identified, the removal/refitting sequences detailed in the following Sections will then allow the appropriate component(s) to be renewed as required.

2 Ignition system – testing

1 If the engine misfires, or runs unevenly, first check that the fault is not due a poor electrical connection. Check the wiring connectors to the ignition coils, and check that the HT side of the coils are firmly connected to the spark plugs. Also check that the fault is not due to poor maintenance (ie, check that the air cleaner filter element is clean, the spark plugs are in good condition and correctly gapped, and that the engine breather hoses are clear and undamaged. If the engine is running very roughly check the compression pressures as described in Chapter 2A.

2 If the engine either will not turn over at all, or only turns very slowly, check the battery and starter motor as described in Chapter 5A. If the engine turns over at normal speed, connect a voltmeter across the battery terminals then note the voltage reading obtained while briefly operating the starter. If the reading obtained is less than approximately 9.5 volts, charge the battery and repeat the check.

3 If these checks fail to reveal the cause of the problem, the vehicle should be taken to a Mercedes-Benz dealer who will use a special test instrument in the diagnostic socket located under the driver's side facia panel, next to the bonnet release lever **(see illustration)**. The test instrument will locate the fault quickly and simply, alleviating the need to test all the system components individually, which is a

time-consuming operation that carries a high risk of damaging the ECU.

3 Ignition coils – removal and refitting

Removal

1 Disconnect the battery negative (earth) lead and position it away from the terminal.

2 The ignition coils are located beneath the plastic cover on top of the camshaft cover **(see illustrations)**.

3 Disconnect the wiring connector from each of the ignition coils **(see illustration)**.

4 Unbolt the ignition coils, and withdraw them out from the camshaft cover, disconnecting them from the spark plugs **(see illustrations)**.

Refitting

5 Refitting is a reversal of removal. Make sure that the ignition coils are fitted correctly.

4 Ignition timing – checking

It is not possible to check the ignition timing without using special instrumentation plugged into the diagnostic socket located under the driver's side facia panel, next to the bonnet release lever. Normally, if a fault occurs in the ignition system, the ECU memory will contain a fault code, and the engine management warning light will be illuminated on the instrument panel. If this occurs, the car should be taken to a Mercedes-Benz dealer who will have the necessary equipment to diagnose the faulty component.

5 Ignition control system components – removal and refitting

The ignition system shares components with the fuel injection system – refer to the information given in Chapter 4A.

3.2a Remove the engine trim cover . . .

3.2b . . . to access the ignition coils

3.3 Disconnect the wiring connectors

3.4a Undo the retaining bolt . . .

3.4b . . . and remove the ignition coil

Chapter 5 Part C:
Preheating system – diesel engines

Contents

Degrees of difficulty

Easy, suitable for novice with little experience	**Fairly easy,** suitable for beginner with some experience	**Fairly difficult,** suitable for competent DIY mechanic	**Difficult,** suitable for experienced DIY mechanic	**Very difficult,** suitable for expert DIY or professional

Specifications

Glow plugs

Nominal operating voltage	11.5 V
Electrical resistance	0.75 to 1.5 ohms (approximately at operating temperature)
Current consumption	14 to 16 amps (per glow plug, after approximately 8 seconds of operation)
After-heating.	180 seconds up to maximum coolant temperature of 40° C

Torque wrench settings

	Nm	lbf ft
Glow plug to cylinder head	20	15
Glow plug wiring terminal.	4	3

1 General information

To assist cold starting, diesel-engined models are fitted with a preheating system, which comprises four glow plugs (one per cylinder), a glow plug control unit, a facia-mounted warning lamp, a coolant temperature sensor and the associated electrical wiring.

The glow plugs are miniature electric heating elements, encapsulated in a metal case with a probe at one end and electrical connection at the other. Each combustion chamber has one glow plug threaded into it. When the glow plug is energised, it heats up rapidly causing the temperature of the air charge drawn into each

of the combustion chambers to rise. The glow plug probe is positioned directly in line with the incoming spray of fuel from the injectors. Hence the fuel passing over the glow plug probe is also heated, allowing its optimum combustion temperature to be achieved more readily. In addition, small particles of the fuel passing over the glow plugs are ignited and this helps to trigger the combustion process.

The duration of the preheating period is governed by the glow plug control unit. This device monitors the temperature of the engine coolant via a sensor threaded into the cylinder head and then alters the preheating time (the length for which the glow plugs are supplied with current) to suit the conditions.

A facia-mounted warning lamp informs the driver that preheating is taking place. The lamp extinguishes when sufficient preheating

has taken place to allow the engine to be started, but power will still be supplied to the glow plugs for a further period until the engine is started. If no attempt is made to start the engine, the power supply to the glow plugs is switched off to prevent battery drain and glow plug burn-out. Note that the warning lamp will also illuminate during normal driving if a preheating system malfunction occurs. The system employs post-glowing (after-heating), which operates as follows. After the engine has been started, the glow plugs continue to operate for a further period of time as given in this Chapter's Specifications. This helps to improve fuel combustion whilst the engine is warming-up, resulting in quieter, smoother running and reduced exhaust emissions. The duration of the after-heating period is dependent on the coolant temperature.

2 Glow plug control unit – removal and refitting

Removal

1 The control unit is located in the front left-hand side of the engine compartment, on the inner wing panel **(see illustration)**.
2 Disconnect the battery negative (earth) lead and position it away from the terminal.
3 Disconnect the wiring connectors from the control unit and move them to one side **(see illustration)**.
4 Undo the retaining nuts and withdraw the bracket, together with the control unit from the engine compartment.

Refitting

5 Refitting is a reversal of removal.

3 Glow plugs – testing, removal and refitting

Testing

1 If the system malfunctions, testing is ultimately by substitution of known good units, but some preliminary checks may be made as described in the following paragraphs.
2 Connect a voltmeter or 12 volt test lamp between the glow plug supply cable and a good earth point on the engine.
Caution: Make sure that the live connection is kept well clear of the engine and bodywork.
3 Have an assistant activate the preheating system with the ignition key and check that battery voltage is applied to the glow plug

2.1 Glow plug control unit

supply cable. Note that the voltage will drop to zero when the preheating period ends.
4 If no supply voltage can be detected at the glow plug supply cable, then either the glow plug relay or the supply cabling must be faulty.
5 To locate a faulty glow plug, first disconnect the supply cabling from all of the glow plug terminals. Connect an ohmmeter between the first glow plug terminal and a good earthing point on the cylinder head and measure the electrical resistance of the glow plug. A reading of anything more than a few ohms indicates that the plug is defective. Repeat the test on the remaining glow plugs.
6 If a suitable ammeter is available, connect it between the glow plug and its supply cable and measure the steady state current consumption (ignore the initial current surge which will be about 50% higher). Compare the result with this Chapter's Specifications – high current consumption (or no current draw at all) indicates a faulty glow plug.
7 As a final check, remove the glow plugs and inspect them visually, as described in the following paragraphs.

2.3 Disconnect the wiring connectors

Removal

8 Disconnect the battery negative (earth) lead and position it away from the terminal. Remove the plastic covers from the top of the engine **(see illustration)**.
9 Pull the wiring connectors from the top of the glow plug terminals to disconnect **(see illustrations)**.
10 Unscrew and remove the glow plug from the cylinder head.
11 Inspect the glow plug probe for signs of damage. A badly burned or charred probe indicates a faulty fuel injector (refer to Chapter 4B).

Refitting

12 Refitting is a reversal of removal, but tighten the glow plug to the specified torque.

4 Engine coolant temperature (ECT) sensor – removal and refitting

1 Refer to Chapter 3, Section 6, for the removal and refitting procedure for the coolant temperature sensor.

3.8 Remove the engine trim cover

3.9a Glow plugs location – two shown

3.9b Pull the connector to disconnect

Chapter 6
Clutch

Contents

Degrees of difficulty

Easy, suitable for novice with little experience	**Fairly easy,** suitable for beginner with some experience	**Fairly difficult,** suitable for competent DIY mechanic	**Difficult,** suitable for experienced DIY mechanic	**Very difficult,** suitable for expert DIY or professional

Specifications

Friction disc

Lining thickness:
  New . . . . 3.6 to 4.0 mm
  Wear limit . . . . 2.6 to 3.0 mm
Lining face run-out . . . . 0.5 mm maximum
Diameter . . . . 228 mm or 240 mm depending on model

Torque wrench settings

	Nm	lbf ft
Clutch pressure plate-to-flywheel bolts	25	18
Clutch release bearing/slave cylinder bolts	10	7
Pedal mounting bracket retaining nuts	20	15

1 General information and precautions

All models are fitted with a single dry plate clutch system. The main components consist of a friction disc, pressure plate (or cover), hydraulic master cylinder and release bearing/ slave cylinder.

The clutch pressure plate is bolted to the rear face of the flywheel, and the friction disc is located between the pressure plate and the flywheel friction surface. The friction disc is splined to the transmission input shaft and is free to slide along the splines. Friction lining material is riveted to each side of the disc, and the disc hub incorporates cushioning springs to absorb transmission shocks and ensure a smooth take-up of drive. The pressure plate incorporates an internal diaphragm spring mounted on a fulcrum ring. When the inner fingers of the spring are depressed, the outer perimeter draws the pressure plate away from the friction disc.

The release bearing is part of the slave cylinder and is operated by the clutch pedal, using hydraulic pressure. The pedal acts on the hydraulic master cylinder pushrod, and hydraulic pressure operates the slave cylinder, which incorporates the release bearing.

When the clutch pedal is depressed, the release bearing is pushed forwards, to bear against the centre of the diaphragm spring, thus pushing the centre of the diaphragm spring inwards.

When the clutch pedal is released, the diaphragm spring forces the pressure plate into contact with the friction linings on the friction disc, and simultaneously pushes the friction disc forwards on its splines, forcing it against the flywheel. The friction disc is now firmly sandwiched between the pressure plate and the flywheel, and drive is taken up.

The clutch is self-adjusting. As wear takes place on the friction disc over a period of time, the pressure plate automatically moves closer to the friction plate to compensate.

 Warning; Dust created by clutch wear and deposited on the clutch components may contain asbestos, which is a health hazard. DO NOT blow it out with compressed air, or inhale any of it. DO NOT use petrol (or petroleum-based solvents) to clean off the dust. Brake *system cleaner or methylated spirit should be used to flush the dust into a suitable receptacle. After the clutch components are wiped clean with rags, dispose of the contaminated rags and cleaner in a sealed, marked container.*

 Warning: Hydraulic fluid is poisonous; wash off immediately and thoroughly in the case of skin contact, and seek immediate medical advice if any fluid is swallowed or gets into the eyes. Certain types of hydraulic fluid are inflammable, and may ignite when allowed into contact with hot components; when servicing any hydraulic system, it is safest to assume that the fluid is inflammable, and to take precautions against the risk of fire as though it is petrol that is being handled. Hydraulic fluid is also an effective paint stripper, and will attack plastics; if any is spilt, it should be washed off immediately, using copious quantities of fresh water. Finally, it is hygroscopic (it absorbs moisture from the air) – old fluid may be contaminated and unfit for further use. When topping-up or renewing the fluid, always use the recommended type, and ensure that it comes from a freshly opened, sealed container.

2.3 Pressure plate retaining bolts

2 Clutch assembly –
removal, inspection
and refitting

Note: *Refer to the precautions given in Section 1 regarding dust.*

Removal

1 Remove the transmission, as described in Chapter 7A.

2 If the original clutch is to be refitted, make alignment marks between the clutch pressure plate assembly and the flywheel, so that the clutch can be refitted in its original position.

3 Progressively unscrew the bolts securing the clutch pressure plate assembly to the flywheel, and recover the washers (where fitted) **(see illustration)**.

4 Withdraw the clutch pressure plate assembly (cover) and disc from the flywheel

2.12a Special tool to adjust pressure plate . . .

2.12c Turn the adjusting ring anti-clockwise . . .

2.4 Note the fitted position of the clutch plate/friction disc

(see illustration). Be prepared to catch the friction disc, and note which way round the friction disc is fitted – the two sides of the disc may be marked *Engine side* and *Transmission side*, or the side with the part number on faces the flywheel. The greater projecting side of the hub faces away from the flywheel.

Inspection

5 Clean the cover, disc, and flywheel. Do not inhale the dust, as it may contain asbestos, which is dangerous to health.

6 Examine the fingers of the diaphragm spring for wear or scoring. If the depth of any scoring is excessive, a new cover assembly must be fitted.

7 Examine the pressure plate for scoring, cracking and discoloration. Light scoring is acceptable, but if excessive, a new assembly must be fitted.

8 Examine the friction disc linings for wear

2.12b . . . which presses down on the diaphragm spring fingers

2.12d . . . and release the pressure on the diaphragm

cracking, and for contamination with oil or grease. Using vernier calipers, check the thickness of the linings and compare with the details given in the Specifications. Check the disc hub and splines for wear by temporarily fitting it on the transmission input shaft. Renew the friction disc as necessary.

9 Examine the flywheel friction surface for scoring, cracking and discoloration (caused by overheating). If excessive, it may be possible to have the flywheel machined by an engineering works, otherwise it should be renewed.

10 Ensure that all parts are clean, and free of oil or grease, before reassembling. Apply just a small amount of high melting-point grease to the splines of the friction disc hub. Note that a new pressure plate may be coated with protective grease. It is only permissible to clean the grease away from the friction disc lining contact area. Removal of the grease from other areas will shorten the service life of the clutch.

11 Check the spigot bearing in the end of the crankshaft or in the centre of the flywheel. Make sure that it turns smoothly and quietly. If the transmission input shaft contact face on the bearing is worn or damaged, fit a new bearing, as described in the relevant part of Chapter 2.

Refitting

12 If you are re-using the pressure plate, the adjustment ring will need to be reset. Position the pressure plate in a hydraulic press (Mercedes technicians use a special tool **(see illustrations)**, with a block of wood placed under the central portion of the pressure plate, directly below the diaphragm spring fingers (not on the friction face). Apply pressure to the diaphragm spring fingers until the adjusting ring is loose. While still applying pressure, use a screwdriver to rotate the adjusting ring anti-clockwise **(see illustrations)**. Hold the adjustment ring in place, and then release the pressure on the diaphragm spring fingers.

13 It is important to ensure that no oil or grease gets onto the friction disc linings, or the pressure plate and flywheel faces. It is advisable to refit the clutch assembly with clean hands, and to wipe down the pressure plate and flywheel faces with a clean rag before assembly begins.

14 Apply a smear of molybdenum disulphide grease to the splines of the friction disc hub, then offer the disc to the flywheel, with the greater projecting side of the hub facing away from the flywheel (most friction discs will have an *Engine side* marking which should face the flywheel). Hold the friction disc against the flywheel while the pressure plate assembly is offered into position, or alternatively use the centralising tool described in paragraph 16 to hold the disc on the flywheel.

15 Fit the clutch pressure plate assembly, where applicable aligning the marks with those on the flywheel. Ensure that the pressure plate assembly locates over the dowels on the flywheel. Insert the securing bolts and washers, and tighten them finger-tight, so that the friction disc is gripped, but can still be moved.

16 The friction disc must now be centralised, to ensure correct alignment of the transmission input shaft with the spigot bearing in the crankshaft/flywheel **(see illustrations)**. To do this, a proprietary tool may be used, or alternatively, use a wooden mandrel made to fit inside the friction disc hub and spigot bearing. Insert the tool through the friction disc into the spigot bearing, and make sure that it is central.

17 Tighten the clutch pressure plate bolts progressively and in diagonal sequence, until the specified torque setting is achieved, and then remove the centralising tool.

18 Check the release bearing in the front of the transmission for smooth operation, and if necessary renew it with reference to Section 3.

19 Refit the transmission with reference to Chapter 7A.

3 Clutch release bearing/ slave cylinder – removal, inspection and refitting

Note: *Refer to the precautions given in Section 1 regarding dust.*

Removal

1 Remove the transmission, as described in Chapter 7A.

2 If not already disconnected, release the retaining clip from the clutch fluid hose on the transmission bellhousing, and remove the hose **(see illustration)**.

3 Undo the retaining bolts and withdraw the release bearing/slave cylinder from the transmission housing, complete with bleed screw connection **(see illustration)**.

Inspection

4 Spin the release bearing, and check it for excessive roughness. If any excessive movement or roughness is evident, renew the bearing. If a new clutch has been fitted, it is wise to renew the release bearing as a matter of course.

Refitting

5 Slide the bearing/slave cylinder into position, and then tighten the retaining bolts to the specified torque setting

6 Refit the transmission as described in Chapter 7A.

4 Hydraulic master cylinder – removal and refitting

Note: *Refer to the precautions given in Section 1 regarding the use of hydraulic fluid.*

Removal

1 The clutch master cylinder is located inside the vehicle, attached to the pedal mounting

2.16a Centralise the clutch plate . . .

2.16b . . . and fit assembly onto the flywheel

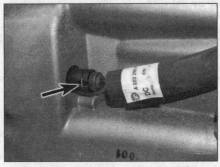
3.2 Clutch fluid line retaining clip

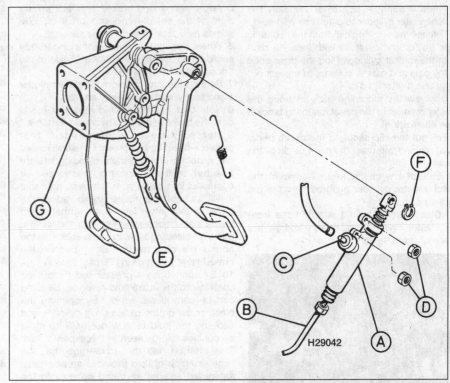
3.3 Release bearing/slave cylinder mounting bolts

bracket **(see illustration)**. Hydraulic fluid for the unit is supplied by a flexible rubber hose connected to the brake fluid reservoir in the engine compartment.

4.1 Clutch master cylinder and pedal assembly

A Master cylinder
B Fluid pipe union
C Fluid hose connection
D Securing nuts
E Clutch assist spring
F Circlip
G Pedal assembly

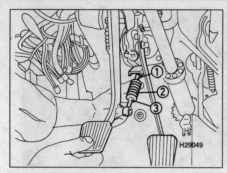

4.8 Pull the pedal upwards, and withdraw the clutch assist spring seat (1), spring (2) and washer (3) from the pushrod

2 Disconnect the battery negative (earth) lead and position it away from the terminal. The battery is located in the rear luggage compartment.

3 Remove the lower facia trim panel from under the steering column for access to the master cylinder and pedal assembly (see Chapter 11).

4 Pull back the floor carpet, and cover the floor beneath the pedals to protect against fluid spillage.

5 To reduce fluid loss, draw off as much fluid as possible from the appropriate chamber of the brake fluid reservoir, using a clean syringe, until the fluid level is below the level of the clutch master cylinder supply pipe. Alternatively, fit a hose clamp to the supply pipe.

6 Place a suitable container beneath the clutch master cylinder to catch any spilt fluid.

7 Release the securing clip from the hydraulic pipe union, and carefully withdraw the pipe from the master cylinder. Plug the open ends of the pipe and master cylinder to prevent dirt entry and further fluid loss.

8 Unscrew the mounting nuts securing the master cylinder to the pedal mounting bracket **(see illustration)**.

9 Pull out the clip securing the clutch pedal pivot pin and withdraw the pivot pin from the pedal.

10 Extract the circlip and disconnect the clutch master cylinder pushrod from the pin on the pedal.

11 Disconnect the fluid supply hose from the master cylinder, and then withdraw the assembly from the footwell.

5.12 Clutch slave cylinder bleed screw

Refitting

12 Refitting is a reversal of removal, making sure that the pivot pins are securely fitted. Finally bleed the hydraulic system as described in Section 5.

5 Hydraulic system – bleeding

Note: *Refer to the precautions given in Section 1 regarding the use of hydraulic fluid.*

1 The correct operation of the hydraulic system is only possible after removing all air from the circuit, and this is achieved by bleeding the system.

2 During the bleeding procedure, add only clean, unused hydraulic fluid of the recommended type. Never re-use fluid that has already been bled from the system. Ensure that sufficient fluid is available before starting work.

3 If there is any possibility of incorrect fluid being already in the system, both the clutch and brake circuits must be flushed completely with uncontaminated, correct fluid, and new seals should be fitted to the various components.

4 If hydraulic fluid has been lost from the system, or air has entered because of a leak, ensure that the fault is cured before proceeding further.

5 Apply the parking brake, then jack up the front of the vehicle and support it on axle stands (see *Jacking and vehicle support*).

6 Where applicable, remove the underbody shield for access to the right-hand side of the transmission bellhousing.

7 Remove the dust cap from the slave cylinder bleed screw, and clean away any dirt.

8 Note that the brake fluid reservoir feeds both the brake and clutch hydraulic systems.

9 Mercedes-Benz recommended that pressure-bleeding equipment be used to bleed the system. Some pressure-bleeding kits are operated by the reservoir of pressurised air contained in a spare tyre; however, note that it will probably be necessary to reduce the pressure to a lower level than normal. Refer to the instructions supplied with the kit. If a pressure-bleeding kit is not available, use the normal bleeding method described for the brake hydraulic circuit in Chapter 9.

10 By connecting a pressurised, fluid-filled container to the brake fluid reservoir, bleeding can be carried out simply by opening the bleed screw on the clutch slave cylinder, and allowing the fluid to flow out until no more air bubbles can be seen in the expelled fluid. This method has the advantage that the large reservoir of fluid provides an additional safeguard against air being drawn into the system during bleeding.

11 Collect a clean glass jar, a suitable length of plastic or rubber tubing which is a tight fit over the bleed screw, and a ring spanner to fit the screw.

12 Fit the spanner and tube to the slave cylinder bleed screw **(see illustration)**, place the other end of the tube in the jar, and pour in sufficient fluid to cover the end of the tube.

13 Connect the pressure-bleeding equipment to the brake/clutch fluid reservoir in accordance with its manufacturer's instructions.

14 Loosen the bleed screw half a turn using the spanner, and allow fluid to drain into the jar until no more air bubbles emerge.

15 When bleeding is complete, tighten the bleed screw, and disconnect the hose and the pressure bleeding equipment.

16 Wash off any spilt fluid, check once more that the bleed screw is tightened securely, and refit the dust cap.

17 Check the hydraulic fluid level in the reservoir, and top-up if necessary (see *Weekly checks*).

18 Discard any hydraulic fluid that has been bled from the system, as it will not be fit for re-use.

19 Check the feel of the clutch pedal. If it feels at all spongy, air must still be present in the system, and further bleeding is required. Failure to bleed satisfactorily after a reasonable repetition of the bleeding procedure may be due to worn master or slave cylinder seals.

20 On completion, lower the vehicle to the ground.

6 Clutch pedal – removal and refitting

Removal

1 Disconnect the battery negative (earth) lead and position it away from the terminal.

2 Remove the driver's side lower facia trim panel to gain access to the master cylinder and pedal assembly.

3 Pull back the floor carpet, and cover the floor beneath the pedals to protect against fluid spillage.

4 To reduce fluid loss, draw off as much fluid as possible from the appropriate chamber of the brake fluid reservoir, using a clean syringe, until the fluid level is below the level of the clutch master cylinder supply pipe.

5 Place a suitable container beneath the clutch master cylinder to catch any spilt fluid.

6 Unscrew the hydraulic pipe union nut from the bottom of the clutch master cylinder, and carefully withdraw the pipe sufficiently far to release it from the cylinder. Plug the open ends of the pipe and master cylinder to prevent dirt entry and further fluid loss.

7 Carefully unhook the brake pedal return spring **(see illustration)**.

8 Disconnect the wiring plug(s) from the pedal switch, and then unclip the switch from the bracket on the pedal assembly.

9 Remove the locking clip from the brake pedal-to-servo pushrod clevis pin, then withdraw the clevis pin.

10 Unscrew the four nuts securing the

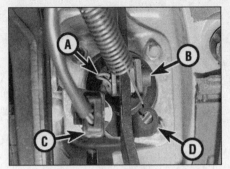

6.7 Brake pedal mounting details

A Clevis pin locking clip
B Clevis pin
C Stop-light switch wiring plug
D Return spring bracket

**6.10a Pedal assembly securing nuts
(arrowed) . . .**

6.10b . . . and securing bolt (arrowed)

pedal assembly to the front of the bulkhead (note that these nuts also secure the brake vacuum servo), and the single bolt securing the assembly to the top of the bulkhead **(see illustrations)**.

11 Pull the pedal assembly back from

the bulkhead until the mounting bracket disengages from the studs, then lower the assembly and disconnect the fluid hose from the clutch master cylinder (be prepared for fluid spillage).

12 Withdraw the assembly from under the facia.

13 Dismantling of the assembly is self-explanatory. Note the locations of all

components to ensure correct refitting **(see illustration)**.

Refitting

14 Refitting is a reversal of removal, but check the adjustment of the stop-light switch as described in Chapter 9, and on completion bleed the clutch hydraulic system as described in Section 5.

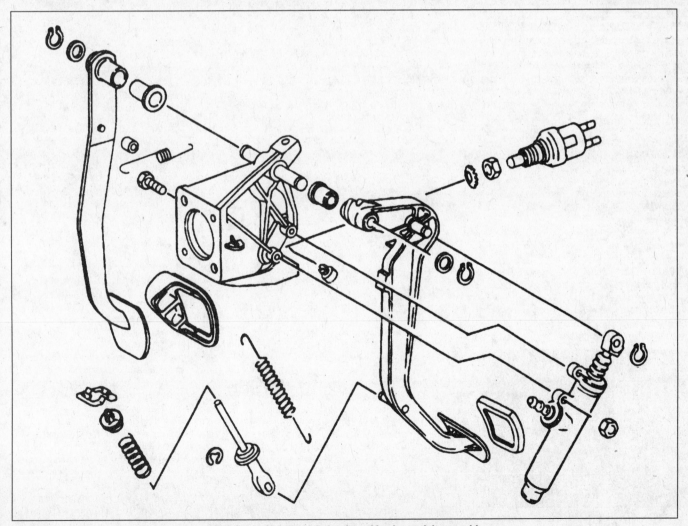

6.13 Exploded view of clutch and brake pedal assembly

Chapter 7 Part A:
Manual transmission

Contents

Degrees of difficulty

Easy, suitable for novice with little experience 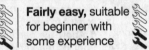	**Fairly easy,** suitable for beginner with some experience	**Fairly difficult,** suitable for competent DIY mechanic	**Difficult,** suitable for experienced DIY mechanic	**Very difficult,** suitable for expert DIY or professional

Specifications

General

Type	6-speed (with an optional sequentronic transmission)
Transmission code*:	
Engine code 111.951	716.620, 716.624 or 716.633
Engine code 111.955	716.620, 716.622, 716.627 or 716.630
Engine code 111.981	716.632, 716.662, 716.663 or 716.668
Engine code 271.921	716.605 or 716.631
Engine codes 271.940, 271.942 and 271.946	716.605, 716.628 or 716.631
Engine code 271.948	716.628
Engine code 611.962	716.601, 716.603, 716.604 or 716.640
Engine code 612.962	716.641
Engine code 646.962	716.604 or 716.606
Engine code 646.963	716.604, 716.606 or 716.654

Refer to Chapter 2A or 2B for engine codes

Transmission fluid

Type	See *Lubricants and fluids* on page 0•16
Capacity:	
Up to transmission code 716.639	1.2 litres
From transmission code 716.640	1.5 litres

Torque wrench settings

	Nm	lbf ft
Fluid filler plug	35	26
Fluid drain plug.	30	22
Engine-to-transmission bolts	40	30
Propeller shaft self-locking nuts:		
M10	40	30
M12	60	44
Propeller shaft centre bearing bolts	30	22
Reversing light switch bolt	10	7
Transmission output flange nut	160	118

2.2a Transmission fluid drain plug location

2.2b Transmission fluid filler/level plug location

Note: *The vehicle must be in a level position.*

5 When the level is correct, refit the plug, and tighten to the specified torque.

3 Gearchange lever assembly – removal, refitting and adjustment

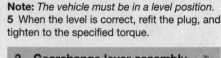

Removal

1 Position the gear lever in the neutral position.

2 Remove the centre console as described in Chapter 11.

3 To remove the gear knob from the gear lever, lift the gaiter from around the lever and turn the gaiter inside out, pulling it upwards over the gear knob. Turn the locking ring, below the gear knob anti-clockwise, and then pull the gear knob upwards to remove it from the gear lever.

4 On models with a gear selector cable fitted (see paragraph 13), push down on the spring-loaded washer at the lower part of the gear lever and remove the retaining pin.

5 Unclip the rubber cover from the gearchange assembly and remove the gear lever. On models without a gear selector cable fitted (see paragraph 13), undo the two retaining screws to remove the gear lever.

6 Apply the parking brake, then jack up the front of the vehicle and support it on axle stands (see *Jacking and vehicle support*).

7 Remove the exhaust front pipe as described in Chapter 4C.

8 Undo the retaining bolts and disconnect the propeller shaft from the rear of the transmission.

9 Undo the retaining bolts and remove the heat shields from under the floor panel.

10 Using a trolley jack support the rear of the transmission. Undo the retaining bolts and remove the mounting and bracket from the rear of the transmission.

11 Working under the vehicle, reach up above the rear of the transmission, unclip the locking clip and slide the gearchange retaining pin out from the transmission **(see illustrations)**.

12 Also at the rear of the transmission, unclip the locking clip from the gear selector rod **(see illustrations)**.

1 General information

A 6-speed manual transmission is bolted to the rear of the engine. Drive is transmitted from the crankshaft via the clutch to the input shaft, which has a splined extension to accept the clutch friction disc. The transmission output shaft transmits the drive via the propeller shaft to the rear differential. The input shaft runs in line with the output shaft. The input shaft and output shaft gears are in constant mesh with the layshaft gear cluster. Selection of gears is by sliding synchromesh hubs, which lock the appropriate output shaft gears to the output shaft.

Gear selection is via a floor-mounted lever and selector mechanism incorporating three gearchange rods. The selector mechanism causes the appropriate selector fork to move its respective synchro-sleeve along the shaft, to lock the gear pinion to the synchro-hub. Since the synchro-hubs are splined to the output shaft, this locks the pinion to the shaft, so that drive can be transmitted. To ensure that gear-changing can be made quickly and quietly, a synchromesh system is fitted to all forward gears, consisting of baulk rings and spring-loaded fingers, as well as the gear pinions and synchro-hubs. The synchromesh cones are formed on the mating faces of the baulk rings and gear pinions.

Some models have an optional Sequentronic six-speed manual transmission that has an electro/hydraulic-operated clutch and shifting system. The result is a transmission that is conventional in its gears and internal components; but which is operated instead in response to commands from the gear lever through the ECU, so when changing gear it operates more like an automatic transmission. Mercedes call it an 'automated manual transmission'.

2 Manual transmission fluid – draining and refilling

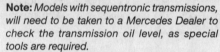

Note: *Models with sequentronic transmissions, will need to be taken to a Mercedes Dealer to check the transmission oil level, as special tools are required.*

1 Apply the parking brake, then jack up the front of the vehicle and support it on axle stands (see *Jacking and vehicle support*).

2 Place a suitable container beneath the transmission drain plug, at the bottom of the casing, then unscrew the plug. Unscrew the level/filler plug, located on the right-hand side of the transmission, to assist draining. A hexagonal key should be used to unscrew the plugs, but a tool can be improvised using a long nut, or a length of hexagonal bar, and a spanner **(see illustrations)**.

3 Once all the fluid has drained, refit and tighten the drain plug.

4 Fill the transmission until fluid runs from the level/filler plug hole. The level should just be up to the bottom of the level/filler plug hole.

3.11a Lift the gearchange securing clip . . .

3.11b . . . and slide it out of the transmission casing . . .

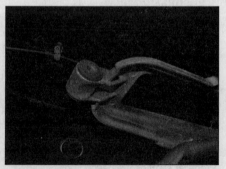

3.11c . . . and out of the gearchange linkage

13 Where fitted, disconnect the selector cable from the lower left-hand corner of the transmission housing. Turn the locking ring anti-clockwise to disconnect the cable.

14 The gearchange assembly can now be removed, by moving it downwards and towards the rear of the vehicle. Check the noise-dampening boot for damage and renew if required.

Refitting

15 Refitting is a reversal of removal, but grease the linkages and locking pins before assembly. Make sure that the gearchange rod securing clips are securely refitted.

4 Output flange oil seal – renewal

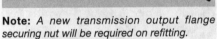

Note: *A new transmission output flange securing nut will be required on refitting.*

1 Disconnect the propeller shaft from the transmission output flange **(see illustration)**, with reference to Chapter 8.

2 Ensure that the transmission is in neutral.

3 Bolt a suitable holding tool to the transmission output flange. A suitable tool can be made up using two pieces of flat bar and bolts – engage the tool with two of the bolts holes in the output flange, and use it to counterhold the flange. Note that it must be possible to gain access to the output flange nut with the tool in place.

4 Counterhold the output flange, then unscrew the flange securing nut. Discard the nut, a new one must be used on refitting **(see illustration)**.

5 Pull the output flange from the shaft, using a suitable puller if necessary.

6 Prise the oil seal from the housing using a screwdriver.

7 Thoroughly clean the oil seal seating in the rear transmission cover.

8 Tap the new seal into position, using a suitable socket or tube, until the outer face of the seal is flush with the end face of the housing.

9 Refit the output flange to the output shaft, and secure using a new nut **(see illustration)**. Tighten the nut to the specified torque.

10 Reconnect the propeller shaft to the output flange, with reference to Chapter 8.

5 Reversing light switch – testing, removal and refitting

Note: *Some models do not have a reversing light switch fitted to the transmission, on these models the ECU controls the operation of the reversing lights.*

Testing

1 Where fitted, the reversing light circuit is controlled by a switch located at the rear of the transmission **(see illustration)**. If a fault

3.12a Pull the locking clip out of the selector rod . . .

develops in the circuit, first ensure that the circuit fuse has not blown.

2 For access to the switch, it will be necessary to apply the parking brake, and then jack up the front of the vehicle and support it on axle stands (see *Jacking and vehicle support*).

3 To test the switch, disconnect the wiring connector, and use a multimeter (set to the resistance function) or a battery-and-bulb test circuit to check that there is continuity between the switch terminals only when reverse gear is selected. If this is not the case, and there are no obvious breaks or other damage to the wires, the switch is faulty, and must be renewed.

Removal

4 Proceed as described in paragraph 2.

5 Unclip the wiring connector from the switch, and then undo the retaining bolt and withdraw the reversing light switch from the transmission.

4.1 Disconnect the propeller shaft

4.9 Renew the transmission output flange securing nut

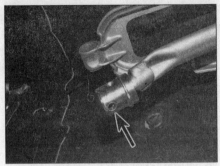

3.12b . . . and the gear lever shaft

Refitting

6 Refitting is a reversal of removal.

6 Manual transmission – removal and refitting

Note: *This is a difficult operation, due to the limited access to the engine-to-transmission bolts. It is suggested that the procedure is read through thoroughly before starting the operation. Suitable ratchet extensions will be required to reach some of the engine-to-transmission bolts.*

Removal

1 Disconnect the battery negative (earth) lead and position it away from the terminal.

2 Raise the bonnet to its fully open position

4.4 Flange securing nut will be tight

5.1 Reversing light switch location

6.2 Raise the bonnet to the vertical position

6.5a Undo the retaining bolts/nuts . . .

6.5b . . . and remove the exhaust bracket

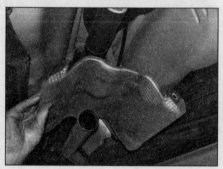

6.6 Remove the heat shield

6.7 Disconnect the propeller shaft

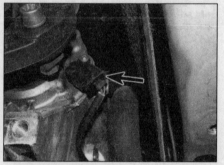

6.8 Disconnect the wiring connector

(see illustration). Take care to protect any brake pipes or wiring at the rear of the engine compartment.

3 Apply the parking brake, then jack up the front of the vehicle and support it on axle stands (see *Jacking and vehicle support*). The vehicle must be raised sufficiently high to enable the transmission to be lowered and removed from under the vehicle. Remove the engine undershield.

4 Drain the transmission fluid with reference to Section 2.

5 Remove the complete exhaust system and catalytic converter as described in Chapter 4C. Also unbolt the exhaust bracket from the rear of the transmission **(see illustrations)**.

6 Where applicable, unbolt the exhaust heat shield from the vehicle floor for access to the propeller shaft intermediate bearing assembly **(see illustration)**.

7 Mark the position of the propeller shaft to

aid refitting and then undo the retaining bolts/nuts and disconnect the propeller shaft from the transmission flange **(see illustration)**.
Note: *It is recommended that the self-locking nuts be renewed.* Fasten the propeller shaft securely under the vehicle to prevent any damage, if required remove the propeller shaft completely with reference to Chapter 8.

8 Where a speedometer transponder is fitted, disconnect the wiring connector **(see illustration)**.

9 Release the securing clip and disconnect the clutch fluid pipe from the transmission **(see illustration),** with reference to Chapter 6. Place a suitable container beneath the pipe to catch the fluid which will be released, and plug or cover the open ends of the pipe and hose.
Note: *The hydraulic fluid pipe from the clutch master cylinder loops over the transmission bellhousing, and an alternative method is to disconnect the union on the side of the*

*transmission **(see illustration),** and leave the pipe and slave cylinder in position while the transmission is being removed. If this course of action is taken, fit a hose clamp to the fluid supply hose leading from the brake fluid reservoir to the clutch master cylinder. Place a suitable container beneath the union to catch the fluid which will be released, and plug or cover the open ends of the pipe and hose.*

10 Prise off the securing clips, and disconnect the gear selector rods from the rear of the transmission. See gearchange lever assembly in Section 3, paragraphs 11 to 13.

11 Unscrew the transmission-to-engine bolt securing the wiring cable mounting bracket across the lower part of the transmission **(see illustration)**. Disconnect any wiring connectors and move the wiring harness and bracket to one side.

12 Remove the starter motor (see Chapter 5A).

13 Support the transmission using a trolley

6.9a Release the securing clip . . .

6.9b . . . or undo the fluid pipe connection

6.11 Remove the wiring harness bracket

jack and interposed block of wood **(see illustration)**.

14 Unbolt the engine/transmission mounting bracket from the rear of the transmission and from the vehicle floor **(see illustration)**. Note the position of the earth cable for refitting.

15 Ensure that the transmission is adequately supported, and then lower the assembly as far as possible until the engine is resting on the crossmember and the sump is supported safely. **Note:** *DO NOT let the complete weight rest on the crossmeber. Take care not to damage any pipes, wiring or any other components on the crossmember and at the rear of the bulkhead as the transmission is lowered. Also make sure the propeller shaft is supported up against the underbody.*

16 Unscrew all the engine-to-transmission bolts, leaving one bolt on either side of the transmission. Access to the upper bolts is very difficult, even with the assembly tilted, and several long socket extensions will be required. Remove the two upper, outer bolts first, removing the retaining brackets and soundproofing from the top of the transmission **(see illustrations)**.

17 Note the position of any mounting brackets, and disconnect any wiring connectors **(see illustrations)**.

 Warning: The transmission is heavy; always have an assistant to help support the transmission.

18 Unscrew the two remaining engine-to-transmission bolts, and then, with the help of an assistant, pull the transmission rearwards and release the transmission input shaft from

6.13 Support the transmission securely

the clutch **(see illustration)**. Take care not to allow the weight of the transmission to hang on the clutch and input shaft, and where applicable take care not to damage the clutch fluid pipe during this procedure. If necessary, rotate the transmission to enable the top of the bellhousing to clear the vehicle body.

19 Once the input shaft is clear of the clutch, lower the transmission to the ground and withdraw from under the vehicle.

Refitting

20 Before refitting the transmission check that the clutch friction disc is centralised as described in Chapter 6. Also check the clutch release components (Chapter 6).

21 Lubricate the transmission input shaft splines with a little molybdenum disulphide grease.

22 Support the transmission using the trolley jack and block of wood, as during removal,

6.14 Remove the transmission mounting bracket

then raise the transmission into position beneath the vehicle. The help of an assistant is recommended.

23 Lift the transmission into position, and if required, lift the fluid pipe over the transmission to ensure that it does not get trapped.

24 Move the transmission forwards, ensuring that the input shaft engages with the clutch friction disc splines (where necessary, turn the transmission to enable the bellhousing to clear the vehicle floor). It may be necessary to rock the engine and transmission slightly and/or turn the crankshaft slightly, to allow the input shaft to engage. Take care not to allow the weight of the transmission to hang on the input shaft.

25 Slide the transmission forwards until the bellhousing contacts the cylinder block, making sure that the bolt holes and location dowels are correctly aligned.

26 Refit and tighten the engine-to-transmission bolts.

6.16a On models with soundproofing . . .

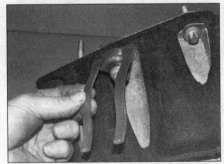
6.16b . . . remove the bolts with brackets first . . .

6.16c . . . and then pull out the soundproofing

6.17a Remove the exhaust bracket

6.17b Disconnect wiring connections

6.18 Separating the transmission from the rear of the engine

27 The remaining procedure is a reversal of removal, bearing in mind the following points.

a) *Where applicable, bleed the clutch hydraulic system as described in Chapter 6.*

b) *Reconnect the propeller shaft to the transmission flange with reference to Chapter 8.*

c) *Refit the exhaust system with reference to Chapter 4C.*

d) *Refill the transmission with fluid as described in Section 2.*

7 Manual transmission overhaul – general information

Overhauling a manual transmission is a difficult and involved job for the DIY home mechanic. In addition to dismantling and reassembling many small parts, clearances must be precisely measured and, if necessary, changed by selecting shims and spacers. Internal transmission components are also often difficult to obtain, and in many instances, extremely expensive. Because of this, if the transmission develops a fault or becomes noisy, the best course of action is to have the unit overhauled by a specialist repairer, or to obtain an exchange reconditioned unit. Be aware that some transmission repairs can be carried out with the transmission in the car.

Nevertheless, it is not impossible for the more experienced mechanic to overhaul the transmission, provided the special tools are available, and the job is done in a deliberate step-by-step manner, so that nothing is overlooked.

The tools necessary for an overhaul include internal and external circlip pliers, bearing pullers, a slide hammer, a set of pin punches, a dial test indicator, and possibly a hydraulic press. In addition, a large, sturdy workbench and a vice will be required.

During dismantling of the transmission, make careful notes of how each component is fitted, to make reassembly easier and more accurate.

Before dismantling the transmission, it will help if you have some idea what area is malfunctioning. Certain problems can be closely related to specific areas in the transmission, which can make component examination and renewal easier. Refer to the *Fault finding* Section at the end of this manual for more information.

Chapter 7 Part B:
Automatic transmission

Contents

Degrees of difficulty

Easy, suitable for novice with little experience	**Fairly easy,** suitable for beginner with some experience	**Fairly difficult,** suitable for competent DIY mechanic	**Difficult,** suitable for experienced DIY mechanic	**Very difficult,** suitable for expert DIY or professional

Specifications

General

Transmission code*:

Engine code 111.951	722.602
Engine code 111.955	722.602 or 722.616
Engine code 111.981	722.616
Engine code 271.921	722.695
Engine code 271.940	722.695
Engine code 271.942	722.628 or 722.695
Engine code 271.946	722.695
Engine code 271.948	722.695
Engine code 611.962	722.619 or 722.699
Engine code 612.962	722.634
Engine code 646.962	722.699
Engine code 646.963	722.699

Refer to Chapter 2A or 2B for engine codes

Torque converter installed height

Distance from transmission housing face:

Transmission code:

722.628	19.5mm (-2)
All except 722.628	7.0mm (-2)

Transmission fluid

Type	See *Lubricants and fluids* on page 0•16
Capacity	7.5 litres

Torque wrench settings

	Nm	lbf ft
Oil drain plug on transmission pan	20	15
Oil pan to transmission	8	6
Propeller shaft self-locking nuts:		
M10 bolt	40	30
M12 bolt	60	44
Selector rod adjustment bolt	12	9
Torque converter drain plug:		
M8 bolt	10	7
M10 bolt	15	11
Torque converter-to-driveplate bolts	42	31
Transmission-to-engine bolts	39	29

2.3 Prise off the clip securing the gear selector lever to the selector rod

1 General information

The vehicles covered in this manual are equipped with a five-speed (model 722) automatic transmission. All transmissions have a torque converter clutch system that improves fuel economy. The TCC engages in drive and overdrive modes. The TCC system consists of a solenoid, controlled by the ECU, which locks the torque converter when the vehicle is cruising on level ground and the engine is fully warmed-up. A transmission oil cooler is also fitted.

The transmission comprises a torque converter, an epicyclic geartrain, and hydraulically-operated brakes and clutches.

The torque converter provides a fluid coupling between the engine and transmission, and acts as a clutch, also providing a degree of torque multiplication when accelerating.

The epicyclic geartrain provides the five forward and one reverse gear ratios, according to which of its component parts are held stationary or allowed to turn. The components of the geartrain are held or released by brakes and clutches, which are activated by a hydraulic control unit. A fluid pump within the transmission provides the necessary hydraulic pressure to operate the brakes and clutches.

Driver control of the transmission is by a selector lever and a two-position switch. This alters the hydraulic control pressure in the transmission, according to throttle position. The 'drive' position (D) provides automatic

3.2a Release the securing clip

2.5 Ignition switch control cable

changing throughout the range of all forward gear ratios, and is the position selected for normal driving. An automatic kickdown facility shifts the transmission down a gear if the accelerator pedal is fully depressed. The 'hold' facility is similar to the 'drive' position, but limits the number of gear ratios available – ie, when the selector lever is in the 3 position, only the first three ratios can be used; in the 2 position, only the first two can be used, and so on. The lower ratio 'hold' is useful when travelling down steep gradients, or for preventing unwanted selection of high gears on twisty roads.

Two driving programs are provided for selection by the switch; 'economy' or 'standard'. With the switch in the 'standard' position, the vehicle will move away from a standstill in 2nd gear with a light throttle, or 1st gear with full throttle. With the switch in the 'economy' position, the vehicle will always move away from a standstill in 2nd gear, and the gearchange points will occur at lower driving speeds.

Due to the complexity of the automatic transmission, any repair or overhaul work must be left to a Mercedes-Benz dealer or automatic transmission specialist with the necessary special equipment for fault diagnosis and repair. The contents of the following Sections are therefore confined to supplying general information, and any service information and instructions that can be used by the owner.

⚠️ **Warning: Before carrying out any operations inside a vehicle with airbag systems, disconnect the battery negative terminal and wait at least**

3.2b Release the securing clip

15 minutes to allow the system capacitors to discharge. When operations are complete, make sure no one is inside the vehicle when the battery is reconnected.

2 Selector lever – removal and refitting

Removal

1 Disconnect the battery negative (earth) lead and position it away from the terminal.
2 Apply the parking brake, then jack up the front of the vehicle, and support securely on axle stands (see *Jacking and vehicle support*). Move the selector lever to position P.
3 Working under the vehicle, prise off the metal retaining clip, and disconnect the selector rod from the bottom of the selector lever **(see illustration)**.
4 Working inside the vehicle, remove the centre console as described in Chapter 11.
5 At the front of the gear lever housing, disconnect the ignition switch control cable from the housing **(see illustration)**. Compress the retaining lug, and pressing against the spring pressure, rotate the collar through 90° and detach the cable.
6 Disconnect the wiring plugs from the selector lever assembly. Depending on model, the wiring connectors are for the illumination, the transmission mode switch and on some models one plug is for the reverse gear/park lock solenoid.
7 Unscrew the mounting bolt at the front of the housing and lift the selector lever assembly from the floor. Recover the gasket and check it for condition. Obtain a new one if necessary.

Refitting

8 Refitting of the selector lever is a reversal of removal, but check the lever/selector rod adjustment, with reference to Section 3.

3 Selector rod – removal, refitting and adjustment

Removal

1 Apply the parking brake, then jack up the front of the vehicle and support it on axle stands (see *Jacking and vehicle support*).
2 Prise the securing clips from the ends of the selector rod, at the bottom of the selector lever and at the lever on the transmission, and then withdraw the rod from under the vehicle **(see illustrations)**.

Refitting

3 Refitting is a reversal of removal, but check and adjust the selector rod as follows.

Adjusting

4 An assistant will be required to hold the selector lever in position D. This needs to be held in this position, throughout the complete procedure.

5 Working under the vehicle, slacken the retaining bolt at the bottom of the selector lever **(see illustration)**.

6 Check that the lever inside the vehicle is still in the D position and tighten the selector lever lower retaining bolt securely. **Note:** *While this bolt is being tightened, make sure that the selector rod to the transmission does not twist.*

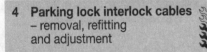

| 4 | Parking lock interlock cables |
| | – removal, refitting and adjustment |

Removal

1 Apply the handbrake, then jack up the front of the vehicle and support it on axle stands (see *Jacking and vehicle support*).

2 Remove the lower facia trim panel from under the steering column, and also remove the steering column shrouds.

3 With the ignition key at position 1, disconnect the interlock cable from the ignition/steering lock switch by compressing the tabs and moving the cable out from the side of the lock.

4 Remove the stop-lamp switch from the brake pedal bracket with reference to Chapter 9.

5 Disconnect the interlock cable from the lever link on the parking brake pedal, then compress the retainers and release the cable from the pedal bracket. Withdraw the steering lock interlock cable.

6 Disconnect the transmission interlock cable from the lever link on the parking brake pedal, then compress the retainers and release cable from the pedal bracket.

7 Move the selector lever to position P, then, working under the vehicle, use a screwdriver to prise open the retaining clip and disconnect the interlock cable from the rear of the transmission.

8 Prise out the rubber grommet from the transmission tunnel, then release the interlock cable from its retainers and withdraw from the vehicle.

Refitting

9 Refitting is a reversal of removal, but adjust the cables as follows before refitting the lower facia trim panel.

Adjustment

10 On most models, there are two cables attached to a bracket on the brake pedal. One cable connects to the ignition/steering lock switch, and the other cable to the transmission. When they are adjusted correctly, the cables prevent the key from turning unless the brake pedal is depressed.

11 Move the gear lever to the Park position.

12 A spring is connected to both sides of the bracket on the brake pedal, and each cable end has a pushbutton lock. Adjust the cable

3.5 Slacken the adjusting bolt

to the steering column, by applying some preload pressure by hand on the spring, then with the key in the off position, push in and release the button on the adjuster located at the cable housing end near the pedal bracket.

13 Carry out the same procedure on the spring and adjuster on the cable that goes to the transmission. The adjuster button is close to the transmission housing.

14 On some models with electronic shift module fitted, there is only one cable fitted, between the gear lever housing and the ignition switch. On this type no mechanical adjustment is available, see your local Mercedes Dealer for information on adjustment for this type.

Gear lever lock override

15 If the park lock interlock cables fail, and the gear lever cannot be moved out of gear, the system is equipped with an override feature.

16 Depending on model, open the

4.16a Open the console compartment . . .

4.16c . . . and insert pen

compartment, withdraw the cup holder and/or coin tray from the centre console at the rear of the gear lever **(see illustrations)**.

17 Depress the footbrake and turn the ignition switch to the ACC position. Using a pen or similar, locate the button through the hole in the centre console (where the cup holder has been removed from), and depress the button. The gear lever will now be able to move out of the Park position.

18 If this operation is required, renew or repair the parking lock interlock system as required.

| 5 | Automatic transmission – removal and refitting |

Note: *This is a difficult operation, due to the limited access to the engine-to-transmission bolts, and to the weight of the transmission assembly. It is suggested that the procedure is read through thoroughly before starting the operation. Suitable ratchet extensions will be required to reach some of the engine-to-transmission bolts.*

Removal

1 Disconnect the battery negative (earth) lead and position it away from the terminal.

2 Raise the bonnet to its fully open position **(see illustration)**. Take care to protect any brake pipes or wiring at the rear of the engine compartment.

3 Apply the parking brake, then jack up the front of the vehicle and support it on axle stands (see *Jacking and vehicle support*).

4.16b . . . lift out the coin tray . . .

5.2 Put the bonnet in the vertical position

5.4a Undo the bolts and nuts . . .

5.4b . . . and remove the mounting bracket

5.5 Remove the heat shield

The vehicle must be raised sufficiently high to enable the transmission to be lowered and removed from under the vehicle. Remove the engine undershield.

4 Remove the complete exhaust system and catalytic converter as described in Chapter 4C. Also unbolt the exhaust bracket from the rear of the transmission **(see illustrations)**.

5 Where applicable, unbolt the exhaust heat shield from the vehicle floor for access to the propeller shaft intermediate bearing assembly **(see illustration)**.

6 Mark the position of the propeller shaft to aid refitting and then undo the retaining bolts/ nuts and disconnect the propeller shaft from the transmission flange **(see illustration)**. **Note:** *It is recommended that the self-locking nuts be renewed.* Fasten the propeller shaft securely under the vehicle to prevent any damage, if required remove the propeller shaft completely with reference to Chapter 8.

7 Remove the starter motor (see Chapter 5A).
8 Working your way around the transmission casing disconnect and unclip any wiring/ connector(s) from the transmission **(see illustration)**.
9 Prise off the securing clip, and disconnect the gear selector rod from the rear of the transmission, see Section 3.
10 Place a suitable container beneath the transmission main fluid drain plug **(see illustration)**, then unscrew the drain plug and drain the transmission fluid. Check the condition of the sealing ring and renew it if necessary, then refit the plug and tighten it to the specified torque.
11 Prise the plastic plug from the transmission bellhousing for access to the torque converter-to-driveplate bolts **(see illustration)**. Mark the torque converter in relation to the driveplate to ensure that their balance is maintained when refitted. **Note:** *The access cover for the torque*

converter bolts is on the right-hand side of the transmission (about half-way up the transmission) on 111.955 engines. On all other engines it is at the bottom of the transmission housing.
12 Unscrew the six torque converter-to-driveplate bolts, turning the crankshaft for access to each pair of bolts in turn **(see illustration)**.
13 Where fitted, select Park and then disconnect the park lock interlock cable from the rear of the transmission using a screwdriver to prise open the retainer.
14 Undo the retaining bolt and remove the fluid level dipstick from the transmission housing.
15 Unscrew the union bolts and disconnect the transmission fluid cooler feed and return pipes from the transmission, be prepared for some oil spillage **(see illustration)**. Recover the sealing washers, and cover or plug the

5.6 Disconnect the propeller shaft

5.8 Disconnect the wiring connector

5.10 Drain the transmission fluid

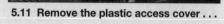

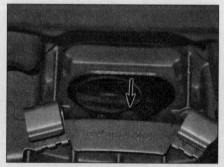

5.11 Remove the plastic access cover . . .

5.12 . . . and undo the torque converter bolts

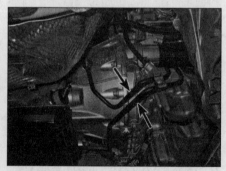

5.15 Disconnect the fluid cooler pipes

open ends of the pipes and transmission to prevent dirt entry and further fluid loss. Tie the pipes to one side.

16 If required, unscrew the bolts securing the wiring cable mounting bracket across the lower part of the transmission. Disconnect any wiring connectors and move the wring harness and bracket to one side.

17 Support the transmission using a trolley jack and interposed block of wood.

18 Unbolt the engine/transmission mounting bracket from the rear of the transmission and from the vehicle floor **(see illustrations)**. Note the position of the earth cable for refitting.

19 Ensure that the transmission is adequately supported, and then lower the assembly as far as possible until the engine is resting on the crossmember and the sump is supported safely. **Note:** *DO NOT let the complete weight rest on the crossmeber. Take care not to damage any pipes, wiring or any other components on the crossmember and at the rear of the bulkhead as the transmission is lowered. Also make sure the propeller shaft is supported up against the underbody.*

20 Unscrew all the engine-to-transmission bolts, leaving one bolt on either side of the transmission. Access to the upper bolts is very difficult, even with the assembly tilted, and several long socket extensions will be required. If soundproof is fitted across the top of the transmission, remove the two upper, outer bolts first, removing the retaining brackets and soundproofing from the top of the transmission first. See Chapter 7A, Section 6, paragraph 16, for the removal of the soundproofing, if fitted.

21 Note the position of any mounting brackets, and disconnect any wiring connectors still attached to the transmission.

⚠ *Warning: The transmission is heavy; always have an assistant to help support the transmission.*

22 Unscrew the two remaining engine-to-transmission bolts, and then, with the help of an assistant, pull the transmission rearwards and release the transmission from the engine. Make sure the torque converter is detached from the driveplate and stays with the transmission as it is removed. If necessary, rotate the transmission slightly to enable the top of the bellhousing to clear the vehicle body.

23 Once the transmission, complete with torque converter, is clear of the driveplate, lower the transmission to the ground and withdraw from under the vehicle.

24 To remove the torque converter, proceed as follows:

a) Support the transmission on wooden blocks in a vertical position, with the bellhousing and torque converter pointing vertically upwards.

5.18a Undo the mounting bracket bolts . . . **5.18b . . . and the two rear mounting bolts**

b) If a bracket is fitted to hold the torque converter in place in the transmission, it can now be removed.

c) Bolt two suitable lifting handles to the torque converter, using long bolts in the torque converter-to-driveplate bolt holes, and use the handles to lift the torque converter from the transmission. Pull evenly on both handles. Alternatively, screw two long bolts into two of the torque converter-to-driveplate bolt holes, and use the bolts to lift out the torque converter. Be prepared for some fluid spillage.

d) Store the torque converter in a safe place, where it cannot be damaged.

Refitting

25 To refit the torque converter, proceed as follows:

a) Lightly grease the torque converter drive flange. Molykote grease is recommended.

b) Using the two bolts, manipulate the converter into position. Move the converter back-and-forth as it is fitted to ensure that it is fully engaged with the transmission input shaft and primary pump. The converter is fully engaged when the distance between the bellhousing face and torque converter driveplate face is as specified at the beginning of this Chapter.

c) Turn the torque converter until two of the torque converter-to-driveplate bolt holes are positioned at the access hole of the transmission bellhousing.

26 Support the transmission using the trolley jack and block of wood, as during removal, then raise the transmission into position beneath the vehicle. Carefully engage the transmission with the rear of the engine; making sure that the bellhousing locates over the two dowels correctly.

27 Refit and tighten the transmission-to-engine bolts, ensuring that the earth strap

and any brackets noted during removal are in place.

28 Insert the torque converter-to-driveplate bolts, and tighten them to the specified torque. Turn the crankshaft as during removal for access to all of the bolts. Make sure that the torque converter is aligned with the driveplate as noted on removal.

29 Further refitting is a reversal of removal, bearing in mind the following points.

a) Use new sealing washers when connecting the transmission fluid cooler pipes.

b) Reconnect the propeller shaft as described in Chapter 8.

c) Tighten all nuts and bolts to the specified torque where given.

d) Ensure that all wiring is correctly reconnected and routed as noted before removal.

e) Refit the starter motor with reference to Chapter 5A.

f) Refit the exhaust system with reference to Chapter 4C.

g) Refill the transmission with fluid with reference to Chapter 1A or 1B.

h) On completion, check the adjustment of the selector rod, as described in Section 3.

6 Automatic transmission overhaul – general information

In the event of a fault occurring with the transmission, it is first necessary to determine whether it is of an electrical, mechanical or hydraulic nature, and to do this special test equipment is required. It is therefore essential to have the work carried out by a Mercedes-Benz dealer or automatic transmission specialist if a transmission fault is suspected. **Do not** remove the transmission from the vehicle for repair before professional fault diagnosis has been carried out, since most tests require the transmission to be in the vehicle.

Chapter 8
Final drive, driveshafts and propeller shaft

Contents

Degrees of difficulty

Easy, suitable for novice with little experience	**Fairly easy,** suitable for beginner with some experience	**Fairly difficult,** suitable for competent DIY mechanic	**Difficult,** suitable for experienced DIY mechanic	**Very difficult,** suitable for expert DIY or professional

Specifications

Final drive
Type . . . . Unsprung casing bolted to rear suspension crossmember

Driveshaft
Type . . . . Steel shafts with ball-and-cage type constant velocity joints at each end

Propeller shaft
Type . . . . Two-piece tubular shaft with centre bearing and universal joint. Rubber coupling at front and rear joints

Torque wrench settings	Nm	lbf ft
Driveshaft		
Driveshaft retaining nut	220	162
Final drive unit		
Mounting bolts:		
Front Allen bolt	45	33
Rear collared bolt	110	81
Oil filler/level plug	50	37
Pinion/flange collar nut	180	133
Propeller shaft		
Propeller shaft self-locking nuts:		
M10	40	30
M12	60	44
Propeller shaft centre bearing bolts	30	22
Roadwheels		
Wheel bolts	110	81

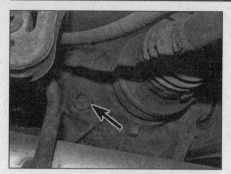

2.3 Final drive unit filler/level plug

2.4 Final drive drain plug

1 General information

Power is transmitted from the transmission to the rear axle by a two-piece propeller shaft, joined in front of the centre bearing by a 'slip joint': a sliding, splined coupling. The slip joint allows slight fore-and-aft movement of the propeller shaft. The propeller shaft is attached to the flanges of the transmission and final drive unit by flexible rubber couplings, a vibration damper being fitted between the front coupling and the shaft. The middle of the propeller shaft is supported by the centre bearing, which is bolted to the vehicle body. A universal joint is located at the rear of the centre bearing, to compensate for movement of the transmission and differential on their mountings, and for any flexing of the chassis.

The final drive assembly includes the drive pinion, the ring gear, the differential and the output flanges. The drive pinion, which drives the ring gear, is also known as the differential input shaft, and is connected to the propeller shaft via an input flange. The differential is bolted to the ring gear and drives the rear wheels through a pair of output flanges bolted to driveshafts. The differential allows the wheels to turn at different speeds when cornering, although only to a limited amount on models fitted with ASD (limited-slip differential).

The driveshafts deliver power from the final drive unit output flanges to the rear wheels. The driveshafts are equipped with constant velocity (CV) joints at each end. The inner CV joints are bolted to the differential flanges; the outer CV joints engage the splines of the wheel hubs, and are secured by a large nut.

Major repair work on the differential assembly components (drive pinion, ring-and-pinion and differential) requires many special tools and a high degree of expertise, and therefore should not be attempted by the home mechanic. If major repairs become necessary, we recommend that they be performed by a Mercedes-Benz service department or other suitably-equipped automotive engineer.

2 Final drive unit – draining and refilling

1 This operation is much quicker and more efficient if the car is first taken on a journey of sufficient length to warm the final drive unit up to normal operating temperature.

2 Park the car on level ground, switch off the ignition and apply the parking brake firmly. For improved access, jack up the rear of the car and support it securely on axle stands (see *Jacking and vehicle support*). Note that the car must be level, to ensure accuracy, when refilling and checking the oil level.

3 Wipe clean the area around the filler/level plug, which is situated on the left-hand side of the final drive unit, next to the driveshaft flange, and unscrew it **(see illustration)**.

4 Position a suitable container under the drain plug, and unscrew the plug from the right-hand side of the housing **(see illustration)**.

5 Allow the oil to drain completely into the container. If the oil is hot, take precautions against scalding. Clean both the filler/level and the drain plugs, being especially careful to wipe any metallic particles off the magnetic inserts.

6 When the oil has finished draining, clean the drain plug threads and those of the final drive casing, and refit the drain plug. If the car was raised for the draining operation, now lower it to the ground.

7 Refilling the final drive unit is an extremely awkward operation. Above all, allow plenty of time for the oil level to settle properly before checking it. Note that the car must be parked on flat level ground when checking the oil level.

8 Refill the final drive unit with the exact amount of the specified type of oil, then check the oil level as described in Chapter 1A or 1B. If the correct amount was poured into the final drive unit and a large amount flows out on checking the level, refit the filler/level plug and take the car on a short journey so that the new oil is distributed fully around the final drive components, then check the level again on your return.

3 Final drive unit – removal and refitting

Note: *New propeller shaft rear coupling nuts, driveshaft joint bolts and final drive unit mounting bolt nuts will be required on refitting.*

Removal

1 Chock the front wheels and loosen the rear wheel bolts. Jack up the rear of the car and support it on axle stands (see *Jacking and vehicle support*). Remove both rear wheels.

2 Drain the oil from the final drive unit, as described in Section 2.

3 With reference to Chapter 4C, remove the rear section of the exhaust system, then unscrew the nuts and lower the exhaust heat shield away from the floorpan **(see illustration)**.

4 Undo the two bolts securing the propeller shaft centre support bearing to the underbody **(see illustrations)**. Note the fitted position of the mounting bolts, as the holes in the bracket are elongated for balance adjustment.

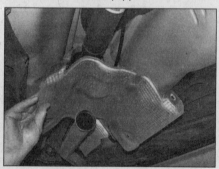

3.3 Remove the heat shield

3.4a Undo the centre bearing mounting bolts . . .

3.4b . . . noting their position

5 Undo the three nuts and remove the bolts securing the propeller shaft rear flexible coupling to the differential pinion flange **(see illustration)**.

6 Push the propeller shaft forwards as far as it will go to disengage the pinion flange centring sleeve **(see illustration)**. Lower the disconnected propeller shaft, and fasten it to one side or support it securely to prevent any damage. Do not let it hang from the rear of the transmission.

7 Remove the rear driveshafts as described in Section 5.

8 Place a jack beneath the final drive housing and just take the weight of the unit.

9 Undo the collared bolts at the rear securing the final drive housing to the subframe, and remove the bolts together with the retaining plate/washers **(see illustration)**.

10 Unscrew the Allen bolt, securing the housing to the subframe at the front **(see illustration)**. When the final drive is removed, note that there are either one or two shims fitted between the Allen bolt and the housing – make sure these are recovered and refitted. Note the fitted order of all the bushes and washers as they are removed.

11 Lower the jack slowly, and remove the final drive housing from under the car.

Refitting

12 To refit the unit, position it centrally within the subframe, and refit the front retaining bolt with a new nut and nut/washer finger-tight.

13 Refit the rear bolts and retaining plate/washers, and tighten to the specified torque. Now tighten the front bolt to the specified torque as well.

14 Further refitting is a reversal of removal, noting the following points:
  a) *Tighten all fasteners to the specified torque, where given.*
  b) *Delay tightening the centre bearing bolts fully until after the propeller shaft has been reconnected.*
  c) *Refit the driveshafts with reference to Section 5.*
  d) *Refit the rear section of the exhaust system with reference to Chapter 4C.*
  e) *On completion, when the car has been lowered to the ground and is level, unscrew the housing filler/level plug and refill the final drive oil to the level of the plug orifice, using the specified lubricant (Section 2). Refit the plug and tighten securely.*

---

4   Final drive unit oil seals – renewal

Right-hand oil seal

1 Renewal of the right-hand final drive unit oil seal is a complex task, requiring the final drive unit to be partially dismantled. This operation should therefore be entrusted to a Mercedes-Benz dealer.

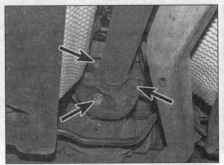

3.5 Rear coupling mounting bolts

3.9 Final drive unit rear mounting bolts

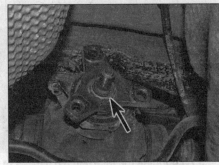

3.6 Pinion flange retaining nut

3.10 Final drive unit front mounting bolt

Left-hand oil seal

2 Chock the front wheels and loosen the left-hand rear wheel bolts. Jack up the rear of the car and support it on axle stands (see *Jacking and vehicle support*). Remove the left-hand rear wheel.

3 Remove the left-hand rear driveshaft as described in Section 5.

4 Note the seal's fitted position in the housing, and then using a lever, carefully prise the seal out of the final drive housing.

5 Clean out the recess in the housing for the seal, and then check the new seal against the old seal to make sure it is the correct one.

6 Using a seal drift/installer or a large deep socket, install the new oil seal into the housing, making sure it is fitted in the same location as noted on removal.

7 Lubricate the lip of the seal with clean gear oil, and then refit the driveshaft with reference to Section 5.

4.11 Remove the rear rubber coupling . . .

8 Check the oil level in the final drive unit as described in Section 2. Lower the vehicle to the ground and tighten the wheel bolts to the specified torque setting.

Pinion oil seal

9 Chock the front wheels and jack up the rear of the car and support it on axle stands (see *Jacking and vehicle support*).

10 Drain the final drive unit oil as described in Section 2.

11 Undo the three nuts and remove the bolts securing the propeller shaft rear flexible coupling to the differential pinion flange **(see illustration)**. Disconnect the propeller shaft from the flange on the differential and fasten it to the underside of the vehicle to prevent it getting damaged.

12 Before attempting to remove the large nut securing the flange to the pinion shaft **(see illustration)**, use a small drift to release the

4.12 . . . and remove the flange retaining nut

5.7 Lubricate the face and the threads of the new driveshaft nut with clean engine oil

staked area of the nut in the depressions on the shaft.

13 Using a tool/bar to prevent the flange from turning, undo the flange retaining nut.

14 Note the seal's fitted position in the housing, and then using a lever, carefully prose the seal out of the final drive housing.

15 Clean out the recess in the housing for the seal, and then check the new seal against the old seal to make sure it is the correct one.

16 Using a seal drift/installer or a large deep socket, install the new oil seal into the housing, making sure it is fitted in the same location as noted on removal.

17 Lubricate the lip of the seal with clean gear oil, and then refit the flange to the pinion shaft and tighten the nut to the specified torque setting. When the nut is tightened, use a drift to stake the nut in place.

18 Refit the propeller shaft, using new retaining nuts, and tighten to the specified torque setting.

6.12a Pack the driveshaft outer joint with the grease supplied with the repair kit

6.12b ... and slide the new gaiter into position

19 Refill the final drive unit with the correct quantity of oil as described in Section 2. Lower the vehicle to the ground and tighten the wheel bolts to the specified torque setting.

5 Driveshaft – removal and refitting

Note: *A new driveshaft retaining nut and bolts will be required on refitting.*

Removal

1 Remove the wheel trim/centre cap (as applicable) and, using a hammer and pointed-nose chisel, carefully relieve the driveshaft retaining nut staking.

2 Slacken the 12-point driveshaft retaining nut with the car resting on its wheels. Note that this nut is extremely tight – ensure that the tools used to loosen it are of good quality, and a good fit. Do not remove the nut at this stage.

3 Chock the front wheels and slacken the rear wheel bolts. Jack up the rear of the car and support it on axle stands (see *Jacking and vehicle support*). Remove the relevant rear roadwheel.

4 If the left-hand driveshaft is to be removed, note that it may be necessary to remove the exhaust system tailpipe to gain the relevant clearance required to manoeuvre the shaft out of position (see Chapter 4C).

5 Remove the rear stub axle as described in Chapter 10.

6 The driveshaft can now be removed from the final drive unit. Carefully lever the driveshaft out from the final drive unit, taking care not to damage the seal in the final drive unit housing. **Note:** *There is a circlip on the driveshaft splined section to locate it in the final drive.*

Refitting

7 Refitting is the reverse of removal, noting the following points.
a) *Slide the driveshaft back into the final drive, making sure that the circlip locates inside the differential securely.*
b) *Lubricate the threads and face of the new driveshaft nut and retaining bolts with clean engine oil prior to fitting (see illustration).*

6.14 Lift the gaiter outer sealing lip to equalise air pressure in the gaiter

c) *Where applicable, tighten the retaining bolts/nuts to their specified torque.*
d) *Once the vehicle is resting on its wheels, tighten the driveshaft retaining nut to the specified torque and stake it firmly into the driveshaft groove using a hammer and punch.*

6 Driveshaft gaiters – renewal

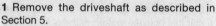

1 Remove the driveshaft as described in Section 5.

2 Secure the driveshaft in a vice equipped with soft jaws, and release the two outer joint gaiter retaining clips. If necessary, the retaining clips can be cut to release them.

3 Cut off the rubber gaiter and discard it, scoop out all the old dirty grease.

4 Using a drift against the inner star part of the joint, carefully tap the joint off the end of the driveshaft, taking care not to damage the joint or splines.

5 Withdraw the joint from the end of the shaft and remove the circlip from the driveshaft groove.

6 Thoroughly clean the constant velocity joint(s) using paraffin, or a suitable solvent, and dry thoroughly. Carry out a visual inspection as follows.

7 Move the inner splined driving member from side-to-side to expose each ball in turn at the top of its track. Examine the balls for cracks, flat spots or signs of surface pitting.

8 Inspect the ball tracks on the inner and outer members. If the tracks have widened, the balls will no longer be a tight fit. At the same time, check the ball cage windows for wear or cracking between the windows.

9 If on inspection any of the constant velocity joint components are found to be worn, or damaged, it will be necessary to renew the complete joint assembly. If the joint is in satisfactory condition, obtain a new gaiter and retaining clips, a constant velocity joint circlip and the correct type of grease. Grease is often supplied with the joint repair kit – if not, use good-quality molybdenum disulphide grease.

10 Slide the new gaiter complete with inner retaining clip onto the end of the driveshaft.

11 Pack the joint with the specified type of grease. Work the grease well into the bearing tracks whilst twisting the joint, until it is full.

12 Fit a new circlip to the driveshaft, then tap the joint onto the driveshaft until the circlip engages in its groove **(see illustrations)**. Make sure that the joint is securely retained by the circlip.

13 Fill the rubber gaiter with the remaining grease.

14 Ease the gaiter over the joint, and ensure that the gaiter lips are correctly located on both the driveshaft and constant velocity joint. Lift the sealing lip of the gaiter to equalise air pressure within the gaiter **(see illustration)**.

15 Fit the large metal retaining clip to the

gaiter. Pull the clip as tight as possible, and locate the hooks on the clip in their slots. Remove any slack in the gaiter-retaining clip by carefully compressing the raised section of the clip. In the absence of the special tool, a pair of side-cutters may be used, taking care not to cut the clip **(see illustrations)**. Secure the small retaining clip using the same procedure.

16 Check the constant velocity joint moves freely in all directions, then refit the driveshaft to the vehicle, as described in Section 5.

7 Propeller shaft – removal and refitting

Note: *New propeller shaft front and rear coupling nuts will be required on refitting.*

Removal

1 Chock the front wheels. Jack up the rear of the car and support it on axle stands (see *Jacking and vehicle support*).

2 Where applicable, release the clips and fasteners, and remove the engine lower cover from under the car.

3 With reference to Chapter 4C, unbolt and remove the rear section of the exhaust system, together with the heat shield(s).

4 Place a jack with a block of wood underneath the transmission and raise the jack so that it is supporting the weight of the unit.

5 To make access easier, unbolt and remove the transmission support bracket, which fits across at the front of the propeller shaft tunnel **(see illustrations)**, and the cross-brace from the propeller shaft tunnel.

6 Make alignment marks between the shaft coupling and transmission flange, then slacken and remove the retaining nuts and bolts securing the flexible coupling to the transmission **(see illustrations)**. Discard the nuts; new ones should be used on refitting.

7 Using paint or a suitable marker pen, make alignment marks between the propeller shaft coupling and final drive unit flange. Unscrew the nuts and bolts securing the coupling to the final drive unit and discard them; new ones must be used on refitting.

8 With the aid of an assistant, support the propeller shaft, then unscrew the centre support bearing bracket retaining bolts **(see**

6.15a Hook the retaining clip tightly around the gaiter . . .

6.15b . . . and remove any slack by compressing the raised section of the clip

illustrations). Mark the fitted position of the mounting bolts, as the holes in the bracket are elongated for balance adjustment.

9 Slide the rear of the shaft forwards and disengage the shaft from the final drive unit. Free the front of the shaft from the transmission, and remove the shaft assembly from underneath the vehicle **(see illustration)**.

Note: *Do not separate the two halves of the shaft without first making alignment marks. If the shafts are incorrectly joined, the propeller shaft assembly may become imbalanced, leading to*

7.5a Remove the transmission rear mounting bracket . . .

7.5b . . . and support bracket

7.6a Make alignment marks . . .

7.6b . . . and then remove the shaft

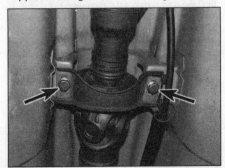

7.8a Undo the centre bearing mounting bolts . . .

7.8b . . . noting their position

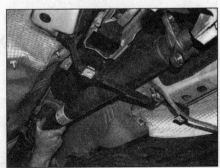

7.9 Remove the propeller shaft

8.6 Inspect the rubber for cracks or wear

noise and vibration during operation. On some models, there are alignment marks already on the shaft; the raised mark on the front section must be positioned in between the two marks on the rear section universal joint.

10 Inspect the rubber couplings, the support bearing and shaft universal joint as described in Sections 8, 9 and 10.

Refitting

11 Lubricate the shaft bushes with multi-purpose grease, and the shaft splines with molybdenum disulphide grease.

12 Manoeuvre the shaft into position, aligning the marks made prior to removal, and engage the shaft with the transmission and final drive unit flanges. With the marks correctly aligned, refit the centre bearing retaining bolts, tightening them lightly only at this stage.

13 Making sure the marks are correctly aligned, insert the retaining bolts securing the rear coupling to the final drive unit and fit the new retaining nuts. Tighten the retaining nuts to the specified torque setting.

14 Make sure the front coupling is correctly aligned with the transmission flange and refit the coupling bolts. Fit the new retaining nuts and tighten them to the specified torque.

15 With both the front and rear couplings correctly tightened, tighten the centre bearing retaining bolts to the specified torque setting.

16 The remainder of refitting is a reversal of removal.

8 Propeller shaft rubber coupling – check and renewal

Check

1 Firmly apply the parking brake, and then jack up the front of the car and support it on axle stands (see *Jacking and vehicle support*).

2 To improve access to the coupling, unscrew the heat shield retaining nuts and manoeuvre the heat shield out from around the exhaust system.

3 Closely examine the rubber couplings which link the propeller shaft to the transmission and final drive, looking for signs of damage such as cracking or splitting or for signs of general deterioration. If necessary, renew the coupling as follows.

Renewal

Note: *New propeller shaft coupling nuts will be required.*

4 Remove the propeller shaft as described in Section 7.

Front coupling

5 Make alignment marks between the coupling and propeller shaft.

6 Unscrew the retaining nuts and washers, then withdraw the bolts and remove the coupling from the propeller shaft. Note carefully any additional markings or wording (which may be in German) for use when refitting. Inspect the vibration damper for signs of wear or damage, and renew if necessary **(see illustration)**.

7 Check the centring sleeve fitted to the centre of the coupling for signs of wear or damage. If necessary, the centring sleeve can be pressed out of position for renewal.

8 Fit the new rubber coupling to the shaft, ensuring that (where applicable) any additional markings or wording are orientated as noted on removal. Insert the retaining bolts then fit the new retaining nuts and washers, and tighten them to the specified torque.

9 Refit the propeller shaft as described in Section 7.

Rear coupling

10 Unscrew the retaining nuts then withdraw the bolts and remove the coupling from the propeller shaft.

11 Fit the new coupling, then fit the retaining bolts and new nuts, tightening them to the specified torque.

12 Refit the propeller shaft as described in Section 7.

9 Propeller shaft support bearing – check and renewal

Check

1 Wear in the support bearing will lead to noise and vibration when the car is driven. The bearing is best checked with the propeller shaft removed (see Section 7).

2 Rotate the bearing and check that it turns smoothly with no sign of free play; if it's difficult to turn, or if it has a gritty feeling, renew it. Also inspect the rubber portion. If it's cracked or deteriorated, renew it.

Renewal

Note: *Bearing renewal requires the use of a puller and hydraulic press, as well as suitable spacers. If access to suitable equipment cannot be gained, entrust the task to your Mercedes-Benz dealer.*

3 Remove the propeller shaft as described in Section 7.

4 Make alignment marks between the front and rear sections of the propeller shaft, noting that on some models there are alignment marks already on the shaft; the raised mark on the front section must be positioned in between the two marks on the rear section universal joint – see Section 7 for details.

5 Separate the two halves of the propeller shaft **(see illustration)**.

6 Remove the rubber gaiter from the rear section of the shaft.

7 Using a suitable puller, draw the centre mounting assembly off the end of the shaft, noting which way around the bracket is fitted.

8 Support the mounting bracket assembly, and carefully press the bearing out of position using a tubular drift.

9 Inspect all components for signs of wear or damage and renew as necessary.

10 Support the mounting bracket securely and press the new bearing fully into position using a tubular drift which bears only on the bearing outer race.

11 Remove all traces of dirt from the propeller shaft, ensure that the mounting bracket is positioned the correct way around, and then press the assembly fully onto the shaft using a tubular drift which bears only on the bearing inner race.

12 Lubricate the propeller shaft splines with molybdenum disulphide grease. Carefully slide the two halves of the propeller shaft together, making sure the alignment marks are correctly positioned (see paragraph 4).

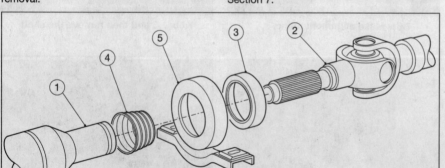

H46642

9.5 Propeller shaft centre bearing components – typical

1 *Propeller shaft*	3 *Bearing*	5 *Centre mounting*
2 *Propeller shaft*	4 *Rubber gaiter*	

13 Refit the propeller shaft as described in Section 7.

10 Propeller shaft universal joint – check and renewal

Check

1 Wear in the universal joint is characterised by vibration in the transmission, noise during acceleration, and metallic squeaking and grating sounds as the bearings disintegrate. The joint can be checked with the propeller shaft still fitted.

2 Hold the front half of the propeller shaft, and try to turn the rear half of the shaft. Free play between the propeller shaft halves indicates excessive wear. If the axial movement is excessive, renew the propeller shaft.

Renewal

3 At the time of writing, no spare parts were available to enable renewal of the universal joints to be carried out. Therefore, if any joint shows signs of damage or wear the propeller shaft assembly must be renewed. Consult your Mercedes-Benz dealer or parts supplier for latest information on parts availability.

4 If renewal of the propeller shaft is necessary, it may be worthwhile seeking the advice of an automotive engineering specialist. They may be able to repair the original shaft assembly, or supply a reconditioned shaft on an exchange basis.

Chapter 9
Braking system

Contents

Degrees of difficulty

Easy, suitable for novice with little experience	**Fairly easy,** suitable for beginner with some experience	**Fairly difficult,** suitable for competent DIY mechanic	**Difficult,** suitable for experienced DIY mechanic	**Very difficult,** suitable for expert DIY or professional

Specifications

Front brakes

Disc thickness:	
Models with 25 mm discs:	
Minimum (before repair)	22.6 mm
Minimum (limit)	22.0 mm
Models with 28 mm discs:	
Minimum (before repair)	26.5 mm
Minimum (limit)	26.0 mm
Maximum disc runout	0.12 mm
Brake pad thickness:	
New (with backing plate)	19.8 mm
Minimum (without backing plate)	2.0 mm
Pad wear indicator actuates at	3.0 mm

Rear brakes

Disc thickness:	
Models with 9 mm discs:	
Minimum (before repair)	7.6 mm
Minimum (limit)	7.3 mm
Models with 10 mm discs:	
Minimum (before repair)	8.8 mm
Minimum (limit)	8.3 mm
Maximum disc runout	0.15 mm
Brake pad thickness:	
New (with backing plate)	15.5 mm
Minimum (without backing plate)	2.0 mm
Pad wear indicator actuates at	3.0 mm

Parking brake

Type	Cable-operated brake shoes with drum machined into rear disc hub
Number of notches on gear segment	5 to 15
Brake shoe friction material thickness:	
New	3.00 mm
Minimum	1.00 mm
Width of shoe	20.00 mm

Torque wrench settings

	Nm	lbf ft
ABS wheel sensor retaining bolts:		
Front sensor	25	18
Rear sensor	8	6
Brake disc retaining screw	10	7
Brake hose unions:		
Caliper unions	18	13
All other pipe unions	14	10
Caliper bleed screws	7	5
Front brake caliper:		
Caliper mounting bracket to steering knuckle	115	85
Guide pin bolts	25	18
Master cylinder mounting nuts	20	15
Parking brake cable bolts at rear wheel	20	15
Parking brake foot pedal bolts	12	9
Rear brake caliper mounting bolts	55	41
Roadwheel bolts	110	81
Servo unit mounting nuts	15	11
Servo unit vacuum hose union nut	30	22
Vacuum pump mounting bolts	14	10

1 General information

The braking system is of the servo-assisted, dual-circuit hydraulic type. The layout is such that under normal circumstances, both circuits operate in unison. Should a hydraulic failure occur in one of the circuits, full braking force will still be available in the other circuit (operating on two diagonally-opposite roadwheels), albeit with increased pedal travel.

All models have disc brakes at the front and rear wheels as standard. An Anti-lock Braking System (ABS) is fitted as standard to all models (refer to the appropriate section for further information on the operation of the ABS). **Note:** *On models equipped with electronic traction control (ASR), this function is also carried out by the ABS.*

Models are equipped with the Mercedes-Benz Brake Assist System (BAS), which ensures that, in an emergency braking situation, full braking effort is applied immediately, reducing stopping distances. Models are also equipped with the Electronic Stability Program (ESP), which uses the braking system to help steer the car in extreme circumstances. Information on these systems was limited at time of writing and, in any case, any problems would have to be referred to a Mercedes-Benz dealer.

The front disc brakes are actuated by sliding single-piston or fixed opposed-piston type calipers. This design of caliper ensures that equal pressure is applied to each disc pad.

On all models, the rear disc brakes are actuated by fixed, opposed-piston calipers.

The parking brake provides an independent, mechanical means of applying the rear brakes. A drum and shoe arrangement is fitted in the centre of each rear brake disc. The parking brake is applied by a foot pedal, and is released by a hand lever on the facia panel; both controls actuate the brake shoes via cables.

Note: *When servicing any part of the system, work carefully and methodically; also observe scrupulous cleanliness when overhauling any part of the hydraulic system. Always renew components (in axle sets, where applicable) if in doubt about their condition, and use only genuine Mercedes-Benz parts, or at least those of known good quality. Note the warnings given in Safety first! and at relevant points in this Chapter concerning the dangers of asbestos dust and hydraulic fluid.*

2 Hydraulic system – bleeding

⚠ *Warning: Hydraulic fluid is poisonous; wash off immediately and thoroughly in the case of skin contact, and seek immediate medical advice if any fluid is swallowed or gets into the eyes.*

⚠ *Warning: Certain types of hydraulic fluid are flammable, and may ignite when brought into contact with hot components. Hence when servicing any part of the hydraulic system, it is safest to assume that the fluid is flammable, and to take precautions against the risk of fire as though it were petrol being handled.*

⚠ *Warning: Hydraulic fluid is also an effective paint stripper, and will attack plastics; if any is spilt, it should be washed off immediately, using copious quantities of fresh water.*

⚠ *Warning: Finally, brake fluid is hygroscopic, which means that if left in an open container, it will absorb moisture from the air. This has the effect of lowering the boiling point of the fluid, rendering it unfit for use. When topping-up or renewing the fluid, always use the recommended type, and ensure that it comes from a sealed, freshly-opened container.*

General

1 The correct operation of any hydraulic system is only possible after removing all air from the components and circuit; this is achieved by bleeding the system.

2 During the bleeding procedure, add only clean, unused hydraulic fluid of the recommended type; never re-use fluid that has already been bled from the system. Ensure that sufficient fluid is available before starting work.

3 If there is any possibility of incorrect fluid being already in the system, the brake components and circuit must be flushed completely with uncontaminated, correct fluid, and new seals should be fitted to the various components.

4 If hydraulic fluid has been lost from the system, or air has entered because of a leak, ensure that the fault is cured before continuing further.

5 Park the car on level ground, switch off the engine and select first or reverse gear, then chock the wheels and release the parking brake.

6 Check that all pipes and hoses are secure, unions tight and bleed screws closed. Clean any dirt from around the bleed screws.

7 Unscrew the master cylinder reservoir cap, and top the master cylinder reservoir up to the MAX level line; refit the cap loosely, and remember to maintain the fluid level at least above the MIN level line throughout the procedure, or there is a risk of further air entering the system.

8 There are a number of one-man, do-it-yourself brake bleeding kits currently available from motor accessory shops. It is recommended that one of these kits is used whenever possible, as they greatly simplify the bleeding operation, and reduce the risk of expelled air and fluid being drawn back into

the system. If such a kit is not available, the basic (two-man) method must be used, which is described in detail below.

9 If a kit is to be used, prepare the car as described previously, and follow the kit manufacturer's instructions, as the procedure may vary slightly according to the type being used; generally, they are as outlined below in the relevant sub-section.

10 Whichever method is used, the same sequence must be followed (paragraphs 11 and 12) to ensure that all air is removed from the system. On completion, test the operation of the braking system exhaustively, before bringing the car back into service on the road.

Bleeding

Sequence

11 If the system has been only partially disconnected, and suitable precautions were taken to minimise fluid loss, it should be necessary only to bleed that part of the system.

12 If the complete system is to be bled, then it should be done working in the following sequence:

  a) *Right-hand rear brake.*
  b) *Left-hand rear brake.*
  c) *Right-hand front brake.*
  d) *Left-hand front brake.*

Basic (two-man) method

13 Collect a clean glass jar, a suitable length of plastic or rubber tubing which is a tight fit over the bleed screw, and a ring spanner to fit the screw. The help of an assistant will also be required.

14 Remove the dust cap from the first screw in the sequence. Fit the spanner and tube to the screw, place the other end of the tube in the jar, and pour in sufficient fluid to cover the end of the tube.

15 Ensure that the master cylinder reservoir fluid level is maintained at least above the MIN level line throughout the procedure.

16 Have the assistant fully depress the brake pedal several times to build-up pressure, and then maintain it on the final downstroke.

17 While pedal pressure is maintained, unscrew the bleed screw (approximately one turn) and allow the compressed fluid and air to flow into the jar. The assistant should maintain pedal pressure, following it down to the floor if necessary, and should not release it until instructed to do so. When the flow stops, tighten the bleed screw again, have the assistant release the pedal slowly, and recheck the reservoir fluid level.

18 Repeat the steps given in paragraphs 16 and 17 until the fluid emerging from the bleed screw is free from air bubbles. If the master cylinder has been drained and refilled, and air is being bled from the first screw in the sequence, allow approximately five seconds between cycles for the master cylinder passages to refill.

19 When no more air bubbles appear, tighten the bleed screw to the specified torque,

remove the tube and spanner, and refit the dust cap. Do not overtighten the bleed screw.

20 Repeat the procedure on the remaining screws in the sequence, until all air is removed from the system and the brake pedal feels firm again.

Using a one-way valve kit

21 As their name implies, these kits consist of a length of tubing with a one-way valve fitted, to prevent expelled air and fluid being drawn back into the system; some kits include a translucent container, which can be positioned so that the air bubbles can be more easily seen flowing from the end of the tube **(see illustration)**.

22 The kit is connected to the bleed screw, which is then opened. The user returns to the driver's seat, depresses the brake pedal with a smooth, steady stroke, and slowly releases it; this is repeated until the expelled fluid is clear of air bubbles.

23 Note that these kits simplify work so much that it is easy to forget the master cylinder reservoir fluid level; ensure that this is maintained at least above the MIN level line at all times.

Using a pressure-bleeding kit

24 These kits are usually operated by the reservoir of pressurised air contained in a spare tyre. However, note that it will probably be necessary to reduce the pressure to a lower level than normal; refer to the instructions supplied with the kit. **Note:** *Mercedes-Benz specify that a pressure of 2 bar (29 psi) should not be exceeded.*

25 By connecting a pressurised, fluid-filled container to the master cylinder reservoir, bleeding can be carried out simply by opening each brake caliper bleed screw in turn (in the specified sequence – see paragraph 12), and allowing the fluid to flow out until no more air bubbles can be seen in the expelled fluid.

26 This method has the advantage that the large reservoir of fluid provides an additional safeguard against air being drawn into the system during bleeding.

27 Pressure-bleeding is particularly effective when bleeding 'difficult' systems, or when bleeding the complete system at the time of routine fluid renewal.

All methods

28 When bleeding is complete, and firm pedal feel is restored, wash off any spilt fluid, tighten the bleed screws to the specified torque, and refit their dust caps.

29 Check the hydraulic fluid level in the master cylinder reservoir, and top-up if necessary (see *Weekly checks*).

30 Discard any hydraulic fluid that has been bled from the system; it will not be fit for re-use.

31 Check the feel of the brake pedal. If it feels at all spongy, air must still be present in the system, and further bleeding is required. Failure to bleed satisfactorily after a reasonable repetition of the bleeding procedure may be due to worn master cylinder seals.

2.21 Bleeding a rear brake caliper

3 Hydraulic pipes and hoses – renewal

Note: *Before starting work, refer to the warnings at the beginning of Section 2.*

1 If any pipe or hose is to be renewed, minimise fluid loss by first removing the master cylinder reservoir cap, then tightening it down onto a piece of polythene to obtain an airtight seal. Alternatively, flexible hoses can be sealed, if required, using a proprietary brake hose clamp; metal brake pipe unions can be plugged (if care is taken not to allow dirt into the system) or capped immediately they are disconnected. Place a wad of rag under any union that is to be disconnected, to catch any spilt fluid.

2 If a flexible hose is to be disconnected, unscrew the brake pipe union nut before removing the spring clip, which secures the hose to its mounting bracket **(see illustration)**.

3 To unscrew the union nuts, it is preferable to obtain a brake pipe spanner of the correct size; these are available from most large motor accessory shops. Failing this, a close-fitting open-ended spanner will be required, though if the nuts are tight or corroded, their flats may be rounded-off if the spanner slips. In such a case, a self-locking wrench is often the only way to unscrew a stubborn union, but it follows that the pipe and the damaged nuts must be renewed on reassembly. Always clean a union and surrounding area before disconnecting it; this helps to prevent the entry of dirt into the hydraulic system. If disconnecting a component with more than one union, make

3.2 Brake hose retaining clip

4.2a Disconnect the wear sensor wiring connector . . .

4.2b . . . and unclip the wiring from the clips under the wheel arch

4.3 Caliper guide pin bolts

a careful note of the connections before disturbing any of them.

4 If a brake pipe is to be renewed, it can be obtained, cut to length and with the union nuts and end flares in place, from Mercedes-Benz dealers. All that is then necessary is to bend it to shape, following the line of the original, before fitting it to the car. Alternatively, most motor accessory shops can make up brake pipes from kits, but this requires very careful measurement of the original, to ensure that the new one is of the correct length. The safest answer is usually to take the original to the shop as a pattern.

5 On refitting, do not overtighten the union nuts. It is not necessary to exercise brute force to obtain a sound joint!

6 Ensure that the pipes and hoses are correctly routed, with no kinks, and that they are secured in the clips or brackets provided. After fitting, remove the polythene from the reservoir, and bleed the hydraulic system as

described in Section 2. Wash off any spilt fluid, and check carefully for fluid leaks.

7 Finally, test the operation of the braking system exhaustively, before bringing the car back into service on the road.

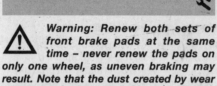

4 Front brake pads – renewal

⚠️ *Warning: Renew both sets of front brake pads at the same time – never renew the pads on only one wheel, as uneven braking may result. Note that the dust created by wear of the pads may contain asbestos, which is a health hazard. Never blow it out with compressed air, and do not inhale any of it. An approved filtering mask should be worn when working on the brakes. DO NOT use petrol or petroleum-based solvents*

to clean brake parts; use brake cleaner or methylated spirit only.

Note: *New caliper guide pin bolts will be required on refitting.*

1 Chock the rear wheels and firmly apply the parking brake. Loosen the front wheel bolts, and then jack up the front of the car and support it on axle stands (see *Jacking and vehicle support*). Remove the appropriate front roadwheel.

Floating calipers

2 Disconnect the wear sensor connector from the caliper housing. Unclip the wear sensor wiring from the clips under the wheel arch **(see illustrations)**.

3 Slacken and remove both caliper guide pin bolts, and remove the caliper from the mounting bracket **(see illustration)**. Tie the caliper up to a convenient point, so that the brake hose is not strained.

4 Withdraw the two brake pads from the caliper mounting bracket, noting the correct fitted location of the wear sensor (on the inner pad). Recover the heat shield fitted around the caliper piston, where applicable, noting how it is fitted **(see illustrations)**.

5 First measure the thickness of each brake pad's friction material (excluding the metal backplate). If either pad is worn at any point to the specified minimum thickness or less, all four pads must be renewed. Also, the pads should be renewed if any of them are fouled with oil or grease. There is no satisfactory way of degreasing friction material, once contaminated. If any of the brake pads are worn unevenly, or are fouled with oil or grease, trace and rectify the cause before reassembly. Inspect the wear sensor for signs of damage, and renew if necessary. New brake pad kits are available from Mercedes-Benz dealers.

6 If the brake pads are still serviceable, carefully clean them using a clean, fine wire brush or similar, paying particular attention to the sides and back of the metal backing. Clean out the grooves in the friction material (where applicable), and pick out any large embedded particles of dirt or debris. Carefully clean the pad locations in the caliper body/mounting bracket.

7 Prior to fitting the pads, check the pins are free to slide easily in the caliper bracket, and are a reasonably tight fit. Ensure that the guide

4.4a Remove the outer brake pad . . .

4.4b . . . and the inner brake pad

4.7a Remove the guide pin . . .

4.7b . . . and lubricate with clean grease

pin gaiters are undamaged. Clean the guide pin and inspect for wear, apply a coat of high-temperature grease and re-assemble. Remove all traces of locking compound from the guide pin threads using a tap of the correct thread size and pitch (see illustrations).

8 Brush the dust and dirt from the caliper and piston, but *do not* inhale it, as it may contain asbestos, which is a health hazard. Inspect the dust seal around the piston for damage, and the piston itself for evidence of fluid leaks, corrosion or damage. If any such deterioration is found, the caliper must be overhauled – refer to Section 8 for details.

9 If new brake pads are to be fitted, the caliper piston must be pushed back into the cylinder to make room for them. Either use a G-clamp or similar tool, or use suitable pieces of wood as levers (see illustration). Provided that the master cylinder reservoir has not been overfilled with hydraulic fluid, there should be no spillage, but keep a careful watch on the fluid level while retracting the piston. If the fluid level rises above the MAX level line at any time, the surplus should be syphoned off or ejected through a plastic tube connected to the bleed screw (see Section 2).

 Warning: Do not syphon the fluid by mouth, as it is poisonous; use a syringe or an old antifreeze tester.

10 Apply a smear of brake grease to the backing plate of each pad (Mercedes-Benz recommend the use of brake paste – number 001 989 10 51); do not apply excess grease or allow the grease to contact the friction material (see illustration).

11 Check that the anti-rattle clips are fitted correctly in the caliper mounting bracket (see illustrations).

12 Clip the pad wear sensor (where removed) securely in position (see illustration), and then fit the pads to the caliper mounting bracket, ensuring that their friction material is against the brake disc. Where applicable, refit the heat shield around the caliper piston.

13 Refit the caliper into position over the pads, passing the wear sensor wiring up through the caliper aperture.

14 Ensure that the pad anti-rattle springs are correctly positioned against the caliper housing, then press down on the caliper and install the guide pin bolts. Tighten the bolts to the specified torque setting while retaining the guide pin with an open-ended spanner.

15 Reconnect the wear sensor wiring connector to the caliper, making sure the excess wiring is wrapped neatly around the connector. Ensure that the connector is correctly fitted, and clip the sensor cover into the caliper aperture.

16 Depress the brake pedal repeatedly, until the pads are pressed into firm contact with the brake disc, and normal (non-assisted) pedal pressure is restored.

17 Repeat the above procedure on the remaining front brake caliper.

18 Refit the roadwheels, then lower the car to

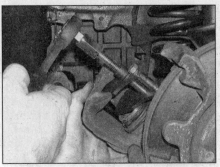

4.9 Using a proprietary tool for pushing the piston back into the caliper

4.10 Apply brake grease to the backing plate

4.11a Check the upper . . .

4.11b . . . and lower clips are secure

the ground and tighten the roadwheel bolts to the specified torque setting.

19 Check the hydraulic fluid level as described in *Weekly checks*. Test the operation of the braking system exhaustively, before bringing the car back into service on the road.

 Warning: New pads will not give full braking efficiency until they have 'bedded in'. Be prepared for this – avoid hard braking, as far as possible, for the first hundred miles or so after pad renewal.

Fixed calipers

20 Where fitted, pull the pad wear sensor wiring connectors out from the caliper body, noting the correct routing of the wiring.

21 Using a hammer and suitable punch, carefully tap out the pad retaining pins towards the inside, and recover the anti-rattle spring, noting its fitted position (see illustration).

22 Slide the pads out from the caliper body, and where applicable, recover the shims, which are fitted between the pads and pistons.

23 Inspect the brake pads as described in paragraphs 5 and 6 of this Section. Renew the anti-rattle spring, pad retaining pin(s) and shims (as applicable) if the pads are to be renewed.

24 Prior to fitting the pads, brush the dust and dirt from the caliper and pistons, but *do not* inhale it, as it is a health hazard. Inspect the dust seals around each piston for damage, and the pistons for evidence of fluid leaks, corrosion or damage. If any such deterioration is found, the caliper must be overhauled – refer to Section 8 for details.

25 If new brake pads are to be fitted, the caliper pistons must be pushed back into the cylinder to make room for them. Carefully

4.12 Check that the sensor wire is fitted

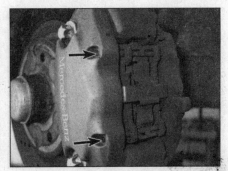

4.21 Brake pad retaining pins

4.25 Carefully lever the piston back

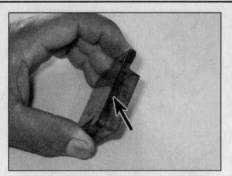

4.26 Apply brake grease along side edges of backing plate

prise the pistons back into position using a suitable lever **(see illustration)**. Provided that the master cylinder reservoir has not been overfilled with hydraulic fluid, there should be no spillage, but keep a careful watch on the fluid level while retracting the piston. If the fluid level rises above the MAX level line at any time, the surplus should be syphoned off or ejected through a plastic tube connected to the bleed screw (see Section 2).

⚠ *Warning: Do not syphon the fluid by mouth, as it is poisonous; use a syringe or an old antifreeze tester.*

26 On brake pads equipped with anti-squeal shims, **do not** apply any lubricant to the pads. Where the pad backing plates are plain and no shim is fitted, apply a smear of copper brake grease to the side edges of the pad backing plate (Mercedes-Benz recommend the use of brake paste – number 001 989 10 51); do not apply excess grease or allow the grease to

contact the friction material **(see illustration)**.
27 Where fitted, ensure that the wear sensors are clipped securely into the backing plate of each pad and fit the shims to the back of each pad.
28 Slide the brake pads and (where applicable) shims into position in the caliper; making sure the friction material of each pad is against the brake disc.
29 Fit the new anti-rattle spring to the top of the pads, making sure it is fitted correctly.
30 Slide in the pad retaining pins over the anti-rattle spring from the inside, and tap fully into place up to the stop.
31 Where fitted ensure that the wiring is correctly routed, and connect the wear sensor connectors to the caliper body.
32 Depress the brake pedal repeatedly, until the pads are pressed into firm contact with the brake disc, and normal (non-assisted) pedal pressure is restored.

33 Repeat the above procedure on the remaining brake caliper.
34 Refit the roadwheels, then lower the car to the ground and tighten the roadwheel bolts to the specified torque setting.
35 Check the hydraulic fluid level as described in *Weekly checks*. Test the operation of the braking system exhaustively, before bringing the car back into service on the road.

⚠ *Warning: New pads will not give full braking efficiency until they have 'bedded in'. Be prepared for this – and avoid hard braking, as far as possible, for the first hundred miles or so after pad renewal.*

5 Rear brake pads – renewal

⚠ *Warning: Renew both sets of rear brake pads at the same time – never renew the pads on only one wheel, as uneven braking may result. Note that the dust created by wear of the pads may contain asbestos, which is a health hazard. Never blow it out with compressed air, and do not inhale any of it. An approved filtering mask should be worn when working on the brakes. DO NOT use petrol or petroleum-based solvents to clean brake parts; use brake cleaner or methylated spirit only.*

1 Chock the front wheels and loosen the rear wheel bolts. Jack up the rear of the car and support it on axle stands (see *Jacking and vehicle support*). Remove the rear roadwheels.
2 Where fitted, pull the pad wear sensor wiring connectors out from the caliper body, noting the correct routing of the wiring.
3 Using a hammer and suitable punch, carefully tap out the pad retaining pin towards the inside, and recover the anti-rattle spring, noting its fitted position **(see illustrations)**.
4 Slide the pads out from the caliper body, and where applicable, recover the shims, which are fitted between the pads and pistons **(see illustrations)**.
5 Inspect the brake pads as described in paragraphs 5 and 6 of Section 4. Renew the anti-rattle spring, pad retaining pin(s) and shims (as applicable) if the pads are to be renewed.
6 Prior to fitting the pads, brush the dust and dirt from the caliper and pistons **(see illustration)**, but *do not* inhale it, as it is a health hazard. Inspect the dust seals around each piston for damage, and the pistons for evidence of fluid leaks, corrosion or damage. If any such deterioration is found, the caliper must be overhauled – refer to Section 9 for details.
7 If new brake pads are to be fitted, the caliper pistons must be pushed back into the cylinder to make room for them. Carefully prise the pistons back into position using a

5.3a Tap out the retaining pin . . .

5.3b . . . and remove the anti-rattle spring

5.4a Withdraw the outer . . .

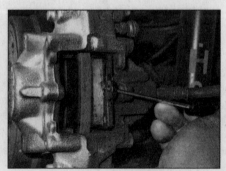

5.4b . . . and inner brake pad

suitable lever **(see illustration)**. Provided that the master cylinder reservoir has not been overfilled with hydraulic fluid, there should be no spillage, but keep a careful watch on the fluid level while retracting the piston. If the fluid level rises above the MAX level line at any time, the surplus should be syphoned off or ejected through a plastic tube connected to the bleed screw (see Section 2).

⚠️ **Warning: Do not syphon the fluid by mouth, as it is poisonous; use a syringe or an old antifreeze tester.**

8 On brake pads equipped with anti-squeal shims, **do not** apply any lubricant to the pads. Where the pad backing plates are plain and no shim is fitted, apply a smear of copper brake grease to the side edges of the pad backing plate (Mercedes-Benz recommend the use of brake paste – number 001 989 10 51); do not apply excess grease or allow the grease to contact the friction material **(see illustration)**.

9 Where fitted, ensure that the wear sensors are clipped securely into the backing plate of each pad and fit the shims to the back of each pad.

10 Slide the brake pads and (where applicable) shims into position in the caliper; making sure the friction material of each pad is against the brake disc.

11 Fit the new anti-rattle spring to the top of the pads, making sure it is fitted the right way up.

12 Slide in the pad retaining pins over the anti-rattle spring from the inside, and tap fully into place up to the stop **(see illustration)**.

13 Where fitted ensure that the wiring is correctly routed, and connect the wear sensor connectors to the caliper body.

14 Depress the brake pedal repeatedly, until the pads are pressed into firm contact with the brake disc, and normal (non-assisted) pedal pressure is restored.

15 Repeat the above procedure on the remaining rear caliper.

16 Refit the roadwheels, then lower the car to the ground and tighten the roadwheel bolts to the specified torque setting.

17 Check the hydraulic fluid level as described in *Weekly checks*. Test the operation of the braking system exhaustively, before bringing the car back into service on the road.

⚠️ **Warning: New pads will not give full braking efficiency until they have 'bedded in'. Be prepared for this – and avoid hard braking, as far as possible, for the first hundred miles or so after pad renewal.**

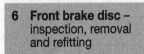

6 Front brake disc –
inspection, removal and refitting

Note: *Before starting work, refer to the note at the beginning of Section 4 concerning the dangers of asbestos dust.*

Inspection

Note: *If either disc requires renewal, BOTH*

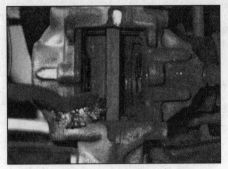

5.6 Clean out the caliper body

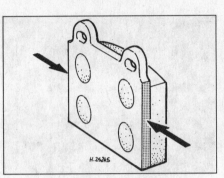

5.8 If the pads have no shims, apply suitable lubricant to the edges of the backing plate (arrowed)

should be renewed at the same time, to ensure even and consistent braking. New brake pads should also be fitted.

1 Chock the rear wheels and firmly apply the parking brake. Loosen the front wheel bolts, and then jack up the front of the car and support on axle stands (see *Jacking and vehicle support*). Remove the appropriate front roadwheel.

2 Slowly rotate the brake disc so that the full area of both sides can be checked; remove the brake pads if better access is required to the inboard surface. Light scoring is normal in the area swept by the brake pads, but if heavy scoring or cracks are found, the disc must be renewed.

3 It is normal to find a lip of loose rust and brake dust around the disc's perimeter; this can be scraped off if required. However, if a lip of solid material has formed due to

6.3 Using a micrometer to measure the brake disc thickness

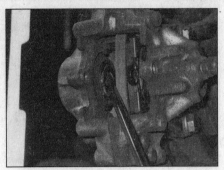

5.7 Lever back the caliper piston

5.12 Tap the pad retaining pin(s) in from the inside

excessive wear of the brake pad swept area, then the disc thickness must be measured using a micrometer **(see illustration)**. Take measurements at several places around the disc, and at the inside and outside edges of the pad swept area; if the disc has worn at *any* point to the specified minimum thickness or less, the disc must be renewed.

4 If the disc is thought to be warped, it can be checked for runout, but first eliminate wheel bearing play as the cause of the problem, with reference to Chapter 10, Section 2.

5 To check the disc runout, fit large, plain washers under the heads of two of the wheel bolts, and then bolt them to the hub through the disc. Position the wheel bolts diagonally opposite each other, to ensure that the disc seats evenly, then tighten the bolts securely. Either use a dial gauge mounted on any convenient fixed point, while the disc is slowly

6.5 Checking disc runout with a dial gauge (rear disc shown – procedure for front disc similar)

6.8 Brake caliper mounting bracket bolts

6.9 Brake disc retaining screw

6.11 Clean out the threads with a tap

6.12a Clean out the inside of the disc . . .

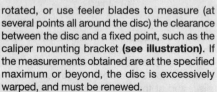

6.12b . . . and the surface of the hub

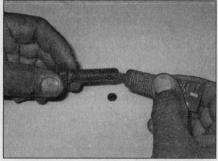

6.14 Apply thread-lock to the bolts

rotated, or use feeler blades to measure (at several points all around the disc) the clearance between the disc and a fixed point, such as the caliper mounting bracket **(see illustration)**. If the measurements obtained are at the specified maximum or beyond, the disc is excessively warped, and must be renewed.

6 Check the disc for cracks, especially around the wheel bolt holes, and any other wear or damage, and renew if necessary.

Removal

Note: *New brake caliper mounting bolts and disc retaining screws will be required on refitting.*

7 Remove the front brake caliper as described in Section 4.

8 Unscrew the two bolts securing the brake caliper mounting bracket to the steering knuckle, then remove the mounting bracket off the disc **(see illustration)**. Discard the bolts; new ones must be used on refitting.

9 Slacken and remove the screw securing the brake disc to the hub **(see illustration)**. Discard the screw, as a new one should be used on refitting.

10 Remove the disc from the hub, noting the correct fitted position. If it is tight, lightly tap its rear face with a hide or plastic mallet.

Refitting

11 Prior to refitting, remove all traces of old locking compound from the caliper bolt hole threads in the mounting bracket by running a tap of the correct thread size and pitch down them **(see illustration)**. Clean the disc retaining screw threads in the hub in the same way.

12 Ensure that the mating surfaces of the disc

and hub are clean and flat **(see illustrations)**. If a new disc has been fitted, use a suitable solvent to wipe any preservative coating from the disc. Apply a thin coat of high-temperature grease to the mating surface of the hub, but ensure that the surface of the disc is not contaminated.

13 Refit the disc to the hub; making sure it is correctly located as noted on removal. Fit the new disc retaining screw and tighten it to the specified torque setting.

14 Refit the caliper mounting bracket over the brake disc and into position on the steering knuckle. Apply some thread-lock to the new bolts and tighten to the specified torque setting **(see illustration)**.

15 Refit the brake caliper with reference to Section 4.

16 Refit the roadwheel, then lower the car to the ground and tighten the roadwheel bolts to the specified torque. On completion, repeatedly depress the brake pedal until normal (non-assisted) pedal pressure returns. Test the operation of the braking system

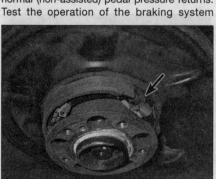

7.5 Parking brake adjusting wheel

exhaustively before bringing the car back into service on the road.

7 Rear brake disc –
inspection, removal
and refitting

Note: *Before starting work, refer to the note at the beginning of Section 4 concerning the dangers of asbestos dust.*

Inspection

Note: *If either disc requires renewal, BOTH should be renewed at the same time, to ensure even and consistent braking. New brake pads should also be fitted.*

1 Firmly chock the front wheels, and then loosen the rear wheel bolts. Jack up the rear of the car and support it on axle stands (see *Jacking and vehicle support*). Remove the appropriate rear roadwheel.

2 Inspect the disc as described in Section 6 (see paragraphs 2 to 6).

Removal

3 Remove the rear brake caliper as described in Section 9.

4 Slacken and remove the screw securing the brake disc to the hub. Discard the screw, as a new one should be used on refitting.

5 Remove the disc from the hub, noting the correct fitted position. Ensure that the parking brake is fully released before trying to remove the disc. If the disc is still tight on the shoes with the brake fully released, slacken the parking brake adjustment as described in Section 13 **(see illustration)**.

Refitting

6 Ensure that the mating surfaces of the disc and hub are clean and flat. If a new disc has been fitted, use a suitable solvent to wipe any preservative coating from the disc. Apply a thin coat of high-temperature grease to the mating surface of the hub, but ensure that the surface of the disc is not contaminated.

7 Refit the disc to the hub; making sure it is correctly located as noted on removal. Fit the new disc retaining screw and tighten it to the specified torque setting.

8 Refit the rear brake caliper with reference to Section 9.

9 Refit the roadwheel, then lower the car to the ground and tighten the roadwheel bolts to the specified torque. On completion, repeatedly depress the brake pedal until normal (non-assisted) pedal pressure returns.

10 On completion, adjust the parking brake as described in Section 13. Test the operation of the braking system exhaustively before bringing the car back into service on the road.

8 Front brake caliper – removal, overhaul and refitting

Note: *Before starting work, refer to the note at the beginning of Section 2 concerning the dangers of hydraulic fluid, and to the warning at the beginning of Section 4 concerning the dangers of asbestos dust.*
Note: *New brake caliper guide pin bolts will be required on refitting.*

Removal

1 Chock the rear wheels and firmly apply the parking brake. Loosen the front wheel bolts, and then jack up the front of the car and support it on axle stands (see *Jacking and vehicle support*). Remove the appropriate front roadwheel.

2 Minimise fluid loss by first removing the master cylinder reservoir cap, and then tightening it down onto a piece of polythene, to obtain an airtight seal. Alternatively, use a brake hose clamp or a similar tool to clamp the flexible hose **(see illustration)**. Do not use a G-clamp or any other device with flat jaws as this may pinch the hose, leading to premature failure.

3 Clean the area around the union, and then loosen the brake hose union nut at the rear of the caliper **(see illustration)**.

4 Remove the brake pads as described in Section 4.

5 On floating calipers, unscrew the caliper and remove it from the end of the brake hose. Be prepared for some fluid spillage and plug the ends of the brake hose and caliper to prevent dirt ingress.

6 On fixed calipers, undo the two caliper retaining bolts and remove the caliper from the brake disc. Unscrew the caliper and remove it from the end of the brake hose. Be prepared for some fluid spillage and plug the ends of the brake hose and caliper to prevent dirt ingress.

8.2 Use a brake hose clamp, a G-clamp or a similar tool to clamp the flexible hose

Overhaul

7 At the time of writing, no parts where available to overhaul the calipers. Consequently, if the calipers are faulty, they must be renewed. It may be possible to get exchange units, check with your local Mercedes dealer or brake specialist.

Refitting

8 Remove all traces of old locking compound from the caliper guide pin/bolt hole threads (as applicable) by running a tap of the correct thread size and pitch down them.

9 Screw the caliper fully onto the flexible hose union, using a new sealing washer, where applicable.

10 Offer the caliper up to the mounting bracket and fit the new retaining/guide pin bolts, tightening it to the specified torque setting.

11 Tighten the brake hose union nut to the specified torque and remove the brake hose clamp or polythene (as applicable).

12 Refit the brake pads as described in Section 4 and bleed the hydraulic system as described in Section 2. Note that, providing the precautions described were taken to minimise brake fluid loss, it should only be necessary to bleed the relevant front brake.

13 Refit the roadwheel, then lower the car to the ground and tighten the roadwheel bolts to the specified torque. On completion, check the hydraulic fluid level as described in *Weekly checks*. Test the operation of the braking system exhaustively before bringing the car back into service on the road.

9.3 Rear brake hose union nut

8.3 Front brake hose union nut

9 Rear brake caliper – removal, overhaul and refitting

Note: *Before starting work, refer to the note at the beginning of Section 2 concerning the dangers of hydraulic fluid, and to the warning at the beginning of Section 4 concerning the dangers of asbestos dust.*
Note: *New caliper mounting bolts will be required on refitting.*

Removal

1 Firmly chock the front wheels, then loosen the rear wheel bolts. Jack up the rear of the car and support it on axle stands (see *Jacking and vehicle support*). Remove the appropriate rear roadwheel.

2 Minimise fluid loss by first removing the master cylinder reservoir cap, and then tightening it down onto a piece of polythene, to obtain an airtight seal. Alternatively, use a proprietary brake hose clamp to seal off the flexible hose leading to the caliper **(see illustration 8.2)**. Do not use a G-clamp, or any other device with flat jaws, as this may pinch the hose, leading to premature failure.

3 Clean the area around the union, and then loosen the brake hose union nut **(see illustration)**.

4 Remove the rear brake pads as described in Section 5.

5 Slacken and remove the caliper mounting bolts **(see illustration)**, then unscrew the caliper from the end of the flexible hose and remove it from the car. Discard the mounting

9.5 Caliper mounting bolts

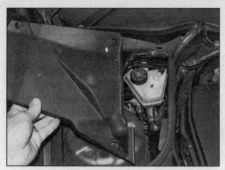

10.2 Remove the trim cover

10.4 Disconnect the wiring connector

10.6 Clutch fluid supply hose

bolts – they should be renewed whenever they are disturbed.
Caution: Never slacken the bolts securing the two halves of the caliper together. If the bolts are slackened and the caliper is body is dismantled, the assembly may leak after reassembly.

Overhaul

6 At the time of writing, no parts where available to overhaul the calipers. Consequently, if the calipers are faulty, they must be renewed. It may be possible to get exchange units, check with your local Mercedes dealer or brake specialist.

Refitting

7 Remove all traces of old locking compound from the caliper bolt hole threads by running a tap of the correct thread size and pitch down them.
8 Screw the caliper fully onto the flexible hose union, using a new sealing washer where applicable.
9 Slide the caliper assembly into position, fit the new mounting bolts, and then tighten them to the specified torque.
10 Tighten the brake hose union nut to the specified torque and remove the brake hose clamp (or the polythene sheet from the fluid reservoir as applicable).
11 Refit the brake pads as described in Section 5 and bleed the hydraulic system as described in Section 2. Note that, providing the precautions described were taken to minimise brake fluid loss, it should only be necessary to bleed the relevant rear brake.

12 Refit the roadwheel, then lower the car to the ground and tighten the roadwheel bolts to the specified torque. On completion, check the hydraulic fluid level as described in *Weekly checks*. Test the operation of the braking system exhaustively before bringing the car back into service on the road.

10 Master cylinder – removal, overhaul and refitting

Note: Before starting work, refer to the warning at the beginning of Section 2 concerning the dangers of hydraulic fluid.

Removal

1 Disconnect the battery negative terminal and then depress the brake pedal several times to remove the vacuum from the brake servo unit.
2 Undo the retaining clips and remove the cover from the top of the brake fluid reservoir **(see illustration)**.
3 Place some absorbent rags below the master cylinder, and clean the area around the master cylinder and brake lines.
4 Disconnect the wiring connector from the brake fluid level sender unit **(see illustration)**.
5 Remove the master cylinder reservoir cap, and syphon the hydraulic fluid from the reservoir. Alternatively, open any convenient bleed screw in the system, and gently pump the brake pedal to expel the fluid through a plastic tube connected to the screw.

⚠ *Warning: Do not syphon the fluid by mouth, as it is poisonous; use a syringe or an old antifreeze tester.*
6 On manual transmission models, disconnect the clutch fluid hose from the side of the reservoir and plug the hose ends to minimise fluid loss **(see illustration)**.
7 Disconnect the wiring connector from the brake pressure sensor in the master cylinder **(see illustration)**. Note: *Some models have two sensors fitted; the second sensor is below the master cylinder and can be disconnected as the master cylinder is removed.*
8 Wipe clean the area around the brake pipe unions on the side and front of the master cylinder, and place absorbent rags beneath the pipe unions to catch any surplus fluid. Make a note of the correct fitted positions of the unions, then unscrew the union nuts and carefully withdraw the pipes. Plug or tape over the pipe ends and master cylinder orifices, to minimise the loss of brake fluid, and to prevent the entry of dirt into the system. Wash off any spilt fluid immediately with cold water.
9 Release the spring clip **(see illustration)**, undo the bracket retaining bolt and remove the mounting bracket from the front of the master cylinder. A new spring clip will be required for refitting.
10 Slacken and remove the nuts and washers securing the master cylinder to the vacuum servo unit, then withdraw the unit forwards and away from servo unit. Note: *Do not tilt the master cylinder until it is disengaged from the servo unit pushrod, otherwise the servo unit will be damaged.* Remove the sealing ring from the rear of the master cylinder.

Overhaul

11 Mercedes-Benz states that this type of master cylinder must not be repaired. It is therefore unlikely that any spare parts or repair kits are available. Consult your Mercedes-Benz dealer or parts supplier for up-to-date information.

Refitting

12 Remove all traces of dirt from the master cylinder and servo unit mating surfaces, and fit a new sealing ring to the rear of the master cylinder body.
13 Fit the master cylinder to the servo unit, ensuring that the servo unit pushrod enters

10.7 Brake pressure sensor

10.9 Master cylinder retaining clip

the master cylinder bore centrally, and keeping the master cylinder horizontal until it is fully engaged. Refit the master cylinder retaining nuts and tighten them to the specified torque.

14 Wipe clean the brake pipe unions, then refit them to the master cylinder ports and tighten them to the specified torque.

15 On manual transmission models, reconnect the clutch fluid hose to the side of the reservoir.

16 Reconnect the wiring connectors to the brake pressure sensor and the fluid level sensor.

17 Refill the master cylinder reservoir with new fluid, and bleed the complete hydraulic system as described in Section 2. Test the operation of the braking system exhaustively before bringing the car back into service on the road.

11 Vacuum servo unit – testing, removal and refitting

Testing

1 To test the operation of the servo unit, depress the footbrake several times with the engine off, to exhaust the vacuum from the servo. Now start the engine whilst keeping the pedal firmly depressed. There should be a noticeable 'give' in the brake pedal as the engine starts and the vacuum builds-up.

2 Allow the engine to run for at least two minutes, and then switch it off. If the brake pedal is now depressed it should feel normal, but further applications should result in the pedal feeling progressively firmer, with the pedal stroke decreasing on each application.

3 If the servo does not operate as described, first inspect the servo unit check valve as described in Section 12.

4 If the servo unit still fails to operate satisfactorily, the fault lies within the unit itself. Repairs to the unit are not possible – if faulty, the servo unit must be renewed.

Removal

Note: *New retaining nuts will be required on refitting.*

5 Remove the master cylinder as described in Section 10.

11.7 Vacuum pipe(s) from servo

11.9b . . . unclip the wiring harness . . .

6 Remove the windscreen wiper motor and linkage as described in Chapter 12.

7 Pull the vacuum pipe to release it from the top of the servo unit (see illustration).

8 Disconnect the wiring connectors from the sensors fitted in the servo unit.

9 Remove the foam insulator, and then release the wiring loom from across the top of the brake servo unit. On some models, it may be necessary to withdraw the ECU from the engine fusebox, so the wiring harness can be moved to one side (see illustrations).

10 Working inside the vehicle, slide the driver's seat backwards, as far as it will go, and then remove the driver's side lower facia panel as described in Chapter 11.

11 Release the retaining clips and remove the plastic cover from the top of the brake pedal (see illustration).

12 Where fitted, disconnect the wiring connector from the brake pedal switch and

11.9a Remove the foam pad . . .

11.9c . . . from the fusebox

remove the switch from the pedal mounting bracket.

13 Carefully release the securing clip (see illustration) from the brake pedal pin that operates the servo pushrod, with the clip removed withdraw the pin from the brake pedal.

14 Slacken and remove the servo unit retaining nuts (see illustration), and then return to the engine compartment and remove the servo unit from the bulkhead.

Refitting

15 Prior to refitting, check the condition of the gasket, which is fitted to the rear of the servo unit. If the gasket shows signs of wear or damage, fit a new one.

16 The remainder of the refitting procedure is a reversal of removal, noting the following points:

a) *Ensure that the servo unit pushrod is correctly engaged with the brake pedal.*

11.11 Remove the plastic cover

11.13 Release the retaining clip

11.14 Brake servo mounting nuts

13.8a Using a screwdriver . . .

13.8b . . . through the stud hole . . .

13.8c . . . to turn the brake adjuster

b) Tighten the servo retaining nuts to the specified torque.
c) Make sure the brake servo pipe is fitted securely in the servo unit.
d) Refit the driver's side lower facia panel with reference to Chapter 11.
e) Refit the master cylinder as described in Section 10.

17 On completion, start the engine and check for air leaks at the vacuum hose-to-servo unit connection; check the operation of the braking system before using the car on the road.

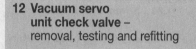

12 Vacuum servo unit check valve – removal, testing and refitting

Removal

1 Pull the vacuum hose connection to disconnect the vacuum hose from the servo unit.
2 Trace the hose back, then disconnect it from the inlet manifold/pump connection (as applicable) and remove the hose and valve assembly from the engine compartment.

Testing

3 Examine the vacuum hose, check the valve for signs of damage, and renew if necessary.
4 The valve may be tested by blowing through the hose in both directions; air should flow through the valve in one direction only – when blown through from the servo unit end of the hose. Renew the hose assembly if this is not the case.

13.13 Undo the cover plate fasteners

Refitting

5 Ensuring that the hose is correctly routed, securely reconnect it to the manifold/pump (as applicable), and the servo unit.
6 On completion, start the engine and check the valve to servo unit connection for signs of air leaks. Test the operation of the braking system exhaustively before bringing the car back into service on the road.

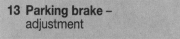

13 Parking brake – adjustment

Note: If the parking brake shoe clearance or cable-adjusting nut requires a significant amount of adjustment, it is advisable to inspect the brake shoe lining thickness.

1 The parking brake cable is self-adjusting on all models. The following procedure is intended merely to compensate for wear of the shoe friction material, which should occur at a very slow and even rate and make routine adjustment unnecessary.
2 The parking brake should be fully applied when five clicks are heard from the ratchet mechanism. Before deciding that shoe adjustment is required, confirm that the cables are operating correctly, and are not broken or seized. After several years' service, it is possible that the parking brake cables may have stretched too far for compensation by the automatic adjuster.
3 One method of checking the parking brake is to park the vehicle on a steep hill with the parking brake applied, and the transmission in

13.14 Adjust the retaining nut

neutral (make sure you stay inside the vehicle for this check). If the parking brake cannot prevent the vehicle from rolling, it is in need of adjustment.
4 There are two areas of adjustment for the parking brake: the star wheel adjuster at the top of the brake shoes on each wheel and the adjusting nut on the front of the handbrake cable. First you will need to carry out the adjustment at the brake shoes.
5 Slacken one of the rear wheel bolts on each rear wheel, before jacking up the car.
6 Firmly chock the front wheels, then jack up the rear of the car and support it on axle stands (see Jacking and vehicle support). Release the parking brake completely. Remove the two wheel bolts (one on each wheel), which had been slackened previously.
7 Turn the wheel so that access can be gained to the parking brake shoe adjuster, situated between the parking brake shoes, at the top.
8 Using a long slim screwdriver engaged in the teeth of the adjuster, turn the adjuster until the parking brake shoes make contact and the wheel can no longer be turned (see illustrations). Repeat the procedure on the other rear wheel. To apply the brake shoes, the adjuster on the left-hand wheel is turned from the bottom upwards, with that on the right-hand wheel being turned from the top downwards.
9 Noting the exact number of strokes required to do so, back off the brake shoe adjuster so that the rear wheel is completely free to turn. Repeat the procedure on the other rear wheel, turning the adjuster by exactly the same amount.
10 Check the operation of the parking brake by gradually applying it, and confirm that the rear wheels both start to 'drag' at the same point. Also check that the parking brake is fully applied when five clicks are heard from the ratchet.
11 Further adjustment can be made at the adjustment nut on the handbrake cable.
12 Remove the rear seat cushion as described in Chapter 11, and then pull back the carpet from the floor panel.
13 Undo the retaining screws and remove the cover from the floor panel (see illustration).
14 Adjust the nut on the adjustment linkage until the correct number of clicks are heard from the parking brake lever (see illustrations).

15 On completion, refit the rear wheel bolts and lower the car to the ground. Tighten the wheel bolts to the specified torque.

14 Parking brake pedal – removal and refitting

Removal

1 Disconnect the parking brake front cable from the cable adjuster under the rear seat cushion as described in Section 15, paragraphs 7 to 8.

2 Remove the driver's side lower facia panel as described in Chapter 11, Section 37, and detach the carpet as required for access to the parking brake pedal.

3 Pull on the cable inner to gain some slack, and then unhook the cable end fitting from the pedal **(see illustration)**. Removing the cable outer completely requires that the clamping ring be destroyed (obtain a new ring for refitting) – also recover the rubber grommet.

4 The pedal bracket can now be withdrawn from its location. The bracket is secured by two or three bolts, depending on model – it is recommended that the lowest bolt is only loosened, not removed **(see illustration)**. Note that the Torx bolts on the pedal bracket should not be loosened. Unhook the pedal bracket from the facia support bar for access to the wiring and hand control cable.

5 Disconnect the parking brake warning light switch wiring connector from the top of the pedal bracket.

6 Unhook the hand control cable outer and end fitting with reference to Section 15, then remove the cable outer from the location next to the warning light switch.

7 Remove the pedal bracket completely from the car, unhooking it from the lower mounting bolt if it was not removed.

Refitting

8 Refitting is a reversal of removal, noting the following points:

a) *Use a new clamping ring to secure the cable outer to the pedal bracket, locating the ring into the groove in the cable.*

b) *To reset the parking brake adjuster, refer to Section 13.*

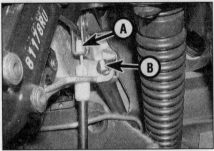

14.3 Parking brake pedal cable end fitting (A) and one of the pedal bracket mounting bolts (B)

c) *Operate the parking brake several times to confirm correct operation.*

15 Parking brake cables – removal and refitting

Hand control cable

Removal

1 Remove the driver's lower facia panel as described in Chapter 11, Section 37.

2 Pull out the parking brake handle to its fullest extent.

3 Release the handle from behind, and unhook it from its location in the facia. Press the cable inner to the right and upwards to release the end fitting from the handle, then disconnect the cable inner and outer from the handle **(see illustrations)**.

15.3a Release the handle from the facia . . .

14.4 Parking brake pedal bracket lower mounting bolt

4 The cable runs over the main foot pedals – trace the line of the cable, releasing it from any clips or cable-ties.

5 The cable outer is secured to the parking brake foot pedal bracket by a clip, which must be prised to the left before the cable can be lifted upwards and removed. Unhook the end fitting from the pedal **(see illustrations)**.

Refitting

6 Refitting is a reversal of removal. Check for correct operation on completion.

Foot pedal cable

Removal

7 Remove the rear seat cushion as described in Chapter 11.

8 Remove the three securing nuts from the access cover under the cushion, and lift out the cover **(see illustration)**.

9 Slacken the adjusting nut and disconnect

15.3b . . . then unhook the cable inner and release the cable outer

15.5a Using a small screwdriver, prise the cable outer locking clip to the left . . .

15.5b . . . then release the cable outer from the pedal bracket

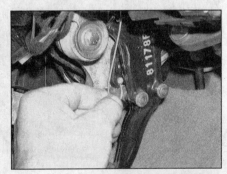

15.5c Unhook the cable end fitting from the pedal

15.8 Removing the access cover . . .

15.9 . . . and slacken the adjuster nut

15.13 Remove the heat shield

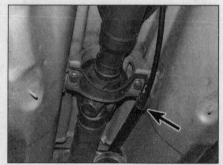

15.14 Handbrake retaining clip

c) Operate the parking brake several times to confirm correct operation.

Rear cables

Removal

16 Remove the relevant set of parking brake shoes as described in Section 16 and detach the expander mechanism from the end of the cable.

17 Remove the cable outer from the rear hub by unscrewing the mounting bolt securing the cable endplate.

18 Remove the rear seat cushion as described in Chapter 11.

19 Remove the securing nuts from the access cover under the cushion, and lift out the cover **(see illustration 15.8)**.

20 Unhook the front cable end fitting from the intermediate lever under the rear seat, then unhook both rear cables from the cable equaliser bracket **(see illustration)**.

21 Remove the rear cable outers from the fittings on the floorpan by releasing the clamping rings (which may have to be destroyed – obtain new rings for refitting) **(see illustration)**. Withdraw the cables from under the vehicle releasing them from any retaining clips.

Refitting

22 Refitting is a reversal of removal, noting the following points:

a) To reset the parking brake adjuster, refer to Section 13.

b) Operate the parking brake several times to confirm correct operation.

the front cable from the linkage **(see illustration)**

10 Remove the driver's side lower facia panel as described in Chapter 11, and detach the carpet as required for access to the parking brake pedal.

11 Unhook the cable end fitting from the parking brake pedal. Remove the cable outer from the pedal bracket by releasing the clamping ring (which may have to be destroyed – obtain a new ring for refitting) – also recover the rubber grommet.

12 Firmly chock the rear wheels, and then jack up the front of the car and support it on axle stands (see *Jacking and vehicle support*).

13 Remove the centre section of exhaust and

heat shields **(see illustration)**, with reference to Chapter 4C.

14 Trace the front brake cable under the vehicle and withdraw it from under the floorpan, disconnecting it from any retaining clips **(see illustration)**.

Refitting

15 Refitting is a reversal of removal, noting the following points:

a) Use new clamping rings to secure the cable outer to the pedal bracket and intermediate lever bracket, locating the ring into the groove in the cable.

b) To reset the parking brake adjuster, refer to Section 13.

<table>
<tr><td>**16 Parking brake shoes –** removal and refitting</td><td></td></tr>
</table>

Removal

1 Remove the rear brake disc as described in Section 7, making a note of the correct fitted position of all components **(see illustration)**.

15.20 Disconnect the front cable

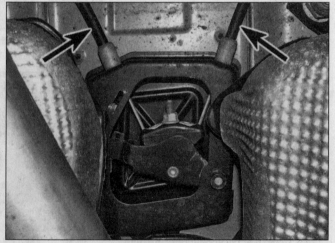

15.21 Remove the rear cables

2 Clean off the parking brake shoe assembly using brake cleaner **(see illustration)**, place rags below the brake assembly to catch any spillage. DO NOT use compressed air to blow out brake dust.

3 Using a pair of thin-nosed pliers, compress the shoe retaining springs then rotate them through 90° and remove them from the backplate. Access to the springs can be gained through the hub flange holes **(see illustration)**.

4 Carefully unhook and remove the parking brake shoe lower return spring, noting which way round the spring is fitted – it is not symmetrical **(see illustration)**.

5 Free the lower ends of the shoes from the lower expander plate, and remove the assembly from the car **(see illustration)**.

6 With the assembly on a bench, note each component's correct fitted location, then unhook the upper return spring and separate the shoes and adjuster assembly.

7 Inspect the parking brake shoes for signs of wear or contamination, and renew if necessary. It is recommended that the return springs are renewed as a matter of course. Check the shoe friction material thickness; shoes with anything less than the minimum friction material given in this Chapter's Specifications should be renewed.

8 With the shoes removed, clean and inspect the condition of the shoe adjuster and expander mechanisms, and renew them if they show signs of wear or damage. If all is well, apply a fresh coat of brake grease (Mercedes-Benz recommend Molykote Paste U or G-Rapid) to the threads of the adjuster and sliding surfaces of the lower expander mechanism. Do not allow the grease to contact the shoe friction material.

Refitting

9 Prior to installation, clean the backplate, and apply a thin smear of high-temperature brake grease (see paragraph 8) or anti-seize compound to all those surfaces of the backplate which bear on the shoes. Do not allow the lubricant to foul the friction material.

10 Assemble the shoes and the adjuster mechanism, noting that the adjuster must be fitted with its knurled ring at the front of the adjuster (facing in the direction of travel). Fully

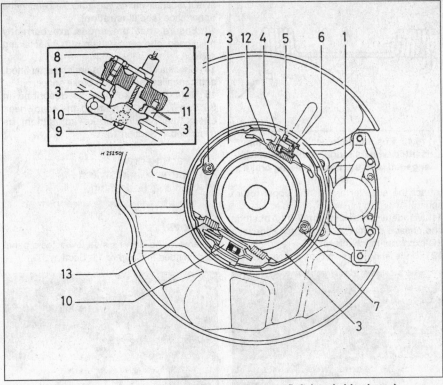

16.1 Layout of parking brake shoe components (left-hand side shown)

1 Brake caliper	5 Adjuster knurled
2 Rear hub carrier	ring
3 Parking brake	6 Adjuster body
shoes	7 Retaining spring
4 Adjuster stud	8 Cable retaining bolt

9 Cable pin
10 Expander mechanism
11 Locating bolts
12 Upper return spring
13 Lower return spring

16.2 Clean off the brake dust

16.3 Release the retaining spring

16.4 Carefully unhook the return spring

16.5a Unhook the lower return spring, noting which way around it is fitted . . .

16.5b . . . and remove the parking brake shoe assembly from the vehicle

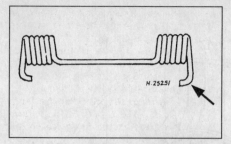

16.12 Ensure the lower return spring is fitted with its longer hook (arrowed) engaged with the upper parking brake shoe

retract the adjuster and fit the upper return spring.

11 Manoeuvre the assembly into position and engage the lower end of each shoe with the expander mechanism.

12 Fit the shoe lower return spring, making

sure it locates with its larger hooked end in the upper shoe **(see illustration)**.

13 Ensure that the shoes are correctly positioned, and secure them with the retaining springs.

14 Check all components are correctly fitted, and centralise the parking brake shoes.

15 Refit the brake disc as described in Section 7. Prior to refitting the roadwheel, check the parking brake adjustment as described in Section 13.

17 Parking brake warning light switch – removal and refitting

Removal

1 Remove the driver's side lower facia panel as described in Chapter 11, Section 37.

17.3 Squeeze the switch retaining lugs to remove it from above the foot pedal

17.4 With the switch removed, disconnect its wiring plug

18.2a Remove the lower wiring plug . . .

18.2b . . . and the upper wiring plug, noting which fits where

18.3 Rotate the switch body, and remove it from the pedal bracket

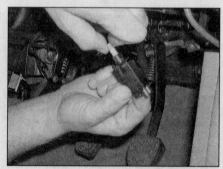

18.4 Pull the switch plunger out fully to reset it

2 The warning light switch is mounted on top of the parking brake pedal bracket.

3 Lift the plastic cover fitted over the switch, then squeeze together the retaining lugs and lift the switch away from the mounting bracket **(see illustration)**.

4 Disconnect the wiring plug from the switch, and remove the switch from the car **(see illustration)**.

Refitting

5 Refitting is a reversal of removal. Check for correct operation on completion.

18 Stop-light switch – removal and refitting

Note: Correct operation of the stop-light switch is essential. Without the signal from the stop-light switch that the brakes have been applied, the ABS will not function. Similarly, if the signal from the switch is delayed (due to the switch plunger sticking, for example), there will be a corresponding delay in operation of the ABS.

Removal

1 Remove the driver's side lower facia panel as described in Chapter 11.

2 Ensure that the ignition is switched off, then disconnect the wiring plug(s) from the stop-light switch **(see illustrations)**.

3 Depress the lug on the side of the switch body, then rotate the switch and withdraw it from the pedal mounting bracket **(see illustration)**.

Refitting

4 Fully extend the stop-light switch plunger from the switch body to reset the switch **(see illustration)**.

5 Fully depress the brake pedal and hold it in position, then manoeuvre the switch into position. Rotate the switch until the locking lug clips into position. Slowly release the brake pedal and allow it to return to its stop. This will automatically adjust the stop-light switch.

6 Reconnect the wiring connector, and check the operation of the stop-lights. The stop-lights should illuminate after the brake pedal has travelled approximately 5 mm. If the switch is not functioning correctly, it is faulty and must be renewed; no other adjustment is possible.

7 On completion, refit the driver's side lower facia panel (see Chapter 11).

19 Anti-lock braking system (ABS) – general information

Note: On models equipped with traction control, the ABS unit is a dual-function unit, and performs both the anti-lock braking system (ABS) and traction control (ASR) system functions. On models with the Electronic

Stability Program (ESP), the ABS unit is also used to modulate the brakes as required.

Without traction control or ESP

1 ABS is fitted to all models as standard. The system comprises the following components:
  a) *A hydraulic unit, which contains four hydraulic solenoid valves (one for each brake) and the electrically-driven return pump.*
  b) *Four roadwheel sensors (one for each wheel) fitted to the wheel hubs.*
  c) *The electronic control unit (ECU), located in the module box at the right-hand rear of the engine compartment (right as seen from the driver's seat).*

2 The purpose of the system is to prevent the wheel(s) locking during heavy braking and/or slippery road conditions. This is achieved by automatic release of the brake on the relevant wheel, followed by re-application of the brake.

3 The solenoids are controlled by the ECU, which itself receives signals from the wheel sensors, which monitor the speed of rotation of each wheel. By comparing these signals with that from the speedometer sensor on the transmission, the ECU can determine the speed at which the vehicle is travelling. It can then use this speed to determine when a wheel is decelerating at an abnormal rate compared to the speed of the vehicle, and therefore predicts when a wheel is about to lock.

4 During normal operation, the system functions in the same way as a non-ABS braking system.

5 If the ECU senses that a wheel is about to lock, it operates the relevant solenoid valve in the hydraulic unit, which then isolates from the master cylinder the relevant brake caliper(s) on the wheel(s) which is/are about to lock – effectively sealing-in the hydraulic pressure.

6 If the speed of rotation of the wheel continues to decrease at an abnormal rate, the ECU switches on the electrically-driven return pump which pumps the hydraulic fluid back into the master cylinder, releasing pressure on the brake caliper(s) so that the brake is released. Once the speed of rotation of the wheel returns to an acceptable rate, the pump stops; the solenoid valve opens, allowing the hydraulic master cylinder pressure to return to the caliper, which then re-applies the brake. This cycle can be carried out at up to 10 times a second.

7 The action of the solenoid valves and return pump creates pulses in the hydraulic circuit. When the ABS system is functioning, these pulses can be felt through the brake pedal.

8 The operation of the ABS system is entirely dependent on electrical signals. To prevent the system responding to any inaccurate signals, a built-in safety circuit monitors all signals received by the ECU. If an inaccurate signal or low battery voltage is detected, the ABS system is automatically shut down, and the warning light on the instrument panel is illuminated to inform the driver that the ABS system is not operational. Normal braking should still be available, however.

9 If a fault does develop in the ABS system, the vehicle must be taken to a Mercedes-Benz dealer for fault diagnosis and repair.

With traction control and/or ESP

10 On models with traction control (ASR) and/or the stability program (ESP), the hydraulic unit performs the traction control and stability program functions as well as the anti-lock braking.

11 On models with ASR and/or ESP, a modified hydraulic unit and electronic control unit is fitted. The ABS electronic control unit (ECU) is linked to the engine management ECU to operate the throttle valve position actuator.

12 The braking side of the system works as described above, and the rear axle speed is monitored solely by the rear wheel ABS sensors.

13 The traction control system prevents the rear wheels from losing traction by either gently applying the brake or by closing the throttle valve, depending on the speed of the vehicle. In extreme cases, a combination of both may be used.

14 On the braking side of the system, if a wheel is about to lose traction, the hydraulic unit uses the hydraulic pressure stored in the accumulator to gently apply the brake on the relevant wheel. Once the risk of wheel spin has passed, the hydraulic unit allows the fluid to return to the accumulator and releases the brake, allowing the wheel to rotate freely again.

15 On the throttle side of the system, if traction is about to be lost, the engine management ECU operates the throttle valve actuator and closes the throttle valve, decreasing the engine power output. Once the risk of wheel spin has passed, the actuator returns the throttle valve to its normal position and returns control of the throttle to the driver.

16 On models with the stability program (ESP), the traction control system is further refined to help retain control of the car during cornering. An accelerometer fitted above the rear axle monitors the lateral (cornering) forces on the car. If the car starts to slide sideways, the system reacts by gently applying one of the brakes to help steer the car – if appropriate, the throttle valve is also closed.

17 In the same way as for the ABS, the vehicle must be taken to a Mercedes-Benz dealer for testing if a fault develops in the traction control (ASR) or ESP systems.

> ⚠ *Warning: Diagnosis of the faults within ABS/ASR/ESP systems requires access to dedicated test equipment. For safety reasons, owners are strongly advised against attempting to investigate complex problems with these systems using standard workshop equipment.*

20 Anti-lock braking system (ABS) components – removal and refitting

> ⚠ *Warning: If any of the ABS system components have been disturbed or renewed, the operation of the system must be verified before the vehicle is brought back into service. This procedure must be carried out using dedicated test equipment, and as such should be entrusted to a Mercedes-Benz dealer.*

Note: *Before starting work, refer to the note at the beginning of Section 2 concerning the dangers of hydraulic fluid.*

Hydraulic unit

Removal

1 Disconnect the battery negative cable and position it away from the terminal.

2 Unscrew the master cylinder reservoir filler cap and top-up the reservoir to the MAX mark. Place a piece of polythene over the filler neck, and securely refit the cap. This will minimise brake fluid loss during subsequent operations. As a precaution, place absorbent rags beneath the hydraulic unit.

3 Disconnect the unit wiring connector(s). The main connector is secured using a sliding locking clip – slide the clip upwards to release the connector pins, and free it from the hydraulic unit **(see illustrations)**.

4 Wipe clean the area around the hydraulic unit brake pipe unions, then make a note of how the pipes are arranged to use as a

20.3a Slide up the locking clip . . .

20.3b . . . and disconnect the wiring connector

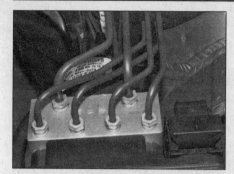

20.4 Note the fitted position of the pipes

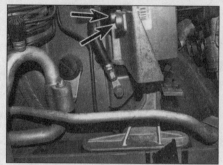

20.5 Hydraulic unit mounting bolts

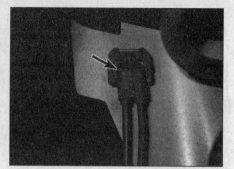

20.9a Prise the wiring plugs from the rear of the wheel arch . . .

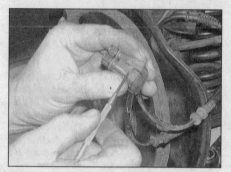

20.9b . . . then prise up the retaining clip with a screwdriver . . .

20.9c . . . and separate the two plugs for removal

20.10 Sensor retaining bolt

reference on refitting. Unscrew the union nuts and carefully withdraw the pipes (see illustration). Plug or tape over the pipe ends and unit orifices, to minimise the loss of brake fluid and to prevent the entry of dirt into the system. Wash off any spilt fluid immediately with cold water.

5 The hydraulic unit mounting bracket is rubber-mounted. Carefully prise the unit complete with mounting bracket upwards, to free it from the mountings. Undo the two retaining bolts to remove the hydraulic unit from the mounting bracket (see illustration). Note: *Do not attempt to dismantle the modulator block hydraulic assembly; overhaul of the unit is not possible.*

Refitting

6 Refitting is the reverse of the removal procedure, noting the following points.
  a) *Examine the mountings for signs of wear or damage, and renew if necessary.*
  b) *Refit the brake pipes to their respective unions, and tighten the union nuts to the specified torque.*
  c) *Ensure that the wiring is correctly routed and securely connected. Slide the locking clip fully into place.*
  d) *On completion prior to refitting the battery, bleed the complete braking system as described in Section 2.*

Front wheel sensor

Note: *New sensor retaining bolt(s) and where applicable, a new plastic centring sleeve, will be required on refitting*

Removal

7 Chock the rear wheels and firmly apply the parking brake. Loosen the front wheel bolts, and then jack up the front of the car and support on axle stands (see *Jacking and vehicle support*). Remove the appropriate front roadwheel.

8 Ensure that the ignition switch is turned off (take out the key), and then trace the wiring back from the sensor to the connector. Free the sensor wiring from any relevant retaining clips or ties, noting its correct routing, so that it is free to be removed.

9 Unclip the wiring connector from its retaining clip and disconnect it from the main harness. The pad wear sensor wiring connector appears at first to be attached to the connector for the ABS sensor, but the two connectors can be prised apart using a small screwdriver (see illustrations).

10 Slacken and remove the bolt securing the sensor to the top of the steering knuckle (see illustration).

11 The sensor itself must now be prised out of its mounting in the brake disc splash shield. Access is not easy, and care must be taken not to damage the rubber seal or plastic sleeve (where fitted). Remove the sensor and lead assembly from the car.

12 Recover the plastic centring sleeve and discard it; a new sleeve must be used on reassembly. Note, however, that some models do not appear to have such a sleeve, and it may have been discontinued in production.

13 Discard the sensor retaining bolt; a new bolt must be fitted whenever they are disturbed.

Refitting

14 Prior to refitting, ensure that the mating surfaces of the sensor and steering knuckle are clean and dry, and apply a thin coat of multi-purpose grease to them (Mercedes-Benz recommend the use of MB long-life grease).

15 Ensure that the sensor tip and reluctor rings are clean and free from debris, and fit the sealing ring or centring sleeve to the sensor, as applicable.

16 Insert the sensor fully into the location in the disc splash shield.

17 Align the sensor mounting plate with the hole in the top of the steering knuckle, and insert the new mounting bolt. Tighten the bolt to the specified torque.

18 Secure the wiring in position with all the necessary clips and ties, making sure it is correctly routed. Ensure that the connector sealing ring is in good condition, then connect the wiring and clip the connector into its retaining clip.

19 On completion, refit the roadwheel(s), and then lower the car to the ground and tighten the roadwheel bolts to the specified torque.

Rear wheel sensor

Removal

20 Loosen the relevant rear wheel bolts, chock the front wheels, then jack up the rear of the car and support it on axle stands (see *Jacking and vehicle support*). Remove the rear wheel.

21 Unclip the sensor wiring from the clip on the suspension arm (see illustration).

20.21 Release the wiring from the retaining clips

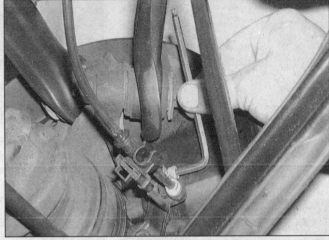

20.22 Using an Allen key to unscrew the sensor retaining bolt

22 Using an Allen key, loosen and remove the sensor retaining bolt **(see illustration)**.
23 Prise the sensor out from its location, noting that it is quite a tight fit. Recover the sealing ring, where applicable **(see illustration)**.
24 Trace the wiring up from the sensor to the floorpan and disconnect the wiring connector **(see illustration)**. Note how the wiring is routed and free it from any retaining clips and remove the sensor.

Refitting

25 Ensure that the sensor and its location are clean and dry, and fit the sealing ring to the sensor.
26 Ease the sensor into position, then fit the new retaining bolt and tighten it to the specified torque setting.
27 Feed the wiring back up into position along the floorpan, and then connect it to the main harness. Ensure that the wiring is correctly routed, and secure it in position with all the relevant clips.
28 On completion, refit the roadwheel(s), and then lower the car to the ground and tighten the roadwheel bolts to the specified torque.

Front reluctor rings

29 The front reluctor rings are fixed onto the rear of wheel hubs. Examine the rings for damage such as chipped or missing teeth. If renewal is necessary, the complete hub assembly must be renewed as described in Chapter 10.

Rear reluctor rings

30 The rear reluctor rings are fixed onto the rear of wheel hubs. Examine the rings for damage such as chipped or missing teeth. If renewal is necessary, the hub carrier must be renewed, as described in Chapter 10.

Over-voltage protection relay

Removal

31 The relay is in the fuse/relay box on the right-hand side of the engine compartment.
32 Prior to removal, ensure that the ignition

is switched off (take out the key). On later models, remove the fusebox cover.
33 Undo the retaining screw (where fitted), then unplug the relay and remove it from the engine compartment.

Refitting

34 On refitting, ensure that the relay and wiring connector terminals are clean and dry.

ABS relays

Removal

35 The ABS relays are in the fuse/relay box on the right-hand side of the engine compartment. A further ABS relay is located in the luggage compartment, and on most models is black or white – do not confuse it with the fuel pump relay which is green and has a fuse attached.
36 To gain access to the relays, remove the driver's side lower facia panel (Chapter 11, Section 37), take off the fusebox lid, or remove the three plastic fasteners and lift up the front section of the boot floor, as applicable.
37 Ensure that the ignition is switched off (take out the key), and then pull the relevant relay out from its location.

Refitting

38 Refitting is a reversal of removal, ensuring that the relays are pushed securely into position.

20.23 Withdrawing the sensor from its location

Note: *The following procedure is for diesel models; some petrol models are also fitted with a vacuum pump.*

Testing

1 The operation of the braking system vacuum pump can be checked using a vacuum gauge.
2 Disconnect the vacuum pipe from the pump, and connect the gauge to the pump union using a suitable length of hose.
3 Start the engine and allow it to idle, and then measure the vacuum created by the pump. As a guide, a minimum of approximately 500 mm Hg should be recorded. If the vacuum registered is significantly less than this, it is likely that the pump is faulty. However, seek the advice of a Mercedes-Benz dealer before condemning the pump.

Removal

4 Disconnect the battery negative cable and position it away from the terminal.
5 Release the retaining clips and disconnect the vacuum hose from the top of the pump, which is mounted on the front of the cylinder head **(see illustration)**.

20.24 Sensor wiring connector in the floor panel

21.5 Disconnect the vacuum pipe

21.6a Disconnect the wiring
connectors . . .

21.6b . . . and unclip the wiring harness

21.7a remove the mounting bracket . . .

21.7b . . . and withdraw the vacuum pump

6 Disconnect the wiring connectors from the switches below the vacuum pump and unhook the wiring harness from across the front of the pump **(see illustrations)**.

7 Undo the retaining bolts and remove the mounting bracket from the vacuum pump, and then withdraw the pump from the front of the cylinder head **(see illustrations)**.

Refitting

8 Refitting is the reverse of removal, using new O-ring seals **(see illustrations)**, and making sure the pump drive flange is correctly engaged.

9 Tighten the vacuum pump mounting bolts to the specified torque.

21.8a Fit new O-ring seals . . .

21.8b . . . to the vacuum pump

Chapter 10
Suspension and steering

Contents

Degrees of difficulty

Easy, suitable for novice with little experience	**Fairly easy,** suitable for beginner with some experience	**Fairly difficult,** suitable for competent DIY mechanic	**Difficult,** suitable for experienced DIY mechanic	**Very difficult,** suitable for expert DIY or professional

Specifications

Front suspension
Type . . . .   Independent, multi-link suspension, with MacPherson struts incorporating coil springs, telescopic shock absorbers and anti-roll bar connected to struts by connecting drop links. Anti-roll bar fitted to all models

Rear suspension
Type . . . .   Independent, multi-link with coil springs and telescopic shock absorbers. Anti-roll bar fitted to all models

Steering
Type . . . .   Hydraulic power-assisted steering with rack-and-pinion, with adjustable tie-rods

Front hub bearing
Endfloat . . . .   0.01 to 0.02 mm

Wheel alignment
Front wheel toe setting (overall) . . . .   0° 06' ± 6' toe-in
Rear wheel toe setting (overall) . . . .   0° 33' ± 15' toe-in

Roadwheels
Type . . . .   Pressed-steel or aluminium alloy (depending on model)
Size. . . . .   6J x 15, 6.5J x 15, 7J x 16, 8J x 16 or 7.5J x 17

Tyres
Roadwheels size:
  6.0J x 15 wheels. . . . .   195/65 R 15
  6.5J x 15 wheels. . . . .   195/65 R 15
  7J x 16 wheels . . . .   205/55 R 16 or 225/50 R 16
  8J x 16 wheels . . . .   225/50 R 16
  7.5J x 17 wheels. . . . .   225/45 R 17
Tyre pressures . . . .   Refer to end of *Weekly checks* on page 0•16

Torque wrench settings

	Nm	lbf ft
Front suspension		
Anti-roll bar body bracket bolts	40	30
Anti-roll bar link rod (balljoint) retaining nuts	60	44
Hub nut clamp bolt.	11	8
Lower suspension arms (cross-strut and torque strut):		
To steering knuckle (balljoint):		
Stage 1	50	37
Stage 2	Angle-tighten a further 60°	
To vehicle chassis (bush):		
Stage 1	80	59
Stage 2	Angle-tighten a further 120°	
Strut upper bearing retaining nut	20	15
Strut upper (inner wing) mounting retaining nut.	60	44
Strut to steering knuckle:		
Upper mounting bolt/nut:		
Stage 1	100	74
Stage 2	Angle-tighten a further 90°	
Lower mounting bolts.	110	81
Rear suspension		
Anti-roll bar:		
Mounting clamp bolts.	30	22
Connecting link (balljoint) nuts	40	30
Rear suspension control arms	70	52
Lower rear (track) arm balljoint nut:		
Stage 1	20	15
Stage 2	Angle-tighten a further 45°	
Lower arm:		
Inner pivot bolt	70	52
Outer pivot bolt.	120	89
Rear axle subframe mounting bolts:		
Stage 1	40	30
Stage 2	Angle-tighten a further 90°	
Shock absorber:		
Upper mounting nut	30	22
Lower mounting bolt nut	55	41
Steering		
Power steering pump:		
Petrol engines:		
Mounting bolts	20	15
Fluid pipe high-pressure connection	40	30
Diesel engines:		
Mounting bolts	20	15
Pulley bolts	25	18
Fluid pipe high-pressure connection	45	33
Steering column:		
Lower coupling to rack.	25	18
Shaft clamp bolt	30	22
Lower mounting bolt.	20	15
Upper mounting bolts.	20	15
Steering rack fluid pipe retaining bolt	18	13
Steering rack mounting bolts:		
Stage 1	50	37
Stage 2	Angle-tighten a further 90°	
Steering rack retaining plate mounting bolts:		
Stage 1	50	37
Stage 2	Angle-tighten a further 60°	
Steering wheel bolt.	80	59
Track rod end balljoint nut:		
Stage 1	50	37
Stage 2	Angle-tighten a further 60°	
Track rod end locknut.	60	44
Track rod inner axial balljoint to rack	110	81
Roadwheels		
Roadwheel bolts.	110	81

1 General information

The independent front suspension is of the MacPherson strut type, incorporating coil springs and integral telescopic shock absorbers. The struts are located by transverse lower suspension arms, which use rubber inner mounting bushes, and incorporate a balljoint at the outer ends. The front wheel bearing housings/steering knuckle, which carry the wheel bearings, brake calipers and the hub/disc assemblies, are attached to the MacPherson struts by clamp bolts, and connected to the lower arms through the balljoints. A front anti-roll bar is fitted to all models. The anti-roll bar is rubber-mounted, and is connected to both lower suspension arms by short drop links.

The independent rear suspension also incorporates coil springs and telescopic shock absorbers. The shock absorbers are located by transverse lower suspension arms, which use rubber mounting bushes. The hub assemblies are fastened to the lower arms, and are joined to the rear subframe by the three control arms; two upper arms and a lower one. Coil springs are fitted between the lower arms and vehicle body **(see illustration)**. A rear anti-roll bar is fitted to all models. The anti-roll bar is rubber-mounted and is connected to the hub carrier by connecting links.

The steering gear is mounted onto the front subframe, and is connected by two track rods, with balljoints at their inner and outer ends, to the steering arms projecting forwards from the wheel bearing housings. The track rod ends are threaded to the track rods in order to allow adjustment of the front wheel toe setting.

Power-assisted steering is standard on all models. The hydraulic steering system is powered by a belt-driven pump which is driven off the crankshaft pulley.

Note: *Many of the suspension and steering components are secured in position with self-locking nuts and bolts. Whenever a self-locking nut or bolt is disturbed, it must be discarded and a new nut/bolt fitted.*

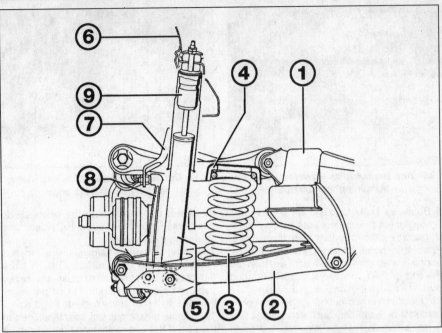

1.2 Cross-sectional view of the rear suspension

1	*Subframe*	*4*	*Spring seat*	*7*	*Anti-roll bar*
2	*Lower arm*	*5*	*Shock absorber*	*8*	*Connecting link*
3	*Coil spring*	*6*	*Body*	*9*	*Bump stop*

2 Front hub bearing – checking and adjustment

1 Mercedes-Benz recommend the use of a dial gauge to check the hub endfloat, as a means of checking the bearing adjustment. While this is certainly the method for assuring the maximum accuracy, a competent mechanic will be able to check and adjust the bearing by feel.

2 If the bearing is worn to the extent that the droning noise can be heard inside the car, there is no point trying to 'adjust' the bearing to reduce the noise. Fit a new bearing as described in Section 3.

Without a dial gauge

3 Chock the rear wheels and firmly apply the parking brake. Jack up the front of the car and support it on axle stands (see *Jacking and vehicle support*).

4 Grasp the wheel at the top and bottom, and shake it to assess free play **(see illustration)**. Repeat the check with the wheel held on the left and right sides. A very small amount of play may be noticed, but if the play is excessive, the bearings should be adjusted as described below.

5 If adjustment is required, the wheel must be removed. This will probably entail lowering the car temporarily to loosen the wheel bolts, then raising the car once more.

6 Taking care not to damage the pad friction material or the disc surface, use a large flat-bladed screwdriver to push the brake pads and pistons back into the caliper, away from the disc so that the pads do not drag.

7 Tap or prise the grease cap out from the centre of the hub **(see illustration)**. If the cap is damaged on removal, it must be renewed.

8 Using an Allen key or socket, slacken the hub nut clamp bolt so that the nut is free to turn **(see illustration)**.

2.4 Shake the wheel to assess play in the bearing

2.7 Tap the grease cap out from the centre of the hub (brake disc removed)

2.8 Unscrew the hub nut clamp bolt using an Allen key

2.9 Turn the hub/disc slowly while lightly tightening the hub nut

2.12 Tap the grease cap back into place, working around the edge

2.19 Using a dial gauge to check the hub bearing endfloat adjustment

9 Rotate the brake disc and at the same time lightly tighten the hub nut until the disc starts to become difficult to turn **(see illustration)**. From this point, slacken the hub nut by approximately one-third of a turn, and then tap the end of the hub spindle with a soft-faced mallet to relieve the tension on the bearing.

10 Slacken the hub nut fully, then very lightly tighten it by hand only until resistance is felt. A few attempts may be required, but there should be a clear point at which, without effort, all free play is eliminated without loading the bearing. Do not tighten the hub nut using tools, or any tighter than described, as this will quickly destroy it.

11 Tighten the hub nut clamp bolt to the specified torque.

12 Pack the grease cap with fresh grease, and tap it fully back into place **(see illustration)**.

13 Refit the wheel, then lower the car to the ground and tighten the wheel bolts to the specified torque. Depress the brake pedal repeatedly until normal pedal pressure returns.

14 If a new bearing has been fitted, recheck the adjustment within approximately 500 miles.

With a dial gauge

15 Chock the rear wheels and firmly apply the parking brake. Loosen the front wheel bolts, and then jack up the front of the car and support it on axle stands (see *Jacking and vehicle support*). Remove the relevant front roadwheel.

16 Using spacers if necessary, refit two of

the wheel bolts (to locate the brake disc), positioning them on opposite sides, and tightening them securely.

17 Taking care not to damage the pad friction material or the disc surface, use a large flat-bladed screwdriver to push the brake pads and pistons back into the caliper, away from the disc so that the pads do not drag.

18 Tap the grease cap out from the centre of the hub. If the cap is damaged on removal, it must be renewed.

19 Mount a dial gauge onto the front face of the hub/disc, and position the gauge probe so that it is in contact with the end of the axle shaft **(see illustration)**. Zero the gauge scale, then grasp the disc at two opposite points and pull it in and out. Note the reading obtained on the gauge, and check that the hub bearing endfloat is within the limits given in the *Specifications* at the start of this Chapter.

20 If all is well, remove the dial gauge. Pack the grease cap with grease, and tap the cap into position. Remove the wheel bolts and refit the roadwheel, then lower the car to the ground and tighten the wheel bolts to the specified torque. Depress the brake pedal several times until normal, non-assisted pedal pressure returns prior to taking the car on the road.

21 If adjustment is required, use an Allen key to slacken the hub retaining nut clamp bolt until the retaining nut is free to turn.

22 Rotate the brake disc while lightly tightening the hub nut, until the disc starts to become difficult to turn. From this point, slacken the hub nut by approximately

one-third of a turn, and then tap the end of the hub spindle with a soft-faced mallet to relieve the tension on the bearing.

23 Check the hub bearing endfloat as described in paragraph 19. If necessary adjust the endfloat by rotating the hub nut as required.

24 Recheck the bearing endfloat, then refit all disturbed components as described in paragraph 20.

25 If a new bearing has been fitted, recheck the adjustment within approximately 500 miles.

3 Front hub and bearing – removal, overhaul and refitting

Note: *The hub assembly should not be removed unless the bearings are to be renewed; the hub bearing inner race is a press-fit on the steering knuckle, and removal of the hub will almost certainly damage the bearings. A press will be required to dismantle and rebuild the assembly; if such a tool is not available, a large bench vice and spacers (such as large sockets) will serve as an adequate substitute. The bearing's inner races are an interference fit on the hub; if the inner race remains on the hub when it is pressed out of the hub carrier, a knife-edged bearing puller will be required to remove it.*

Removal

1 Remove the front brake disc, disc shield and ABS sensor as described in Chapter 9.

2 Tap the grease cap out from the centre of the hub. If the cap is damaged on removal, it must be renewed.

3 Slacken the hub nut clamp bolt, then slacken and remove the hub nut from the axle **(see illustration)**. Remove the thrustwasher (where fitted).

4 Take off the hub outer bearing, and place it to one side where it can be kept clean **(see illustration)**.

5 The front hub assembly can now be withdrawn from the steering knuckle. If the hub assembly is a tight fit on the axle, a puller will be required to draw it off.

6 If the inner bearing race remains on the

3.3 Slacken and remove the hub nut

3.4 Remove the hub outer bearing

steering knuckle, a knife-edge type puller will be required to remove it. With the race removed, slide off the hub oil seal.

7 Inspect the steering knuckle axle shaft for signs of damage, and renew if necessary (see Section 4).

Overhaul

8 Remove the inner race from the outer bearing.

9 Where necessary, carefully lever out the oil seal from the rear of the hub assembly and drift out the inner bearing.

10 Support the front of the hub assembly and tap the outer bearing inner race out of position using a hammer and punch passed through the hub.

11 Turn the hub over and remove the inner bearing outer race in the same way **(see illustration)**.

12 Thoroughly clean the hub, removing all traces of dirt and grease, and polish away any burrs or raised edges, which might hinder reassembly. Check for cracks or any other signs of wear or damage, and renew if necessary. Ensure that the ABS sensor ring is in good condition.

13 On reassembly, apply a light coating of grease to the bearing outer race and hub contact surfaces. Also work the grease well into the inner bearing tracks.

14 Securely support the hub, and locate the inner bearing outer race in the hub. Press the race fully into position, ensuring that it enters the hub squarely, using a tubular spacer (such as a large socket), which bears only on the outer edge of the race.

15 Turn the hub over and fit the outer bearing inner race in the same way.

16 Fit the inner bearing to the inner race. Fit the oil seal into the rear of the hub, making sure its sealing lip is facing inwards, and press it squarely into position **(see illustration)**.

17 Pack the hub assembly about two-thirds full of grease. The outer bearing is best fitted once the hub assembly has been fitted to the steering knuckle.

Refitting

18 Apply a smear of grease to the hub rear oil seal lip, and locate the hub assembly onto the steering knuckle shaft.

19 Pack the outer bearing with grease, working it well into the bearing tracks. Fit the outer bearing into position over the steering knuckle pin, and slide it fully into the hub location.

20 Screw on the hub nut. Rotate the hub assembly whilst using the hub nut to press the hub assembly onto the steering knuckle axle. Once the hub assembly is correctly seated, adjust the hub bearing endfloat as described in Section 2 and tighten the hub nut clamp bolt to the specified torque.

21 Pack the grease cap with grease, then tap it squarely into position.

22 Refit the brake disc and shield, and the ABS front wheel sensor, as described in Chapter 9.

3.11 Tap out the inner bearing outer race using a suitable punch

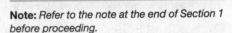

3.16 Tap the rear oil seal squarely into the hub, using a suitable socket

| 4 | **Front steering knuckle assembly** – removal and refitting |

Note: *Refer to the note at the end of Section 1 before proceeding.*

Removal

1 Chock the rear wheels and firmly apply the parking brake. Loosen the front wheel bolts, and then jack up the front of the car and support it on axle stands (see *Jacking and vehicle support*). Remove the relevant front roadwheel.

2 If the steering knuckle is to be renewed, remove the hub assembly as described in Section 3. With the hub and brake disc removed, the brake dust shield can also be removed, which greatly improves access for removing the steering knuckle.

3 If the steering knuckle assembly is to be refitted, slacken and remove the two bolts securing the brake caliper mounting bracket to the knuckle, then slide the caliper assembly off the disc. **Note:** *Discard the caliper bolts, new ones must be used on refitting.* Using a piece of wire or string, tie the caliper to the front suspension coil spring, to avoid placing any strain on the hydraulic brake hose. Also remove the ABS wheel sensor as described in Chapter 9.

4 Slacken and remove the nut securing the track rod balljoint to the steering knuckle, and release the balljoint tapered shank using a universal balljoint separator **(see illustration)**.

5 Similarly, release the balljoints securing the steering knuckle to the two suspension lower arms **(see illustrations)**.

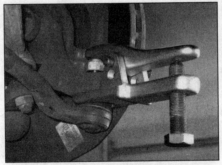

4.4 Release the balljoint taper using a separator tool

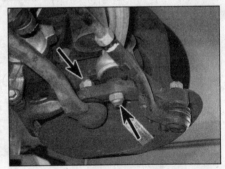

4.5a Unscrew the lower arm balljoint nuts . . .

4.5b . . . release the balljoint taper using a separator tool . . .

4.5c . . . and use drift to release taper if required

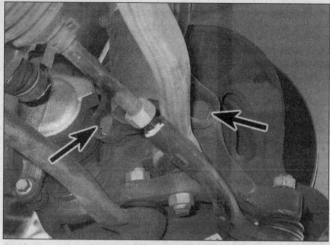

4.6 Strut lower mounting bolts

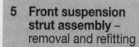

4.7 Steering knuckle upper mounting bolt

6 Loosen and remove the two mounting bolts from the bottom of the suspension strut **(see illustration).**

7 Remove the upper steering knuckle mounting bolt **(see illustration)**, and then remove the steering knuckle from the vehicle. Inspect the knuckle for signs of wear or damage, and renew as necessary.

Refitting

8 Refitting is the reversal of the removal procedure, noting the following points:

a) Clean any threads by running a tap of the correct thread size and pitch down them.

b) Thoroughly clean the balljoint tapers and their locating holes, also clean the balljoint threads if necessary, using a wire brush.

c) Check all the balljoint rubbers for signs of damage or perishing. If the rubber has split, this will lead to loss of lubricant and dirt entry, which will destroy the joint. If any balljoints are suspect, take the opportunity to fit new components.

d) Fit a new locking nuts, where required.

e) Tighten bolts and nuts to the specified torque setting where applicable.

f) Refer to Chapter 9, when refitting the discs, calipers and ABS wheel sensors.

g) Where removed, refit the hub assembly as described in Section 3.

h) Refit the roadwheel, then lower the car to the ground and tighten the wheel bolts to the specified torque.

i) Where new parts have been fitted, it is advisable to have the front wheel toe setting ('tracking') checked on completion.

5 Front suspension strut assembly – removal and refitting

Note: Refer to the note at the end of Section 1 before proceeding. Shock absorbers should always be renewed in pairs on the same axle, to preserve safe handling.

Removal

1 Chock the rear wheels, and firmly apply the parking brake. Loosen the front wheel bolts, and then jack up the front of the car and support it on axle stands (see Jacking and vehicle support). Remove the relevant front roadwheel.

2 Unclip the wiring and/or hoses from the strut/body bracket from the steering knuckle **(see illustration)**. Note it may be necessary to remove the front brake caliper hose, as it passes through the mounting bracket. Refer to Chapter 9, to remove brake hose.

3 Unscrew the nut and disconnect the anti-roll bar link from the strut **(see illustration)**.

4 Loosen and remove the two mounting bolts from the bottom of the suspension strut **(see illustration).**

5 Note which way round the upper bolt is fitted, then unscrew the nut and remove the clamp bolt securing the steering knuckle to the bottom of the strut **(see illustration)**. Using wire or similar tie the wheel bearing housing up to the inner wing panel to prevent any strain on the brake hose or wiring harness.

6 Working inside the engine compartment, remove the plastic cap from the top of the suspension strut **(see illustration)**.

7 With the aid of an assistant to support the strut assembly, unscrew the upper mounting nut and lower the strut from under the wheel

5.2 Unclip the wires and hoses from the strut

5.3 Drop link upper retaining nut

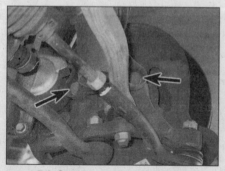

5.4 Strut lower mounting bolts

5.5 Steering knuckle upper mounting bolt

arch. Remove the positioning washer from the top of the strut, noting its fitted position (see illustration).

Refitting

8 Check the strut body for leaking fluid, dents, cracks and other obvious signs of damage. Also check the coil spring for any cracks and inspect the spring seat for any general deterioration. Renew any faulty components.

9 With the aid of an assistant manoeuvre the strut assembly back into position so that the threaded top section passes through the hole in the inner wing.

10 Fit the strut positioning washer, in the position noted on removal (see illustration 5.7), and then fit the strut upper securing nut. Do not tighten at this point; this can be tightened once the vehicle is lowered down onto the ground.

11 Refit the steering knuckle to the lower part of the strut, and then tighten the bolts/nut to the specified torque setting.

12 Refit the anti-roll bar link rod balljoint back onto the strut and tighten to the specified torque.

13 Refit the brake hose and wiring connectors and clip them into their retaining clips.

14 Refit the wheel, lower the car to the ground, and tighten the wheel bolts to the specified torque.

15 With the car resting on its wheels, push down on the front wing, and then release it. Repeat this a few times, to settle the components.

16 Tighten the strut assembly upper mounting nut to the specified torque, making sure the piston rod does not turn. Fit the plastic cap to the top of the strut.

17 Where new parts have been fitted, it is advisable to have the front wheel toe setting ('tracking') checked on completion.

6 Front suspension coil spring – removal and refitting

Note: *Refer to the note at the end of Section 1 before proceeding. Springs should always be renewed in pairs on the same axle, to preserve safe handling.*

⚠ **Warning: Before attempting to dismantle the suspension strut, a suitable tool to hold the coil spring in compression must be obtained. Adjustable coil spring compressors are readily available, and are recommended for this operation. Any attempt to dismantle the strut without such a tool is likely to result in damage or personal injury.**

1 With the strut removed from the car as described in Section 5, clean away all external dirt. If necessary, mount it upright in a vice during the dismantling procedure.

2 Fit the spring compressor, and compress the coil spring until all tension is relieved from the upper spring seat.

5.6 Remove the plastic cap

3 Unscrew and remove the upper centre retaining nut, whilst retaining the strut piston with a suitable Allen key. Make sure the spring is securely located in the spring compressor before removing the centre bearing retaining nut.

4 Remove the upper bearing and washers, including the bump stop and protective sleeve, from the strut, noting their fitted positions.

5 Withdraw the coil spring from the strut, noting its fitted position for refitting.

6 With the strut assembly now completely dismantled, examine all the components for wear, damage or deformation, and check the bearing for smoothness of operation. Renew any of the components as necessary and grease upper bearing.

7 Examine the strut for signs of fluid leakage. Check the strut piston for signs of pitting along its entire length, and check the strut body for signs of damage. While holding it in an upright position, test the operation of the strut by moving the piston through a full stroke, and then through short strokes of 50 to 100 mm. In both cases, the resistance felt should be smooth and continuous. If the resistance is jerky, or uneven, or if there is any visible sign of wear or damage to the strut, renewal is necessary.

8 If any doubt exists about the condition of the coil spring, carefully remove the spring compressors, and check the spring for distortion and signs of cracking. Renew the spring if it is damaged or distorted, or if there is any doubt as to its condition.

9 Inspect all other components for signs

7.2 Using a balljoint separator tool

5.7 Note the position of the upper washer/ plate

of damage or deterioration, and renew as necessary.

10 Fit the coil spring (together with the compressor tool) onto the strut, making sure its lower end is correctly located against the spring seat stop, as noted on removal.

11 Refit the protective sleeve, bump stop, upper plate and bearing mounting, and washer, and then screw on a new retaining nut. Tighten the nut to the specified torque while holding the piston rod with an Allen key.

12 Refit the strut assembly to the vehicle as described in Section 5.

7 Front suspension lower arms – removal, overhaul and refitting

Note: *There are two lower suspension arms fitted to this model, the front one is called the torque strut, and the rear one is called the cross-strut. The inner mounting bushes have elongated bolt holes to allow for adjusting wheel alignment.*

Removal

1 Chock the rear wheels, and firmly apply the parking brake. Loosen the front wheel bolts, and then jack up the front of the car and support it on axle stands (see *Jacking and vehicle support*). Remove the relevant front roadwheel.

Torque strut

2 Slacken and remove the nut securing the torque strut (front lower arm) to the steering knuckle, and release the balljoint tapered shank using a universal balljoint separator (see illustration).

3 Slacken and remove the strut-to-steering knuckle mounting bolts and move the steering knuckle to one side, taking care not to damage the brake hose or wiring. It should now be possible to disconnect the torque strut balljoint from the bottom of the steering knuckle.

4 Undo the retaining bolts from the anti-roll bar mounting bracket and move the anti-roll bar down to access the torque strut-to-chassis mounting bolt (see illustration).

5 At the vehicle chassis end of the torque strut, undo the retaining nut and withdraw

7.4 Anti-roll bar mounting bracket bolts

7.5 Note the lugs on the inside of the bush on the strut arm

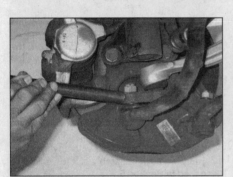

7.7 Tap the arm to release the balljoint taper

7.8 Strut arm inner retaining bolt

the bolt from the mounting bracket. **Note:** *Some mounting bolts have grooves running down the length of them, to hold the inner mounting in position; this is used for wheel alignment adjustment.* **DO NOT** *turn the bolt as this could damage the lugs inside the bush in the torque strut* **(see illustration).** *Undo the retaining nut and mark the position of the bolt for refitting, and then withdraw the bolt.*

6 The torque strut can then be removed from underneath the car.

Cross-strut

7 Slacken and remove the nut securing the cross-strut (rear lower arm) to the steering knuckle, and release the balljoint tapered shank using a universal balljoint separator **(see illustration).**

8 At the vehicle chassis end of the cross-strut, undo the retaining nut and withdraw the bolt from the mounting bracket **(see illustration).** **Note:** *Some mounting bolts have grooves*

running down the length of them, to hold the inner mounting in position; this is used for wheel alignment adjustment. **DO NOT** *turn the bolt as this could damage the lugs inside the bush in the cross-strut. Undo the retaining nut and mark the position of the bolt for refitting, and then withdraw the bolt.*

9 The cross-strut can then be removed from underneath the car.

Overhaul

10 Thoroughly clean the lower arm and the area around the arm mountings, removing all traces of dirt and underseal if necessary. Check carefully for cracks, distortion or any other signs of wear or damage, paying particular attention to the mounting bushes and balljoints.

11 In theory, the lower arm can be mounted in a large vice (with protected jaws), and the bushes pressed or driven out using a suitable drift. The new bushes can then be pressed or drawn in

using a long bolt and several large washers and spacers. If carrying out this procedure at home, make sure the rubber bushes are marked and fitted in the arm in the correct position as noted on removal. This is important, as the bushes have an elongated bolt hole to provide wheel alignment adjustment.

12 In practice, if either bush requires renewal, it may be best to take the lower arm to a Mercedes-Benz dealer or suitably-equipped garage. On a car which has covered many miles, removing the old bushes may be extremely difficult without appropriate tools.

13 Inspect the balljoints for signs of wear, and for damage to the balljoint gaiters. If damaged, a new suspension strut/arm will be required as the balljoint cannot be renewed separately.

14 Thoroughly clean the balljoint tapers and their locating holes, making sure that no lubricant is present, which would prevent the tapers from locking firmly into position. Clean the balljoint threads, if necessary using a wire brush.

15 Check the threads on the pivot bolts, and clean using a wire brush if necessary.

Refitting

16 Refitting is the reversal of the removal procedure, noting the following points:
a) Fit the new nuts, tightening them to the specified torque.
b) Fit the inner mounting bolts in the position noted on removal.
c) Refit the roadwheel, then lower the car to the ground and tighten the wheel bolts to the specified torque.
d) It is recommended that the front steering angles (camber and castor) and wheel alignment (toe-in, or 'tracking') are checked at the earliest possible opportunity by a Mercedes-Benz dealer or other suitably-equipped garage.

---

8   Front suspension anti-roll bar –
removal and refitting

Note: *Refer to the note at the end of Section 1 before proceeding.*

Removal

1 Chock the rear wheels, and firmly apply the parking brake. Loosen the front wheel bolts, and then jack up the front of the car and support it on axle stands (see *Jacking and vehicle support*). Remove both the front roadwheels.

2 Make alignment marks between the mounting bushes and anti-roll bar.

3 Slacken and remove the nut securing the drop link, and then release the balljoint from the anti-roll bar **(see illustration).**

4 Slacken and remove the bolts securing the mounting clamps to the body brackets, and remove the clamps **(see illustration).**

5 Free the anti-roll bar and manoeuvre it out from underneath the car.

8.3 Drop link lower balljoint retaining nut

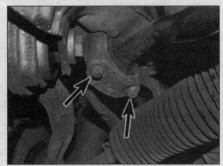

8.4 Anti-roll bar mounting bracket bolts

9.5 Rear arm protective cover

9.6 Support the suspension lower arm

9.7 Lower suspension arm-to-hub carrier bolt

6 Inspect the mounting rubbers for signs of damage or deterioration, and renew as necessary.

Refitting

7 Align the mounting rubbers with the marks made prior to removal, and manoeuvre the anti-roll bar into position.

8 Engage the mounting rubbers with the mounting clamps. Insert the clamp bolts and tighten them lightly only at this point.

9 Locate the outer ends of the anti-roll bar with the balljoints on the drop links, then fit the new retaining nuts.

10 Ensure that the marks made prior to removal are correctly aligned, and then tighten all the clamp bolts and balljoint nuts to the specified torque setting.

11 Fit the roadwheels, and then lower the car to the ground and tighten the wheel bolts to the specified torque.

9 Rear hub carrier – removal and refitting

Note: *Refer to the note at the end of Section 1 before proceeding.*

Removal

1 Remove the wheel trim or hub cap, then using a hammer and pointed-nose chisel, carefully relieve the driveshaft retaining nut staking (where applicable).

2 Slacken the driveshaft retaining nut with the car resting on its wheels. Note that this nut is extremely tight – ensure that the tools used to loosen it are of good quality, and a good fit. Do not remove the nut at this stage.

3 Chock the front wheels, and loosen the rear wheel bolts. Jack up the rear of the car and support it on axle stands (see *Jacking and*

vehicle support). Remove the relevant rear roadwheel.

4 With reference to Chapter 9, carry out the following:

a) *Unbolt the brake caliper and suspend it out of the way.*

b) *Remove the brake disc.*

c) *Unhook the relevant rear parking brake cable from the equaliser bracket.*

5 Undo the retaining screws and unclip the protective cover from the base of the suspension lower arm **(see illustration)**.

6 Position a jack and block of wood underneath the lower arm, and raise the jack until it is supporting the weight of the arm **(see illustration)**.

7 Slacken and remove the nut and pivot bolt securing the lower arm to the hub carrier **(see illustration)**.

8 Support the hub carrier assembly, then slacken and remove the nuts and pivot bolts

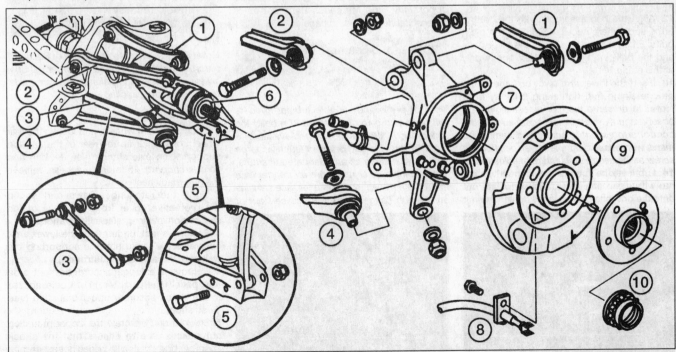

9.8 Rear suspension and hub carrier details

1	Camber control arm	3	Track control arm	5	Lower arm
2	Torque control arm	4	Thrust control arm	6	Driveshaft

7	Hub carrier	9	Disc splash shield
8	Parking brake cable	10	Driveshaft nut

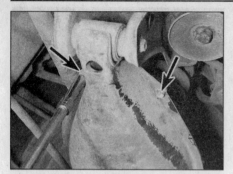

11.2a Undo the retaining screws (arrowed) . . .

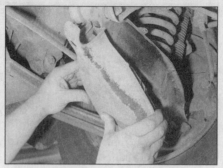

11.2b . . . and remove the protective cover from the base of the lower arm

securing the upper and lower control arms to the hub carrier, with reference to Section 14 **(see illustration). Note:** *To preserve the rear wheel alignment settings, mark the position of the eccentric screw and cam before removing the upper and lower control arms.*

9 Remove the driveshaft retaining nut completely, and withdraw the hub assembly from the end of the driveshaft joint. If necessary, tap the joint out of the hub using a soft-faced mallet. If this fails to free it from the hub, the joint will have to be pressed out using a suitable tool which is bolted to the hub.

10 Remove the hub assembly and support the driveshaft by hanging it from the vehicle underbody using a piece of wire. **Note:** *Do not allow the driveshaft to hang under its own weight, as the CV joint may be damaged.*

Refitting

11 Manoeuvre the hub assembly into position, and engage it with the driveshaft joint.

12 Align the hub assembly with the control arms and (where necessary) insert the pivot bolts. Fit a new nut to each of the pivot bolts and the balljoint, tightening them lightly only at this stage.

13 Insert the lower arm pivot bolt and fit the new retaining nut, tightening it lightly only. **Note:** *To preserve the rear wheel alignment, observe the alignment markings made on the control arm eccentric screw and cam. If no marks were made during removal, position the screw at the centre of its range of adjustment.*

14 Lubricate the threads of the new driveshaft nut with clean engine oil, and screw the nut onto the driveshaft end. Lightly tighten the nut

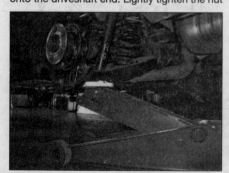

11.3 Support the suspension lower arm

at this stage – it is safer to tighten and stake the nut once the car is resting on its wheels.

15 Refit the brake disc and caliper, and reconnect the parking brake cable, as described in Chapter 9.

16 Refit the protective cover to the lower arm, and securely tighten its retaining screws.

17 Refit the roadwheel, then lower the car to the ground and tighten the wheel bolts to the specified torque.

18 With the car resting on its wheels, rock it to settle the hub carrier in position, then tighten the control arm and lower arm outer pivot bolt/balljoint nuts to their specified torque settings.

19 Tighten the driveshaft retaining nut to the specified torque (see Chapter 8 Specifications) and stake it firmly into the driveshaft groove using a hammer and punch.

Note: *It is recommended that the rear wheel alignment is checked at the earliest possible opportunity by a Mercedes-Benz dealer or other suitably-equipped garage.*

10 Rear hub bearing – renewal

Note: *A press and suitable tubular spacers will be required to dismantle and rebuild the assembly; if such a tool is not available, a large bench vice and spacers (such as large sockets) will serve as an adequate substitute. The bearing's inner races are an interference fit on the hub flange; if the inner race remains on the hub flange when it is pressed out of*

11.4 Rear shock absorber upper mounting (Estate)

position, a knife-edged bearing puller will be required to remove it.

1 Remove the rear hub carrier as described in Section 9.

2 Securely support the hub carrier and carefully press the hub flange out from the centre of the bearing. If the bearing inner race remains on the flange, remove it with a knife-edge bearing puller.

3 Remove the hub bearing retaining circlip from the hub carrier.

4 Support the hub carrier, and press the hub bearing out of position using a suitable tubular spacer.

5 Thoroughly clean the hub carrier bore, removing all traces of dirt and grease. Polish away any burrs or raised edges which might hinder reassembly. Renew the circlip if there is any doubt about its condition.

6 On reassembly, apply a light film of clean engine oil to the bearing outer race, to aid installation.

7 Locate the bearing in the hub carrier and press it fully into position, ensuring that it enters the carrier squarely, using a suitable tubular spacer which bears only on the bearing outer race.

8 Secure the bearing in position with the circlip, making sure it is correctly located in the hub carrier groove.

9 Securely support the bearing inner race, and press the hub flange fully into the bearing.

10 Check the bearing rotates freely, then refit the rear hub carrier as described in Section 9.

11 Rear suspension shock absorber – removal, testing and refitting

Note: *Refer to the note at the end of Section 1 before proceeding. Shock absorbers should always be renewed in pairs on the same axle, to preserve safe handling.*

Removal

1 Chock the front wheels, and loosen the rear wheel bolts. Jack up the rear of the car and support it on axle stands (see *Jacking and vehicle support*). To improve access, remove the rear roadwheel.

2 Undo the retaining screws and unclip the protective cover from the base of the suspension lower arm **(see illustrations)**.

3 Position a jack underneath the lower arm, and raise the jack until it is supporting the weight of the arm **(see illustration)**.

4 Remove the luggage compartment side trim panel (see Chapter 11) to gain access to the shock absorber upper mounting **(see illustration)**.

5 Slacken and unscrew the upper mounting nut, taking care to ensure that the shock absorber body/piston rod does not rotate, and lift off the large washer and rubber bush. Note, on some models there may be two nuts at the top of the shock absorber, the upper one being a locknut.

Warning: Do not attempt to remove the shock absorber upper mounting nuts unless the lower arm is securely supported by the jack.

6 From underneath the car, slacken and remove the shock absorber lower mounting bolt nut **(see illustration)**, and withdraw the bolt and washers.

7 Carefully lower the suspension arm slightly, and then manoeuvre the shock absorber out from underneath the wheel arch. Take off the dust cover, and recover the spacer sleeve and bump stop from the top of the shock absorber **(see illustration)**.

Testing

8 Examine the shock absorber for signs of fluid leakage. Check the piston for signs of pitting along its entire length, and check the body for signs of damage.

9 While holding it in an upright position, test the operation of the shock absorber by moving the piston through a full stroke, and then through short strokes of 50 to 100 mm. In both cases, the resistance felt should be smooth and continuous. If the resistance is jerky, or uneven, or if there is any visible sign of wear or damage, renewal is necessary.

10 Inspect all other components for signs of damage or deterioration, and renew any that are suspect.

Refitting

11 If a new shock absorber is being fitted, gently compress and release the unit a few times, to prime it before fitting.

12 Slide the bump stop onto the shock absorber piston, then refit the dust cover and spacer.

13 Manoeuvre the unit into position so that the threaded top section passes through the hole at the top of the wheel arch. Raise the lower arm slightly if necessary, and engage the lower mounting loosely with the mounting point on the lower arm; fully insert the lower mounting bolt with its washer.

14 Working from above, fit the rubber bush and large washer, then screw on the upper mounting nut, and tighten by hand only.

15 Fit the new nut and washer (where fitted) to the lower mounting bolt, and tighten it by hand only.

16 Refit the roadwheel, then lower the car to the ground and tighten the wheel bolts to the specified torque.

17 With the car resting on its wheels, push down on the wing, and then release it. Repeat this a few times, to settle the components.

18 Tighten the shock absorber upper mounting nut to the specified torque, making sure the piston rod does not turn. Where fitted, fit a new locknut, and tighten it to its specified torque while counter-holding the first nut.

19 Refit the luggage compartment trim panel with reference to Chapter 11.

20 Tighten the lower mounting nut to the specified torque, holding the bolt against rotation if necessary.

11.6 Shock absorber lower mounting bolt

21 Refit the protective cover to the lower arm, and securely tighten its retaining screws.

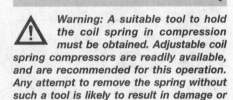

12 Rear suspension coil spring – removal and refitting

Warning: A suitable tool to hold the coil spring in compression must be obtained. Adjustable coil spring compressors are readily available, and are recommended for this operation. Any attempt to remove the spring without such a tool is likely to result in damage or personal injury.

Note: Refer to the note at the end of Section 1 before proceeding.

Removal

1 Chock the front wheels, and loosen the rear wheel bolts. Jack up the rear of the car and support it on axle stands (see Jacking and vehicle support). Remove the relevant rear roadwheel.

2 Fit the spring compressor, and compress the coil spring until all tension is relieved from the spring seats.

3 Undo the retaining screws and remove the protective cover from the base of the lower suspension arm.

4 Position a jack beneath the lower arm, and raise the jack head until the arm is securely supported.

5 Slacken and remove the nut, and withdraw the pivot bolt securing the lower suspension arm to the rear subframe. Also slacken and remove the nut and bolt securing the shock absorber mounting to the lower arm.

6 Carefully lower the lower suspension arm until it is possible to remove the coil spring and upper spring seat **(see illustration)**.

7 Inspect the coil spring for signs of wear or damage, and renew if necessary. The upper spring seat should also be renewed if it is damaged or shows signs of deterioration.

Refitting

8 Ensure that the lower arm spring seat is clean, then fit the upper spring seat to the coil spring and manoeuvre the spring into position.

9 Locate the lower end of the spring correctly against the stop on the lower arm seat. Align

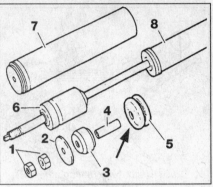

11.7 Rear shock absorber upper mounting components

1 *Locknut and mounting nut*	5 *Mounting rubber*
2 *Washer*	6 *Bump stop*
3 *Mounting rubber*	7 *Dust cover*
4 *Spacer*	8 *Shock absorber*

the upper spring seat with the body mounting, and carefully raise the lower arm whilst also aligning it with the subframe.

10 Check that the spring is correctly located, and then insert the lower arm pivot bolt. Fit a new nut to the pivot bolt, tightening it lightly only at this stage. Refit the shock absorber mounting bolt, and tighten the new retaining nut to the specified torque.

11 Remove the jack from beneath the lower arm, and then carefully release the spring compressor whilst making sure both its upper and lower ends are correctly located.

12 Refit the roadwheel, then lower the car to the ground and tighten the wheel bolts to the specified torque.

13 With the car resting on its wheels, rock it to settle the spring and lower arm in position.

14 Tighten the lower arm pivot bolt nut to the specified torque setting.

15 Refit the protective cover to the lower arm, and securely tighten its retaining screws.

13 Rear suspension control arms – removal and refitting

Note: Refer to the note at the end of Section 1 before proceeding.

12.6 Carefully remove the rear coil spring

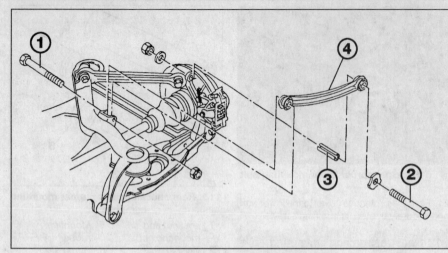

13.2 Upper camber control arm fixings

1 *Inner pivot bolt*   2 *Outer pivot bolt*   3 *Locating sleeve*   4 *Control arm*

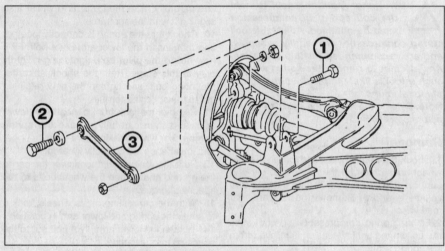

13.5 Upper torque control arm fixings

1 *Inner pivot bolt*   2 *Outer pivot bolt*   3 *Control arm*

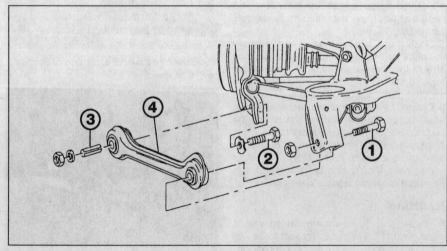

13.6 Lower thrust control arm fixings

1 *Inner pivot bolt*   2 *Outer pivot bolt*   3 *Locating sleeve*   4 *Control arm*

Note: *If more than one control arm is to be removed at the same time, support the lower arm with a jack and block of wood.*

Removal

1 Chock the front wheels, and loosen the rear wheel bolts. Jack up the rear of the car and support it on axle stands (see *Jacking and vehicle support*). Remove the relevant rear roadwheel.

Upper camber control arm

2 Slacken and remove the nut, and withdraw the pivot bolt securing the arm to the hub carrier **(see illustration)**.

3 Slacken and remove the nut and pivot bolt securing the control arm to the subframe, and remove the arm from the car. If necessary, tap out the locating sleeve from the control arm hub carrier bush.

4 Inspect the control arm for signs of damage, paying particular attention to the rubber bushes, and renew if necessary. Also renew the pivot bolts if they show signs of wear.

Upper torque control arm

5 Remove the arm as described in paragraphs 2 to 4, ignoring the remark about the locating sleeve **(see illustration)**.

Lower thrust control arm

6 Remove the arm as described in paragraphs 2 to 4 **(see illustration)**.

Lower track control arm

7 Prior to removal, make alignment marks between the arm inner pivot bolt, the eccentric washers and the subframe. This will be necessary to ensure that the rear wheel toe setting remains correct on refitting.

8 Slacken and remove the nut and eccentric washer, and withdraw the pivot bolt securing the arm to the subframe **(see illustration)**.

9 Unscrew the nut from the balljoint shank, then free the balljoint from the hub carrier and remove the arm from the car. If necessary, use a balljoint separator to free the balljoint shank from the carrier.

10 Inspect the control mounting bush for signs of damage or deterioration. Also check that the balljoint is free to move easily, and that its gaiter is undamaged. Renew the control arm if necessary.

Refitting

Note: *It is recommended that the rear wheel alignment is checked at the earliest possible opportunity after arm refitting.*

Upper camber control arm

11 Where necessary, tap the locating sleeve back into position in the arm hub carrier bush.

12 Locate the arm in position and insert the pivot bolts. Fit the new nuts to the pivot bolts, tightening them lightly only at this stage.

13 Refit the rear roadwheel, then lower the car to ground and tighten the wheel bolts to the specified torque.

14 With the car resting on its wheels, rock

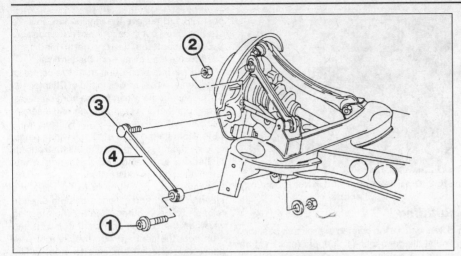

13.8 Lower track control arm fixings

1 *Inner pivot bolt*	3 *Outer pivot bolt*
2 *Outer retaining nut*	4 *Control arm*

it to settle the control arm in position, then tighten both pivot bolt nuts to the specified torque setting.

Upper torque control arm

15 Refit the arm as described in paragraphs 11 to 14.

Lower thrust control arm

16 Refit the arm as described in paragraphs 11 to 14.

Lower track control arm

17 Manoeuvre the arm into position, then insert the inner pivot bolt, eccentric washer and fit the new retaining nut. Align the marks made prior to removal and lightly tighten the nut.

18 Fit the new retaining nut to the balljoint shank, and tighten it to the specified torque setting.

19 Refit the rear roadwheel then lower the car to ground and tighten the wheel bolts to the specified torque.

20 With the car resting on its wheels, rock it to settle the control arm in position.

21 Check that the marks on the subframe, pivot bolt and eccentric washer are still correctly aligned, then tighten the pivot bolt nut to the specified torque setting.

14 Rear suspension lower arm – removal, overhaul and refitting

Note: *Refer to the note at the end of Section 1 before proceeding.*

Removal

1 Chock the front wheels, and loosen the rear wheel bolts. Jack up the rear of the car and support it on axle stands (see *Jacking and vehicle support*). Remove the relevant rear roadwheel.

2 Remove the rear coil spring as described in Section 12.

3 Unscrew the nut, then withdraw the inner pivot bolt and washers and remove the lower arm from underneath the car **(see illustration)**.

Overhaul

4 Thoroughly clean the lower arm and the area around the arm mountings, removing all traces of dirt and underseal.

5 Check carefully for cracks, distortion or any other signs of wear or damage, paying particular attention to the mounting bushes. If either bush requires renewal, the lower arm should be taken

to a Mercedes-Benz dealer or suitably equipped garage. A hydraulic press and suitable spacers are required to press the bushes out of position and install the new ones.

Refitting

6 Offer up the lower arm, and insert the inner pivot bolt and washers. Fit the new nut to the bolt, tightening it lightly only at this stage.

7 Refit the coil spring with reference to Section 12.

8 Refit the rear roadwheel, then lower the car to ground and tighten the wheel bolts to the specified torque.

9 With the car resting on its wheels, rock it to settle all disturbed components in position.

10 Tighten the lower arm pivot bolts and shock absorber lower mounting nut to there specified torque settings.

11 Refit the protective cover to the lower arm, and securely tighten its retaining screws.

15 Rear suspension anti-roll bar – removal and refitting

Note: *Refer to the note at the end of Section 1 before proceeding.*

Removal

1 Chock the front wheels, and loosen the rear wheel bolts. Jack up the rear of the car and support it on axle stands (see *Jacking and vehicle support*). To improve access, remove the rear roadwheels.

2 Slacken and remove the nut securing each connecting link to the anti-roll bar **(see illustration)**.

3 Make alignment marks between the mounting bushes and anti-roll bar, then slacken the two anti-roll bar mounting clamp retaining bolts and remove the clamps **(see illustration)**. If required, remove the rubber mountings from the anti-roll bar, noting which way around they are fitted. Manoeuvre the anti-roll bar out of position from underneath the car.

Refitting

4 Manoeuvre the anti-roll bar into position, and engage it with the connecting links.

5 If removed, fit the mounting rubbers to the

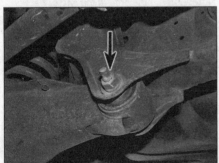

14.3 Lower suspension arm inner mounting bolt

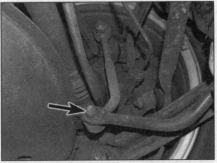

15.2 Drop link to anti-roll bar retaining nut

15.3 Anti-roll bar retaining clamp bolts

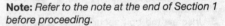

anti-roll bar, and align them with the marks made prior to removal. Then refit the mounting clamps and screw in the new clamp bolts.

6 Fit the new securing nuts to the connecting links at the ends of the anti-roll bar, tighten them to the specified torque setting, then tighten the mounting clamp bolts to the specified torque setting.

7 Refit the rear roadwheels, and then lower the car to the ground and tighten the wheel bolts to the specified torque settings.

16 Rear suspension anti-roll bar connecting link – removal and refitting

Note: *Refer to the note at the end of Section 1 before proceeding.*

Removal

1 Chock the front wheels, and then jack up the rear of the car and support it on axle stands (see *Jacking and vehicle support*). If required, to make access easier remove the relevant rear roadwheel.

2 Slacken and remove the nut securing the connecting link to the anti-roll bar **(see illustration)**.

3 Unscrew the bolt securing the upper part of the connecting link to the hub carrier and remove it from the car.

4 Inspect the connecting link mounting bush for signs of damage or deterioration. Also check that the balljoint is free to move easily, and that its gaiter is undamaged. Renew the connecting link if necessary.

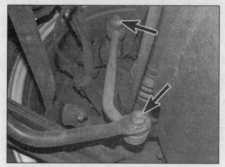

16.2 Drop link upper and lower mounting points

Refitting

5 Manoeuvre the connecting link into position, and fit the connecting link upper retaining bolt to the hub carrier.

6 Fit the lower part of the connecting link to the anti-roll bar and fit a new retaining nut, tighten it to the specified torque.

7 Refit the roadwheel (if removed), then lower the car to the ground and tighten the wheel bolts to the specified torque.

17 Steering wheel – removal and refitting

Note: *A new steering wheel retaining bolt will be required for refitting.*

Removal

1 Set the front wheels in the straight-ahead

position, and remove the ignition key. Pull the steering wheel out to its fully-extended position.

2 Disconnect the battery earth lead, and position the lead away from the terminal.

3 Remove the airbag unit from the centre of the steering wheel as described in Chapter 12.

4 Disconnect the wiring for the horn contacts, airbag contact unit and steering angle sensor (models with Electronic Stability Program – ESP). Note the position of all the wiring plugs, or label them to aid refitting **(see illustration)**.

5 Slacken and remove the steering wheel retaining bolt **(see illustration)**.

6 If marks do not already exist, mark the steering wheel and steering column shaft in relation to each other, then lift the steering wheel off the column splines. If it is tight, tap it up near the centre, using the palm of your hand, or twist it from side-to-side, whilst pulling upwards to release it from the shaft splines **(see illustration)**.

Refitting

7 Refitting is the reverse of removal, noting the following points:

a) *Coat the steering wheel horn contact ring with a smear of petroleum jelly and refit the wheel, making sure the contact unit wiring is correctly routed.*

b) *Ensure that the steering wheel locates correctly with the contact unit as the steering wheel is refitted.*

c) *Engage the wheel with the column splines, aligning the marks made on removal, and tighten the steering wheel retaining bolt to the specified torque setting.*

d) *Reconnect the wiring using the notes made on dismantling.*

e) *Refit the airbag unit as described in Chapter 12.*

f) *If the ESP warning light flashes when the ignition is switched on, turn the steering wheel fully from lock-to-lock. This should reset the steering wheel sensor, and extinguish the warning light.*

18 Steering column – removal, inspection and refitting

Note: *Refer to the note at the end of Section 1 before proceeding.*

Removal

1 Disconnect the battery earth lead, and position the lead away from the terminal.

2 Remove the steering wheel as described in Section 17.

3 Take off the airbag wiring contact unit with reference to Chapter 12.

4 Remove the steering lock as described in Section 19.

5 Remove the steering column combination switches as described in Chapter 12, and lift off the steering column upper trim **(see illustration)**.

17.4 Disconnect the wiring around the steering wheel

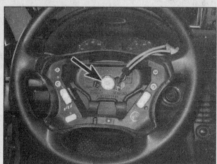

17.5 Removing the steering wheel retaining bolt

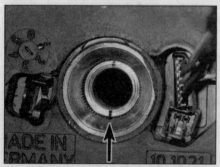

17.6 Mark the steering wheel and shaft for refitting

18.5 Remove the steering column upper switch assembly

18.9 Heat shield retaining bolts

18.10 Steering column shaft lower mounting bolt

18.11 Release the locking lever

6 Remove the instrument panel with reference to Chapter 12.

7 Chock the rear wheels, and then jack up the front of the car and support it on axle stands (see *Jacking and vehicle support*).

8 Working under the vehicle, remove the plastic shield from under the engine compartment.

9 Undo the two retaining bolts and remove the heat shield from the lower steering column joint **(see illustration)**.

 Warning: Make sure the exhaust system has cooled down before working on the lower part of the steering column.

10 Using paint or a suitable marker pen, make alignment marks between the lower end of the steering column and the coupling **(see illustration)**.

11 Working back inside the vehicle, release the locking lever on the steering column to disengage the adjustment lever from the steering column **(see illustration)**.

12 Release the clip from the top of the steering column and withdraw the trim from the vehicle **(see illustrations)**.

13 Release the wiring harness from the steering column, noting its fitted position. It may be necessary to cut through some of the cable-ties used.

14 Slacken and remove the bolt at the lower end of the steering column **(see illustration)**.

15 Slacken and remove the steering column upper mounting bolts **(see illustration)**.

16 Free the steering column gaiter bush from the bulkhead, and carefully pull the column and shaft into the car. Do not use excessive force, or the steering column may be damaged.

Inspection

17 The steering column incorporates a telescopic safety feature. In the event of a front-end crash, the lower section of the shaft collapses and prevents the steering wheel injuring the driver. Before refitting the steering column, examine the column and mountings for signs of damage and deformation, and renew as necessary.

18 Check the steering shaft for signs of free play in the column bushes. If any damage or wear is found on the steering column bushes, the column should be overhauled. Overhaul of the column is a complex task requiring several

special tools, and should be entrusted to a Mercedes-Benz dealer.

Refitting

19 Prior to refitting, lubricate the column lower bush with multipurpose grease.

20 Aligning the marks made on removal, manoeuvre the steering column into position, feeding the lower end through the bulkhead and engaging the lower shaft with the coupling. Make sure that the wiring harness is routed correctly as the column is fitted.

21 Ensure that the column gaiter bush is correctly located in the bulkhead, then refit and tighten the steering column lower mounting bolts/nuts, then the upper mounting bolts.

22 Fit a new clamp bolt to the coupling, and tighten it to the specified torque.

23 Where necessary, secure the wiring harness to the column, using new cable-ties.

24 Refit the column trim, then refit the

18.12a Release the securing clip . . .

18.14 Steering column housing lower retaining bolt

combination switches and instrument panel as described in Chapter 12.

25 Refit the steering lock as described in Section 19.

26 Refit the airbag contact unit as described in Chapter 12.

27 Refit the steering wheel as described in Section 17.

19 Steering lock/ignition switch
– removal and refitting

Ignition switch

1 Disconnect the battery negative terminal, and position the lead away from the terminal.

2 Remove the driver's lower facia panel as described in Chapter 11.

3 Unscrew the chrome trim ring from the front of the switch, by using some long-nose pliers

18.12b . . . and remove the trim panel

18.15 Steering column upper retaining bolts

19.3a Use a small screwdriver . . .

19.3b . . . or a pair of long-nose pliers . . .

19.3c . . . to unscrew and remove the switch trim ring

or by tapping it round with a small screwdriver if necessary (take care not to damage the finish) **(see illustrations)**.

4 Release the switch from the facia panel, and then disconnect the wiring plugs from the rear of the switch, noting their locations.

5 Refitting is a reversal of removal, noting the following points:

a) *Make sure that the switch wiring is correctly and securely reconnected.*

b) *Engage the lug on the right-hand rear of the switch aperture with the cut-out on the front face of the switch, then screw on the trim ring to secure.*

Steering lock

6 Disconnect the battery negative terminal, and position the lead away from the terminal.

7 Remove the driver's lower facia panel as described in Chapter 11.

8 Unscrew the nut and tap out the lock retaining bolt, noting how it is fitted.

9 Disengage the lock from the column, and disconnect the wiring plug. Note that the lock is electrically-activated, via a signal from the keyfob.

10 Refitting is a reversal of removal.

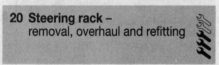

20 Steering rack – removal, overhaul and refitting

Note: *Refer to the note at the end of Section 1 before proceeding.*

Removal

1 Chock the rear wheels, firmly apply the

parking brake, then jack up the front of the car and support on axle stands (see *Jacking and vehicle support*).

2 Set the front wheel in the straight-ahead position, and lock the column in position using the steering lock (take out the ignition key). **Note:** *Do not rotate the column whilst the steering rack is removed, or the airbag contact unit will be damaged.*

3 Where possible, Use a brake hose clamp to clamp the power steering fluid supply and return hoses near the steering rack to minimise fluid loss.

4 Mark the fluid hose unions to ensure that they are correctly positioned on reassembly, then slacken and remove the hose union nuts/bolts **(see illustration)**. Be prepared for fluid spillage, and position a suitable container beneath the hoses whilst unscrewing the nuts. Plug the hose ends and steering rack orifices to prevent fluid leakage and to keep dirt out of the hydraulic system.

5 Using paint or a suitable marker pen, make alignment marks between the lower end of the steering column shaft, coupling/clamp, and the steering rack pinion. Note that on some models it will be necessary to unbolt the steering rack heat shield(s) to gain access to the coupling.

6 Slacken and remove the clamp bolt, and then separate the steering column shaft from the coupling **(see illustration)**.

7 Unscrew the nuts securing the track rod ends to the steering knuckle. Free the balljoints, if necessary, using a universal balljoint separator.

8 From underneath the vehicle, slacken and remove the two steering rack mounting bolts and the two retaining plate bolts **(see**

illustration). Also it will be necessary to remove the screws from around the base of the retaining/support plate and remove it.

9 Manoeuvre the rack out from underneath the car. **Note:** *On models with speed-sensitive power steering, disconnect the wiring connector from the sensor on the pinion housing.*

Overhaul

10 Examine the steering rack assembly for signs of wear or damage. If overhaul of the steering rack assembly is necessary, the task must be entrusted to a Mercedes-Benz dealer.

Refitting

11 Manoeuvre the steering rack assembly into position. Align the marks made on removal or ensure that the pinion remains correctly centred, and engage the pinion with the coupling.

12 Engage the lower end of the steering column shaft with the coupling; taking care not to use force, otherwise the shaft lower section may be damaged.

13 Fit the steering rack mounting bolts and retaining plate screws, and tighten them to the specified torque.

14 Fit a new coupling clamp bolt, and tighten it to the specified torque.

15 Insert the track rod balljoints into the steering knuckle. Fit new balljoint retaining nuts and tighten them to the specified torque.

16 Reconnect the power steering fluid pipes to the steering rack, renewing any seals, and tighten the bolt securely. If used, remove the fluid hose clamps. On completion, refill and bleed the hydraulic system as described in Section 22.

20.4 Power steering fluid pipe retaining bolt

20.6 Steering column lower coupling joint bolt and nut

20.8 Steering rack mounting bolts and retaining plate bolts

21 Power steering pump – removal and refitting

1 Open the bonnet and remove the plastic trim covers from the top of the engine.
2 To reduce the amount of fluid spillage, syphon off as much of the power steering fluid from the reservoir as possible, taking care not to introduce dirt into the system. Alternatively, attach fluid hose clamps to the rubber supply and return hoses before disconnecting the unions.
3 Working as described in Chapter 1A or 1B, release the drivebelt tension and unhook the drivebelt from the pump pulley, noting that on diesel models, the pulley retaining bolts should be slackened prior to releasing the tension.

Removal

Diesel engines

4 To make access easier remove the throttle valve actuator (646 engines) or EGR valve (611 & 612 engines), as described in 4B.
5 Unscrew the retaining bolts and remove the pulley from the power steering pump, noting which way round it is fitted **(see illustration)**.
6 Wipe clean the area around the pump unions, and make identification marks between the hydraulic pipes and hoses and the pump.
7 Slacken the retaining clip and disconnect the hose from the pump (or fluid reservoir). Also undo the securing nut and disconnect the high-pressure pipe from the pump. Be prepared for fluid spillage, and position a suitable container beneath the hose whilst removing **(see illustration)**. Plug the hose ends and steering pump orifices to prevent fluid leakage and to keep dirt out of the hydraulic system.
8 Slacken and remove the power steering pump mounting bolts, and remove the pump assembly from the engine compartment **(see illustrations)**. Note that the upper two mounting bolts also secure a mounting bracket.
9 If the power steering pump is faulty, seek the advice of your Mercedes-Benz dealer as to the availability of spare parts. If spares

21.5 Remove the pulley

are available, it may be possible to have the pump overhauled by a suitable specialist or alternately obtain an exchange unit. If not, the pump must be renewed.

Petrol engines

10 Wipe clean the area around the pump unions, and make identification marks between the hydraulic pipes and hoses and the pump.
11 Slacken the union nut and disconnect the high-pressure pipe from the pump. Be prepared for fluid spillage, and position a suitable container beneath the pipe whilst unscrewing the nut. Plug the pipe end and steering pump orifices to prevent fluid leakage and to keep dirt out of the hydraulic system.
12 Slacken the retaining clip and disconnect the feed hose from the reservoir. Be prepared for fluid spillage, and position a suitable container beneath the hose whilst disconnecting. Plug the hose end and reservoir orifices to prevent fluid leakage and to keep dirt out of the hydraulic system.
13 Undo the retaining screws and remove the heat shield from the rear of the fluid reservoir.
14 Slacken and remove the power steering pump mounting bolts, and remove the pump assembly from the engine compartment **(see illustration)**. Note that the fluid reservoir will be removed with the pump.
15 The reservoir can be separated if wished, after removing the locking clip which secures the reservoir supply pipe.
16 If the power steering pump is faulty, seek the advice of your Mercedes-Benz dealer as to the availability of spare parts. If spares

21.7 Disconnect the fluid hose and pressure pipe

are available, it may be possible to have the pump overhauled by a suitable specialist or alternately obtain an exchange unit. If not, the pump must be renewed.

Refitting

17 Refit the pump and tighten the mounting bolts to the specified torque.
18 Using the marks made on removal, reconnect the hoses to the pump, tightening the union nuts to the specified torque.
19 Where applicable, refit the pulley to the pump, making sure it is fitted the correct way round and tighten the retaining bolts to the specified torque.
20 Fit the drivebelt and tension as described in Chapter 1A or 1B.
21 On completion, refill the reservoir and bleed the hydraulic system as described in Section 22.

22 Power steering system – bleeding

1 With the engine stopped, fill the fluid reservoir to within 10 mm of the top of the reservoir. Use only the specified type of fluid (see end of *Weekly checks*).
2 With the engine stopped, slowly move the steering from lock-to-lock several times to purge out the trapped air, then top-up the level in the fluid reservoir. Repeat this procedure until the fluid level in the reservoir does not drop any further.
3 Have an assistant start the engine, whilst

21.8a Undo the pump mounting bolts . . .

21.8b . . . and remove the bracket

21.14 Removing the power steering pump/reservoir

24.2a Slacken the locknut . . .

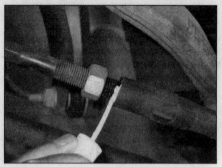

24.2b . . . and mark the position on the threads

you keep watch on the fluid level. Be prepared to add more fluid as the engine starts, as the fluid level is likely to drop quickly. The fluid level must not be allowed to drop too far, or more air will be drawn into the system.

4 With the engine running at idle speed, turn the steering wheel slowly two or three times approximately 45° to the left and right of the centre, then turn the wheel twice from lock-to-lock. Do not hold the wheel on either lock, as this imposes strain on the hydraulic system. Repeat this procedure until bubbles cease to appear in fluid reservoir.

5 If, when turning the steering, an abnormal noise is heard from the fluid lines, it indicates that there is still air in the system. Check this by turning the wheels to the straight-ahead position and switching off the engine. If the fluid level in the reservoir rises, then air is present in the system and further bleeding is necessary.

6 Once all traces of air have been removed from the power steering hydraulic system, turn the engine off and allow the system to cool. Once cool, check that fluid level is up to the maximum mark, topping-up if necessary (see Chapter 1A or 1B).

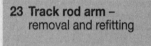

23 Track rod arm – removal and refitting

Note: *Refer to the note at the end of Section 1 before proceeding.*

1 Chock the rear wheels, firmly apply the

parking brake, and then jack up the front of the car and support on axle stands (see *Jacking and vehicle support*).

2 Remove the relevant track rod end and steering rack rubber gaiter as described in Section 24.

3 Hold the steering rack stationary with one spanner on the flats provided, then loosen the balljoint nut with another spanner. Fully unscrew the nut and remove the track rod from the rack.

4 Locate the new track rod on the end of the steering rack and screw on the nut. Hold the rack stationary with one spanner and tighten the balljoint nut to the specified torque. A crow's-foot adapter may be required since the track rod prevents access with a socket, and care must be taken to apply the correct torque in this situation.

5 Refit the rubber gaiter and track rod end with reference to Section 24.

6 On completion check and, if necessary, adjust the front wheel alignment as described in Section 25.

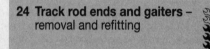

24 Track rod ends and gaiters – removal and refitting

Note: *Refer to the note at the end of Section 1 before proceeding.*

Removal

1 Chock the rear wheels, and loosen the front wheel bolts. Jack up the front of the car and

support it on axle stands (see *Jacking and vehicle support*). Remove the relevant front roadwheel.

2 Clean the end of the track rod and slacken the locknut **(see illustrations)**. Make a mark on the track rod arm threads to aid refitting. It will be needed to ensure that the wheel alignment remains correctly set when the balljoint is installed.

3 Slacken and remove the balljoint nut, and free the balljoint from the steering knuckle. If necessary, free the balljoint tapered shank using a universal balljoint separator **(see illustration)**.

4 Counting the **exact** number of turns necessary to do so, unscrew the balljoint from the track rod end.

5 To remove the steering rack gaiter, unscrew the locking nut from the track rod arm, after noting its position on the threads. Release the retaining clips and withdraw the gaiter from the track rod arm **(see illustration)**. Check the rubber gaiter for splits or cracking and renew if required.

6 Carefully clean the balljoint and the threads – the balljoint taper must not have any lubricant on it, otherwise it will not lock into position. Renew the balljoint if its movement is sloppy or too stiff, is excessively worn, or is damaged in any way; carefully check the stud taper and threads.

Refitting

7 If removed, refit the steering rack gaiter to the track rod arm and fit new securing clips. Position the gaiter as previously noted on removal, making sure that it is not twisted. Before fitting the outer securing clip, lift the outer sealing lip of the gaiter to equalise air pressure within the gaiter. Screw the locking nut back into position on the track rod arm.

8 Screw the balljoint back onto the track rod by the number of turns noted on removal, and tighten the locknut. This should position the balljoint at the relevant marks made on removal.

9 Refit the balljoint shank to the steering knuckle, then fit a new retaining nut and tighten it to the specified torque.

10 Refit the roadwheel, then lower the car to the ground and tighten the roadwheel bolts to the specified torque.

11 Check and, if necessary, adjust the front wheel toe setting as described in Section 25. After the wheel alignment is set, make sure the locknut is securely tightened.

25 Wheel alignment and steering angles – general information

Definitions

A car's steering and suspension geometry is defined in four basic settings – all angles are defined in degrees; the steering axis is defined as an imaginary line drawn through the axis of the suspension strut, extended where necessary to contact the ground.

24.3 Using a universal balljoint separator

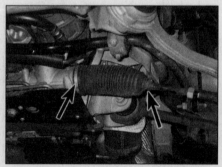

24.5 Steering rack gaiter retaining clips

Camber is the angle between each roadwheel and a vertical line drawn through its centre and tyre contact patch, when viewed from the front or rear of the car. Positive camber is when the roadwheels are tilted outwards from the vertical at the top; negative camber is when they are tilted inwards.

The front camber angle is adjusted by slackening and rotating the lower arm front pivot bolt, and can be adjusted using a camber angle gauge. The rear wheel camber is not adjustable.

Castor is the angle between the steering axis and a vertical line drawn through each roadwheel's centre and tyre contact patch, when viewed from the side of the car. Positive castor is when the steering axis is tilted so that it contacts the ground ahead of the vertical; negative castor is when it contacts the ground behind the vertical.

The front castor angle is adjusted by slackening and rotating the lower arm rear pivot bolt, and can be adjusted using a castor angle gauge. The rear wheel castor is not adjustable.

Toe is the difference, viewed from above, between lines drawn through the roadwheel centres and the car's centre-line. 'Toe-in' is when the roadwheels point inwards, towards each other at the front, while 'toe-out' is when they splay outwards from each other at the front.

The front wheel toe setting is adjusted by screwing the track rod in or out of its balljoints, to alter the effective length of the track rod assembly.

Rear wheel toe setting is also adjustable. The toe setting is adjusted by slackening and rotating the lower rear (track) control arm inner pivot bolt.

Checking and adjustment

Due to the special measuring equipment necessary to check the wheel alignment and steering angles, and the skill required to use it properly, the checking and adjustment of these settings is best left to a Mercedes-Benz dealer or similar expert. Note that most tyre-fitting shops now possess sophisticated checking equipment.

Chapter 11
Bodywork and fittings

Contents

Degrees of difficulty

Easy, suitable for novice with little experience | **Fairly easy,** suitable for beginner with some experience | **Fairly difficult,** suitable for competent DIY mechanic | **Difficult,** suitable for experienced DIY mechanic | **Very difficult,** suitable for expert DIY or professional

Specifications

Torque wrench settings	Nm	lbf ft
Bonnet hinge bolts	8	6
Boot lid/tailgate hinge bolts	11	8
Bumper mounting nuts	20	15
Door check strap bolt	25	18
Door hinge bolts	37	27
Front seat belt mounting bolts	35	26
Front seat mounting bolts	50	37
Rear seat belt mounting bolts	30	22
Tailgate lock/catch mounting bolts	9	7

1 General description

The body is of unitary all-steel construction, and incorporates computer-calculated impact crumple zones at the front and rear, with a central safety cell passenger compartment. During manufacture the body is dip-primed, fully sealed and undercoated, then painted with multi-layered base and top-coats.

The bodyshell on all models covered by this manual is of two-door Coupe, four-door Saloon or five-door Estate configuration.

A number of structural components and body panels are made of galvanised steel to provide a high level of protection against corrosion. Extensive use is also made of plastic materials, mainly in the interior, but also in exterior components. The front and rear bumpers are moulded from a synthetic material that is very strong and yet light. Plastic components such as wheel arch liners are fitted to the underside of the vehicle to further improve corrosion resistance.

2 Maintenance – bodywork and underframe

The general condition of a vehicle's bodywork is the one thing that significantly affects its value. Maintenance is easy but needs to be regular. Neglect, particularly after minor damage, can lead quickly to further deterioration and costly repair bills. It is important also to keep watch on those parts of the vehicle not immediately visible, for instance the underside, inside all the wheel arches and the lower pan of the engine compartment.

The basic maintenance routine for the bodywork is washing – preferably with a lot of water, from a hose. This will remove all the loose solids, which may have stuck to the vehicle. It is important to flush these off in such a way as to prevent grit from scratching the finish. The wheel arches and underframe need washing in the same way to remove any accumulated mud, which will retain moisture and tend to encourage rust. Paradoxically, the best time to clean the underframe and wheel arches is in wet weather when the mud is thoroughly wet and soft. In very wet weather the underframe is usually cleaned of large accumulations automatically and this is a good time for inspection.

Periodically, except on vehicles with a wax-based underbody protective coating, it is a good idea to have the whole of the underframe of the vehicle steam cleaned, engine compartment included, so that a thorough inspection can be carried out to see what minor repairs and renovations are necessary. Steam cleaning is available at many garages and is necessary for removal of the accumulation of oily grime, which sometimes is allowed to become thick in certain areas. If steam-cleaning facilities are not available, there are some excellent grease solvents available which can be brush applied. The dirt can then be simply hosed off. Note that these methods should not be used on vehicles with wax-based underbody protective coating or the coating will be removed. Such vehicles should be inspected annually, preferably just prior to winter, when the underbody should be washed down and any damage to the wax coating repaired. Ideally, a completely fresh coat should be applied. It would also be worth considering the use of such wax-based protection for injection into door panels, sills, box sections, etc, as an additional safeguard against rust damage where such protection is not provided by the vehicle manufacturer.

After washing paintwork, wipe off with a chamois leather to give an unspotted clear finish. A coat of clear protective wax polish will give added protection against chemical pollutants in the air. If the paintwork sheen has dulled or oxidised, use a cleaner/polisher combination to restore the brilliance of the shine. This requires a little effort, but such dulling is usually caused because regular washing has been neglected. Care needs to be taken with metallic paintwork, as special non-abrasive cleaner/polisher is required to avoid damage to the finish. Always check that the door and ventilator opening drain holes and pipes are completely clear so that water can be drained out. Bright work should be treated in the same way as paintwork. Windscreens and windows can be kept clear of the smeary film that often appears by the use of a proprietary glass cleaner. Never use any form of wax or other body or chromium polish on glass.

3 Maintenance – upholstery and carpets

Mats and carpets should be brushed or vacuum cleaned regularly to keep them free of grit. If they are badly stained remove them from the vehicle for scrubbing or sponging and make quite sure they are dry before refitting. Seats and interior trim panels can be kept clean by wiping with a damp cloth. If they do become stained (which can be more apparent on light coloured upholstery) use a little liquid detergent and a soft nail brush to scour the grime out of the grain of the material. Do not forget to keep the headlining clean in the same way as the upholstery. When using liquid cleaners inside the vehicle do not over-wet the surfaces being cleaned. Excessive damp could get into the seams and padded interior causing stains, offensive odours or even rot. If the inside of the vehicle gets wet accidentally it is worthwhile taking some trouble to dry it out properly, particularly where carpets are involved. *Do not leave oil or electric heaters inside the vehicle for this purpose.*

4 Minor body damage – repair

Minor scratches

If the scratch is very superficial, and does not penetrate to the metal of the bodywork, repair is very simple. Lightly rub the area of the scratch with a paintwork renovator, or a very fine cutting paste, to remove loose paint from the scratch and to clear the surrounding bodywork of wax polish. Rinse the area with clean water.

In the case of metallic paint, the most commonly found scratches are not in the paint, but in the lacquer top coat, and appear white. If care is taken, these can sometimes be rendered less obvious by very careful use of paintwork renovator (which would otherwise not be used on metallic paintwork); otherwise, repair of these scratches can be achieved by applying lacquer with a fine brush.

Apply touch-up paint to the scratch using a fine paintbrush; continue to apply fine layers of paint until the surface of the paint in the scratch is level with the surrounding paintwork. Allow the new paint at least two weeks to harden, and then blend it into the surrounding paintwork by rubbing the scratch area with a paintwork renovator or a very fine cutting paste. Finally, apply wax polish.

Where the scratch has penetrated right through to the metal of the bodywork, causing the metal to rust, a different repair technique is required. Remove any loose rust from the bottom of the scratch with a penknife, and then apply rust-inhibiting paint to prevent the formation of rust in the future. Using a rubber or nylon applicator, fill the scratch with bodystopper paste. If required, this paste can be mixed with cellulose thinners to provide a very thin paste, which is ideal for filling narrow scratches. Before the stopper-paste in the scratch hardens, wrap a piece of smooth cotton rag around the top of a finger. Dip the finger in cellulose thinners, and then quickly sweep it across the surface of the stopper-paste in the scratch; this will ensure that the surface of the stopper-paste is slightly hollowed. The scratch can now be painted over as described earlier in this Section.

Dents

When deep denting of the vehicle's bodywork has taken place, the first task is to pull the dent out, until the affected bodywork almost attains its original shape. There is little point in trying to restore the original shape completely, as the metal in the damaged area will have stretched on impact and cannot be reshaped fully to its original contour. It is better to bring the level of the dent up to a point which is about 3 mm below the level of the surrounding bodywork. In cases where the dent is very shallow anyway, it is not worth trying to pull it out at all. If the underside of the dent is accessible, it can be hammered out gently from behind, using a mallet with a wooden or plastic head. Whilst doing this, hold a suitable block of wood firmly against the outside of the panel to absorb the impact from the hammer blows and thus prevent a large area of the bodywork from being 'belled-out'.

Should the dent be in a section of the bodywork, which has a double skin or some other factor making it inaccessible from behind, a different technique is called for. Drill several small holes through the metal inside the area – particularly in the deeper section. Then screw long self-tapping screws into the holes just sufficiently for them to gain a good purchase in the metal. Now the dent can be pulled out by pulling on the protruding heads of the screws with a pair of pliers.

The next stage of the repair is the removal of the paint from the damaged area, and from an inch or so of the surrounding 'sound' bodywork. This is accomplished most easily by using a wire brush or abrasive pad on a power drill, although it can be done just as effectively by hand using sheets of abrasive paper. To complete the preparation for filling, score the surface of the bare metal with a screwdriver or the tang of a file, or alternatively, drill small holes in the affected area. This will provide a really good 'key' for the filler paste.

To complete the repair see the Section on filling and re-spraying.

Rust holes or gashes

Remove all paint from the affected area and from an inch or so of the surrounding 'sound' bodywork, using an abrasive pad or a wire brush on a power drill. If these are not available a few sheets of abrasive paper will do the job just as effectively. With the paint removed you will be able to gauge the severity of the corrosion and therefore decide whether to renew the whole panel (if this is possible) or to repair the affected area. New body panels are not as expensive as most people think and it is often quicker and more satisfactory to fit a new panel than to attempt to repair large areas of corrosion.

Remove all fittings from the affected area except those, which will act as a guide to the original shape of the damaged bodywork. Then, using tin snips or a hacksaw blade, remove all loose metal and any other metal badly affected by corrosion. Hammer the edges of the hole inwards in order to create a slight depression for the filler paste.

Wire-brush the affected area to remove the powdery rust from the surface of the remaining metal. Paint the affected area with rust -inhibiting paint – if the back of the rusted area is accessible, treat this also.

Before filling can take place it will be necessary to block the hole in some way. This can be achieved by the use of aluminium or plastic mesh, or aluminium tape.

Aluminium or plastic mesh is probably the best material to use for a large hole. Cut a piece to the approximate size and shape of the hole to be filled, then position it in the hole so that

its edges are below the level of the surrounding bodywork. It can be retained in position by several blobs of filler paste around its periphery.

Aluminium tape should be used for small or very narrow holes. Pull a piece off the roll and trim it to the approximate size and shape required, then pull off the backing paper (if used) and stick the tape over the hole; it can be overlapped if the thickness of one piece is insufficient. Burnish down the edges of the tape with the handle of a screwdriver or similar, to ensure that the tape is securely attached to the metal underneath.

Filling and re-spraying

Before using this Section, see the Sections on dent, deep scratch, rust holes and gash repairs.

Many types of bodyfiller are available, but generally speaking those proprietary kits which contain a tin of filler paste and a tube of resin hardener are best for this type of repair. A wide, flexible plastic or nylon applicator will be found invaluable for imparting a smooth and well-contoured finish to the surface of the filler.

Mix up a little filler on a clean piece of card or board – measure the hardener carefully (follow the maker's instructions on the pack) otherwise the filler will set too rapidly or too slowly. Using the applicator, apply the filler paste to the prepared area; draw the applicator across the surface of the filler to achieve the correct contour and to level the filler surface. As soon as a contour that approximates to the correct one is achieved, stop working the paste – if you carry on too long, the paste will become sticky and begin to 'pick up' on the applicator. Continue to add thin layers of filler paste at twenty-minute intervals until the level of the filler is just proud of the surrounding bodywork.

Once the filler has hardened, excess can be removed using a metal plane or file. From then on, progressively finer grades of abrasive paper should be used, starting with a 40-grade production paper and finishing with 400-grade (or higher) wet-and-dry paper. Always wrap the abrasive paper around a flat rubber, cork, or wooden block – otherwise the surface of the filler will not be completely flat. During the smoothing of the filler surface, the wet-and-dry paper should be periodically rinsed in water. This will ensure that a very smooth finish is imparted to the filler at the final stage.

At this stage the 'dent' should be surrounded by a ring of bare metal, which in turn should be encircled by the finely 'feathered' edge of the good paintwork. Rinse the repair area with clean water, until all of the dust produced by the rubbing-down operation has gone.

Spray the whole repair area with a light coat of primer – this will show up any imperfections in the surface of the filler. Repair these imperfections with fresh filler paste or bodystopper, and once more smooth the surface with abrasive paper. If bodystopper is used, it can be mixed with cellulose thinners to form a really thin paste, which is ideal for

filling small holes. Repeat this spray-and-repair procedure until you are satisfied that the surface of the filler, and the feathered edge of the paintwork are perfect. Clean the repair area with clean water, and allow to dry fully.

The repair area is now ready for final spraying. Paint spraying must be carried out in a warm, dry, windless and dust-free atmosphere. This condition can be created artificially if you have access to a large indoor working area, but if you are forced to work in the open, you will have to pick your day very carefully. If you are working indoors, dousing the floor in the work area with water will help to settle the dust that would otherwise be in the atmosphere. If the repair area is confined to one body panel, mask off the surrounding panels; this will help to minimise the effects of a slight mis-match in paint colours. Bodywork fittings (e.g. rubbing strips, door handles, etc) will also need to be masked off. Use genuine masking tape and several thicknesses of newspaper for the masking operations.

Before commencing to spray, agitate the aerosol can thoroughly, and then spray a test area (an old tin, or similar) until the technique is mastered. Cover the repair area with a thick coat of primer; the thickness should be built up using several thin layers of paint rather than one thick one. Using 400-grade (or higher) wet-and-dry paper, rub down the surface of the primer until it is really smooth. While doing this, the work area should be thoroughly doused with water, and the wet-and-dry paper periodically rinsed in water. Allow to dry before spraying on more paint.

Spray on the top coat, again building up the thickness by using several thin layers of paint. Start spraying at the top of the repair area and then, using a side-to-side motion, work downwards until the whole repair area and about 2 inches of the surrounding original paintwork is covered. Remove all masking material 10 to 15 minutes after spraying on the final coat of paint.

Allow the new paint at least two weeks to harden, then, using a paintwork renovator or a very fine cutting paste, blend the edges of the paint into the existing paintwork. Finally, apply wax polish.

Plastic components

With the use of more and more plastic body components by the vehicle manufacturers (e.g. bumpers, spoilers, and in some cases major body panels), rectification of more serious damage to such items has become a matter of either entrusting repair work to a specialist in this field, or renewing complete components. Repair of such damage by the DIY owner is not really feasible, owing to the cost of the equipment and materials required for effecting such repairs. The basic technique involves making a groove along the line of the crack in the plastic using a rotary burr in a power drill. The damaged part is then welded back together by using a hot-air gun to heat up and fuse a plastic filler rod into the groove.

**6.2 Grille panel retaining screw –
one shown**

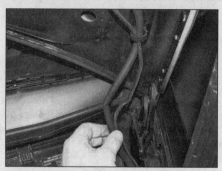

6.5 Unclip the wiring and washer hose

Removal

1 Raise the bonnet to the vertical position.
2 Working under the rear of the bonnet, undo the three retaining bolts from the grille panel **(see illustration)**.
3 Lower the bonnet (do not close completely), and lift the grille panel to release the locking clips from outside the rear of the bonnet.
4 Put a clean piece of cloth across the paintwork on the bonnet and lift out the grille panel and lay it upside down on the piece of cloth.
5 Unclip the washer hoses **(see illustration)** from the bonnet and release them from the washer nozzles from the right and left-hand side of the grille panel.
6 Where fitted, disconnect the wiring connector from the sun sensor fitted to the centre of the grille panel.
7 With the grille panel removed, open the bonnet to the vertical position.
8 Mark the position of the hinge bolts on both sides **(see illustration)**, so that the bonnet can be refitted in its original position.
9 With the aid of an assistant to support the bonnet, extract the strut upper retaining clip, then unhook and remove the strut from the bonnet on both sides **(see illustration)**.
10 With the help of an assistant, loosen and withdraw the hinge bolts, and carefully lift off the bonnet. Store the bonnet in a safe place to prevent any damage.

Refitting

11 Refitting is a reversal of removal, noting the following points:
a) *Reconnect the wiring plug(s) and hose(s) securely.*
b) *Lower the bonnet and check its fit and alignment. If necessary, adjust the bonnet position as described in Section 7.*
c) *Tighten the bonnet hinge bolts to the specified torque.*

6.8 Bonnet hinge retaining bolts

6.9 Strut upper retaining clip

Any excess plastic is then removed and the area rubbed down to a smooth finish. It is important that a filler rod of the correct plastic is used, as body components can be made of a variety of different types (e.g. polycarbonate, ABS, polypropylene).

Damage of a less serious nature (abrasions, minor cracks etc) can be repaired by the DIY owner using a two-part epoxy filler repair material. Once mixed in equal proportions, this is used in similar fashion to the bodywork filler used on metal panels. The filler is usually cured in twenty to thirty minutes, ready for sanding and painting.

If the owner is renewing a complete component himself, or if he has repaired it with epoxy filler, he will be left with the problem of finding a suitable paint for finishing which is compatible with the type of plastic used. At one time the use of a universal paint was not possible, owing to the complex range of plastics encountered in body component applications. Standard paints, generally speaking, will not bond to plastic or rubber satisfactorily. However, it is now possible to obtain a plastic body parts finishing kit, which consists of a pre-primer treatment, a primer and coloured top coat. Full instructions are normally supplied with a kit, but basically the method of use is to first apply the pre-primer to the component concerned and allow it to dry for up to 30 minutes. Then the primer is applied and left to dry for about an hour before finally applying the special coloured top coat. The result is a correctly coloured component where the paint will flex with the plastic or rubber, a property that standard paint does not normally possess.

Where serious damage has occurred, or large areas need renewal due to neglect, it means that complete new panels will need welding in, and this is best left to professionals. If the damage is due to impact, it will also be necessary to completely check the alignment of the bodyshell, and this can only be carried out accurately by a Mercedes-Benz dealer using special jigs. If the body is left misaligned, it is primarily dangerous as the car will not handle properly, and secondly, uneven stresses will be imposed on the steering, suspension and possibly transmission, causing abnormal wear, or complete failure, particularly to such items as the tyres.

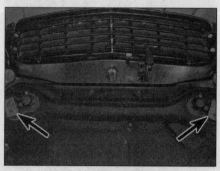

7.2 Lock striker plates

1 With the bonnet closed, check the gap between the bonnet and front wings on both sides (transverse adjustment), the alignment of the front edge of the bonnet with the front edge of the wing when looking down (longitudinal adjustment), and the height of the bonnet front edge and top edge in relation to the wing (height adjustment). The help of an assistant would be useful when adjusting the bonnet.
2 Open the bonnet and slacken the two bolts securing the lock striker plate to the bonnet. There are two striker plates fitted to the bonnet, one on the left and one on the right **(see illustration)**.

3 By trial and error, move the striker plate until an equal gap exists between the bonnet and the front wings on each side.

4 From within the engine compartment, slacken the locknut and screw down the bonnet rubber buffer **(see illustration)**.

5 Slacken the hinge retaining bolts.

6 By trial and error, move the bonnet as necessary, tightening the hinge bolts each time until the bonnet upper edge and front wing edge are aligned.

7 Now raise the rubber buffer a few turns at a time until the front edge of the bonnet and the edge of the wing, when viewed from the front, are aligned. Tighten the buffer locknut when adjustment is correct.

8 Bonnet support strut – removal and refitting

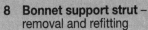

Removal

1 Raise the bonnet to the vertical position and have an assistant support the bonnet

2 Extract the strut retaining clip, then unhook and remove the strut from the bonnet **(see illustration)**.

3 Working at the lower end of the strut, extract the retaining clip, then unhook and remove the strut from the inner wing panel **(see illustration)**.

Refitting

4 Refitting is the reverse sequence to removal.

9 Bonnet release cables – removal and refitting

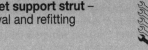

1 There are three bonnet release cables fitted. The rear one is from the bonnet release lever inside the vehicle to the connection box at the front right-hand side of the engine compartment. The two front cables are from the connection box to the two bonnet catches bolted to the front crossmember.

Removal

2 Open the bonnet. If the bonnet release cable has broken, it is probably best to seek the advice of a Mercedes-Benz dealer as to the best course of action.

3 Remove the bonnet lock catches from the front crossmember as described in Section 10.

4 Open the connector box and disconnect the rear bonnet release cable from the cable connection box **(see illustration)**.

5 Release the securing clips on the front crossmember and withdraw the front cables from the engine compartment, complete with the cable connection box.

6 Set the wiper arms to the vertical position and disconnect the battery negative lead, with reference to Chapter 5A.

7.4 Bonnet height adjuster

7 Unclip the washer nozzle cable and hose from the plastic water guard at the rear of the fusebox. Place the cable and hose to one side.

8 Release the locking clips and remove the cover from the fusebox, in the right-hand rear corner of the engine compartment.

9 Depending on model, lift out the engine control unit(s), release the locking clip and disconnect the wiring connectors.

10 Undo the retaining bolts and lift out the fuse/relay box.

11 Working inside the vehicle, undo the retaining screw from the bonnet release lever and pass the lever through the lower trim panel **(see illustration)**.

12 Undo the three retaining screws and remove the lower trim panel from under the driver's side of the facia panel. Disconnect the wiring connector from the data link connector as it is removed.

9.4 Disconnect the bonnet release cable

13 Unclip the bonnet release cable from the lever inside the vehicle and tie string to the release cable so that, as the cable is pulled through the bulkhead, it will pull the string with it.

14 Moving to the engine compartment, trace the route of the cable for use when refitting.

15 Pull out the cable in a forward direction. When the drawstring appears through the bulkhead, untie it and remove the cable from the car, leaving the string in place.

Refitting

16 Refitting is the reverse sequence to removal – use the string to draw the new cable through the bulkhead into the car. With the help of an assistant, make sure that the lock is working satisfactorily before closing the bonnet.

10 Bonnet lock catches – removal and refitting

1 There are two bonnet lock catches fitted, one on the left-hand side of the front cross-member and one on the right-hand side.

Removal

2 Open the bonnet.

3 Working inside the engine compartment, undo the retaining bolts on the left and right-hand bonnet lock catches in the crossmember **(see illustration)**.

4 Withdraw the plastic covers and remove

8.2 Strut upper retaining clip . . .

8.3 . . . and strut lower retaining clip

9.11 Undo the bonnet lever retaining screws

10.3 Bonnet catch retaining bolts

10.4 Disconnect the wiring connector

11.1 Undo the grille retaining screws

11.3 Remove the retaining screws

the lock catches from the crossmember, releasing them from the front bonnet release cable (**see illustration**). On later models, disconnect the wiring connectors from the lock catches.

11.4a Release the sides of the grille . . .

11.4b . . . and unclip it from the bumper

12.1 Bonnet emblem retaining clip

12.2 Remove the emblem from the bonnet

Refitting

5 Refitting is the reverse sequence to removal. Minor adjustment of the closing action can be carried out by adjusting the position of the lock striker on the underside of the bonnet.

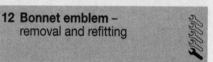

11 Radiator grille – removal and refitting

Removal

Bonnet-mounted grille

1 Open the bonnet and, from the inside at the front, undo the grille retaining screws (**see illustration**).
2 Remove the grille surround and grille from the bonnet, taking care not to damage the paintwork.

Bumper-mounted grille

3 Open the bonnet and undo the two centre grille retaining screws (**see illustration**).
4 Release each end of the grille from the retaining clips and withdraw the grille from the bumper (**see illustrations**), taking care not to damage the paintwork.

Refitting

5 Refitting is the reverse sequence to removal.

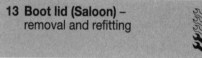

12 Bonnet emblem – removal and refitting

Removal

1 From the underside of the bonnet, turn the emblem retaining clip 90° anti-clockwise – the clip has raised sides to make it easier to grip with pliers (**see illustration**).
2 Pull the emblem upwards out of the bonnet to remove (**see illustration**).

Refitting

3 Refitting is the reverse sequence to removal, ensuring that the retaining clip is securely engaged.

13 Boot lid (Saloon) – removal and refitting

Removal

1 Disconnect the battery negative terminal.
2 Unclip and remove the trim panel from inside the boot lid for access to the hinges and wiring, etc. Prise out the plastic retaining clips using a wide-bladed screwdriver or forked tool.
3 Remove the clips securing the wiring harness duct to the left-hand hinge, and disconnect the wiring connectors (**see illustrations**).
4 Mark the outline of the hinges on the boot lid using a pencil.
5 Place some rags beneath the lower corners of the boot lid and, with the help of an assistant, undo the hinge retaining bolts.

Remove the boot lid upwards out of the restraining hooks, and out from the car.

Refitting

6 Refitting is the reverse sequence to removal, but align the hinges with the outline marks made prior to removal before tightening the bolts. Adjust the lock striker plate as necessary to achieve satisfactory opening and closing of the boot lid.

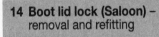

14 Boot lid lock (Saloon) – removal and refitting

Removal

1 Unclip and remove the trim panel from inside the boot lid. Prise out the plastic retaining clips using a wide-bladed screwdriver or forked tool. Where applicable, the mountings for the warning triangle are removed by depressing the catch with a small screwdriver.

2 Working inside the boot lid undo the eight retaining screws from the number plate panel. From the outside of the boot lid remove the number plate, and then undo the retaining nut from the centre of the number plate panel.

3 Disconnect the wiring connectors from the lock assembly, undo the retaining bolts and remove the lock catch from the lower edge of the boot lid **(see illustration)**.

4 Working on the outside of the boot lid, undo the lock barrel mounting bolts and withdraw the lock. Remove the plastic cover from the

13.3a release the retaining clips . . .

lock assembly and disconnect the control cable **(see illustration)**.

5 If required, the lock striker plate can be removed from the rear crossmember by removing the two retaining bolts **(see illustration)**.

Refitting

6 Refitting is the reverse sequence to removal. Adjust the lock striker plate as necessary to achieve satisfactory opening and closing of the boot lid.

15 Tailgate and support struts (Estate and Coupe) – removal and refitting

Removal

1 Disconnect the battery negative terminal with reference to Chapter 5A.

13.3b . . . and unclip the trim from the hinge

2 With the tailgate open, on Estate models, unclip the plastic trim from the rear edge of the roof lining inside the vehicle. On Coupe models, unclip the rear of the headlining and insert spacers (approximately 65 mm) to hold the rear of the headlining down.

3 Working around the sides and lower edge of the rear tailgate, remove the inner panel securing screws/clips.

4 Carefully unclip the lower trim panel from the tailgate **(see illustration)**, releasing it from the two side trim panels.

5 Unclip the plastic upper trim panel and two side trim panels from the top of the tailgate, taking care not to damage the panels **(see illustrations)**.

6 On Coupe models undo the retaining screws and remove the plastic trim panel from across the centre of the tailgate panel **(see illustration)**.

7 Disconnect the wiring connectors and

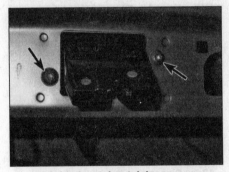

14.3 Lock catch retaining screws

14.4 Lock control cable

14.5 Lock striker retaining screws

15.4 Unclip the trim panel from the tailgate (Coupe)

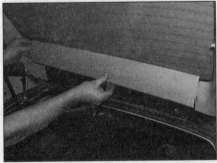

15.5a Unclip the plastic trim panel . . .

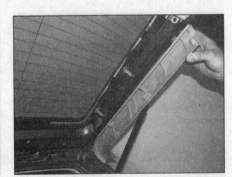

15.5b . . . and the side trim panels

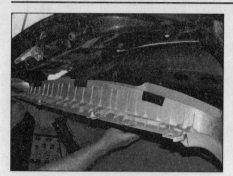

15.6 Remove plastic centre trim panel (Coupe)

15.9 Remove the strut lower balljoint

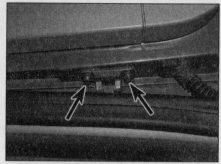

15.10 Hinge retaining bolts

washer hose from their connections in the tailgate. Where necessary, tie string to the hoses/wiring, so that as the hoses/wiring are pulled out of the tailgate, it will pull the string with it, leaving the string in position.

8 Mark the fitted positions of the hinges on the tailgate, so that the tailgate can be accurately aligned when refitting.

9 Have an assistant support the tailgate, then prise off the tailgate strut upper retaining clips, and remove the tailgate support struts, pulling them off their lower ball fittings on the body if required (see illustrations).

10 Still supporting the tailgate, loosen and remove the tailgate hinge bolts (see illustration), and with the help of an assistant, remove the tailgate from the car.

Refitting

11 Refitting is a reversal of removal. If necessary, adjust the tailgate to achieve a good fit. The hinge and lock striker plate can be loosened and the components moved as required; there are also two adjustable rubber buffers fitted to the lower edge of the tailgate.

16 Tailgate lock (Estate and Coupe) – removal and refitting

1 Disconnect the battery negative terminal.
2 With the tailgate open, work around the sides and lower edge of the rear tailgate and remove the inner panel securing screws/clips.
3 Carefully unclip the lower trim panel from the tailgate, releasing it from the two side trim panels.
4 On Estate models, working inside the boot lid undo the retaining nut from the middle of the number plate panel. From the outside of the boot lid unclip and remove the number plate panel (see illustrations).
5 Disconnect the wiring connector from the tailgate lock assembly (see illustrations).
6 On Coupe models, undo the two retaining bolts and then remove the lock from inside the tailgate.
7 On Estate models, undo the two retaining bolts on the outside of the tailgate, and then remove the lock from inside the tailgate (see illustration).
8 Disconnect the wiring connector from the tailgate catch, undo the two bolts on the lower edge of the tailgate and remove the catch (see illustrations).
9 If required, the lock striker plate can be removed from the rear crossmember by removing the trim panel and then removing the two retaining bolts (see illustrations).

16.4a Undo the retaining nut . . .

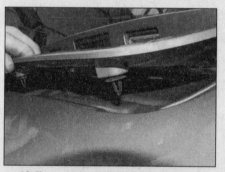

16.4b . . . and unclip the tailgate trim

16.5a Disconnect the wiring connector (Coupe)

16.5b Disconnect the wiring connector (Estate)

16.7 Tailgate lock retaining bolts

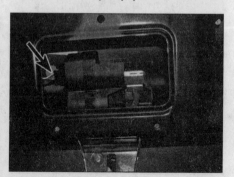

16.8a Disconnect the wiring connector . . .

16.8b . . . and undo the tailgate catch retaining bolts

16.9a Remove the rear trim retaining clips

16.9b Lock striker retaining bolts

Refitting

10 Refitting is a reversal of removal. If necessary, adjust the tailgate lock striker on completion to achieve satisfactory operation.

17 Bumpers –
removal and refitting

Front bumper

1 Chock the rear wheels and firmly apply the parking brake, then jack up the front of the car and support it on axle stands (see *Jacking and vehicle support*).

2 Remove the front section of the wheel arch liner, for access to the bumper side mounting nuts.

3 Working under each side of the bumper, unscrew and remove the two bolts which secure the bumper to the mounting brackets, and then swivel the brackets away from the bumper (see illustrations).

4 On models equipped with front foglights, disconnect the foglight wiring from the light units, and fasten it up out of the way.

5 Where the outside air temperature sensor is fitted, trace the wiring harness from the sensor fitted to the inside of the bumper, and disconnect it at the connector (see illustration).

6 Open the bonnet, and remove the two bumper securing bolts visible in the radiator grille aperture. Immediately below these two bolts are two further bolts, accessed through

the front of the bumper trim panel apertures (see illustration).

7 With all mounting nuts and bolts removed, make sure the side retaining brackets have been released (see paragraph 3) and with the help of an assistant, pull the bumper forwards off its guides.

8 Refitting is a reversal of removal.

Rear bumper

9 Remove the rear light unit as described in Chapter 12.

10 Working inside the luggage compartment, remove the panelling from the left and right-hand inner wing panels. Where applicable, undo the retaining screws and remove the rear speakers.

11 On Estate models, remove the rear loading floor and panelling. Also undo the retaining

bolts and remove the tool holder from inside the left-hand rear wing panel.

12 Where the Parktronic parking aid system is fitted, working inside the right-hand side of the luggage compartment, trace the wiring harness from the sensors fitted to the bumper, and disconnect it at the connector.

13 Unscrew the inner retaining nuts and retaining screws from the inner wing panels at each side (see illustration).

14 On level ground, chock the front wheels, and then jack up the rear of the car and support it on axle stands (see *Jacking and vehicle support*).

15 Working under the rear wheel arches, undo the retaining screws and clips and remove the inner wheel arch liners from both sides.

16 Remove the two retaining clips and one

17.3a Remove the retaining screw . . .

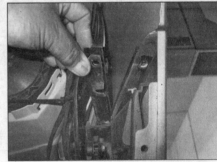

17.3b . . . and swivel the bracket

17.5 Air temperature sensor connector

17.6 Bumper retaining screws – one side shown

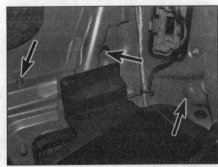

17.13 Bumper inner mounting bolts (Estate)

retaining bolt from under each side of the rear bumper **(see illustration)**.

17 Release the rear exhaust silencer rubber mounting from its mounting bracket and lower the rear of the exhaust. Use an axle stand or similar to support the weight of the exhaust to prevent damage.

18 Slacken and remove the retaining nuts/ bolts on the two rear mounting brackets from under the vehicle.

19 With the help of an assistant, carefully pull the bumper rearwards to release it from the side mounting guides, and remove it from the car.

20 Refitting is a reversal of removal.

18 Door trim panel – removal and refitting

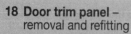
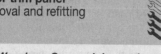

⚠ **Warning: On models equipped with side airbags, one airbag unit is housed in each front door trim panel. Although removing the door trim panel should not involve disturbing the airbag unit in any way, it is still wise to be aware of the precautions to be observed when working with the airbag system.**

● **Before carrying out any operations on the airbag system, disconnect the battery negative terminal and wait at least 15 minutes to allow the system capacitors to discharge. When operations are complete, make sure no one is inside the vehicle when the battery is reconnected.**

● **Airbags must not be subjected to**

17.16 Wheel arch inner mounting bolt

temperatures in excess of 90°C. When an airbag is removed, ensure that it is stored the correct way up to prevent possible inflation.

● *Do not allow any solvents or cleaning agents to contact the airbag assemblies. They must be cleaned using only a damp cloth.*

● *Airbags are sensitive to impact. If they are dropped or damaged, they should be renewed.*

Removal

1 On models equipped with side airbags, ensure that the ignition switch is off (take out the key). Disconnect the battery negative lead, and position the lead away from the battery terminal (Mercedes-Benz recommend covering up the terminal, to prevent accidental reconnection). Wait for at least 15 minutes before proceeding.

2 Carefully unclip the trim panel from the door grab handle **(see illustration)**.

3 On front doors, unclip the airbag trim emblem from the door trim panel **(see illustration)**.

4 Remove the screw at the rear of the door and remove the door lock trim panel **(see illustration)**.

5 Remove the retaining screw from the door grab handle recess **(see illustration)**.

6 On front doors, unclip the mirror inner trim panel and disconnect the wiring connectors as it is removed **(see illustration)**.

7 Where fitted, unclip the door-open light unit from the bottom of the door trim panel **(see illustration)**.

8 Using a wide-bladed or wedge tool, carefully prise off the door trim panel, working progressively around the edge of the panel until all the clips have been released **(see illustrations)**. Do not use excessive force; otherwise the clips will be broken.

9 Lift the trim panel slightly, and free it from the window channel at the top. Further lift the panel, to clear the lock-operating knob at the top

10 Carefully withdraw the panel from the door, sufficiently to gain access to the lock handle operating mechanism. Unhook the lock operating cable **(see illustration)**.

11 Where applicable, disconnect the wiring plug(s) from the window switch(es) **(see illustration)**. Check that there is nothing else attached to the door trim panel, then remove it from the car.

12 If desired (if the door internal components

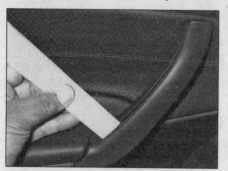

18.2 Unclip the trim panel

18.3 Unclip the SRS airbag trim

18.4 Remove trim retaining screw

18.5 Undo the retaining screw inside the handle

18.6 Unclip the mirror inner trim

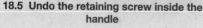

18.7 Unclip the door-open light unit

18.8a Carefully unclip the door trim panel . . .

18.8b . . . and remove from the door

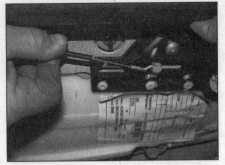

18.10 Unclip the operating cable

18.11 Disconnect the wiring connectors

18.12a Remove the grab handle bracket . . .

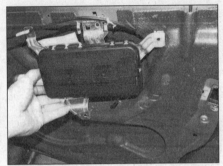

18.12b . . . and the airbag unit

are to be worked on), the waterproofing sheet must now be removed from the door. To remove the sheet completely, first remove the door speaker as described in Chapter 12. Also drill out the rivets and remove the grab handle support bracket and the airbag unit from the door. If great care is taken, the sheet can simply be peeled off, and re-used **(see illustrations)**.

Refitting

13 Refitting is the reverse sequence to removal. On models with side airbags, close the front doors, making sure that no-one is inside the car, and check that the ignition switch is still off before reconnecting the battery negative lead.

19 Front door window glass and regulator – removal and refitting

Removal

1 Remove the door inner trim panel and waterproofing sheet, as described in Section 18.
2 Prise up and remove the inner and outer window channel sealing strips at the top of the door, taking care not to damage the door paintwork.
3 Lower the window until the bolts securing the window glass to the window regulator are accessible through the apertures **(see illustrations)**.

4 Disengage the window from the regulator and guide channel, then tilt it forwards before lifting it up and removing it to the outside of the door.
5 Drill out the regulator and guide channel pop-rivets, then manoeuvre the regulator downwards and out through the door aperture **(see illustration)**.
6 Disconnect the wiring plug from the window motor as it becomes accessible, then remove the regulator completely.

Refitting

7 Refitting is the reverse sequence to removal. Lubricate the regulator sliding channels when reassembling.

19.3a Align front guide mounting bolt . . .

19.3b . . . and the rear guide mounting bolt

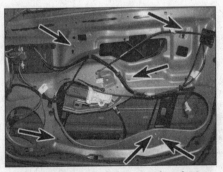

19.5 Window regulator securing rivets

20.3 Align the guide mounting bolt

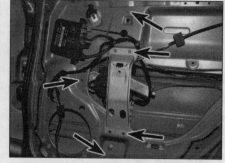

20.5 Window regulator securing rivets

20 Rear door window glass and regulator – removal and refitting

Removal

1 Remove the door inner trim panel as described in Section 18.
2 Carefully prise up the inner and outer sealing strips at the top of the door panel, taking care not to damage the paintwork.
3 Lower the window until the bolt securing the window glass to the window regulator is accessible through the aperture (**see illustration**).
4 Disengage the window from the regulator and guide channel, then tilt it forwards before lifting it up and removing it to the outside of the door.
5 Drill out the regulator and guide channel pop-rivets, then manoeuvre the regulator

downwards and out through the door aperture (**see illustration**).
6 Disconnect the wiring plug from the window motor as it becomes accessible, then remove the regulator completely.

Refitting

7 Refitting is the reverse sequence to removal. Lubricate the regulator sliding channels when reassembling.

21 Front door exterior handle – removal and refitting

Removal

1 Open the door, pull off the door seal in the area around the door lock, and then undo the door button/lock cylinder retaining screw (**see illustration**).

2 Withdraw the door lock cylinder/button from the door handle and where applicable, disconnect the wiring connector (**see illustrations**).
3 Push the door exterior handle to the rear, while at the same time pulling outwards, then disengage the tangs at the front from the mounting bracket; recover the rubber gaskets from the front and rear of the handle (**see illustrations**).

Refitting

4 Refitting is the reverse sequence to removal.

22 Front door lock assembly – removal and refitting

Removal

1 Remove the door window glass and regulator as described in Section 19.
2 Trace the wiring connectors and cables and unclip them from the door panel.
3 Remove the front door exterior handle as described in Section 21.
4 Working on the outside of the door, remove the rubber gasket and undo the outer retaining screw (**see illustration**).
5 Remove the three lock securing screws from the rear edge of the door, and withdraw the lock assembly down the rear edge of the door until it can be withdrawn through the door aperture (**see illustration**). Where applicable, disconnect the anti-theft alarm wiring plug as

21.2a Pull out the door lock cylinder . . .

21.2b . . . and disconnect the wiring connector

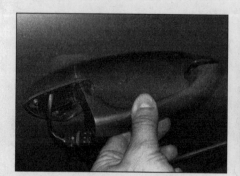

21.1 Undo the securing screw

21.3a Pull the door handle out . . .

21.3b . . . and remove the rubber gaskets

22.4 Undo the outer retaining screw

22.5 Undo the three lock mounting bolts

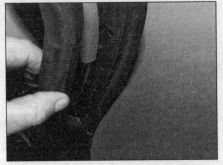

23.1a Pull back the door seal . . .

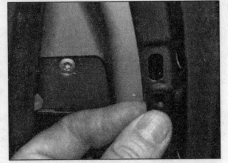

23.1b . . . and remove the rubber grommet

the lock is removed, and separate the cover from the lock assembly.

Refitting

6 Refitting is the reverse sequence to removal. Check the lock operation before refitting the door inner trim panel.

23 Rear door exterior handle – removal and refitting

Removal

1 Open the door, pull off the door seal in the area around the door lock button, and remove the rubber grommet **(see illustrations)**.
2 Insert a Torx 20 screwdriver and undo the door button retaining screw **(see illustrations)**. Depending on which door is being worked on, the screw may need to be turned clockwise or anti-clockwise. **Note:** *This screw does not need to be removed completely, it just needs to be slackened to release the inner retaining clips.*
3 Withdraw the door button from the door handle **(see illustration)**.
4 Push the door exterior handle to the rear, while at the same time pulling outwards, then disengage the tangs at the front from the mounting bracket; recover the rubber gaskets from the front and rear of the handle **(see illustrations)**.

Refitting

5 Refitting is the reverse sequence to removal.

24 Rear door lock assembly – removal and refitting

Removal

1 Remove the door inner trim panel as described in Section 18. Make sure the window is in the fully closed position.
2 Trace the wiring connectors and cables and unclip them from the door panel.
3 Remove the rear door exterior handle as described in Section 23.
4 Working on the outside of the door, remove

23.2a Slacken the retaining screw . . .

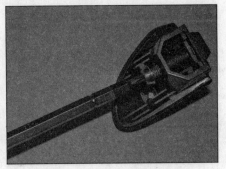

23.2b . . . in the door button . . .

the rubber gaskets and undo the outer retaining screws **(see illustration)**.
5 Remove the three lock securing screws from the rear edge of the door, and withdraw the lock assembly down the rear edge of the

door until it can be withdrawn through the door aperture **(see illustration)**. Where applicable, disconnect the anti-theft alarm wiring plug as the lock is removed, and separate the cover from the lock assembly.

23.3 . . . and remove from the door handle

23.4b . . . and remove the rubber gaskets

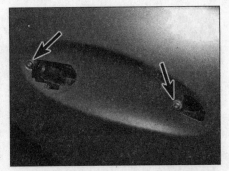

24.4 Door lock outer retaining screws

23.4a Release the door handle . . .

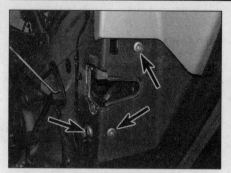

24.5 Remove the door lock retaining screws

25.3 Actuator retaining screws

25.8a Front door control module

25.8b Rear door control module

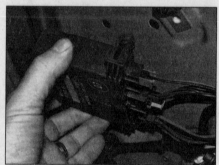

25.12a Release the retaining clips . . .

25.12b . . . and remove from the door

Refitting

6 Refitting is the reverse sequence to removal. Check the lock operation before refitting the door inner trim panel.

25 Central locking system components – removal and refitting

Lock switches and actuators

1 The switches and actuators are all part of the door lock assemblies. On most models, only the front door locks have switches which activate the complete system when either front door is locked/unlocked. Remove the lock assemblies as described in the relevant Section. See your local Mercedes dealer for availability of components for the lock assembly.

Fuel filler flap

2 Open the boot lid or tailgate, and remove the inner trim panel from the right-hand side of the luggage area for access to the fuel filler flap actuator.
3 Loosen but do not remove the two bolts on the actuator bracket (see illustration).
4 Detach the actuator and its bracket from the support strut, then press down the raised tab between the actuator body and bracket to release the actuator.
5 Refitting is a reversal of removal. Check the operation of the flap before refitting the trim.

Infra-red receivers

6 The receivers are only fitted to those locks which are equipped with lock switches, ie, the front doors.
7 The receivers for the front doors are incorporated into the lock cylinders, and may be removed as described in Section 21.

Control module

8 There are control modules located behind the door trim panels (see illustrations). Note that, where applicable, the other 'modules' in the front doors are the side airbag, which are riveted in position.
9 Disconnect the battery negative lead.
10 Remove the door trim panel as described in Section 18.
11 Disconnect the wiring plugs from the module.
12 Release the retaining lugs (they either squeeze together, or are pressed apart), and remove the module from the car (see illustrations).
13 Refitting is a reversal of removal.

26 Doors – removal and refitting

Front doors

1 Remove the door trim panel as described in Section 18.
2 Pull off the door seal from around the door aperture. Remove the A-pillar kick panel to access the front door wiring harness or the B-pillar lower trim to access the rear door wiring harness.
3 With the lower trim panel removed, open the cover on the wiring harness inside the pillar, and disconnect the wiring connectors.
4 Detach the rubber gaiter (see illustration), either from the door or the body and pull the wiring out through the aperture.
5 Undo the two retaining bolts from the door check strap (see illustration).

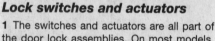

26.4 Unclip the rubber gaiter

26.5 Check strap retaining bolts

26.6a Upper hinge retaining nut . . .

26.6b . . . and lower hinge retaining nut

6 Remove the upper and lower hinge retaining nuts **(see illustrations)**, and then with the aid of an assistant lift the door off the hinges and away from the vehicle, taking care not to damage the paintwork.

7 Refitting is the reverse sequence to removal, noting the following points:
a) Locate the door onto the centring bolts on each hinge when fitting initially, prior to inserting and tightening the hinge bolts.
b) Tighten the hinge bolts and door check strap bolt to the specified torque.
c) Make sure that all wiring connectors are secure and correctly reconnected.
d) Adjustments can be made at the hinges and at the door striker to provide an equal gap all round the door, and to align the contour of the door panel with that of the front wing.

27 Windscreen and fixed glass – removal and refitting

Due to the methods of attachment, and the special equipment required to complete the task successfully, removal and refitting of the windscreen, rear/tailgate window (and rear side windows on Estate models) should be entrusted to a dealer or an automotive glass specialist.

28 Door mirror glass and housing – removal and refitting

Mirror glass

Note: The mirror glass is clipped into place with a spring clip. Wear protective gloves and glasses to prevent personal injury.

1 Press in the bottom of the mirror glass so that the top edge is furthest from the housing. Then insert a small screwdriver and release the mirror glass retaining spring clip and unclip the mirror. Take great care when removing the glass; do not use excessive force, as the glass is easily broken **(see illustrations)**.

2 Disconnect the wiring connectors from the rear of the mirror glass as it is removed **(see illustration)**.

3 Refitting is the reverse of the relevant removal procedure. When refitting the mirror glass, make sure the spring clip is located correctly on the rear of the glass before pressing into position. Fit the spring clip over the lug at the top of the glass, and when the mirror glass is in position, use a small screwdriver to hook the spring to secure the top of the glass **(see illustrations)**. Press firmly at the centre taking care not to use excessive force, as the glass is easily broken. Make sure the wiring inside the mirror housing is connected securely, before refitting the mirror glass.

Mirror housing

4 Remove the mirror glass as described in paragraphs 1 and 2.

5 Fold the mirror inwards towards the door and insert a screwdriver inside the back of the mirror to release the retaining clip **(see illustrations)**.

6 Withdraw the cover from the mirror motor mechanism; disconnect the wiring connectors if required **(see illustration)**.

28.1a Release the retaining clip . . .

28.1b . . . and remove the mirror glass

28.2 Disconnect the wiring connector(s)

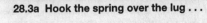

28.3a Hook the spring over the lug . . .

28.3b . . . and then release it (cover removed for clarity)

28.5a Insert a screwdriver . . .

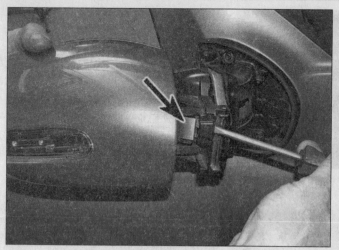

28.5b . . . and release the locking clip

28.6 Lugs locate into cover

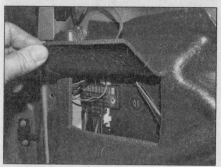

29.2 Wiring connectors in control unit

29.3 Mirror retaining screws

7 Refitting is the reverse of the relevant removal procedure.

29 Door mirror assembly – removal and refitting

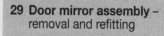

1 Remove the door trim panel as described in Section 18.
2 Open the flap in the weather sheet and disconnect the wiring connector from the control unit **(see illustration)**.
3 Working outside the vehicle, fold the mirror inwards towards the door and undo the three retaining screws **(see illustration)**.
4 Withdraw the mirror from the door while guiding the wiring through the hole.
5 Refitting is a reversal of removal. Before refitting the mirror cover, return the cover retaining spring plate to its original position. The cover also has a retaining lug inside, which must engage correctly with the mirror body when it is fitted.

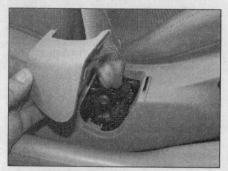

30.1 Unclip the trim panel . . .

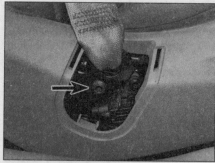

30.2 . . . and remove the retaining bolt

30 Front seats – removal and refitting

Removal

1 Move the seat fully forward and carefully unclip the trim from the end of the seat belt attachment to the seat **(see illustration)**.
2 Unscrew the seat belt mounting bolt from the seat, and recover any washers and spacers, noting their order of fitting **(see illustration)**.
3 Unscrew the bolts at the rear of each seat slide rail **(see illustration)**.
4 Move the seat fully backwards, and unscrew the bolts at the front of each seat slide rail **(see illustrations)**.
5 Disconnect the seat wiring connector at the front of the seat, noting its location for refitting **(see illustration)**. Depending on the level of equipment fitted, there may be more

30.3 Seat rear mounting bolts

30.4a Front right-hand mounting bolt . . .

than one plug – make sure that all wiring is disconnected before lifting the seat out.

6 Lift the seat and remove it from the car.

Refitting

7 Refitting is the reverse sequence to removal. Tighten the seat belt end fittings and seat mounting bolts to the specified torque.

31 Rear seat –
removal and refitting

30.4b . . . and left-hand mounting bolt

30.5 Disconnect the wiring connector(s)

Seat cushion

1 Slide both front seats as far forward as possible.

2 On models with split rear seats for loading, release the locking catches and tilt the rear seat cushion forward. Undo the retaining nuts and disconnect the seat cushion support straps from the floor panel **(see illustrations)**.

3 Unclip the plastic caps from along the front edge of the seat cushion **(see illustration)**.

4 Undo the retaining nuts, and lift out the seat cushion from the vehicle.

5 Refitting is the reverse sequence to removal, noting the following points.

a) *Make sure the seat belts are not trapped as the seat is installed, and that the belt buckles are fed through the seat properly.*

b) *Ensure that the seat catches engage securely.*

Seat back

6 Remove the headrests from the seat back.

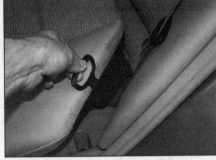

31.2a Lift up the rear seat cushion . . .

31.2b . . . and undo the strap retaining nuts

7 Release the locking catches and tilt the rear seat cushions forward **(see illustration)**.

8 Where applicable, undo the retaining bolts, and then unclip the side cushion from the body panel **(see illustrations)**.

9 Release the securing clips and unclip the

seat pads from the lower end of the seat back **(see illustrations)**.

10 Undo the retaining bolts and remove the seat belt anchorage points from the floor panel **(see illustration)**.

11 Undo the two retaining nuts from the

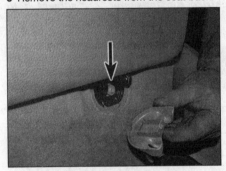

31.3 Undo the retaining nuts

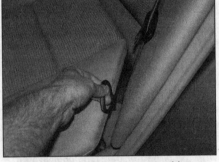

31.7 Lift up the rear seat cushion

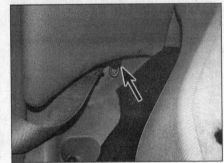

31.8a Undo the retaining bolts . . .

31.8b . . . and remove the side cushions

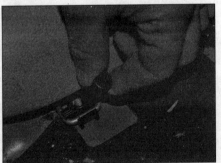

31.9a Release the securing clips . . .

31.9b . . . and remove the lower pads

31.10 Seat belt anchorage bolt

31.14a Remove the retaining screw . . .

31.14b . . . the hook and trim . . .

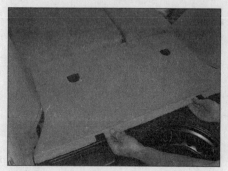

31.14c . . . and then remove the trim floor panel

31.15a Seat inner mounting nuts

31.15b Seat outer mounting bolts

hinge bracket, where the split seat back joins.

12 Release the locking catches and tilt the rear seat back forwards, so they lie flat.

13 Release the loading compartment blind from the rear of the seats by sliding it to the side.

14 Where applicable, undo the cargo holding hooks from the floor of the luggage compartment and remove the floor covering to access the seat back hinges **(see illustrations)**.

15 Undo the two retaining nuts and bolts from the hinge brackets **(see illustrations)**, and carefully withdraw the seat backs from the vehicle.

16 Refitting is the reverse sequence to removal, noting the following points:

 a) Tighten the hinge nuts and bolts securely.

 b) Ensure that the seat belts are not trapped as the seat is installed, and that the belts and buckles are fed through properly.

 c) Ensure that the seat catches engage securely.

32 Seat belts – removal and refitting

⚠️ **Warning: All models are equipped with spring-loaded automatic tensioning devices fitted to the front seat belt inertia reel assemblies. The belt tensioners are triggered by the airbag system in the event of an accident. For safety reasons, no attempt should be made to dismantle the front seat belt inertia reels, and no electrical testing should be performed on any of the wiring associated with the airbag or belt tensioner system – work of this nature must be entrusted to a Mercedes-Benz dealer.**

• *Although no specific precautions are given by the manufacturer, it seems prudent to treat the seat belt tensioner with as much care as an airbag unit (see Chapter 12). Therefore, do not drop or strike the tensioner, nor subject it to extremes of heat. If there is any doubt about the condition of the seat belt or tensioner, refer to a Mercedes-Benz dealer – DO NOT attempt to dismantle the belt reel or tensioner, as this could be highly dangerous. If any noise has been noted from the seat belt mechanism, do not attempt to cure this by applying lubricants of any kind. A noise from the tensioner may indicate an internal fault, or it may be that the unit has 'fired', and is therefore no longer operative.*

Front belts

1 Disconnect the battery negative lead, and position the lead away from the battery terminal.

2 Pull off the door rubber sealing weatherstrip around the centre pillar **(see illustration)**.

3 Remove the B-pillar trim panels as described in Section 36.

4 Carefully unclip the trim surrounding the end of the seat belt attachment to the seat.

5 Unscrew the seat belt mounting bolt from the seat, and recover any washers and spacers, noting their order of fitting **(see illustration)**.

6 Feed the end of the seat belt through the upper section of the trim panel, and remove the panel completely.

32.2 Unclip the door seal

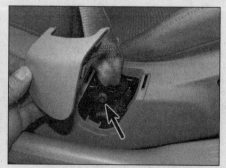

32.5 Undo the seat belt bolt

32.7 Seat belt upper mounting nut

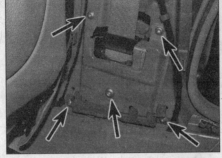

32.8 Inertia reel mounting bracket bolts

32.21 Unbolt and remove the seat belt lower mounting

7 Unscrew and remove the seat belt upper mounting bolt, and recover the washers and spacers fitted around it, noting their fitted sequence **(see illustration)**.
8 Unscrew and remove the inertia reel mounting bracket bolts **(see illustration)**, and recover any washers or spacers used, noting their fitted sequence.
9 Disconnect the wiring plug as the seat belt inertia reel/belt tensioner assembly is removed.
10 Remove the seat belt from the car, noting the precautions listed at the start of this Section.
11 Refitting is the reverse sequence to removal, noting the following points:
  a) *Tighten the seat belt mounting bolts to the specified torque.*
  b) *When refitting the B-pillar trim panel, engage the seat belt height adjuster lug with the inside of the adjuster lever. Where applicable, refit the screws and wiring plug to the alarm sensor before fitting the panel over it.*

Front belt stalks

12 Remove the relevant front seat as described in Section 30.
13 Unscrew the bolt at the rear securing the stalk side trim panel, and remove the panel.
14 Release the wiring from the cable-ties as necessary, and then unclip the inner cover from the belt stalk.
15 Disconnect the wiring plug from the seat belt stalk.
16 Unscrew the seat belt stalk mounting bolt, noting the fitted sequence of any washers, and remove the stalk from the car.
17 Refitting is a reversal of removal. Tighten the stalk mounting bolt to the specified torque, and secure the wiring using new cable-ties.

Rear belts

Note: *Where fitted, the centre seat belt is incorporated into the seat itself, and can only be removed by dismantling the seat, which includes removing the seat covering. This job is considered beyond the scope of this manual, and is best entrusted to a Mercedes-Benz dealer.*

32.22 Feed the seat belt through the C-pillar trim panel

Saloon models

18 Remove the rear seat cushion and backrest as described in Section 31.
19 Pull off the door rubber sealing weatherstrip around the front edge of the C-pillar trim panel.
20 Remove the C-pillar trim panels as described in Section 36.
21 Unscrew the seat belt end fitting bolt from the floor, recovering any washers or spacers used. Unhook the endplate from the recess in the car body **(see illustration)**.
22 Feed the end of the seat belt through the trim panel, and remove the panel completely **(see illustration)**.
23 Unbolt and remove the seat belt upper mounting bolt, recovering any washers or spacers used **(see illustration)**.
24 Unscrew and remove the bolts securing

32.23 Unscrew and remove the seat belt upper mounting bolt

the seat belt guide to the rear pillar, and remove the guide.
25 Unscrew and remove the inertia reel mounting bolt, and remove the seat belt from the car, feeding the belt through the sound insulation panel.
26 If required, the rear seat belt stalks can be unbolted from the floor and removed.
27 Refitting is a reversal of removal. Tighten the seat belt mounting bolts to the specified torque.

Estate and Coupe models

28 Remove the rear seat bench and backrest as described in Section 31.
29 Unclip the cover fitted over the seat belt upper mounting bolt, and then unscrew and remove **(see illustrations)**.
30 Unclip and remove the luggage compartment side trim panels as described in Section 36.

32.29a Remove the plastic trim . . .

32.29b . . . and seat belt upper mounting bolt

32.31 Inertia reel mounting bracket bolts

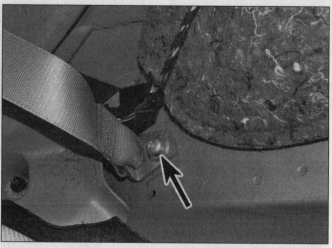

32.32 Seat belt lower anchorage bolt

32.33 Seat belt stalk bolt

31 Unscrew and remove the seat belt inertia reel mounting bracket bolts **(see illustration)**.
32 Undo the seat belt lower anchorage-mounting bolt **(see illustration)**. In all cases, note the fitted sequence of any washers or spacers used. Remove the seat belt from the car.
33 If required, the rear seat belt stalks can be unbolted from the floor and removed **(see illustration)**, once the insulating mat is lifted out.
34 Refitting is a reversal of removal. Tighten the seat belt mounting bolts to the specified torque.

33 Sunroof – general information

A sliding sunroof, either mechanically- or electrically-operated, is available as a factory-fitted option. Adjustment or repair of the sunroof or its component parts should be left to a dealer, as the complexity of the unit and the need for special tools and equipment renders these operations beyond the scope of the average owner.

34 Centre console – removal and refitting

Removal

1 Disconnect the battery negative lead, and position the lead away from the battery terminal.
2 Prise out and release the gear lever boot from the console cover, and slide the boot up the lever **(see illustration)**.
3 On automatic transmission models, prise up the plastic frame surrounding the selector level panel. Disconnecting the wiring plug as this is removed **(see illustration)**.
4 On manual transmission models, operate the clutch pedal and select 2nd gear. On automatic transmission models, move the selector lever towards the rear of the vehicle. If lever is in the locked position, insert a pen or similar inside the compartment behind the gear lever to release the switch **(see illustrations)**.
5 Open the small storage compartment lid at the rear of the gear lever and remove the cup holder (where fitted). Remove the rubber mat and undo the retaining screw from inside the cup holder.
6 Unclip the trim cover from the top of the centre console **(see illustration)**.
7 Open the ashtray and release the two tabs

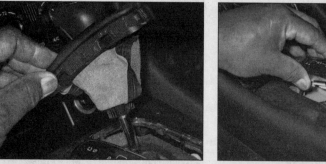

34.2 Release the gaiter from around the lever

34.3 Unclip the selector panel

34.4a Unclip the coin holder . . .

34.4b . . . and insert a pen

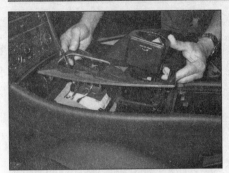

34.6 Remove the upper trim cover

34.7 Removing the ashtray

34.8a Remove the plastic covers . . .

34.8b . . . and turn the locking clips

34.9 Undo the two retaining bolts

34.10 Console front locating peg – one side shown

at the lower part of the ashtray. Withdraw the ashtray, disconnecting the wiring connector as this is done **(see illustration)**.

8 Unclip the plastic covers from inside the left and right-hand sides of the front edge of the console **(see illustrations)**. Then turn the locating screws approximately half a turn anti-clockwise to release the front edge of the console.

9 Open up the centre armrest and remove the piece of carpet from the inside the storage compartment. Undo the two retaining bolts from inside the bottom of the compartment **(see illustration)**.

10 Lift and tilt the console to separate the sliding joint connections **(see illustration)** at the front, where it joins the facia panel. Lift the console over the gear/selector lever, and remove it from the car. Disconnect any wiring from the centre console as it is removed, noting its fitted position.

Refitting

11 Refitting is the reverse sequence to removal.

35 Glovebox –
removal and refitting

Removal

1 Disconnect the battery negative terminal and remove the centre console as described in Section 34.

2 Release the lower locking clips at each end of the centre air vents and position the vents in the upward position **(see illustration)**. Then undo the two retaining screws from inside the lower part of the air vents.

3 Release the upper locking clips at each

end of the centre air vents and position the vents in the downward position. Then release the two retaining clips from inside the upper part of the centre air vent and unclip from the facia panel. Where applicable, disconnect the wiring connector from the vent panel.

4 Undo the retaining screws and remove the radio/display unit with reference to Chapter 12.

5 Undo the retaining screws and remove the centre panel and unclip it from the facia. Disconnect the wiring connectors from the rear of the centre panel as it is removed.

6 Working under the glovebox, unscrew the two retaining screws, and remove the lower cover **(see illustration)**.

7 Pull the cover to remove it from the left-hand end of the facia panel, and undo the two retaining screws **(see illustrations)**.

8 Open the glovebox and undo the retaining screws from the facia panel.

35.2 Release the locking clips inside vent

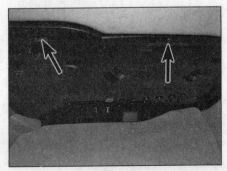

35.6 Lower cover retaining screws

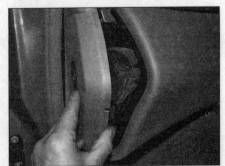

35.7a Unclip the facia end cover . . .

9 Undo the retaining screws from the centre console left-hand panel and remove it complete with glovebox assembly.

Refitting

10 Refitting is the reversal of the removal procedure.

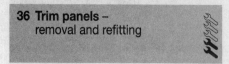

36 Trim panels –
removal and refitting

A-pillar trim panel

1 Pull away the door seal weatherstrip on the front body pillar on both sides.
2 Remove both front pillar trim panels by pushing the panel in the area of the retaining clips away from the pillar using a plastic wedge or small screwdriver – four clips are

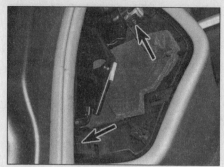

35.7b . . . and remove retaining screws

used altogether **(see illustration)**. Take care not to damage or mark the panel.
3 When the main clips have been released, slide the panel upwards to release from the facia panel, and remove it from the car **(see illustration)**.

36.2 Prise the trim panel away from its retaining clips

36.3 Release the upper clip, and remove the A-pillar trim

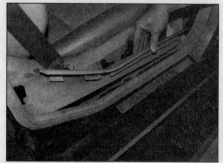

36.7a Unclip the sill trim . . .

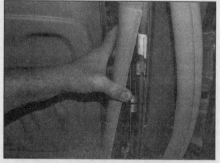

36.7b . . . and the lower pillar trim

36.8 Unclip the pillar upper trim panel . . .

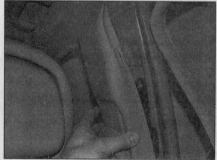

36.9 . . . and remove it from the seat belt adjuster

4 Refitting is a reversal of removal.

B-pillar trim panel

5 Pull off the door rubber sealing weatherstrip around the centre pillar.
6 Where applicable, unclip the cover from the alarm system interior sensor at the top of the pillar.
7 Unclip the sill trim panel and the lower section of the B-pillar trim panel **(see illustrations)**.
8 Using a screwdriver, release the four upper clips securing the B-pillar upper trim panel to the car body **(see illustration)**.
9 Pull the upper section of the trim panel upwards, to release it from the seat belt adjuster **(see illustration)**.
10 Loosen and remove the alarm sensor retaining screws (where fitted), then disconnect the sensor unit and remove it from the car.
11 Refitting is the reverse sequence to removal, noting the following points:
  a) *When refitting the B-pillar trim panel, engage the seat belt height adjuster lug with the inside of the adjuster lever.*
  b) *Where applicable, refit the screws and wiring plug to the alarm sensor before fitting the panel.*

C-pillar trim panel

Saloon

12 Removing the panel is made easier if the rear seat side cushion is removed first, as described in Section 31.
13 Pull off the door rubber sealing weatherstrip around the front edge of the panel.
14 Using a screwdriver, and taking care not to damage the panel or surrounding trim, release the three securing clips at the front edge of the panel.
15 Release the panel retaining clip at the top rear corner of the panel by moving the panel sideways, towards the centre of the car.
16 Finally, release the panel lower securing clips by lifting the panel upwards **(see illustration)**. Recover the insulation panel fitted inside the trim panel.
17 Unscrew the seat belt lower mounting bolt with reference to Section 32, recovering any washers or spacers used, feed the end of the seat belt through the trim panel, and remove the panel completely.

36.16 Removing the C-pillar trim panel

18 Refitting is a reversal of removal. Tighten the seat belt mountings to the specified torque.

Estate

19 Unclip the cover from the seat belt upper mounting bolt, then unscrew and remove the bolt, noting the fitted sequence of the washers and spacers **(see illustration)**.
20 Pull off the tailgate rubber seal from the door aperture, around the side of the trim panel to be removed **(see illustration)**.
21 Using a thin wedge or slim screwdriver, and taking care not to mark the panel, unclip the panel retaining clips and remove the panel, releasing its lower edge from the side trim panel **(see illustrations)**.
22 Refitting is a reversal of removal. Tighten the seat belt mountings to the specified torque.

D-pillar trim panel (Estate)

23 Unscrew and remove the bolt that secures the hook for the luggage net, and remove the hook from the trim panel.
24 Pull off the tailgate rubber seal from the tailgate aperture, around the side of the trim panel to be removed.
25 Using a thin wedge or slim screwdriver, and taking care not to mark the panel, unclip the panel retaining clips and remove the panel. If difficulty is experienced, it will be necessary to locally remove the C-pillar trim panel and luggage area side trim panel, using the appropriate removal procedures in this Section.
26 Refitting is a reversal of removal.

Door trim panels

27 See Section 18.

Trim panels – general

28 The interior trim panels are secured using either screws or various types of trim fasteners, usually studs or clips.
29 Check that there are no other panels overlapping the one to be removed, or other components hindering removal; usually there is a sequence that has to be followed, and this will only become obvious on close inspection.
30 Some of the interior panels will additionally be retained by the screws, which are used to secure other items, such as the grab handles.
31 Remove all visible retainers such as screws, noting that these may be hidden under small plastic caps. If the panel will not come free, it is held by internal clips or fasteners. These are usually situated around the edges of the panel, and can be prised up to release them; note, however, that they can break quite easily, so new ones should be available. The best way of releasing such clips is to use a large flat-bladed screwdriver or other wide-bladed tool. Note that in many cases, the adjacent sealing strip must be prised back to release a panel.
32 When removing a panel, **never** use excessive force or the panel may be damaged; always check carefully that all

36.19 Seat belt upper mounting bolt

36.21a Remove the upper trim panel . . .

fasteners or other relevant components have been removed or released before attempting to withdraw a panel.
33 Refitting is a reversal of removal; secure the fasteners by pressing them firmly into place and ensure that all disturbed components are correctly secured to prevent rattles.

Carpets

34 Carpet removal and refitting is reasonably straightforward, but is very time-consuming because all adjoining trim panels must be removed first, as must components such as the seats, centre console and seat belt lower anchorages.

Headlining

35 The headlining is clipped to the roof, and can be withdrawn only once all fittings such as grab handles, sunvisors, sunroof (if fitted), fixed window glass, and related trim panels

37.5 Diagnostic socket

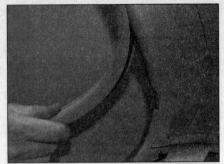

36.20 Pull back the door seal

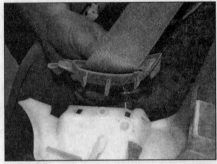

36.21b . . . and unclip the seat belt guide

have been removed and the relevant sealing strips have been prised clear.
36 Note that headlining removal and refitting requires considerable skill and experience if it is to be carried out without damage, and is therefore best entrusted to a dealer or automotive upholstery specialist.

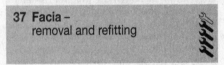

37 Facia –
    removal and refitting

Removal

1 Release the locking levers and move the steering column all the way out and downwards.
2 Remove the glovebox as described in Section 35.
3 Remove the steering wheel as described in Chapter 10.
4 Remove the instrument panel and the radio/CD player as described in Chapter 12.
5 Working in the driver's side footwell, undo the retaining screws and unclip the on board diagnostic (OBD) socket from the lower trim panel **(see illustration)**.
6 Undo the retaining screw from the bonnet release lever and pass the lever through the lower trim panel.
7 Undo the three retaining screws and remove the lower trim panel from under the driver's side of the facia panel. Disconnect any wiring connectors as it is removed.
8 Unclip the cover from the right-hand end of the facia panel **(see illustration)**.

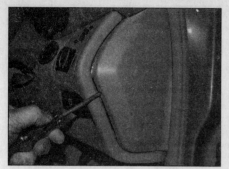

37.8 Unclip the facia end cover

37.9a Undo the retaining screw . . .

37.9b . . . and remove the light switch unit

37.11 Release the securing clips

37.14 Unclip the facia end cover . . .

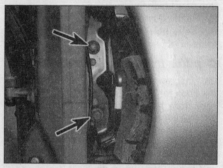

37.14 . . . and remove the facia mounting bolts

9 Undo the securing screw from behind the parking brake release lever **(see illustrations)** in the facia panel and then unclip the lighting switch module from the facia panel. Disconnect the wiring connectors as it is removed.

10 Working around the instrument panel lower trim panel, undo the five retaining screws and carefully unclip the trim panel from the facia. When accessible, disconnect the parking brake cable from the release lever in the trim panel. Also unscrew the lock cover plate and release the ignition/starter switch from the trim panel.

11 Release the lower locking clips at each end of the centre air vents and position the vents in the upward position (see illustration). Then undo the two retaining screws from inside the lower part of the air vents. Release the upper locking clips at each end of the centre air vents and position the vents in the downward position. Then release the two retaining clips from inside the upper part of the centre air vent and unclip from the facia panel. Where applicable, disconnect the wiring connector from the vent panel.

12 Working inside the centre of the facia panel, undo the four retaining screws.

13 Release the lower locking clips at each end of the centre air vents and position the vents in the upward position. Then undo the two retaining screws from inside the lower part of the air vents.

14 Unclip the cover from the left-hand end of the facia panel, and undo the two upper facia mounting bolts **(see illustrations).**

15 Undo the retaining screws from the centre of the facia panel, below the central air vent.

16 Remove the A-pillar trim panels as described in Section 36.

17 Working inside the glovebox aperture, break out the plastic covers and remove the bolts from the passenger airbag.

18 Remove the fusebox from the end of the facia panel and move it to one side with all the wiring still connected.

19 Undo the four retaining screws from inside the lower part of the instrument panel aperture.

20 Slacken the securing bolt in the upper part of the steering column; do not remove.

21 Working inside the instrument panel aperture once again, remove the two mounting bolts from the upper steering column bracket.

22 Where applicable, disconnect the wiring connectors from the left and right-hand air vents in the facia panel.

23 Disconnect the wiring connector(s) from the passenger airbag.

24 With the aid of an assistant, lift the facia panel slightly and withdraw it rearwards.

25 Take care not to damage the passenger airbag as the facia panel is withdrawn.

26 As the facia panel is removed, take care to ensure that nothing is still attached, and feed any wiring carefully through the various apertures, noting how it is routed for refitting.

Refitting

27 Refitting is the reverse of removal, noting the following points:
   a) *Ensure that all wiring is correctly routed, and is not trapped as the facia is refitted. The aid of an assistant will be useful.*
   b) *When reconnecting the battery, make sure that no-one is inside the car because of the potential risk of airbag deployment.*
   c) *On completion, check that all the electrical components and switches function correctly.*

Chapter 12
Body electrical system

Contents

Degrees of difficulty

Easy, suitable for novice with little experience	**Fairly easy,** suitable for beginner with some experience	**Fairly difficult,** suitable for competent DIY mechanic	**Difficult,** suitable for experienced DIY mechanic	**Very difficult,** suitable for expert DIY or professional

Specifications

System type .... 12 volt, negative earth

Battery
Type .... 12 volt lead-acid, 46 to 100 Ah depending on model

Bulbs

Wattage

Exterior lights

Headlight:
Dipped beam	55 (H7 halogen type) or D2S-35 (xenon bulb)
Main beam	55 (H7 type)
Front foglight	55 (H1 type)
Front sidelight	W 5
Direction indicator	PY 21 (amber)
Direction indicator side repeater	5 (amber)
Stoplight	P 21
High-level stop-light	LEDs (light-emitting diodes)
Rear foglight/tail light	P 21/4
Reversing light	P 21
Rear sidelight	R 5
Number plate light	C 5 (festoon)

Interior lights
Front courtesy lights	10
Rear courtesy lights	10
Luggage compartment light	10

Instrument panel:
Illumination bulbs	3
Warning light bulbs	1.5

Torque wrench settings

	Nm	lbf ft
Driver's airbag screws	6	4
Windscreen wiper motor:		
Mounting bolts	5	4
Spindle nut	19	14

1 General information and precautions

⚠️ **Warning: Before carrying out any work on the electrical system, read through the precautions given in Safety first! at the beginning of this manual and in Chapter 5A.**

The electrical system is of the 12 volt negative-earth type. Power for the lights and all electrical accessories is supplied by a lead-acid type battery, which is located in the right-hand rear corner of the engine compartment, and is charged by the alternator.

This Chapter covers repair and service procedures for the various electrical components not associated with the engine. Information on the battery, alternator and starter motor can be found in Chapter 5A.

It should be noted that prior to working on any component in the electrical system, the battery negative terminal should first be disconnected to prevent the possibility of electrical short-circuits and/or fires.

2 Electrical fault finding – general information

Note: Refer to the precautions given in Safety first! and in Chapter 5A before starting work. The following tests relate to testing of the main electrical circuits, and should not be used to test delicate electronic circuits (such as anti-lock braking systems), particularly where an electronic control module (ECU) is used.

General

1 A typical electrical circuit consists of an electrical component; any switches, relays, motors, fuses, fusible links or circuit breakers related to that component, and the wiring and connectors which link the component to both the battery and the chassis. To help to pin-point a problem in an electrical circuit, wiring diagrams are included at the end of this Chapter.

2 Before attempting to diagnose an electrical fault, first study the appropriate wiring diagram to obtain a complete understanding of the components included in the particular circuit concerned. The possible sources of a fault can be narrowed down by noting if other components related to the circuit are operating properly. If several components or circuits fail at one time, the problem is likely to be related to a shared fuse or earth connection.

3 Electrical problems usually stem from simple causes, such as loose or corroded connections, a faulty earth connection, a blown fuse, a melted fusible link, or a faulty relay (refer to Section 3 for details of testing relays). Visually inspect the condition of all fuses, wires and connections in a problem circuit before testing the components. Use the wiring diagrams to determine which terminal connections will need to be checked in order to pin-point the trouble spot.

4 The basic tools required for electrical fault finding include a circuit tester or voltmeter (a 12 volt bulb with a set of test leads can also be used for certain tests); a self-powered test light (sometimes known as a continuity tester); an ohmmeter (to measure resistance); a battery and set of test leads; and a jumper wire, preferably with a circuit breaker or fuse incorporated, which can be used to bypass suspect wires or electrical components. Before attempting to locate a problem with test instruments, use the wiring diagram to determine where to make the connections.

5 To find the source of an intermittent wiring fault (usually due to a poor or dirty connection, or damaged wiring insulation), a 'wiggle' test can be performed on the wiring. This involves wiggling the wiring by hand to see if the fault occurs as the wiring is moved. It should be possible to narrow down the source of the fault to a particular section of wiring. This method of testing can be used in conjunction with any of the tests described in the following sub-Sections.

6 Apart from problems due to poor connections, two basic types of fault can occur in an electrical circuit – open-circuit, or short-circuit.

7 Open-circuit faults are caused by a break somewhere in the circuit, which prevents current from flowing. An open-circuit fault will prevent a component from working, but will not cause the relevant circuit fuse to blow.

8 Short-circuit faults are caused by a 'short' somewhere in the circuit, which allows the current flowing in the circuit to 'escape' along an alternative route, usually to earth. Short-circuit faults are normally caused by a breakdown in wiring insulation, which allows a feed wire to touch either another wire, or an earthed component such as the bodyshell. A short-circuit fault will normally cause the relevant circuit fuse to blow.

Finding an open-circuit

9 To check for an open-circuit, connect one lead of a circuit tester or voltmeter to either the negative battery terminal or a known good earth.

10 Connect the other lead to a connector in the circuit being tested, preferably nearest to the battery or fuse.

11 Switch on the circuit, bearing in mind that some circuits are live only when the ignition switch is moved to a particular position.

12 If voltage is present (indicated either by the tester bulb lighting or a voltmeter reading, as applicable), this means that the section of the circuit between the relevant connector and the battery is problem-free.

13 Continue to check the remainder of the circuit in the same fashion.

14 When a point is reached at which no voltage is present, the problem must lie between that point and the previous test point with voltage. Most problems can be traced to a broken, corroded or loose connection.

Finding a short-circuit

15 To check for a short-circuit, first disconnect the load(s) from the circuit (loads are the components which draw current from a circuit, such as bulbs, motors, heating elements, etc).

16 Remove the relevant fuse from the circuit, and connect a circuit tester or voltmeter to the fuse connections.

17 Switch on the circuit, bearing in mind that some circuits are live only when the ignition switch is moved to a particular position.

18 If voltage is present (indicated either by the tester bulb lighting or a voltmeter reading, as applicable), this means that there is a short-circuit.

19 If no voltage is present, but the fuse still blows with the load(s) connected, this indicates an internal fault in the load(s).

Finding an earth fault

20 The battery negative terminal is connected to 'earth' – the metal of the engine/transmission and the car body – and most systems are wired so that they only receive a positive feed, the current returning through the metal of the car body. This means that the component mounting and the body form part of that circuit. Loose or corroded mountings can therefore cause a range of electrical faults, ranging from total failure of a circuit, to a puzzling partial fault. In particular, lights may shine dimly (especially when another circuit sharing the same earth point is in operation), motors (eg, wiper motors or the heater fan motor) may run slowly, and the operation of one circuit may have an apparently unrelated effect on another.

21 Note that on many vehicles, earth straps are used between certain components, such as the engine/transmission and the body, usually where there is no metal-to-metal contact between components due to flexible rubber mountings, etc.

22 To check whether a component is properly earthed, disconnect the battery and connect one lead of an ohmmeter to a known good earth point. Connect the other lead to the wire or earth connection being tested. The resistance reading should be zero; if not, check the connection as follows.

23 If an earth connection is thought to be faulty, dismantle the connection and clean back to bare metal both the bodyshell and the wire terminal or the component earth connection mating surface. Be careful to remove all traces of dirt and corrosion, and then use a knife to trim away any paint, so that a clean metal-to-metal joint is made.

24 On reassembly, tighten the joint fasteners securely; if a wire terminal is being refitted, use serrated washers between the terminal and the bodyshell to ensure a clean and secure connection. When the connection is remade, prevent the onset of corrosion in the future by applying a coat of petroleum jelly or

3.1a Engine compartment fusebox

3.1b Facia fusebox

**3.1c Luggage compartment fusebox –
Estate model**

silicone-based grease or by spraying on (at regular intervals) a proprietary ignition sealer or a water-dispersant lubricant.

3 Fuses and relays –
general information

Main fuses

1 Most of the fuses are situated in the main fusebox, located at the rear right-hand corner of the engine compartment; there is also another fusebox at the right-hand end of the facia panel. An additional fusebox is located in the left-hand inner panel of the luggage compartment **(see illustrations)**.
2 To gain access to the fuses, unclip and remove the fusebox cover. On the fusebox in the engine compartment release the two locking levers and then unclip the cover.
3 A list of the circuits each fuse protects is given on a diagram sheet inside of the fusebox cover on the left-hand end of the facia panel **(see illustration)**.
4 To remove a fuse, first switch off the circuit concerned (or the ignition), and then pull the fuse out of its terminals. The wire within the fuse should be visible; if the fuse is blown it will be broken or melted.
5 Always renew a fuse with one of an identical rating; never use a fuse with a different rating from the original or substitute anything else. Never renew a fuse more than once without tracing the source of the trouble. The fuse rating is stamped on top of the fuse; note

that the fuses are also colour-coded for easy recognition.
6 If a new fuse blows immediately, find the cause before renewing it again; a short to earth as a result of faulty insulation is most likely. Where a fuse protects more than one circuit, try to isolate the defect by switching on each circuit in turn (if possible) until the fuse blows again. Always carry a supply of spare fuses of each relevant rating on the vehicle; a spare of each rating should be clipped into the base of the fusebox.

Relays

7 Most of the relays are situated in the main fusebox, located at the rear of the engine compartment on the right-hand side. Additional relays may be located in the fusebox situated at the left-hand rear of the luggage compartment **(see illustrations)**.
8 To gain access to the relays in the engine

compartment, the fusebox cover must first be unclipped. Remove the screws securing the fusebox cover surround a quarter of a turn, and lift off the larger cover **(see illustrations)**.
9 If a circuit or system controlled by a relay develops a fault and the relay is suspect, operate the system; if the relay is functioning it should be possible to hear it click as it is energised. If this is the case the fault lies with the components or wiring of the system. If the relay is not being energised then either the relay is not receiving a main supply or a switching voltage or the relay itself is faulty. Testing is by the substitution of a known good unit but be careful; while some relays are identical in appearance and in operation, others look similar but perform different functions.
10 To renew a relay, first ensure that the ignition switch is off. The relay can then simply be pulled out from the socket and the new relay pressed in.

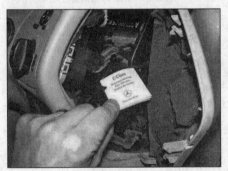

3.3 Fuse allocation sheet

3.7a Relays fitted to main fusebox

**3.7b Relays fitted in luggage compartment
fusebox – Saloon model**

3.8a Remove upper plastic trim . . .

3.8b . . . and then unclip fusebox cover

4.5 Remove the three switch securing screws

4.6 Withdraw the switch assembly

4.7 Disconnect the switch multiplug

4.8 Unclip the airbag contact unit wiring plug

4.9 Removing the column upper surround

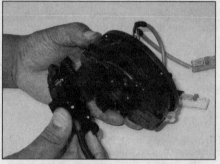

4.10 Disconnect the switch

4 Steering column combination switch – removal and refitting

Removal

1 Disconnect the battery negative terminal.
2 Remove the driver's side lower facia panel as described in Chapter 11.
3 Remove the steering wheel as described in Chapter 10.
4 Remove the airbag contact unit/clockspring as described in Section 23.

On models up to 23-04-2004

5 Undo the three screws securing the combination switch to the steering column (see illustration).
6 Partially remove the combination switch (and cruise control switch, where applicable)

for access to the wiring multiplug (see illustration).
7 Release the switch multiplug from its location, and separate the connector halves (see illustration). On models with cruise control, similarly release and disconnect the multiplug connector for the cruise control switch.
8 Unclip the wiring plug for the airbag contact unit, and move it to one side (see illustration).
9 If required, lift off the column surround, and remove it (see illustration).

On models from 23-04-2004

10 Release the retaining clips and remove the switch from the rear of the contact unit/clockspring (see illustration).

Refitting

11 Refitting is the reverse sequence to removal.

5 Facia, console and door switches – removal and refitting

1 Before removing any switches, disconnect the battery negative terminal, and reconnect on completion.

Facia switches

2 Remove the vents from the centre of the facia panel as described in Chapter 11, Section 37.
3 Remove the two screws from above the switch panel, and then unclip it from the facia (see illustrations).
4 Refitting is a reversal of removal.

Headlight and mirror main switch

5 Undo the securing screw from behind the parking brake release lever (see illustrations)

5.3a Undo the retaining screws . . .

5.3b . . . and unclip the switch panel

5.5a Undo the retaining screw . . .

in the facia panel and then unclip the lighting switch module from the facia panel. Disconnect the wiring connectors as it is removed.

6 Refitting is a reversal of removal.

Centre console switches

7 Remove the centre console upper trim panel as described in Chapter 11.

8 Unclip the switch from the trim panel and disconnect the wiring connector.

9 Refitting is the reverse sequence to removal.

Door switches

10 Remove the door trim panel as described in Chapter 11.

11 Release the retaining clip and withdraw the switch from the door trim panel **(see illustrations)**.

12 Refitting is the reverse sequence to removal.

Roof console switches

13 Prise out the light lenses from the roof console.

14 Release the console retaining catches using a screwdriver in the prise points provided, and then remove from the roof panel **(see illustration)**.

15 Disconnect the wiring plugs from the roof console, noting their locations for refitting.

16 Some of the switches can be unclipped and removed from the console, while others are integral with it.

17 Refitting is a reversal of removal.

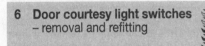

---

6 Door courtesy light switches – removal and refitting

Removal

1 It is possible to prise out the switches from their locations without any preliminary dismantling, but this carries a high risk of damaging the surrounding paintwork or damaging the switch locating lugs, which would mean the switch would not fit back into position. It is recommended that the removal procedures are followed, to avoid these problems.

6.4 Disconnect the wiring connector

5.5b . . . and remove the switch unit

5.11b . . . and remove the switch

2 Disconnect the battery negative terminal.

3 Remove the inner pillar trim panels as described in Chapter 11.

4 Disconnect the wiring plug from the rear of the switch **(see illustration)**.

5 Depress the upper securing lug, and release the switch from the body **(see illustration)**.

Refitting

6 Refitting is the reverse sequence to removal. Check for correct operation on reassembly.

---

7 Instrument panel – removal and refitting

Removal

1 Disconnect the battery negative terminal.

2 Adjust the steering column to its lowest

6.5 Remove the door switch

5.11a Slide the retaining clip . . .

5.14 Remove the light console

position to give better access to the instrument panel.

3 Using two hooked tools, insert them into the slots in the lower part of the instrument panel surround **(see illustration)**. Push the hooks into the slots and turn them 90-degrees, and then pull the surround from the facia panel.

4 Using the same hooked tools, release the retaining clips at each side of the instrument panel and withdraw the instrument panel from the facia **(see illustration)**

5 When they are accessible, release the locking levers securing the two wiring connectors, and disconnect the wiring from the rear of the panel.

Refitting

6 Offer the panel into position, and reconnect the wiring plugs, securing each with its locking clip.

7 Make sure the panel is lined up squarely

7.3 Remove the instrument panel surround

7.4 Unclip instrument panel from facia

with the facia aperture, and press it gently into place until the securing clips are felt to engage.

8 Refit the instrument panel surround, making sure it fits securely.

9 Reset the steering wheel height to the correct position.

10 On completion, check for correct operation of all instruments and warning lights.

8 Bulbs (exterior lights) – renewal

General

1 Whenever a bulb is renewed, note the following points:

a) *Disconnect the battery negative lead before starting work.*

b) *Remember that if the light has just been in use, the bulb may be extremely hot.*

c) *Always check the bulb contacts and holder, ensuring that there is clean metal-to-metal contact between the bulb and its live(s) and earth. Clean off any corrosion or dirt before fitting a new bulb.*

d) *Wherever bayonet-type bulbs are fitted, ensure that the live contact(s) bear firmly against the bulb contact.*

e) *Always ensure that the new bulb is of the correct rating and that it is completely clean before fitting it; this applies particularly to headlight/foglight bulbs (see below).*

f) *With quartz halogen bulbs (headlights and similar applications), use a tissue or clean cloth when handling the bulb; do not touch the bulb glass with the fingers. Even small quantities of grease from the fingers will cause blackening and premature failure. If a bulb is accidentally touched, clean it with methylated spirit and a clean rag.*

Headlight (halogen bulbs)

Note: *DO NOT remove xenon headlight bulbs: some models use High Intensity Discharge (HID) bulbs instead of conventional halogen bulbs. According to the manufacturer, the high voltages produced by this system can be fatal in the event of a shock. The voltage can remain in the circuit after the light unit has been switched off and the key removed. Therefore, for your safety, it is recommended that these type of bulbs are renewed by a* Mercedes dealer or other qualified service department.

2 From within the engine compartment, release the clip(s) securing the light unit cover in place, and remove it. There are two separate covers – the main beam bulb is behind the inner cover **(see illustration)**.

3 Carefully pull off the wiring connector from the relevant bulb.

4 Release the bulb retaining clip by turning it anti-clockwise **(see illustration)**.

5 Withdraw the bulb from the light unit, take care not to touch the glass with your fingers.

6 Refitting is the reverse sequence to removal, but ensure that the tags on the bulb plate engage with the recesses in the light unit.

Sidelight

7 Remove the headlight unit cover as described in paragraph 2. On models with two covers, the sidelight bulb is located behind the outer cover.

8 Pull out the sidelight bulbholder **(see illustration)**.

9 Pull out the wedge-base bulb from its holder.

10 Refitting is the reverse sequence to removal.

Foglight

11 To improve access, make sure that the parking brake is firmly applied, then jack up the front of the car and support on axle stands (see *Jacking and vehicle support*).

12 Unclip and remove the cover from under the wheel arch to access the rear of the light unit.

13 Turn the bulbholder to release it from the light unit, and then disconnect the wiring connector **(see illustration)**.

14 Refitting is a reversal of removal.

Direction indicator

15 At the rear of the light unit, turn the bulbholder anti-clockwise to release it from the top of the headlight unit **(see illustration)**.

16 Depress and turn the bulb anti-clockwise to remove it from the bulbholder **(see illustration)**.

17 Refitting is a reversal of removal.

8.2 Cover for main beam bulb

8.4 Turn the locking ring to release the bulb

8.8 Sidelight bulb

8.13 Remove the foglight bulb

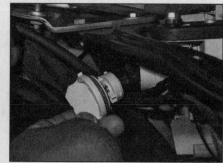

8.15 Remove the indicator bulbholder

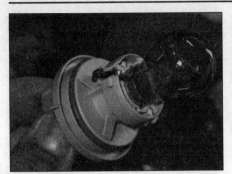

8.16 Remove the bulb from the holder

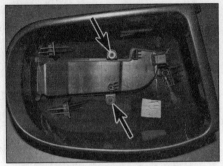

8.19 Light unit retaining screws

8.21 Pull back the carpet panel . . .

8.22a . . . release the locking catch . . .

8.22b . . . and remove the bulbholder

8.23 Push bulb in and twist to remove

Mirror-mounted

18 Remove the mirror housing as described in Chapter 11.
19 Undo the retaining screws and remove the LED light unit from the mirror housing **(see illustration)**.
20 Refitting is the reverse sequence to removal.

Rear light cluster bulbs

Saloon

21 From inside the luggage compartment, release the retaining clip and open the panel behind the light unit **(see illustration)**.
22 Turn the bulbholder catch, and then withdraw the bulbholder from the light unit **(see illustrations)**.
23 Remove the relevant bulb by turning anti-clockwise slightly **(see illustration)**.
24 Refitting is the reverse sequence to removal.

Coupe

25 From inside the luggage compartment, release the retaining clip and open the panel behind the light unit.
26 Release the retaining clip, and then withdraw the bulbholder from the light unit **(see illustrations)**.
27 Remove the relevant bulb by turning anti-clockwise slightly **(see illustration)**.
28 Refitting is the reverse sequence to removal.

Estate

29 From inside the luggage compartment, release the trim clips, and remove the carpeted

trim panel from the area around the rear light **(see illustration)**.
30 Release the retaining clips, and then withdraw the bulbholder from the rear of the light unit **(see illustration)**.

31 Remove the relevant bulb by turning anti-clockwise slightly **(see illustration)**.
32 Refitting is the reverse sequence to removal.

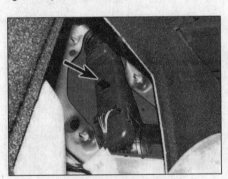

8.26a Release the securing clip . . .

8.26b . . . and withdraw the bulbholder

8.27 Push the bulb in and twist to remove

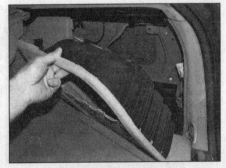

8.29 Remove the inner wing compartment . . .

8.30 Unclip the and remove the bulbholder

8.31 Push the bulb in and twist to remove

8.33 Number plate light bulb

9.2 Unclip the lens . . .

Number plate light

33 Undo the two retaining screws and withdraw the lens unit (see illustration).
34 Unclip the festoon-type bulb from the light lens.

9.3 . . . and remove the bulb

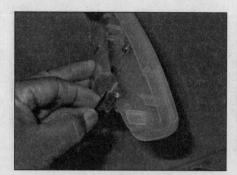

9.7a Open the reflector plate . . .

35 Refitting is the reverse sequence to removal.

High-level stop-light

36 The 'bulbs' in the high-level stop-light are

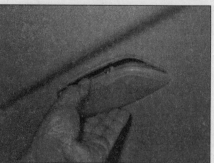

9.6 Unclip the light unit

9.7b . . . and remove the bulb

LEDs, and are not available separately. If the light unit stops working, check the wiring and fuse first. If the light unit is defective, remove it as described in Section 10 for renewal.

9 Bulbs (interior lights) – renewal

General

1 Whenever a bulb is renewed, note the following points:
   a) *Disconnect the battery negative lead before starting work.*
   b) *Remember that if the light has just been in use, the bulb may be extremely hot.*
   c) *Always check the bulb contacts and holder, ensuring that there is clean metal-to-metal contact between the bulb and its live(s) and earth. Clean off any corrosion or dirt before fitting a new bulb.*
   d) *Wherever bayonet-type bulbs are fitted, ensure that the live contact(s) bear firmly against the bulb contact.*
   e) *Always ensure that the new bulb is of the correct rating and that it is completely clean before fitting it; this applies particularly to headlight/foglight bulbs (see below).*

Interior courtesy lights

Front

2 Carefully prise out the relevant lens unit, taking care only to prise at the points on the inner edges of the lens (see illustration).
3 Release the festoon-type bulb from its contacts (see illustration).
4 To remove the map reading light bulbs, remove the unit as described in Section 5, and then twist the bulbholder to remove it from the rear of the light unit.
5 Refitting is the reverse sequence to removal.

Rear

6 Carefully prise out the light unit from the headlining (see illustration).
7 Where applicable, open the hinged cover inside the light unit for access to the bulb. Spread the bulb contacts and remove the festoon-type bulb (see illustrations).
8 Refitting is a reversal of removal.

Glovebox light

9 Open the glovebox and then prise the light lens unit down out of its location.
10 Spread the contacts and remove the festoon-type bulb (see illustration).
11 Refitting is the reverse sequence to removal.

Luggage compartment light

12 Carefully prise off the lens for access to the festoon-type bulb.
13 Spread the bulb contacts and remove the bulb.

14 Refitting is a reversal of removal.

Selector lever illumination light

15 Remove the upper part of the centre console as described in Chapter 11.
16 Remove the illumination bulb from its holder.
17 Refitting is a reversal of removal.

Door entry lights

18 Prise out the light unit from the lower edge of the door **(see illustration)** and disconnect the wiring plug.
19 Unclip the bulb from light unit.
20 Refitting is a reversal of removal.

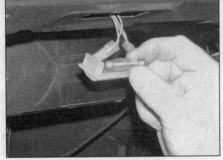

9.10 Remove the festoon-type bulb from its contacts

9.18 Prise out the door light

---

10 Exterior lights –
removed and refitting

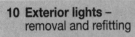

Note: *Disconnect the battery negative lead before removing any light unit.*

Front direction indicator light

1 The front indicator light unit is built into the headlight unit and cannot be removed separately, see following paragraphs.

Headlight unit

  Warning: DO NOT remove xenon headlight bulbs; some models use High Intensity discharge (HID) bulbs instead of conventional halogen bulbs. According to the manufacturer, the high voltages produced by this system can be fatal in the event of a shock. The voltage can remain in the circuit after the light unit has been switched off and the key removed. Therefore, for your safety, it is recommended that these type of bulbs are renewed by a Mercedes dealer or other qualified service department.

2 Open the bonnet and remove the two upper headlight mounting bolts **(see illustration)**.
3 Working under the wheel arch remove the inner wheel arch liner.
4 Undo the lower bolt from the headlight unit situated under the inner wheel arch **(see illustration)**.
5 Pull the headlight forwards and remove it from the car, taking care not to scratch the bumper.

6 Disconnect the wiring multiplug at the rear of the light unit; on models with Xenon lights, also disconnect the vacuum hose – this may need to be prised off, using a suitable screwdriver.
7 Refitting is the reverse sequence to removal. Have the headlight beam alignment checked on completion.

Front foglight

8 To improve access, make sure that the parking brake is firmly applied, then jack up the front of the car and support on axle stands (see *Jacking and vehicle support*).
9 Remove the front bumper as described in Chapter 11. Note the bumper only requires moving forward at each end to allow for the removal of the foglight unit.
10 Disconnect the wiring from the rear of the light unit, then remove the retaining bolts and

withdraw the light unit from the rear of the bumper **(see illustration)**.
11 Refitting is a reversal of removal. On completion, have the beam alignment checked and adjusted if necessary.

Rear light cluster

Saloon

12 Remove the bulbholder from the rear of the light unit as described in Section 8. Alternatively, disconnect the wiring plug from the bulbholder.
13 Unscrew and remove the four nuts at the rear of each light unit. Make sure all nuts are removed before removing the light unit. Note one is at the side of the light unit, and is in an elongated slot, to aid refitting **(see illustrations)**.
14 Withdraw the light unit from the rear of the vehicle, and recover the rubber seal, which

10.2 Headlight upper mounting bolts

10.4 Headlight lower mounting bolt

10.10 Disconnect the wiring connector

10.13a Rear light unit mounting bolts

10.13b Note elongated hole

10.14 Check seal is not damaged

10.15 Check the side bolt is located correctly

10.16 Disconnect the wiring connector

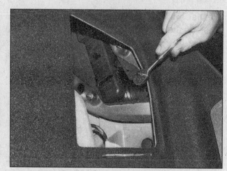

10.17 Undo the four retaining nuts

Alternatively, disconnect the wiring plug from the bulbholder (see illustration).

17 Unscrew and remove the four nuts at the rear of each light unit (see illustration). Make sure all nuts are removed before removing the light unit.

18 Withdraw the light unit from the rear of the vehicle, and recover the rubber seal, which should come away with the light unit.

19 Refitting is the reverse sequence to removal. Ensure that the seal is correctly located on the rear of the light unit – fit a new one, if necessary, to prevent leaks into the boot.

Estate

20 Remove the bulbholder from the rear of the light unit as described in Section 8. Alternatively, disconnect the wiring plug from the bulbholder (see illustration).

21 Unscrew the three nuts at the rear of the light unit, and withdraw it from the car (see illustrations). Recover the seal fitted between the light unit and the body.

22 Refitting is the reverse sequence to removal. Ensure that the seal is correctly located on the rear of the light unit – fit a new one, if necessary, to prevent leaks into the boot.

High-level stop-light

Saloon and Coupe

23 Open the boot/tailgate and remove the inner trim panel as described in Chapter 11 (see illustration).

24 Disconnect the wiring plug, then undo the two retaining screws and remove the light unit from the boot lid/tailgate (see illustrations).

should come away with the light unit (see illustration).

15 Refitting is the reverse sequence to removal. Ensure that the seal is correctly located on the rear of the light unit – fit a new one, if necessary, to prevent leaks into the

boot. Make sure the side bolt locates correctly in the wing panel (see illustration).

Coupe

16 Remove the bulbholder from the rear of the light unit as described in Section 8.

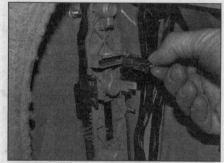

10.20 Disconnect the wiring connector

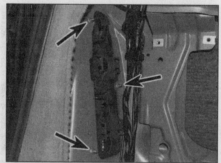

10.21a Undo the three retaining nuts . . .

10.21b . . . and remove the light unit

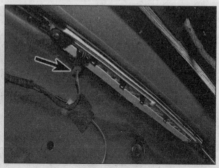

10.23 Remove the tailgate inner trim panel

10.24a Disconnect the wiring connector . . .

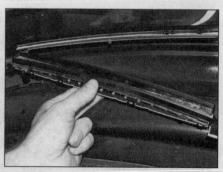

10.24b . . . and remove the light unit

10.27 Remove the upper trim panel

10.28a Disconnect the wiring connector . . .

10.28b . . . undo the retaining nuts . . .

10.28c . . . undo the retaining screws . . .

10.28d . . . and remove the spoiler

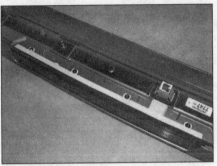

10.29 To remove the light unit undo the four retaining screws

25 Refitting is a reversal of removal.

Estate

26 The high-level stop-light is incorporated in the rear spoiler, which must first be removed.
27 Using the information in Chapter 11, unclip the tailgate upper trim panel **(see illustration)**.
28 Disconnect the wiring plug for the light unit, then remove the nuts securing the spoiler to the tailgate **(see illustrations)**, and lift the spoiler off the rear of the car.
29 The light unit is secured by four screws – remove the screws and separate the light from the spoiler **(see illustration)**.
30 Refitting is a reversal of removal.

Number plate light

Saloon and Coupe

31 Gain access to the inside of the light unit, as described for bulb removal in Section 8. The bulb does not have to be removed, but there is less chance of damaging the bulb if it is.
32 The light unit is secured by two clips, which must be released from inside the boot lid – withdraw the light from its location.
33 Disconnect the wiring connectors when they become accessible, and remove the light unit from the car.
34 Refitting is a reversal of removal.

Estate

35 Remove the lens and bulb as described in Section 8.
36 The rear halves of the two light units are incorporated in the tailgate behind the number plate trim **(see illustration)**.

37 Remove the tailgate inner trim panel as described in Chapter 11.
38 Disconnect the two wiring connectors **(see illustration)**, from behind each number plate light (note how they are fitted).
39 Release the retaining clips and remove the light units from the outside of the tailgate.
40 Refitting is a reversal of removal.

11 Headlights –
alignment

Accurate adjustment of the headlight beam is only possible using optical beam-setting equipment, and a Mercedes-Benz dealer or service station should therefore carry out this work with the necessary facilities.

10.36 Remove the number plate trim

12 Headlight height adjustment
system – description and component renewal

Description

1 On some models, the headlights are provided with a beam height adjustment system to enable the driver to regulate the beam height from inside the car to cater for different vehicle loading. Later models with xenon headlight bulbs have an automatic adjuster facility, and the manual control is not fitted.
2 Control of the system is by a three-position switch built into the main lighting switch on the right-hand side of the facia. The vacuum supplied to the headlight adjusting unit is regulated according to switch position. The

10.38 Number plate light wiring connectors

12.6a Twist the adjusting unit clockwise . . .

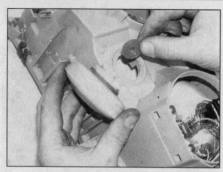

12.6b . . . and remove it from the headlight, recovering the spacer

12.7a Refitting the adjusting unit

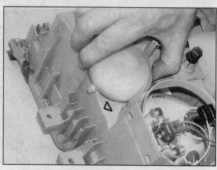

12.7b Turn the adjusting unit until the arrow mark is aligned with the vacuum hose connection

adjusting unit consists of a diaphragm which is connected to the movable headlight lens by means of a pull-rod having a stroke of approximately 3.0 mm. Vacuum applied to the diaphragm causes it to deflect, which in turn moves the pull-rod to raise or lower the headlight beams.

3 Apart from periodically checking the condition of the vacuum hoses, the system does not require any maintenance or adjustment in service.

Component renewal

Adjuster switch

4 The adjuster switch is part of the main headlight switch; refer to Section 5, for the removal and refitting procedure.

Headlight adjusting unit

5 Remove the headlight unit as described in Section 10.

6 To remove the adjusting unit, twist it to release the bayonet fitting on the rear of the headlight, then pull firmly outwards to disengage the ball fitting. Recover the orange aligning spacer, which will probably fall off as the unit is removed **(see illustrations)**.

7 Refitting is a reversal of removal, noting the following points:

a) *Reconnecting the ball fitting is a tricky operation, and will probably require several attempts **(see illustration)**. Grease the fittings to aid assembly.*

b) *When refitting the adjusting unit, note that it should be turned anti-clockwise so that the arrow marks on the rear of the headlight comes into alignment with the vacuum connection **(see illustration)**.*

c) *Refit the headlight as described in Section 10.*

13 Wiper arms – removal and refitting

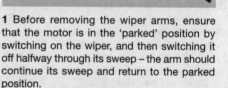

1 Before removing the wiper arms, ensure that the motor is in the 'parked' position by switching on the wiper, and then switching it off halfway through its sweep – the arm should continue its sweep and return to the parked position.

Windscreen wiper

2 Open the bonnet to access the wiper arm retaining nuts **(see illustrations)**.

3 Undo the retaining nuts and withdraw the wiper arms from the spindle, noting their fitted position. Hold the spring-loaded lower section of the arm as this is done, otherwise it may strike the glass with some force.

4 Refitting is a reversal of removal. Tighten the wiper arm retaining nuts securely, and then check for correct operation.

Tailgate wiper

5 Prise up the cover from the end of the wiper arm, for access to the arm retaining nut **(see illustration)**.

6 Remove the nut, and then pull the wiper arm away from the tailgate and remove it **(see illustrations)**. Take care not to damage the washer jet. If the arm is a tight fit, then a puller will be required to withdraw the wiper arm from the spindle.

13.2a Right-hand wiper blade nut

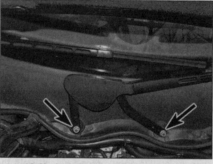

13.2b Left-hand wiper blade nuts

13.5 Lift up the plastic cover

13.6a Remove the rear wiper arm

13.6b If a tight fit, use a puller to remove

7 Refitting is a reversal of removal. Tighten the wiper arm retaining nut securely, then check for correct operation.

14 Windscreen wiper motor and linkage – removal and refitting

Removal

1 Remove the wiper arm as described in the previous Section.
2 Raise the bonnet to the vertical position by releasing the catch on the side of the bonnet strut **(see illustration)**.
3 Release the clips and remove the trim panel from above the fusebox **(see illustration)**.
4 Remove the cover from the fusebox and trace the wiring harness back from the wiper

motor, and disconnect its wiring plug from inside the fusebox. Lift out the harness, and release the grommet from the side of the fusebox so that it can be removed with the motor **(see illustration)**.
5 Working your way along the water collector across the top of the bulkhead, undo the retaining screws and carefully unclip the plastic trim from the bottom of the windscreen **(see illustrations)**.
6 Undo the three mounting bolts from the wiper linkage **(see illustration)**.
7 Release any wiring clips from the mounting brackets and note their fitted position.
8 Carefully withdraw the wiper assembly from its mountings, taking care not to damage either the bonnet or the windscreen.
9 To remove the motor from the linkage, pry off the linkage rods and undo the mounting bolts **(see illustration)**. Mark the position of any linkage rods to aid refitting.

Refitting

10 Refitting is a reversal of removal.
11 On completion, check the wiper linkage does not come into contact with anything when it is operated. Make sure that all wiring is routed correctly as noted on removal.

15 Washer system components – removal, refitting and adjustment

1 The windscreen washer system consists of a water reservoir located at the front left-hand

14.2 Raise the bonnet to the vertical position

side of the engine compartment, an electric pump attached to the reservoir and two double nozzle jets located on each side of the bonnet. A water level indicator is also fitted to the reservoir to inform the driver of low water supply in the reservoir.

Removal

2 To remove the reservoir, first remove the inner wheel arch liner from the left-hand front wing panel.
3 Open the bonnet and pull the washer reservoir filler neck upwards to disengage it from the reservoir.
4 Disconnect the wiring connectors from the washer pump(s) and fluid level switch, and fasten them to one side. Release any wiring clips noting their fitted position for refitting **(see illustration)**.
5 Disconnect the washer hose(s) from the

14.3 Remove the plastic trim cover

14.4 Wiper motor wiring connector

14.5a Undo the retaining screws . . .

14.5b . . . and unclip the trim panel

14.6 Wiper assembly mounting bolts

14.9 Wiper motor-to-linkage bolts

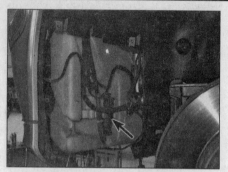

15.4 Washer motor location

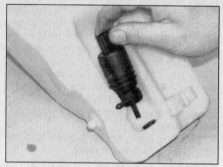

15.7 Prise out the washer pump, and remove it

washer pump(s), placing a container to catch any fluid that flows out of the reservoir/pump.

6 Undo the two retaining bolts from the top of the reservoir and manoeuvre it out from under the wheel arch.

7 The washer pump is a push-fit in the reservoir, and can be removed by carefully prising it out (drain the reservoir first) **(see illustration)**. The pump is a sealed unit, and cannot be repaired.

8 To remove the water level sensor prise it out of its location. Recover the rubber seal.

9 To remove the jets disconnect the water hose and electrical connection from within the aperture on the inside of the bonnet.

10 Release the retaining lugs, then push the jet upwards and withdraw it from the bonnet.

Refitting and adjustment

11 Refitting all the components is the reverse sequence to removal.

12 Adjust the jets using a pin, so that the water contacts the windscreen/tailgate centrally. When adjusting the windscreen jets, allow for the downforce created by the airflow over the bonnet and windscreen when the car is in forward motion.

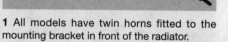

16 Rain sensor – removal and refitting

1 Some later models are equipped with a rain sensor – an infra-red device mounted on the inside of the windscreen (above the interior mirror) which detects the presence of rain droplets on the windscreen and activates the windscreen wipers automatically.

Removal

2 Carefully unclip the cover from the rear of the sensor.

3 Unhook the retaining clips at either side by prising them outwards, and remove the sensor from its lens.

4 The lens is glued to the inside of the windscreen, and no attempt should be made to remove it. If it is damaged, seek the advice of a Mercedes-Benz dealer.

Refitting

5 Refitting is a reversal of removal. On completion, check the operation of the sensor by turning the ignition on and spraying some water onto the windscreen.

17 Tailgate wiper motor – removal and refitting

Removal

1 Remove the wiper arm as described in Section 13.

2 Remove the tailgate inner trim panel as described in Chapter 11.

3 Disconnect the wiper motor wiring plug, and pull off the washer hose **(see illustrations)**.

4 Remove the three motor mounting bolts, and withdraw the motor from the tailgate **(see illustration)**. Recover the rubber sealing grommet from the tailgate glass.

Refitting

5 Refitting is a reversal of removal. Fit a new sealing grommet if necessary when refitting the motor.

18 Horns – removal and refitting

1 All models have twin horns fitted to the mounting bracket in front of the radiator.

2 Open the bonnet and then disconnect the wiring connectors from both horns. Then unscrew the mounting nut and remove the horn unit from the front of the car **(see illustration)**.

3 Refitting is the reverse sequence to removal. Check for correct operation on completion.

19 Radio/audio unit – removal and refitting

Note: *This Section relates principally to radio equipment fitted as standard by Mercedes-Benz, or supplied and fitted by Mercedes-Benz dealers.*

Removal

1 Disconnect the battery negative terminal.

2 Remove the upper part of the centre console and ashtray as described in Chapter 11.

Audio 10 or Audio 30 unit

3 Undo the two retaining screws from the

17.3a Disconnect the wiring connector . . .

17.3b . . . and the washer hose

17.4 Undo the wiper mounting bolts

18.2 Horn bracket retaining nut

19.5 Remove the heater controls

19.6 Radio/audio retaining screws

19.7 Disconnect the wiring connectors

lower part of the radio and withdraw it from the facia panel, taking care not to damage the wiring. When wiring comes into view disconnect it from the rear of the radio.

Audio 20 unit

4 Remove the facia switch panel from across the top of the radio as described in Section 5.
5 Remove the heater control panel **(see illustration)** from across the bottom of the radio as described in Chapter 3.
6 Undo the two upper and lower retaining screws from the facia centre panel **(see illustration)**.
7 Withdraw the radio from the facia panel **(see illustration)**, taking care not to damage the wiring. When wiring comes into view disconnect it from the rear of the radio.

Refitting

8 Refitting is the reverse sequence to removal.
9 Reconnect the wiring to the radio, making sure that all connectors and aerial is secure. Push the radio/audio unit back into its aperture and fit the retaining screws.
10 On models with a coded unit, it will be necessary to re-activate the code once the battery has been reconnected. The code will have been provided (like the removal tools) with the car when new. Again, a Mercedes-Benz dealer or car audio specialist may be able to help if the code has been lost.

20 Speakers –
removal and refitting

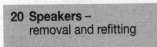

Removal

Facia-mounted speakers

1 The front speaker is located in the centre of the facia at the top.
2 Carefully unclip the speaker from the top of the facia, taking care not to damage the top of the facia.
3 Lift up the speaker and disconnect the wiring plug.

Front door speakers

4 Remove the front door trim panel as described in Chapter 11.

5 Disconnect the speaker wiring connector **(see illustration)**.
6 Unscrew and remove the speaker retaining screws, then withdraw the speaker from its location **(see illustration)**.

Rear door speakers

7 Remove the rear door trim panel as described in Chapter 11.
8 Disconnect the speaker wiring connector.
9 Unscrew and remove the speaker retaining screws, then withdraw the speaker from its location **(see illustration)**.

Mirror trim speakers

10 Unclip the trim panel from the top of the door panel.
11 Disconnect the speaker wiring connector and remove **(see illustration)**.

Rear shelf speakers

12 On Saloon models, remove the rear shelf trim panel as described in Chapter 11.

20.5 Disconnect the wiring connector . . .

20.6 . . . and remove the speaker

13 Unclip the speaker housing from the rear shelf, and remove complete with the speaker.
14 Disconnect the speaker wiring, labelling it if necessary to ensure correct refitting.

Refitting

15 Refitting is the reverse sequence to removal.

21 Anti-theft alarm system –
general information

Note: *This information is applicable only to the anti-theft alarm system fitted by Mercedes-Benz as standard equipment.*

All models are fitted with an anti-theft alarm system as standard equipment. The alarm has switches on all the doors (including the boot lid), the bonnet, the

20.9 Speaker retaining screws

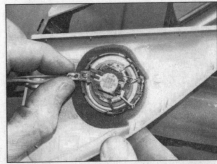

20.11 Disconnect the wiring connector

23.2 Undo the airbag retaining screws

audio unit and the ignition switch, and also a tilt switch, which is sensitive to shocks. If the boot lid, bonnet or either of the doors are opened, the ignition switch or audio unit are switched on whilst the alarm is set, or if the tilt switch senses the vehicle is being tampered with, the alarm horn will sound and the hazard warning lights will flash. The alarm also has an immobiliser function, which makes the ignition/starter (as applicable) system inoperable whilst the alarm is triggered.

On later models, the scope of alarm functions is increased, with switchable interior motion sensors and anti-jacking/tilt sensor.

The alarm is set using the key in the front door lock or boot/tailgate lock; on later models, the alarm is also set when the doors are locked using the remote central locking device. The LED on the centre console will flash to indicate that the alarm system is operational.

Models are equipped with the Mercedes-Benz Driver Authorisation System (DAS). This advanced security system does away with a conventional key for locking and unlocking the doors and, instead, a sophisticated electronic remote-control handset/electronic key is provided. Without this handset, the engine cannot be started.

Should the alarm system become faulty, the vehicle should be taken to a Mercedes-Benz dealer for examination. They will have access to a special diagnostic tester, which will quickly trace any fault present in the system.

23.3 Disconnect the airbag wiring connectors

22 Airbag system – general information and precautions

A driver's airbag, passenger airbag and front side airbags are fitted as standard to all models – the side airbags are fitted in the front door trim panels.

Airbag units have the word AIRBAG or SRS-AIRBAG stamped on them. The airbag system comprises of the airbag unit(s) (each with a gas generator), the control unit (with an integral impact sensor) and a warning light in the instrument panel. The airbag control unit features 'intelligent' software, and also operates the front seat belt tensioner mechanisms at the same time as the airbag (see Chapter 11).

The driver's and passenger's front airbags will only be triggered in the event of a heavy frontal impact above a predetermined force; depending on the point of impact (rear impacts will not usually trigger the airbag system). The side airbags will only be triggered if the car is hit from the side, and only on the side from which the car has been hit. The passenger airbags and seat belt tensioner will only be triggered if the passenger seat is occupied – a sensor built into the seat cushion informs the control unit of this. Light impacts, such as those which might be sustained when parking, will not trigger the system.

The airbag is inflated within milliseconds, and forms a safety cushion between the driver, steering wheel and door, or between the passenger, facia and door, depending on the severity of the accident. This prevents contact between the upper body and wheel/facia/door, and therefore greatly reduces the risk of injury. The airbag then deflates almost immediately.

Every time the ignition is switched on, the airbag control unit performs a self-test. The self-test takes approximately 4 seconds and during this time the airbag warning light in the instrument panel is illuminated. After the self-test has been completed the warning light should go out. If the warning light fails to come on, remains illuminated after the initial period or comes on at any time when the vehicle is being driven, there is a fault in the airbag system. The vehicle should be taken to a Mercedes-Benz dealer for examination at the earliest possible opportunity.

⚠ *Warning: Before carrying out any operations on the airbag system, first switch off the ignition (ideally, take out the key). Disconnect the battery negative terminal, and position the lead away from the battery terminal (Mercedes-Benz recommend covering up the terminal, to prevent accidental reconnection). Wait 15 minutes after disconnecting the battery for the capacitive charge in the system to dissipate. When operations are complete, make sure no one is inside the vehicle when the battery is reconnected.*

• *Note that the airbag(s) must not be subjected to temperatures in excess of 100°C. When an airbag is removed, ensure that it is stored with the airbag upwards to prevent possible inflation.*
• *Do not allow any solvents or cleaning agents to contact the airbag assemblies. They must be cleaned using only a damp cloth.*
• *The airbags and control unit are both sensitive to impact. If dropped or damaged, they should be renewed.*
• *Disconnect the airbag control unit wiring plug prior to using arc-welding equipment on the vehicle.*

23 Airbag system components – removal and refitting

Note: *Refer to the warnings given in Section 22 before carrying out the following operations.*

1 Turn the ignition key to position 0, then disconnect the battery negative cable, and position it away from the terminal.

Driver's airbag

Removal

2 Slacken and remove the two airbag retaining screws from the rear of the steering wheel, rotating the wheel as necessary to gain access to the screws **(see illustration)**.

3 Return the steering wheel to the straight-ahead position, then carefully lift the airbag assembly away from the steering wheel and disconnect the wiring connector from the rear of the unit **(see illustration)**. Note that the airbag must not be knocked or dropped, and should be stored the correct way up (padded surface uppermost).

Refitting

4 Ensure that the wiring connector is securely reconnected (it should engage audibly), and seat the airbag unit centrally in the steering wheel, making sure the wire does not become trapped.

5 Fit the retaining screws and tighten them to the specified torque setting, noting the left-hand retaining screw should be tightened first.

6 Ensure no one is inside the vehicle, and reconnect the battery. Turn on the ignition switch and check the operation of the airbag warning light, whilst turning the steering wheel from full left lock to full right lock.

7 Mercedes-Benz states that, if the airbag has been deployed, a new steering wheel should be fitted.

Passenger airbag

Removal

8 Remove the glovebox from the facia panel as described in Chapter 11.

9 Disconnect the airbag wiring plug at the side of the unit, then unscrew the securing bolts and remove the airbag unit from the facia **(see illustration)**.

Refitting

10 Refitting is a reversal of removal. Tighten the airbag retaining nuts securely, and ensure that the wiring plug is fully reconnected. Refit the glovebox as described in Chapter 11.

11 Mercedes-Benz state that, if the airbag has been deployed, a new facia panel should be fitted.

Side airbag

Removal

12 Remove the door trim panel as described in Chapter 11.

13 Drill out the retaining rivets and remove the airbag unit from the door panel **(see illustrations)**. Disconnect the airbag wiring plug as the unit is removed.

Refitting

14 Refitting is a reversal of removal. Secure the airbag using new pop-rivets, and ensure that the wiring plug is fully reconnected. Refit the door trim panel as described in Chapter 11.

Airbag control unit

15 Removal and refitting of the control unit should be entrusted to a Mercedes-Benz dealer. On refitting, the control unit must be tested using special Mercedes-Benz diagnostic equipment to ensure that the system is operating correctly. For reference, the control unit is mounted underneath the centre console.

Airbag wiring contact unit

Removal

16 Remove the steering wheel as described in Chapter 10.

17 Note the position of the contact unit, as it will need to be refitted in the same position. Undo the retaining screw and withdraw the contact unit complete with switches from the top of the steering column **(see illustrations)**.

18 Undo the retaining screws and remove the contact unit from the steering column shroud.

19 With the contact unit removed, complete with switches, put some tape around the contact unit to prevent it from turning **(see illustration)**.

20 Release the retaining clips and remove the switches from the rear of the contact unit **(see illustration)**.

Refitting

21 Refitting is a reversal of removal, ensure that the contact unit is correctly centralised as noted on removal.

24 Parktronic system – general information

Available as an option, the Parktronic system is an ultrasonic parking aid. The system uses sensors in the front and rear bumpers to transmit a signal which then bounces off any objects in range in front of or behind the car. The sensors receive the reflected signal, and the control unit can then calculate the distance of the object from the car. The system works at speeds up to 9 mph. The resulting distance information is conveyed to the driver by visual display and audio signal.

There are six sensors in the front bumper, and four at the rear. The control unit is located under the luggage area floor. The audio/visual

23.9 Passenger airbag mounting bolts

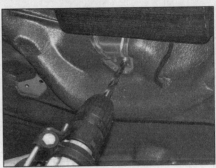

23.13a Drill out the rivets . . .

23.13b . . . remove the airbag unit . . .

23.13c . . . and disconnect the wiring connector

23.17a Undo the retaining screw . . .

23.17b . . . and withdraw the switch assembly

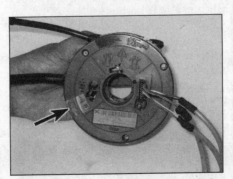

23.19 Using tape to hold contact switch in place

23.20 Remove the switches from the contact unit

25.2 Wiring connector for ambient air temperature sensor

warning units are located in the instrument panel incorporated in the rear interior light.

When the ignition is switched on, the system performs a self-test. If the system develops a fault, this will be indicated by just the red sections of the visual warning units staying on. In the event of a fault, first check the connections at the bumper-mounted sensors, as these may be subject to dirt and water entry. After checking this, and the wiring as far as possible, it is advisable to take the car to a Mercedes-Benz dealer for testing using diagnostic equipment.

25 Outside temperature sensor – removal and refitting

Removal

1 The outside temperature sensor is clipped to the right-hand side of the grille below the front bumper, and the sensor display is incorporated into the instrument panel.

2 To remove the sensor, unclip the trim panel from the bumper and disconnect the sensor wiring plug **(see illustration)**.

3 Unclip the sensor from its location on the trim panel, and remove it.

Refitting

4 Refitting is a reversal of removal.

5 Note that, if the sensor display is faulty, renewal is a job for a Mercedes-Benz dealer or automotive electrician. The sensor is part of the instrument panel, which can be removed as described in Section 7, but removing the display completely requires that its wiring is separated from the instrument panel wiring multiplug, which is a delicate operation.

Mercedes-Benz C-Class wiring diagrams

Diagram 1

 WARNING: This vehicle is fitted with a supplemental restraint system (SRS) consisting of a combination of driver (and passenger) airbag(s), side impact protection airbags and seatbelt pre-tensioners. The use of electrical test equipment on any SRS wiring systems may cause the seatbelt pre-tensioners to abruptly retract and airbags to explosively deploy, resulting in potentially severe personal injury. Extreme care should be taken to correctly identify any circuits to be tested to avoid choosing any of the SRS wiring in error.

For further information see airbag system precautions in body electrical systems chapter.

Note: The SRS wiring harness can normally be identified by yellow and/or orange harness or harness connectors.

Key to symbols

Dashed outline denotes part of a larger item, containing in this case an electronic or solid state device. 7/10 denotes connector 7 pin 10.

Solenoid actuator

Heating element

Earth point & location

Wire colour (red with yellow tracer)

Bulb

Switch

Fuse/fusible link

Resistor

Variable resistor

Variable resistor

Wire splice, soldered joint, or unspecified connector

Connecting wires

Diode

Light-emitting diode

Item number

Motor/pump

Earth locations

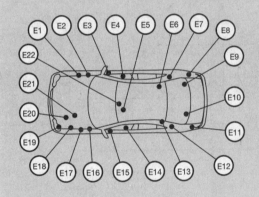

Engine fusebox

Fuse	Rating	Circuit protected
F43a	15A	LH & RH horn
F43b	15A	LH & RH horn
F44	5A	Telephone
F45	7.5A	Safety restraint system (SRS) control unit
F46	40A	Wiper on/off relay, wiper speed 1 & 2 relay
F47	15A	Glovebox light, cigar lighter
F48	15A	Oxygen sensor, headlight range adjustment (HRA)
F49	7.5A	Restraint system control unit
F50	5A	Light switch control unit
F51	7.5A	LH front light unit, RH front light unit, instrument cluster, convenience automatic air conditioning (C-AAC) multifunction & sun sensors
F52	15A	Starter
F53	15A	Starter relay, rear fusebox, engine management control unit
F54	15A	Automatic air conditioning (ACC), exhaust gas recirculation (EGR)
F55	7.5A	Electric controller unit
F56	5A	Electronic stability program (ESP) & brake assist system (BAS) control unit
F57	5A	Electronic ignitoin switch control unit
F58	-	Spare
F59	50A	Electronic stability program (ESP) & brake assist system (BAS) control unit
F60	40A	Electronic stability program (ESP) & brake assist system (BAS) control unit
F61	-	Spare
F62	5A	Diagnostic connector, stop lights
F63	5A	Light switch control unit
F64	10A	Audio navigation & cockpit management system (COMAND)
F65	40A	Electric air pump

R1	Horn relay
R2	Terminal 87 relay chassis
R3	Wiper speed 1 & 2 relay
R4	Terminal 15R relay
R5	Sequentronic automated manual transmission (SEQ) pump relay
R6	Air pump relay
R7	Terminal 15 relay
R8	Wiper on/off relay
R9	Terminal 87 relay engine
R10	Starter relay

Engine maxi-fuse box

Fuse	Rating	Circuit protected
F1	125A	Passenger fusebox
F2	200A	Rear fusebox
F3	-	Spare
F4	200A	Engine fusebox
F5	125A	Automatic air conditioning (AAC), glow plugs
F6	60A	Engine fusebox

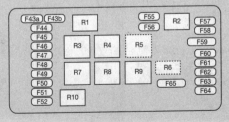

H33868

Mercedes-Benz C-Class wiring diagrams

Diagram 2

Passenger fusebox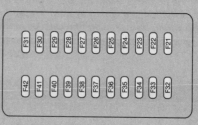

Fuse	Rating	Circuit protected
F21	30A	LH front door control unit
F22	30A	RH front door control unit
F23	-	Spare
F24	7.5A	CD player
F25	30A	Upper control panel control unit
F26	25A	Audio amplifier
F27	-	Spare
F28	-	Spare
F29	30A	RH front seat adjustment control unit
F30	40A	Heating system recirculation unit
F31	20A	EIS control unit, electric steering lock control unit
F32	-	Spare
F33	-	Spare
F34	30A	LH front seat adjustment control unit
F35	30A	Stationary heater unit (STH)
F36	10A	Telephone
F37	-	Spare
F38	-	Spare
F39	-	Spare
F40	7.5A	Phone
F41	7.5A	Automatic air conditioning (AAC)
F42	7.5A	Instrument cluster

Rear fusebox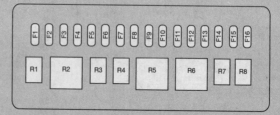

Fuse	Rating	Circuit protected
F1	30A	LH front seat adjustment control
F2	30A	RH front seat adjustment control
F3	7.5A	Rear interior light, parktronic system (PTS) control unit
F4	20A	Fuel pump
F5	20A	Spare relay 2
F6	-	Spare
F7	7.5A	Head restraint system
F8	7.5A	Alarm, aerial amplifier
F9	25A	Overhead control panel control unit
F10	40A	Heated rear window
F11	-	Spare
F12	-	Spare
F13	5A	Voice control system control unit
F14	-	Spare
F15	10A	Fuel filler cap motor
F16	20A	Voice control system control unit
F17	-	Spare
F18	-	Spare
F19	-	Spare
F20	-	Spare

R1	Fuel pump relay
R2	Terminal 15R relay 2
R3	Reserve relay 2
R4	Reserve relay 1
R5	Heated rear window relay
R6	Terminal 15R relay 1
R7	Filler cap polarity reversing relay 1
R8	Filler cap polarity reversing relay 2

H33869

Wire colours

Bk	Black	**Pk**	Pink
Bn	Brown	**Rd**	Red
Bu	Blue	**Vt**	Violet
Gn	Green	**Wh**	White
Gy	Grey	**Ye**	Yellow
Og	Orange		
Tr	Transparent		

Key to items

1 Battery
2 Starter motor
3 Alternator
4 Maxifusebox
5 Engine fusebox
    R1 = horn relay
    R7 = terminal 15 relay
    R9 = terminal 87 relay chassis
    R10 = starter relay
6 Horn
7 Ignition switch control unit

8 Horn switch
9 Steering column control unit
10 Steering wheel clock springs
11 LH m/f steering wheel push button group
12 RH m/f steering wheel push button group
13 Passenger fusebox
14 Rear fusebox
    R5 = heated rear window relay
15 AAC control unit
    a = heated rear window/mirror switch
16 Heated rear window

17 Reversing light switch
18 Stop light switch
19 EPS/BAS control unit
20 LH rear light unit
    a = stop light
    b = reversing light
21 RH rear light unit
    (as above)
22 High level stop light
23 Instrument cluster
    a = alternator warning light

Diagram 3

H33870

Typical starting & charging

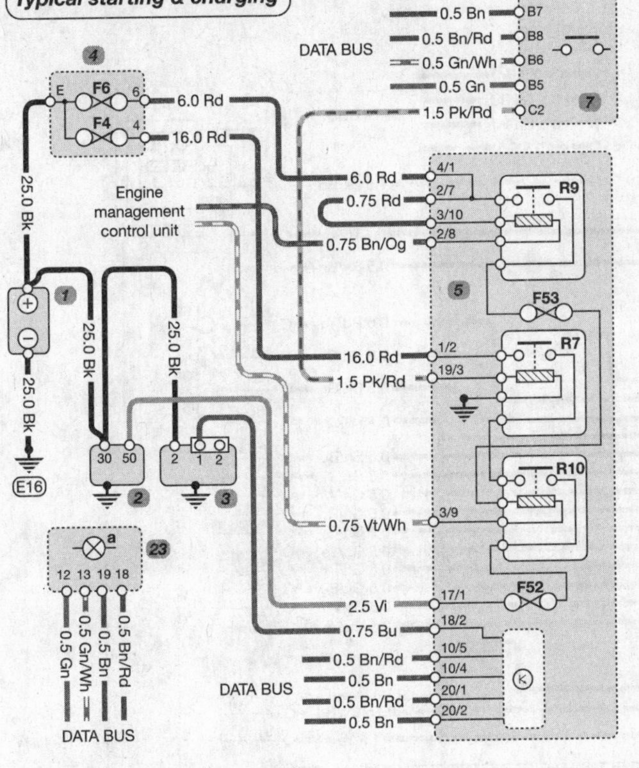

Typical horn

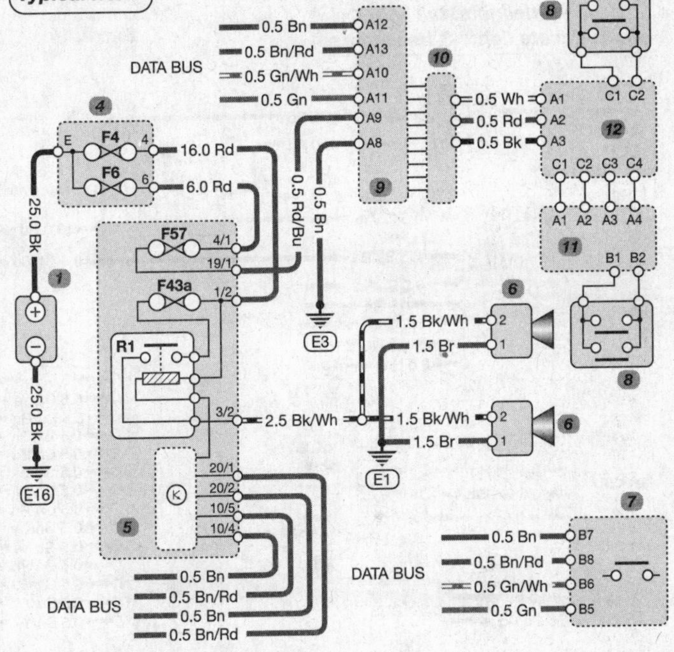

Typical heated rear window

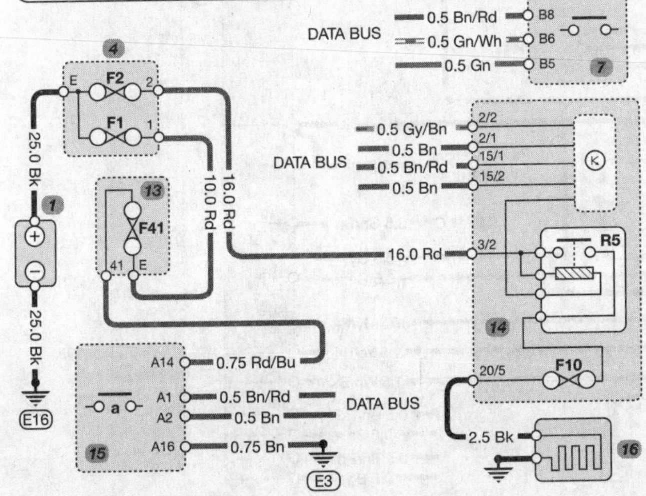

Typical stop & reversing lights

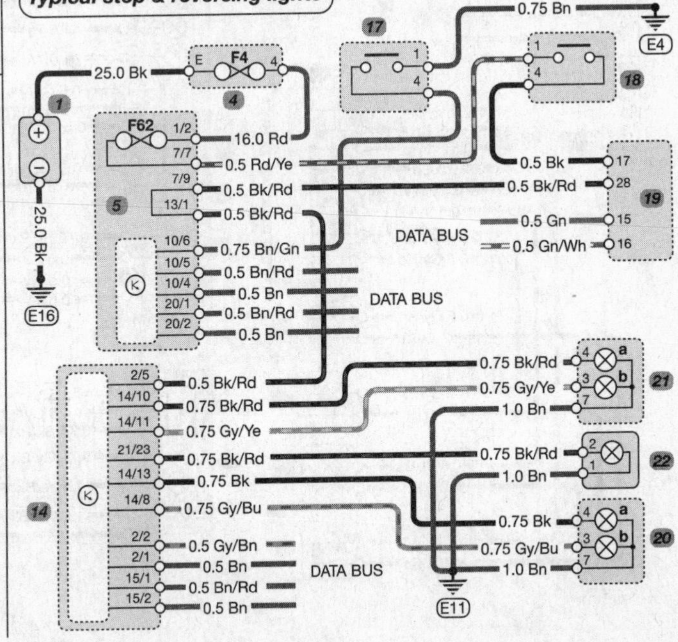

Wire colours

Bk	Black	Pk	Pink
Bn	Brown	Rd	Red
Bu	Blue	Vt	Violet
Gn	Green	Wh	White
Gy	Grey	Ye	Yellow
Og	Orange		
Tr	Transparent		

Key to items

1 Battery
4 Maxifusebox
5 Engine fusebox
  R7 = terminal 15 relay chassis
7 Electronic ignition switch control unit
9 Steering column control unit
13 Passenger fusebox
14 Rear fusebox
20 LH rear light unit
  c = tail light
21 RH rear light unit
  (as above)

23 Instrument cluster
  b = main beam warning light
25 LH front light unit
  a = side light
  b = dip beam
  c = main beam warning light
  d = xenon headlight
26 RH front light unit
  (as above)
27 Light switch control unit
  a = side/headlight switch

28 LH number plate light
29 RH number plate light
30 Front headlight levelling level sensor
31 Rear headlight levelling level sensor
32 Combination switch
  a = direction indicator switch
  b = headlight dip/main switch
  c = headlight flasher switch
33 Overhead panel control unit
34 Automatic lighting daylight sensor
35 Diagnostic connector

Diagram 4

H33871

Typical sidelights, tail lights, number plate lights & headlights

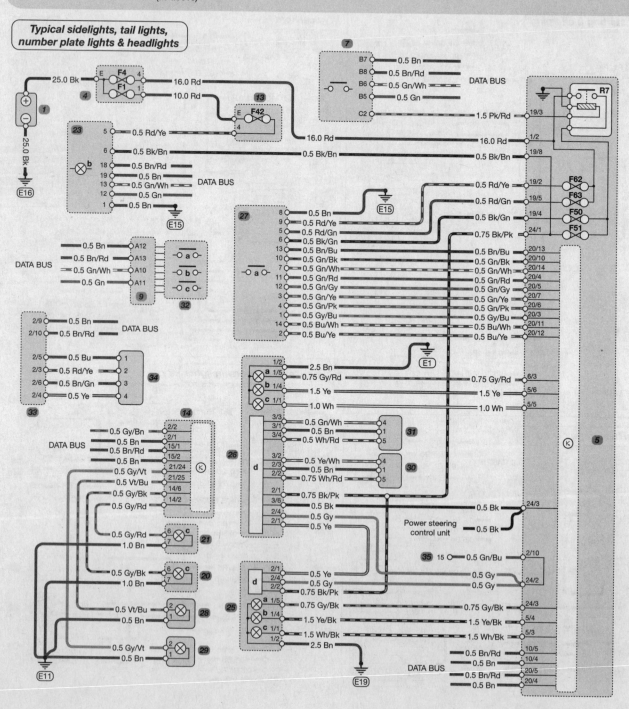

Wire colours

Bk	Black	Pk	Pink
Bn	Brown	Rd	Red
Bu	Blue	Vt	Violet
Gn	Green	Wh	White
Gy	Grey	Ye	Yellow
Og	Orange		
Tr	Transparent		

Key to items

1 Battery
4 Maxifusebox
5 Engine fusebox
7 Electronic ignition switch control unit
9 Steering column control unit
10 Steering wheel clock springs
11 LH m/f steering wheel push button group
12 RH m/f steering wheel push button group
14 Rear fusebox
20 LH rear light unit
   e = direction indicator
21 RH rear light unit
   d = foglight
   e = direction indicator
23 Instrument cluster
   c = LH direction indicator waring light
   d = RH direction indicator warning light
   c = direction indicator warning buzzer
   d = multifunction display

25 LH front light unit
   e = direction indicator
26 RH front light unit
   (as above)
27 Light switch control unit
   b = front foglight switch
   c = rear foglight switch
32 Instrument cluster
38 Upper panel control unit
   a = hazard warning switch
39 LH front foglight
40 RH front foglight
41 LH front door control unit
42 RH front door control unit
43 LH door mirror
   a = direction indicator side repeater
44 RH door mirror
   (as above)
45 Audio unit

46 CD changer
47 Auxiliary input
48 LH front door speaker
49 LH front tweeter
50 LH rear speaker
51 RH front door speaker
52 RH front tweeter
53 RH rear speaker

Diagram 5

H33872

Typical foglights, direction indicators & hazard warning lights

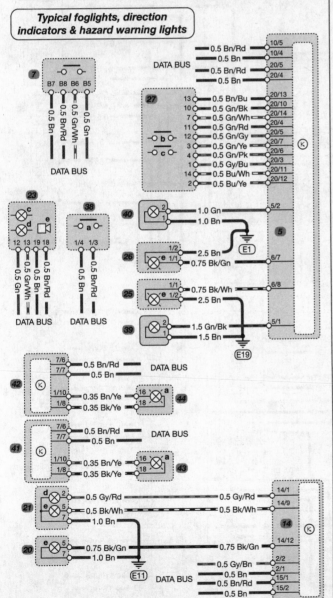

Typical audio system

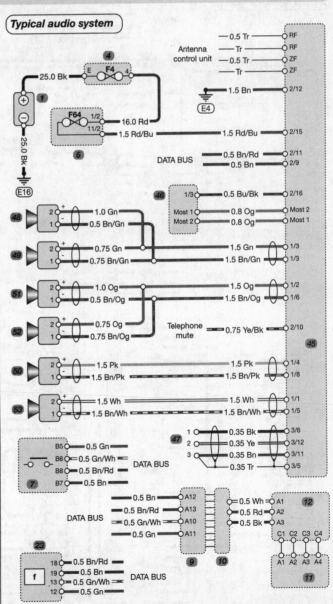

Wire colours

Bk	Black	Pk	Pink
Bn	Brown	Rd	Red
Bu	Blue	Vt	Violet
Gn	Green	Wh	White
Gy	Grey	Ye	Yellow
Og	Orange		
Tr	Transparent		

Key to items

1 Battery
4 Maxifusebox
5 Engine fusebox
   R4 = terminal 15R relay
7 Electronic ignition switch control unit
14 Rear fusebox
23 Instrument cluster
   g = instrument illumination
27 Light switch control unit
   a = side/headlight switch
41 LH front door control unit
42 RH front door control unit
55 Overhead panel control unit
   a = interior light
   b = LH reading light
   c = RH reading light

d = interior light switch
e = LH reading light switch
f = RH interior light switch
56 Glovebox light/switch
57 Cigar lighter
58 Ashtray light
59 LH air outlet illumination
60 RH air outlet illumination
61 Centre air outlet illumination
62 LH vanity mirror light
63 RH vanity mirror light
64 Rear interior light
   a = warning display
   b = reading light
   c = interior light
65 Main luggage compartment light

66 LH luggage compartment light
67 RH luggage compartment light
68 LH front door switch
69 LH rear door switch
70 RH front door switch
71 RH rear door switch
72 LH front door entry light
73 RH front door entry light
74 LH rear door entry light
75 RH rear door entry light
76 LH rear door control unit
77 RH rear door control unit

Diagram 6

H33873

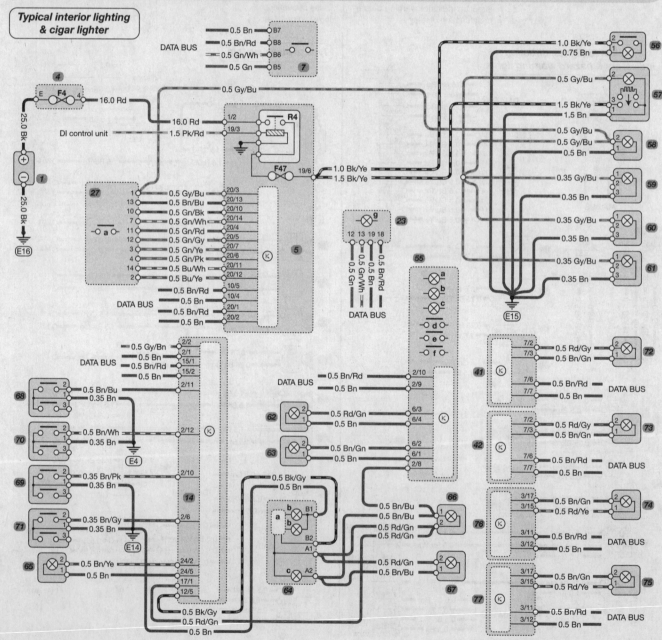

Typical interior lighting & cigar lighter

Wire colours

Bk Black Pk Pink
Bn Brown Rd Red
Bu Blue   Vt Violet
Gn Green Wh White
Gy Grey   Ye Yellow
Og Orange
Tr Transparent

Key to items

1 Battery
4 Maxifusebox
5 Engine fusebox
  R7 = terminal 15 relay chassis
7 Electronic ignition switch control unit
9 Steering column control unit
13 Passenger fusebox
14 Rear fusebox
  R6 = terminal 15R relay 1
23 Instrument cluster
  a = alternator warning light
  b = main beam warning light
  c = LH direction indicator warning light
  d = RH direction indicator warning light
  e = direction indicator buzzer
  f = multifunction indicator
  g = instrument illumination
  h = illumination rheostat
  i = trip meter reset button
  j = preheater warning light
  k = ABS warning light
  l = SRS warning light
  m = brake fluid/handbrake warning light
  n = speed limiter warning light
  o = gear display
  p = tachometer
  q = speedometer
  r = fuel gauge
  s = low fuel warning light
  t = warning buzzer
  u = engine management warning light
  v = ESP warning light
  w = seatbelt warning light
32 Combination switch
  d = front washer switch
  e = front wiper switch
  f = rear washer switch
  g = rear wiper switch
55 Overhead panel control unit
80 Front wiper motor
81 Rear wiper motor
82 Accessory socket
83 Rain sensor
84 Front washer pump
85 Rear washer pump
86 LH washer nozzle heater
87 RH washer nozzle heater
88 Washer nozzle hose heater
89 Low coolant level sensor
90 Low washer fluid level sensor
91 DI control unit

Diagram 7

H33874

Typical wash/wipe & accessory socket

Typical instrument cluster

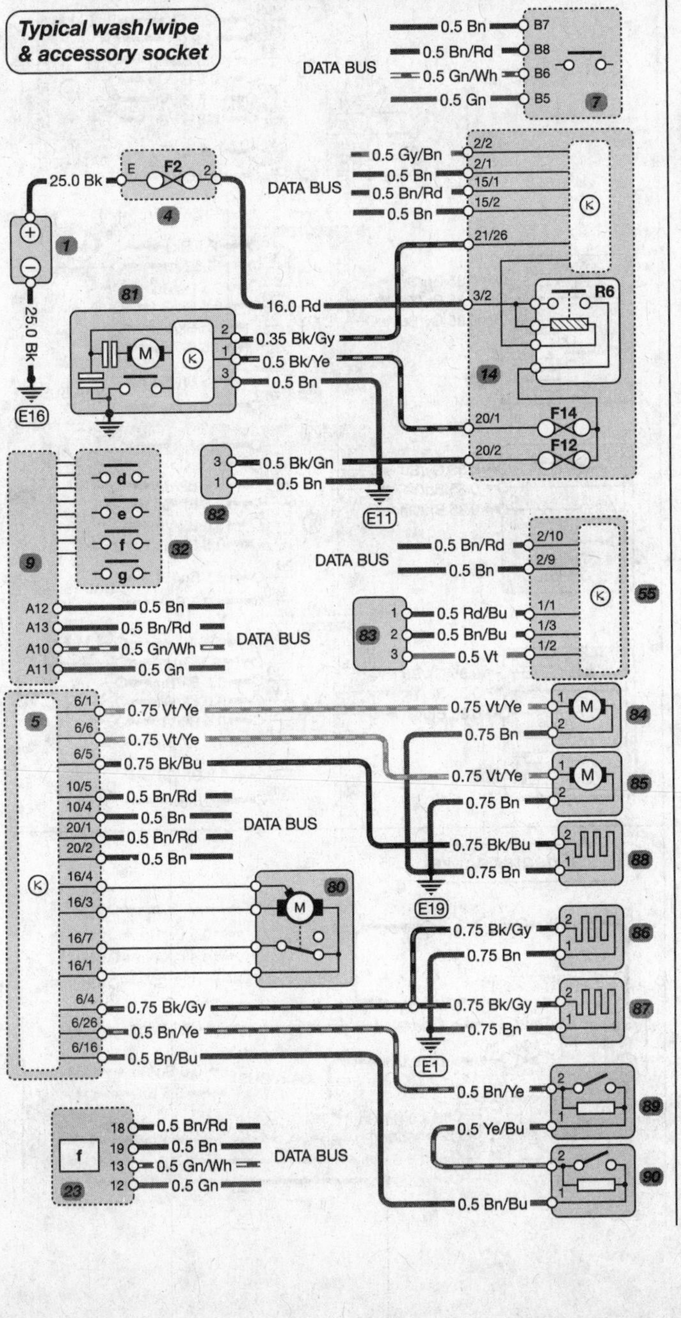

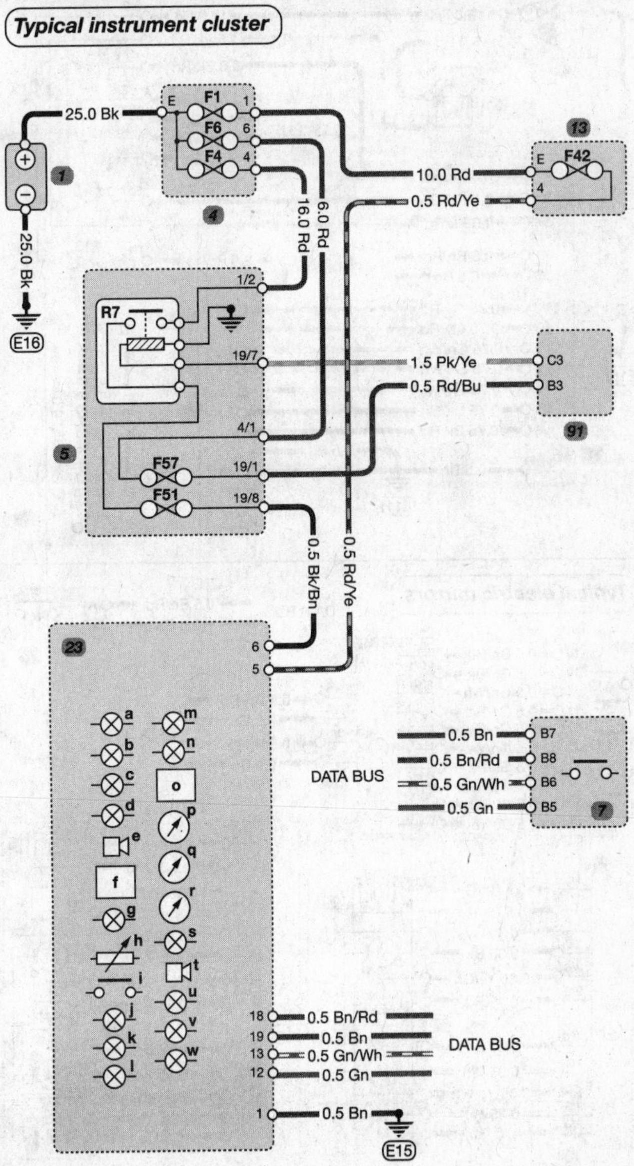

Wire colours

Bk	Black	Pk	Pink
Bn	Brown	Rd	Red
Bu	Blue	Vt	Violet
Gn	Green	Wh	White
Gy	Grey	Ye	Yellow
Og	Orange		
Tr	Transparent		

Key to items

1 Battery
4 Maxifusebox
5 Engine fusebox
7 Electronic ignition switch control unit
13 Passenger fusebox
14 Rear fusebox
15 AAC control unit
  a = heated rear window/mirror switch
27 Light switch control unit
  d = mirror fold-in switch
  e = mirror fold-out switch
  f = LH mirror selector switch
  g = RH mirror selector switch
  h = mirror adjustment switch

41 LH front door control unit
42 RH front door control unit
43 LH door mirror
  b = heating element
  c = automatic mirro dimming sensor
  d = UP/DOWN motor
  e = L/R motor
  f = folding mirror motor
44 RH door mirror
  (as above)
76 LH rear door control unit
77 RH rear door control unit
95 Trailer socket
96 Trailer recognition control unit

97 Heater blower motor
98 LH front window motor
99 RH front window motor
100 LH rear window motor
101 RH rear window motor
102 LH front window switch
103 RH front window switch
104 LH rear window switch
105 RH rear window switch

Diagram 8

H33875

Typical trailer socket

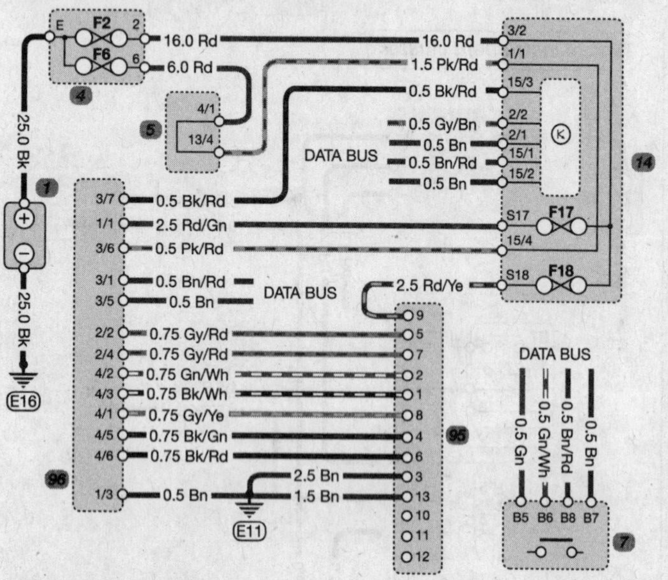

Typical electric windows

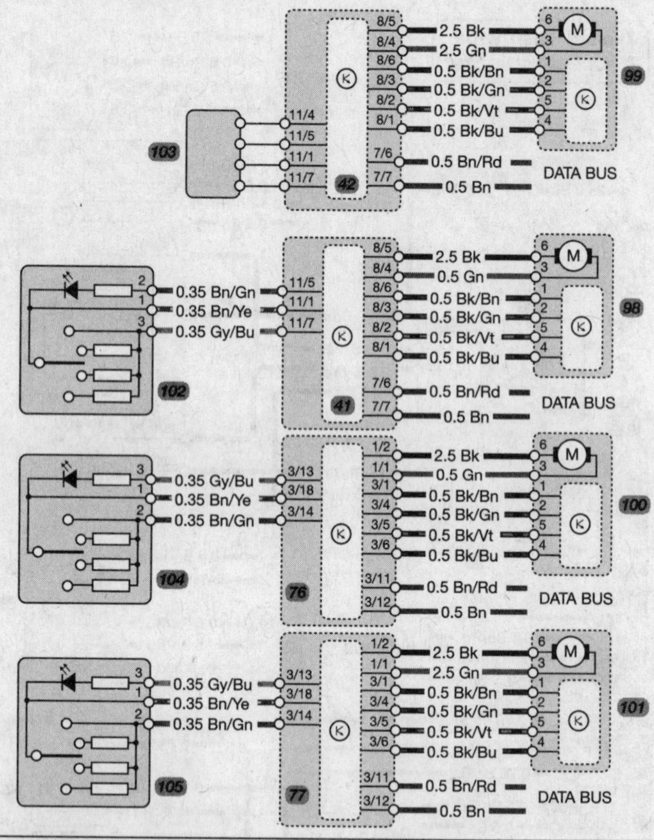

Typical electric mirrors

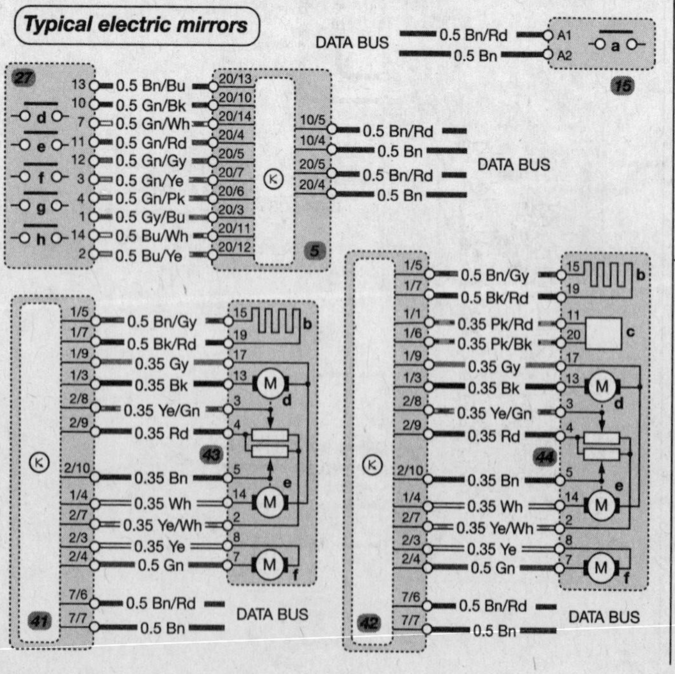

Typical heater blower

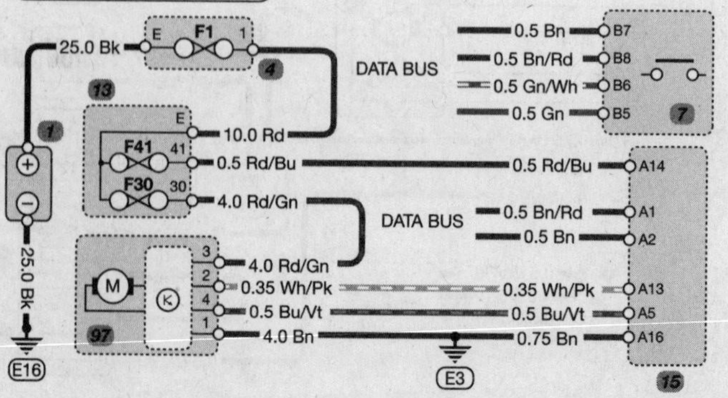

Wire colours

Bk	Black	**Pk**	Pink
Bn	Brown	**Rd**	Red
Bu	Blue	**Vt**	Violet
Gn	Green	**Wh**	White
Gy	Grey	**Ye**	Yellow
Og	Orange		
Tr	Transparent		

Key to items

1 Battery
4 Maxifusebox
5 Engine fusebox
13 Passenger fusebox
14 Rear fusebox
   R7 = filler cap polarity reversing relay 1
   R8 = filler cap polarity reversing relay 2
19 ESP/BAS control unit
23 Instrument cluster
   f = multifunction display
33 Overhead panel control unit
38 Upper panel control unit
   b = passenger's central locking switch

41 LH front door control unit
42 RH front door control unit
68 LH front door switch
69 LH rear door switch
70 RH front door switch
71 RH rear door switch
76 LH rear door control unit
77 RH rear door control unit
103 RH front window switch
   a = tailgate release switch
108 SRS control unit
109 Sunroof assembly
110 Filler flap lock motor

111 Tailgate release switch
112 Tailgate lock motor & key switch
113 Tailgate push button switch
114 LH front door lock motor
115 RH front door lock motor
116 LH rear door lock motor
117 RH rear door lock motor
118 LH I/R sensor
119 RH I/R sensor

Diagram 9

H33876

Typical central locking

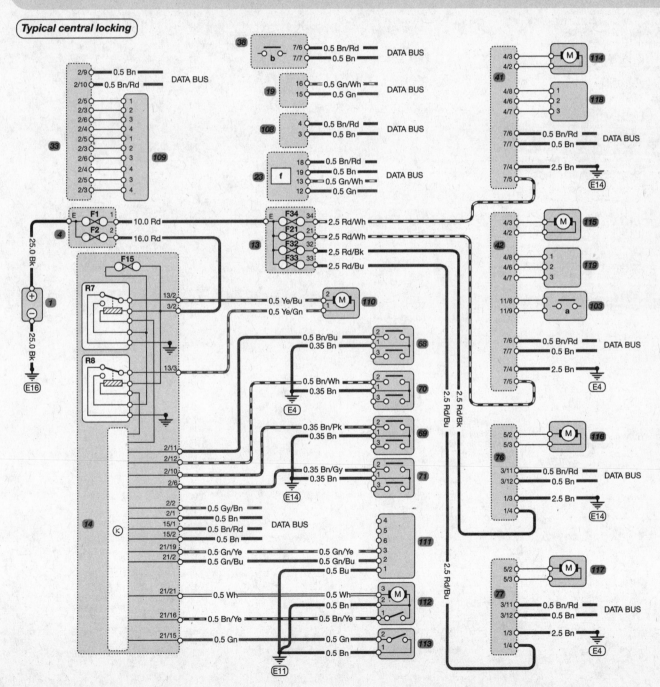

Dimensions and weights

Note: *All figures are approximate, and may vary according to model. Refer to manufacturer's data for exact figures.*

Dimensions	Coupe	Saloon	Estate
Overall length.	4343 mm	4526 mm	4541 mm
Overall width.	1728 mm	1728 mm	1728 mm
Overall height	1406 mm	1426 mm	1465 mm
Wheelbase	2715 mm	2715 mm	2715 mm

Weights	Coupe	Saloon	Estate
Unladen weight*:			
C180.	1445 kg	1475 kg	1525 kg
C200.	1480 kg	1475 kg	1525 kg
C230.	1500 kg		
C220 CDI	1505 kg	1520 kg	1570 kg
C270 CDI		1600 kg	1650 kg
Maximum gross vehicle weight:			
C180.	1870 kg	1955 kg	2050 kg
C200.	1905 kg	1955 kg	2050 kg
C230.	1925 kg		
C220 CDI	1930 kg	2000 kg	2095 kg
C270 CDI		2080 kg	2175 kg
Maximum front axle load:			
C180.	940 kg	960 kg	970 kg
C200.	965 kg	960 kg	970 kg
C230.	980 kg		
C220 CDI	985 kg	990 kg	1005 kg
C270 CDI		1060 kg	1065 kg
Maximum rear axle load:			
C180.	955 kg	1025 kg	1120 kg
C200.	965 kg	1025 kg	1120 kg
C230.	970 kg		
C220 CDI	970 kg	1040 kg	1130 kg
C270 CD.		1050 kg	1150 kg
Trailer towing – maximum rear axle load:			
C180.	1000 kg	1065 kg	1155 kg
C200.	1010 kg	1065 kg	1155 kg
C230.	1015 kg		
C220 CDI	1015 kg	1080 kg	1570 kg
C270 CDI		1090 kg	1650 kg

* Unladen weight – incudes driver (68kg), luggage (7kg) and all fluids with fuel tank 90% full.

Fuel economy

Although depreciation is still the biggest part of the cost of motoring for most car owners, the cost of fuel is more immediately noticeable. These pages give some tips on how to get the best fuel economy.

Working it out

Manufacturer's figures

Car manufacturers are required by law to provide fuel consumption information on all new vehicles sold. These 'official' figures are obtained by simulating various driving conditions on a rolling road or a test track. Real life conditions are different, so the fuel consumption actually achieved may not bear much resemblance to the quoted figures.

How to calculate it

Many cars now have trip computers which will

display fuel consumption, both instantaneous and average. Refer to the owner's handbook for details of how to use these.

To calculate consumption yourself (and maybe to check that the trip computer is accurate), proceed as follows.

1. Fill up with fuel and note the mileage, or zero the trip recorder.
2. Drive as usual until you need to fill up again.
3. Note the amount of fuel required to refill the tank, and the mileage covered since the previous fill-up.
4. Divide the mileage by the amount of fuel used to obtain the consumption figure.

For example:

Mileage at first fill-up (a) = 27,903
Mileage at second fill-up (b) = 28,346
Mileage covered (b - a) = 443
Fuel required at second fill-up = 48.6 litres

The half-completed changeover to metric units in the UK means that we buy our fuel

in litres, measure distances in miles and talk about fuel consumption in miles per gallon. There are two ways round this: the first is to convert the litres to gallons before doing the calculation (by dividing by 4.546, or see Table 1). So in the example:

48.6 litres ÷ 4.546 = 10.69 gallons
443 miles ÷ 10.69 gallons = 41.4 mpg

The second way is to calculate the consumption in miles per litre, then multiply that figure by 4.546 (or see Table 2).

So in the example, fuel consumption is:

443 miles ÷ 48.6 litres = 9.1 mpl
9.1 mpl x 4.546 = 41.4 mpg

The rest of Europe expresses fuel consumption in litres of fuel required to travel 100 km (l/100 km). For interest, the conversions are given in Table 3. In practice it doesn't matter what units you use, provided you know what your normal consumption is and can spot if it's getting better or worse.

Table 1: conversion of litres to Imperial gallons

litres	1	2	3	4	5	10	20	30	40	50	60	70
gallons	0.22	0.44	0.66	0.88	1.10	2.24	4.49	6.73	8.98	11.22	13.47	15.71

Table 2: conversion of miles per litre to miles per gallon

miles per litre	5	6	7	8	9	10	11	12	13	14
miles per gallon	23	27	32	36	41	46	50	55	59	64

Table 3: conversion of litres per 100 km to miles per gallon

litres per 100 km	4	4.5	5	5.5	6	6.5	7	8	9	10
miles per gallon	71	63	56	51	47	43	40	35	31	28

Maintenance

A well-maintained car uses less fuel and creates less pollution. In particular:

Filters

Change air and fuel filters at the specified intervals.

Oil

Use a good quality oil of the lowest viscosity specified by the vehicle manufacturer (see *Lubricants and fluids*). Check the level often and be careful not to overfill.

Spark plugs

When applicable, renew at the specified intervals.

Tyres

Check tyre pressures regularly. Under-inflated tyres have an increased rolling resistance. It is generally safe to use the higher pressures specified for full load conditions even when not fully laden, but keep an eye on the centre band of tread for signs of wear due to over-inflation.

When buying new tyres, consider the 'fuel saving' models which most manufacturers include in their ranges.

Driving style

Acceleration

Acceleration uses more fuel than driving at a steady speed. The best technique with modern cars is to accelerate reasonably briskly to the desired speed, changing up through the gears as soon as possible without making the engine labour.

Air conditioning

Air conditioning absorbs quite a bit of energy from the engine – typically 3 kW (4 hp) or so. The effect on fuel consumption is at its worst in slow traffic. Switch it off when not required.

Anticipation

Drive smoothly and try to read the traffic flow so as to avoid unnecessary acceleration and braking.

Automatic transmission

When accelerating in an automatic, avoid depressing the throttle so far as to make the transmission hold onto lower gears at higher speeds. Don't use the 'Sport' setting, if applicable.

When stationary with the engine running, select 'N' or 'P'. When moving, keep your left foot away from the brake.

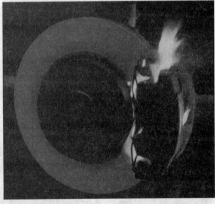

Braking

Braking converts the car's energy of motion into heat – essentially, it is wasted. Obviously some braking is always going to be necessary, but with good anticipation it is surprising how much can be avoided, especially on routes that you know well.

Carshare

Consider sharing lifts to work or to the shops. Even once a week will make a difference.

Electrical loads

Electricity is 'fuel' too; the alternator which charges the battery does so by converting some of the engine's energy of motion into electrical energy. The more electrical accessories are in use, the greater the load on the alternator. Switch off big consumers like the heated rear window when not required.

Freewheeling

Freewheeling (coasting) in neutral with the engine switched off is dangerous. The effort required to operate power-assisted brakes and steering increases when the engine is not running, with a potential lack of control in emergency situations.

In any case, modern fuel injection systems automatically cut off the engine's fuel supply on the overrun (moving and in gear, but with the accelerator pedal released).

Gadgets

Bolt-on devices claiming to save fuel have been around for nearly as long as the motor car itself. Those which worked were rapidly adopted as standard equipment by the vehicle manufacturers. Others worked only in certain situations, or saved fuel only at the expense of unacceptable effects on performance, driveability or the life of engine components.

The most effective fuel saving gadget is the driver's right foot.

Journey planning

Combine (eg) a trip to the supermarket with a visit to the recycling centre and the DIY store, rather than making separate journeys.

When possible choose a travelling time outside rush hours.

Load

The more heavily a car is laden, the greater the energy required to accelerate it to a given speed. Remove heavy items which you don't need to carry.

One load which is often overlooked is the contents of the fuel tank. A tankful of fuel (55 litres / 12 gallons) weighs 45 kg (100 lb) or so. Just half filling it may be worthwhile.

Lost?

At the risk of stating the obvious, if you're going somewhere new, have details of the route to hand. There's not much point in achieving record mpg if you also go miles out of your way.

Parking

If possible, carry out any reversing or turning manoeuvres when you arrive at a parking space so that you can drive straight out when you leave. Manoeuvering when the engine is cold uses a lot more fuel.

Driving around looking for free on-street parking may cost more in fuel than buying a car park ticket.

Premium fuel

Most major oil companies (and some supermarkets) have premium grades of fuel which are several pence a litre dearer than the standard grades. Reports vary, but the consensus seems to be that if these fuels improve economy at all, they do not do so by enough to justify their extra cost.

Roof rack

When loading a roof rack, try to produce a wedge shape with the narrow end at the front. Any cover should be securely fastened – if it flaps it's creating turbulence and absorbing energy.

Remove roof racks and boxes when not in use – they increase air resistance and can create a surprising amount of noise.

Short journeys

The engine is at its least efficient, and wear is highest, during the first few miles after a cold start. Consider walking, cycling or using public transport.

Speed

The engine is at its most efficient when running at a steady speed and load at the rpm where it develops maximum torque. (You can find this figure in the car's handbook.) For most cars this corresponds to between 55 and 65 mph in top gear.

Above the optimum cruising speed, fuel consumption starts to rise quite sharply. A car travelling at 80 mph will typically be using 30% more fuel than at 60 mph.

Supermarket fuel

It may be cheap but is it any good? In the UK all supermarket fuel must meet the relevant British Standard. The major oil companies will say that their branded fuels have better additive packages which may stop carbon and other deposits building up. A reasonable compromise might be to use one tank of branded fuel to three or four from the supermarket.

Switch off when stationary

Switch off the engine if you look like being stationary for more than 30 seconds or so. This is good for the environment as well as for your pocket. Be aware though that frequent restarts are hard on the battery and the starter motor.

Windows

Driving with the windows open increases air turbulence around the vehicle. Closing the windows promotes smooth airflow and

reduced resistance. The faster you go, the more significant this is.

And finally . . .

Driving techniques associated with good fuel economy tend to involve moderate acceleration and low top speeds. Be considerate to the needs of other road users who may need to make brisker progress; even if you do not agree with them this is not an excuse to be obstructive.

Safety must always take precedence over economy, whether it is a question of accelerating hard to complete an overtaking manoeuvre, killing your speed when confronted with a potential hazard or switching the lights on when it starts to get dark.

Conversion factors

Length (distance)

Inches (in)	x 25.4	= Millimetres (mm)	x 0.0394	= Inches (in)
Feet (ft)	x 0.305	= Metres (m)	x 3.281	= Feet (ft)
Miles	x 1.609	= Kilometres (km)	x 0.621	= Miles

Volume (capacity)

Cubic inches (cu in; in³)	x 16.387	= Cubic centimetres (cc; cm³)	x 0.061	= Cubic inches (cu in; in³)
Imperial pints (Imp pt)	x 0.568	= Litres (l)	x 1.76	= Imperial pints (Imp pt)
Imperial quarts (Imp qt)	x 1.137	= Litres (l)	x 0.88	= Imperial quarts (Imp qt)
Imperial quarts (Imp qt)	x 1.201	= US quarts (US qt)	x 0.833	= Imperial quarts (Imp qt)
US quarts (US qt)	x 0.946	= Litres (l)	x 1.057	= US quarts (US qt)
Imperial gallons (Imp gal)	x 4.546	= Litres (l)	x 0.22	= Imperial gallons (Imp gal)
Imperial gallons (Imp gal)	x 1.201	= US gallons (US gal)	x 0.833	= Imperial gallons (Imp gal)
US gallons (US gal)	x 3.785	= Litres (l)	x 0.264	= US gallons (US gal)

Mass (weight)

Ounces (oz)	x 28.35	= Grams (g)	x 0.035	= Ounces (oz)
Pounds (lb)	x 0.454	= Kilograms (kg)	x 2.205	= Pounds (lb)

Force

Ounces-force (ozf; oz)	x 0.278	= Newtons (N)	x 3.6	= Ounces-force (ozf; oz)
Pounds-force (lbf; lb)	x 4.448	= Newtons (N)	x 0.225	= Pounds-force (lbf; lb)
Newtons (N)	x 0.1	= Kilograms-force (kgf; kg)	x 9.81	= Newtons (N)

Pressure

Pounds-force per square inch (psi; lbf/in²; lb/in²)	x 0.070	= Kilograms-force per square centimetre (kgf/cm²; kg/cm²)	x 14.223	= Pounds-force per square inch (psi; lbf/in²; lb/in²)
Pounds-force per square inch (psi; lbf/in²; lb/in²)	x 0.068	= Atmospheres (atm)	x 14.696	= Pounds-force per square inch (psi; lbf/in²; lb/in²)
Pounds-force per square inch (psi; lbf/in²; lb/in²)	x 0.069	= Bars	x 14.5	= Pounds-force per square inch (psi; lbf/in²; lb/in²)
Pounds-force per square inch (psi; lbf/in²; lb/in²)	x 6.895	= Kilopascals (kPa)	x 0.145	= Pounds-force per square inch (psi; lbf/in²; lb/in²)
Kilopascals (kPa)	x 0.01	= Kilograms-force per square centimetre (kgf/cm²; kg/cm²)	x 98.1	= Kilopascals (kPa)
Millibar (mbar)	x 100	= Pascals (Pa)	x 0.01	= Millibar (mbar)
Millibar (mbar)	x 0.0145	= Pounds-force per square inch (psi; lbf/in²; lb/in²)	x 68.947	= Millibar (mbar)
Millibar (mbar)	x 0.75	= Millimetres of mercury (mmHg)	x 1.333	= Millibar (mbar)
Millibar (mbar)	x 0.401	= Inches of water (inH₂O)	x 2.491	= Millibar (mbar)
Millimetres of mercury (mmHg)	x 0.535	= Inches of water (inH₂O)	x 1.868	= Millimetres of mercury (mmHg)
Inches of water (inH₂O)	x 0.036	= Pounds-force per square inch (psi; lbf/in²; lb/in²)	x 27.68	= Inches of water (inH₂O)

Torque (moment of force)

Pounds-force inches (lbf in; lb in)	x 1.152	= Kilograms-force centimetre (kgf cm; kg cm)	x 0.868	= Pounds-force inches (lbf in; lb in)
Pounds-force inches (lbf in; lb in)	x 0.113	= Newton metres (Nm)	x 8.85	= Pounds-force inches (lbf in; lb in)
Pounds-force inches (lbf in; lb in)	x 0.083	= Pounds-force feet (lbf ft; lb ft)	x 12	= Pounds-force inches (lbf in; lb in)
Pounds-force feet (lbf ft; lb ft)	x 0.138	= Kilograms-force metres (kgf m; kg m)	x 7.233	= Pounds-force feet (lbf ft; lb ft)
Pounds-force feet (lbf ft; lb ft)	x 1.356	= Newton metres (Nm)	x 0.738	= Pounds-force feet (lbf ft; lb ft)
Newton metres (Nm)	x 0.102	= Kilograms-force metres (kgf m; kg m)	x 9.804	= Newton metres (Nm)

Power

Horsepower (hp)	x 745.7	= Watts (W)	x 0.0013	= Horsepower (hp)

Velocity (speed)

Miles per hour (miles/hr; mph)	x 1.609	= Kilometres per hour (km/hr; kph)	x 0.621	= Miles per hour (miles/hr; mph)

Fuel consumption*

Miles per gallon, Imperial (mpg)	x 0.354	= Kilometres per litre (km/l)	x 2.825	= Miles per gallon, Imperial (mpg)
Miles per gallon, US (mpg)	x 0.425	= Kilometres per litre (km/l)	x 2.352	= Miles per gallon, US (mpg)

Temperature

Degrees Fahrenheit = (°C x 1.8) + 32   Degrees Celsius (Degrees Centigrade; °C) = (°F - 32) x 0.56

It is common practice to convert from miles per gallon (mpg) to litres/100 kilometres (l/100km), where mpg x l/100 km = 282

Spare parts are available from many sources, including maker's appointed garages, accessory shops, and motor factors. To be sure of obtaining the correct parts, it will sometimes be necessary to quote the vehicle identification number. If possible, it can also be useful to take the old parts along for positive identification. Items such as starter motors and alternators may be available under a service exchange scheme – any parts returned should be clean.

Our advice regarding spare parts is as follows.

Officially-appointed garages

This is the best source of parts which are peculiar to your car, and which are not otherwise generally available (e.g. badges, interior trim, certain body panels, etc). It is also the only place at which you should buy parts if the vehicle is still under warranty.

Accessory shops

These are very good places to buy materials and components needed for the maintenance of your car (oil, air and fuel filters, light bulbs, drivebelts, greases, brake pads, touch-up paint, etc). Components of this nature sold by a reputable shop are usually of the same standard as those fitted by the car manufacturer.

Besides components, these shops also sell tools and general accessories, usually have convenient opening hours, charge lower prices, and can often be found close to home. Some accessory shops have parts counters where components needed for almost any repair job can be purchased or ordered.

Motor factors

Good factors will stock all the more important components, which wear out comparatively quickly, and can sometimes supply individual components needed for the overhaul of a larger assembly (e.g. brake seals and hydraulic parts, bearing shells, pistons, valves). They may also handle work such as cylinder block re-boring, crankshaft regrinding, etc.

Tyre and exhaust specialists

These outlets may be independent, or members of a local or national chain. They frequently offer competitive prices when compared with a main dealer or local garage, but it will pay to obtain several quotes before making a decision. When researching prices, also ask what 'extras' may be added – for instance, fitting a new valve and balancing the wheel are both commonly charged on top of the price of a new tyre.

Other sources

Beware of parts or materials obtained from market stalls, car boot sales or similar outlets. Such items are not invariably sub-standard, but there is little chance of compensation if they do prove unsatisfactory. In the case of safety-critical components such as brake pads, there is the risk not only of financial loss, but also of an accident causing injury or death.

Second-hand components or assemblies obtained from a car breaker can be a good buy in some circumstances, but this sort of purchase is best made by the experienced DIY mechanic.

Modifications are a continuing and unpublicised process in vehicle manufacture, quite apart from major model changes. Spare parts manuals and lists are compiled upon a numerical basis, the individual vehicle identification numbers being essential to correct identification of the component concerned.

When ordering spare parts, always give as much information as possible. Quote the model number, chassis number, engine number and, where applicable, the spare parts number, as appropriate.

Vehicle Identification Number

The *Vehicle Identification Number (VIN)* plate appears at the base of the B-pillar, and is visible with the driver's door open **(see illustration).** The VIN also appears on a small plate visible from outside, through the passenger side of the windscreen **(see illustration).**

Body number and paint code

The *body number and paint code* are marked on a coloured plate attached to the bonnet crossmember.

Engine number and type code

The *engine number* is either stamped onto the rear of the cylinder block, near the transmission mounting face, or onto the front of the left-hand face of the cylinder block, depending on engine type. The engine number can also be found on the car's registration document (V5C or log book) **(see illustration).** The engine code is the first part of the engine number.

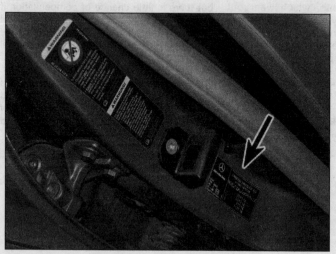

VIN plate on driver's door pillar

VIN visible through windscreen

[D.4]	Wheelplan	2-AXLE-RIGID BODY
J	Vehicle Category	M1
K	Type approval number	e1*95/54*0039*10 *
P.2	Max. net power (kW)	
E	VIN/Chassis/Frame No.	WDB17044271923985
P.5	Engine Number	11165932167725
F.1	Max. permissible mass (exc. m/c)	

The engine number also appears on the registration document

The first part of the number is the engine code (eg, 111)

Whenever servicing, repair or overhaul work is carried out on the car or its components, observe the following procedures and instructions. This will assist in carrying out the operation efficiently and to a professional standard of workmanship.

Joint mating faces and gaskets

When separating components at their mating faces, never insert screwdrivers or similar implements into the joint between the faces in order to prise them apart. This can cause severe damage which results in oil leaks, coolant leaks, etc upon reassembly. Separation is usually achieved by tapping along the joint with a soft-faced hammer in order to break the seal. However, note that this method may not be suitable where dowels are used for component location.

Where a gasket is used between the mating faces of two components, a new one must be fitted on reassembly; fit it dry unless otherwise stated in the repair procedure. Make sure that the mating faces are clean and dry, with all traces of old gasket removed. When cleaning a joint face, use a tool which is unlikely to score or damage the face, and remove any burrs or nicks with an oilstone or fine file.

Make sure that tapped holes are cleaned with a pipe cleaner, and keep them free of jointing compound, if this is being used, unless specifically instructed otherwise.

Ensure that all orifices, channels or pipes are clear, and blow through them, preferably using compressed air.

Oil seals

Oil seals can be removed by levering them out with a wide flat-bladed screwdriver or similar implement. Alternatively, a number of self-tapping screws may be screwed into the seal, and these used as a purchase for pliers or some similar device in order to pull the seal free.

Whenever an oil seal is removed from its working location, either individually or as part of an assembly, it should be renewed.

The very fine sealing lip of the seal is easily damaged, and will not seal if the surface it contacts is not completely clean and free from scratches, nicks or grooves. If the original sealing surface of the component cannot be restored, and the manufacturer has not made provision for slight relocation of the seal relative to the sealing surface, the component should be renewed.

Protect the lips of the seal from any surface which may damage them in the course of fitting. Use tape or a conical sleeve where possible. Lubricate the seal lips with oil before fitting and, on dual-lipped seals, fill the space between the lips with grease.

Unless otherwise stated, oil seals must be fitted with their sealing lips toward the lubricant to be sealed.

Use a tubular drift or block of wood of the appropriate size to install the seal and, if the seal housing is shouldered, drive the seal down to the shoulder. If the seal housing is unshouldered, the seal should be fitted with its face flush with the housing top face (unless otherwise instructed).

Screw threads and fastenings

Seized nuts, bolts and screws are quite a common occurrence where corrosion has set in, and the use of penetrating oil or releasing fluid will often overcome this problem if the offending item is soaked for a while before attempting to release it. The use of an impact driver may also provide a means of releasing such stubborn fastening devices, when used in conjunction with the appropriate screwdriver bit or socket. If none of these methods works, it may be necessary to resort to the careful application of heat, or the use of a hacksaw or nut splitter device.

Studs are usually removed by locking two nuts together on the threaded part, and then using a spanner on the lower nut to unscrew the stud. Studs or bolts which have broken off below the surface of the component in which they are mounted can sometimes be removed using a stud extractor. Always ensure that a blind tapped hole is completely free from oil, grease, water or other fluid before installing the bolt or stud. Failure to do this could cause the housing to crack due to the hydraulic action of the bolt or stud as it is screwed in.

When tightening a castellated nut to accept a split pin, tighten the nut to the specified torque, where applicable, and then tighten further to the next split pin hole. Never slacken the nut to align the split pin hole, unless stated in the repair procedure.

When checking or retightening a nut or bolt to a specified torque setting, slacken the nut or bolt by a quarter of a turn, and then retighten to the specified setting. However, this should not be attempted where angular tightening has been used.

For some screw fastenings, notably cylinder head bolts or nuts, torque wrench settings are no longer specified for the latter stages of tightening, "angle-tightening" being called up instead. Typically, a fairly low torque wrench setting will be applied to the bolts/nuts in the correct sequence, followed by one or more stages of tightening through specified angles.

Locknuts, locktabs and washers

Any fastening which will rotate against a component or housing during tightening should always have a washer between it and the relevant component or housing.

Spring or split washers should always be renewed when they are used to lock a critical component such as a big-end bearing retaining bolt or nut. Locktabs which are folded over to retain a nut or bolt should always be renewed.

Self-locking nuts can be re-used in non-critical areas, providing resistance can be felt when the locking portion passes over the bolt or stud thread. However, it should be noted that self-locking stiffnuts tend to lose their effectiveness after long periods of use, and should then be renewed as a matter of course.

Split pins must always be replaced with new ones of the correct size for the hole.

When thread-locking compound is found on the threads of a fastener which is to be re-used, it should be cleaned off with a wire brush and solvent, and fresh compound applied on reassembly.

Special tools

Some repair procedures in this manual entail the use of special tools such as a press, two or three-legged pullers, spring compressors, etc. Wherever possible, suitable readily-available alternatives to the manufacturer's special tools are described, and are shown in use. In some instances, where no alternative is possible, it has been necessary to resort to the use of a manufacturer's tool, and this has been done for reasons of safety as well as the efficient completion of the repair operation. Unless you are highly-skilled and have a thorough understanding of the procedures described, never attempt to bypass the use of any special tool when the procedure described specifies its use. Not only is there a very great risk of personal injury, but expensive damage could be caused to the components involved.

Environmental considerations

When disposing of used engine oil, brake fluid, antifreeze, etc, give due consideration to any detrimental environmental effects. Do not, for instance, pour any of the above liquids down drains into the general sewage system, or onto the ground to soak away. Many local council refuse tips provide a facility for waste oil disposal, as do some garages. If none of these facilities are available, consult your local Environmental Health Department, or the National Rivers Authority, for further advice.

With the universal tightening-up of legislation regarding the emission of environmentally-harmful substances from motor vehicles, most vehicles have tamperproof devices fitted to the main adjustment points of the fuel system. These devices are primarily designed to prevent unqualified persons from adjusting the fuel/air mixture, with the chance of a consequent increase in toxic emissions. If such devices are found during servicing or overhaul, they should, wherever possible, be renewed or refitted in accordance with the manufacturer's requirements or current legislation.

OIL CARE
FOLLOW THE CODE

OIL BANK LINE
0800 66 33 66
www.oilbankline.org.uk

Note: It is antisocial and illegal to dump oil down the drain. To find the location of your local oil recycling bank, call this number free.

The jack supplied with the vehicle tool kit should **only** be used for changing the roadwheels in an emergency – see *Wheel changing* at the front of this book. When carrying out any other kind of work, raise the vehicle using a heavy-duty hydraulic (or 'trolley') jack, and always supplement the jack with axle stands positioned under the vehicle jacking points. If the roadwheels do not have to be removed, consider using wheel ramps – these can be placed under the wheels once the vehicle has been raised using a hydraulic jack, and the vehicle lowered onto the ramps so that it is resting on its wheels.

Only ever jack the vehicle up on a solid, level surface. If there is even a slight slope, take great care that the vehicle cannot move as the wheels are lifted off the ground. Jacking up on an uneven or gravelled surface is not recommended, as the weight of the vehicle will not be evenly distributed, and the jack may slip as the vehicle is raised.

As far as possible, do not leave the vehicle unattended once it has been raised, particularly if children are playing nearby.

Before jacking up the front of the car, ensure that the parking brake is firmly applied, and engage first gear (or P). When jacking up the rear of the car, place wooden chocks in front of the front wheels.

The jack supplied with the vehicle locates in the holes provided in the sill. Unscrew the access plug and insert the jack fully into the hole in the sill. Ensure that the jack head is correctly engaged before attempting to raise the vehicle.

When using a hydraulic jack or axle stands, the jack head or axle stand head may be placed directly under one of the jacking points – a large rubber support block is provided on the base of the sill, at the front and rear, for this purpose **(see illustrations)**. It is still advisable to use a block of wood between the jack head or axle stand, and the rubber block, to avoid damage to the sill. **Do not** jack the vehicle under any other part of the sill, engine sump, floor pan, or directly under any of the steering or suspension components.

To raise the front of the vehicle, position a block of wood on the jack head and position the jack underneath the centre of the front suspension subframe crossmember (where applicable, remove the plastic undertray first). If one side of the vehicle is to be raised, the jack can be positioned to one side of the crossmember, but **not** under the front suspension arms **(see illustration)**. Lift the vehicle to the required height and support it on axle stands positioned underneath the front rubber support blocks, which are located directly underneath the vehicle jack location holes in the sill. The vehicle can also be lifted under the front rubber support blocks, and supported under the front crossmember.

To raise the rear of the vehicle, position a block of wood on the jack head, and position the jack underneath one of the rear rubber support blocks directly underneath the vehicle jack location holes in the sill. Lift the vehicle to the required height and support it on axle stands positioned underneath the triangular-shaped flanges just behind and inboard of the rubber support blocks **(see illustration)** – do not confuse the metal flanges with the plastic fuel tank! Although not necessarily recommended by Mercedes, it is generally accepted that a jack or axle stand (with a block of wood) may be placed directly under the final drive unit – ie that, with care, the final drive may be used as a jacking or support point.

Providing care is taken (and a block of wood is used to spread the load), reinforced areas of the floorpan, particularly those in the region of suspension mountings, and may be used as support points. Consult a Mercedes dealer for advice before using anything other than the approved jacking points, however.

Never work under, around, or near a raised vehicle, unless it is adequately supported on stands. Do not rely on a jack alone, as even a hydraulic jack could fail under load. Makeshift methods should not be used to lift and support the car during servicing work.

Jack head positioned under rubber support block

Axle stand under rubber support block

Axle stand under one side of the front suspension crossmember

Axle stand under rear flange, inboard of rubber support block (arrowed)

Several of the systems require battery power to be available at all times (permanent live). This is either to ensure their continued operation (such as the clock), or to maintain electronic memory settings, which would otherwise be erased. Whenever the battery is to be disconnected therefore, first note the following points, to ensure there are no unforeseen consequences:

a) *Firstly, on any vehicle with central door locking, it is a wise precaution to remove the key from the ignition, and to keep it with you. This avoids the possibility of the key being locked inside the car, should the central locking engage when the battery is reconnected.*

b) *The radio/audio unit fitted as standard equipment by Mercedes is equipped with a built-in security code to deter thieves. If the power source to the unit is cut, the anti-theft system will activate. Even if the power source is immediately reconnected, the radio/audio unit will not function until the correct security code has been entered. Therefore, if you do not know the correct security code for the radio/audio unit,* **do not** *disconnect either of the battery terminals, or remove the radio/audio unit from the vehicle. The code appears on a code card supplied with the car when new. Details for entering the code appear in the vehicle handbook. Should the code have been misplaced or forgotten, on production of proof of ownership a Mercedes dealer or in-car entertainment specialist may be able to help.*

c) *The engine management system ECU is of the 'self-learning' type, meaning that, as it operates, it adapts to changes in operating conditions, and stores the optimum settings found (this is especially true for idle settings). When the battery is disconnected, these 'learned' settings are lost, and the ECU reverts to the base factory settings. When the engine is restarted, it may idle and run roughly until the ECU has 'relearned' the best settings. To further this 'learning' process, take the car for a road test of at least 15 minutes' duration, covering as many engine speeds and loads as possible, and concentrating on the 2000 to 4000 rpm range. On completion, let the engine idle for at least 10 minutes, turning the steering wheel occasionally and switching on high-current-draw equipment such as the heater fan or heated rear window.*

d) *After the battery has been reconnected, the electric windows and sunroof closed positions must be reprogrammed by closing the windows and sunroof, and holding the operating switch in the closed position for a few seconds.*

e) *After the battery has been reconnected, the ESP system needs to be set up by turning the steering wheel fully from one lock to the other three or four times.*

Devices known as 'memory-savers' or 'code-savers' can be used to avoid some of the above problems. Precise details of use vary according to the device used. Typically, it is plugged into the cigar lighter socket, and is connected by its own wiring to a spare battery; the vehicle battery is then disconnected from the electrical system, leaving the memory-saver to pass sufficient current to maintain audio unit security codes and other memory values, and also to run permanently-live circuits such as the clock.

⚠️ **Warning: Some of these devices allow a considerable amount of current to pass, which can mean that many of the vehicle's systems are still operational when the main battery is disconnected. If a memory-saver is used, ensure that the circuit concerned is actually 'dead' before carrying out any work on it!**

Introduction

A selection of good tools is a fundamental requirement for anyone contemplating the maintenance and repair of a motor vehicle. For the owner who does not possess any, their purchase will prove a considerable expense, offsetting some of the savings made by doing-it-yourself. However, provided that the tools purchased meet the relevant national safety standards and are of good quality, they will last for many years and prove an extremely worthwhile investment.

To help the average owner to decide which tools are needed to carry out the various tasks detailed in this manual, we have compiled three lists of tools under the following headings: *Maintenance and minor repair, Repair and overhaul,* and *Special.* Newcomers to practical mechanics should start off with the *Maintenance and minor repair* tool kit, and confine themselves to the simpler jobs around the vehicle. Then, as confidence and experience grow, more difficult tasks can be undertaken, with extra tools being purchased as, and when, they are needed. In this way, a *Maintenance and minor repair* tool kit can be built up into a *Repair and overhaul* tool kit over a considerable period of time, without any major cash outlays. The experienced do-it-yourselfer will have a tool kit good enough for most repair and overhaul procedures, and will add tools from the *Special* category when it is felt that the expense is justified by the amount of use to which these tools will be put.

Maintenance and minor repair tool kit

The tools given in this list should be considered as a minimum requirement if routine maintenance, servicing and minor repair operations are to be undertaken. We recommend the purchase of combination spanners (ring one end, open-ended the other); although more expensive than open-ended ones, they do give the advantages of both types of spanner.

- ☐ Combination spanners:
  Metric - 8 to 19 mm inclusive
- ☐ Adjustable spanner - 35 mm jaw (approx.)
- ☐ Spark plug spanner (with rubber insert) - petrol models
- ☐ Spark plug gap adjustment tool - petrol models
- ☐ Set of feeler gauges
- ☐ Brake bleed nipple spanner
- ☐ Screwdrivers:
  Flat blade - 100 mm long x 6 mm dia
  Cross blade - 100 mm long x 6 mm dia
  Torx - various sizes (not all vehicles)
- ☐ Combination pliers
- ☐ Hacksaw (junior)
- ☐ Tyre pump
- ☐ Tyre pressure gauge
- ☐ Oil can
- ☐ Oil filter removal tool
- ☐ Fine emery cloth
- ☐ Wire brush (small)
- ☐ Funnel (medium size)
- ☐ Sump drain plug key (not all vehicles)

Repair and overhaul tool kit

These tools are virtually essential for anyone undertaking any major repairs to a motor vehicle, and are additional to those given in the *Maintenance and minor repair* list. Included in this list is a comprehensive set of sockets. Although these are expensive, they will be found invaluable as they are so versatile - particularly if various drives are included in the set. We recommend the half-inch square-drive type, as this can be used with most proprietary torque wrenches.

The tools in this list will sometimes need to be supplemented by tools from the *Special* list:

- ☐ Sockets (or box spanners) to cover range in previous list (including Torx sockets)
- ☐ Reversible ratchet drive (for use with sockets)
- ☐ Extension piece, 250 mm (for use with sockets)
- ☐ Universal joint (for use with sockets)
- ☐ Flexible handle or sliding T "breaker bar" (for use with sockets)
- ☐ Torque wrench (for use with sockets)
- ☐ Self-locking grips
- ☐ Ball pein hammer
- ☐ Soft-faced mallet (plastic or rubber)
- ☐ Screwdrivers:
  Flat blade - long & sturdy, short (chubby), and narrow (electrician's) types
  Cross blade - long & sturdy, and short (chubby) types
- ☐ Pliers:
  Long-nosed
  Side cutters (electrician's)
  Circlip (internal and external)
- ☐ Cold chisel - 25 mm
- ☐ Scriber
- ☐ Scraper
- ☐ Centre-punch
- ☐ Pin punch
- ☐ Hacksaw
- ☐ Brake hose clamp
- ☐ Brake/clutch bleeding kit
- ☐ Selection of twist drills
- ☐ Steel rule/straight-edge
- ☐ Allen keys (inc. splined/Torx type)
- ☐ Selection of files
- ☐ Wire brush
- ☐ Axle stands
- ☐ Jack (strong trolley or hydraulic type)
- ☐ Light with extension lead
- ☐ Universal electrical multi-meter

Sockets and reversible ratchet drive

Brake bleeding kit

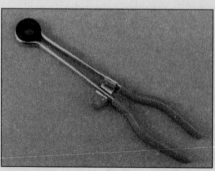

Torx key, socket and bit

Hose clamp

Angular-tightening gauge

Special tools

The tools in this list are those which are not used regularly, are expensive to buy, or which need to be used in accordance with their manufacturers' instructions. Unless relatively difficult mechanical jobs are undertaken frequently, it will not be economic to buy many of these tools. Where this is the case, you could consider clubbing together with friends (or joining a motorists' club) to make a joint purchase, or borrowing the tools against a deposit from a local garage or tool hire specialist. It is worth noting that many of the larger DIY superstores now carry a large range of special tools for hire at modest rates.

The following list contains only those tools and instruments freely available to the public, and not those special tools produced by the vehicle manufacturer specifically for its dealer network. You will find occasional references to these manufacturers' special tools in the text of this manual. Generally, an alternative method of doing the job without the vehicle manufacturers' special tool is given. However, sometimes there is no alternative to using them. Where this is the case and the relevant tool cannot be bought or borrowed, you will have to entrust the work to a dealer.

- ☐ Angular-tightening gauge
- ☐ Valve spring compressor
- ☐ Valve grinding tool
- ☐ Piston ring compressor
- ☐ Piston ring removal/installation tool
- ☐ Cylinder bore hone
- ☐ Balljoint separator
- ☐ Coil spring compressors (where applicable)
- ☐ Two/three-legged hub and bearing puller
- ☐ Impact screwdriver
- ☐ Micrometer and/or vernier calipers
- ☐ Dial gauge
- ☐ Stroboscopic timing light
- ☐ Dwell angle meter/tachometer
- ☐ Fault code reader
- ☐ Cylinder compression gauge
- ☐ Hand-operated vacuum pump and gauge
- ☐ Clutch plate alignment set
- ☐ Brake shoe steady spring cup removal tool
- ☐ Bush and bearing removal/installation set
- ☐ Stud extractors
- ☐ Tap and die set
- ☐ Lifting tackle
- ☐ Trolley jack

Buying tools

Reputable motor accessory shops and superstores often offer excellent quality tools at discount prices, so it pays to shop around.

Remember, you don't have to buy the most expensive items on the shelf, but it is always advisable to steer clear of the very cheap tools. Beware of 'bargains' offered on market stalls or at car boot sales. There are plenty of good tools around at reasonable prices, but always aim to purchase items which meet the relevant national safety standards. If in doubt, ask the proprietor or manager of the shop for advice before making a purchase.

Care and maintenance of tools

Having purchased a reasonable tool kit, it is necessary to keep the tools in a clean and serviceable condition. After use, always wipe off any dirt, grease and metal particles using a clean, dry cloth, before putting the tools away. Never leave them lying around after they have been used. A simple tool rack on the garage or workshop wall for items such as screwdrivers and pliers is a good idea. Store all normal spanners and sockets in a metal box. Any measuring instruments, gauges, meters, etc, must be carefully stored where they cannot be damaged or become rusty.

Take a little care when tools are used. Hammer heads inevitably become marked, and screwdrivers lose the keen edge on their blades from time to time. A little timely attention with emery cloth or a file will soon restore items like this to a good finish.

Working facilities

Not to be forgotten when discussing tools is the workshop itself. If anything more than routine maintenance is to be carried out, a suitable working area becomes essential.

It is appreciated that many an owner-mechanic is forced by circumstances to remove an engine or similar item without the benefit of a garage or workshop. Having done this, any repairs should always be done under the cover of a roof.

Wherever possible, any dismantling should be done on a clean, flat workbench or table at a suitable working height.

Any workbench needs a vice; one with a jaw opening of 100 mm is suitable for most jobs. As mentioned previously, some clean dry storage space is also required for tools, as well as for any lubricants, cleaning fluids, touch-up paints etc, which become necessary.

Another item which may be required, and which has a much more general usage, is an electric drill with a chuck capacity of at least 8 mm. This, together with a good range of twist drills, is virtually essential for fitting accessories.

Last, but not least, always keep a supply of old newspapers and clean, lint-free rags available, and try to keep any working area as clean as possible.

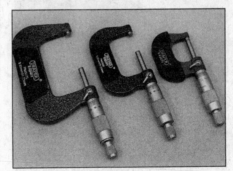

Micrometers

Dial test indicator ("dial gauge")

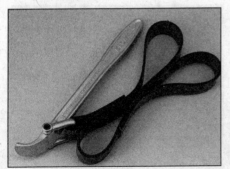

Strap wrench

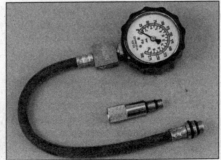

Compression tester

Fault code reader

This is a guide to getting your vehicle through the MOT test. Obviously it will not be possible to examine the vehicle to the same standard as the professional MOT tester. However, working through the following checks will enable you to identify any problem areas before submitting the vehicle for the test.

It has only been possible to summarise the test requirements here, based on the regulations in force at the time of printing. Test standards are becoming increasingly stringent, although there are some exemptions for older vehicles.

An assistant will be needed to help carry out some of these checks.

The checks have been sub-divided into four categories, as follows:

1 Checks carried out **FROM THE DRIVER'S SEAT**

2 Checks carried out **WITH THE VEHICLE ON THE GROUND**

3 Checks carried out **WITH THE VEHICLE RAISED AND THE WHEELS FREE TO TURN**

4 Checks carried out on **YOUR VEHICLE'S EXHAUST EMISSION SYSTEM**

---

1 Checks carried out **FROM THE DRIVER'S SEAT**

Handbrake

☐ Test the operation of the handbrake. Excessive travel (too many clicks) indicates incorrect brake or cable adjustment.
☐ Check that the handbrake cannot be released by tapping the lever sideways. Check the security of the lever mountings.

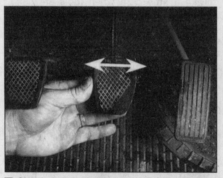

Footbrake

☐ Depress the brake pedal and check that it does not creep down to the floor, indicating a master cylinder fault. Release the pedal, wait a few seconds, then depress it again. If the pedal travels nearly to the floor before firm resistance is felt, brake adjustment or repair is necessary. If the pedal feels spongy, there is air in the hydraulic system which must be removed by bleeding.

☐ Check that the brake pedal is secure and in good condition. Check also for signs of fluid leaks on the pedal, floor or carpets, which would indicate failed seals in the brake master cylinder.
☐ Check the servo unit (when applicable) by operating the brake pedal several times, then keeping the pedal depressed and starting the engine. As the engine starts, the pedal will move down slightly. If not, the vacuum hose or the servo itself may be faulty.

Steering wheel and column

☐ Examine the steering wheel for fractures or looseness of the hub, spokes or rim.
☐ Move the steering wheel from side to side and then up and down. Check that the steering wheel is not loose on the column, indicating wear or a loose retaining nut. Continue moving the steering wheel as before, but also turn it slightly from left to right.
☐ Check that the steering wheel is not loose on the column, and that there is no abnormal

movement of the steering wheel, indicating wear in the column support bearings or couplings.

Windscreen, mirrors and sunvisor

☐ The windscreen must be free of cracks or other significant damage within the driver's field of view. (Small stone chips are acceptable.) Rear view mirrors must be secure, intact, and capable of being adjusted.

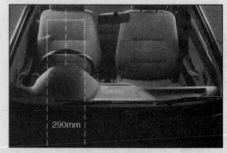

290mm

☐ The driver's sunvisor must be capable of being stored in the "up" position.

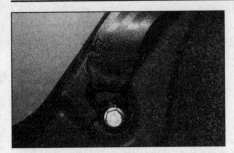

Seat belts and seats

Note: *The following checks are applicable to all seat belts, front and rear.*

☐ Examine the webbing of all the belts (including rear belts if fitted) for cuts, serious fraying or deterioration. Fasten and unfasten each belt to check the buckles. If applicable, check the retracting mechanism. Check the security of all seat belt mountings accessible from inside the vehicle.

☐ Seat belts with pre-tensioners, once activated, have a "flag" or similar showing on the seat belt stalk. This, in itself, is not a reason for test failure.

☐ The front seats themselves must be securely attached and the backrests must lock in the upright position.

Doors

☐ Both front doors must be able to be opened and closed from outside and inside, and must latch securely when closed.

2 Checks carried out WITH THE VEHICLE ON THE GROUND

Vehicle identification

☐ Number plates must be in good condition, secure and legible, with letters and numbers correctly spaced – spacing at (A) should be at least twice that at (B).

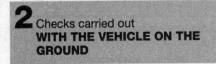

☐ The VIN plate and/or homologation plate must be legible.

Electrical equipment

☐ Switch on the ignition and check the operation of the horn.

☐ Check the windscreen washers and wipers, examining the wiper blades; renew damaged or perished blades. Also check the operation of the stop-lights.

☐ Check the operation of the sidelights and number plate lights. The lenses and reflectors must be secure, clean and undamaged.

☐ Check the operation and alignment of the headlights. The headlight reflectors must not be tarnished and the lenses must be undamaged.

☐ Switch on the ignition and check the operation of the direction indicators (including the instrument panel tell-tale) and the hazard warning lights. Operation of the sidelights and stop-lights must not affect the indicators - if it does, the cause is usually a bad earth at the rear light cluster.

☐ Check the operation of the rear foglight(s), including the warning light on the instrument panel or in the switch.

☐ The ABS warning light must illuminate in accordance with the manufacturers' design. For most vehicles, the ABS warning light should illuminate when the ignition is switched on, and (if the system is operating properly) extinguish after a few seconds. Refer to the owner's handbook.

Footbrake

☐ Examine the master cylinder, brake pipes and servo unit for leaks, loose mountings, corrosion or other damage.

☐ The fluid reservoir must be secure and the fluid level must be between the upper (**A**) and lower (**B**) markings.

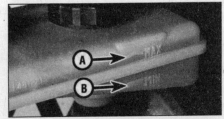

☐ Inspect both front brake flexible hoses for cracks or deterioration of the rubber. Turn the steering from lock to lock, and ensure that the hoses do not contact the wheel, tyre, or any part of the steering or suspension mechanism. With the brake pedal firmly depressed, check the hoses for bulges or leaks under pressure.

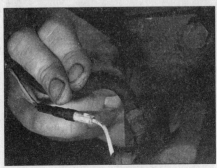

Steering and suspension

☐ Have your assistant turn the steering wheel from side to side slightly, up to the point where the steering gear just begins to transmit this movement to the roadwheels. Check for excessive free play between the steering wheel and the steering gear, indicating wear or insecurity of the steering column joints, the column-to-steering gear coupling, or the steering gear itself.

☐ Have your assistant turn the steering wheel more vigorously in each direction, so that the roadwheels just begin to turn. As this is done, examine all the steering joints, linkages, fittings and attachments. Renew any component that shows signs of wear or damage. On vehicles with power steering, check the security and condition of the steering pump, drivebelt and hoses.

☐ Check that the vehicle is standing level, and at approximately the correct ride height.

Shock absorbers

☐ Depress each corner of the vehicle in turn, then release it. The vehicle should rise and then settle in its normal position. If the vehicle continues to rise and fall, the shock absorber is defective. A shock absorber which has seized will also cause the vehicle to fail.

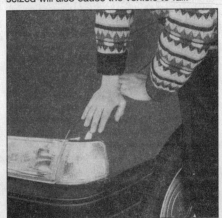

Exhaust system

☐ Start the engine. With your assistant holding a rag over the tailpipe, check the entire system for leaks. Repair or renew leaking sections.

3 Checks carried out **WITH THE VEHICLE RAISED AND THE WHEELS FREE TO TURN**

Jack up the front and rear of the vehicle, and securely support it on axle stands. Position the stands clear of the suspension assemblies. Ensure that the wheels are clear of the ground and that the steering can be turned from lock to lock.

Steering mechanism

☐ Have your assistant turn the steering from lock to lock. Check that the steering turns smoothly, and that no part of the steering mechanism, including a wheel or tyre, fouls any brake hose or pipe or any part of the body structure.
☐ Examine the steering rack rubber gaiters for damage or insecurity of the retaining clips. If power steering is fitted, check for signs of damage or leakage of the fluid hoses, pipes or connections. Also check for excessive stiffness or binding of the steering, a missing split pin or locking device, or severe corrosion of the body structure within 30 cm of any steering component attachment point.

Front and rear suspension and wheel bearings

☐ Starting at the front right-hand side, grasp the roadwheel at the 3 o'clock and 9 o'clock positions and rock gently but firmly. Check for free play or insecurity at the wheel bearings, suspension balljoints, or suspension mountings, pivots and attachments.
☐ Now grasp the wheel at the 12 o'clock and 6 o'clock positions and repeat the previous inspection. Spin the wheel, and check for roughness or tightness of the front wheel bearing.

☐ If excess free play is suspected at a component pivot point, this can be confirmed by using a large screwdriver or similar tool and levering between the mounting and the component attachment. This will confirm whether the wear is in the pivot bush, its retaining bolt, or in the mounting itself (the bolt holes can often become elongated).

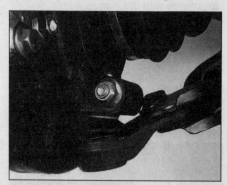

☐ Carry out all the above checks at the other front wheel, and then at both rear wheels.

Springs and shock absorbers

☐ Examine the suspension struts (when applicable) for serious fluid leakage, corrosion, or damage to the casing. Also check the security of the mounting points.
☐ If coil springs are fitted, check that the spring ends locate in their seats, and that the spring is not corroded, cracked or broken.
☐ If leaf springs are fitted, check that all leaves are intact, that the axle is securely attached to each spring, and that there is no deterioration of the spring eye mountings, bushes, and shackles.

☐ The same general checks apply to vehicles fitted with other suspension types, such as torsion bars, hydraulic displacer units, etc. Ensure that all mountings and attachments are secure, that there are no signs of excessive wear, corrosion or damage, and (on hydraulic types) that there are no fluid leaks or damaged pipes.
☐ Inspect the shock absorbers for signs of serious fluid leakage. Check for wear of the mounting bushes or attachments, or damage to the body of the unit.

Driveshafts (fwd vehicles only)

☐ Rotate each front wheel in turn and inspect the constant velocity joint gaiters for splits or damage. Also check that each driveshaft is straight and undamaged.

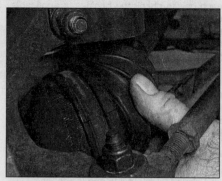

Braking system

☐ If possible without dismantling, check brake pad wear and disc condition. Ensure that the friction lining material has not worn excessively, (A) and that the discs are not fractured, pitted, scored or badly worn (B).

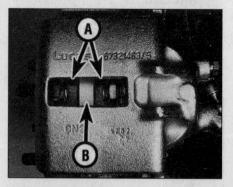

☐ Examine all the rigid brake pipes underneath the vehicle, and the flexible hose(s) at the rear. Look for corrosion, chafing or insecurity of the pipes, and for signs of bulging under pressure, chafing, splits or deterioration of the flexible hoses.
☐ Look for signs of fluid leaks at the brake calipers or on the brake backplates. Repair or renew leaking components.
☐ Slowly spin each wheel, while your assistant depresses and releases the footbrake. Ensure that each brake is operating and does not bind when the pedal is released.

□ Examine the handbrake mechanism, checking for frayed or broken cables, excessive corrosion, or wear or insecurity of the linkage. Check that the mechanism works on each relevant wheel, and releases fully, without binding.

□ It is not possible to test brake efficiency without special equipment, but a road test can be carried out later to check that the vehicle pulls up in a straight line.

Fuel and exhaust systems

□ Inspect the fuel tank (including the filler cap), fuel pipes, hoses and unions. All components must be secure and free from leaks.

□ Examine the exhaust system over its entire length, checking for any damaged, broken or missing mountings, security of the retaining clamps and rust or corrosion.

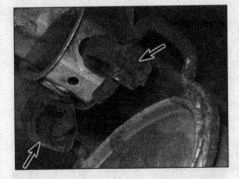

Wheels and tyres

□ Examine the sidewalls and tread area of each tyre in turn. Check for cuts, tears, lumps, bulges, separation of the tread, and exposure of the ply or cord due to wear or damage. Check that the tyre bead is correctly seated on the wheel rim, that the valve is sound and properly seated, and that the wheel is not distorted or damaged.

□ Check that the tyres are of the correct size for the vehicle, that they are of the same size

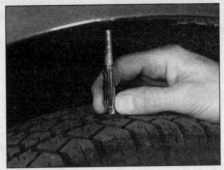

and type on each axle, and that the pressures are correct.

□ Check the tyre tread depth. The legal minimum at the time of writing is 1.6 mm over at least three-quarters of the tread width. Abnormal tread wear may indicate incorrect front wheel alignment.

Body corrosion

□ Check the condition of the entire vehicle structure for signs of corrosion in load-bearing areas. (These include chassis box sections, side sills, cross-members, pillars, and all suspension, steering, braking system and seat belt mountings and anchorages.) Any corrosion which has seriously reduced the thickness of a load-bearing area is likely to cause the vehicle to fail. In this case professional repairs are likely to be needed.

□ Damage or corrosion which causes sharp or otherwise dangerous edges to be exposed will also cause the vehicle to fail.

4 Checks carried out on **YOUR VEHICLE'S EXHAUST EMISSION SYSTEM**

Petrol models

□ The engine should be warmed up, and running well (ignition system in good order, air filter element clean, etc).

□ Before testing, run the engine at around 2500 rpm for 20 seconds. Let the engine drop to idle, and watch for smoke from the exhaust. If the idle speed is too high, or if dense blue or black smoke emerges for more than 5 seconds, the vehicle will fail. Typically, blue smoke signifies oil burning (engine wear); black smoke means unburnt fuel (dirty air cleaner element, or other fuel system fault).

□ An exhaust gas analyser for measuring carbon monoxide (CO) and hydrocarbons (HC) is now needed. If one cannot be hired or borrowed, have a local garage perform the check.

CO emissions (mixture)

□ The MOT tester has access to the CO limits for all vehicles. The CO level is measured at idle speed, and at 'fast idle' (2500 to 3000 rpm). The following limits are given as a general guide:

At idle speed – Less than 0.5% CO
At 'fast idle' – Less than 0.3% CO
Lambda reading – 0.97 to 1.03

□ If the CO level is too high, this may point to poor maintenance, a fuel injection system problem, faulty lambda (oxygen) sensor or catalytic converter. Try an injector cleaning treatment, and check the vehicle's ECU for fault codes.

HC emissions

□ The MOT tester has access to HC limits for all vehicles. The HC level is measured at 'fast idle' (2500 to 3000 rpm). The following limits are given as a general guide:

At 'fast idle' – Less then 200 ppm

□ Excessive HC emissions are typically caused by oil being burnt (worn engine), or by a blocked crankcase ventilation system ('breather'). If the engine oil is old and thin, an oil change may help. If the engine is running badly, check the vehicle's ECU for fault codes.

Diesel models

□ The only emission test for diesel engines is measuring exhaust smoke density, using a calibrated smoke meter. The test involves accelerating the engine at least 3 times to its maximum unloaded speed.

Note: *On engines with a timing belt, it is VITAL that the belt is in good condition before the test is carried out.*

□ With the engine warmed up, it is first purged by running at around 2500 rpm for 20 seconds. A governor check is then carried out, by slowly accelerating the engine to its maximum speed. After this, the smoke meter is connected, and the engine is accelerated quickly to maximum speed three times. If the smoke density is less than the limits given below, the vehicle will pass:

Non-turbo vehicles: 2.5m-1
Turbocharged vehicles: 3.0m-1

□ If excess smoke is produced, try fitting a new air cleaner element, or using an injector cleaning treatment. If the engine is running badly, where applicable, check the vehicle's ECU for fault codes. Also check the vehicle's EGR system, where applicable. At high mileages, the injectors may require professional attention.

Engine

- ☐ Engine fails to rotate when attempting to start
- ☐ Engine rotates, but will not start
- ☐ Engine difficult to start when cold
- ☐ Engine difficult to start when hot
- ☐ Starter motor noisy or excessively-rough in engagement
- ☐ Engine starts, but stops immediately
- ☐ Engine idles erratically
- ☐ Engine misfires at idle speed
- ☐ Engine misfires throughout the driving speed range
- ☐ Engine hesitates on acceleration
- ☐ Engine stalls
- ☐ Engine lacks power
- ☐ Engine backfires
- ☐ Oil pressure warning light illuminated with engine running
- ☐ Engine runs-on after switching off
- ☐ Engine noises

Cooling system

- ☐ Overheating
- ☐ Overcooling
- ☐ External coolant leakage
- ☐ Internal coolant leakage
- ☐ Corrosion

Fuel and exhaust systems

- ☐ Excessive fuel consumption
- ☐ Fuel leakage and/or fuel odour
- ☐ Excessive noise or fumes from exhaust system

Clutch

- ☐ Pedal travels to floor – no pressure or very little resistance
- ☐ Clutch fails to disengage (unable to select gears)
- ☐ Clutch slips (engine speed increases, with no increase in vehicle speed)
- ☐ Judder as clutch is engaged
- ☐ Noise when depressing or releasing clutch pedal

Manual transmission

- ☐ Noisy in neutral with engine running
- ☐ Noisy in one particular gear
- ☐ Difficulty engaging gears
- ☐ Jumps out of gear
- ☐ Vibration
- ☐ Lubricant leaks

Automatic transmission

- ☐ Fluid leakage
- ☐ Transmission fluid brown, or has burned smell
- ☐ General gear selection problems
- ☐ Transmission will not downshift (kickdown) with accelerator pedal fully depressed
- ☐ Engine will not start in any gear, or starts in gears other than Park or Neutral
- ☐ Transmission slips, shifts roughly, is noisy, or has no drive in forward or reverse gears

Differential and propeller shaft

- ☐ Vibration when accelerating or decelerating
- ☐ Low-pitched whining, increasing with road speed

Braking system

- ☐ Vehicle pulls to one side under braking
- ☐ Noise (grinding or high-pitched squeal) when brakes applied
- ☐ Excessive brake pedal travel
- ☐ Brake pedal feels spongy when depressed
- ☐ Excessive brake pedal effort required to stop vehicle
- ☐ Judder felt through brake pedal or steering wheel when braking
- ☐ Brakes binding
- ☐ Rear wheels locking under normal braking

Suspension and steering

- ☐ Vehicle pulls to one side
- ☐ Wheel wobble and vibration
- ☐ Excessive pitching and/or rolling around corners, or during braking
- ☐ Wandering or general instability
- ☐ Excessively-stiff steering
- ☐ Excessive play in steering
- ☐ Lack of power assistance
- ☐ Tyre wear excessive

Electrical system

- ☐ Battery will not hold a charge for more than a few days
- ☐ Ignition/no-charge warning light remains illuminated with engine running
- ☐ Ignition/no-charge warning light fails to come on
- ☐ Lights inoperative
- ☐ Instrument readings inaccurate or erratic
- ☐ Horn inoperative, or unsatisfactory in operation
- ☐ Windscreen wipers inoperative, or unsatisfactory in operation
- ☐ Windscreen washers inoperative, or unsatisfactory in operation
- ☐ Electric windows inoperative, or unsatisfactory in operation
- ☐ Central locking system inoperative, or unsatisfactory in operation

Introduction

The vehicle owner who does his or her own maintenance according to the recommended service schedules should not have to use this section of the manual very often. Modern component reliability is such that, provided those items subject to wear or deterioration are inspected or renewed at the specified intervals, sudden failure is comparatively rare. Faults do not usually just happen as a result of sudden failure, but develop over a period of time. Major mechanical failures in particular are usually preceded by characteristic symptoms over hundreds or even thousands of miles. Those components that do occasionally fail without warning are often small and easily carried in the vehicle.

With any faultfinding, the first step is to decide where to begin investigations. Sometimes this is obvious, but on other occasions, a little detective work will be necessary. The owner who makes half a dozen haphazard adjustments or replacements may be successful in curing a fault (or its symptoms), but will be none the wiser if the fault recurs, and ultimately may have spent more time and money than was necessary. A calm and logical approach will be found to be more satisfactory in the long run. Always take into account any warning signs or abnormalities that may have been noticed in the period preceding the fault – power loss, high or low gauge readings, unusual smells,

etc – and remember that failure of components such as fuses or spark plugs may only be pointers to some underlying fault.

The pages which follow provide an easy-reference guide to the more common problems which may occur during the operation of the vehicle. These problems and their possible causes are grouped under headings denoting various components or systems, such as Engine, Cooling system, etc. The general Chapter which deals with the problem is also shown in brackets; refer to the relevant part of that Chapter for system-specific information. Whatever the fault, certain basic principles apply. These are as follows:

Verify the fault. This is simply a matter of

being sure that you know what the symptoms are before starting work. This is particularly important if you are investigating a fault for someone else, who may not have described it very accurately.

Don't overlook the obvious. For example, if the vehicle won't start, is there fuel in the tank? (Don't take anyone else's word on this particular point, and don't trust the fuel gauge either!) If an electrical fault is indicated, look for loose or broken wires before digging out the test gear.

Cure the disease, not the symptom. Substituting a flat battery with a fully charged one will get you off the hard shoulder, but if the underlying cause is not attended to, the new battery will go the same way. Similarly, changing oil-fouled spark plugs for a new set will get you moving again, but remember that the reason for the fouling (if it wasn't simply an incorrect grade of plug) will have to be established and corrected.

Don't take anything for granted. Particularly, don't forget that a 'new' component may itself be defective (especially if it's been rattling around in the boot for months), and don't leave components out of a fault diagnosis sequence just because they are new or recently fitted. When you do finally diagnose a difficult fault, you'll probably realise that all the evidence was there from the start.

Consider what work, if any, has recently been carried out. Many faults arise through careless or hurried work. For instance, if any work has been performed under the bonnet, could some of the wiring have been dislodged or incorrectly routed, or a hose trapped? Have all the fasteners been properly tightened? Were new, genuine parts and new gaskets used? There is often a certain amount of detective work to be done in this case, as an apparently unrelated task can have far-reaching consequences.

Diesel fault diagnosis

The majority of starting problems on small diesel engines are electrical in origin. The mechanic who is familiar with petrol engines but less so with diesel may be inclined to view the diesel's injectors and pump in the same light as the spark plugs and distributor, but this is generally a mistake.

When investigating complaints of difficult starting for someone else, make sure that the correct starting procedure is understood and is being followed. Some drivers are unaware of the significance of the preheating warning light – many modern engines are sufficiently forgiving for this not to matter in mild weather, but with the onset of winter, problems begin.

As a rule of thumb, if the engine is difficult to start but runs well when it has finally got going, the problem is electrical (battery, starter motor or preheating system). If poor performance is combined with difficult starting, the problem is likely to be in the fuel system. The low-pressure (supply) side of the fuel system should be checked before suspecting the injectors and high-pressure pump. The most common fuel supply problem is air getting into the system, and any pipe from the fuel tank forwards must be scrutinised if air leakage is suspected. Normally the pump is the last item to suspect, since unless it has been tampered with, there is no reason for it to be at fault.

Engine

Engine fails to rotate when attempting to start

- ☐ Battery terminal connections loose or corroded *(Weekly checks)*
- ☐ Battery discharged or faulty (Chapter 5A)
- ☐ Broken, loose or disconnected wiring in the starting circuit (Chapter 5A)
- ☐ Defective starter solenoid or switch (Chapter 5A)
- ☐ Defective starter motor (Chapter 5A)
- ☐ Starter pinion or flywheel ring gear teeth loose or broken (Chapters 2A, 2B or 2C and 5A)
- ☐ Engine earth strap broken or disconnected (Chapter 2C)

Engine rotates, but will not start

- ☐ Fuel tank empty
- ☐ Battery discharged (engine rotates slowly) (Chapter 5A)
- ☐ Battery terminal connections loose or corroded *(Weekly checks)*
- ☐ Immobiliser fault (Chapter 12)
- ☐ Ignition components damp or damaged – petrol models (Chapters 1A and 5B)
- ☐ Broken, loose or disconnected wiring in the ignition circuit – petrol models (Chapters 1A and 5B)
- ☐ Worn, faulty or incorrectly-gapped spark plugs – petrol models (Chapter 1A)
- ☐ Preheating system faulty – diesel models (Chapter 5C)
- ☐ Fuel injection system faulty – petrol models (Chapter 4A)
- ☐ Stop solenoid faulty – diesel models (Chapter 4B)
- ☐ Air in fuel system – diesel models (Chapter 4B)
- ☐ Major mechanical failure (eg camshaft drive) (Chapter 2A, 2B or 2C)

Engine difficult to start when cold

- ☐ Battery discharged (Chapter 5A)
- ☐ Battery terminal connections loose or corroded *(Weekly checks)*
- ☐ Worn, faulty or incorrectly-gapped spark plugs – petrol models (Chapter 1A)
- ☐ Preheating system faulty – diesel models (Chapter 5C)
- ☐ Fuel injection system faulty – petrol models (Chapter 4A)
- ☐ Other ignition system fault – petrol models (Chapters 1A and 5B)
- ☐ Low cylinder compressions (Chapter 2A, 2B or 2C)

Engine difficult to start when hot

- ☐ Air filter element dirty or clogged (Chapter 1A or 1B)
- ☐ Fuel injection system faulty – petrol models (Chapter 4A)
- ☐ Low cylinder compressions (Chapter 2A, 2B or 2C)

Starter motor noisy or excessively-rough in engagement

- ☐ Starter pinion or flywheel ring gear teeth loose or broken (Chapters 2A, 2B or 2C and 5A)
- ☐ Starter motor mounting bolts loose or missing (Chapter 5A)
- ☐ Starter motor internal components worn or damaged (Chapter 5A)

Engine starts, but stops immediately

- ☐ Loose or faulty electrical connections in the ignition circuit – petrol models (Chapters 1A and 5B)
- ☐ Vacuum leak at the throttle body or inlet manifold – petrol models (Chapter 4A)
- ☐ Blocked injector/fuel injection system faulty – petrol models (Chapter 4A)
- ☐ Stop solenoid faulty – diesel models (Chapter 4B)
- ☐ Air in fuel system – diesel models (Chapter 4B)

Engine idles erratically

- ☐ Air filter element clogged (Chapter 1A or 1B)
- ☐ Vacuum leak at the throttle body, inlet manifold or associated hoses – petrol models (Chapter 4A)
- ☐ Worn, faulty or incorrectly-gapped spark plugs – petrol models (Chapter 1A)
- ☐ Uneven or low cylinder compressions (Chapter 2A, 2B or 2C)
- ☐ Camshaft lobes worn (Chapter 2A, 2B or 2C)
- ☐ Timing chain incorrectly fitted (Chapter 2A or 2B)
- ☐ Blocked injector/fuel injection system faulty – petrol models (Chapter 4A)
- ☐ Faulty injector(s) – diesel models (Chapter 4B)

Engine (continued)

Engine misfires at idle speed

- ☐ Worn, faulty or incorrectly-gapped spark plugs – petrol models (Chapter 1A)
- ☐ Vacuum leak at the throttle body, inlet manifold or associated hoses – petrol models (Chapter 4A)
- ☐ Blocked injector/fuel injection system faulty – petrol models (Chapter 4A)
- ☐ Faulty injector(s) – diesel models (Chapter 4B)
- ☐ Uneven or low cylinder compressions (Chapter 2A, 2B or 2C)
- ☐ Disconnected, leaking, or perished crankcase ventilation hoses (Chapter 4C)

Engine misfires throughout the driving speed range

- ☐ Fuel filter choked (Chapter 1A or 1B)
- ☐ Fuel pump faulty, or delivery pressure low – petrol models (Chapter 4A)
- ☐ Fuel tank vent blocked, or fuel pipes restricted (Chapter 4A, 4B or 4C)
- ☐ Vacuum leak at the throttle body, inlet manifold or associated hoses – petrol models (Chapter 4A)
- ☐ Worn, faulty or incorrectly-gapped spark plugs – petrol models (Chapter 1A)
- ☐ Faulty ignition coils – petrol models (Chapter 5B)
- ☐ Faulty injector(s) – diesel models (Chapter 4B)
- ☐ Uneven or low cylinder compressions (Chapter 2A, 2B or 2C)
- ☐ Blocked injector/fuel injection system fault – petrol models (Chapter 4A)

Engine hesitates on acceleration

- ☐ Worn, faulty or incorrectly-gapped spark plugs – petrol models (Chapter 1A)
- ☐ Vacuum leak at the throttle body, inlet manifold or associated hoses (Chapter 4A)
- ☐ Blocked injector/fuel injection system fault – petrol models (Chapter 4A)
- ☐ Faulty injector(s) – diesel models (Chapter 4B)

Engine stalls

- ☐ Vacuum leak at the throttle body, inlet manifold or associated hoses – petrol models (Chapter 4A)
- ☐ Fuel filter choked (Chapter 1A or 1B)
- ☐ Fuel pump faulty, or delivery pressure low – petrol models (Chapter 4A)
- ☐ Fuel tank vent blocked, or fuel pipes restricted (Chapter 4A, 4B or 4C)
- ☐ Blocked injector/fuel injection system fault – petrol models (Chapter 4A)
- ☐ Faulty injector(s) – diesel models (Chapter 4B)

Engine lacks power

- ☐ Timing chain incorrectly fitted (Chapter 2A, 2B or 2C)
- ☐ Fuel filter choked (Chapter 1A or 1B)
- ☐ Fuel pump faulty, or delivery pressure low – petrol models (Chapter 4A)
- ☐ Uneven or low cylinder compressions (Chapter 2A, 2B or 2C)
- ☐ Worn, faulty or incorrectly-gapped spark plugs – petrol models (Chapter 1A)
- ☐ Vacuum leak at the throttle body, inlet manifold or associated hoses – petrol models (Chapter 4A)
- ☐ Blocked injector/fuel injection system fault – petrol models (Chapter 4A)
- ☐ Faulty injector(s) – diesel models (Chapter 4B)
- ☐ Injection pump timing incorrect – diesel models (Chapter 4B)
- ☐ Brakes binding (Chapters 1A or 1B and 9)
- ☐ Clutch slipping (Chapter 6)

Engine backfires

- ☐ Timing chain incorrectly fitted (Chapter 2A, 2B or 2C)
- ☐ Vacuum leak at the throttle body, inlet manifold or associated hoses – petrol models (Chapter 4A)
- ☐ Blocked injector/fuel injection system fault – petrol models (Chapter 4A)

Oil pressure warning light illuminated with engine running

- ☐ Low oil level, or incorrect oil grade (Weekly checks)
- ☐ Faulty oil pressure sensor
- ☐ Worn engine bearings and/or oil pump (Chapter 2C)
- ☐ High engine operating temperature (Chapter 3)
- ☐ Oil pressure relief valve defective (Chapter 2A, 2B or 2C)
- ☐ Oil pick-up strainer clogged (Chapter 2A, 2B or 2C)

Engine runs-on after switching off

- ☐ Excessive carbon build-up in engine (Chapter 2C)
- ☐ High engine operating temperature (Chapter 3)
- ☐ Fuel injection system fault – petrol models (Chapter 4A)
- ☐ Faulty stop solenoid – diesel models (Chapter 4B)

Engine noises

Pre-ignition (pinking) or knocking during acceleration or under load

- ☐ Ignition timing incorrect/ignition system fault – petrol models (Chapters 1A and 5B)
- ☐ Incorrect grade of spark plug – petrol models (Chapter 1A)
- ☐ Incorrect grade of fuel (Chapter 4A)
- ☐ Vacuum leak at the throttle body, inlet manifold or associated hoses – petrol models (Chapter 4A)
- ☐ Excessive carbon build-up in engine (Chapter 2C)
- ☐ Blocked injector/fuel injection system fault – petrol models (Chapter 4A)

Whistling or wheezing noises

- ☐ Leaking inlet manifold or throttle body gasket – petrol models (Chapter 4A)
- ☐ Leaking exhaust manifold gasket or pipe-to-manifold joint (Chapter 1A or 1B and 4C)
- ☐ Leaking vacuum hose (relevant parts of Chapters 4, 5 and 9)
- ☐ Blowing cylinder head gasket (Chapter 2A, 2B or 2C)

Tapping or rattling noises

- ☐ Worn valve gear or camshafts (Chapter 2A, 2B, or 2C)
- ☐ Ancillary component fault (water pump, alternator, etc) (Chapters 3, 5A, etc)

Knocking or thumping noises

- ☐ Worn big-end bearings (regular heavy knocking, perhaps less under load) (Chapter 2C)
- ☐ Worn main bearings (rumbling and knocking, perhaps worsening under load) (Chapter 2C)
- ☐ Piston slap (most noticeable when cold – engine worn) (Chapter 2C)
- ☐ Ancillary component fault (water pump, alternator, etc) (Chapters 3, 5A, etc)

Cooling system

Overheating

- [ ] Insufficient coolant in system (Weekly checks)
- [ ] Thermostat faulty – not opening (Chapter 3)
- [ ] Radiator core blocked, or grille restricted (Chapter 3)
- [ ] Cooling fan faulty (Chapter 3)
- [ ] Inaccurate temperature gauge sender unit (Chapter 3)
- [ ] Airlock in cooling system (Chapter 3)
- [ ] Pressure cap faulty (Chapter 3)

Overcooling

- [ ] Thermostat faulty – not closing, or thermostat missing (Chapter 3)
- [ ] Inaccurate temperature gauge sender unit (Chapter 3)
- [ ] Cooling fan faulty (Chapter 3)

External coolant leakage

- [ ] Deteriorated or damaged hoses or hose clips (Chapter 1A or 1B and 3)
- [ ] Radiator core or heater matrix leaking (Chapter 3)
- [ ] Pressure cap faulty (Chapter 3)
- [ ] Coolant pump internal seal leaking (Chapter 3)
- [ ] Coolant pump gasket leaking (Chapter 3)
- [ ] Boiling due to overheating (Chapter 3)
- [ ] Core plug leaking (Chapter 2C)

Internal coolant leakage

- [ ] Leaking cylinder head gasket (Chapter 2A or 2B)
- [ ] Cracked cylinder head or cylinder block (Chapter 2C)

Corrosion

- [ ] Infrequent draining and flushing (Chapter 1A or 1B)
- [ ] Incorrect coolant mixture or inappropriate coolant type (Weekly checks)

Fuel and exhaust systems

Excessive fuel consumption

- [ ] Air filter element dirty or clogged (Chapter 1A or 1B)
- [ ] Fuel injection system fault – petrol models (Chapter 4A)
- [ ] Faulty injector(s) – diesel models (Chapter 4B)
- [ ] Ignition timing incorrect/ignition system fault – petrol models (Chapters 1A and 5B)
- [ ] Tyres under-inflated (Weekly checks)

Fuel leakage and/or fuel odour

- [ ] Damaged or corroded fuel tank, pipes or connections (Chapter 4A, 4B or 4C)

Excessive noise or fumes from exhaust system

- [ ] Leaking exhaust system or manifold joints (Chapters 1A or 1B and 4C)
- [ ] Leaking, corroded or damaged silencers or pipe (Chapters 1A or 1B and 4C)
- [ ] Broken mountings causing body or suspension contact (Chapter 1A or 1B)

Clutch

Pedal travels to floor – no pressure or very little resistance

- [ ] Hydraulic fluid level low/air in the hydraulic system (Chapter 6)
- [ ] Broken clutch release bearing (Chapter 6)
- [ ] Broken diaphragm spring in clutch pressure plate (Chapter 6)

Clutch fails to disengage (unable to select gears)

- [ ] Clutch disc sticking on gearbox input shaft splines (Chapter 6)
- [ ] Clutch disc sticking to flywheel or pressure plate (Chapter 6)
- [ ] Faulty pressure plate assembly (Chapter 6)
- [ ] Clutch release mechanism worn or incorrectly assembled (Chapter 6)

Clutch slips (engine speed increases, with no increase in vehicle speed)

- [ ] Clutch disc linings excessively worn (Chapter 6)
- [ ] Clutch disc linings contaminated with oil or grease (Chapter 6)
- [ ] Faulty pressure plate or weak diaphragm spring (Chapter 6)

Judder as clutch is engaged

- [ ] Clutch disc linings contaminated with oil or grease (Chapter 6)
- [ ] Clutch disc linings excessively worn (Chapter 6)
- [ ] Faulty or distorted pressure plate or diaphragm spring (Chapter 6)
- [ ] Worn or loose engine or gearbox mountings (Chapter 2A, 2B or 2C)
- [ ] Clutch disc hub or gearbox input shaft splines worn (Chapter 6)

Noise when depressing or releasing clutch pedal

- [ ] Worn clutch release bearing (Chapter 6)
- [ ] Worn or dry clutch pedal bushes (Chapter 6)
- [ ] Faulty pressure plate assembly (Chapter 6)
- [ ] Pressure plate diaphragm spring broken (Chapter 6)
- [ ] Broken clutch disc cushioning springs (Chapter 6)

Manual transmission

Noisy in neutral with engine running

☐ Input shaft bearings worn (noise apparent with clutch pedal released, but not when depressed) (Chapter 7A)*
☐ Clutch release bearing worn (noise apparent with clutch pedal depressed, possibly less when released) (Chapter 6)

Noisy in one particular gear

☐ Worn, damaged or chipped gear teeth (Chapter 7A)*

Difficulty engaging gears

☐ Clutch fault (Chapter 6)
☐ Worn or damaged gearchange linkage (Chapter 7A)
☐ Incorrectly-adjusted gearchange linkage (Chapter 7A)
☐ Worn synchroniser units (Chapter 7A)*

Vibration

☐ Lack of oil (Chapter 1A or 1B)
☐ Worn bearings (Chapter 7A)*

Jumps out of gear

☐ Worn or damaged gearchange linkage (Chapter 7A)
☐ Incorrectly-adjusted gearchange linkage (Chapter 7A)
☐ Worn synchroniser units (Chapter 7A)*
☐ Worn selector forks (Chapter 7A)*

Lubricant leaks

☐ Leaking differential output oil seal (Chapter 7A)
☐ Leaking housing joint (Chapter 7A)*
☐ Leaking input shaft oil seal (Chapter 7A)*

*Although the corrective action necessary to remedy the symptoms described is beyond the scope of the home mechanic, the above information should be helpful in isolating the cause of the condition, so that the owner can communicate clearly with a professional mechanic.

Automatic transmission

Note: *Due to the complexity of the automatic transmission, it is difficult for the home mechanic to properly diagnose and service this unit. For problems other than the following, the vehicle should be taken to a dealer service department or automatic transmission specialist. Do not be too hasty in removing the transmission if a fault is suspected, as most of the testing is carried out with the unit still fitted.*

Fluid leakage

☐ Automatic transmission fluid is usually dark red in colour. Fluid leaks should not be confused with engine oil, which can easily be blown onto the transmission by airflow.
☐ To determine the source of a leak, first remove all built-up dirt and grime from the transmission housing and surrounding areas using a degreasing agent, or by steam-cleaning. Drive the vehicle at low speed, so airflow will not blow the leak far from its source. Raise and support the vehicle, and determine where the leak is coming from. The following are common areas of leakage:
a) *Transmission fluid pan (Chapter 1A or 1B and 7B)*
b) *Dipstick tube (Chapter 1A or 1B and 7B)*
c) *Transmission-to-fluid cooler pipes/unions (Chapter 7B)*

Transmission fluid brown, or has burned smell

☐ Transmission fluid level low, or fluid in need of renewal (Chapter 1A or 1B)

Transmission will not downshift (kickdown) with accelerator pedal fully depressed

☐ Low transmission fluid level (Chapter 1A or 1B)
☐ Incorrect selector rod adjustment (Chapter 7B)

General gear selection problems

☐ Chapter 7B deals with checking and adjusting the selector rod on automatic transmissions. The following are common problems, which may be caused by a poorly adjusted selector rod:
a) *Engine starting in gears other than Park or Neutral.*
b) *Indicator panel indicating a gear other than the one actually being used.*
c) *Vehicle moves when in Park or Neutral.*
d) *Poor gear shift quality or erratic gear changes.*
☐ Refer to Chapter 7B for the selector rod adjustment procedure.

Engine will not start in any gear, or starts in gears other than Park or Neutral

☐ Incorrect starter/inhibitor switch adjustment (Chapter 7B)
☐ Incorrect selector rod adjustment (Chapter 7B)

Transmission slips, shifts roughly, is noisy, or has no drive in forward or reverse gears

☐ There are many probable causes for the above problems, but the home mechanic should be concerned with only one possibility – fluid level. Before taking the vehicle to a dealer or transmission specialist, check the fluid level and condition of the fluid as described in Chapter 1. Correct the fluid level as necessary, or change the fluid and filter if needed. If the problem persists, professional help will be necessary.

Differential and propeller shaft

Vibration when accelerating or decelerating

- [ ] Worn universal joint (Chapter 8)
- [ ] Bent, distorted or unbalanced propeller shaft (Chapter 8)

Low-pitched whining, increasing with road speed

- [ ] Worn differential (Chapter 8)

Braking system

Note: *Before assuming that a brake problem exists, make sure that the tyres are in good condition and correctly inflated, that the front wheel alignment is correct, and that the vehicle's load is distributed evenly. Apart from checking the condition of all pipe and hose connections, any faults occurring on the anti-lock braking system should be referred to a Mercedes-Benz dealer for diagnosis.*

Vehicle pulls to one side under braking

- [ ] Worn, defective, damaged or contaminated brake pads on one side (Chapters 1A or 1B and 9)
- [ ] Seized or partially-seized brake caliper piston (Chapters 1A or 1B and 9)
- [ ] A mixture of brake pad lining materials fitted between sides (Chapters 1A or 1B and 9)
- [ ] Brake caliper mounting bolts loose (Chapter 9)
- [ ] Worn or damaged steering or suspension components (Chapters 1A or 1B and 10)

Noise (grinding or high-pitched squeal) when brakes applied

- [ ] Brake pad friction lining material worn down to metal backing (Chapters 1A or 1B and 9)
- [ ] Excessive corrosion of brake disc (may be apparent after the vehicle has been standing for some time (Chapters 1A or 1B and 9)
- [ ] Foreign object (stone chipping, etc) trapped between brake disc and shield (Chapters 1A or 1B and 9)

Brake pedal feels spongy when depressed

- [ ] Air in hydraulic system (Chapters 1A or 1B and 9)
- [ ] Deteriorated flexible rubber brake hoses (Chapters 1A or 1B and 9)
- [ ] Master cylinder mounting nuts loose (Chapter 9)
- [ ] Faulty master cylinder (Chapter 9)

Excessive brake pedal travel

- [ ] Faulty master cylinder (Chapter 9)
- [ ] Air in hydraulic system (Chapters 1A or 1B and 9)
- [ ] Faulty vacuum servo unit (Chapter 9)

Excessive brake pedal effort required to stop vehicle

- [ ] Faulty vacuum servo unit (Chapter 9)
- [ ] Disconnected, damaged or insecure brake servo vacuum hose (Chapter 9)
- [ ] Primary or secondary hydraulic circuit failure (Chapter 9)
- [ ] Seized brake caliper piston (Chapter 9)
- [ ] Brake pads incorrectly fitted (Chapters 1A or 1B and 9)
- [ ] Incorrect grade of brake pads fitted (Chapters 1A or 1B and 9)
- [ ] Brake pad linings contaminated (Chapters 1A or 1B and 9)
- [ ] Faulty vacuum pump – diesel models (Chapter 9)

Judder felt through brake pedal or steering wheel when braking

- [ ] Excessive run-out or distortion of discs (Chapters 1A or 1B and 9)
- [ ] Brake pad linings worn (Chapters 1A or 1B and 9)
- [ ] Brake caliper mounting bolts loose (Chapter 9)
- [ ] Wear in suspension or steering components or mountings (Chapters 1A or 1B and 10)

Brakes binding

- [ ] Seized brake caliper piston (Chapter 9)
- [ ] Incorrectly-adjusted parking brake mechanism (Chapter 9)
- [ ] Faulty master cylinder (Chapter 9)

Rear wheels locking under normal braking

- [ ] Rear brake pad linings contaminated (Chapters 1A or 1B and 9)
- [ ] Rear brake discs warped (Chapters 1A or 1B and 9)

Suspension and steering

Note: *Before diagnosing suspension or steering faults, be sure that the trouble is not due to incorrect tyre pressures, mixtures of tyre types, or binding brakes.*

Vehicle pulls to one side

- [ ] Defective tyre *(Weekly checks)*
- [ ] Excessive wear in suspension or steering components (Chapters 1A or 1B and 10)
- [ ] Incorrect front wheel alignment (Chapter 10)
- [ ] Accident damage to steering or suspension components (Chapter 1A or 1B)

Wheel wobble and vibration

- [ ] Front roadwheels out of balance (vibration felt mainly through the steering wheel) (Chapters 1A or 1B and 10)
- [ ] Rear roadwheels out of balance (vibration felt throughout the vehicle) (Chapters 1A or 1B and 10)
- [ ] Roadwheels damaged or distorted (Chapters 1A or 1B and 10)
- [ ] Faulty or damaged tyre *(Weekly checks)*
- [ ] Worn steering or suspension joints, bushes or components (Chapters 1A or 1B and 10)
- [ ] Wheel bolts loose (Chapters 1A or 1B and 10)

Excessive pitching and/or rolling around corners, or during braking

- [ ] Defective shock absorbers (Chapters 1A or 1B and 10)
- [ ] Broken or weak spring and/or suspension component (Chapters 1A or 1B and 10)
- [ ] Worn or damaged anti-roll bar or mountings (Chapter 10)

Wandering or general instability

- [ ] Incorrect front wheel alignment (Chapter 10)
- [ ] Worn steering or suspension joints, bushes or components (Chapters 1A or 1B and 10)
- [ ] Roadwheels out of balance (Chapters 1A or 1B and 10)
- [ ] Faulty or damaged tyre *(Weekly checks)*
- [ ] Wheel bolts loose (Chapters 1A or 1B and 10)
- [ ] Defective shock absorbers (Chapters 1A or 1B and 10)

Excessively-stiff steering

- [ ] Seized steering linkage joints or suspension balljoint (Chapters 1A or 1B and 10)
- [ ] Broken or incorrectly-adjusted auxiliary drivebelt – power steering (Chapter 1A or 1B)
- [ ] Incorrect front wheel alignment (Chapter 10)
- [ ] Faulty steering rack (Chapter 10)

Excessive play in steering

- [ ] Worn steering column intermediate shaft coupling joint (Chapter 10)
- [ ] Worn steering linkage balljoints (Chapters 1A or 1B and 10)
- [ ] Worn steering or suspension joints, bushes or components (Chapters 1A or 1B and 10)
- [ ] Faulty steering rack (Chapter 10)

Lack of power assistance

- [ ] Broken or incorrectly-adjusted auxiliary drivebelt (Chapter 1A or 1B)
- [ ] Incorrect power steering fluid level *(Weekly checks)*
- [ ] Restriction in power steering fluid hoses (Chapter 1A or 1B)
- [ ] Faulty power steering pump (Chapter 10)
- [ ] Faulty steering rack (Chapter 10)

Tyre wear excessive

Tyres worn on inside or outside edges

- [ ] Tyres under-inflated (wear on both edges) *(Weekly checks)*
- [ ] Incorrect camber or castor angles (wear on one edge only) (Chapter 10)
- [ ] Worn steering or suspension joints, bushes or components (Chapters 1A or 1B and 10)
- [ ] Excessively-hard cornering
- [ ] Accident damage

Tyre treads exhibit feathered edges

- [ ] Incorrect toe setting (Chapter 10)

Tyres worn in centre of tread

- [ ] Tyres over-inflated *(Weekly checks)*

Tyres worn on inside and outside edges

- [ ] Tyres under-inflated *(Weekly checks)*

Tyres worn unevenly

- [ ] Tyres/wheels out of balance (Chapter 1A or 1B)
- [ ] Excessive wheel or tyre run-out (Chapter 1A or 1B)
- [ ] Worn shock absorbers (Chapters 1A or 1B and 10)
- [ ] Faulty tyre *(Weekly checks)*

Electrical system

Note: *For problems associated with the starting system, refer to the faults listed under 'Engine' earlier in this Section.*

Battery will not hold a charge more than a few days

- ☐ Battery defective internally (Chapter 5A)
- ☐ Battery terminal connections loose or corroded *(Weekly checks)*
- ☐ Auxiliary drivebelt worn or incorrectly adjusted (Chapter 1A or 1B)
- ☐ Alternator not charging at correct output (Chapter 5A)
- ☐ Alternator or voltage regulator faulty (Chapter 5A)
- ☐ Short-circuit causing continual battery drain (Chapters 5A and 12)

Ignition/no-charge warning light remains illuminated with engine running

- ☐ Auxiliary drivebelt broken, worn, or incorrectly adjusted (Chapter 1A or 1B)
- ☐ Alternator brushes worn, sticking, or dirty (Chapter 5A)
- ☐ Alternator brush springs weak or broken (Chapter 5A)
- ☐ Internal fault in alternator or voltage regulator (Chapter 5A)
- ☐ Broken, disconnected, or loose wiring in charging circuit (Chapter 5A)

Ignition/no-charge warning light fails to come on

- ☐ Warning light bulb blown (Chapter 12)
- ☐ Broken, disconnected, or loose wiring in warning light circuit (Chapter 12)
- ☐ Alternator faulty (Chapter 5A)

Lights inoperative

- ☐ Bulb blown (Chapter 12)
- ☐ Corrosion of bulb or bulbholder contacts (Chapter 12)
- ☐ Blown fuse (Chapter 12)
- ☐ Faulty relay (Chapter 12)
- ☐ Broken, loose, or disconnected wiring (Chapter 12)
- ☐ Faulty switch (Chapter 12)

Instrument readings inaccurate or erratic

Instrument readings increase with engine speed

- ☐ Faulty voltage regulator (Chapter 12)

Fuel or temperature gauges give no reading

- ☐ Faulty gauge sender unit (Chapters 3 and 4A, 4B or 4C)
- ☐ Wiring open-circuit (Chapter 12)
- ☐ Faulty gauge (Chapter 12)

Fuel or temperature gauges give continuous maximum reading

- ☐ Faulty gauge sender unit (Chapters 3 and 4A, 4B or 4C)
- ☐ Wiring short-circuit (Chapter 12)
- ☐ Faulty gauge (Chapter 12)

Horn inoperative, or unsatisfactory in operation

Horn operates all the time

- ☐ Horn push either earthed or stuck down (Chapter 12)
- ☐ Horn cable-to-horn push earthed (Chapter 12)

Horn fails to operate

- ☐ Blown fuse (Chapter 12)
- ☐ Cable or cable connections loose, broken or disconnected (Chapter 12)
- ☐ Faulty horn (Chapter 12)

Horn emits intermittent or unsatisfactory sound

- ☐ Cable connections loose (Chapter 12)
- ☐ Horn mountings loose (Chapter 12)
- ☐ Faulty horn (Chapter 12)

Windscreen wiper inoperative, or unsatisfactory in operation

Wiper fails to operate, or operates very slowly

- ☐ Wiper blade stuck to screen, or linkage seized or binding (Weekly checks and Chapter 12)
- ☐ Blown fuse (Chapter 12)
- ☐ Cable or cable connections loose, broken or disconnected (Chapter 12)
- ☐ Faulty relay (Chapter 12)
- ☐ Faulty wiper motor (Chapter 12)

Wiper blade sweeps over too large or too small an area of the glass

- ☐ Wiper arm incorrectly positioned on spindles (Chapter 1)
- ☐ Excessive wear of wiper linkage (Chapter 12)
- ☐ Wiper motor or linkage mountings loose or insecure (Chapter 12)

Wiper blade fails to clean the glass effectively

- ☐ Wiper blade rubber worn or perished *(Weekly checks)*
- ☐ Wiper arm tension spring broken, or arm pivot seized (Chapter 12)
- ☐ Insufficient windscreen washer additive *(Weekly checks)*

Windscreen washers inoperative, or unsatisfactory in operation

One or more washer jets inoperative

- ☐ Blocked washer jet (Chapter 1A or 1B and 12)
- ☐ Disconnected, kinked or restricted fluid hose (Chapter 12)
- ☐ Insufficient fluid in washer reservoir *(Weekly checks)*

Washer pump fails to operate

- ☐ Broken or disconnected wiring or connections (Chapter 12)
- ☐ Blown fuse (Chapter 12)
- ☐ Faulty washer switch (Chapter 12)
- ☐ Faulty washer pump (Chapter 12)

Washer pump runs for some time before fluid is emitted from jets

- ☐ Faulty one-way valve in fluid supply hose (Chapter 12)

Electric windows inoperative, or unsatisfactory in operation

Window glass will only move in one direction

- ☐ Faulty switch (Chapter 12)

Window glass slow to move

- ☐ Regulator seized or damaged (Chapter 11, Sections 19 and 21)
- ☐ Door internal components or trim fouling regulator (Chapter 11)
- ☐ Faulty motor (Chapter 11)

Window glass fails to move

- ☐ Blown fuse (Chapter 12)
- ☐ Faulty relay (Chapter 12)
- ☐ Broken or disconnected wiring or connections (Chapter 12)
- ☐ Faulty motor (Chapter 11, Sections 19 and 21)

Note: *References throughout this index are in the form* "Chapter number" • "Page number". *So, for example, 2C•15 refers to page 15 of Chapter 2C.*

Note: *References throughout this index are in the form "Chapter number" • "Page number". So, for example, 2C•15 refers to page 15 of Chapter 2C.*

Note: *References throughout this index are in the form* **"Chapter number"** • *"Page number". So, for example, 2C•15 refers to page 15 of Chapter 2C.*

Note: *References throughout this index are in the form "***Chapter number***" • "***Page number***". So, for example, 2C•15 refers to page 15 of Chapter 2C.*

Haynes Manuals – The Complete **UK Car** List

Title	Book No.
ALFA ROMEO Alfasud/Sprint (74 - 88) up to F *	0292
Alfa Romeo Alfetta (73 – 87) up to E *	0531
AUDI 80, 90 & Coupe Petrol (79 – Nov 88) up to F	0605
Audi 80, 90 & Coupe Petrol (Oct 86 – 90) D to H	1491
Audi 100 & A6 Petrol & Diesel (May 91 – May 97) H to P	3504
Audi A3 Petrol & Diesel (96 – May 03) P to 03	4253
Audi A3 Petrol & Diesel (June 03 – Mar 08) 03 to 08	4884
Audi A4 Petrol & Diesel (95 – 00) M to X	3575
Audi A4 Petrol & Diesel (01 – 04) X to 54	4609
Audi A4 Petrol & Diesel (Jan 05 – Feb 08) 54 to 57	4885
AUSTIN A35 & A40 (56 – 67) up to F *	0118
Mini (59 – 69) up to H *	0527
Mini (69 – 01) up to X	0646
Austin Healey 100/6 & 3000 (56 – 68) up to G *	0049
BEDFORD/Vauxhall Rascal & Suzuki Supercarry (86 – Oct 94) C to M	3015
BMW 1-Series 4-cyl Petrol & Diesel (04 – Aug 11) 54 to 11	4918
BMW 316, 320 & 320i (4-cyl)(75 – Feb 83) up to Y *	0276
BMW 3- & 5- Series Petrol (81 – 91) up to J	1948
BMW 3-Series Petrol (Apr 91 – 99) H to V	3210
BMW 3-Series Petrol (Sept 98 – 06) S to 56	4067
BMW 3-Series Petrol & Diesel (05 – Sept 08) 54 to 58	4782
BMW 5-Series 6-cyl Petrol (April 96 – Aug 03) N to 03	4151
BMW 5-Series Diesel (Sept 03 – 10) 53 to 10	4901
BMW 1500, 1502, 1600, 1602, 2000 & 2002 (59 – 77) up to S *	0240
CHRYSLER PT Cruiser Petrol (00-09) W to 09	4058
CITROEN 2CV, Ami & Dyane (67 – 90) up to H	0196
Citroen AX Petrol & Diesel (87- 97) D to P	3014
Citroen Berlingo & Peugeot Partner Petrol & Diesel (96 – 10) P to 60	4281
Citroen C1 Petrol (05 – 11) 05 to 11	4922
Citroen C3 Petrol & Diesel (02 – 09) 51 to 59	4890
Citroen C4 Petrol & Diesel (04 – 10) 54 to 60	5576
Citroen C5 Petrol & Diesel (01 – 08) Y to 08	4745
Citroen C15 Van Petrol & Diesel (89 – Oct 98) F to S	3509
Citroen CX Petrol (75 – 88) up to F	0528
Citroen Saxo Petrol & Diesel (96 – 04) N to 54	3506
Citroen Visa Petrol (79 – 88) up to F	0620
Citroen Xantia Petrol & Diesel (93 – 01) K to Y	3082
Citroen XM Petrol & Diesel (89 – 00) G to X	3451
Citroen Xsara Petrol & Diesel (97 – Sept 00) R to W	3751
Citroen Xsara Picasso Petrol & Diesel (00 – 02) W to 52	3944
Citroen Xsara Picasso (Mar 04 – 08) 04 to 58	4784
Citroen ZX Diesel (91 – 98) J to S	1922
Citroen ZX Petrol (91 – 98) H to S	1881
FIAT 126 (73 – 87) up to E *	0305
Fiat 500 (57 – 73) up to M *	0090
Fiat 500 & Panda (04 – 12) 53 to 61	5558
Fiat Bravo & Brava Petrol (95 – 00) N to W	3572
Fiat Cinquecento (93 – 98) K to R	3501
Fiat Panda (81 – 95) up to M	0793
Fiat Punto Petrol & Diesel (94 – Oct 99) L to V	3251
Fiat Punto Petrol (Oct 99 – July 03) V to 03	4066
Fiat Punto Petrol (03 – 07) 03 to 07	4746

Title	Book No.
Fiat Punto Petrol (Oct 99 – 07) V to 07	5634
Fiat X1/9 (74 – 89) up to G *	0273
FORD Anglia (59 – 68) up to G *	0001
Ford Capri II (& III) 1.6 & 2.0 (74 – 87) up to E *	0283
Ford Capri II (& III) 2.8 & 3.0 V6 (74 – 87) up to E	1309
Ford C-Max Petrol & Diesel (03 – 10) 53 to 60	4900
Ford Escort Mk I 1100 & 1300 (68 – 74) up to N *	0171
Ford Escort Mk I Mexico, RS 1600 & RS 2000 (70 – 74) up to N *	0139
Ford Escort Mk II Mexico, RS 1800 & RS 2000 (75 – 80) up to W *	0735
Ford Escort (75 – Aug 80) up to V *	0280
Ford Escort Petrol (Sept 80 – Sept 90) up to H	0686
Ford Escort & Orion Petrol (Sept 90 – 00) H to X	1737
Ford Escort & Orion Diesel (Sept 90 – 00) H to X	4081
Ford Fiesta Petrol (Feb 89 – Oct 95) F to N	1595
Ford Fiesta Petrol & Diesel (Oct 95 – Mar 02) N to 02	3397
Ford Fiesta Petrol & Diesel (Apr 02 – 08) 02 to 58	4170
Ford Fiesta Petrol & Diesel (08 – 11) 58 to 11	4907
Ford Focus Petrol & Diesel (98 – 01) S to Y	3759
Ford Focus Petrol & Diesel (Oct 01 – 05) 51 to 05	4167
Ford Focus Petrol (05 – 09) 54 to 09	4785
Ford Focus Diesel (05 – 09) 54 to 09	4807
Ford Fusion Petrol & Diesel (02 – 11) 02 to 61	5566
Ford Galaxy Petrol & Diesel (95 – Aug 00) M to W	3984
Ford Galaxy Petrol & Diesel (00 – 06) X to 06	5556
Ford Granada Petrol (Sept 77 – Feb 85) up to B *	0481
Ford Ka (96 – 08) P to 58	5567
Ford Mondeo Petrol (93 – Sept 00) K to X	1923
Ford Mondeo Petrol & Diesel (Oct 00 – Jul 03) X to 03	3990
Ford Mondeo Petrol & Diesel (July 03 – 07) 03 to 56	4619
Ford Mondeo Petrol & Diesel (Apr 07 – 12) 07 to 61	5548
Ford Mondeo Diesel (93 – Sept 00) L to X	3465
Ford Sierra V6 Petrol (82 – 91) up to J	0904
Ford Transit Connect Diesel (02 – 11) 02 to 11	4903
Ford Transit Diesel (Feb 86 – 99) C to T	3019
Ford Transit Diesel (00 – Oct 06) X to 56	4775
Ford 1.6 & 1.8 litre Diesel Engine (84 – 96) A to N	1172
HILLMAN Imp (63 – 76) up to R *	0022
HONDA Civic (Feb 84 – Oct 87) A to E	1226
Honda Civic (Nov 91 – 96) J to N	3199
Honda Civic Petrol (Mar 95 – 00) M to X	4050
Honda Civic Petrol & Diesel (01 – 05) X to 55	4611
Honda CR-V Petrol & Diesel (02 – 06) 51 to 56	4747
Honda Jazz (02 to 08) 51 to 58	4735
JAGUAR E-Type (61 – 72) up to L *	0140
Jaguar Mk I & II, 240 & 340 (55 – 69) up to H *	0098
Jaguar XJ6, XJ & Sovereign, Daimler Sovereign (68 – Oct 86) up to D	0242
Jaguar XJ6 & Sovereign (Oct 86 – Sept 94) D to M	3261
Jaguar XJ12, XJS & Sovereign, Daimler Double Six (72 – 88) up to F	0478
JEEP Cherokee Petrol (93 – 96) K to N	1943
LAND ROVER 90, 110 & Defender Diesel (83 – 07) up to 56	3017
Land Rover Discovery Petrol & Diesel (89 – 98) G to S	3016

Title	Book No.
Land Rover Discovery Diesel (Nov 98 – Jul 04) S to 04	4606
Land Rover Discovery Diesel (Aug 04 – Apr 09) 04 to 09	5562
Land Rover Freelander Petrol & Diesel (97 – Sept 03) R to 53	3929
Land Rover Freelander (97 – Oct 06) R to 56	5571
Land Rover Series II, IIA & III 4-cyl Petrol (58 – 85) up to C	0314
Land Rover Series II, IIA & III Petrol & Diesel (58 – 85) up to C	5568
MAZDA 323 (Mar 81 – Oct 89) up to G	1608
Mazda 323 (Oct 89 – 98) G to R	3455
Mazda B1600, B1800 & B2000 Pick-up Petrol (72 – 88) up to F	0267
Mazda MX-5 (89 – 05) G to 05	5565
Mazda RX-7 (79 – 85) up to C *	0460
MERCEDES-BENZ 190, 190E & 190D Petrol & Diesel (83 – 93) A to L	3450
Mercedes-Benz 200D, 240D, 240TD, 300D & 300TD 123 Series Diesel (Oct 76 – 85) up to C	1114
Mercedes-Benz 250 & 280 (68 – 72) up to L *	0346
Mercedes-Benz 250 & 280 123 Series Petrol (Oct 76 – 84) up to B *	0677
Mercedes-Benz 124 Series Petrol & Diesel (85 – Aug 93) C to K	3253
Mercedes-Benz A-Class Petrol & Diesel (98 – 04) S to 54	4748
Mercedes-Benz C-Class Petrol & Diesel (93 – Aug 00) L to W	3511
Mercedes-Benz C-Class (00 – 07) X to 07	4780
Mercedes-Benz Sprinter Diesel (95 – Apr 06) M to 06	4902
MGA (55 – 62)	0475
MGB (62 – 80) up to W	0111
MGB 1962 to 1980 (special edition) *	4894
MG Midget & Austin-Healey Sprite (58 – 80) up to W *	0265
MINI Petrol (July 01 – 06) Y to 56	4273
MINI Petrol & Diesel (Nov 06 – 13) 56 to 13	4904
MITSUBISHI Shogun & L200 Pick-ups Petrol (83 – 94) up to M	1944
MORRIS Minor 1000 (56 – 71) up to K	0024
NISSAN Almera Petrol (95 – Feb 00) N to V	4053
Nissan Almera & Tino Petrol (Feb 00 – 07) V to 56	4612
Nissan Micra (83 – Jan 93) up to K	0931
Nissan Micra (93 – 02) K to 52	3254
Nissan Micra Petrol (03 – Oct 10) 52 to 60	4734
Nissan Primera Petrol (90 – Aug 99) H to T	1851
Nissan Qashqai Petrol & Diesel (07 – 12) 56 to 62	5610
OPEL Ascona & Manta (B-Series) (Sept 75 – 88) up to F *	0316
Opel Ascona Petrol (81 – 88)	3215
Opel Ascona Petrol (Oct 91 – Feb 98)	3156
Opel Corsa Petrol (83 – Mar 93)	3160
Opel Corsa Petrol (Mar 93 – 97)	3159
Opel Kadett Petrol (Oct 84 – Oct 91)	3196
Opel Omega & Senator Petrol (Nov 86 – 94)	3157
Opel Vectra Petrol (Oct 88 – Oct 95)	3158
PEUGEOT 106 Petrol & Diesel (91 – 04) J to 53)	1882
Peugeot 107 Petrol (05 – 11) 05 to 11	4923
Peugeot 205 Petrol (83 – 97) A to P	0932
Peugeot 206 Petrol & Diesel (98 – 01) S to X	3757

* Classic reprint

Title	Book No.
Peugeot 206 Petrol & Diesel (02 – 06) 51 to 06	4613
Peugeot 207 Petrol & Diesel (06 – July 09) 06 to 09	4787
Peugeot 306 Petrol & Diesel (93 – 02) K to 02	3073
Peugeot 307 Petrol & Diesel (01 – 08) Y to 58	4147
Peugeot 308 Petrol & Diesel (07 – 12) 07 to 12	5561
Peugeot 405 Diesel (88 – 97) E to P	3198
Peugeot 406 Petrol & Diesel (96 – Mar 99) N to T	3394
Peugeot 406 Petrol & Diesel (Mar 99 – 02) T to 52	3982
Peugeot 407 Diesel (04 -11) 53 to 11	5550
PORSCHE 911 (65 – 85) up to C	0264
Porsche 924 & 924 Turbo (76 – 85) up to C	0397
RANGE ROVER V8 Petrol (70 – Oct 92) up to K	0606
RELIANT Robin & Kitten (73 – 83) up to A *	0436
RENAULT 4 (61 – 86) up to D *	0072
Renault 5 Petrol (Feb 85 – 96) B to N	1219
Renault 19 Petrol (89 – 96) F to N	1646
Renault Clio Petrol (91 – May 98) H to R	1853
Renault Clio Petrol & Diesel (May 98 – May 01) R to Y	3906
Renault Clio Petrol & Diesel (June 01 – 05) Y to 55	4168
Renault Clio Petrol & Diesel (Oct 05 – May 09) 55 to 09	4788
Renault Espace Petrol & Diesel (85 – 96) C to N	3197
Renault Laguna Petrol & Diesel (94 – 00) L to W	3252
Renault Laguna Petrol & Diesel (Feb 01 – May 07) X to 07	4283
Renault Megane & Scenic Petrol & Diesel (96 – 99) N to T	3395
Renault Megane & Scenic Petrol & Diesel (Apr 99 – 02) T to 52	3916
Renault Megane Petrol & Diesel (Oct 02 – 08) 52 to 58	4284
Renault Scenic Petrol & Diesel (Sept 03 – 06) 53 to 06	4297
Renault Trafic Diesel (01 – 11) Y to 11	5551
ROVER 216 & 416 Petrol (89 – 96) G to N	1830
Rover 211, 214, 216, 218 & 220 Petrol & Diesel (Dec 95 – 99) N to V	3399
Rover 25 & MG ZR Petrol & Diesel (Oct 99 – 06) V to 06	4145
Rover 414, 416 & 420 Petrol & Diesel (May 95 – 99) M to V	3453
Rover 45 / MG ZS Petrol & Diesel (99 – 05) V to 55	4384
Rover 618, 620 & 623 Petrol (93 – 97) K to P	3257
Rover 75 / MG ZT Petrol & Diesel (99 – 06) S to 06	4292
Rover 820, 825 & 827 Petrol (86 – 95) D to N	1380
Rover 3500 (76 – 87) up to E *	0365
Rover Metro, 111 & 114 Petrol (May 90 – 98) G to S	1711
SAAB 95 & 96 (66 – 76) up to R *	0198
Saab 90, 99 & 900 (79 – Oct 93) up to L	0765
Saab 900 (Oct 93 – 98) L to R	3512
Saab 9000 4-cyl (85 – 98) C to S	1686
Saab 9-3 Petrol & Diesel (98 – Aug 02) R to 02	4614
Saab 9-3 Petrol & Diesel (92 – 07) 52 to 57	4749
Saab 9-3 Petrol & Diesel (07-on) 57 on	5569
Saab 9-5 4-cyl Petrol (97 – 05) R to 55	4156
Saab 9-5 (Sep 05 – Jun 10) 55 to 10	4891
SEAT Ibiza & Cordoba Petrol & Diesel (Oct 93 – Oct 99) L to V	3571
Seat Ibiza & Malaga Petrol (85 – 92) B to K	1609
Seat Ibiza Petrol & Diesel (May 02 – Apr 08) 02 to 08	4889

Title	Book No.
SKODA Fabia Petrol & Diesel (00 – 06) W to 06	4376
Skoda Felicia Petrol & Diesel (95 – 01) M to X	3505
Skoda Octavia Petrol (98 – April 04) R to 04	4285
Skoda Octavia Diesel (May 04 – 12) 04 to 61	5549
SUBARU 1600 & 1800 (Nov 79 – 90) up to H *	0995
SUNBEAM Alpine, Rapier & H120 (68 – 74) up to N *	0051
SUZUKI SJ Series, Samurai & Vitara 4-cyl Petrol (82 – 97) up to P	1942
Suzuki Supercarry & Bedford/Vauxhall Rascal (86 – Oct 94) C to M	3015
TOYOTA Avensis Petrol (98 – Jan 03) R to 52	4264
Toyota Aygo Petrol (05 – 11) 05 to 11	4921
Toyota Carina E Petrol (May 92 – 97) J to P	3256
Toyota Corolla (80 – 85) up to C	0683
Toyota Corolla (Sept 83 – Sept 87) A to E	1024
Toyota Corolla (Sept 87 – Aug 92) E to K	1683
Toyota Corolla Petrol (Aug 92 – 97) K to P	3259
Toyota Corolla Petrol (July 97 0 Feb 02) P to 51	4286
Toyota Corolla Petrol & Diesel (02 – Jan 07) 51 to 56	4791
Toyota Hi-Ace & Hi-Lux Petrol (69 – Oct 83) up to A	0304
Toyota RAV4 Petrol & Diesel (94 – 06) L to 55	4750
Toyota Yaris Petrol (99 – 05) T to 05	4265
TRIUMPH GT6 & Vitesse (62 0 74) up to N *	0112
Triumph Herald (59 – 71) up to K *	0010
Triumph Spitfire (62 – 81) up to X	0113
Triumph Stag (70 – 78) up to T *	0441
Triumph TR2, TR3, TR3A, TR4 & TR4A (52 – 67) up to F *	0028
Triumph TR5 & TR6 (67 – 75) up to P *	0031
Triumph TR7 (75 – 82) up to Y *	0322
VAUXHALL Astra Petrol (Oct 91 – Feb 98) J to R	1832
Vauxhall/Opel Astra & Zafira Petrol (Feb 98 – Apr 04) R to 04	3758
Vauxhall/Opel Astra & Zafira Diesel (Feb 98 – Apr 04) R to 04	3797
Vauxhall/Opel Astra Petrol (04 – 08)	4732
Vauxhall/Opel Astra Diesel (04 – 08)	4733
Vauxhall/Opel Astra Petrol & Diesel (Dec 09 – 13) 59 to 13	5578
Vauxhall/Opel Calibra (90 – 98) G to S	3502
Vauxhall Cavalier Petrol (Oct 88 0 95) F to N	1570
Vauxhall/Opel Corsa Diesel (Mar 93 – Oct 00) K to X	4087
Vauxhall Corsa Petrol (Mar 93 – 97) K to R	1985
Vauxhall/Opel Corsa Petrol (Apr 97 – Oct 00) P to X	3921
Vauxhall/Opel Corsa Petrol & Diesel (Oct 03 – Aug 06) 53 to 06	4617
Vauxhall/Opel Corsa Petrol & Diesel (Sept 06 – 10) 56 to 10	4886
Vauxhall/Opel Corsa Petrol & Diesel (00 – Aug 06) X to 06	5577
Vauxhall/Opel Frontera Petrol & Diesel (91 – Sept 98) J to S	3454
Vauxhall/Opel Insignia Petrol & Diesel (08 – 12) 08 to 61	5563
Vauxhall/Opel Meriva Petrol & Diesel (03 – May 10) 03 to 10	4893
Vauxhall/Opel Omega Petrol (94 – 99) L to T	3510
Vauxhall/Opel Vectra Petrol & Diesel (95 – Feb 99) N to S	3396

Title	Book No.
Vauxhall/Opel Vectra Petrol & Diesel (Mar 99 – May 02) T to 02	3930
Vauxhall/Opel Vectra Petrol & Diesel (June 02 – Sept 05) 02 to 55	4618
Vauxhall/Opel Vectra Petrol & Diesel (Oct 05 – Oct 08) 55 to 58	4887
Vauxhall/Opel Vivaro Diesel (01 – 11) Y to 11	5552
Vauxhall/Opel Zafira Petrol & Diesel (05 -09) 05 to 09	4792
Vauxhall/Opel 1.5, 1.6 & 1.7 litre Diesel Engine (82 – 96) up to N	1222
VW Beetle 1200 (54 – 77) up to S	0036
VW Beetle 1300 & 1500 (65 – 75) up to P	0039
VW 1302 & 1302S (70 – 72) up to L *	0110
VW Beetle 1303, 1303S & GT (72 – 75) up to P	0159
VW Beetle Petrol & Diesel (Apr 99 – 07) T to 57	3798
VW Golf & Jetta Mk 1 Petrol 1.1 & 1.3 (74 – 84) up to A	0716
VW Golf, Jetta & Scirocco Mk 1 Petrol 1.5, 1.6 & 1.8 (74 – 84) up to A	0726
VW Golf & Jetta Mk 1 Diesel (78 – 84) up to A	0451
VW Golf & Jetta Mk 2 Petrol (Mar 84 – Feb 92) A to J	1081
VW Golf & Vento Petrol & Diesel (Feb 92 – Mar 98) J to R	3097
VW Golf & Bora Petrol & Diesel (Apr 98 – 00) R to X	3727
VW Golf & Bora 4-cyl Petrol & Diesel (01 – 03) X to 53	4169
VW Golf & Jetta Petrol & Diesel (04 – 09) 53 to 09	4610
VW LT Petrol Vans & Light Trucks (76 – 87) up to E	0637
VW Passat 4-cyl Petrol & Diesel (May 88 – 96) E to P	3498
VW Passat 4-cyl Petrol & Diesel (Dec 96 – Nov 00) P to X	3917
VW Passat Petrol & Diesel (Dec 00 – May 05) X to 05	4279
VW Passat Diesel (June 05 – 10) 05 to 60	4888
VW Polo Petrol (Nov 90 – Aug 94) H to L	3245
VW Polo Hatchback Petrol & Diesel (94 – 99) M to S	3500
VW Polo Hatchback Petrol (00 – Jan 02) V to 51	4150
VW Polo Petrol & Diesel (02 – May 05) 51 to 05	4608
VW Transporter 1600 (68 – 79) up to V	0082
VW Transporter 1700, 1800 & 2000 (72 – 79) up to V *	0226
VW Transporter (air cooled) Petrol (79 – 82) up to Y *	0638
VW Transporter (water cooled) Petrol (82 – 90) up to H	3452
VW Type 3 (63 – 73) up to M *	0084
VOLVO 120 & 130 Series (& P1800) (61 – 73) up to M *	0203
Volvo 142, 144 & 145 (66 – 74) up to N *	0129
Volvo 240 Series Petrol (74 – 93) up to K	0270
Volvo 440, 460 & 480 Petrol (87 – 97) D to P	1691
Volvo 740 & 760 Petrol (82 – 91) up to J	1258
Volvo 850 Petrol (92 – 96) J to P	3260
Volvo 940 Petrol (90 – 98) H to R	3249
Volvo S40 & V40 Petrol (96 – Mar 04) N to 04	3569
Volvo S40 & V50 Petrol & Diesel (Mar 04 – Jun 07) 04 to 07	4731
Volvo S60 Petrol & Diesel (01 – 08) X to 09	4793
Volvo S70, V70 & C70 Petrol (96 – 99) P to V	3573
Volvo V70 / S80 Petrol & Diesel (98 – 07) S to 07	4263
Volvo V70 Diesel (June 07 – 12) 07 to 61	5557
Volvo XV60 / 90 Diesel (03 – 12) 52 to 62	5630

* Classic reprint

Preserving Our Motoring Heritage

< The Model J Duesenberg Derham Tourster. Only eight of these magnificent cars were ever built – this is the only example to be found outside the United States of America

Almost every car you've ever loved, loathed or desired is gathered under one roof at the Haynes Motor Museum. Over 300 immaculately presented cars and motorbikes represent every aspect of our motoring heritage, from elegant reminders of bygone days, such as the superb Model J Duesenberg to curiosities like the bug-eyed BMW Isetta. There are also many old friends and flames. Perhaps you remember the 1959 Ford Popular that you did your courting in? The magnificent 'Red Collection' is a spectacle of classic sports cars including AC, Alfa Romeo, Austin Healey, Ferrari, Lamborghini, Maserati, MG, Riley, Porsche and Triumph.

A Perfect Day Out

Each and every vehicle at the Haynes Motor Museum has played its part in the history and culture of Motoring. Today, they make a wonderful spectacle and a great day out for all the family. Bring the kids, bring Mum and Dad, but above all bring your camera to capture those golden memories for ever. You will also find an impressive array of motoring memorabilia, a comfortable 70 seat video cinema and one of the most extensive transport book shops in Britain. The Pit Stop Cafe serves everything from a cup of tea to wholesome, home-made meals or, if you prefer, you can enjoy the large picnic area nestled in the beautiful rural surroundings of Somerset.

John Haynes O.B.E., Founder and Chairman of the museum at the wheel of a Haynes Light 12.

< Graham Hill's Lola Cosworth Formula 1 car next to a 1934 Riley Sports.

The Museum is situated on the A359 Yeovil to Frome road at Sparkford, just off the A303 in Somerset. It is about 40 miles south of Bristol, and 25 minutes drive from the M5 intersection at Taunton.
Open 9.30am - 5.30pm (10.00am - 4.00pm Winter) 7 days a week, *except Christmas Day, Boxing Day and New Years Day*
Special rates available for schools, coach parties and outings Charitable Trust No. 292048